OUR
G

BY LE
TV Mov
Movie Con
Behind the C
The Great Mo
The Disney Fil
Carole Lombard
BY RICHARD W.
Laurel & Hardy, Fi
The Laurel & Hardy

OUR GANG

THE LIFE AND TIMES OF THE LITTLE RASCALS

by Leonard Maltin and Richard W. Bann

CROWN PUBLISHERS, INC., NEW YORK

© 1977 by Leonard Maltin and Richard W. Bann

Inquiries should be addressed to Crown Publishers, Inc., One Park Avenue, New York, N.Y. 10016.

Printed in the United States of America
Published simultaneously in Canada by
General Publishing Company Limited

Library of Congress Cataloging in Publication Data

Maltin, Leonard.
Our gang: the life and times of the Little rascals.

Includes index.
1. Our Gang films.   I. Bann, Richard W., joint author.   II. Title.
PN1995.9.08M3 1976   791.43'7   76-14951

ISBN 0-517-52675-1

Designed by Shari de Miskey

Third Printing, March 1978

ACKNOWLEDGMENTS

Researching any branch of films lost to history always presents special problems, but little did we imagine *how* difficult it would be to solve some of them for this book. Fortunately, we received gracious assistance in all quarters, at all turns.

First, grateful acknowledgment is extended to *our* gang, the friends and organizations that have generously shared their knowledge, helped us fill the gaps in our own private collections by contributing rare stills and prints to screen, and provided us much-needed encouragement during the incredibly long and painstaking five years this book was in preparation.

Alphabetically, they are:

Allied Artists, Gordon Berkow, Block-Heads Tent of Sons of the Desert, Eddie Brandt, British Film Institute, John Brunas, Ralph Celentano, John Cocchi, Susan Dalton of the Wisconsin Center for Theatre Research, Bill Diehl, Gordon Dishington, William K. Everson, James F. Foster, John Gallos of WCCO-TV, Mr. and Mrs. Ed Glass, Lester Glassner, Herb Graff, Gerald Haber, Hal Roach Studios, Ron Hall, Harry Jones and his staff (Claude Heisch & Co.) at WCCO-TV, Al Kilgore, Michael G. King of King World Productions, Larry Edmunds Bookshop, Lincoln Center and its Theatre Collection staff, John McCabe, Andrew C. McKay, Milton Menell of Select Film Library, Michael Merrick (not his real name), Metro-Goldwyn-Mayer, Monogram Pictures, Movie Star News, Maureen Murphy of Blackhawk Films, The Museum of Modern Art, Charles Pavlicek of Select Film Library, Jack Roth, David Shepard of Blackhawk Films, Samuel M. Sherman, Lou Valentino, Jerry Vermilye, Jordan Young, the late Robert Youngson, and Fred Zentner of Cinema Bookshop.

Credit for most of the book's marvelous photographs goes to unsung Hal Roach Studios still cameramen Gene Kornman and Bud "Stax" Graves. Many of the stills taken at M-G-M were by Graybill.

We would also like to express thanks to the filmmakers and grown Our Gangers who worked at Hal Roach Studios and M-G-M and who graciously shared with us their time, their insight, and their reminiscences of Hollywood's Golden Era, and who also kindly supplied us with some of the photographs reprinted in our book:

Stymie Beard, Tommy Bond, Joe Cobb, Jackie Cooper, Bob Davis, Gordon Douglas, the late Lewis Foster, Herbert Gelbspan, Dorothy Granger, T. Marvin Hatley, Darla Hood, Dick Hurley, the late Stan Laurel, the late George Marshall, George Spanky McFarland, Shirley Jean Rickert Measures, Dick Moore, Hal Roach, Sr., George Sidney, the late George Stevens, Sr., George Stevens, Jr.

For their many courtesies, and the fruits of their work, we will be always in their debt. The recollections of Mr. Hal Roach, Sr. (without whom there'd be no *Our Gang* to write about) were particularly invaluable.

Finally, personal sets of thanks from the two authors:

To my parents, who bought the television set that brought Clellan Card (starring as "Axel") into our home, introducing the mostly marvelous *Our Gang* comedies . . . with deepest gratitude.

Richard W. Bann

To my wonderful wife, Alice, who lived through the final stages of this long project . . . and to Pippin, who added moral support during the last two weeks.

Leonard Maltin

CONTENTS

* The nomenclature involving the series' original twin names of *Our Gang* and *Hal Roach's Rascals,* and also the more recently coined *The Little Rascals* (for television syndication) is set out briefly in the Introduction, and more fully in the chapter on the Television Revival.

INTRODUCTION AND KEY TO FILM ENTRIES

This book is intended as a film history, a chronology, a reference, and sometimes a celebration of the *Our Gang* comedies, now known through television as *The Little Rascals.* As such, the book is also an account of the lives and times of Hollywood movie-makers, especially those at Hal Roach Studios.

With at least lip service to objectivity, we have tried to appraise the films in a then and now perspective. And indeed the focus is on the *films:* how they were made, why they succeeded (when they did), and what makes them so much fun to view today.

It's just not possible, however, to judge films with absolute detachment, and each critical evaluation is inevitably a personal response to the film at hand, colored by many variables. Print quality, for instance, is enormously important to the appreciation and enjoyment of any film. And viewing a pristine, tinted and scored 35mm print of "The Champeen" in the grandeur of an old movie palace with a large and responsive audience would have had far greater impact than seeing a cut print of "The Champeen," duped nearly white, projected at the wrong speed on a tiny TV screen, and interrupted by loud commercials for hemorrhoid preparations, of which we'll not be buying many.

It is our hope that for those whose recollections of the *Our Gang* comedies are only fading happy memories, a trip through these pages will rekindle past affections. For those who've more recently seen a few or even many of the films, we feel confident this book will serve as the catalyst for seeking out the rest and for viewing special favorites over again. After all, the tenth rerun of "Teacher's Pet" is certainly better than the first run of most anything else.

Specifically, what this book offers is a complete, illustrated *Our Gang* filmography, with selected production credits, comprehensive cast listings and character roles, plot synopses, gag highlights, critical evaluations, related esoterica, interviews, pertinent and impertinent anecdotes, tidbits, transitional material, and now and then some published contemporary reviews.

The domestic release date for each film is disclosed, but it is important to know that the film entries are ordered according to production sequence, not by release dates or copyright dates. For instance, the entry for "Divot Diggers," a February release, comes ahead of the entry for "The Pinch Singer," a January release, since "Divot Diggers" was made first. Hal Roach shorts were generally released in the same order they were made, but there are a good number of exceptions.

Production credits were obtained by consulting trade publications and, of course, the films themselves. Cast credits and related character parts were similarly gathered through research and repeated screenings, although finding out who's who has been a lifelong inquiry. There is no published or private source for either cast credits or character parts; Hal Roach Studios did not keep such records, and with but two exceptions none of the kids was ever given on-screen billing. Luckily, lots of times the kids and character actors would use their real names in films; rare old casting directories and the sometimes sharp memories of Hal Roach staffers helped confirm our findings and fill in the rest. Two kids we know only by their nicknames ("Uh-Huh," early 1930s, and "Leonard," late 1930s); otherwise we've successfully identified virtually every bit player, character actor, and *Our Gang* kid appearing in the films.

While a most difficult task was merely corroborating and synthesizing the massive amount of trade paper and interview material gathered, a more important task was tracking down prints of the films to screen. It wasn't easy. We were able to screen all the sound films, but at the present time, sadly, the silent films are mostly reposing in archives and private collections, and we were unable to find prints to view for about fifteen of the silents, as the entries for these films so indicate. Hopefully the general unavailability of the silents will be rectified, though some of the Pathés appear not to have been preserved and may be irretrievably lost.

The authors split evenly the actual writing chores, each having the right of approval on the other's views: changing things, deleting things, but mostly adding things. The manuscript's thickness was half tape and glue from the hundreds of revisions and additions—just one of the many reasons this volume took so long to complete.

Finally, two clarifications.

A source of real confusion is the name of the series this book is about. Originally, the series was conceived as "The Hal Roach Rascals" or "Hal Roach's Rascals," but the very first film made was entitled "Our Gang." That caught on. The trade press and motion picture exhibitors treated to southern California previews of this pilot film asked Roach for "lots more of those *Our Gang* comedies." It was this kind of popular usage that resulted in the series being officially known by two names right from the outset: "The Our Gang Comedies" featuring "Hal Roach's Rascals."

It wasn't until television sets were being plugged in that the Roach talkies were renamed *The Little Rascals* in the early 1950s.* The title *Our Gang* had been sold to M-G-M when Roach discontinued production of the series in 1938 and M-G-M churned out the final fifty-two entries. All this is more fully covered in the chapter on the television revival.

To try to simplify things, this book's nomenclature treats Our Gang, Hal Roach's Rascals, and The Little Rascals pretty much interchangeably.

Another important distinction is the one between director Robert Francis "Bob" McGowan and his considerably less talented nephew, who directed the weakest Roach *Our Gang* films under the pseudonym of Anthony Mack and who, after his uncle had more or less retired, also collaborated on the screenplays for the even weaker Metro-produced *Our Gangs* under the name of Robert A. (for Anthony) McGowan.

---

* Though, coincidentally, the year the series was launched, 1922, Century Comedies released a two-reel short entitled *The Little Rascal*.

1 HAL ROACH STUDIOS

Probably no producer's work has brought the world more laughter than that of movie pioneer Hal Roach. Dating from 1914, Hal Roach Studios has produced silent motion pictures, sound short subjects and feature length films, radio and television. The best of it is still in great demand on television, in theaters, and in home-movie form. With each passing year, in fact, the effortless style and finesse of films starring Our Gang, Harold Lloyd, Laurel & Hardy, and Charley Chase makes them look better and better.

As a boy, Hal Roach seemed to have been everywhere and done everything. His own youth was as colorful as anything ever depicted in his films. He had met Mark Twain, and his grandfather lived on a plantation in Virginia adjoining one owned by Robert E. Lee. He was an adventurous drifter turned Alaskan prospector turned mule skinner when he saw an ad offering a dollar a day for experienced cowboys to serve as technical advisors on movies being made at Universal Studios. It was 1912. Roach journeyed to the film capital and rose rapidly from movie extra to movie producer, with short stops at all the posts in between.

On the strength of a small inheritance Hal Roach launched his first production unit in 1914, using the fresh, rolling Los Angeles parks for locations and the stories he wrote while en route for scripts. The stories were always elastic enough to fit any circumstance.

The first star Roach created was Harold Lloyd, whose pictures during the 1920s grossed more than anyone else's in Hollywood. With Roach as his producer and often his director, Harold Lloyd developed an exciting, sophisticated style of comedy.

One couldn't build a successful studio on just a single star though, and Roach spun off supporting characters, like Snub Pollard (into his own series) and later Sunshine Sammy (into *Our Gang*). Stan Laurel was signed from vaudeville and given a series, too.

By 1919, on the threshold of comedy's golden age, Roach had prospered and built his own fun factory, nestled in the low green hills of Culver City, not very far from Hollywood. The administration building was covered with ivy, and the picturesque little comedy plant became known as the green ivy studio. It would be comedy's home for nearly half a century.

During the 1920s and 1930s, among those who starred in their own series under the Roach banner were Harold Lloyd, Harold's brother Gaylord Lloyd, Charley Chase, Chase's brother James "Paul" Parrott, Mabel Normand, Snub Pollard, Thelma Todd and ZaSu Pitts, Thelma Todd and Patsy Kelly, Stan Laurel, Laurel & Hardy, Max

Hal Roach, *left,* with Harold Lloyd.

Davidson, Theda Bara, Harry Langdon, Irvin S. Cobb, and Will Rogers. There were other series, not named for their individual stars, including, of course, *Our Gang, The Boy Friends,* The Hal Roach Comedy *All Stars* (meaning no stars), *The Taxi Boys, The Dippy Doo Dads,* and others.

Some of the notable writers, directors, and photographers who got their start and learned their craft working on these same Roach pictures were Leo McCarey, George Stevens, Frank Tashlin, Gordon Douglas, William Beaudine, Tay Garnett, Frank Capra, Hal Mohr, George Marshall, Clyde Bruckman, and Frank Butler.

Among the performers who graduated from Roach comedies on their way to stardom elsewhere were Jean

Stan Laurel, Hal Roach, and Oliver Hardy on the occasion of their Academy Award for *The Music Box* in 1932.

Our Gang's famous red bus, parked in front of Hal Roach Studios, set to take the Gang on location. The bus driver (not visible) is Bob Davis, for more than *fifty* years a friend and neighbor of Joe Cobb (pictured next to Pete the Pup). Note the multiple doors and the running board.

Harlow, Lupe Velez, Janet Gaynor, Jean Arthur, Bebe Daniels, Fay Wray, Paulette Goddard, and Boris Karloff.

People like these who worked at Roach during its first quarter century have characterized the studio as a wonderfully warm place, with a lighthearted close-knit ''family'' atmosphere unique even among movie studios. It was ''family'' in more ways than one. The extras in Roach pictures were often the friends and real family of both stars and the studio stock company of character actors. Everyone from the directors to the grips loved comedy, loved what they were doing, and worked in remarkable harmony to create the most endearing, enduring short films ever made.

The love showed, and the care showed; Roach comedies have unmistakable charm and style. They're comedies not only of slapstick and spectacular gags, but often of tender feeling and whimsy, too.

Although Roach had made some serials and dramatic features, the studio's first twenty years had won Roach renown as producer of the finest short comedies in the industry. By 1934, however, the looming twin menaces of double bills in exhibition and block booking in distribution were slowly smothering the short subject.

The depression had given birth to the double-feature concept, offering audiences more for their money, and the traditional movie program of one feature film supported by various comedies, musicals, cartoons, and newsreels

was being disarranged as a result. The whole thing was an economics-related proposition. Short subjects were not being dislodged because as a group they were less popular or of lesser quality than the second feature. It was instead a matter of dollars and cents. Shorts were costing more and more to make, while due to double bills the potential for increased rentals was dwindling.

Then there was block booking. For a good while, major studio powers like M-G-M, Warner Bros., and Columbia could continue to subsidize short subjects that they could both produce under the same roof with features, and distribute in the same sealed package, forcing theater owners to take the short subjects in order to play the features.

A short comedy specialist like Hal Roach could use neither industry trend to his advantage. He made features only incidentally, and so he couldn't cash in on double bills. And since he was a producer, not a distributor, he couldn't engage in block booking. The only course was to begin making features instead of shorts, or perish as a producer. Reluctantly, the studio tested its short subject stars in features, while at the same time acquiring new and different properties to develop as features.

At first, Roach imprinted the same stamp of quality on his features that had characterized his short subjects: good production values, technical gloss, strong casts, etc. Such wonderful Laurel & Hardy features as *Sons of the*

Desert and *Way Out West* were critical and commercial successes, as was the trilogy of droll *Topper* features, and also the film version of John Steinbeck's powerful *Of Mice and Men,* probably Roach's masterwork. *One Million B.C.* was notable since Hal Roach and D. W. Griffith (to some degree) codirected. Roach's foray into the genre of screwball comedies gave us such diverting features as *Turnabout* and *Merrily We Live.* Fast and lively swashbucklers included *Captain Fury* and *Captain Caution.*

While all this was going on in the late 1930s, Roach had an idea that edging back to shorter length features, "streamliners" he called them, would be successful as an answer to the double-feature problem. They were moderately so, and a couple dozen were released, but the concept never really took hold.

The Air Force was encamped on the studio back lot during World War II, engaged in specialized film projects. Roach himself, then in his early fifties, was called back into service as a lieutenant colonel and stationed in England. He even saw action in the Normandy invasion. Coincidentally, before the war, he'd been a business partner of Mussolini for some projected Italian films that were never made.

After the war Roach admits he'd lost some of his movie-making zest. United Artists, which was then distributing his pictures, was not doing very well, which made producing for theatrical consumption a shaky proposition. All this, coupled with Roach's desire to return to short comedies, brought him to the field of television, where he pioneered once more.

Besides being the first Hollywood motion-picture com-

pany whose product was photographed entirely in color (Cinecolor), Roach was also then the only studio devoted exclusively to producing films for television. Beginning in 1948, among the scores of early TV series produced by Hal Roach (or filmed at his studio) were *Amos 'n' Andy Screen Director's Playhouse, My Little Margie, The Lone Ranger, Blondie, Groucho Marx De Soto, Abbott and Costello, Beulah, The George Raft Show, The Life of Riley, Racket Squad, Trouble With Father* (The Stu Erwin Show), *Oh Susannah, Fireside Theatre,* and *Topper.* John Ford, Buster Keaton, and John Wayne were among the many big name stars and directors who worked on Roach television programs.

Sadly, planned TV series to revive both *Our Gang* and *Laurel & Hardy* never reached the air.

In 1955 Hal Roach sold the studio to his less creative son, Hal, Jr. Soon after, it became part of an industrial combine that in time crumbled, bringing down the last of the small studio empires in the financial collapse.

In 1959 the studio declared bankruptcy. After reorganization, Hal Roach Studios produced a number of features (Al Kilgore and Chuck McCann's *The World of Hans Christian Andersen,* and *The Groundstar Conspiracy* in 1972), but mostly the studio has been content with global distribution and licensing of its many literary properties, remake rights, and motion picture and television films backlog.

Hal Roach, Sr., has lived comfortably in Hollywood through the troubles of his studio, and remains hale and hearty; within two months of this writing he will celebrate his 84th birthday. He doesn't seem to want to retire completely, and one wonders where he will pioneer next.

High-powered talent: some of the creative artists behind the scenes at Hal Roach Studios. *Left to right,* Fred Guiol, associated with Hal Roach and George Stevens through most of his career; Bob McGowan; Hal Roach; Leo McCarey, who'd served a stint as *Our Gang* writer before his ascension to the front ranks of Hollywood directors;

Hal Yates, who was still directing for Hal Roach in the 1950s on such TV shows as *My Little Margie* and *Life of Riley;* James Parrott, Charley Chase's brother and director of Laurel & Hardy's finest short comedies; and Clyde Bruckman, later a writer and director on features starring Harold Lloyd, Buster Keaton, and W. C. Fields.

II   AN OUR GANG OVERVIEW

"Our Gang" has a nice ring. The two words strike each other engagingly. Apart they don't mean much, but together they stand for all the best of the collective American boyhood. From a kid's point of view. As timeless as childhood itself, *Our Gang* represents the kind of adventures kids yearn for, and the ones grownups wish they *could* have had.

The series' foundation was pitting scruffy, mischievous have-not kids against pretentious rich kids, sissy kids, and in general a hardened, rule-governed, class-conscious adult world that would stand between them and the only thing they were interested in—making their own fun. On their side, these enterprising kids had wit, common sense, and mettle as their only assets, and usually a neighborhood Grandma as their only ally, but in Our Gang's world, that was usually enough.

From 1922 through 1944 a total of two hundred and twenty-one *Our Gang* comedies were made—more films than in any other movie series ever produced. *Our Gang* became an American tradition, with the same kind of once in a lifetime impact made by the likes of a Babe Ruth, a Charlie Chaplin, or a Harry Houdini. Why do these few names of the past live vibrantly on while millions of others have faded with time?

Our Gang was something special right from the start, and the series remains unique more than a half century after its inception. Why has *Our Gang* never once been successfully copied? Why is it that even Hal Roach, whose brainchild the series was, could not revive a new *Our Gang* in the more than thirty years since the series fizzled out? What other movies from the early 1930s are still shown every day to children as entertainment of the 1970s? For that matter, how many feature films of the same period could be shown to a mass audience without prior explanations about the films' age?

Luck, timing, skilled and creative filmmakers, talented yet unaffected youngsters, ambition and hard work all contributed to the successful creation of *Our Gang*.

The early Pathés are easily the best silent *Our Gang* comedies. Certainly there are plenty of rough edges, but that's part of the charm. There is no definitive *Our Gang* film, but entries like "The Big Show," "The Champeen," "Derby Day," "A Quiet Street," "Seein' Things," "High Society," "The Sun Down Limited," "Ask Grandma," "Mary Queen of Tots," and "Thundering Fleas" are typical of the spirited inventive outdoors comedy that characterized the series' first few years.

Important in the sweeping triumph of these early Pathés was Hal Roach's active participation in all phases of the films' production. So much so, in fact, that it upset Harold Lloyd, who felt Roach was giving *Our Gang* both too much time and too many great gags that Lloyd felt should have been reserved for his pictures. Indeed, it was

Our Gang in 1925: *top row,* Mickey Daniels, Johnny Downs, Jackie Condon; *next row,* Joe Cobb, Mary Kornman, Jay R. Smith; and, *below,* Allen "Farina" Hoskins.

Our Gang in 1928: *left to right,* Jay R. Smith, Allen "Farina" Hoskins, Jackie Condon, Jean Darling, Pete the Pup, Harry Spear, Mildred Kornman, Bobby "Wheezer" Hutchins, and Joe Cobb.

Our Gang in 1931: *left to right,* Allen "Farina" Hoskins, Norman "Chubby" Chaney, Dorothy De Borba, Mary Ann Jackson, Pete the Pup, Shirley Jean Rickert, Bobby "Wheezer" Hutchins, Jackie Cooper, and Matthew "Stymie" Beard.

Roach's preoccupation with *Our Gang* to the neglect of Harold Lloyd that eventually led to a parting (amicable) of the producer and his first major star.

Midway through the silents, however, Roach began devoting time to his polo ponies, and taking trips around the world. His energies at the studio were increasingly swallowed up by executive chores and developing new properties, like the *Laurel & Hardy* series. Charley Chase was by then starring in his own Roach series, and had long relinquished his *Our Gang* association. Bob McGowan, too, was either ill and away from the series entirely or detached from it and serving in a "supervisory" capacity, turning over the directorial reins to his same-named nephew who took screen credit as Anthony Mack. Evidence would indicate Mack was not an inspired comedy director, but in fairness it should also be noted that he took over direction at a time when the series and the studio were experiencing growing pains.

Perhaps what hurt *Our Gang* as much as anything else at this point was the loss of Mickey Daniels after four years, and the inability to find a suitable replacement for him throughout the remaining Pathés, the M-G-M silents, and up until the early talkies when Jackie Cooper filled the void.

Watching Mickey Daniels at work in the early Pathés, one would think he was a movie comic of long experience, instead of the unaffected preadolescent he really was. Like all the best *Our Gang* kids, whatever he's doing on screen, he communicates the experience and one shares the feeling. Mickey had a wide range of wonderfully natural expressions that always told an audience exactly what he was thinking. He was a leader, a scrapper, an underdog—and always quite vulnerable, making it easy to identify with him.

When Mickey Daniels outgrew the series (an occupational hazard) there was no one left in the gang to really "pull" for. The rest of the troops were fine at what they did, most always fresh, spontaneous, and appealing, but their specialties were all best served when supporting the one "take charge" guy that could command audience empathy.

The post-Mickey Daniels silents and pre-Jackie Cooper talkies were also more mechanical, and had neither the charm, characterization nor energy of the early Pathés.

Still, though the series was faltering, its popularity did not diminish during this period.

The advent of talkies was a turning point, a creative impetus, and after a few false starts the gang quickly regained its stride and enjoyed its greatest success ever. Sound had impelled a cast turnover, and rekindled a sense of novelty and imagination. Clever dialogue, sound-effects, and music were all swiftly mastered and used to advantage. The early 1930s talkies are especially enchanting, as the recharged Bob McGowan successfully combined quips, slapstick, and sight gags with sentiment, finding that the most effective way to reach an audience's funny bone was through its heart.

After creating a few years more worth of filmic gems, the strain finally forced McGowan to bow out. A fine director, Gus Meins, was there to take over, and after Meins, Gordon Douglas, whose very first *Our Gang* effort, "Bored of Education," won the Academy Award as best short subject of 1936.

In the *Our Gang* canon of two hundred and twenty-one films, there are lots of bad films, mediocre films, and good films. There's also a handful of imperishable comedy classics, full of heart and warmth, and they're all Roach talkies from the 1930s. If *Our Gang* had made only a dozen films like "Dogs Is Dogs," "Mama's Little Pirate," "Hi'-Neighbor!," "Free Wheeling," "The Kid From Borneo," "Teacher's Pet," "Bedtime Worries," "Divot Diggers," "Our Gang Follies of 1938," "Glove Taps," "Fly My Kite," and "Pups Is Pups," the series would be worthy of comparison with the best short films of Chaplin, Keaton, Laurel & Hardy, W. C. Fields, and anyone else who's come before or since, in theaters or on television.

Filmmakers should be judged by their best works, and there's little doubt *Our Gang's* finest years are represented by the Roach sound films from mid-1930 through 1937. During those years, fresh new faces like Jackie Cooper, Dickie Moore, Scotty Beckett, Stymie, Spanky and Alfalfa kept turning up to continue revitalizing the series. All were incredibly natural and gifted performers. Hal Roach says that Cary Grant, while he was on the lot making the first *Topper* film, "used to sit and watch *Our*

Our Gang in 1935: *left to right,* Harold and Alfalfa Switzer, Darla Hood, Spanky McFarland, Billie "Buckwheat" Thomas, Scotty Beckett, and Baby Patsy.

Gang for half an hour at a time, marvelling at their ability to convey an idea even though they were such little kids. He was amazed at how convincing they could be.

In the mid-1930s, however, motion-picture distribution and exhibition were changing, forcing Hal Roach to produce feature length films like *Topper,* and to test his units in features or drop them. Shorts were dying. Curiously, the quality and popularity of a short subject series like *Our Gang* had very little to do with the situation. Double bills and block booking were simply shoving shorts made by all but the industry giants right off the screen.

Our Gang's feature test, "General Spanky," was not a success, as a film or as a moneymaker. But Hal Roach was not about to abandon his favorite series just yet, and produced two seasons of shorter length one-reel films before finally selling the entire *Our Gang* unit—director, writers, talent contracts, and all—to M-G-M in 1938.

The final 52 Metro-produced *Our Gang* efforts were steadily deteriorating films that varied from bad to worse, but somehow the series managed to survive for another six years. Hal Roach Studios was geared to making nothing but good comedy shorts, while M-G-M was geared to making everything *but*. The result was a strictly-for-kids mixture of ten minute morality plays and pep talks pushing American virtues during wartime. No one liked these "comedies" very much, but they continued to be made on the basis of inertia, and with block booking, a power like M-G-M simply forced theater owners to play its short subjects, like them or not. Exhibitors had to pay for and play the shorts, or else they couldn't also rent the big ticket Metro features. It was a package deal.

It's too bad that Robert Blake, who appeared in these last *Our Gangs,* and is so outspoken today, didn't tell M-G-M producers what lousy films they were making. Possibly, he did, and most likely, they didn't care.

Fortunately, the best *Our Gang* comedies are still very much around, in home-movie form, playing on television as *The Little Rascals* (occasionally in mutilated form), and sometimes even back up on theater screens in their pictorially flawless original form.

No matter how often one has seen the films, it's nice to escape for a while from the uncertain future we all face, and retreat to the more leisurely joys of a certain past. Whatever pleases long, and pleases many, pleases best. And indeed the *Our Gang* comedies have pleased long, many, and best.

III OTHER KID SERIES, AND LOTS OF THEM

Our Gang was not the first series of kid pictures. Sidney Franklin's Fox *Sunshine Kiddies* predated Hal Roach's Rascals by about seven years. These shorts and features, though, in no way gave rise to *Our Gang.* The two series' likeness ends with the average age of their casts. The principal difference is that the Franklin pictures ("Jack and the Beanstalk," "Babes in the Wood," "Treasure Island," etc.) were lavishly mounted costume adventures designed for a children's audience, whereas Roach hoped to entertain everyone who bought a theater ticket and targeted his back yard *Our Gang* capers at the entire movie-going public: adults and kids alike.

The Franklin kid pictures were made first in association with D. W. Griffith, then production headquarters moved to Fox, where this unique series ended in 1917. Among those featured were Francis Carpenter, Virginia Lee Corbin, Raymond Lee, and Buddy and Gertrude Messinger (later a star of Roach's teen-aged *Our Gang* series, *The Boy Friends*).

Just about the time *Our Gang* was being launched as a part of American folklore, Pathé inaugurated another kid series starring Johnny Jones (for whom the series was named) and again Gertrude Messinger.

With that, the *Our Gang* sweepstakes were off in high dudgeon. The beauty of the series was that it looked so easy and natural, everyone thought he could copy it. No imitator would match the gang's popularity or durability, but lots tried.

On July 7, 1923 Mack Sennett announced that he was assigning one or more units to work on kids-and-animals comedies, once more for Pathé. "The decision to make this type of comedy was reached," it was announced, "because of the tremendous and increasing popular vogue of this type of comedy in which the natural gifts of children and the comic effects secured through expert training of animals is obtained." Which is about as polite a way as possible of saying that Sennett wanted to cash in on the *Our Gang* bonanza. Although the series never got rolling, Sennett did spoof the genre in a 1924 short called "The Hollywood Kid."

In England, British Screen Productions Limited called their *Our Gang* adaptation *Hoo-Ray Kids,* starring Jackie Ray and featuring a fat kid, a black kid, and a freckled kid, just like the rest of the *Our Gang* copies.

States-side *Our Gang* spin-offs (and their fast-buck producers) included *Buddy Messinger Comedies* (Broadway Distributing Corp.); *Hey Fella's* (Davis Dist. Division); *Kid Noah* (Pinellas Films); *The Reg'lar Kids* (M. J. Winkler); *Kiddie Kute Komedies* (Eureka Productions); *The Kiddie Troupers* (producer not known); *The*

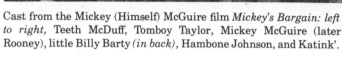

Cast from the Mickey (Himself) McGuire film *Mickey's Bargain: left to right,* Teeth McDuff, Tomboy Taylor, Mickey McGuire (later Rooney), little Billy Barty *(in back),* Hambone Johnson, and Katink'.

Shirley Temple and Georgie Smith in *The Pie Covered Wagon,* a Baby Burlesks episode.

McDougal Alley Kids (Bray Prod., Inc., who were bold enough to name *their* black kid "Oatmeal"); and an outrageous copy, *The Us Bunch Comedies.*

Just as nervy was Educational Pictures' 1924 announcement that they had "a real innovation in the comedy field" called *Juvenile Comedies.* Something new. Featured was one of the original Our Gang, Peggy Cartwright, and also Bennie Alexander, later Jack Webb's sidekick on *Dragnet.* Some of these shorts were directed by Norman Taurog, whose association with children extended to later hits like *Skippy* (a role incarnated by nephew Jackie Cooper), *Boys Town,* and many other films starring such adolescents as Mickey Rooney, Deanna Durbin, and Jerry Lewis.

More successful were Educational's dimly amusing *Big Boy* comedies of 1927–28. Malcolm Sebastian as Big Boy was himself an interesting performer, but filmmakers Jules White (later producer of *The Three Stooges* shorts), Jack White, and Charles Lamont gave him only feeble stories and gags to work with.

After sound, Educational did try one last *Our Gang* imitation, the soporific *Baby Burlesks.* They were largely unfunny takeoffs on adult movies. Shirley Temple was the star of this one-gag series in which everybody wore diapers held up by oversized safety pins. Hilarious, right? One need only see a *Baby Burlesks* episode to appreciate the expertise behind *Our Gang.* Shirley Temple was as good as she could be with the paper-thin material she had, but the rest of the kids stood around alternately gaping into the camera and delivering stilted dialogue they obviously didn't understand.

Stern Bros., too, tried several *Our Gang* imitations. Like the rest, there's little to be said about or for them.

First came the *Baby Peggy* series, then *The Newlyweds and Their Baby* (Snookums) series, and the best of the three, the *Buster Brown* comedies, derived from the famous comic strip. Interestingly, Gus Meins and Francis Corby (both later associated with *Our Gang*) alternated direction. Doreen Turner and the original Pete the Pup were featured.

Cast in the *Smitty* comedies were Jackie Searle, and some past and future Our Gangers: George Ernest, Eugene Jackson, Donald Haines, Artye Folz, and Kendall McComas.

Probably the closest *Our Gang* equivalent, and the only one to carry over into talkies, was Larry Darmour's *Mickey McGuire* series, starring a young Mickey Rooney, and based on Fontaine Fox's popular comic strip *Toonerville Folks.* Besides Roguish Mickey (Himself) McGuire, the folks who lived along the Toonerville Trolley Line included Tomboy Tailor, Stinky Davis, Hambone Johnson, Katink', Teeth McDuff, and little Billy Barty, a midget still active in television and movies.* Mickey's Kid Brudder was sometimes played by Kendall McComas, later *Our Gang's* "Breezy Brisbane." The misadventures of Mickey McGuire, though, depended on the magnetic

---

* Shirley Jean Rickert left *Our Gang* in 1931 to work in the *Mickey McGuire* series. She remembers the time her parents brought her to the Darmour studio to audition. Inside they met tiny Billy Barty, who was made up as a baby. He promptly jumped out of a baby carriage, lit a cigar and did some hand springs. Astonished, Shirley Jean's mom left the set and wearily told Dad back out in the car, "Let's go home. There is a baby in there doing cartwheels—my child can't do things like that." Dad, though, talked her into taking Shirley Jean back inside where she was cast as Tomboy Tailor.

Mickey Rooney. When the brash youngster left the series after six years, it folded.

Mickey Rooney had originally come to Hollywood with his mother to audition for *Our Gang.* He didn't make it. Hal Roach tells why: "I remember the kid; I remember seeing him. We could've had him, I just didn't think he'd fit into the Gang. Then when I saw the *Mickey McGuire* pictures, I mean right from the time he started, he overacted. He'd lost his naturalness. To my mind he was acting more like an adult than a kid. He was a very good little actor, and maybe somebody could have worked on him to tone him down, but that was also work."

Someone else who tried out for *Our Gang,* got turned down, and went to a competing series was Mighty Moppet, Shirley Temple. That she attempted to audition and failed illustrates one of the gang's mixed blessings: Roach and his staff were surfeited by vest-pocket movie hopefuls. Hal Roach explains: "We were very fortunate in starting out with a good group, and then all the kids who came to Hollywood after that, including Shirley Temple, were knocking on our door trying to get into the gang. So we got the pick of the best kids that came along. If somebody had a kid or two they thought was cute, they'd send them to the studio. So with all these kids, lots would get lost in the shuffle. About Shirley Temple, her mother brought her in five or six times I understand, and nobody'd let her get beyond the outer office. But bear in mind there would usually be dozens of kids out there every single day. You couldn't see them all, and the casting director apparently didn't think Shirley Temple had anything to offer the gang. So she didn't get chosen."

More than anything else, Hal Roach is asked why he doesn't produce another *Our Gang,* or at least a derivative series. He's half tried—as long ago as some late 1940s features Bob McGowan helped produce, and as recently as the summer of 1971. In between, there were periodic announcements in *Variety* that Roach was attempting to revive the *Our Gang* idea. At one point, plans for a new *Little Rascals* series gave birth to a merchandising boom which encompassed comic books, toys, and games based on cartoon-caricatures of Spanky, Alfalfa, and other now-famous kids. No new *Our Gang* series of any quality was forthcoming though.

It seems quite possible that a major problem in reestablishing *Our Gang* is that the idea belonged to a certain time, and that time is past. If one were to be generous, one might even consider that M-G-M could have turned out better shorts if not for timing. After all, *Our Gang* was conceived in the 1920s on the basis of its members being poor, rural children. The Depression of 1930s was a perfect format to continue this idea. But the streamlined 1940s, with suburban America consolidating and the communications media changing our way of life, didn't seem to suit *Our Gang* as well.

When *Our Gang* alumnus Jackie Cooper became production chief of Screen Gems, the television division of Columbia Pictures in the 1960s, he tried to launch a revival of *Our Gang,* and worked very hard to bring the idea to life, without success. Aside from the problems of working with kids under modern-day labor laws, and the near impossiblility of being as flexible and informal as Bob McGowan had been in Cooper's day, the actor-turned-producer discovered what was perhaps the essence of *Our Gang,* something sadly lacking in today's kids: innocence. He credits or blames television for the change in American youth over the years.

Hal Roach says the difficulty of reviving *Our Gang* has been finding those four or five great kids with the right chemistry at one time. "In the old days," he says, "they would come to us, and we would look at hundreds of kids to find one who qualified. Today you'd have to stage a nationwide search. It would be a tremendous job to find kids talented and natural enough who also photographed well. They're not around anymore."

If there be any doubt, one need only look at the singularly unappealing children being paid big money for television commercials these days. Especially those toy blurb screamers. No thank you. The age of innocence that fostered something like *Our Gang* has long passed by.

"Children *can* be exciting performers," Hal Roach says. "There was never any star bigger than Shirley Temple, and maybe Jackie Coogan in his day. I mean in the old days, starting with Baby Marie Osborn,* decades before you were born, there were many kid stars that captured the public's imagination. But in the last thirty years, nobody's come up with even one kid that means a thing. Yet there's great talent in kids if somebody'd go to the trouble to dig 'em up. *Our Gang,* modernized, would go as well today as when they were made, *if* you could find the right kids."†

Finding the right kids, incidentally, is what gave Hal Roach the biggest kick in making the *Our Gang* comedies. "Picking the kids that turned out to be good," he explains, "and also figuring the kind of a kid it was, bringing out whatever the kid had that might make him special, or the type of thing that kid could do that would be funny. Mickey Daniels with all the freckles was irrepressible, a scrapper. Alfalfa was the kid who couldn't sing but thought he could. That was original. Kids with character like those were will always have great appeal."

Happily the original *Our Gang* comedies are still in circulation, as delightful as ever, and as long as they are, we needn't be too concerned that a wide screen Technicolor imitation hasn't come along to replace them.

---

* Star of a pre-1920s Pathé series.

† Producer Charles Mortimer thinks he's found such a group of kids for his new *Little Rascals* feature film, which is in production at the time of this writing.

IV SERIES GENESIS: BIRTH OF A NOTION

By 1921 Hal Roach had an ample supply of bathing beauty comedies, and chalk-faced slapstick was being manufactured in abundance by units starring Harold Lloyd, Snub Pollard, and others. That same year Hollywood was shaken to its foundations by disclosures of drug addiction, sordid scandals, and murder among its vaunted ranks. Roach wanted to try something novel to eclipse Mack Sennett, something fresh and wholesome, too. 1921 was also the year Jackie Coogan nearly stole one of Charlie Chaplin's early masterworks in the title role for *The Kid*.

From these variegated circumstances—and one precipitative audition—was crystallized the idea for Hal Roach's Rascals: *Our Gang*.

The producer who fathered the series, Hal Roach, reminisces: "In those early days, film actors used a great deal of makeup, and the child actors did too. Every one of them looked like a Sarah Bernhardt with heavy lipstick, false eyelashes, and the whole works. I was sick of it. One time for an audition, a woman brought an overrehearsed little girl in to me. The kid came in all made up, and I had to listen to her speak some kind of a piece, do a dance, and sing a song. The kid thought she was a child prodigy but all she could do was what they'd trained her to do. I was unimpressed. When finally she left I walked over to the window. There's a lumber yard across the street and out of my office window I saw this bunch of five or six little kids. They had picked up these sticks of lumber and then began arguing over them. Now *this* amused me. The littlest kid claimed the biggest stick, and the oldest kid wanted it. Now they were going to throw the sticks away as soon as they walked another block, but the most important thing in the world right then was who could have which stick. All of a sudden I realized I'd been watching this silly argument over the sticks for fifteen minutes. I'd spent fifteen minutes because these are *real* kids, I mean they're on the square. They're just kids being kids. So I thought if I could find some clever street kids to just play themselves in films and show life from a kid's angle, maybe I could make a dozen of these things before I wear out the idea."

Casting this brainstorm of a series was a surprisingly casual affair.

As "Sunshine Sammy," Ernie Morrison had long been contributing mischief and worse to the Harold Lloyd and Snub Pollard comedies around the lot. Here was a proven favorite to build on. One talented black boy.

In late 1921 Ernie Morrison and his sister had worked in Marshall Neilan's filmization of Booth Tarkington's *Penrod* for First National, which had so impressed Hal Roach that he went out and recruited two of the many unbilled kids from this picture, Jackie Condon and Peggy

Cartwright. One tiny imp with irrepressible gusto, and one pretty girl of every boy's dreams.

Jackie Davis was the younger brother of Harold Lloyd's leading lady Mildred Davis. One good-looking tough guy.

One-year-old Allen (dubbed "Farina") Hoskins reportedly followed Ernie Morrison's bare footsteps to the studio one day and walked into a ten-year job. One infant tag-along.

Still photographer Gene Kornman volunteered his daughter Mary and recommended a friend's son, Mickey Daniels. One more adorable little blond-haired girl, and one freckle-faced rough-and-tumble all-American boy.

Joe Cobb was not a charter member, but would soon join the ensemble. One good-natured fat boy.

Throw an aggregation of neighborhood pets into this eclectic pool of mischief and talent and the nucleus of the original *Our Gang* is complete.

At first most of Roach's associates had tried to dissuade him from making comedies about a nondescript collection of meddlesome street kids, warning that they couldn't be managed, there were legal constraints, it would cost a lot of money, etc. But *Our Gang* was a novelty Hal Roach liked, and in his own words, "I have always had a simple idea of humor. I go by what makes *me* laugh. Sometimes I'd be right and sometimes I'd be wrong, and sometimes the things that I liked and were funny to me weren't funny to anybody else. I was almost notorious for disregarding some of the business details at the studio; they were always telling me I was spending too much money. But if I liked the idea, I didn't care, I made the picture anyway."

So he went ahead and made "Our Gang," with "a cast of just kids, tattered and full of spirits," as an early trade ad read.

The series was to be an instant, resounding success. If Jackie Coogan was tugging the country's heart strings, *Our Gang* would make the nation laugh, bringing Hal Roach and his Rascals swift and remunerative fame.

Engaged to organize the new unit, under the supervision of director-general Charley Chase, were Tom McNamara, Hiram Walker, Charley Oelze, and Bob McGowan.

Tom McNamara had originated the *Us Boys* comic strip, and was signed as a writer.

Hiram "Beanie" Walker had been a cartoonist and sports editor with the Los Angeles *Examiner*. He'd also written a book called *The Wisdom of Blinky Ben*. Hal Roach thought he was "funny with words," and persuaded him to join the Roach staff in 1916. The fertile-witted Walker would write all the amusing subtitles and name each picture.

Charley Oelze had worked on a circus and a cattle ranch before catching on with Universal, where in 1913 he was placed in charge of the bullpen extras used for cowboy movies. He became close friends with some of those extras hoping to be picked for scenes: Fred Newmeyer, Hal Roach, George Marshall, and Harold Lloyd. When Roach founded his own studio soon thereafter, he brought Oelze along, first as property man, then as technical assistant and assistant director, having responsibility for all the magical contraptions and gadgetry in the *Our Gang* and other Roach comedies. Like Walker, Oelze was unsung but indispensable, and would stay with Roach for nearly forty years.

Bob McGowan was a Denver fireman who'd had an accident, claimed a pension, and came to Hollywood to break into the movie business—where else but as a prop man working with Charley Oelze at Universal! He didn't join forces with Roach as soon as the rest, though. First he graduated to directing comedy shorts over at Christie. He even piloted a series of children's films there. After some free-lancing he wrote short subject scenarios that Charley Chase directed at Paramount, one of them called *Kids Is Kids* (not pups or dogs, but "kids"). Then in 1920 McGowan wrote a two-reeler William A. Seiter directed for Goldwyn entitled *The Little Dears*. The following year McGowan signed with Roach as a gagman, and when *Our Gang* was conceived, he was a natural to develop and direct stories. McGowan was a big teddy bear of a man who loved kids, and realized immediately that the best

Summit meeting: *Our Gang* producer Hal Roach with his director, Bob McGowan.

way to preserve their spontaneity was to turn the filmmaking process into something of a game. The kids regarded it as play, and McGowan would become a favorite uncle to them.

All in all it was a perfect blending of ingredients—a bunch of pretty nice kids, just full of talent, and an expert staff of comedy craftsmen given a free hand to guide their destinies. Together they'd pave the way to a screen institution that would delight generation after generation.

V   THE ROACH PATHÉ SILENTS

1 · OUR GANG

Two Reels · Produced by Hal Roach · Supervised by Charles Parrott (Charley Chase) · Directed by Robert F. McGowan · Titles by H. M. Walker · Story by Hal E. Roach · Released on November 5, 1922, by Pathé Exchange · The original Our Gang: Ernie "Sunshine Sammy" Morrison, Jackie Condon, Peggy Cartwright, and perhaps Monty O'Grady and Winston Doty, with Dinah the Mule

The following official synopsis was taken from Pathé's home-movie catalogue: "One member of the gang has a widowed mother who keeps the village store. A rival merchant opens a shop across the street and by questionable methods lures the widow's customers away from her. The gang decides to take a hand and, with the help of all the pet animals in town, it stages such a show that the widow's business is restored and her

competitor seeks his fortune in a more peaceful town."

The first film made starring Hal Roach's Rascals was conceived in midwinter of 1922, shot sometime during the late spring, previewed extensively around Los Angeles test theaters during the summer, officially announced to the trade papers in August, copyrighted in October, and released in November. Obviously, great care and patience were exercised to ensure the series' success. But this first film produced and entitled "Our Gang" was held out of distribution for unknown reasons and finally released to exhibitors as the third entry in the series. (For the record, director Fred Newmeyer and writer Tom McNamara both worked on "Our Gang," but their contribution is not known.)

As the picture premiered in movie palaces across the country, audiences little dreamed that the Pathé rooster trademark introducing "Our Gang" was also trumpeting a silent prelude to what would become one of filmdom's most beloved, enduring series.

Sadly, no negatives or prints of "Our Gang" are known to survive; it's unavailable for reappraisal, and is considered a lost film.

Critical response was enthusiastic at the time of the film's release, but imprecise. A news column in the April 8, 1922, edition of *Moving Picture World* carried this item: "The Los Angeles dramatic critics and trade press were the guests of Hal Roach at a studio luncheon, after which a projection room preview was held of the 'Kiddie Animal' picture 'Our Gang.' Both were very well received by the hungry scribes. The picture contains novelties that will bring a pleasant surprise to the exhibitor."

The same trade paper printed this review when the film was finally released seven months later: "A cast of interesting children has been directed with unusual appreciation of their capabilities, in this third number of the new Hal Roach series. The motive is light and mischievous, with an undercurrent of burlesque. For instance, the leading lady has a few big emotional moments, and her triangular romance is treated with a mock seriousness that results in very enjoyable entertainment. The children decide to do something noble and with the aid of the pony and mule save the heroine and her mother from the threatened mortgage foreclosure. A number of highly amusing incidents are included and the trend as a whole is decidedly entertaining."

For historical purposes, "Our Gang" would be fascinating to view today, but all indications are that the film is no lost classic. Archivists, though, are earnestly invited to retrieve a preservation copy somewhere and hopefully prove our expectations wrong.

2 · FIRE FIGHTERS

Two Reels · Produced by Hal Roach · Supervised by Charles Parrott (Charley Chase) · Directed by Robert F. McGowan and Tom McNamara · Titles by H. M. Walker and Tom McNamara · Story by Hal E. Roach and Robert F. McGowan · Released on October 8, 1922, by Pathé Exchange · The original Our Gang: Jackie "Rosie" Condon, Ernie "Booker T." Morrison, Peggy Cartwright, Allen "Farina" Hoskins, Winston Doty, Monty O'Grady, and Dinah the Mule · Bootlegger, George Rowe; Officer, Charles Stevenson; Ernie's dad, Ernie Morrison, Sr.

As the flimsy shack hiding a moonshine still collapses, the kids think the giant boiler-tank would be a great excuse to form a fire department. Besides, little Jackie has a fireman's hat. So they set to work and build a horse-propelled, steam-engine truck, a hook-and-ladder division, and a separate vehicle to carry the chief, this one under dog-power. The firemen go to sleep in their barn headquarters, waiting for the lookout on the roof to report a fire. Steam coming out of a nearby kitchen window looks like smoke to the lookout (it's just a kettle boiling on the stove) and the fire brigade plunges into action. After dousing the "fire," they realize that the liquid coming out of their tank smells somehow funny—it certainly isn't water. The smell is picked up by a passing policeman as well. He sits down with Jackie on his dog-cart to ask what's been going on; just then a cat passes by and the dog takes off, pulling the cop with him. By a happy coincidence, the cop-cart runs smack into the escaping bootlegger, solving the mystery and bringing justice. Meanwhile, the barnyard animals who have sipped the moonshine covering the ground outside the house are on a drunken spree!

"Fire Fighters" was the second *Our Gang* comedy made. Hal Roach ran a preview for it at Ocean Park way back in early May, then designated it the second *Our Gang* release (following "One Terrible Day") in October. "Fire Fighters" is also the earliest entry available for reappraisal.

Director Bob McGowan used to be a fireman, so the story here is a natural. The trouble is "Fire Fighters" has only one reel's worth of material, and the padding shows in its two-reel form. The film begins with a totally irrelevant animal-comedy sequence, one presaging Hal Roach's *The Dippy Doo Dads* series. *Our Gang*'s original concept was kids and pets, and while the animals are funny, the material is not well integrated. When this sequence concludes, there is another introductory segment on Ernie Morrison (called Booker T. Bacon in these very early shorts instead of the more familiar moniker, Sunshine Sammy). It takes a good long time before we even approach some semblance of plot with the introduction of the fireman idea.

Here, too, there is a general laziness about the film, setting up the possibilities for gags but never realizing them. The three fire-trucks are ingeniously put together, and the firehouse itself has many imaginative touches, including a unique alarm system that crashes a hammer against a frying pan and tugs on Chief Jackie's leg in order to alert the crew that it's time to go to work.

But the gag-filled chase or fire scenes one would expect never occur, and instead the filmmakers utilize what would become a standard gag, showing supposedly drunken animals in slow motion. This sequence is particularly well done, but still a letdown. As with the opening section of the short, the focus is on animals and not on the gang.

There is also very little of what could be called characterization in this short. Only two kids stand out from the crowd—Ernie Morrison and Jackie Condon, the half-pint of the crew who gets to be chief only because he owns the fireman's hat. His scenes are delightful, including one funny gag where the whole fire company must stand and wait because the chief needs help getting his pants on correctly.

All in all, "Fire Fighters" is a weak endeavor; had it been tightened to one reel, its best moments telescoped, the effect could have been different. But at this stage of the game McGowan and company had not yet found all the young personalities whose personal charm would carry even flimsy material along. This particular group of kids needed strong support from gags and situations, and "Fire Fighters" couldn't deliver the goods.

Hal Roach's innovative idea of funny-looking animals doing funny things foreshadowed the revolutionary success of animal cartoon characters (Mickey Mouse, Daffy Duck, Woody Woodpecker, etc.) during the 1930s and 1940s, but the notion suffers in that it detracts from what would become the primary focus of the series—the kids.

Still, it's unfair to dismiss the animal sequences, which today might be easily taken for granted, in view of the continuing onslaught of animated cartoons. In 1922, the funny animals concept was new, and the short scored highly with critics and audiences. *Moving Picture World* said, "Here is a picture that should prove a wonderful delight for the children and which because of its clean clever comedy should highly amuse grown-ups as well. It is a two reeler distributed by Pathé and is the second of the *Our Gang* comedies introducing a clever cast of children headed by Sunshine Sammy and also a lot of laugh-getting animals. The opening scenes showing a duck, all dressed up, with walking cane, derby hat and everything, strutting around and trying to make love to a hen, is a scream." *Exhibitor's Herald* reported, " 'Fire Fighters' is one of the best comedies we have ever seen. Appeals to

The Goat Alley Fire Department in a scene from the second *Our Gang* comedy made, "Fire Fighters." On the far left is Jackie Condon, then Peggy Cartwright. Monty O'Grady is pictured third from right, and Ernie Morrison is on the extreme right.

all and has a wonderful variety of talent. The pet duck is a knockout." And *Motion Picture News* observed that " 'Fire Fighters' is so spontaneous the high jinks seem to evolve from the youngsters themselves. . . . There is real humor here. There is also a place on every exhibitor's program for such wholesome ideas."

3 · YOUNG SHERLOCKS

Two Reels · Produced by Hal Roach · Supervised by Charles Parrott (Charley Chase) · Directed by Robert F. McGowan and Tom McNamara · Titles by H. M. Walker · Story by Hal E. Roach · Released on November 26, 1922, by Pathé Exchange · The original Our Gang: Ernie "Sunshine Sammy" Morrison, Jackie Condon, Peggy Cartwright, Mickey Daniels, Jackie Davis, Allen "Farina" Hoskins, Mary Kornman, and Dinah the Mule · Officer, Charles Stevenson; Motorist, Dick Gilbert; Baker, George Rowe; Mary Jane's rich father, Charley Young; Her mother, Dot Farley; Bank extra, Ernie Morrison, Sr.; Giovanna de Bullochi, criminal, Charles Stevenson; Kidnapper's Gang, Dick Gilbert, William Gillespie, Roy Brooks, Ed Brandenberg, Wallace Howe

Jackie and Ernie are aspiring detectives—when Jackie isn't earning money selling newspapers, and Ernie isn't busy finding food and drink for his baby "sister" Farina. When a newspaper sale brings Jackie a big tip, the little trio drops everything and heads for the bakery. Ernie loses their coin down a sidewalk grating, however, and as he peers into the grill to retrieve their money, gas fumes float to the surface, and Ernie finds himself becoming entranced, soon loping in slow motion across the street. He falls through a cellar door and into the basement meet-

ing place of the Mystic J.J.J.'s (the Jesse James Juniors). The juvenile society informs him that only the brave and fearless enter here—and what has *he* ever done? Still dazed, Ernie declares, "You is gazin' at the bravest guy that ever traveled on feet—listen . . ." Then, in flashback, we see how an escaped criminal kidnaps a rich young girl and holds her for $10,000 ransom. With the aid of their brainy mule Dinah, Ernie and Jackie find the hide-out; Ernie stays and tries to subdue the villains, clumsily working a rifle he's latched onto, while Jackie

A Young Sherlock himself, Mickey Daniels. The beautiful thing about Mickey was his wide range of wonderfully natural expressions that always revealed exactly what he was thinking. It made Mickey easy to identify with and "pull" for.

received, he tells his avid audience, he bought a whole city and named it Freetown, a kiddie paradise where everything is free and plentiful. Farina has it best of all, with a direct line to several cows for milk whenever he wants it.

This early entry has its rambling moments at the outset, but pretty soon gets down to business with a definite idea that provides the catalyst for a string of action sight gags. The story line turns out to be the film's major strength, as opposed to the improvised and often meandering nature of other early *Our Gangs*.

While the plot elements do not flow as smoothly as they might, the idea of a basic chase premise with the two youngsters taking after the adult kidnappers is a perfect framework for gag ideas. Riding horseback to the hideout, Jackie keeps slipping towards the rear of the horse, always managing to pull back in the nick of time. Using a similar methodology (you can't see the wires but you know they're being pulled) every time Ernie fires his rifle, the force of the blast knocks him back several feet—the first time around conveniently kayoing a thug approahing from behind.

In the climactic battle with the villains, Ernie finds himself on the wrong end of a group of flying swords. This and all the other gags in the film are masterfully executed, so they seem completely real—or at least, real enough to make the gag work, as in a succession of shots where Dinah mule-kicks most of the kidnap gang in the derriere.

Another rather spectacular sight gag finishes off the film, with tiny Farina obtaining some helium balloons in Freetown and quickly floating into the heavens.

The Freetown sequence is all too brief, considering the possibilities of such an idea. This is perfect *Our Gang* fodder, making a dreamlike idea come true in perfect detail. A sidewalk beanery called the Digg Inn exemplifies the spirit of Freetown, with hundreds of kids, dressed in the finest clothes, frolicking along Main Street and greeting their Mayor (Ernie) and Chief of Police (Jackie), along with the Mayor's charge, Farina.

stumbles onto the worried parents who are on their way to pay the ransom money. The young sleuths and their mule make short order of the crooks and save the damsel in distress. The girl's father gratefully rewards them by turning over the money he was going to pay the kidnappers. At this point, Ernie finishes spinning his yarn, and we cut back to the clubhouse, where still in a stupor, he's got a topper for his own tall tale. With the money he

4 · ONE TERRIBLE DAY

Two Reels · Produced by Hal Roach · Supervised by Charles Parrott (Charley Chase) · Directed by Robert F. McGowan and Tom McNamara · Titles by H. M. Walker and Tom McNamara · Story by Hal E. Roach and Tom McNamara · Released on September 10, 1922, by Pathé Exchange · The original Our Gang: Jack Davis, Mickey Daniels, Ernie "Booker T." Morrison, Jackie Condon, Allen "Farina" Hoskins, Peggy Cartwright, and Winston Doty · James, the chauffeur, William Gillespie; Butler, Charles Stevenson; Officer, Wallace Howe; Carlene Culpepper, Helen Gilmore; Alvira, Clara Guiol; Cook, Ed Brandenberg; Secretary, Lincoln Stedman

In order to maintain her position as a leader of local society, Mrs. Pennington Van Renssalaer concocts the novel idea of sponsoring a children's outing. The high-strung matron has no idea of what's in store for her as her small group of five invitees gradually swells and makes the automobile trip a nightmare for her, her pet monkey, her secretary, and her chauffeur. When the group finally arrives at her country estate, the youngsters become even rowdier, using a decorative fountain as a swimming hole, taunting the local farm animals, and generally making a wreck of the place, as well as its owner. When day is done, everyone clambers back in the open-topped car for

the return trip; just as they get started, the front tire goes flat, for the second time that day. This is too much for Mrs. Van Renssalaer, who faints dead away.

The genesis of "One Terrible Day" is a theme that recurred many times throughout *Our Gang's* history, with the mischievous Rascals being turned loose in plush surroundings. This early attempt doesn't begin to explore the real possibilities of the situation, but it has its moments.

What weakens the film after a promising start is extended and seemingly improvised scenes of the kids playing with various animals out in the country. Scenes featuring chickens, geese, cows, and such, are predictable and largely unfunny; but back to back as in this film, they undermine the overall comedy at hand.

Furthermore, plumpish Mrs. Van Renssalaer and her prissy secretary are perfect targets for slapstick indignities, yet they escape nearly scot-free. Later *Our Gang* films, like "Washee Ironee" and "Honkey Donkey," knew there were big laughs to be had at the expense of haughty society matrons who clashed with the gang.

One of the best aspects of this short is the chauffeur's mounting frustration as the steadily increasing number of frisky passengers makes the joy-ride a pain in the neck. When the car gets a flat tire on the way to the country, the kids interfere with the poor driver so much that he nearly goes crazy. One funny sequence has the nerve-ridden man putting the kids out of his way by lifting them aside. As he does, one by one, the kids run around and get back in line, turning the procedure into a game as the driver keeps moving kids aside, never reaching the end of his task!

In this portion of the film one sees a very direct line to another more famous Hal Roach comedy made at the end of the decade, Laurel & Hardy's *Perfect Day,* and there's even a title card during the closing moments of "One Terrible Day" that announces "The end of a perfect day."

Shot in early July, "One Terrible Day" was the fourth comedy made starring Hal Roach's Rascals, but the first to be released. No one remembers why. Throughout the summer, all four comedies had been extensively previewed around Los Angeles (to smash critical reaction), and for whatever reasons, "One Terrible Day" was designated to see general release before any of the others.

In retrospect, it was a perfect choice, for "One Terrible Day" served to introduce the aspects of *Our Gang* that perhaps more than any other solidified its success: poor but fun-loving kids getting the better of adults in general, and stuck-up society types in particular. This was something that both kids and grownups could identify with and enjoy (after all, how many movie-going adults in America had mansions and chauffeurs?), and it helped to make the film, and the series, an instant hit.

From the outset, the series was advertised dually as "two-part [reel] comedies" featuring "Our Gang" and/or "Hal Roach's Rascals." Though it had been an open secret around Hollywood for many months, the series' first official announcement came in August with Hal Roach's commitment to deliver at least thirteen "kids-and-pets" comedies to Pathé for distribution, beginning in September.

According to press releases, the series was designed to play up the "spontaneous pranks of unspoiled boyhood" and its natural alliance with "petted animal comrades," meaning the zoo that had come into being around Hal Roach Studios in the form of assorted mules, hens, ponies, bulldogs, goats, geese, and monkeys.

Our Gang's trade-paper advertisement put it this way: "Take a dozen or so typical kids, ragged and neat, clean and dirty, just as they come from street and yard. Add one very particular society woman, anxious for publicity. Mix in a few animals who don't give a darn for anybody. Stir in a flossy motor car and a fine mansion. Then you have the first 'Our Gang' comedy, a veritable classic of comicality. Big laughs from little kids."

Some critical response to *Our Gang's* debut: *The New York Post* said, "The best thing on the Rivoli Theater program this week is the funniest comedy shown for some time, 'One Terrible Day,' bringing forth screams of laughter." The *New York Herald* reported, "The outstanding hit of the bill at the Rivoli is a rollicking Pathé comedy, 'One Terrible Day.'" The *New York World* remarked it was "extremely funny."

The trade press was equally enthusiastic. *Moving Picture World* observed, "A distinctive comedy of the broad type, 'One Terrible Day' will excite the risibilities from the time the first scene is flashed upon the screen. If the succeeding releases may be judged from the first, they will go big. 'Sunshine Sammy' is among the actors." The *Exhibitor's Trade Review* commented, 'One Terrible Day' is funny beyond question. . . . Fun in chunks." While *Exhibitor's Herald* had this to say, "Let Hal Roach maintain the same high quality of production in the remainder of the *Our Gang* series as in 'One Terrible Day,' and Pathé will have added another short subject worthy of the widest circulation. They have a freshness and originality that captivates."

5 · A QUIET STREET

Two Reels · Produced by Hal Roach · Directed by Robert F. McGowan and Tom McNamara · Titles by H. M. Walker · Story by Hal E. Roach · Released on December 31, 1922, by Pathé Exchange · Our Gang: Mickey Daniels, Ernie "Booker T." Morrison, Jack Davis, Peggy Cartwright, Jackie Condon, and Dinah the Mule · "Red Mike," Jack Hill; Officers, Charles Stevenson, Dick Gilbert; Man who gets mugged, Dick Gilbert; Police dispatcher, William Gillespie; New kid's mother, Clara Guiol; Ernie's father, Ernie Morrison, Sr.

There's great excitement in the neighborhood; a new kid's just moved in. His father is a policeman, but the scruffy street urchins of Our Gang are going to beat him up anyway. While that's going on, a police dragnet is closing in on Red Mike, notorious bad guy. When the gang is nearly captured administering a licking to the new kid on the block, they mistakenly think the police patrols are after *them,* and scatter. Wherever they turn, a squad of police walks out of nowhere towards them, but the kids finally take refuge where Red Mike is coincidentally also hiding out. The gang's dog takes offense when ill-tempered Red Mike begins shooting at him, precipitating a fantastic chase that culminates in Red Mike's eventual apprehension, with the police department showing grateful thanks to the gang.

The frenetically paced "A Quiet Street" is anything

Across the curb, Jack Davis, Farina Hoskins, Jackie Condon, Mickey Daniels, Hal Roach and simian friend, Mary Kornman, Joe Cobb, and Sunshine Sammy Morrison. All cherubs they're not.

but quiet, and while not deserving hymns of praise, like lots of other early Pathés surfacing recently, the film *is* a rediscovered delight.

"A Quiet Street" takes place entirely out-of-doors, with its many lively chase sequences through the busy streets of Los Angeles offering us a variety of glimpses at life-style trappings that have long since perished from the scene: horse-drawn milk wagons, picket fences, trolley cars, etc. One leg of the chase carries its participants over (presumably) the same huge flight of terraced stairs Laurel & Hardy would later use in *Hats Off* and *The Music Box*.

Wrapped around the chases are some few quiet moments and typical *Our Gang* material, with the Rascals using their ingenuity to solve boyhood problems and escape boyhood chores. The film's payoff gag illustrates the consequences of their ill-advised ingenuity, in this instance involving Ernie and the mule he tricked into beating a rug for him. It's ripped to shreds—which is how Ernie will be if his father can catch him.

Adding to the enjoyment are some first-rate sight gags and some amusingly written and wonderfully illustrated (even animated) titles.

Ferreting through old trade magazines and newspaper clippings, one stands in awe of the acclaim *Our Gang* received in the early 1920s. Reviewers combed their dictionaries for new adjectives to describe their delight with the series, and for once in the history of movies it would have been difficult to distinguish studio-prepared publicity from trade press and newspaper criticism. They *all* praised *Our Gang*. Theater owners across the country sent in their comments on the new series to various trade papers, and these too reflected nothing but grateful praise. Many exhibitors pointedly referred to the fact that *Our Gang* seemed to please both children and adults at the same time—no mean feat. One enterprising showman in Hudson, Wisconsin, reported, "Drawing more than any feature, these are the best two-reel comedies we know of. We raise the admission price every time we play one of them." Another theater manager in Los Angeles hailed "A Quiet Street" as "the funniest show-stopping short of the best comedy series on the market in recent years." Which is interesting (if perhaps debatable) because by 1923 Charlie Chaplin, Buster Keaton, and Harold Lloyd had all recently completed their legacies of silent short subjects.

Noteworthy too is that Pathé recognized the series' great impact in 1923 by selecting it along with the Mack Sennett and Ben Turpin comedies as the only short subjects with sufficient audience interest to warrant the production of coming-attractions trailers—an unusual practice indeed.

6 · SATURDAY MORNING

Two Reels · Produced by Hal Roach · Supervised by Charles Parrott (Charley Chase) · Directed by Robert F. McGowan and Tom McNamara · Titles by H. M. Walker · Story by Hal E. Roach · Released on December 3, 1922, by Pathé Exchange · Our Gang: Mickey Daniels, Ernie "Sorghum" Morrison, Allen "Maple" Hoskins, Jack "Waldemar" Davis, Jackie Condon, and Dinah the Mule · Waldemar's father, William Gillespie; Aunty Jackson, Ernie Morrison, Sr.; Maid, Katherine Grant; One of the parents, Richard Daniels

Saturday morning means different things to different kids. To wealthy Waldemar, it's another day of pampering by countless maids and butlers. To Mickey, it's a day of nagging from his mother for him to practice his bass violin. For Sorghum and little Maple, it's the day they deliver laundry from their mule-drawn wagon. All four kids eventually converge when they spot freewheeling Jackie fishing in the local river. Complaining that no one loves them at home, the four "big kids" decide to become pirates, with Maple tagging along. They build a Huck Finn-inspired raft, and when it crashes on shore, they set up camp and continue the masquerade. Meanwhile, Mickey's mother, Sorghum's Aunty Jackson, and Waldemar's valet are searching for the missing boys with the aid of several cops. They discover the gang on a river bank, but before they can get around to discipline, a bear the "pirates" were stalking comes out of the bushes to chase everyone off into the distance.

Made only a few months after Cecil B. DeMille's feature *Saturday Night* (but four years before Harry Langdon's *Saturday Afternoon*), "Saturday Morning" was being sold to exhibitors with catch lines like "If you had to pay per laugh, you'd pay feature prices for these comedies." But reviewers said as much, too, with the critic for *The New York Globe* reporting that " 'Saturday Morning' took all the picture honors at the Capitol," and *The New York Sun* calling the short "a hilarious outpouring of mirth."

"Saturday Morning" cleverly contrasts the different life styles of different kids in the gang. The longest episode features Mickey, who dreams of taking an ax and smashing his bass fiddle into smithereens. In order to catch some more shuteye and convince his mother that he's continuing to practice "Humoresque," he rigs up a contraption where his dog operates the bow by swinging on a rocking chair. Later, his bass meets a sorry fate when he throws it off a bridge for the other kids to catch below. So much for "Humoresque."

Sorghum (the odd name given to Ernie "Sunshine Sammy" Morrison in this film) takes care of the infant Maple in their all-purpose room (with a picture of Abraham Lincoln on the wall), treating her to a makeshift shower and a watermelon breakfast before setting out for the day's chores. As in many later silents, Maple (actually Farina, and actually a "him") provides comic punctuation for many scenes. While the gang sails down the river on their raft, Maple follows behind, sitting in Mickey's floating bass fiddle.

One of the closing gags involving Sunshine Sammy and Farina was repeated nine years later by Farina and Stymie in the talkie "Fly My Kite"; it's one of those

Pouty-faced Jackie Condon, always disheveled, always getting into trouble, but somehow quiet just long enough to sit for this portrait. He's the only Rascal who would appear in every one of the sixty-six Pathé shorts.

curiously tasteless gags that produces an instant laugh and simultaneous embarrassment at finding it funny. The gang is wading waist-deep in the river when someone asks what happened to Maple. "She's right here," says Sorghum, apparently standing alone, "I got hold of her hand."

Another sight gag comes near the end of the film when two cops dive off the bridge into the river below to capture the kids . . . and land smack on their heads in water six inches deep. This elaborate gag is quite funny, but totally wasted as a throwaway here. It would have better served a Snub Pollard comedy being shot elsewhere on the Roach lot that week.

Built on an elastic theme, "Saturday Morning" highlights several staple elements that ran through the series: the beleaguered kids think their parents don't really love them; the one rich kid in the group is smothered by overattention and eagerly trades places with Ernie, driving the laundry wagon; and most importantly, all kids find a common meeting ground in playing make-believe together.

7 · THE BIG SHOW

Two Reels · Produced by Hal Roach · Directed by Robert F. McGowan · Photographed by Len Powers · Titles by H. M. Walker · Story by Hal E. Roach · Released on February 25, 1923, by Pathé Exchange · Our Gang: Jackie Davis, Mickey Daniels, Jackie Condon, Billy Lord, Allen "Farina" Hoskins, Ernie "Booker T." Morrison, Joe Cobb, Mary Kornman, Andy Samuels, and Dinah the Mule · Security guard, Dick Gilbert; DeRues, Lincoln Stedman

"Small boys pass up only one thing at a county fair—the box office," reads the opening title, as the gang does its best to sneak a free look at the local festivities. Jackie Condon tries to join in the fun, but the gang pushes him away, telling him he's too young. Meanwhile, the cruel head of DeRues Trained Animal Show ("Two jumps ahead of the last feed bill") sends his browbeaten young

helper to exercise two of the horses. He meets the gang and wows them with his animals' talents, so together they devise their own county fair, collecting cigar coupons and marbles for admission. There are animal exhibits, a makeshift merry-go-round propelled by a dog chasing a cat inside a suspended cage, a shooting gallery, and a telescope. But the featured event is the gang's special free movie show, actually a live performance on stage inside a movielike frame. Various kids imitate Charlie Chaplin, Harold Lloyd, Douglas Fairbanks, William S. Hart, and even Uncle Tom in a rousing movie that has the kiddie audience cheering. The show over, all seems well until Jackie creeps onto the fairground, and, seeking revenge, sets all the animals in the menagerie loose. To add to the chaos, angry DeRues shows up and whips his young apprentice. One of the enraged dogs takes after DeRues, who painfully exits amidst the shower of rocks and bricks as the gang cheers its canine defender into the horizon.

A typical, and enjoyable entry with a characteristic format: a real county fair is shown during the opening scenes, giving Our Gang an inspiration to devise their own carnival. Paraphrasing one of H. M. Walker's titles, Edison had nothing on these kids. They even imitate the security guard who chased them away from their peepholes, appointing little Farina a "speshal kop," who administers his duty with great enthusiasm, and an ever-active billy club. The workings of the fair are based on stalwart *Our Gang* gimmicks—dog-chasing-cat propulsion, for instance. The animals in the menagerie are cleverly conceived as well: the "lion" is a dog with a fur collar, the "camel" a goat with two derbies tied to his back. Familiar as these gags may seem, they drew laughs in *Our Gang* comedies throughout the 1920s, and never fail to bring audiences to life today.

There is a nice indication that the game of pretend extends to the kiddie audience as well, when a girl examining the caged "ferocious wild man" makes a face that scares *him* off. Her smile of satisfaction indicates that, at least for the moment, she had the desire to burst the bubble of make-believe when it strained her credibility a bit too far.

The movie show is the most ingenious portion of the film, with the kids doing quite creditable imitations of various film stars. The enactments are hinged to a "plot" that wanders aimlessly; basically the movie heroes are contesting over the favors of the gang's heroine, Mary Kornman. To maintain the illusion that this is really a movie, one of the kids periodically bursts into view holding dialogue and narrative title-cards, and hard-working Joe Cobb acts as projectionist, hand-cranking his makeshift machine.

The Chaplin takeoff is quite deft. The Little Tramp's mannerisms are duplicated with notable comic effect: the splay feet, twirling cane, jaunty walk, even his one-legged off-balance skidding turn around corners. And to confirm the mime, a famous Chaplin gag is reprised from *Shoulder Arms,* in which the Tramp disguises himself as a walking tree!

Playing his part to the hilt, Mickey Daniels makes for a bungling but most appealing Doug Fairbanks, mimicking the swashbuckling artistry of Fairbanks's *The Three Musketeers.* Tumbling down hills, tripping over fences and his own feet, Mickey trundles about with sword held high, all to such rousing titles as "All for one, and two by four!" Most effective is Mickey's pointed parody of Fairbanks's gleaming smile and special wink, which he flashes toward the camera at every possible opportunity.

The Harold Lloyd caricature is made most convincing by drawing on gags and plot elements from the popular Lloyd feature *Grandma's Boy,* made by Hal Roach the year before. While the spoof is amusing on its own, its full effect could only be appreciated by those familiar with the original Lloyd film. Curiously enough, although there is a marvelous poster on view for Chaplin's *The Idle Class* at the gang's movie theater, no similar plug was made for *Grandma's Boy,* which was, after all, a Roach film.

Bookings for "The Big Show" exceeded those for all previous *Our Gang* comedies. Trade press reaction is typified by this excerpt from Lillian Gale's review for *Moving Picture World:* "Every child will find delight in this amusing two-reeler, which may serve, also, as a panacea for the grouch, the tired businessman, and the busy housewife. There are laughs for every member of the family, from baby to grandpa, laughs that are not forced by overdone, unnatural things, but sparkling, fast and merry comedy. 'The Big Show' is the kind of two-reeler that may safely be advertised as an 'added attraction.'" And *The New York Times* raved, " 'The Big Show' is wonderful, great fun, a half hour's delight for young and old."

8 · THE COBBLER

Two Reels · Produced by Hal Roach · Directed by Tom McNamara · Titles by H. M. Walker · Story by Hal E. Roach · Released on February 18, 1923, by Pathé Exchange · Our Gang: Mickey Daniels, Jack Davis, Ernie "Sunshine Sammy" Morrison, Jackie Condon, Allen "Farina" Hoskins, Mary Kornman, and Pete the Pup · The cobbler, Mr. Tuttle, Richard Daniels; Shoe repair customer, Clara Guiol; Postman, Charley Young; Mary's nursemaid, Katherine Grant; Dandy Dick, Dick Gilbert

The gang likes to hang around Mr. Tuttle's shoe-repair shop; he doesn't seem to mind their mischief too much. But they get an unexpected eyeful this particular morning when a limousine drives up and a nursemaid steps out with her young charge, little Mary, who needs to have a shoe repaired. The young boys compete for her attention, and as she leaves she deposits a small vase of flowers on the counter for her male admirers. But the best is yet to come: the morning mail brings news of Mr. Tuttle's long-awaited back pension. He and the gang set out to celebrate with a picnic, but Mr. Tuttle's temperamental car moves in fits and starts before coming to a stop in the middle of an open field. While some of the kids try to repair the auto, others scamper in and around a hayloft, interfering with a shady character who's hiding out there. Pete eventually chases the villain away, enabling the kids to return to their disabled car, where they find Farina fresh from a visit to the nearby watermelon patch. It seems as if his stomach has swelled in size, but it's really a spare melon that he's tucked under his shirt. They grab the delicacy and dig in for a happy finale to their would-be picnic.

"The Cobbler" is a disjointed short with no plot, but it does move, and that seems to have been the main idea behind this two-reeler. The sequence with rich-girl Mary is just a throwaway, the kids' relationship with the cobbler is never explored, and even the "celebration" resulting from his back-pension payment is rather half-baked. The title character disappears from the film two-thirds of the way through, leaving Farina to grab what's left of the spotlight with his never-ending antics. That the film works at all is a tribute to the kids' personalities and the wisdom of nonstop movement.

Ernie "Sunshine Sammy" Morrison, star of his own short-lived Roach series before *Our Gang* began.

9 · THE CHAMPEEN

Two Reels · Produced by Hal Roach · Directed by Robert F. McGowan · Photographed by Len Powers · Titles by H. M. Walker · Story by Hal Roach · Released on January 28, 1923, by Pathé Exchange · Our Gang: Mickey Daniels, Ernie "Sunshine Sammy" Morrison, Jackie "Tuffy" Davis, Mary Kornman, Jackie Condon, Allen "Farina" Hoskins, Johnny Downs, Billy Lord, Andy Samuels, and Joe Cobb · Officer, Charles Stevenson; Smoker, Wallace Howe

A cop catches Sammy stealing apples from the local store, and warns him that he'll go to jail and have to work on a rock pile unless he pays the grocery man one dollar. Sammy notices that a fight promoter carries a thick wad of money with him, and decides that this is how he can earn his dollar. Taking advantage of a feud between Mickey and Jackie over the affections of Mary, he schedules a championship bout between "Knockout Mickey, the Irish Giant" and "Terribul Jackie, the Bone Crusher." The two opponents put on a good exhibition, but the proceedings change course when Mary ditches both of them for a well-dressed newcomer (obviously a sissy—no one in the gang is well-dressed on a weekday). The intruder offers to buy her a soda. When she tries to leave with him, the two combatants suddenly unite and trounce the newcomer till he turns tail, sniffling and sobbing. After his licking, the sissy meets up with the cop, and together they return to the scene of the brawl, causing the gang, and a frenzied Sammy who fears another brush with the law, to scatter down the road.

A delightful outing, "The Champeen" benefits from a story line that flows naturally from beginning to end, but more so from a string of ingenious gag and cinematic ideas. The two-reeler is brimming with inventive touches that add a special luster to this early classic.

After a rousing chase through the neighborhood back yards, the cop catches Sammy and paints a vivid picture of his inevitable punishment; the picture dissolves to a prison yard where Sammy, bound and chained, is cracking rocks under the watchful eyes of three gun-toting guards. Later, when it seems he'll never get the required dollar, Sammy pictures himself in prison stripes. He has to get that dollar!

In training for the fight, Mickey sees his opponent's face in the punching bag, and lets go a special wallop. During the actual fight, when he is knocked onto the canvas, Mickey blinks his eyes and sees fireworks. One kid cheats Sammy out of his admission charge by viewing the fight from a hole in the gymnasium roof, and the camera shows us his overhead view for a brief sequence. These devices help make "The Champeen" consistently bright and entertaining.

The characters are nicely drawn, as well. Mickey, especially, seems to relish the opportunity to be a street fighter. He is liable to battle anyone over anything, daring an opponent with a ritual of rolling up his ragged sleeves, spitting on the ground, and tugging at his cap. His pugilistic prowess vanishes with the first blow, however, and Jackie Davis polishes him off with regularity.

A title card introduces Mary as "the innocent cause of many a black eye." In this film, Jackie Condon plays her younger brother, and it is Jackie Davis's bullying that prompts Mary to sic Mickey on him. Our first view of Condon shows him gleefully driving a real car, his trusty

Pugs Mickey and Jack, *left*, go at it while "crooked" promoter Sunshine Sammy shrinks in apprehension.

dog by his side; then the camera slowly pulls back to reveal that it is merely the body of an automobile being transported on a flat-bed truck.

Sammy does his best to play up the role of fight promoter, appointing tiny Farina as special guard to watch out for rough stuff and make sure each customer pays his admission fee (one sack or one bottle). When Mickey seems to be backing off, Sammy tells Mick that his opponent has agreed to lie down in the second round. This done, he tells Jackie the same thing about Mickey. When the two boxers find out they've been double-crossed later on, they both sock Sammy on the kisser.

Near the end of the fight we get a glimpse of a chubby but pint-sized fellow at ringside—it's a very young Joe Cobb, making what amounts to a cameo appearance in the short.

"The Champeen" is a winner in every respect—one of the best silent comedies in the *Our Gang* series.

10 · BOYS TO BOARD

Two Reels · Produced by Hal Roach · Directed by Tom McNamara · Titles by H. M. Walker and Tom McNamara · Story by Hal E. Roach and Tom McNamara · Released on April 8, 1923, by Pathé Exchange · Our Gang: Ernie "Sunshine Sammy" Morrison, Jack Davis, Mickey Daniels, Jackie Condon, Andy Samuels, Allen "Farina" Hoskins, Joe Cobb, and Dinah the Mule · Mother Malone, Helen Gilmore; Pop Malone, Richard Daniels; Bootlegger, Charles Stevenson; Sheriff, Wallace Howe; Household helper, Clara Guiol

Mother Malone's School promises fresh air, recreation, and other niceties, but all the young boarders get is skimpy meals and crabby scoldings from hawk-faced Mother Malone. Kindly Pop Malone acts as schoolteacher and general buffer between mother and the kids; he'd much rather read Wild West pulp fiction than do any serious teaching, but he hasn't got the gumption to answer back his shrewish wife. When the kids plan an escape late one night, Pop joins them, but the fugitives soon find themselves inside the elaborately booby-trapped house of a bootlegger, who ties up the kids as they slide through trap doors into his hide-out. Pop coasts down the chute and lands right on top of the criminal, subduing him just in time for the sheriff to arrive and collar his man. He proclaims Pop a hero, and so in keeping with his new stature, Pop returns home with the children and demands that his wife institute a new policy: good meals, and a strict understanding that *he's* the boss. Amazingly enough, it works, and in a festive dinner table close-up, Jackie Condon winks at the camera to let us know they'll all eat happily ever after.

"Boys to Board" is based on fairly obvious material, with no belly-laughs to be had, but an amiable outing nonetheless. As often happens in these early Pathés, the casual *Our Gang* by-play is generally more rewarding than gags or action anyhow.

Mother Malone's school is similar to later boarding school/prisons depicted in *Our Gang* films, with an appropriately harsh old woman in charge, and a docile husband or caretaker to offset her meanness. Yet the emotions inherent in this setup are not particularly well realized in "Boys to Board," as if the filmmakers were acknowledging that the unoriginal situation speaks for itself and doesn't require elaboration.

Flawed technically as well, the "nighttime" escape is shot in broad daylight, and it's difficult to see how, even with dark filters, it could convince anyone otherwise.

"Boys to Board" was Tom McNamara's second solo directing effort, and Bob McGowan's deft touch was missed. No one seems to remember much about McNamara, who made varied contributions to the earliest *Our Gang* comedies. Like many Roach staffers, he was a newspaper cartoonist* and was hired to help create this series on the strength of his syndicated comic strip *Us Boys*. Besides writing and directing, McNamara drew caricatures and illustrations for the card titles of the films; they often constituted individual comic panels in themselves.

---

* George Herriman, creator of Krazy Kat, was never on the studio payroll but spent much of his free time there; he introduced Roach to many of his colleagues. Harry Langdon was a cartoonist, and he continued his syndicated comic strip even while working for Roach during the 1930s. Gus Meins, *Our Gang*'s most sophisticated director, moved into films from newspaper comic strips. As a nod to Herriman, Krazy Kat stuffed dolls were often used on-screen in *Our Gang* shorts, "Fire Fighters" being the earliest instance.

Unfortunately, in the 1960s a television syndicator cut up many of the Pathé silent shorts, renaming them *The Mischief Makers* (another company dubbed its series *Those Lovable Scallawags, with Their Gangs*). Besides scrambling the continuity of these shorts, sometimes combining two or more together, they deleted all card titles, obliterating McNamara's delightful art titles, not to mention H. M. Walker's witty prose. Sadly, these prints are often the only versions that survive of certain Pathé titles.

McNamara and William Beaudine left the Hal Roach studio at the same time; later they collaborated on two notable Mary Pickford films, *Little Annie Rooney* and *Sparrows*, both full of kids, including two *Our Gang* grads, Monty O'Grady and Eugene Jackson.

11 · A PLEASANT JOURNEY

Two Reels · Produced by Hal Roach · Directed by Robert F. McGowan · Titles by H. M. Walker and Tom McNamara · Story by Hal E. Roach · Released on March 18, 1923, by Pathé Exchange · Our Gang: Ernie Morrison, Mickey Daniels, Jack Davis, Jackie Condon, Allen "Farina" Hoskins, Joe Cobb, Mary Kornman, Winston Doty, and Monty O'Grady · Tilford, the bachelor, William Gillespie; Inebriated novelties salesman, Roy Brooks; Railroad train passengers, George K. French, Jules Mendel, Richard Daniels; Porter, Ernie Morrison, Sr.; Passenger with gout, Wallace Howe; Welfare physician, Wallace Howe; Cabdriver, Sam Lufkin; Conductors, Charley Young, Charles Stevenson; Officers, Charles Stevenson, Charles A. Bachman; Pedestrian who bumps into Farina, Bob McGowan; Chief of Police, Lincoln Stedman

A title tells us that every day, in every way, the gang keeps the fat policeman busier and busier. Mickey's engaged in a freckle-counting contest; somehow, he loses. Elsewhere, Ernie and Farina are in the shoeshine business, brushing up a little extra trade by painting unsuspecting pedestrians' shoes white when they're not looking. Enterprising Farina surreptitiously whitewashes the inspection-ready shoes of a lineup of police officers standing at rigid attention. Ernie wins the job of cleaning and repolishing everybody's shoes, but Farina gives the game away when he comes to administer a second coating! The police force gives chase, but the wily pair manages to elude the law at the railway station. There they rejoin the rest of the gang, and meet up with some runaway boys from San Francisco who have been intercepted by welfare authorities, and ticketed back home—for a licking. Before they board a return train, however, the fugitive youngsters talk the gang into switching places with them, telling the gang that they'd planned to stop off in Mexico on the way and shoot some wild Indians. Ernie's skeptical, arguing that there aren't any more wild Indians— "They're all in the movies." But the inducement works, and the twin mobs of street urchins change places. The welfare lady who is supposed to escort them back, though, sprains her ankle, and imposes on her boyfriend to take over. He hates children ("They're so sticky"), and for this poor man, the long railway trek becomes one rolling world of hurt, with the rascals wreaking havoc on everyone in the unprotected coach, and causing special commotion when they get their hands on a novelty salesman's kit full of samples for magic tricks, practical jokes,

A rare moment of repose in "A Pleasant Journey." The slumbering Rascals are Jack Davis, Mary Kornman, Joe Cobb, Ernie Morrison, Jackie Condon, and Mickey Daniels. That's Farina front and center.

and fireworks! The hapless escort's admonitions prove to be insufficient, and the kids all but destroy the pullman car and contents. Arriving in San Francisco, some attendants in white coats collect the frazzled guardian in a van bound for the funny farm. Not knowing what to do with the young mischief makers, they load the kids into the truck too, lock the door and drive away.

A relatively unknown *Our Gang* picture, "A Pleasant Journey" is a fine comedy, rich in both visual and situational gags, full of amusing titles, but still carried largely by the ingratiating personalities of the kids, perhaps never again in the entire series so collectively appealing as in these early Pathés.

Against a backdrop of trolley cars, Tin Lizzies, and a bright young city full of real people doing real things, the first half of "A Pleasant Journey" spotlights the fresh outdoors comedy so typical of Hal Roach's early work, distinguishing it from much of the crude knockabout Mack Sennett was still doing (with pancake-faced "people" so heavily made-up they looked like they belonged in a circus).

Hal Roach though, like Sennett, was guilty of casting actors in multiple parts, underestimating the sophistication of his audience. Wallace Howe and Charles Stevenson (one of Harold Lloyd's favorite character performers) both have two parts in "A Pleasant Journey."

The early shoeshine routine is quite funny, and stands out for its clever direction and photography. It's material that was repeated successfully in "Every Man for Himself," and again in "General Spanky" thirteen years later.

One of the paintbrush encounters has a curious improvised look to it. A trucking shot follows Farina down the sidewalk as he paints the town white. A pedestrian walks into view, pauses, and stoops over to say something; as he does, tiny Farina slaps white paint all over his shoes, causing the pedestrian to do a little dodge-the-dabs dance, and then point Farina in the opposite direction before continuing on his way. Predating even Hitchcock cameos, the man on the street is played by director Bob McGowan, who walks away from the camera with a slight limp caused by an injury sustained while he was a young fire fighter back in Denver.

The film's coach-demolition second half is a blueprint for "Choo-Choo!" of nine years later, though sound added little to the same material.

As for contemporary critical response, an August issue of *Motion Picture News* ran this unusual item: "James W. Dean, the well-known reviewer whose opinions are widely syndicated, in his current list of the 'Ten Best Pictures' places the Hal Roach *Our Gang* two-reel comedy 'A Pleasant Journey' well towards the top of his list of selections. He explains his choice as follows: ' "A Pleasant Journey" is only two reels long. I place it in my list because it is the most entertaining comedy I ever saw.' " Quite an eloquent fellow, this well-known widely syndicated James W. Dean—but he sure knows his comedies!

12 · GIANTS VS. YANKS

Two Reels · Produced by Hal Roach · Directed by Robert F. McGowan · Titles by H. M. Walker · Story by Hal E. Roach · Released on May 13, 1923, by Pathé Exchange · Our Gang: Mickey Daniels, Allen "Farina" Hoskins, Jackie Condon, Ernie "Sunshine Sammy" Morrison, Jackie Davis, Andy Samuels, Joe "Squeaky" Cobb, and Dinah the Mule · Mr. Reddy, William Gillespie; Mrs. Reddy, Clara Guiol; Physician, Wallace Howe; Ernie Morrison, Sr., Himself; Woodcutter, Dick Gilbert; Mickey's mother, Fanny Kelly

Our Gang's Sultan of Swat, Mickey Daniels, takes a turn in the batting cage in this scene from "Giants vs. Yanks." What a slugger!

The gang's baseball game is held up as Mickey, Jackie, and Sunshine Sammy connive to get out of doing chores at home. Just as the game gets underway, however, the owner of the empty lot that serves as the playing field chases the kids away. They retreat to a nearby house where a wealthy, child-loving couple has been babysitting with Jackie's little sister Imogene. At the same time, a doctor is upstairs examining the couple's baby; he discovers that she has a contagious fever, and places the house under quarantine for one week. That means that the gang can't leave the premises, and it doesn't take long for the husband and wife to learn to despise children. The kids make a wreck of the elegant home, as well as wearing the adults' nerves to a frazzle, before the doctor returns to announce that he was wrong—the fever *isn't* contagious after all. With this, the Rascals are quickly ejected from the house, only to be greeted by a crowd of angry parents who are looking to punish the kids who ran away from their chores.

Since the 1921, 1922 and 1923 World Series all pitted Casey Stengel and the New York Giants against Babe Ruth and the New York Yankees, the title "Giants vs. Yanks" would imply a two-reeler centered around baseball, but after a few minutes of engaging footage of the ball game (with little Farina an incongruous choice as umpire), the story takes an unexpected turn into the sub-plot of a quarantined household. Unfortunately, it is a turn for the worse.

The idea of the gang systematically destroying a large house, starting in the living room and working their way up, is good for a few laughs, but doesn't provide sufficient impetus for fully half of a film's running time. The adults' reactions become increasingly repetitive, and the premise increasingly slim.

The gang's sand-lot baseball game is fun, but the most ingenious thing in the whole film is the washday routine at Mickey's house. A stationary bicycle propels a revolving clothesline where Mickey's mother hangs out the wash; Mickey must sit on the bike and pedal continuously. This looks like the kind of device that the gang would concoct, and it's rare to see an adult sponsoring such an idea in an *Our Gang* film. Of course, Mickey gets one up on his mother by rigging up a companion piece of machinery so a goat can operate the bike by running on a treadmill, leaving him free to head for the ball park.

Playing baseball should have been the core of this film; instead, it is used as an almost incidental sidelight. The result is a slightly disappointing two-reeler.

13 · BACK STAGE

Two Reels · Produced by Hal Roach · Directed by Robert F. McGowan · Titles by H. M. Walker · Story by Hal E. Roach · Released on June 3, 1923, by Pathé Exchange · Our Gang: Mickey Daniels, Allen "Farina" Hoskins, Joe Cobb, Ernie Morrison, Jackie Condon, Jack Davis, Andy Samuels, and Dinah the Mule · Startled pedestrian, Bob McGowan; Head of the touring show, William Gillespie; Manager of the theater, Wallace Howe; Outside workers, Charley Young, Dick Gilbert; Audience extra, Jack Hill; Man in box-seat disrupted by Farina, James W. Cobb; Man in audience trying to slap spider, Richard Daniels

"The gang: On their good behavior all week—reaction has started to set in." While operating a donkey-powered double-decker bus of their own contrivance, the gang chances to meet the head of a second-rate vaudeville troupe, who engages them to assist in his performance that night at a local theater. Without half trying, the rascals manage to wreck the entire show, and have a grand time in the bargain.

"Back Stage" is a mildly amusing two-reeler whose delightful highlight scenes have nothing to do with the crux of the story. The film's opening segment deals with the gang's double-decker touring bus, one of the most awe-inspiring contraptions in a long line of remarkable *Our Gang* machinery. Built on the foundation of an old car—old even then—the bus is propelled by a mule situated somewhere inside the huge surrounding frame. Ernie rides atop the animal, signalling by telephone to motorman Farina, who pulls a string to open the feed box that activates the donkey. When Ernie wants to sound his "horn," he pulls another string that brushes a feather duster against the animal, resulting in a loud "hee-haw!"

In one case Ernie sounds the horn to alert a pedestrian trying to cross the street in their path. Startled at first, the pedestrian—who happens to be director Bob McGowan—reacts with a broad smile as he steps back to observe this crazy contraption that trundles by.

For engineer Ernie to put the makeshift bus into reverse, another strap pulls the mule's tail, indicating the need to walk backward for a while. Requiring fuel, Ernie stops at a local gas station and pours water into a tiny trough near Dinah's feed box.

Best of all, when Ernie phones Farina but gets no response (since Farina has dozed off inside his sealed compartment) he walks to the front of the bus and turns a crank, which jiggles the floor of Farina's cubicle and wakes him up.

"Megaphone" Mickey is the silver-tongued announcer and tour guide, who with a pair of binoculars (Coke bottles glued together) looks for interesting sights to point out to passengers. Grabbing his funnel, he reports, "On my left . . . the schoolhouse. I hope it burns."

Disarming in their simplicity, all these scenes benefit tremendously from having been shot out of doors in the bright, sunny streets of Culver City, rich in 1920s detail and an ideal backdrop for comedy filmmakers.

After this fascinating opening segment, the heart of the film, shot indoors back on the lot and dealing with the evening show, seems anticlimactic and not half as interesting. The cheapskate producer who hired the gang puts on a virtual one-man show. As The Great Bicepto, his strongman routine is undermined when tiny Farina wanders on stage behind him and plays with the phony "weights." The crowd loves it. For the magic act, Jackie and Mickey hide under each of two tables, helping to make objects—usually the wrong ones—suddenly appear from below, but revealing their hands in the process!

Finally, they give "drinking water" to several horses for the animal-act finale, but use a basin that Farina has just filled with liquor. The expected results: a group of drunken horses cavorting across stage in slow motion!

Some of the kids have been sitting in the balcony for the show, and they make their presence felt as well, dropping popcorn and part of their insect collection onto the crowd below. The spectators (which include the real-life fathers of Mickey Daniels and Joe Cobb) are so busy itching and contending with bugs that they pay no attention to the crummy tap-dancers who open the show.

"Back Stage" has few belly-laughs, although Farina's capers and upstaging, and William Gillespie's performance as the tacky vaudevillian are quite funny. The film as a whole is certainly above average and up to the high standard set in the series' early years.

With the release of "Back Stage," *Moving Picture World* carried this headlined story: "Pathé has announced that in view of the steadily increasing demand for *Our Gang* comedies, it has renewed its contract with Hal

Roach, which will insure a supply of these two-reel kid and animal laughmakers, one every four weeks, for this and next season.

"According to reports from Pathé, no screen comedies irrespective of length have so quickly and firmly established themselves with exhibitors and patrons. Although the first one was released less than a year ago, the natural and hilarious doings of this bunch of juvenile actors and their animal co-conspirators have helped fatten box office records throughout the country.

"In the latest comedy, Mickey Daniels with his tremendous crop of freckles and additional juvenile deviltry assisted by the full strength of Our Gang appear in 'Back Stage,' which as a special attraction heads the Pathé program of eight subjects for June 3."

14 · DOGS OF WAR

Two Reels · Produced by Hal Roach · Directed by Robert F. McGowan · Titles by H. M. Walker · Story by Hal E. Roach · Released on July 1, 1923, by Pathé Exchange · Our Gang: Mickey Daniels, Mary Kornman, Jack Davis, Ernie "Sunshine Sammy" Morrison, Jackie Condon, Joe Cobb, Allen "Farina" Hoskins, Monty O'Grady, and Andy Samuels · Studio guard, Dick Gilbert; Officer, Jack Hill; The director of *Should Husbands Work?*, William Gillespie; The film's assistant director, Ernie Morrison, Sr.; The film's photographer, Charley Young; Actor, "Dan," Charles Stevenson; Actress, mother of "Little Clarice," Clara Guiol; Other actors around the lot, Roy Brooks, Wallace Howe, Leo White; The director of *Why Worry?*, Fred Newmeyer; The film's photographer, Walter Lundin; Harold Lloyd, Himself; Jobyna Ralston, Herself; Truck driver, Bob Davis; Casting director, Lincoln Stedman

Near the site of West Coast Studios, the Great Battle of Kelly's Tomato Patch is raging, fought by five commanding officers and one private. Our Gang's principal munitions are some dated vegetables. Jack and Mickey lead their troops in trench fighting and then retreat to battle each other over the attentions of Red Cross nurse Mary Kornman at the field hospital behind the lines. Farina's fascination with skunks ("Here kittie—kittie") disrupts the warfare, however, and as the opposing sides confer over who's winning, Mary is called away to do some acting at the nearby movie studio. She's to earn five dollars, which prompts the gang to reverse their strategy and redirect their invasion at the motion picture studio. They present themselves at the main office of West Coast Studios, but the casting director takes one look and throws them out. Meanwhile, Farina has wandered into the studio, so the other kids have to sneak past a studio guard to get inside and retrieve him. A long and winding chase ensues, through indoor sets and exterior streets, in and out of prop doors, across a treadmill, until the gang ends up on a set where a scene is being filmed for a weepy adult drama. When the leading man seems to be "strangling" little Mary, they run to her rescue, upsetting the director and hastening a call for lunch. When the set is deserted, the gang decides to make movies themselves, using the same set, the same camera, and giving their interpretation of the same scene they just witnessed. Returning from lunch, the director has the exposed film developed, and watches in horror in a screening room as his scene is suddenly double-exposed with the mocking of the gang, and their subsequent filmed tomfoolery. The agonized filmmaker chases after them, with the studio guard joining in and finally prodding them past the studio gate for a final exit.

A two-part subject, "Dogs of War" abounds in fast-action slapstick and first-rate sight gags, and for its behind-the-scenes look at Hal Roach Studios manages to remain one of *Our Gang*'s most interesting silent comedies.

Scene from the early Hal Roach feature *Dr. Jack*, with Harold Lloyd and the Gang's Mickey Daniels. Lloyd returns the favor with a cameo appearance in *Our Gang*'s "Dogs of War."

The opening battlefield scenes are totally unrelated to what follows, and far less amusing—though Mickey and Mary's underplayed romanticizing is certainly a highlight. Actually, the only link between the film's two disparate episodes is the skunk, with Farina having flushed out the animal during the kiddie warfare. Later, as the film's sure-fire punch line, when the gang is finally being chased out of the studio, Farina goes roaming again and latches onto the skunk for a second time, sending everyone scurrying toward the horizon.

Despite a clumsy segue from battlefield to studio back lot, "Dogs of War" is fun all the way, following a foolproof premise: turn Our Gang loose in a movie studio. The proliferation of various standing sets provides a perfect setting for an elaborate chase sequence, as the guard at the studio gate takes after our heroes.

On the shooting stage, we see a production unit at work on a typical film in progress, *Should Husbands Work?*, a neat satire on the sappy love triangles so popular then with audiences. The leading players, clinching or grimacing in close-up, read such title cards as "No! No! Not that, Dan. Think of our little Clarice!" and "Why did you follow me from Tasmania?"

Naturally, the gang sees right through this mush, and gives it a good send-off when they make their film a few minutes later. "Kiss me, my boob," says Jackie in an approximation of the dialogue he heard the actors mouth.

After lunch, the real cast and crew adjourn to the projection room to view the rushes of their morning's work. As each scene unfolds, the schmaltzy director begins reaching over the seats to congratulate his hammy actors, but then everyone recoils in shock when the gang intrudes on their super-feature.

Double-exposed over the real-life thespians, the pint-sized actors provide some funny juxtapositions. The following scenes of the gang alone are blurry, warped; they expand and contract, and are covered with patterned splotches (effects which, ironically enough, come out rather intriguingly, not unlike a great many experimental films of later years! Perhaps Our Gang had more going for themselves as filmmakers than anyone at the time could have guessed).

While spoofing dramatic films of the day, "Dogs of War" also gives us some invaluable glimpses of the Hal Roach studio property, its two big stages, the administration building, the writer's bungalow, the casting office, the studio gate, even the parking lot, and the standing city streets, office and store fronts, interior hallways, dressing rooms, and mechanical devices like the rotating scenery-backed treadmill—all recognizable in so many Hal Roach shorts and feature films down through the years. One house front is the same one used in virtually every episode of Roach's *Topper* television series during the 1950s.

Best of all, we get a look at Hal Roach's reigning star, Harold Lloyd, in a "preview" of his next feature. Lloyd and his co-star, Jobyna Ralston, are in costume and filming a scene for *Why Worry?* which wasn't released for another two months after "Dogs of War." Unperturbed by the kids running through his set, Harold Lloyd takes a moment off from shooting to help his real-life brother-in-law Jack Davis and the rest of the gang elude the studio cop by disguising them as Mexican peasants with huge sombreros for a scene in his film, sending them on their way with a smile after the guard passes by.

15 · LODGE NIGHT

Two Reels · Produced by Hal Roach · Directed by Robert F. McGowan · Titles by H. M. Walker · Story by Hal E. Roach · Released on July 29, 1923, by Pathé Exchange · Our Gang: Joe Cobb, Jack Davis, Ernie Morrison, Mickey Daniels, Mary Kornman, Allen "Farina" Hoskins, Jackie Condon, Winston Doty, Mary Murphy, Richard Billings, and Andy Samuels · Jackie and Mickey's dad, Richard Daniels; Prof. T. Jefferson Culpepper, Ernie Morrison, Sr.; Auto thieves, Lincoln Stedman, Charles Stevenson

When a new boy (Joe Cobb) comes to town, the Gang immediately recruits him for their fraternal order, the Cluck Cluck Klams. During the initiation ceremony in the loft of Jones's barn, some notorious auto thieves break in below and use the barn as a temporary hide-out. When they drive off, Jackie and Farina are in the back seat, so the rest of the gang sets out to rescue their pals, finding themselves behind the wheel of a runaway car! A crash finally brings the two parties together, and a policeman in pursuit nabs the crooks and presents the gang with a $500 reward for their capture.

"Lodge Night" is an average entry from the early-silent period, distinguished (or perhaps "hampered" is the word) by a subplot involving a black lecturer that provides some uncomfortable moments today. Professor T. Jefferson Culpepper, supposedly offering a philosophy lecture, speaks only in double-talk (sprinkled with a Negro dialect), much to the bewilderment of his black audience. In shaking his fist to make a point, the professor is reminded of a more pleasant pastime, and within minutes the lecture has been transformed into an evening of dice-rolls and gambling.

While the gang footage is innocuous enough, here too there is the disconcerting reminder of the Ku Klux Klan, as the kids wear white sheets and pay homage to their "Xsalted Ruler." Ernie and Farina are members, erasing any doubt that this is just a club, but even a spoof of the KKK is enough to put a damper on the film's humorous intent. Of Farina one title explains, "[He] Doesn't know what the lodge is about—but is in favor of anything."

As this is a male organization, Mary and the girls are hardly seen in the course of the two-reeler, although the schoolroom segment introduces Mary as "not yet a vamp—but give her time." When Joe comes to class for the first time, Mickey refers to him as "the balloon," but the girls seem to find him cute, clustering around and prompting the gang to label him "a sheek," a nod to the passionate Valentino craze engulfing the nation.

Title writer H. M. Walker is in good form for most of the proceedings, heralding the schoolmarm with the title: "The teacher admits that she is 20—it's her second time around." Typical Hal Roach studio inside-joking gets a brief workout when a "wanted" poster for the auto thieves is signed by a bogus sheriff named Big "Bob" McGowan.

Despite its occasional moments of humor, and a pretty

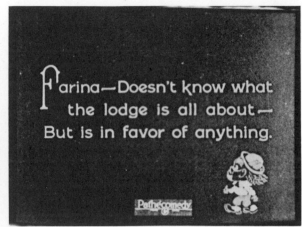

Descriptive title cards from *Lodge Night*.

good chase sequence for a finale, "Lodge Night" suffers today from the problems of trying to watch an innocent 1923 offering under the pressures and values of the 1970s.

While the black-lecture sequence represents an unfortunate lapse into stereotype humor, it's worth noting that this scene is played out by adults and not by the gang. These kids are always ahead of their grown-up counterparts in terms of tolerance and understanding. Although they call their group the Cluck Cluck Klams, they have no idea what the organization they "emulate" really stands for, since they have two black youngsters as members!

Of further interest is the fact that contemporary reviewers felt no discomfort whatever about the subject matter of "Lodge Night." *Moving Picture World* reported, "More delightful entertainment from *Our Gang* is forthcoming in this. Hal Roach seems to have unlimited resources for making these comedies different from the ordinary run and this one is another decided success. 'Inishiashun' night at the Cluck Cluck Klams headquarters is treated in a fashion that will amuse everybody. A few thrills are brought in at the close. A very good number."

16 · FAST COMPANY

Two Reels · Produced by Hal Roach · Directed by Robert F. McGowan · Titles by H. M. Walker · Story by Hal E. Roach · Released on November 16, 1924, by Pathé Exchange* · Our Gang (presumed): Mickey Daniels, Joe Cobb, Allen "Farina" Hoskins, Jackie Condon, Jack Davis, and Ernie "Sunshine Sammy" Morrison

This film was not available for viewing. It was described and critiqued in *Motion Picture News* by T. C. Kennedy:

"The Hal Roach Rascals cut up some exceptionally amusing hi-jinks in this two-reel offering from Pathé. By way of variety, and it is most welcome, they get away from ambitions to run railroads or organize profitable shoe-shining establishments and deliver themselves wholeheartedly to the business of having a glorious adventure at a fashionable hotel, where Mickey gets himself installed as a guest in a handsome and finely appointed suite. The titles are in Mr. Walker's best style and their humor is matched letter for letter by the incidents which Robert McGowan—that most consistent of leading comedy directors—has contrived for his temperamental troupe.

"'Fast Company' shows the gang starting out on a swimming expedition. Mickey, however, meets a poor little rich boy on his way to a hotel, where he is to await his mother. They swap hats and jackets and Mickey moves into the hotel. The rest of the gang also gain entrance, bringing a goat which vies with a monkey to produce bang-up laughs when the kids themselves are not doing that very thing. Farina has some corking scenes at a hose nozzle at which he seeks a most desired drink. And Mickey does some fine work in his dressed-up masquerade as the rich boy. This is a particularly good *Our Gang* and its success is therefore assured."

The film generated even greater enthusiasm from an unnamed reviewer in *Exhibitor's Daily Review:* "Any of Hal Roach's *Our Gang* comedies is well worth a trip to the local theater alone, and 'Fast Company' is just as hilarious as any of its predecessors, if not more so. To anyone who knows anything about kids these comedies are bound to ring true, for the types are perfect examples of the old adage 'boys will be boys.' The fun is fast and furious and if you are one of those laugh-proof folks, go to see 'Fast Company' and you'll split your sides."

* Inexplicably, this film was held out of release for the better part of a year.

17 · STAGE FRIGHT

Two Reels · Produced by Hal Roach · Directed by Robert F. McGowan · Titles by H. M. Walker · Story by Hal E. Roach · Released on October (?), 1923, by Pathé Exchange · Our Gang: Joe Cobb, Ernie "Sunshine Sammy" Morrison, Jack Davis, Mickey Daniels, Mary Kornman, Jackie Condon, Allen "Farina" Hoskins, Jannie Hoskins, and Andy Samuels · Dalmar El Faro, William Gillespie; Mickey Daniels's father, Richard Daniels; Mickey's mother, Helen Gilmore; Tony the fruit vendor, Charles Stevenson; Miss Fawn Ocheltree, Clara Guiol; Audience, Jack Hill, Roy Brooks, Sam Lufkin

Prince Dalmar El Faro isn't exactly a crook, we're told, but honesty annoys him. He comes to this sucker-filled community with a tale of starving Trombonians and claims that they "do not ask for charity—all they want is money." To raise this money, local authoress Fawn Ocheltree writes an original playlet to be performed by the kids, taking place in ancient Rome. The kids want no part of it, but they are egged on by their doting mothers standing in the wings. As it's past their bedtime, they have little patience for the lines they don't understand, and to liven up the proceedings, Jackie ties some firecrackers to the tail of a cow posing as a bull in the final act. The crackers ignite and really give the people a good show—until a whole box of fireworks is set ablaze, sending everyone scurrying for the hills, and bringing the performance to a welcome end.

"Stage Fright" is a fast-moving, completely entertaining comedy based on typical, tried-and-true *Our Gang* precepts. Naturally, it's the adults of the town who fall for the double-talking Prince El Faro, and not the kids, who see right through him, especially when he has the nerve to present Sammy and Farina (in costume) as two supposed cannibals!

Still, the townspeople seem to prefer laughing at the ineptitude of Miss Ochletree's production than trying to take it seriously. In one scene where Mary appears as a slave girl pleading for mercy from Emperor Nero (Joe), Mickey just can't help giggling, setting off a chain reaction with the whole audience joining in. Similarly, when some of the kids onstage begin to yawn (it's past their bedtime) the people down front pick up the cue and start to stretch sleepily.

Nothing goes right in this play. Two guards announce, "Behold th' conkerin' hero comes," but Jackie makes his entrance from the opposite side of the set. Miss Ochletree stage-whispers, "Wrong side!" so both the guards *and* Jackie dutifully switch positions, and are left right back where they started. Later, a clever stage effect using a wall to give the impression that Mickey is on horseback, followed by rows of bayoneted troops, is exposed when the wall topples forward to reveal that Mickey and a horse-facade are riding piggyback atop an adult stagehand, and the bayonetted troops are really kids carrying pitchforks!

Interrupting the proceedings from time to time is Little Irma, whose mother is determined that she should recite in this play. At various intervals, Irma is shooed onstage, where she declares, "Twinkle, twinkle . . ." only to be shooed right off again by the angry Miss Ocheltree. After the fireworks episode, when the audience has left and

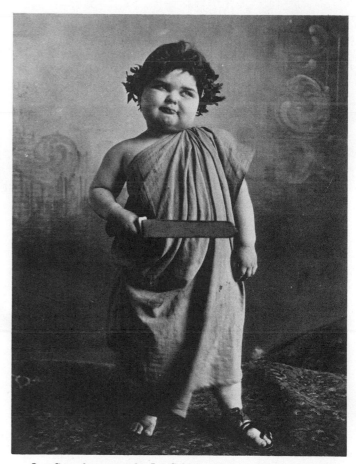

Our Gang heavyweight Joe Cobb, as Nero in "Stage Fright."

only the actors and their mothers remain, Little Irma finally gets her chance to recite the poem all the way through. "Twinkle, twin——" she begins, stopping to call, "Ma-MAH! I forget!"

Roger Ferri in *Motion Picture News* thought "Stage Fright" "worth its weight in gold, for it is one long laugh from beginning to end, without a single letup."

The film *is* beautifully paced, which is more than could be said for its slow-moving early-talkie remake, "Shivering Shakespeare," which substituted pie-throwing for the firecrackers that disrupt this production. It would have been nice, however, to see Miss Ocheltree receive her comeuppance with a well-aimed custard pie.

18 · JULY DAYS

Two Reels · Produced by Hal Roach · Directed by Robert F. McGowan · Titles by H. M. Walker · Story by Hal E. Roach · Released on August 26, 1923, by Pathé Exchange · Our Gang: Mickey Daniels, Mary Kornman, Jack Davis, Joe Cobb, Ernie Morrison, Jackie "Duster-Head" Condon, Allen "Farina" Hoskins, and Dinah the Mule · "Dad" Anderson, Richard Daniels; Businessman, William Gillespie

Mary and Mickey in a scene from "July Days." When a boy falls in love, no sacrifice is too great—Mickey would willingly have combed his hair, a title tells us.

"Dad" Anderson, the village blacksmith, loves the boys of the gang and builds them sail-propelled scooters to play with. But the scooters take a back seat when a pretty young girl moves into the neighborhood. Mickey takes a shine to Mary and tries his best to court her, first imitating his big sister's beau by pulling up in his "car" with candy and flowers, and then taking a cue from Mary herself when she yearns for a knight in shining armor to come and serenade her. Mickey does his best, with Dad helping him assemble a suit of armor from pots and pans, but when the other fellows make fun of him, Mickey reverts to type and sheds his outerwear to engage in a fist fight. He retains his neighborhood supremacy, and Dad is rewarded for his kindness by getting word that a manufacturer wants to pay him a lot of money for his scooters!

"July Days" is a typical *Our Gang* outing, with some marvelous characterization, sticking close to by-now familiar territory with delightful results.

Given these ingredients, one can imagine how the film comes together: The ragamuffin, ever-scrapping gang . . . a friendly father-figure . . . neat-looking scooters sailing down the sedate Culver City residential streets . . . little Farina wandering where he shouldn't . . . pretty Mary moving into the neighborhood . . . rivalry between Mickey and Jack, the bully ("wants to grow up and be tough—he has a wonderful start"), and of course, a happy ending for all.

This formula works so well, and the participants are so engaging to watch, it hardly matters that "July Days" is really an assembly-line product quite similar to the films that preceded it, and those that would follow.

"July Days" remains enjoyable today, and one can readily understand how its gentle humor contributed to the young series' enormous popularity in the 1920s.

19 · SUNDAY CALM

Two Reels · Produced by Hal Roach · Directed by Robert F. McGowan · Titles by H. M. Walker · Story by Hal E. Roach · Released on December 16, 1923, by Pathé Exchange · Our Gang: Ernie Morrison, Jackie Condon, Jack Davis, Joe Cobb, Mickey Daniels, and Allen "Farina" Hoskins · Mr. Tucker, Richard Daniels; Mrs. Tucker, Clara Guiol; Mrs. McTeeter, Helen Gilmore

On a quiet Sunday, two neighboring families plan a picnic outing in the country. Hitching horsepower to their wagon, everybody piles on for the trek. Unknown to his parents, Jackie has arranged for Ernie and Farina to accompany the picnickers, by tying their little wagon to the big one as the trip begins. That's not all he's done. He has loosened the lug bolt on the front wheel, and when the wheel works its way off the axle, all the grownups get out to repair it. When the wheel's been replaced, the Little Rascals race off with the horse and rig, leaving the angry parents to hoof it for themselves. Then somewhere in nowhere, the gang selects a tranquil spot for their picnic, where uninvited guests include frogs, field mice, turtles, baby bruins, and pigs. After a swim in a nearby stream, the gang's parents finally arrive on the scene, greeting their little darlings with affection. As the dust settles, everyone prepares at last to dig into their picnic lunch . . . just in time for a cloudburst.

Somewhat of a misfire, "Sunday Calm" is one of those lukewarm comedies where its assets are offset by such

Every day was a school day, whether the *Our Gang* unit was shooting or not. Here, a Roach stage serves as schoolroom, and teacher Fern Carter puts the Gang through their paces while director Bob McGowan looks on. Reading and writing, *from left to right*, are Jackie Condon, Joe Cobb, Jack Davis, Mary Kornman, and Mickey Daniels. Where's Farina? He was yet a little too young for lessons.

things as sub-par locations, lame pacing, and a meandering story thread.

Anecdotes concerning Hal Roach in story conference are legion. (This is not about to be one of them.) In retirement, Harold Lloyd said of his one-time boss, "Hal had an excellent mind, a very fertile mind for thinking of comedy ideas. He had a mind that drew ideas seemingly out of thin air. He was not always the one to develop these ideas, but he had the good sense to encourage initiative in others once he had started them on their way."

On the subject of story creation, Hal Roach explains that most often he'd conceive an idea, call in his battery of *Our Gang* writers (which during the coming year included Frank Capra and Leo McCarey), and develop along with them the basic story line and attendant gags he had in mind. "Always I would have the Gang writers work up the *kind* of a story and the particular angle of comedy I wanted to do that time," Mr. Roach explains. Whichever writers showed the best grasp of the project were then assigned the task of polishing the "treatment" (generally just a page or two of notes explicating key notions and gags), as Roach himself obviously hadn't the time to personally supervise everything that was happening at the studio. "All right, that's the idea, boys," Mr.

Roach would say in leaving with a wink. "Now it's in your lap, go ahead with it from there, know what I mean?"

"Sunday Calm" appears to be an instance where they didn't know what he meant. Small boys innocent of any good intentions that set out to disrupt a quiet family picnic was the basic idea, and it's a premise rich in potential, but like the picnic itself, it never quite works out as planned.

The film's most pleasing moments, unfold at the outset, with the gang (and Mickey Daniels's real-life father) leisurely reading through the Sunday newspaper comic strips on the front stoop. Beyond this point, however, inspiration flags, and "Sunday Calm" tramples aimlessly through its two reels much the same way the countryside fauna later track through the picnic spread.

The Our Gangers are roguishly appealing as always, but their talented antics just aren't enough to bind up mediocre material and a loosely connected series of gags.

Hal Roach's picnic premise was resurrected five years later in another story conference, however, at a time we're *certain* Leo McCarey was listening, and the upshot was Laurel & Hardy's delightful and infinitely better *Perfect Day*.

20 · NO NOISE

Two Reels · Produced by Hal Roach · Directed by Robert F. McGowan · Titles by H. M. Walker · Story by Hal E. Roach · Released on September 23, 1923, by Pathé Exchange · Our Gang: Mickey Daniels, Jack Davis, Ernie "Sunshine Sammy" Morrison, Mary Kornman, Joe Cobb, Jackie Condon, Allen "Farina" Hoskins, Andy Samuels, Lewis De Vore, and Dinah the Mule · Mickey's nurse, Beth Darlington; Other nurses, Clara Guiol, Helen Gilmore; Officer, Charles Bachman; Physicians, Charley Young, Charles Stevenson, Lincoln Stedman

Daniel may have had his troubles in the lions' den, a title tells us, but Mickey figures he's up against something worse—a nurse wrestling to feed him castor oil. Having

his tonsils removed wasn't so bad, but Mickey reasons a dose of castor oil calls for an anaesthetic. Meanwhile, the rest of Our Gang is practicing football; there's a big game

Farina seems to be saying, "Operate? On who, me? Oh no you don't!" *Left to right,* the "No Noise" surgical team consists of Jackie Condon, Ernie Morrison, Mickey Daniels, Jack Davis (who really became a physician), Mary Kornman, and Joe Cobb.

coming up with the Goose Alley Juniors. Mickey's the team captain. The squad imagines they can play without him, "but we're sure gonna miss him when it comes to fightin'." Mary strolls by on her way to the hospital, announcing she's bringing some candy and fireworks down to Mickey. The gridiron behemoths forsake practice to come along. During their "visit," the gang sweeps through the hospital like a plague, engulfing the institution in a seige of mayhem—practicing football in Mickey's room, gobbling up his ice cream, racing around the halls on a gurney, taking X rays, ruining medical instruments, spilling chemicals, and sampling the laughing gas—until at last they're all bounced out on their ears. The kids want to get back inside though, and stay as long as the ice cream lasts, so they persuade some youngsters on their way in to swap vaccination orders. But the hospital staff catches on and sets out to teach these rascals a lesson, giving a faulty prognosis for each patient's "illness." Sunshine Sammy is told he has hay fever, and a meal of baled hay is prescribed as the antidote. The gang is scared stiff. An extended chase through the hospital ensues, and

when everyone is finally rounded up, it's time once again . . . for Mickey's castor oil.

A breezy recital of precision-timed gags, sometimes delivered at breakneck speed, "No Noise" is quite appealing. Hal Roach's stylistic shift toward concentrating on character and situation was already beginning to pay big dividends, and when combined with as many rapid-fire visual gags as there are here, the result is a fresh, funny comedy.

As often happens, Mickey Daniels steals the film. He has the knack of being able to mirror furious and utter disgust at his various misfortunes—taking castor oil being one of them. In that suffering facial pantomime, Mickey can register the kind of look that makes us so happy that the apparent problems are Mickey's and not our own that we *have* to laugh.

An early scene has Mickey switching his breakfast pancake syrup with castor oil while the nurse isn't looking, an artifice that backfires somewhat as it did when Dickie Moore tried the same thing in "Free Wheeling" a decade later.

Farina has his difficulties, too, eating nails, needles, and bits of tin and wire, as revealed by an X ray of his stomach. Before the gang can operate, however, laughing gas and chloroform send Farina gliding through the halls in a slow motion state of bliss. Sunshine Sammy grabs a pair of electrodes, then accidentally flips the power switch, and as the frightened kids link arms they form a vibrating human chain. Only when tipsy Farina joins hands with the rest is he shocked back to reality from his daze.

Not the least of the film's delights is Sunshine Sammy's lengthy encounter with a demonstration skeleton (which has a seemingly motorized jaw) during the film's wrap-up chase footage.

In another pleasant Roach device, the ivy-covered entrance to "Municipal Hospital" is actually the front of the Hal Roach studio.

21 · DERBY DAY

Two Reels · Produced by Hal Roach · Directed by Robert F. McGowan · Titles by H. M. Walker · Story by Hal E. Roach · Released on November (?), 1923, by Path'e Exchange · Our Gang: Ernie "Sunshine Sammy" Morrison, Allen "Farina" Hoskins, Mickey Daniels, Jack Davis, Joe Cobb, Mary Kornman, Jackie Condon, Billy Lord, Sing Joy, and Dinah the Mule · Mary's father, the horse owner, William Gillespie; Gate attendant, Wallace Howe; Trainer, Richard Daniels; Officer, Charles A. Bachman

The Gang has "established a big business on borrowed capital—someone loaned them fifty cents." They're doing OK selling hot dogs and lemonade across the street from the big race track, but when Mary, the daughter of a horse-owner, offers to let them in for free, they jump at the chance. The kids get such a thrill out of watching the race that they decide to mount their own Blue Grass Derby, with various members of the gang as jockeys, and

riding such noble steeds as a mule, cow, goat, and dog. All the accouterments of a great race are provided: a brass band, a betting window (with odds up to 1000-to-1), an official weigh-in (it had been rumored in betting circles that Joe was overweight), a newsreel camera (from "Path" News), a purse ($5 offered by Mary's father), and even a society box for the most elite spectators. When the race starts to fall apart, however, as the jockeys keep

"Derby Day": Lemonade merchants take time out from their thriving concession ("The Filling Station") to gawk at adorable Mary Kornman—or is it Dinah the Mule who's caught their attention?

tumbling off their thoroughbreds and the sulkies become temperamental, the competition turns into a foot race, with little Farina leading the way, having lasted the longest on his well-oiled tricycle and now coming down to the finish line just ahead of his pals. He wins by a neck, before the timely arrival of some cops sends the participants and spectators alike running off into the distance amid a cyclone-size cloud of dust and smoke.

Full of wonderful throwaway gags, witty titles, and whirlwind action, "Derby Day" runs sure and steady all the way. As might be expected, the format neatly divides into two sections: in the first the gang watches a real horse race, and in the second they try to copy the same idea in kiddie fashion.

The actual "adult" race is presented in such a way that no kid could resist its magnetic attraction. The sequence is masterfully edited with a variety of shots showing the race from the stands, from the sidelines, from closeups of the horses' hooves, and in particularly exciting trucking shots following the horses head-on as they gallop around the track.

The gang's own race is presented in the same manner . . . except that unlike the professional jockeys, Farina keeps overturning his tricycle, and Mickey falls out of his sulky every time it hits a bump, only to run ahead and hop right on again. As usual, the gang does its best to simulate reality, from "borrowing" shirtwaists and making their own leggings to create jockey uniforms, to announcing its derby as part of the "Southern Racing Association."

Although rules for admission are flexible (one guy gets in by donating a baseball, another offers a live turtle), no cheating is allowed, and the gang's dog is appointed as watchman, literally dragging away freeloaders by the seat of their pants.

As fun as "Derby Day" is to watch today, it really went over big in 1923, especially with *Motion Picture News* critic Roger Ferri, who exulted, "Hal Roach's company of clever juvenile comedians makes Zev,

Morich, and Man O'War look like 'also rans' in 'Derby Day,' about the funniest thing this mob has done for cinematographic entertainment. With the air hopped with turf gossip this travesty on horse racing comes at an opportune time. . . . For originality, 'Derby Day' can't be beat—you can't touch it. It's in a class by itself. . . . [A] description of the theme does the comedy no justice—it's got to be seen, and once your audience see it they won't forget it."

While similar enthusiasm was shown for many other 1920s *Our Gang* releases, "Derby Day" has stood the test of time better than many, and remains today a most enjoyable two-reeler.

Footnote: As fate would have it, in real life Mary Kornman grew up and married a man who owned a stable of horses.

22 · TIRE TROUBLE

Two Reels · Produced by Hal Roach · Directed by Robert F. McGowan · Titles by H. M. Walker · Story by Hal E. Roach · Released on January 13, 1924, by Path'e Exchange · Our Gang: Mickey Daniels, Joe Cobb, Jackie Condon, Ernie "Sunshine Sammy" Morrison, Mary Kornman, and Allen "Farina" Hoskins; Officer, Noah Young

This film was not available for viewing. It was very well received by the trade magazines when first shown in early 1924, however.

Tomham in *Motion Picture News* wrote, "Everybody loves Our Gang, and Hal Roach has presented us with another 'humdinger.' Here we have the inventive genius of the boys in bringing a flivver up to date according to

their own peculiar and weird conceptions. This vehicle enables the kids to inject a continuous line of comedy while carrying Farina's laundry to the rich Mr. McAllister. The wealthy gentleman is coerced by his wife, doctor and servants into believing that he is actually sick with the gout and whatnot. But when he sights the gang of kids he promptly goes along with them and treats the kids to the

various joy-devices of an up-to-date amusement park and many thrills are provided to embellish the comedy. This is a safe bet for any program.''

Film Daily headlined its review ''Excellent amusement'' and went on to say, ''Hal Roach's ingenuity never fails him when it comes to thinking up new stunts for his gang of rascals to romp through. This time it is a real automobile of their own construction. The trick appliances, self starters, etc., are marvelous in themselves, but when you see them in action they are bound to bring forth plenty of laughs. In addition to this intriguing feature there is a revel at an amusement park where the kids, from freckle-faced Mickey down to little Farina chute the chutes to their hearts' content. If you haven't been booking these most excellent comedies, don't fail to get them for 1924.''

Mischievous Jackie Condon grabs a fistful of Mary's hair. It always seemed they "combed" Jackie's hair with an eggbeater.

23 · BIG BUSINESS

Two Reels · Produced by Hal Roach · Directed by Robert F. McGowan · Titles by H. M. Walker · Story by Hal E. Roach · Released on February 10, 1924, by Pathé Exchange · Our Gang: Mickey Daniels, Mary Kornman, Joe Cobb, Ernie "Sunshine Sammy" Morrison, Jackie Condon, Allen "Farina" Hoskins, Andy Samuels, Jannie "Mango" Hoskins, and Sing Joy · Mickey's father, William Gillespie; Mickey's mother, Lyle Tayo; Office worker, Allen Cavan; Gardener, Charley Young

The Gang opens a deluxe barbershop, with Joe as head barber, gum-chewing Mary as cashier, Sammy as engineer for the mechanical works, Farina as shoeshine boy, Jackie as "superintendent of exploitation" (wearing a sandwich sign to advertise the shop), and Sing Joy running the cleaning and pressing concession. Little Mango sits on the sidelines, often the victim of stray shaving cream, while a manicurist practices her art with a pair of pinking shears. What these self-styled beauticians do to their customers is astounding: some young men are left completely bald, while another young man emerges looking like a Mohawk Indian. When they spot Mickey walking by in Little Lord Fauntleroy curls, they see their chance for greatness, and Mickey becomes the victim of a complete overhaul. Shaven and shorn, he is invited to join the gang, which he does with pleasure, even getting into a brawl with his first customer. When Mickey's parents come looking for him, his doting mother faints at the sight, but Dad is overjoyed that his son is no longer a sissy. Meanwhile, Farina's latest "customer," a skunk, sends the assembled crowd in all directions for a finale, as Farina and Jackie bury their clothes from the odorous encounter.

As always, the gang's enthusiasm for a make-believe world is shared by other kids. In addition to the elaborate gimmicks employed in the barbershop, the local youngsters get into the spirit of things, as when a "bearded" ditch-digger and a mustachioed banker patronize the establishment, one ten-year-old telling the other, "A man sure needs a shave after a hard day's work."

In addition to makeshift cutting implements, such as garden shears, there is the expected array of ingenious inventions in the shop: an overhead fan and barber pole propelled by a squirrel in a cage (when one of the customers catches the squirrel's attention and he stops running, engineer Sammy yells, "Keep away from that power plant!"), a hand-pumped vacuum hose for picking up clipped hair, etc. And when shoeshine boy Farina is confronted with a barefoot customer, he merely paints the fellow's feet to *look* like shoes. Meanwhile, Mary plays her part of the cashier to the hilt, Jackie explaining, "She's a widow," when Mickey is attracted by her flirtatious behavior.

In contrast to the scruffiness of the gang is poor-little-rich-boy Mickey, who wears a velvet coat and has two maids fussing over his long curls. He hates it, of course, and his father does too. Naturally, all it takes is one run-in with the gang to transform this Buster Brown into a regular guy. At the same time, the other neighborhood kids who go along with the barber routine bring on an angry crowd of unamused mothers.

As in some other *Our Gang* films from this period, Little Mango's role, as a somewhat manipulated observer, prompts a disconcerting reaction today, particularly in watching scenes of her casually chewing on a razor!

In most respects, ''Big Business'' is a typical and typically enjoyable entry from this era.

Long unavailable for screening and reevaluation, it was hoped that this film might be an antecedent for Laurel & Hardy's reciprocal destruction masterwork *Big Business*, made five years later. But alas, discounting Lyle Tayo's character role in each film, the only tie is simply that both sets of Hal Roach stars are trying to crash "the seething whirlpool of modern big business," with predictably spectacular failure!

However, a scrap of paper dated November, 1923, would seem to indicate that Stan Laurel sold Hal Roach the story for this *Our Gang* short. Stan's title was "A Close Shave," and his fee was ten dollars!

24 · THE BUCCANEERS

Two Reels · Produced by Hal Roach · Directed by Robert F. McGowan and Mark Haldane · Titles by H. M. Walker · Story by Hal E. Roach · Released on March 9, 1924, by Pathé Exchange · Our Gang: Mickey Daniels, Mary Kornman, Ernie "Sunshine Sammy" Morrison, Jackie Condon, Joe Cobb, Allen "Farina" Hoskins, Andy Samuels, and Pal the Dog · Officer, Dick Gilbert

"The Buccaneers": First Mate Andy Samuels, Captain Mickey Daniels, Mary Kornman, Seaman Jackie Condon (deep-water expeŕience: reluctant trips to the Saturday Night Bath Tub Club), peg-leg Joe Cobb, and Captain Whelan.

As would-be pirates, the gang enjoys only moderate success. Their full-fledged ship is christened with a bottle of ketchup, and immediately sinks to the bottom of the harbor. Then, after an episode with the cops involving some stolen watermelon, they hide out on a scow belonging to friendly old Captain Whalen, and inadvertently find themselves drifting out to sea. A nearby Navy ship sends a launch to pick up the gang, who consider the rescuers to be deadly foes and therefore engage them in a short but vigorous battle. Brought back to the ship, the kids are put to work by the Captain, determined to teach these "pirates" a lesson, while he contacts their parents on shore. But the gang is too slippery for the Navy; they manage to jump ship and return to their own vessel, where they remain until the police pull alongside in a motorboat carrying the kids' mothers and fathers. The parents are eager to punish their offspring, but the young seafarers are too busy leaning over the railing, feeling the ill effects of the bounding main!

Somehow, "The Buccaneers" misses the mark, although all the ingredients for an enjoyable pirate romp are here. The problem seems to be an overabundance of activity, and far too little footage devoted to the prime purpose of the short: showing the kids as pirates.

The heart of the film should have been a meaty sequence of the kids at sea, their misadventures in running a ship, and their attempts to enact their pirate fantasies. Instead, the film is fragmented in such a way that no individual sequence is truly fulfilled, from an early dispute over Mary's participation in the all-male pirate crew, to the climactic conflict with the Navy personnel. One can just picture a colorful, gag-filled chase in and around the battleship, with the kids ducking in and out of cabins and portholes—but such an obvious, sure-fire scene is not to be found in this film.

Instead, there are extraneous sequences, such as one where Joe goes to buy fish for his mother and systematically attracts every stray cat in the neighborhood by dropping the fish one by one while walking back home.

As to the battleship climax, one can plainly see the real-life sailors and officers standing in the background of several shots, watching Hal Roach's crew film their comedy on board. Apparently, in the excitement of obtaining permission to shoot the scenes on this ship, director McGowan forgot to make the setting seem realistic. Perhaps he was denied permission to make wider use of the ship's facilities for a chase sequence, but there is no excuse for allowing gawking sailors to appear on-camera, thereby destroying any feeling of authenticity for the story.

Depicting Our Gang as a group of kiddie pirates is an ideal premise for a comedy short; unfortunately, "The Buccaneers" doesn't live up to this idea.

Footnote: The same month that "The Buccaneers" was released to theaters the Our Gang troupe (excepting Mary Kornman) also appeared in a very entertaining Charley Chase comedy called "The Fraidy Cat," as an incorrigible band of rowdies who taunt cowardly Chase. This film is sometimes mistakenly identified as an *Our Gang* comedy.

25 · SEEIN' THINGS

Two Reels · Produced by Hal Roach · Directed by Robert F. McGowan · Photographed by Harry V. Gerstad · Edited by Thomas J. Crizer · Titles by H. M. Walker · Story by Hal E. Roach · Released on April 6, 1924, by Pathé Exchange · Our Gang: Allen "Farina" Hoskins, Ernie Morrison, Florence Morrison, Mickey Daniels, Andy Samuels, Jackie Condon, Joe Cobb, and Mary Kornman · Dancer in top hat and tails, Ernie Morrison Sr.; Officer, Silas D. Wilcox

Every time Farina eats meat, he has strange nightmares. After being chased away from the gang's "barbercooe," he comes upon a toppled picnic basket in the street with enough food to fill an army. Farina downs it all, from fried chicken to ice cream, and that night he has a dream to end all dreams, being chased by giant-size versions of the gang kids through city streets, diving underwater, then returning to shore where a dynamite blast sends him flying through the air, landing on the ledge of a tall building, which he climbs to the top as the gang pursues him, following this with a shimmy up a roof-top flagpole, and after that's been chopped down, toppling precariously on a plank many stories above the pavement. Finally the gang manages to saw off the board, and Farina plummets to the ground—or rather, his bed, for at this point he awakens from his dream and vows, "Ah eat mush from now on!"

Until its climactic nightmare sequence, "Seein' Things" is a pleasant but disjointed comedy. The final dream sequence makes up for everything.

Farina's dream strays into the surreal to produce an uncanny mixture of comedy and thrills. The technical effects range from crude to astounding. In an almost indescribable sequence, Farina glides around beneath the surface of the water as he's chased by a startlingly realistic swordfish. Though the TNT blast that sends him flying through the air is patently phony, the subsequent kids-as-giants routine is disturbingly authentic. Borrowing miniature sets from Roach's monkey comedy series *The Dippy Doo Dads,* the enraged gangsters tower above absolutely lifelike buildings as they stalk tiny Farina through the city streets in King Kong fashion—and the illusion is phenomenal.

Similarly, it's impossible to detect how the climactic building sequences were filmed, for it seems that just like Harold Lloyd in *Safety Last,* Farina is really climbing up a skyscraper wall, really perched atop a wobbling flagpole, and then really seated on a long plank suspended in midair over a bustling city street far, far below. Even if as in Lloyd's films, it *was* real, with a safety platform and cushion underneath, it is still amazing that this could have been accomplished with an infant like Farina—or even with Sunshine Sammy, who doubles for Farina in some of the "human spider" scenes.

One mystery looms above all others, however, and that is the continuing puzzle over Farina's gender. Several times in the film, the gang threatens to capture "her," yet when Farina is dreaming, he imitates a Dapper Dan seen earlier in the film, flirting with a pretty girl, and this is definitely a "him." This curious Julian Eltinge aspect of *Our Gang* repeated itself a decade later with Buckwheat. Both characters were boys, decidedly, but those upswept pigtails and ragamuffin outfits made it difficult to tell. Also, Farina and Buckwheat were each named for breakfast foods, which, as nine of ten doctors will testify, have no gender, thus further contributing to the mystery.

Actually, what happened was that the studio had been deluged with mail inquiring whether Farina was a boy or a girl—a puzzled movie-going audience really didn't know, and for some reason wanted to find out. So Hal Roach seized upon this widespread curiosity as a publicity gimmick, resulting in news releases that failed to disclose the lad's real name, Allen Clayton Hoskins, and avoided the matter of sex, instead describing Farina with incredible appellations such as "that chocolate-coated fun drop of Hal Roach's Rascals."

26 · COMMENCEMENT DAY

Two Reels · Produced by Hal Roach · Directed by Robert F. McGowan and Mark Haldane · Titles by H. M. Walker · Story by Hal E. Roach · Released on May 4, 1924, by Pathé Exchange · Our Gang: Mary Kornman, Mickey Daniels, Joe Cobb, Ernie "Sunshine Sammy" Morrison, Jackie Condon, Allen "Farina" Hoskins, Andy

Samuels, Billy Lord, Wadell Carter,* Jannie "Mango" Hoskins, and Dinah the Mule • School teacher, George K. French; Mickey's mother, Dorothy Vernon; Mary's mother, Lyle Tayo; Joe's mother, Helen Gilmore; Parent with ear-horn, Gus Leonard; Another parent, Charley Young

Ganging up: After having been splattered with mud by Mickey, Joe lets him know that it's a "good thing my maw don't let me fight." A scene from "Commencement Day."

The fact that it's the last day of school doesn't make life any less hectic for the gang. Brothers Jackie and Joe continue to fight, Ernie still has trouble keeping track of Farina and Mango, and Mickey gets involved in a battle royal with bully Snoozer. At commencement day ceremonies, Mary tries to recite but can't remember the third line of "Mary Had a Little Lamb," Joe plays his saxophone, which Jackie has filled with pepper (setting off a flurry of sneezes), and Mickey attempts "Humoresque" on the violin with a frog squirming in the back of his shirt. Proceedings are interrupted when Farina falls into a well outside, but even this can't bring the important ceremony to a halt. What finally sets the lid off is Snoozer's revenge for taking a licking from Mickey; he lets loose a beehive in the classroom, sending the kids and parents scattering in all directions.

Highlighted by "Beanie" Walker's text titles, "Commencement Day" is pretty standard stuff, with the basic theme of school graduation being just enough framework for a disjointed but entertaining series of vignettes.

One particularly nice sequence shows Mickey walking to school; as he nears a corner, he sees Mary approaching from the other side, and deliberately waits so he will "coincidentally" bump into her. Every time he starts out, however, he finds her lagging behind, distracted by a neighborhood goat. Since her back is turned, he's able to scamper back into place and try again. He's forced to retrace his steps four times before finally making contact—with Snoozer, not with Mary. There was always some neighborhood tough guy one never wanted to run into on his way to school, and for Mickey, this was the guy.

These readily identifiable childhood thoughts and schemes are a vital part of *Our Gang*'s timelessness; it is often the lack of such touches that distinguishes a run-of-the-mill entry from a creative and successful short.

27 • IT'S A BEAR

Two Reels • Produced by Hal Roach • Directed by Robert F. McGowan • Titles by H. M. Walker • Story by Hal E. Roach • Released on July 27, 1924, by Pathé Exchange • Our Gang: Mickey Daniels, Mary Kornman, Joe Cobb, Allen "Farina" Hoskins, Ernie "Sunshine Sammy" Morrison, Jackie Condon, and Dinah the Mule • Sheriff, Noah Young; Farmer's wife, Helen Gilmore

"Give a small boy an air gun or a slingshot. And then have an ambulance ready." Joe is busy with his rifle, enjoying target practice. Jackie is hunting wild game, with Dick acting the role of the animals. Ernie has a bow and arrow, with Farina as his equipment carrier. Then Mickey comes along in his milk wagon and offers the kids a chance to see some *real* animals on his farm. Mary joins them for the jaunt, and once in the wilds the kids go after everything, any way they can, from lassoing a pig to shooting down a rooster weather vane. Things get a bit

* Identification provided by Joe Cobb, who explains that the young lady is the daughter of Fern Carter, Our Gang's lifelong on-the-set school instructor.

Scene from "It's a Bear," with Joe, Jackie, the midget, the bear, Ernie, Farina, Mickey, and Mary . . . with pistol.

too realistic, however, when a bear appears at the end of Ernie's lasso rope. A second bear gives the gang a double scare, and the chase is on. Meanwhile, Joe has settled down to rest under a shady tree, tired of running around with his pants continually falling down. When the gang flies by and tells him a bear is close behind, he suddenly jumps into action—losing his pants along the way.

"It's a Bear" has no real plot; the hunting theme merely provides a peg for gags involving animals. The best moments, however, come during the first half of the film, which merely introduces the kids. Mickey drives a rickety milk wagon, and has his dog trained to do all the heavy work—delivering the bottles, returning the empties, and collecting the money. Mary is introduced by the title: "Her love is blind—she thinks Mickey looks like Tommy Meighan," a reference to one of the 1920s' handsome leading men. Meanwhile, Farina's purposely and perpetually confusing gender is again noted when older brother Sunshine Sammy scolds "her," saying, "Quit chasin' things—be a lady."

In another deliberate contrivance, Joe Cobb recalls today that the kid known as Dick in "It's a Bear" was *Our Gang*'s only genuine ringer, a nineteen-year-old midget who smoked cigars between scenes.

28 · CRADLE ROBBERS

Two Reels · Produced by Hal Roach · Directed by Robert F. McGowan · Titles by H. M. Walker · Story by Hal E. Roach · Released on June 1, 1924, by Pathé Exchange · Our Gang: Joe Cobb, Mickey Daniels, Ernie "Sunshine Sammy" Morrison, Allen "Farina" Hoskins, Mary Kornman, Jackie Condon, Sonny Loy Warde, Jannie Hoskins, Peggy Ahearn, and Nanette Fabray (?) · Officer chasing Joe, William Gillespie; Gypsy, William Gillespie; Another officer, Allen Cavan; Baby Show officials, Allen Cavan, Clara Guiol; Jackie's mother, Helen Gilmore; Girl with bald boyfriend, Beth Darlington; Angry mothers, Lyle Tayo, Dorothy Vernon

The gang is forced to babysit with its younger brothers and sisters instead of going fishing. But when they learn that there's a baby show in town, they try to turn their drudgery into a profitable enterprise. Alas, the only prize yet to be awarded when they arrive is the one for Fattest Baby. Mickey decides to dress up Joe as an infant and cop the prize, but Joe gets cold feet when he sees a pediatrician about to undress him for inspection, and heads for the hills, with a police officer in hot pursuit. Meanwhile, the gang stages its own exhibition ("Their First Annual Baby Show—and probably their last"), with a special section for baby animals in the barn loft. When a group of irate mothers heads toward the barn with several policemen, hoping to locate their "lost" babies, the gang ducks into the back of a gypsy wagon parked outside. As the wagon takes off, the cops and mothers follow, thinking that the gypsy—and not the gang—is responsible for the kidnappings. The runaways are rounded up, but when they step down from the wagon, the original baby-show cop spies Joe, still in his infant clothes, and resumes his chase, with the bogus baby leading him off into the distant horizon.

Of the gang it is said, "All of them were 'beautiful babies' once—but they've outgrown it." With that typical H. M. Walker introduction, "Cradle Robbers" gets off to a brisk start, and never lets up. The film follows a by-now traditional formula of having the gang experience an adult activity (here, a baby show), allowing them to imitate the grownups with their own version of the same enterprise.

While "Cradle Robbers" is not wildly inventive, it embellishes this formula with a fair share of amusing gags, and a good sampling of funny title cards. As we first meet the gang, they are sitting on what appears to be a river bank, fishing poles outstretched toward the camera. Moving back, we see the whole picture, however, and discover that they are on the edge of a bluff, dangling milk bottles and playthings at the end of their lines to amuse and quiet their baby brothers and sisters in perambulators parked below. This gag was repeated some years later in the talkie short "Forgotten Babies," where succeeding Rascals faced the same problem of being stuck with babysitting chores.

Joe is the only one without a baby to look after, and he expresses impatience with his pals. "Let's go fishin'," he says. "This is the bunk." A short time later, he finds himself volunteered to win the gang a prize at the baby show; the camera takes Mickey's point of view as he looks at Joe and pictures him as a toddler—a camera dissolve neatly executed. After their run-in with the cops, assorted mothers, and one excited gypsy, Joe turns to his friends and complains, "I told you this was the bunk—we oughtta went fishin'."

At the gang's own baby show, Mickey and Mary walk about in high-society fashion, noses in the air and lor-

"Cradle Robbers": the opening gag, reworked nine years later in "Forgotten Babies."

gnettes held against their eyes as they inspect the precious youngsters on display. Two of the kids operate an elevator to the mezzanine floor (a large wash basin on a rope pulley), but Joe is too heavy to lift that high. A "Calfateeria" barrel of milk has hoses running from its spout to deliver milk to babies around the room, causing Farina some anguish as he tries to get the liquid flowing at just the right moment.

Somewhat superfluous is a sequence in which Farina spills a bottle of ammonia, the fumes sending everyone into a slow-motion stupor. Why Bob McGowan and his gagsters felt that audiences wouldn't ever tire of this well-worn gag device is a mystery, but it remained prominent in the *Our Gang* bag of tricks for years to come.

If nothing to shout about, "Cradle Robbers" is certainly an amusing entry in the series.

29 · JUBILO, JR.

Two Reels · Produced by Hal Roach · Directed by Robert F. McGowan · Titles by H. M. Walker · Story by Hal E. Roach · Released on June 29, 1924, by Pathé Exchange · Our Gang: Mickey "Jubilo, Jr." Daniels, Mary Kornman, Joe Cobb, Jackie Condon, Andy Samuels, and Allen "Farina" Hoskins · Jubilo, Will Rogers; Emil, Jubilo's father, Noah Young; Mother, Lyle Tayo; Hat vendor, Allen Cavan; Grocer, Richard Daniels; Tramp pal of Jubilo, Leo Willis; Extra outside church, Joy Winthrop; Photographer, Otto Himm; Director, Charley Chase

Jubilo (Will Rogers) runs across three fellow tramps who are harmonizing on "That Old Gang of Mine." The song sets Jubilo to reminiscing. It's his mother's birthday, and he recalls that same date many years ago, via flashback. His father grumbles that he can't afford to buy birthday presents, leaving his mother heartbroken. Little Jubilo decides to get his mother the best gift he can find, and he eyes a $3 hat in a store window. He desperately searches for work that will earn him the money, but all of his odd-job schemes backfire (a man who offered one dollar if he would dig a six-foot hole turns out to be an escaped lunatic). Finally he hits on the idea of running a circus, and this nets him $2.70. For the balance he borrows his mother's pin money, and buys the hat; before he can explain, however, his father whips him for taking the money. After presenting the hat, all is forgiven, and his mother proudly wears the somewhat flamboyant headgear to church that Sunday. When Jubilo finishes telling this story, he is revealed to be Will Rogers, shooting a film on location at the railroad tracks. His mother, now well taken care of, comes to visit him and displays the same hat which she's kept all these years. Looking at it again, Rogers says that he can still see his old gang, as if it were today—and they appear on the horizon to wave hello once more.

A standard *Our Gang* story is presented in most unusual surroundings in "Jubilo, Jr." Jubilo was the title character in one of Will Rogers's most famous silent features; Hal Roach merely "borrowed" the name to use when the comedian came to work for him in the mid-1920s. And since Rogers's best pictures for Roach were lively collections of movie spoofs, it's only fitting that he'd turn his rapierlike wit on one of his own films, having fun with the folksy philosophizing tramp characterization he'd created in *Jubilo*.

The flashback technique works pretty well, allowing for a generous dose of sentiment as Rogers and the other tramps mistily recall their youth. Mickey Daniels plays Will as a boy, and even this is somehow palatable in the context of the film. What is surprising, and somewhat baffling, is the final sequence where suddenly Jubilo is not Jubilo at all, but Will Rogers on a movie location. His director, played by Charley Chase (who really did direct Rogers for Hal Roach), sets up a scene, after which Will's mother, appropriately matronly by now, arrives in a limousine to say hello to her son on the occasion of her birthday. After conjuring up the gang's image once more, Will turns back to her and introduces her to the film crew as the picture fades out.

This leaves unclear whether the whole film is supposed

Mickey Daniels as the youthful impresario in "Jubilo, Jr."

One almost suspects that the footage was taken from, or intended for, another film entirely and spliced into this one as an afterthought. Furthermore, the bareback rider introduced as "Mademoiselle Mary" turns out to be Mickey in drag, indicating that some backstage plot is missing.

Significantly, the plot peg of Mickey struggling to buy a birthday present for his neglected mother was the basis for a talkie two-reeler, "Birthday Blues," with Dickie Moore. Without the confusion of flashbacks and meandering ideas, the story was fully developed and quite successful. Clearly, Bob McGowan learned from the experience.

Thus, the real claim of "Jubilo, Jr." to importance in the chronology of *Our Gang* is for its use of Will Rogers and the film-within-a-film framework, and not for its central plot.

"Jubilo, Jr." takes some interesting movie liberties, borrowing a page from *Tom Sawyer* as Mickey convinces the other kids that digging dirt is loads of fun. Instances like this one, and others found in "Beanie" Walker's titles, suggest the admiration Roach staffers had for Mark Twain. Coincidentally, as a boy growing up in Elmira, New York, Hal Roach had known Mark Twain. The writer's wife's sister lived in Elmira, and when Twain visited her, Roach saw him each time he brought something to the house in his job as a delivery boy.

Finally, Joe Cobb has some recollections of Will Rogers around the Roach lot: "He liked to be with the kids, and talk to us, always had something humorous to say. He seemed real interested in the gang, asked us lots of questions about different things. He usually had his knife out, and he was always whittling for somebody, making a little something for you. Boats and canoes, mostly. He'd cut it right out for you, didn't take any time, then he'd get a big kick to see what you'd do with it. He was really a down-to-earth kind of guy. He'd eat in Roach's cafe with all of us at the studio, and he didn't want you to go to any special trouble for him. He wanted to be treated just like everybody else. We all liked him; he kept everybody laughing."

to be regarded as a film-within-a-film, or if Rogers was merely reminiscing on the sidelines with some friends between scenes. The construction of the short leaves the audience up in the air.

As for the *Our Gang* portions of the narrative, these are well done, but somewhat fragmented by the flashback technique. After trying to earn money digging a ditch, pushing a wheelbarrow for a construction company, and running errands for a grocer, little Jubilo abruptly opens a circus, and in the passing of one title card has set up a fantastically elaborate big-top, filled to the brim with kids. There is a full-scale trapeze act (!), Joe Cobb as the strong-man, Farina with his trained dog, and a sideshow outside. This would seem to be meat for an entire two-reeler, not a disembodied segment in a rambling story.

30 · HIGH SOCIETY

Two Reels · Produced by Hal Roach · Directed by Robert F. McGowan · Titles by H. M. Walker · Story by Hal E. Roach · Released on August 24, 1924, by Pathé Exchange · Our Gang: Mickey Daniels, Mary Kornman, Joe Cobb, Andy Samuels, Allen "Farina" Hoskins, Jackie "Percy" Condon, and Sonny Loy Warde · Pat Kelly, Himself; Police detectives, Sam Lufkin, Charles Bachman, Jack Gavin

Mickey is separated from his uncle Pat—and from the gang—when his wealthy aunt Kate adopts him. Kate, and her harried butler, try to make him a little gentleman, but he hates it, and having to live with his despicable cousin Percy doesn't make life any sweeter. One day Uncle Pat and the gang come to call on Mickey, while Aunt Kate is out, and they take over the mansion to have a day-long party. Pat keeps the butler out of the way so the kids can have fun—and they do, turning the house into a shambles! The kids ride in the dumbwaiter, pile sofa cushions at the foot of the bannister to create a sliding chute, pour liquid soap all over the kitchen to make a funhouse floor, etc. When the butler finally frees himself, he sets off a

police alarm, but Farina plays with the knob and unwittingly sends for the fire department and an ambulance as well! This crowd converges on the house just as Aunt Kate walks up to the front door herself; seeing the mess, she says that she's sorry she brought Mickey here, and tells Uncle Pat to take him away. Mickey, Pat, and the gang are jubilant, and all's well that ends well.

"High Society" is a pip: a fast-paced entertainment that never strays from tried-and-true territory.

Mickey and his uncle Pat are poor but happy; their idea of luxury is cooking corned beef. The other kids in the gang contrive to steal fruit from a local merchant (with the aid of an awesome contraption using a funnel and a drainpipe) but even the cop doesn't really get angry—he just wants to teach them a lesson, and then sits down for corned beef dinner with Uncle Pat.

Contrast this with the life style of Aunt Kate and her bratty son Percy ("Not naturally mean—he had to practice for three years"). Mickey complains that they think every day is Saturday night, as the butler, wearing a raincoat, battles his way toward giving him a bath. Mickey's hair is slicked down, and he is made to wear a little Lord Fauntleroy suit.

When the gang comes to pay a visit, the air is alive with fun and laughter. Mary peeks into Aunt Kate's room, and has a ball dressing herself up in jewelry and other finery. Downstairs, Farina is curious about other things, getting his kicks by pouring a bottle of booze into the goldfish bowl, then watching the drunken fish bump into each other!

It's only natural that Aunt Kate would be horrified at all this, and her announcement that Mickey should leave is music to his ears.

"High Society" does not stress the sentimental aspect of Mickey's leaving home as much as some of McGowan's early talkies might have, but the sequence is effective nonetheless. Mickey bids a formal good-bye to his friends, and the neighborhood cop, and then gets into Aunt Kate's chauffeured car and looks through the rear window, crying and waving as he is taken away.

There's also an inside joke to Mickey's adoption, as the official papers are signed by a judge named L. A. French—actually, the studio purchasing agent and later production manager (and no relation to long-time comedy writer-director Lloyd French).

"High Society": Mickey Daniels, Mary Kornman, and Jackie Condon.

McGowan and his successors learned that there were certain plot themes and story elements that never failed for *Our Gang,* and a basic one—poor-but-happy vs. rich-but-stuffy—was among the best, as seen here in "High Society."

31 · THE SUN DOWN LIMITED

Two Reels · Produced by Hal Roach · Directed by Robert F. McGowan · Tiltes by H. M. Walker · Story by Hal E. Roach · Released on September 21, 1924, by Pathé Exchange · Our Gang: Mickey Daniels, Joe Cobb, Mary Kornman, Jackie Condon, Andy Samuels, Allen "Farina" Hoskins, and Sonny Loy Warde

The gang enjoys hanging around the railroad yard, but after Mickey and Joe set off a runaway locomotive, two formerly friendly engineers chase them away. Left to their own devices, the kids build *their* railroad line on an abandoned piece of track. The train itself is a whiz, and there is no lack of passengers, but this steals the thunder from Toughy, who'd been running his own train nearby, and he vows to destroy the gang's operation. First he sets a piano crate on the tracks and causes a crash; then he uncouples three of the cars; finally he removes a piece of track, derailing the train and sending it rolling onto the city streets, where it causes considerable havoc before crashing to a halt. All the kids manage to bail out before the final tumble, except Farina, who survives the crash but emerges in a daze, seeing stars and holding his aching head.

"The Sun Down Limited" realizes a great childhood fantasy of the 1920s—not to mention the subject of many an adult fancy ever since—to ride and run your own railroad. One can readily share the excitement of Mickey and Joe in opening scenes as they ride in the engine car of a real train—but this is only the beginning.

"Engineering is a cinch," Mickey tells Joe. "All you gotta do is shove one thingamajigg and pull 'nother." By pulling and shoving the wrong things, however, their train suddenly lurches forward, and for the next few hair-raising minutes, the two would-be railroadmen run their train back and forth, back and forth, unable to stop it but doing their best to avoid hitting something on either end of the track. Complicating matters, Farina has gotten his foot stuck in the middle of the track; as the engine nears, the kids help him run for cover, but Farina ducks, the train riding over him without causing a scratch. Once is bad enough for this harrowing experience, but with Mickey and Joe at the controls, the train continues to run over the hapless Farina again and again, until a watchful engineer comes by and pulls him free just as the train is about to hit the mark—a neat bit of seriallike cliff hanging. When someone tells Farina how lucky he is, since he almost got run over, he replies, "Almos'! Ah did!"

As for the gang's home-built train, a subtitle declares, "There had only been seven wonders of the world—until now." And indeed, the finished setup *is* quite a wonder, with a miniature Union Station, taxi service, telegraph

Derailment in "The Sun Down Limited."

around a large expanse of lawn, and carrying a group of eager passengers. Needless to say, the propulsion for this vehicle is provided by one-dog-power: the canine is situated inside the "engine" on a treadmill, with caged cats on either end to get him to run forward and reverse. Flour is used to create the effect of steam, and when the train stops to take on water, the mighty flow drains down into a dog dish inside the locomotive.

As if this isn't enough to create a dream-come-true for any child (young-at-heart, or railroad buff) in the audience, the film's finale sends this same train out onto the streets for an even greater thrill-session, narrowly escaping collisions with cars, racing through a blacksmith's garage, plowing into a vendor's wagon, pulling four cops along who try to lasso the runaway engine, and finally coming to a stop after careening down a hill and overturning. The best part of this sequence, like the whole film, is that it's *real*. There are no miniatures or process-screens to dull the excitement, or the comedy; and as always, it's fascinating to see chases take place on the undeveloped Culver City streets outside the Hal Roach studio.

office, mail pickup, and all the trimmings one would expect at a major depot, for the gang's train is not just a ramshackle engine, but a full five-car train, circling

32 · EVERY MAN FOR HIMSELF

Two Reels · Produced by Hal Roach · Directed by Robert F. McGowan · Titles by H. M. Walker · Story by Hal E. Roach · Released on October 19, 1924, by Pathé Exchange · Our Gang: Mickey Daniels, Mary Korman, Allen "Farina" Hoskins, Joe Cobb, Andy Samuels, Jackie Condon, and Monty O'Grady · Second man whose shoes get sprayed, Dick Gilbert; Man seated at the shoeshine stand, Rolfe Sedan; One of the ladies with rings around her eyes, Martha Sleeper

The Gang comes to Farina's rescue at the close of "Every Man for Himself."

pedestrians' shoes at one end of the block, then corner them for a shine farther down the street. The money they earn goes toward boxing gloves, but gloves are nowhere in sight when Mickey plunges the group into a major battle with a newcomer to the neighborhood. At first, the well-dressed sissy runs from Mickey's assault, but then he seemingly turns on his assailant and flattens him. It develops that there are twins, one tough and one timid. After the war is over, the gang welcomes the two new kids, who have proven their mettle with their fists, to the club.

"Every Man for Himself" is a string of unresolved situations, one having little to do with the other. The film opens on a boxing match in the Athletic Club, with views of the homemade equipment (a bicycle-powered shower, a pinwheel billed as a lung-tester, etc.). The next sequence deals with the shoeshine operation; Mickey is in charge, with Powder Puff manning the power-plant and Mary acting as the flirtatious cashier. Another particularly meaningless segment shows the entire population of the city sporting black eye rings, having fallen for the gang's peephole practical joke alongside the shoeshine stand. Finally there is the cat-and-mouse battle with the new twins, Scrappy and Sissy, including some good mistaken-identity situations. The film ends with Farina, having eluded Scrappy, emerging from a cactus field covered with needles from head to toe, which the other kids pitch in to remove.

The gang supports its well-equipped Athletic Club by running a sidewalk shoeshine parlor, using a Rube Goldbergish contraption to give the appearance of automation. When business gets slow, the kids spray paint on

Like many other two-reelers along the *Our Gang* assembly line, this one has no structure, and is clearly a case of odds and ends being thrown together in the hope that the kids' personalities, and occasional gags, would carry the short. In this instance, it almost works.

It should be noted that occasional mediocrities like "Every Man for Himself" were readily—even eagerly—forgiven in 1924 by *Our Gang* devotees, who were legion. Such was the enthusiasm over the series that Pathé could claim very little exaggeration in the wording of this ad, which appeared in *Film Daily* on November 23: "Two years of unequaled popularity! In September of this year the Hal Roach *Our Gang* comedies had their second an-

niversary. It is doubtful if the business has ever seen such an amazing record of popularity, for certainly no pictures have played in such a large number of houses. Star names did not do it, for the *Our Gang*s have no stars; the whole company of remarkable little kids stars. Quality did it. Laughs did it. Human interest did it. Are you profiting through big laughs from little kids?"

Many readers of *Film Daily* could answer yes: *Our Gang* comedies were then being shown in 10,000 theaters!

33 · THE MYSTERIOUS MYSTERY!

Two Reels · Produced by Hal Roach · Directed by Robert F. McGowan · Titles by H. M. Walker · Story by Hal E. Roach · Released on December 14, 1924, by Pathé Exchange · Our Gang: Mickey Daniels, Jackie "Little Adelbert" Condon, Joe Cobb, Andy Samuels, Allen "Hawkeye" Hoskins, Eugene "Pineapple" Jackson, and Sing Joy · Mr. Wallingford, William Gillespie; Kidnap henchmen, Sam Lufkin, Dick Gilbert; Detective Jinks, mistaken "suspeck," Charles Bachman; Adelbert's Grandfather, Allen Cavan; Butler, Charley Young

Little rich boy Adelbert Wallingford is kidnapped, so Mickey the Mastermind, otherwise known as Sherlock Hawkshaw, goes to work with his team of detectives. First they capture a suspicious-looking character, who turns out to be Detective Jinks of the police force. Then they earn a dollar for delivering a package to Mr. Wallingford, unaware that they've just transmitted the head kidnapper's ransom note! Wallingford is to attach $5,000 to an accompanying carrier pigeon; if the bird returns without the money, the worst may happen. Just then, the pigeon breaks loose, flies out of the house, and sends Wallingford and the gang on a desperate chase that soon takes to the air, with Mickey, Joe, and Farina (as Hawkeye) stowing away aboard a plane that tries to catch the elusive bird. The pilot falls out during a mishap (landing in the river below), leaving a nervous Mickey at the controls, with Joe on the wing and Farina on the tail, both having climbed there to capture the pigeon. Somehow Mickey manages to follow the bird to the barn hide-out of the kidnappers, crashing the plane right into the roof, thus exposing the criminals to Wallingford and Jinks, who were following by car, rescuing Adelbert, and earning the gang a well-deserved reward.

"The Mysterious Mystery!" is a misleading title for this fine two-reeler, which is jam-packed with action and excitement.

The opening segment, after introducing Little Adelbert, focuses on supersleuth Mickey and his gang. Using such camouflage disguises as a barber pole, a sandwich sign, a mannequin, and a grocery sack, they stalk their victim (Detective Jinks), lure him to their hide-out, pull a trap-door lever and send him into their basement headquarters where he is suddenly manacled at the waist, arms, and ankles by a ready-made thief-capturing contraption. This impressive handiwork is all for naught, as Joe brings a policeman who reveals that their "crook" is also a cop.

Then the scene shifts to the Wallingford home and the pigeon quest. After a brief but exciting car ride, at high speeds over California hills, the action takes to the air, combining surprisingly convincing shots of the plane dangling in front of a moving cyclorama with bona fide aerial views of the city below. The effect is such that one becomes unaware of any trickery, and shares the intended excitement of Joe stranded on the wing and Farina

balancing precariously on the tail flap as Mickey tries to figure out the steering mechanism.

Best of all is the climactic crash, executed with an impressive set of miniatures as the plane soars straight into the roof of the barn, cutting to a real-life scene of the rubble on the ground. Such meticulous effects were rare in Hal Roach comedies.

An introductory title reveals Adelbert as a rich boy who would much rather be playing with kids like the gang than being pampered by a series of tutors. His current instructor becomes the target of a pea-shooter, and has a tack placed on his seat while trying to give the boy some education.

Mickey, on the other hand, has rigged up a detective hide-out second to none, with disguise kits, machinery for camouflaging his basement entrance, an alarm system to gather the gang together, etc. His manual is an edition of Conan Doyle's Sherlock Holmes stories.

In fact, the only real weakness in "The Mysterious Mystery!" is that the opening half, with the kids capturing Detective Jinks, strays so far from the matter at hand—rescuing the kidnapped boy. That aside, the film has pace, excitement, and fun, a perfect combination for a first-rate *Our Gang* comedy.

There's something mysterious here, but Mickey isn't telling.

34 · THE BIG TOWN

Two Reels · Produced by Hal Roach · Directed by Robert F. McGowan · Photographed by Art Lloyd · Edited by
T. J. Crizer · Titles by H. M. Walker · Story by Hal E. Roach · Released on January 11, 1925, by Pathé Exchange
· Our Gang: Mickey Daniels, Mary Kornman, Joe Cobb, Jackie Condon, Allen "Farina" Hoskins, and Eugene
Jackson · Entomologist, Gus Leonard; Train passengers, William Gillespie, Helen Gilmore, Lyle Tayo; The
Gang's escort, Jack Gavin

Leave it to the Gang to get front-row seats for a bus tour of New
York.

A postcard from Skinny, vacationing in New York, sets
the gang to thinking about the excitement of a trip to the
big city. But they get their wish sooner than expected:
while they are sitting in an empty boxcar at the railroad
yard, the door suddenly closes, and the next morning they
find themselves in New York City. After crossing the
Brooklyn Bridge, the kids take a ferry past the Statue of
Liberty to Manhattan, where Mickey commandeers a
double-decker bus up Fifth Avenue. Meanwhile, an alert
has gone out from Elmira for the missing children, and
some New York cops find the gang, pull them off the
stolen bus, and send them back home on an overnight
train. Here the gang manages to get into still more mischief, with the help of a flock of insects which have escaped
from the collection of an entomologist on board. When
they arrive home in Elmira, their greeting committee
consists of four angry mothers, who welcome their offspring home with a round of spankings.

"There are two kinds of little boys that want to travel
and see the world," explains an introductory title. "Those

under 12—And those over 12." The gang certainly fits
into those categories, and their excitement at visiting
New York is contagious . . . especially today, looking
back at the city more than fifty years ago.

Actually, the New York footage in "The Big Town" is
tantalizingly brief, and one yearns for more extensive shots
of Fifth Avenue as the gang's bus drives through the
Washington Square arch (now blocked to traffic) and up
the two-way street (now limited to downtown motorists).
Before the kids have much of a chance to see the town,
their freewheeling bus is boarded by a motorcycle
policeman who turns them in, ending their adventure and
cheating the audience of more sightseeing footage.

Most of the turmoil on the train ride home is not caused
by the gang, but by the bugs that escape from the sleeping entomologist (played by Gus Leonard, best remembered as "Old Cap" in the later *Our Gang* short "Mush
and Milk"). Admittedly, Farina helps distribute the
creepy crawlers around the Pullman car, but he is just an
accessory to the fact. The humor of this sequence is
tinged with a bit of shock value, since the insects in question are not standard slapstick-comedy ants-on-the-loose,
but large and frightening specimens of all sorts, eventually managing to awaken every sound sleeper on the train.
"The end of a perfect nightmare" is the coming of morning, and the first call for breakfast, where the gang
chooses breakfast food from the menu by picking blindly,
then having to negotiate the proper approach to eating
spaghetti, oysters on half shell, and artichokes (which
Mickey declares are "all outside and no inside").

An incidental subplot involves the owner of a barn
where the kids are playing at the outset of the film. He
chases them away, but in the process drops a lit cigarette
into a pile of hay. When the barn catches fire, the gang
runs inside and grabs the nearest fire extinguisher; how
are they to know that the barn-owner keeps this cylinder
filled with bootleg liquor? Their sincere attempt to douse
the fire only enhances the flames. At the end of the film,
the same barn-owner is on hand when the kids arrive. As
the mothers administer their whippings, the jubilant old
man shouts, "Spank 'em good—they need it!" But
Farina is hiding behind a barrel nearby; he grabs a slat of
wood (with two nails in it!) and whacks the barn-owner in
the behind to give him a taste of his own medicine.

One brief inside joke features a telegram to the New
York police from the kids' home town police chief. The
message to be on the lookout for six missing children is
signed "C. H. Roach, Chief of Police, Elmira, New
York." Elmira was, of course, producer Hal Roach's
home town, and C. H. Roach was Hal Roach's father.

"The Big Town" went into production under the title
"In New York," and regained that name for home-movie
release. A fast-moving and delightful two-reeler, it nevertheless leaves us hungry for more on-location footage of
the gang running loose in New York City.

35 · CIRCUS FEVER

Two Reels · Produced by Hal Roach · Directed by Robert F. McGowan · Photographed by Art Lloyd · Edited by Thomas J. Crizer · Titles by H. M. Walker · Story by Hal E. Roach · Released on February 8, 1925, by Pathé Exchange · Our Gang: Mickey Daniels, Mary Kornman, Joe Cobb, Allen "Farina" Hoskins, Jackie Condon, Johnny Downs, Peggy Ahearn, Eugene Jackson, and Wadell Carter · Dr. Royal Sorghum, Ernie Morrison, Sr.; Physician, Charley Young

The one day a year the circus comes to town, Farina and older brother Gene are stuck in bed with "speckled fever." Mickey, Jackie, and Joe are equally upset, because they must go to school instead of attending the afternoon performance. When they learn that Farina and Gene will be out of school for six weeks because of their spotted faces, the three schemers dot their faces with red paint and go home, moaning with pain. Their mothers are fooled by the trick, but the family doctor is not, calling the case a familiar round of "circus symptoms." Just then, Mary comes by and tells the boys that the teacher has given the class free tickets for the circus that afternoon; but a pair of angry mothers want to make sure that the three fakers learn their lesson, and they are given a dose of castor oil and ordered to stay in bed "until they learn to grow up."

It's difficult to isolate a film like "Circus Fever" and give it a fair hearing, since the plot elements are so familiar from the more popularly shown *Our Gang* talkies like "Three Smart Boys," "Fish Hooky," "Spooky Hooky," "Bored of Education," and other comedy films as well, which all use the same material. One is prompted to wonder if it was fresh and original even in 1925.

Be that as it may, "Circus Fever" moves briskly and enjoyably despite the viewer's familiarity with everything that's happening on-screen . . . from the black kids' faces sprayed with white paint to the parents' inevitable reactions.

There are a number of bright moments throughout the film that are only marginally related to the plot. A slow-motion shot of children lumbering along a street at a snail's pace is described as a scene of young students "rushing madly, joyously to their lessons."

It's pretty easy to identify with a troupe of (as a title says) "Little Rascals" who talk themselves into believing they can learn more at a circus than they can at school.

Mary Kornman, who appears only fleetingly in the film, is introduced with a title that says she believes in long engagements—she's promised to marry Mickey in 1944.

Another sequence involves the black doctor Sorghum who comes to call on Gene and Farina in his colorful, explosive car, which attracts the attention of the other kids passing by.

Best of all, however, is a communications system rigged by Joe and Mickey, who live next door to each other. A long-distance rope pulls a cowbell to alert one party that the other is about to speak; then Mickey opens a secret panel in a picture on the wall, revealing a hose, which presumably burrows underground to a similar location in Joe's bedroom. This is their makeshift yet workable telephone system. The message conveyed indicates that Joe wants to join his cohorts, so Mickey and younger brother Jackie lower a plank from outside their second-story window that provides a ramp for Joe to crawl over.

This is the kind of material that appeals to the child in

Joe Cobb has "Circus Fever."

every viewer, no matter how old. Doubtless for many of us, it was a fond wish as a youngster to live directly next door to another kid so that we could have rigged a system like the one shown in this and other, later, *Our Gang* films. It's the stuff that dreams are made of . . . and it's one sequence that helps set "Circus Fever" slightly apart from other similar ventures in the series.

Miscellany: It is worth noting one "inside" joke. The name of the performing troupe is Crizer's Colossal Circus . . . borrowing the monicker of film editor T. J. Crizer, who also served as scenarist and gagman for Hal Roach on the Harold Lloyd and *Our Gang* pictures.

36 · DOG DAYS

Two Reels · Produced by Hal Roach · Directed by Robert F. McGowan · Titles by H. M. Walker · Story by Hal E. Roach · Released on March 8, 1925, by Pathé Exchange · Our Gang: Mickey Daniels, Joe Cobb, Allen "Farina" Hoskins, Mary Kornman, Eugene Jackson, and Jackie Condon

This film was unavailable for viewing.

Film Daily called it "another excellent comedy," going on to say, "Hail, hail, the gang's all here—Mickey, Farina, Jackie, Joe, and Gene again produce the laughs. This time the gang has pet dogs which are trained. Each thinks his dog the best. The slogan they use is 'Let's see your dog p'form that trick.' Mary is a little society lady and when Mickey's dog stops her runaway pony, she invites all the gang to her party, where a good time is had by all. However, in the midst of the fun, one of the dogs is missing. After a hunt he is discovered with a litter of new puppies. And the proud owner says 'Let's see your dog p'form that trick.' "

Moving Picture World said, " 'Dog Days' is par value for an *Our Gang* comedy. Mickey, Farina, and the rest of the kids are as good and as funny as ever but their story does not possess all of the ingenuity and novel little twists of some of the past scripts. The poorest and most hackneyed type of plot outline would pass 100% with these clever youngsters in the frame, we feel certain the thousands of *Our Gang* enthusiasts will concede." Concerning the highbrow party, the review concludes, "Needless to say what takes place when the little roughnecks mix in with the silk stockings except that it is great entertainment."

Exhibitor's Daily Review was somewhat less enthusiastic. "While not quite as amusing as some of the earlier releases of this series, 'Dog Days' is quite entertaining screen fare. . . . The situations at times are a little strained, and the comedy not as spontaneous as in some of the earlier releases, but nonetheless 'Dog Days' is one of the *Our Gang* series and as such will more than justify the faith of any exhibitor. These Hal Roach sketches of kid life are deservedly popular with the fans."

The message is clear: at this time, *Our Gang* could do no wrong.

37 · THE LOVE BUG

Two Reels · Produced by Hal Roach · Directed by Robert F. McGowan · Titles by H. M. Walker · Story by Hal E. Roach · Released on April 5, 1925, by Pathé Exchange · Our Gang: Mickey Daniels, Mary Kornman, Joe Cobb, Jackie Condon, Allen "Farina" Hoskins, Johnny Downs, Eugene "Pineapple" Jackson, Peggy Ahearn, and Wadell Carter · Manager at the beauty parlor, William Gillespie; Father of Farina's girl friend, Ernie Morrison, Sr.

The gang turns to Grandma for advice and help, especially when love matches aren't working out too well for Farina and Joe. Then the kids go off on their own to visit Pineapple at the beauty salon where he's working as a page. It's a super-deluxe establishment, and since no one is around at the end of the afternoon, the gang goes to work fiddling with the various cosmetics and machinery on display: Joe gets stuck in a steam cabinet, Mickey gives himself a mudpack, Farina gives his pigtails a permanent wave, and Jackie fools with various hoses, which don't seem to work until he finds the central controls and sends steam, air, and water through the now runaway tubes. The boss happens to come by just at this moment and calls in a cop to remove the kids and keep his beauty parlor from being wrecked. The cop does his duty and is about to turn in the kids when Grandma comes to the rescue, distracting the officer's attention as the gang runs away—then taking it on the lam herself!

"The Love Bug" is a pleasing if disjointed two-reeler, a forerunner of several talkie shorts featuring a kindly old woman who becomes a "grandma" to the entire gang. Although the film opens with sequences of Joe, Farina,

Mickey and Mary . . . out for a ride.

and Mickey in various encounters with their girl friends, romance is abruptly dismissed about a third of the way through,* in order to move on to the beauty parlor segment.

This has surefire slapstick potential which is never

* At least in the only print available for screening, which appears to have been cut for television syndication.

realized. Jackie's discovery of how to turn on the steam-and-water hoses is supposed to be the gag climax, but the major holocaust one expects never arrives. The fact that there are no customers present severely restricts the idea's possibilities and keeps "The Love Bug" well below par for the Hal Roach gag team: mild fun, but nothing special.

38 · ASK GRANDMA

Two Reels · Produced by Hal Roach · Directed by Robert F. McGowan · Titles by H. M. Walker · Story by Hal E. Roach · Released on May 31, 1925, by Pathé Exchange · Our Gang: Mickey Daniels, Mary Kornman, Johnny Downs, Joe Cobb, Allen "Farina" Hoskins, Jackie Condon, and David Sharpe · Martha, Mickey's mother, Lyle Tayo; Johnny's "Daddy," Noah Young

Mickey's plagued by his overly protective mother, who wants to raise her boy as a "hothouse flower," while he'd prefer to be a weed. When he is dressed like a sissy and made to stay indoors for dancing lessons, Mickey's spirits plummet to a new low when he catches a glimpse out the window of the gang's airplane ride in the next yard. Everybody's having a great time but him. . . . Grandma is his only pal. They confide in one another, play ball together, even spar together. When Mickey lets Grandma know that he likes Mary (she thinks he's cute between freckles), Grandma encourages his romantic inclinations, and helps him sneak outside to join in the fun with the gang. Neighborhood tough guy Johnny Downs—who also has eyes for Mary— counts that day lost when he fails to pound somebody, and he's picking on Joe Cobb when Mickey comes along. The two rivals square off, and Mickey's getting the worst of it till he begins asking advice from Grandma, who is watching at the window. "Get up, and slam him, and keep on slammin,' " she urges. Rolling in dust and glory, Mickey manages to do all three, and pretty successfully, too, until Johnny yells for his daddy, a big bruiser who's just come home from work. When this muscle-bound pug-ugly and his bully son start pummeling Mickey together, that's Grandma's cue to join the action! Even Mother, alarmed at first, begins cheering, and when Mickey and Grandma polish off their two adversaries, Mom promises to let Mickey be a "regular boy" from now on.

A companion piece to "The Love Bug," "Ask Grandma" is an excellent comedy in every way, besides being one of the few silent *Our Gangs* to really tell a story, and a good one. For a change, tangential gags and meandering story threads are eschewed in favor of a straightforward tale where the comedy follows from solid situations and characterizations. One wonders about the possible involvement of a Frank Capra or a Leo McCarey, both Roach scenarists at the time. The youngsters, too, are every bit as appealing as ever.

As a bonus, there's a flashback scene where Grandma tries to remind Mickey's demure mom what a tomboy *she* was. Of course, it's Mickey in drag. Nimbly skipping along in pigtails, "she" stops to flirt with a bunch of boys, subtly heaving rocks at them and precipitating a shoving match with the biggest of them, who's none other than David Sharpe, soon to be A.A.U. tumbling champion and

Eugene Jackson, Jackie Condon, Mary Kornman, Mickey Daniels, and Joe Cobb.

later one of movies' all-time greatest stunt men and second-unit directors (which he remains today). In the early 1930s, he costarred in Hal Roach's *The Boy Friends* series with grown-up Mickey Daniels and Mary Kornman, blending comedy and acrobatics in his likable performances.

Several standard *Our Gang* routines originate in "Ask Grandma." In the most notable, scenes indoors of Mickey and his sprightly grandma romping around together are a dry run for the identical sequence in "Fly My Kite"—with the Wild West pulp fiction episode, the warm-up exercises, the backflips, the front-flips, the boxing match, and everything virtually the same. Not so coincidentally, Dave Sharpe doubled for the Grandma in "Fly My Kite."

Outdoors, the gang (with the help of technical wizard Charley Oelze) has conceived one of their most ingenious fun devices, a merry-go-round apparatus supporting two biplanes. The twin airships are suspended above the ground by wires attached to long poles that are made to revolve in a circle by a connected motorized go-cart that Johnny Downs drives around beneath the same "flight pattern" traveled by the planes. Few commercial amusement parks could hope to do as well!

39 · SHOOTIN' INJUNS

Two Reels · Produced by Hal Roach · Directed by Robert F. McGowan · Photographed by Alvin V. Knetchel · Titles by H. M. Walker · Story by Hal E. Roach · Released on May 3, 1925, by Pathé Exchange · Our Gang: Mickey Daniels, Jackie Condon, Allen "Farina" Hoskins, Joe Cobb, Johnny Downs, and Eugene Jackson · W. R. Jones, inventor, Richard Daniels; Joe's dad, "Tonnage" Martin Wolfkeil; Other dads, Jack Gavin, William Gillespie

The Gang obliges studio still photographer Gene Kornman (Mary's father) and apprehensively stares off camera at absolutely nothing for this Christmas publicity photo.

The gang has been Western-ized; they plan to run away from home and spend their time shooting Indians. Parents' warnings to the contrary, they decide to meet that night and run away "to some foreign country." Traveling at night proves to be pretty eerie, and when it rains the kids seek refuge at a nearby house, which just happens to be the inventor's model for a gimmicked-up "magnetic house" about to be sold to an amusement park entrepreneur. The gang is scared witless by all the frightening contraptions, but when their parents arrive to "rescue" them, the adults get caught in the gimmickry just as much as the kids!

"Shootin' Injuns" keeps moving, but does not rank as one of the more coherent *Our Gang* outings. What's more, the "spook stuff" is prolonged from the kids' initial nighttime rendezvous through the lengthy haunted-house sequence. While there is some fine material here, it's just too much of a good thing.

The "crazy house" is perhaps the most impressive of many such mansions seen in *Our Gang* comedies over the years. This one has more going on, in a more bizarre fashion, than any other that comes to mind. Paintings are suddenly imbued with life, chairs collapse, stairways turn into sliding chutes, a corps of skeletons resurges, the floor moves, the walls are full of sliding panels, bodies pop out of closets, etc.

There is also some striking trick photography, credited to Alvin V. Knetchel. In one sequence, an array of skeletons appears, emanating one at a time from the body of an initial figure. Then, all spread out along the top of a staircase, they slide down the bannister, reconverging into one bony being at the bottom of the stairs. This impressive scene is a matter of carefully timed and executed multiple exposures, much like Buster Keaton's nine-man minstrel show (all nine participants being himself) in *The Playhouse* (1922).

Another memorable shot involves Farina, who in running away from a skeleton pauses in midflight and remains motionless while he seemingly leaps out of his skin and continues, putting two Farinas on screen at the same time.

This camerawork serves as a fascinating ancestor to more sophisticated examples like Gene Kelly's alter-ego dance in *Cover Girl* (1944) or Norman McLaren's classic ballet film *Pas de Deux* (1967). It all goes to show that there's nothing on film that hasn't been tried before.

Unfortunately, one is hard pressed to find the same enthusiasm for "Shootin' Injuns" as a whole. The opening sequences in the gang's secret underground hide-out (which "Pancho Farina" can't find through its camouflage of hay) are fun, and nicely express the idea of kids' romantic fantasies about the Wild West, gleaned mostly from dime novels. But the rest of the film gets into more standard scare comedy that is anything but original or unique to *Our Gang*.

40 · OFFICIAL OFFICERS

Two Reels · Produced by Hal Roach · Directed by Robert F. McGowan · Titles by H. M. Walker · Story by Hal E. Roach · Released on June 28, 1925, by Pathé Exchange · Our Gang: Mickey Daniels, Mary Kornman, Allen "Farina" Hoskins, Joe Cobb, Johnny Downs, Jackie Condon, Peggy Ahearn, Jackie Hanes, Jannie Hoskins, and Pal the Dog · "Hard-Boiled" McManus, Jack Gavin; Angry motorist, James Finlayson; Cross-eyed motorist, George Rowe; Construction worker, Chet Brandenberg; Officer, Dick Gilbert; Tony, the fruit vendor, Charley Young

In the tenement district, the gang has no place to play, so they improvise on the city streets, where their baseball game is constantly interrupted by passing cars. Mickey decides that the best solution is to block off the street, and he thereby incurs the wrath of "Hard-Boiled" McManus, the cop on the beat, who gives chase and threatens to arrest the kids. This is duly noted by kindly Inspector Malone, who sends McManus away and replaces him with a "human being," Officer Mac. He appoints the gang as special deputies, whose first job is to maintain law and order, and whose second job is to make people happy. The gang takes the task seriously, setting up their own paddy wagon and jail, but their first major encounter is with their old nemesis McManus, who's been fired from the police force. They harass the towering meanie, who fights back and causes quite a ruckus. When Officer Mac arrives on the scene, McManus knocks him cold with a nightstick and runs away. The gang, with the help of some vigilant canines, manages to capture the culprit and effect their first bona fide arrest.

"Official Officers" is a pleasant, well-paced short with plenty of action—obscuring the fact that the sum total falls short of the bull's eye.

Introductory titles note that in the teeming city, "everybody seems to have forgotten the small boy—the little fellow who wants a chance, and a place, to play." But the gang (including one little *girl*, Mary) is nothing if not resourceful, and they attempt to carry on a baseball game amid a constant stream of whirring cars—one of which runs over Farina but leaves him unscratched.

"Hard-Boiled" McManus, we are told, "likes nobody—nobody likes him—that makes it a tie game." He can see no good in the antics of the gang, shooing them off the street, reacting unsympathetically when a stray ball breaks a store window, and growing madder still when they accidentally pelt him with a tomato during a brawl with their rival gang, the Man Eating Tiger Cubs of Wildcat Alley. Even so, he *is* a cop, and hardly the meanest ogre the gang has ever faced, so it seems odd that the kids would pounce on him so mercilessly at the end of the film, just because he's no longer wearing a uniform. Their actions are somewhat justified, however, when McManus deliberately knocks out Officer Mac, proving that he was a no-good character all along, and eminently worthy of the gang's hostility.

The main problem with "Official Officers" is that neither of its two plot elements is fully developed. One can envision an entire two-reeler devoted to the problems of playing in the streets, and even more logically, an entire short based on the gang playing policemen. As it stands, the junior-cop segment is much too abbreviated, with fleeting glimpses of the gang in action (including Farina's encounter with a violent group of black men shooting craps) and hauling lawbreakers to their makeshift jail.

The only aspect of this sequence that is fully explored is Joe's continuing attempt to mooch free bananas from Tony, the local fruit-vendor.*

But following the doctrine of keeping things moving, "Official Officers" never stands still, and provides diverting enough entertainment to blur most criticism . . . until one stops and takes a closer look.

* Identified by way of a sign above his stand which reads "Antonio Campanaro, Fruits and Vegetables," Campanaro is yet another inside joke, since he spent much of his unsung career working for Hal Roach, managing the studio's menagerie of dogs, cats, chickens, horses, mules, and monkeys that were kept down the road at Roach's favorite location site, the picturesque Arnaz Ranch (where, also, Hal Roach, Harold Lloyd, and others around the lot used to get together for physical fitness workouts in the mornings). But while Tony Campanaro's *Our Gang* contributions spanned the entire Roach period, he would also loan out trained animals to other motion picture studios on behalf of Hal Roach. One noted customer was Buster Keaton, for whom Campanaro supplied the monkey used in *The Cameraman*, and the progressively larger canines needed for the marvelous four seasons prologue gag at the outset of *Seven Chances*.

41 · MARY, QUEEN OF TOTS

Two Reels · Produced by Hal Roach · Supervised by F. Richard Jones · Directed by Robert F. McGowan · Photographed by Art Lloyd · Edited by Richard Currier · Titles by H. M. Walker · Story by Hal E. Roach · Released on August 23, 1925, by Pathé Exchange · Our Gang: Mary Kornman, Mickey Daniels, Joe Cobb, Allen "Farina" Hoskins, Jackie Condon, and Pal the Dog · Mrs. Newman, Mary's mother, Lyle Tayo; Kindly gardener, Richard Daniels; Radio station actor, James Finlayson; Governess, May Beatty; Officer, Charles Bachman; Doll-maker, Charley Young; Doll-maker's wife, Helen Gilmore

Rich-girl Mary is ignored by her parents, and kept from having much fun by a stuffy governess. Her only friend is the gardener on the estate, who buys her some home-made dolls. Mary loves the dolls, and as she naps, she dreams that they come to life and play with the "giant" furniture in her room. During her sleep, however, the

Mary Kornman.

governess finds the dolls and throws them out. Meanwhile, four boys who amazingly resemble the miniature dolls come to Mary's house delivering laundry. Mary thinks that the toys have come to life, full-size, but when she learns the truth, she decides to play a trick on her governess. When the snippy woman brings a policeman to throw the gang out of the house, she finds only the tiny doll likenesses of the youngsters. She can't believe her eyes, while the cop presumes that she's lost her marbles, giving Mary, the boys, and the gardener the last laugh.

"Mary, Queen of Tots" is an amusing and frustrating film—"frustrating" because the wonderful fantasy sequence in the middle of the film is tossed away so casually.

Mary goes to sleep on the floor of her room, resting on a pillow. She is shown in the foreground of the picture, while behind her (via split-screen) the *Our Gang* dolls come to life, one by one, cavorting on the giant chairs, bed, rocker, and bureau, with startling results. The photography is excellent and the illusion is beautifully maintained.

There are some ingenious scenes using perspective and relative size: a toy donkey is perfectly in proportion to the toy children, so when the humans come alive, they are able to play with the live mule—a miniature from the audience's point of view. But Mary's toy dog is larger, so when *it* comes to life it somewhat dwarfs the doll-children; some of the effectiveness here is diminished by the fact that the dog is clearly a man inside an animal suit. (In 1925 though, there was a sturdy precedent for movie-goers that Roach might have been counting on. The previous year's filmic adaptation of Barrie's *Peter Pan* had similarly featured a man-in-animal-costume for the fetching role of Nana the Dog.)

In one scene Joe combs his hair with a comb that's bigger than he is. And there is a marvelous reverse-angle

shot as Farina, on the floor, talks to Mickey, who's sitting on top of Mary's bureau. First we see the conversation from Mickey's point of view, looking all the way down at Farina, and then the angle switches, the camera moving *under* a clear-glass floor to catch Farina's point of view looking way up at Mickey!

When Mary wakes up and finds the dolls gone, the film progresses to other plot situations, and spends far too much time on conventional humor about the four poor children running rampant in the opulent mansion. There is a superfluous gag about the kids encountering a radio for the first time, and being frightened by disembodied voices telling them to take off their hats (explained somewhat improbably by the fact that station KHJ is presenting a playlet entitled "Take off That Hat").

Mary's confusion about the resemblance between the dolls and the boys is also logically explained as Mickey indelicately declares, "Aw, a wop makes those dolls to look like us—we get $1 a week for modeling."

Thus, every possibility for a charming *Our Gang* fantasy film is abruptly thrown out the window. Having gone to the trouble and expense of building authentic giant-size sets, and carried out the superb split-screen photography, one would think director McGowan and his staff might have seized the opportunity to create a full-fledged dreamlike frolic, with Mary turning herself into a miniature doll, and running through the house with her friends, eluding the witchy governess.

There is even a brief storybook sequence in which Mary starts to tell her dolls about a make-believe princess, visualized in a brief swashbuckling segment, which like the doll dream is blithely tossed aside after a few minutes. McGowan seems to be more intrigued with the comic prospects of the kids encountering a slippery throw-rug in Mary's living room! Did the production staff really think it necessary to keep the gang on solid, realistic ground rather than permitting themselves one offbeat flight of fantasy?

Apparently, such was the case, and we are left with a pleasant two-reeler revealing tantalizing glimpses of something *very* special that might have been.

Audiences often don't laugh at enchanting sequences, and perhaps Roach found that preview audiences simply admired the technique, instead of laughing, so that the whimsy and magiclike elements had to be relegated to incidental status. But even if McGowan and company failed to fully exploit the fantasy possibilities offered, one can be thankful for the sequences that remain—sequences that disarm criticism.

One does find it easy, however, to admire a different aspect of McGowan's direction. For a 1925 comedy (*Our Gang* or otherwise), it concentrates especially well on the kids and their personalities (Mary's particularly, of course), rather than merely on gags or situations that somehow coincidentally involve the kids.

Winsome Mary Kornman, as always, is cuter than any doll could *ever* be, and effortlessly mirrors the range of emotions her characterization calls for: from scenes where she makes mud pies to feed her governess to scenes where she discovers life-size replicas of her stuffed dolls, and, believing they've come to life, tries to kiss them all. Naturally, the gang will have no quarter with this nonsense, and when it comes Farina's turn, he gives her such an open-mouthed look of "Don't try it, sister," that it should have stopped the camera!

On their way to see Mr. Pan-American, the surveyor, or, as Mickey says, "the big survivor."

42 · BOYS WILL BE JOYS

Two Reels · Produced by Hal Roach · Supervised by F. Richard Jones · Directed by Robert F. McGowan · Photographed by Art Lloyd · Edited by Richard Currier · Titles by H. M. Walker · Story by Hal E. Roach · Released on July 26, 1925, by Pathé Exchange · Our Gang: Mickey Daniels, Mary Kornman, Johnny Downs, Allen "Farina" Hoskins, Joe Cobb, Jackie Condon, Jay R. Smith, Jannie Hoskins, Andy Samuels, Dinah the Mule, and Pal the Dog · Henry Mills, board chairman, Paul Weigel; Officer, Noah Young; Surveyor, Charles Bachman; Board of directors, George K. French, Allen Cavan, William Gillespie, William A. Orlamond, Charley Young

The gang has big plans for an amusement park, but a surveyor tells them that their plot of land is being used for a new factory. Undaunted, the kids go to see the president of the company that owns the land. He turns out to be a sixty-year-old with a heart aged ten, and after hearing the youngsters' story, he walks out on a board of directors meeting and helps them set up their amusement park. The board of directors, determined to meet with their chairman to try to vote him out of office, follow close behind. When the kids get tired of operating their own rides, they enlist the services of these men, and at the end of the day, the president tells them that they can *have* the company—he's going to retire and stay young, like the gang.

Overly familiar plot elements, realized with greater success in other films, leave this a pleasant but unexceptional entry. The gang's amusement park is not, as one would expect, a shoestring affair, but incredibly elabo-rate, with a ferris wheel, merry-go-round, roller coaster, water slide, and a wide array of fun house staples. While there is some attempt to show the makeshift nature of these rides, the whole affair is far too sophisticated to be believable as a creation of the gang—even with the aid of a fun-loving financier. Additionally, a great deal of footage is devoted to the operation of these rides, with no gags in sight.

Even the subplot about the aging executive helping the gang is curiously flat. An introductory title explains his young-at-heart outlook, so his decision to help the gang is perfectly natural.

For a finale, the film falls back on a skunk gag with Farina, which despite its surefire nature must have been rather timeworn even in 1925. The executive's flashback recollection of a circus was also familiar: stock footage from "Jubilo, Jr."

43 · BETTER MOVIES

Two Reels · Produced by Hal Roach · Supervised by F. Richard Jones · Directed by Robert F. McGowan · Edited by Richard Currier · Titles by H. M. Walker · Story by Hal E. Roach · Released on November 1, 1925, by Pathé Exchange · Our Gang: Jackie Condon, Mary Kornman, Billy Lord, Jay R. Smith, Mickey Daniels, Johnny Downs, Joe Cobb, Allen "Farina" Hoskins, Jackie Hanes, Bobby "Bonedust" Young, and Pal the Dog · Billy's mother, Lyle Tayo; The teen-aged "vamp," Martha Sleeper; Officer, William Gillespie

The gang has organized a full-fledged motion picture enterprise, with only one missing ingredient: a camera. When Billy sees what's going on, he abandons his violin practicing and brings his home-movie camera to join the kids as cinematographer. When filming is completed, the gang stages a premiere engagement, which comes to an abrupt finale when Jackie and Jay R., spiteful because they were left out of the fun, bring a cop around to clear out the barn.

"Better Movies" is, unfortunately, *not* one of the gang's better movies, but it does have certain elements that are undeniably intriguing.

The most striking aspect of "Better Movies" is just how the gang has managed to assemble such elaborate

Director Bob McGowan watches as the Gang mimics fellow Hal Roach star Jimmie Finlayson, very much out of character and practically unrecognizable in glasses, without his walrus mustache, and wearing a straw hat to cover his bald dome. Mary Kornman and Scooter Lowry are clinging to McGowan, while fashioning Finsquints are Jackie Condon, Joe Cobb, Johnny Downs, and Farina.

sets and costumes to make their film. Settings range from Egypt to Africa for their seriallike adventure, and the trappings are far beyond the capabilities of most eight-year-olds. An ersatz alligator which attacks Joe in one scene is rather impressively constructed, as is the outdoor shooting stage on which the young filmmakers operate. Thus, while the gang's movie-making enterprise is makeshift, it loses certain appeal because it isn't makeshift *enough*.

The only print available for review appears to have been rather severely cut by a television syndicator, leaving the subject incomplete and minus inter-titles. Judging from other *Our Gangers* cast in the same mold, originally an opening sequence could have tied in with a premiere for a real movie (which would be fascinating to view), or shooting on the set for a real movie (possibly a chapter play), which inspires the gang to see if they can do as well, or *better*.

As it is, the subject is awkwardly constructed, beginning with sequences of the film being made, then moving on to its initial showing, where we cut from on-screen activities to reactions in the audience, periodically showing Billy in the projection booth, where he has some sideline fun by running sequences backwards or stopping them in midaction.

Although elements of the gang's finished film are fun to see, this is really a one-joke comedy—and not a terribly funny joke at that. The actions on-screen are somewhat protracted, except for highlights like a cliffhanger ending to one "chapter" where spies Mickey and Joe are tied to a position directly facing a cannon about to go off. Their escape is effected by the cannonball itself, which in Rube Goldbergish fashion misses its target, and knocks a sword off the wall above, which on its way to the ground splits the ropes holding our heroes helpless.

The filming itself is relatively uneventful, except for some harried script conferences, and the pranks played by disgruntled Jackie and Jay R., who hurl tomatoes and pepper-bombs at the cast and crew (even this slapstick sidetrip is thrown away, instead of being built into a funny filmmaking disaster).

"Better Movies" features two older kids prominently: Billy Lord as a neighborhood rich-kid whose doting mother insists that he practice the violin instead of playing with the other children; and Martha Sleeper who is recruited as leading lady for the film when the gang spots her mimicking a sultry siren from a magazine photo. Her comic aggressiveness and know-how seem a bit too slick for an *Our Gang* film, where the rest of the "actors" are supposedly amateurs. Indeed, within a year she was working as Charley Chase's love interest in things such as *Crazy Like a Fox*.

As with many other *Our Gang* silents, "Better Movies" presents a situation that seems tailor-made for this series, but that somehow goes awry and doesn't hit the target. This kind of material was handled much better in earlier comedies like "The Big Show" and "Dogs of War."

Footnote: According to studio publicity, the gang actually produced their own film-within-the-film, to celebrate the industry-wide "Greater Movie Season" promotion. Our Gang's contribution was supposedly this polite satire of what the studio blurb described as "the oldtime movies of ten years ago."

44 · YOUR OWN BACK YARD

Two Reels · Produced by Hal Roach · Supervised by F. Richard Jones · Directed by Robert F. McGowan · Edited by Richard Currier · Titles by H. M. Walker · Story by Hal E. Roach · Released on September 27, 1925, by Pathé Exchange · Our Gang (presumed): Mickey Daniels, Joe Cobb, Jackie Condon, Allen "Farina" Hoskins, Johnny Downs, and Mary Kornman

This film was unavailable for viewing. A thorough description and critique is provided from a write-up of the day in *Exhibitor's Daily Review:* "Farina, dusky juvenile of *Our Gang,* is very lonesome and wants to play with the white boys, but is rebuffed continually. Mammy tells him to stay in his 'own back yard.' Life there is too monotonous for him and he strays out again and runs into all sorts of difficulties and pranks played by the other boys. The gang get free samples of dental cream and not only go into a tooth drill for themselves but insist on brushing the mouths of three dogs, who give the appearance of foaming at the mouth. They are taken for mad dogs; chased by the police and shot at, Farina thinking he is the victim. Finally he falls asleep in a beggar's seat and gets contributions with which he outfits himself with new clothes, in triumph.

"Farina has come into his own in this Hal Roach comedy, being given the major portion of the action, and boy, he takes it like a trouper. Formerly his very appearance was a signal for the laughs to begin, but now in addition, he is exhibiting a choice brand of histrionics. The comedy is excellent and the gags likewise. The contrivance of the camera that squirts water on the unsuspecting; the episode of the dental cream and the mad dogs; the stunt of the revolving doors, with Farina emerging dizzy; the chase of the dogs by the police and the use of novograph and slow-motion photography; the Mexican jumping beans and the jumping chickens and eggs; all go far toward upholding the reputation of these comedies for originality and uniqueness."

Farina ties into director Bob McGowan and seems to be winning approval from the rest of the Rascals. In the background is the Roach studio tank, eventually dubbed Lake Laurel & Hardy.

"Your Own Back Yard" is unique in another way: the two-reeler stands out in Hal Roach's mind today as his all-time favorite *Our Gang* comedy. One always has high hopes for any film so long unseen, and Hal Roach's endorsement makes us particularly anxious for its rescue from the growing list of lost films.

45 · ONE WILD RIDE

Two Reels · Produced by Hal Roach · Supervised by F. Richard Jones · Directed by Robert F. McGowan · Edited by Richard Currier · Titles by H. M. Walker · Story by Hal E. Roach · Released on December 6, 1925, by Pathé Exchange · Our Gang: Allen "Farina" Hoskins, Mickey Daniels, Joe Cobb, Mary Kornman, Johnny Downs, and Jackie Condon · Horse owner, Richard Daniels; Sprinter, Ed Brandenberg; Man with bird cage, Al Hallet

Take one abandoned car, minus engine, add one unused horse, and you've got what passes for a "sightseeing taxi," until Johnny's angry father comes to reclaim his horse, leaving the gang without a means of propulsion. A friendly motorist offers to give them a tow up the hill, enabling them to coast down from there. When they park the taxi temporarily, Farina, who's been left out of the fun, decides to take it out for a spin himself. He manages to get a tow, but then breaks loose and embarks on a long, scary ride, out of control—around corners, down steep hills, narrowly missing cars and people, encountering all sorts of obstructions along the way, before knocking over a watermelon cart and overturning halfway down a hill, watermelons in hot pursuit. When Farina emerges from the mess, he is literally covered with watermelons as a souvenir of his first solo flight!

Obviously, the main attraction in "One Wild Ride" is just that—Farina's wild and woolly auto excursion. The fright aspects of this out-of-control journey are expertly handled by the Hal Roach technicians, combining authentic close-ups of Farina in the runaway car with long shots on actual city streets, some hair-raising first-person shots from Farina's point-of-view, and a handful of medium shots with artificial backdrops. The end result is a memorable collage of film, bringing the excitement of this ride to the audience with maximum impact—unlike so many later comedy chases in the talkie era that settled for patently phony rear projection and long shots where it was clear that a stuntman was driving.

For comic purposes, there are various and sundry obstacles in Farina's path. At the bottom of one hill he bumps a man carrying a birdcage and a fishbowl. The bowl goes flying and lands on Farina's head, while the fish sails down the back of his shirt! Later an organ grinder's monkey hops aboard to give Farina additional grief, wrapping its tail around his neck and generally being a nuisance. Another sidetrip takes the car through a mudpuddle where a group of birds are converged; the impact sends thousands of feathers flying, most of them landing on the hapless Farina! The watermelon cart provides a final comic calamity, with the loose melons rolling down the hill after Farina, and piling up against the overturned car.

(Interestingly enough, this gag was echoed many years later in Ossie Davis's spirited movie *Cotton Comes to Harlem,* where a crash into a fruit stand brings a car chase by the two black detective heroes to an abrupt halt. Of course, the 1970 movie brought an element of irony and satire to the association of blacks and watermelons missing from the 1920s Hal Roach comedy.)

While ''One Wild Ride'' is fun, and the prolonged car chase is masterfully executed, director McGowan made better use of the idea some years later in his talkie ''Free Wheeling,'' where the runaway car was worked into the framework of a story and given a real purpose, instead of standing on its own as the raison d'être for an entire film.

46 · GOOD CHEER

Two Reels · Produced by Hal Roach · Supervised by F. Richard Jones · Directed by Robert F. McGowan · Edited by Richard Currier · Titles by H. M. Walker · Story by Hal E. Roach · Released on January 10, 1926, by Pathé Exchange · Our Gang: Mary Kornman, Mickey Daniels, Johnny Downs, Joe Cobb, Allen "Farina" Hoskins, Jackie Condon, Jay R. Smith, Jannie Hoskins, Dinah the Mule, and Pal the Dog · Old man, Richard Daniels; Motorist, Charlie Hall; First officer, Gene Morgan; Second officer, Noah Young; Store window assistant, Ed Brandenberg; Inebriated Santa Claus, Sam Lufkin; Store window Santa, "Tonnage" Martin Wolfkeil; Pedestrians, Chet Brandenberg, Jack Hill; Crooked Santas, Jack Gavin, Al Hallet, Jack Ackroyd, William A. Orlamond, Jules Mendel, Wallace Howe, Charlie Hall

It's the day before Christmas, ''down where poverty shakes hands with sorrow, and they both smile.'' The poor street kids have sadly concluded that there is no Santa Claus—they've seen one too many phonies. Then two of the older kids, Mickey and Johnny, are visited by the spirit of the real Santa Claus, who inspires them to earn money so they can play Santa for the others. They hit upon the idea of selling hot bricks to keep people's feet warm, and collect enough money to celebrate Christmas in style. Together (piggyback) they disguise as Kris Kringle, dress up Dinah the Mule as a makeshift reindeer, and make their entrance via the chimney with a fine array of presents. Meanwhile, a band of bootleggers is in the area, all disguised as Santa; Mickey and Johnny help the police capture these impostors, and manage to collect their booty as additional gifts for the awestruck gang.

The opening sequence of this film features a heavier dose of sentiment than one is accustomed to in *Our Gang.* The florid opening title leads to a series of wintertime vignettes: two gift-laden pedestrians crashing into each other, a cat and mouse whose whiskers have frozen stiff, a silk-hatted poet whose chapeau is immediately plastered with a snowball, etc.

While in tempo and tone still a moderately funny short, there is a definite element of pathos in the film's portrait of the gang as street urchins who live alone and can't afford a real Christmas. Fortunately, all of the simpering is in the point-of-view of the filmmakers; the kids are never shown feeling sorry for themselves. They take what they can, as always, and make the best of it, as when Joe discovers an iron grating in the sidewalk just above a bakery, where you can smell hot bread—for free.

The sentimental overtones of several scenes are most unusual for this series. Mickey helps cheer a one-legged

Our Ganger Jackie Condon visits Harold Lloyd, who's in costume for his 1927 feature *The Kid Brother*.

youngster on the street, who complains about keeping his foot warm, by saying, "You gotta lot to be thankful for. You only got one foot—I got two."

There is an equally offbeat element of whimsy in this short, in the depiction of the Spirit of Father Christmas, a cheerful specter who oversees the goodwill enterprise of Mickey and Johnny.

"Good Cheer" features a special-effects sequence that is treated almost as a throwaway. The so-called wind-up toys in a store window display are actually live actors in miniature, much like Dr. Praetorius's creations in *Bride of Frankenstein*. These little clowns dance and frolic, with Santa looking on, and for a finale they hoist a banner which reads "Next Show in 20 Minutes."

The sentiment in "Good Cheer" is forgivable, considering its timing as a seasonal release. Yet even so, it must have struck audiences of that time as unusual to place the boisterous, nothing-sacred *Our Gang* kids into a Little Match Girl framework. Fortunately, this was a rare exception, and not a rule. The following year, Hal Roach left the studios' yuletide release to Charley Chase, and the resulting "There Ain't No Santa Claus" went straight for laughs and proved to be a better film.

"Good Cheer," however, does showcase some bizarre gags—particularly scenes where everyone in town is nonchalantly walking about with heavy bricks attached to the bottoms of their shoes, or when the gang hoses down a Model T, literally whitewashing it with a sheath of icy decorations. These, together with the novelty of viewing the gang in a wintry setting, offset somewhat the melancholy aspects of the film.

47 · BURIED TREASURE

Two Reels · Produced by Hal Roach · Supervised by F. Richard Jones · Directed by Robert F. McGowan · Photographed by Art Lloyd · Edited by Richard Currier · Titles by H. M. Walker · Story by Hal E. Roach · Released on February 14, 1926 by Pathé Exchange · Our Gang: Mickey Daniels, Mary Kornman, Joe Cobb, Jackie Condon, Johnny Downs, Jay R. "Specks" Smith, and Allen "Farina" Hoskins · Man in gorilla suit, Charlie Hall; Johnny's mother, Lyle Tayo; Mother of one of the gang members, Dorothy Vernon

"In 1698, Captain Kidd buried his treasure," a title card reads. "Since then, 14,987,652,376,456,983 little boys have started out to find it." The latest group of would-be millionaires has gleaned its inspiration from wealthy Johnny's yacht, building a makeshift replica that at least stays afloat, and from a so-called treasure map proffered by salty Cap' Tuttle, who has merely torn a section from a real estate brochure describing Catalina Island. The kids take off for high adventure but run out of gas sooner than expected. Overnight the tide brings them to a nearby island, however, which appears to be the exact location spotted on the map! The excited youngsters begin to dig up the beach, while elsewhere on the island a movie company on-location, with men dressed as cannibals and assorted wild animals, decides to have fun with the unsuspecting kids by giving them a good scare. They underestimate the gang, however; before long the kids have the last laugh, outwitting, outrunning, and generally out-

doing the movie crew with the help of some coconuts, Roman candles, and fancy footwork.

This pleasant two-reeler only scratches the surface of possibilities inherent in an *Our Gang* pirate film. A lengthy sequence with Farina and a baboon and a climax with the gang encountering lions, gorillas, and cannibals could have found their way into any *Our Gang* outing. An introductory device with the kids reading passages from *Treasure Island* is thrown overboard rather quickly, diminishing further the effectiveness of the pirate premise.

The best scenes are on-board the gang's yacht, one of those wondrous *Our Gang* devices that no kids could really have built—amazingly elaborate and surprisingly seaworthy. Aside from this, the major asset of "Buried Treasure" is the location shooting, first at sea and then on a magnificently picturesque Pacific island. It's a shame the action on-screen doesn't match the scenery behind it or live up to the film's enticing title.

48 · MONKEY BUSINESS

Two Reels · Produced by Hal Roach · Supervised by F. Richard Jones · Directed by Robert F. McGowan · Edited by Richard Currier · Titles by H. M. Walker · Story by Hal E. Roach · Released on March 21, 1926, by Pathé Exchange · Our Gang: Allen "Farina" Hoskins, Joe Cobb, Mickey Daniels, Jackie Condon, Johnny Downs, Jannie "Mango" Hoskins, Mary Kornman, and Jay R. Smith · First officer, Robert A. (Anthony Mack) McGowan; Man repairing auto, Harry Bowen; Balloons vendor, Charlie Hall; Patrol wagon driver, Ed Brandenberg; Other officers, William Gillespie, Charles A. Bachman

Posed shot from *Monkey Business.*

The gang has been beating up Farina, and his parents' constant battles make home life just as hectic, so he decides to run away. At the same time, a mischievous monkey has the same idea, fleeing from his trainers, who run a vaudeville act called "The Missing Link." The two fugitives meet, and when Farina discovers that his monkey pal can fight the pants off anybody, he returns to the gang and earns a new respect because of his simian friend. With peace restored, the kids decide to build a tent and charge admission to see the talented animal. While they're working, however, the monkey is left on his own, and after drinking some bootleg liquor, he goes on a rampage, terrorizing the town with giant-size pranks and sending the cops after the ape and the gang, who are responsible for his actions. The cops decide to give the kids a scare, and load them into a patrol wagon, but in a flash, the monkey boots the driver out of his seat and starts the wagon himself, careening through city streets and causing more commotion than ever. When the truck smashes into a building, the kids and their monkey pal hop out and start running, as four very angry cops chase them into the distance.

Decidedly no inspiration for the later Marx Brothers film (they didn't even use a monkey—unless he was a fifth stowaway, never discovered), *Our Gang's* "Monkey Business" was timely, if little else. Today, we could never understand the film's impact, but at the time, movie audiences really had monkeys on their minds. The year 1925 had been the year of the famous Scopes monkey trial, concerning the right to teach Darwin's theory of evolution in the schools.

"Monkey Business" wisely skirts controversy, though Beanie Walker opens the film on a topical note: "Darwin says—Man sprang from monkey. Will Rogers says—Some of them didn't spring far enough."

In "Monkey Business," unlike your typical chimpanzee, The Missing Link is quite powerful, and when he plays rough, it's wise to duck. One of the "destruction" gags, during the monkey's drunken spree, begins with a shot of an amateur mechanic pulling a broken part from under the hood of his automobile. He walks away to repair the pipe, and as soon as he leaves, the monkey hops onto the hood and starts pulling out other gadgets, right and left. When the owner returns, he finds the monkey proudly sitting atop the heap of rubble that used to be his car!

The hyperactive chimp opens a fire hydrant, beats up a policeman and steals his uniform, overturns a fruit vendor's cart, yanks down the pants of an innocent pedestrian, and shoots off two loaded pistols in the middle of a busy street. Just playful, that's all.

Another foolproof gag is pulled into the proceedings when the monkey downs an entire keg of homemade hooch, and suddenly does backflips in ultra slow motion.

In fact, "Monkey Business" is hardly more than an excuse to fill two reels with quite literal monkeyshines. The chimp is fun to watch, and the film moves briskly, but as an *Our Gang* comedy, it falls short of its mark, not only in subordinating the kids to second bananas (bad pun unintended) but in failing to realize the slapstick potential of its situations, opting for destruction instead of comic chaos.

Still, it's difficult to argue with success, and from the 1920s to the present day, playful monkeys remain crowd pleasers. Hal Roach and his *Our Gang* filmmakers knew this as well as anyone, and saw to it that chimpanzees appeared with great frequency throughout the gang's career.

Bob McGowan cast his nephew Robert A. (Anthony Mack) McGowan in "Monkey Business" as a cop. He's no more an actor than he'd be a writer or director later, but at least when he was acting he couldn't write or direct.

49 · BABY CLOTHES

Two Reels · Produced by Hal Roach · Supervised by F. Richard Jones · Directed by Robert F. McGowan · Photographed by Art Lloyd · Edited by Richard Currier · Titles by H. M. Walker · Story by Hal E. Roach · Released on April 25, 1926, by Pathé Exchange · Our Gang: Joe Cobb, Mickey Daniels, Mary Kornman, Johnny Downs, Allen "Farina" Hoskins, Jackie Condon, and Bobby "Bonedust" Young · House detective, Stanley (Tiny) Sandford; Bellboys, Charlie Hall, Ed Brandenberg; William Weedle, William Gillespie; Mrs. Weedle, Charlotte Mineau; Man telling Irish joke, Rolfe Sedan; Man listening to Irish joke, Lee Phelps; Joe's mother, Helen Gilmore; The midget, Harry Earles; Midget's guardian, Fay Holderness; Leggy lady, Martha Sleeper

A conniving couple has been collecting $50 a week for the support of two nonexistent children from a rich uncle who lives out of town. Now the uncle is coming to visit, and they must produce two kids for his approval. Joe's mother has him wearing baby clothes as punishment for getting into so many fights, but this becomes an asset when he's hired to play the part of a two-year-old. Mickey obligingly dons a dress and curly-haired wig to portray the eight-year-old daughter. But lurking about the hotel where the couple lives is a twenty-seven-year-old midget who dresses as a baby in order to play practical jokes on people. He joins Joe and Mickey while the couple is out, and just at that point, Uncle arrives unexpectedly, and finds *three* kids instead of two. The couple returns and tries to explain, but the situation becomes more suspicious when Joe leaves and Jackie tries to take his place, thinking that no one will know the difference. The final straw comes when Farina wanders in, hoping to pass himself off as yet another baby brother! Uncle is furious, the couple is flustered, and the gang is on the run—while Joe, still in baby clothes, gets into another fight with a tough guy on the corner.

"Baby Clothes" is a somewhat jumbled but generally amusing two-reeler that has enough good moments to make one overlook some of its flaws.

The familiar Hal Roach hotel lobby set is given a brief workout, with several twists one doesn't find in other films using this locale. As Jackie and Farina come to call on their pals, they are greeted by the burly doorman, and the camera takes their point of view, looking up at the unfriendly fellow. Then they run into the elevator and command control of it themselves, with the camera taking us on an exciting ride all the way up and then all the way down the elevator shaft at top speed, filmed so that we're looking upward at the seesawlike excursion. When the two mischief makers are thrown out the front door, we see them against the background of a real street, with cars passing behind—a neat bit of movie trickery to hide the fact that they've just been on a studio interior set.

The midget gags, and the unoriginal idea of Joe donning baby clothes are handled in ordinary fashion, or perhaps it's just that one has seen the same idea executed so much better in the talkie "Free Eats" that colors one's opinion. In the 1931 film, the two midgets are crooks, and their infant disguises have a definite purpose—to enable them to attend a charity party and steal jewelry from the matrons who fondle them. The only explanation we have for the bizarre actions of this midget in "Baby Clothes" is that he's been playing practical jokes for twenty-six of his twenty-seven years.

Mickey(!), Mary, and *Our Gang*'s All-American Boy, Johnny Downs, in a scene cut from extant prints of "Baby Clothes."

This is not the only aspect of the film that raises questions; characters appear and disappear without rhyme or reason, and actions take place off-screen that are never explained to the audience, from Mickey's decision to dress as a girl to the sudden appearance of Mary Kornman when Mickey and Joe first arrive at the hotel.

Still, there are good contributions from Hal Roach stock company players like Charlie Hall, as the bellboy, Tiny Sandford, as the house detective, shifty William Gillespie, as the "father," and pert Martha Sleeper, as a flapper whose silk-stockinged legs deservedly attract the twenty-seven-year-old "baby."

And there are some enjoyable descriptive titles. "Dempsey gets $1,000,000 a fight," we're told. "Joe fights six times a day and doesn't get a nickel."

Even better, there's an introduction to the gang that could well describe their entire existence: "Nothing to do—and the whole neighborhood to do it in."

50 · UNCLE TOM'S UNCLE

Two Reels · Produced by Hal Roach · Supervised by F. Richard Jones · Directed by Robert F. McGowan · Photographed by Art Lloyd · Edited by Richard Currier · Titles by H. M. Walker · Story by Hal E. Roach · Released on May 30, 1926, by Pathé Exchange · Our Gang: Joe Cobb, Mickey Daniels, Mary Kornman, Allen "Farina" Hoskins, Jackie Condon, Johnny Downs, Jay R. Smith, Jannie Hoskins, Bobby "Bonedust" Young, Peggy Eames, Scooter Lowry, Jackie Hanes, Bobby Green, David Durand, Bobby Mallon, Billy Butts, Billy Naylor, and Dinah the Mule

Mickey's barn is the setting for Our Gang's reenactment of *Uncle Tom's Cabin.* Joe is cast as Uncle Tom, but it seems he's plagued by a conflict of interests: Joe's mother would rather see him cleaning out their back yard than acting in Mickey's barn. That isn't the only problem the company faces. A huge crowd of neighborhood kids has gathered to watch the play, and apparently all of them are rooting for a flop so they can bombard the stage with the arsenal of firecrackers, rotten fruits and vegetables they just happen to have with them. If the show isn't a flop, these kids are going to make it a messy success. Once the little melodrama is under way, the unusually boisterous crowd begins cheering and roaring at every foul-up, and soon the garbage is flying. Perched in the hayloft overhead, Farina's younger sister joins in the fun too, pelting the thespians beneath her with an inexhaustible supply of eggs. But if not very dramatic, the gang is persistent, and somehow they muddle through the chase across the icebergs to the scene where a dying Uncle Tom is to be taken up to heaven—if the rope doesn't break. Heaven is depicted overhead by an angelic Mary Kornman floating among the clouds (with "clowd" scrawled across each one so nobody can mistake the locale). Joe's mother still thinks he should finish cleaning up the yard, so he balks at finishing the scene, "I can't die now, my mother is calling me!" *That* is all the audience is waiting for, and the camera reveals a huge throng of practically rabid kids, now standing, massed together, poised with ammunition in hand, primed to heave it in unison and crush Mickey on stage with an avalanche of garbage!

Motion pictures, especially silent ones, are meant to *move,* and this fast-paced comedy certainly does that. A fine second-echelon Rascals film, "Uncle Tom's Uncle" has a very physical quality and depends upon a variety of skillful mime, funny costuming, and traditional slapstick for its considerable laughs. The steady stream of accomplished visual gags is often up to the gang's best standards, with Joe Cobb and Mickey Daniels scoring especially well. Throughout the play, Mickey—dressed as Simon Legree—steps out between the curtains to try and introduce the next act, declaring "Now this is very serious." Each time, the audience responds by pelting him with some well-thrown gook or garbage, and each time Mickey doubles the laugh with an assortment of comic business—one time exchanging sick looks off-scene with someone else in the gang, reacting broadly another time, stomping around and gesturing wildly still another, or maybe just dead-panning his assailant. It works every time. Once, seeking suitable protection from all these assaults, he tries wearing a catcher's mask. Fending off missile after missile, Mickey is confident he's hit upon the solution until some smart guy plasters him with an egg,

Posed still from "Uncle Tom's Uncle" depicting absolutely nothing that happens in the film.

which successfully truncates the introduction to the next "ack." Mickey reacts calmly and blankly, turns, and walks back through the curtains.

The opening title reads, "*Uncle Tom's Cabin* had been translated and played in forty-two languages—the gang decided to make it forty-three." The same year, D. W. Griffith was offered what turned out to be Universal's $2,000,000 production of *Uncle Tom's Cabin,* but the director turned down the assignment—perhaps he had seen *Our Gang*'s version. In any case, there had been many, many dramatic adaptations of Harriet Beecher Stowe's novel *Uncle Tom's Cabin; Or, Life Among The Lowly*—why, though, this comedy treatment on the back lot of Hal Roach Studios? Hal Roach explains: "This kind of thing is all a matter of story construction. Really, it doesn't make a lot of difference whether a story idea is comic or dramatic to *begin* with. For instance, when I was a little kid, every night after supper we'd all gather around in the sitting room, and my grandfather, who had become totally blind, would tell us these wonderful stories. He allowed me and my brother to invite kids in from around the neighborhood. And all of us, I mean we couldn't wait for him to begin. He would tell us the most dramatic things you could ever imagine kids hearing, and he kept us spellbound. We'd keep asking for more and more of it, saying, 'What happened then?' You know what I mean. Well, it wasn't until I got much older that I would read books or see plays having the very stories he'd told us as kids, and I realized that what he was doing was taking classics, or stories that were common knowledge to everyone at that time, and then retelling them in such a way so that kids could understand them. Now outstanding filmed stories are the same. And I think that much of the success I have had in pictures is due to an ability to adapt ideas and create a dramatic or humorous situation that works on film in just the same way. You break the thing down into its basic elemental appeal, and try and fit the material to the characters you have, and then develop all the natural gags along a certain line that grow out of what you're trying to build on . . . that's story contruction.

"Now there's a very slight distinction between comedy and drama, anyway. That's why with the proper story development, we could take something like *Uncle Tom's Cabin* and work out the routines to make a comedy with it. Many of the things I did in comedy that were humorous I got from dramatic pictures. You'd wonder, well, if they twisted that idea and did it from a different slant, how would that work out for a comedy? And you'd develop it from there."

51 · THUNDERING FLEAS

Two Reels · Produced by Hal Roach · Supervised by F. Richard Jones · Directed by Robert F. McGowan · Edited by Richard Currier · Titles by H. M. Walker · Story by Hal E. Roach · Released on July 18, 1926, by Pathé Exchange · Our Gang: Allen "Farina" Hoskins, Mickey Daniels, Joe Cobb, Mary Kornman, Johnny Downs, Jay R. Smith, Bobby "Bonedust" Young, Jackie Condon, Mildred Kornman, Jannie Hoskins, and Scooter Lowry · Officer, Oliver Hardy; Sheldon, the groom, Jerry Mandy; Prof. Clements, George K. French; Pedestrian without fleas, Lyle Tayo; Father of the bride, Allen Cavan; Justice of the Peace, James Finlayson; Musicians, Alex Finlayson, Charlie Hall; Watching the flea circus, Harry Bowen, Charley Young; Extras at the wedding, Sam Lufkin, Ham Kinsey; Mustachioed wedding guest, Charley Chase; Bride, Martha Sleeper

Prof. Clements's Trained Flea and Insect Circus is in town, and when Farina goes to examine the sidewalk show with his dog Magnolia, the Professor's star flea, Garfield, decides to go AWOL and live with the pooch for a while. When the entrepreneur discovers that his star is gone, he offers the gang a dollar if they can find Garfield. In the confusion that follows, the entire Flea Circus is tipped over, and Garfield invites his cronies to "come on up" and join him on Magnolia's back. Meanwhile, Mary's older sister is getting married, and the gang is in attendance; the little kids, Farina and Scooter, also show up, however, and Magnolia is with them. As the dog wanders around the home where the ceremony is about to begin, she drops fleas hither and yon, first sending the musicians into itching spasms and eventually infecting the entire room. When Farina drops a whole jar of additional fleas the situation becomes impossible, and the party is violently disrupted, with everyone running outside for relief. The fleas continue to wreak their havoc, however, even on a nearby statue of a discus thrower that goes into convulsions and runs off its pedestal when the insects get to him!

"Thundering Fleas" is pure and delightful sight-gag comedy, expertly served by the Hal Roach team for maximum effect.

Garfield, the star flea, is an animated cartoon character, combined with some live-action movement to provide at least a minimal illusion of reality—although "minimal" is certainly the only goal of this far-fetched comedy.

The real highlights of "Thundering Fleas" are the appearances of members of the Hal Roach comedy troupe in featured roles. First, we see Oliver Hardy as a cop who becomes Magnolia's first transfer-victim, going into amusing contortions as his body is covered with fleas. He eventually rips off his pants, causing considerable embarrassment when Farina runs off with the trousers and unwittingly leaves the policeman stranded. His solution to the problem, in true silent comedy style, is to paint his bright white long johns black and simulate pants legs!

The next cameo features Charley Chase, somewhat hidden behind a giant walrus mustache, as a wedding guest. When he feels an itch under his nose, his mustache twitches from side to side with hilarious results, before he plucks the intruder out of his hair and relaxes. Not for long, however—since another small army of fleas is assembling under his shirt front. Chase's "guest appearance" was apparently filmed during a spare moment from his own shooting schedule on the Roach lot, since he appears alone on-screen as a cutaway from the party.

Then there is James Finlayson, *sans* mustache (Charley Chase must have worn it) as the justice of the peace. His performance is conventional until the actual moment of truth, when he asks the groom the Big Question and the fellow, covered with fleas, jerks his head from side to side as if to say "No!" Then Fin gives him his famous fisheye look and repeats the question; when the same result occurs, his reaction is even funnier, until the preacher gets bitten himself and becomes a victim of itching.

Pert Martha Sleeper is also seen to good advantage in her brief scenes as the bride, who is among the last to suffer from fleadom.

Although the gang is on hand throughout the proceed-

A shot from "Thundering Fleas": you said a mouthful!

Oliver Hardy and Charley Chase in frames from "Thundering Fleas." ›

ings, they really take a back seat to these "guest stars" and sight gags. As if to compensate, McGowan opens the film with a junior version of the wedding, allowing us to spend time with the kids before moving on to the grown-up wedding.

Some viewers might find it odd that the wedding is never resolved in this film and the "story" never comes to a close. But "Thundering Fleas" is more concerned with gags than with plot, and it scores as a completely satisfying comedy because the laughs never let up.

52 · SHIVERING SPOOKS

Two Reels · Produced by Hal Roach · Supervised by F. Richard Jones · Directed by Robert F. McGowan · Edited by Richard Currier · Titles by H. M. Walker · Story by Hal E. Roach · Released on August 8, 1926, by Pathé Exchange · Our Gang: Allen "Farina" Hoskins, Joe Cobb, Mary Kornman, Johnny Downs, Scooter Lowry, Bobby Young, Jay R. Smith, and Jackie Condon · Detective, Stanley (Tiny) Sandford; Professor Fleece, George K. French; His assistants, also the "spookers," Ham Kinsey, Harry Bowen; "Suckers" at the seance, Clara Guiol, Dorothy Walbert

The gang has been annoying Professor Fleece, a fake spiritualist whose activities have been disrupted by the kids' boisterous baseball games nearby. So when the kids tunnel from their underground cave headquarters into the professor's emporium, he and his cohorts decide to give the youngsters a good scare. The kids get the last laugh, however, when they realize what's been going on and drop vases onto the heads of Fleece and his gang—just in time for a police detective to round up the fakers for a ride in the paddy wagon.

"Shivering Spooks" is an extremely entertaining, admirably fast-paced comedy.

The main problem with "scare comedy" is that it follows obvious formulas; what sets this film apart from many others (even within the *Our Gang* series) is the lightning tempo, both within each scene and in moving from one shot to the next. There are also some ingenious comic embellishments to the routine pattern of such sequences.

For instance, it's no special novelty to watch Farina turn white when confronted by a ghost (this admittedly remarkable gag having been used time and time again throughout the 1920s)—but "Shivering Spooks" follows up this gimmick with a sequence printed in negative form, as Farina is pursued by a dazzlingly phosphorescent ghost!

In another scene Farina unwittingly crawls underneath the professor's levitation table; someone pulls the appropriate switch and the table goes flying in the air, up and down, with Farina hanging on. The camera follows this action, whirling up and down with the table for an unpolished but vivid result.

Earlier in the film, as Mary starts to read a ghost story to Farina and Scooter, Farina asks why there are nothing but *white* ghosts. "Colored people can't be ghosts," Mary replies logically. "How could you see them in the dark?" Farina replies, just as thoughtfully, "They could carry lanterns—couldn't they?" This exchange is typical of the nonmalicious innocence with which *Our Gang* always treated the black-white situation.

The gang's headquarters is a cave burrowed underneath a field; and like most of the kids' hide-outs, this one has an instant camouflage system whereby a couple of "doors" consisting of tall grass can be pulled shut, completely obscuring the existence of the clubhouse. When a minor cave-in occurs, however, they are forced to burrow through a nearby wall into Professor Fleece's basement, with amusing results.

The professor has gathered a healthy crowd of "suckers" who swallow his fake theatrics hook, line, and sinker. But the professor and his aides get a taste of their own medicine when noises and voices mysteriously appear from underneath their very feet. Naturally, it's the gang, tunneling underground. When their candles go out, leaving them in the dark, there are shouts of dismay, one of which times perfectly with part of the professor's ceremony above. A gullible customer rises and asks the medium, "What must I do to be successful?" And from underground one of the kids shouts to another, "Stop blubbering and sit down," which is mistaken as the answer to the customer's query!

The professor's "parlor" is rigged with an astounding array of mechanical devices, all of which are put to use in trying to scare the gang: rugs pulled out from underfoot, a skeleton popping out from a wardrobe, eerie voices piercing the silence, a flying table, etc.

But "Shivering Spooks" manages to surround the basic notion of this "scare sequence" with a well-constructed comedy short that moves beautifully and provides real laughs along with its fright quotient.

53 · THE FOURTH ALARM

Two Reels · Produced by Hal Roach · Supervised by F. Richard Jones · Directed by Robert F. McGowan · Photographed by Art Lloyd · Edited by Richard Currier · Titles by H. M. Walker · Story by Hal E. Roach and Robert F. McGowan · Released on September 12, 1926, by Pathé Exchange · Our Gang: Joe Cobb, Mary Kornman, Mildred Kornman, Allen "Farina" Hoskins, Johnny Downs, Jackie Condon, Bobby "Bonedust" Young, Jay R. Smith, Jannie Hoskins, Billy Naylor, Scooter Lowry, Pal the dog, and Dinah the mule · Officer, Charles Bachman; Chemist, George K. French; Crowd extra, Sam Lufkin; Firemen, Gene Morgan, Ed Brandenberg, Ham Kinsey

It's a hot day out, but the gang finds relief playing water games around the fire station. The fire chief never had any kids of his own, so he's adopted the neighborhood. Their frolicking is interrupted, however, by a real fire alarm. As the firemen answer the call, the gang tags along in their swimsuits, and by God's grace alone—what else could it be—they manage to help squelch a kitchen fire, earning the respect of the chief, who helps them found their own junior department. They convert a barn into their station house, duplicating all the fire house accouterments, including the between-floors slide pole. Now with the whole world safe from fire, as a title tells us, the junior firemen set about to emulate their adult heroes, beginning by playing checkers, napping, and snoring. Meanwhile, downtown (on the Hal Roach back lot), there's a fire blazing in a building that houses a chemist's lab. Both sets of hook-and-ladder companies respond to the call, but the police chase the gang back into the alley, where unknown to everyone, the fire is creeping dangerously toward the high explosives in the laboratory. In yet another miracle, Mary and Farina battle the flames and succeed in rescuing all the powder and dynamite before the threatened explosion deposits everyone across Kansas.

Every kid dreams about being a fireman, but never content to dream about things, it figures that the gang would try and become *real* firemen. It would also figure that sooner or later Bob McGowan would make another film about a fire department, since he used to *be* a fireman. Joe Cobb recalls that McGowan's old friends from the fire station used to visit him on the Roach lot now and then.

Somewhat regrettably, however, "The Fourth Alarm" plays up the trappings and conventions of a firehouse and fire fighting, while neglecting to allow for individual characterization by the kids. The result is a cluttered comedy that satisfies in some individual sequences, but disappoints elsewhere. "Beanie" Walker's titles save more than a few scenes. The streamlined and much subtler sound equivalent of six years later, "Hook and Ladder," is frankly much funnier stuff.

"The Fourth Alarm" does feature one interesting gag, though, that was not reworked into "Hook and Ladder," perhaps because it was the kind of gag indigenous to silent comedy. In one of the big fire-fighting scenes, Farina is struggling trying to control a fire hose, and as he gradually loses the battle, the powerful jet of water begins dousing everything in town but the fire. Then as he loses all control, the force of the water stream carries Farina high into the air, whipping him around on the end of the hose like a tree branch in a blizzard.

A running gag which was transferred intact to "Hook and Ladder" had Joe stopping every fifteen minutes to give his little sister her medicine, saying, "Gobble this." A title lets us know he's been working on this assignment for three weeks, but he "can't get her filled."

Side-note: Motion Picture News reported, " 'The Fourth Alarm' is being edited in five reels for the European market because of the demand for the kiddie comedies in this length, claim the Pathé offices." The brief item does not indicate if additional footage was filmed especially for European audiences or if, as Hal Roach did in the early 1930s, several comedies were spliced together in a makeshift "story" in order to create so-called feature-length films. Coincidentally, just one month earlier Roach had done the same thing with one of his Theda Bara comedies, "Madame Mystery."

54 · WAR FEATHERS

Two Reels · Produced by Hal Roach · Supervised by F. Richard Jones · Directed by Robert F. McGowan · Edited by Richard Currier · Titles by H. M. Walker · Story by Hal E. Roach · Released on November 21, 1926, by Pathé Exchange · Our Gang: Allen "Farina" Hoskins, Joe Cobb, Johnny Downs, Jackie Condon, Jannie "Mango" Hoskins, Jay R. Smith, Bobby "Bonedust" Young, Scooter Lowry, Mildred Kornman, and Peggy Ahearn · Sheriff, Sam Lufkin; One of the conductors, Ham Kinsey; Train passenger, Allen Cavan; Ranchers at the Whistling Clam, Chet Brandenberg, George K. French

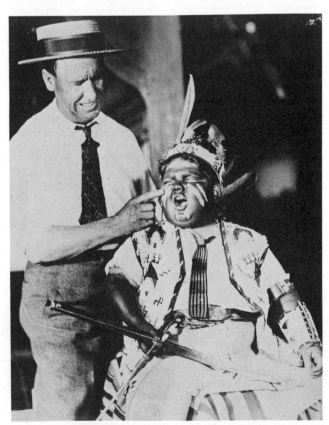

Preparing for a scene in *War Feathers,* director Bob McGowan checks the makeup for Joe Cobb, or, as the title identifies him, "Leaping Lollipop, the only living successor to Sitting Bull."

"There are 104 ways to discourage a small boy—but none of them work." This rule of thumb is particularly evident on a cross-country train ride, where the gang takes over an entire car to play cowboys and Indians, making a shambles of the place and driving the conductor crazy. When the train pulls in at Red Dog, the kids decide to get a close-up look at a real Western town, where the shootouts are no laughing matter. Stowing away in a covered wagon, they are taken to the ranch hide-out of a bandit trio and joined by Farina who, disguised as an Indian boy, has narrowly escaped from the clutches of an angry tribe. Just as the bandits threaten to lock up the kids, an aptly timed series of chain reactions sends all three bad guys into a nearby well, where they remain while the gang reports their capture to the sheriff. The kids' reward is a silver half-dollar, which Mango promptly swallows!

The only thing wrong with "War Feathers" is its incoherence. All the elements of a sure-fire comedy are here, putting the kids in a real-life Western setting, but the "story" is so fragmented that the viewer has a difficult time figuring out who's doing what to whom, and why. Moreover, the results aren't very funny.

This is particularly disappointing because considerable effort went into making this short. The locations are eye-filling and authentic, and the camera work unusually good, with some impressive tracking shots of men on horseback, and the gang on foot running along a dusty road. Another sequence with one of the kids doing some bronco busting is apparently filmed with a hand-held camera, for equally striking effect.

But instead of complementing the Western locale with a simple, solid story line, the film runs off in several directions at once, never bothering to establish motives or identities for the characters who later turn out to be bandits. A sequence with Farina mistaken for an Indian papoose is abruptly resolved with one sight gag, killing off another promising story angle and adding to the jumble.

55 · SEEING THE WORLD

Two Reels · Produced by Hal Roach · Supervised by F. Richard Jones · Directed by Robert F. McGowan · Photographed by Art Lloyd · Edited by Richard Currier · Titles by H. M. Walker · Story by Hal E. Roach · Released on February 13, 1927, by Pathé Exchange · Our Gang: Joe Cobb, Allen "Farina" Hoskins, Jackie Condon, Johnny Downs, Peggy Eames, Scooter Lowry, Jay R. Smith, and Jean Darling · Teacher James Finlayson, "Old Buzz-Fuzz," Himself; English chauffeur, Charlie Hall; Window washer, Ed Brandenberg; Pair of English pedestrians, Stan Laurel, Frank Butler; Extras at the pier, Charley Young, Dorothy Hamilton Darling; Ship's officials, Ham Kinsey, Charles McMurphy; Prince of Wales, Himself; Sultan of Morocco, Himself; President of France, Himself

Schoolteacher Finlayson wants to win a popularity contest sponsored by the town newspaper, so he can collect first prize: a trip to Europe. He doesn't count on the gang coming with him, however, turning his excursion into a hectic sightseeing tour. After stopping in Naples, Pompeii, Rome, Venice, and London, they arrive in Paris, and take an elevator to a landing high on the Eiffel Tower. Farina climbs out on a board tottering over the ledge and falls off, with Finlayson following him, holding on to the other end of the board! Just then, he wakes up from what has been a quite vivid daydream, induced by one of the classroom pranksters who put sleeping potion in the drinking water.

"Seeing the World" is not one of the funniest Our Gang silents, but it certainly rates as one of the most unusual. Combining elements of a conventional two-reeler with first-rate travelogue footage, it remains a fascinating novelty today.

Unfortunately, Bob McGowan and his writers apparently had difficulty developing ideas for making comic use of this great scenery; most of the travel gags in the film are dialogue jokes, conveyed via "Beanie" Walker's card titles. Amazingly little happens on-screen other than panoramic vistas of such sights as the Roman Colosseum, the Vatican, the ruins at Pompeii, the canals of Venice, Notre Dame, Napoleon's tomb, and the magnificent view from the Eiffel Tower.

Squint-eyed Roach star Jimmy Finlayson—he of the glowering double take—was wisely borrowed from the All Star series and carries the greatest measure of the film's visual humor, often saving what might have been rather dull scenes for Our Gang fans expecting the usual fare.

There are occasional attempts to work in bits of business, but most of them are weak. Farina "almost" falls into smoking Mt. Vesuvius, the kids go fishing in the Venice canal, landing a very slippery fish, and, in Paris, Fin and the kids lean back so far to look at the gigantic tower that they fall over onto their backs, and continue to lie on the sidewalk admiring the view.

One odd aspect of this short is the combination of authentic and doctored footage of the kids frolicking against the varied backdrops of the Continent. While Finlayson is shown to be in a gondola actually riding along a canal, when the picture cuts to the kids, seated in the rear of the boat, they are clearly matted in against a prefilmed backdrop. In France, there are seemingly bona fide shots of the kids and their teacher riding in a car and later admiring the Eiffel Tower, but then there is a very complicated optical-process shot of them watching a parade.

Why all this trickery if the gang was there on location? Because the kids weren't there after all! Joe Cobb explains, "No, we didn't get to go. They took our clothes,

Of course we're not supposed to notice, but teacher Finlayson's desk is covered with Hal Roach Studios press releases. And how did the movie trade paper with Tyler Brooke's photo get there? At the time, Brooke was a recently signed Roach star.

though, and they got these other kids over there to wear them, and then they photographed those kids in all the long, long shots you see, so you can't tell it isn't really us. And then we made the rest back in the studio. A lot of people say, 'Oh, you went to Europe, and I saw that picture and you were there.' No, well, I wasn't, but they thought I was anyway. Sure fooled a lot of smart people, though! And it was a pretty good story, too, I thought."

The film's press book actually tipped off the illusion, explaining, "There are no fake movie settings in 'Seeing the World,' as it was filmed in the real cities of the story. James Finlayson . . . [and director] Robert McGowan went abroad on a vacation. Combining business with pleasure, they took along a cameraman and spent two months in Europe shooting the exteriors for what was destined to be the most novel comedy in Our Gang history. Only in this way could such a comedy have been made, for the cost of bringing an entire cast to Europe would have been prohibitive."

The effects are incredibly cunning, but apparently McGowan and crew didn't really know what kind of footage they needed while they were traveling through Europe, and were forced to do the less convincing optical-effect scenes later in order to fashion some plot and gag footage in the film.

Some of the match-ups are interesting for other reasons. In London a head-on view of the touring car shows the chauffeur to be the ubiquitous Roach player Charlie Hall, sporting a monocle. Yet a rear view of Finlayson and the same driver reveals him to be clearly someone else. Obviously, the close-up shots of Fin and Hall were added after the trip, in California.

Similarly, there is a shot of two Englishmen standing in front of a store; one of them is the victim of a gang member's peashooter. His friend laughs at the sight, only to have a second piece of ammunition fly into his open mouth. The two actors in this scene *were* native Britons: Frank Butler and Stan Laurel.

Butler (whose name appears on-screen along with Roach casting director Mollie Thompson in a newspaper article about leading entrants in the European-trip contest) was a top Hollywood comedy writer whose credits ranged from Hal Roach shorts and features (such as *Babes in Toyland*) to the Crosby-Hope *Road* pictures and *Going My Way,* for which he won an Academy Award in 1944.

Stan Laurel, interestingly enough, had no recollection of doing this cameo appearance in later years. In a 1963 letter he wrote, "I don't recall ever appearing in a film titled 'Seeing the World' with *Our Gang* . . . sounds phony to me! Plain ridiculous—I never even appeared in any of the *Our Gang* films, PERIOD!"

Of course, it could be that this scene was shot for another film and simply lifted by McGowan, for "Seeing the World" is full of newsreel footage pulled from various sources. In Paris the kids watch a parade; as a black regiment of soldiers marches by, Farina smiles proudly and proclaims, "Alabama, we is here!" Then Finlayson identifies two dignitaries as the president of France and the sultan of Morocco. In London the gang's touring car supposedly pulls up alongside that of the Prince of Wales, who looks at the camera and says (in a title card), "Carry on." One wonders whether or not the prince's permission was obtained to make him seem part of the action of this short . . . probably not!

The most exciting shots are the final ones in Paris; the camera actually shows the ascension in an Eiffel Tower elevator, as well as views not only from the tower, but of the kids themselves from below and above the landing where they are staying.

Considering all the fakery that has preceded it, the various and intricate shots of Farina teetering along the ledge of the tower railing are breathtaking, and a bit curious as well. Even if there were a mattress a few feet below, it seems unlikely that anyone would have risked having a youngster fall from a ledge. Yet the railing and background scenery do not look like a small-scale mock-up. When Farina and Finlayson fall over the rail, it's quite a jolt to the audience, prolonged by several special-effects scenes of their long, long descent . . . but at this point it becomes clear that something is amiss, and sure enough Finlayson wakes up from his dream.

Although it could never rank as a comedy classic, "Seeing the World" is unique in *Our Gang* history, and it remains an interesting curio today.

56 · TELLING WHOPPERS

Two Reels · Produced by Hal Roach · Supervised by F. Richard Jones · Directed by Robert F. McGowan and Anthony Mack · Edited by Richard Currier · Titles by H. M. Walker · Story by Hal E. Roach · Released on December 19, 1926, by Pathé Exchange · Our Gang: Johnny "Toughey" Downs, Jay R. Smith, Jackie Condon, Scooter Lowry, Bobby "Bonedust" Young, Joe Cobb, Allen "Farina" Hoskins, Peggy Eames, and Billy Naylor · Toughey's mother, Dorothy Vernon; Officers, Silas D. Wilcox, Gene Morgan, Charles McAvoy; Man near swimming hole, Charley Young

A bully named Toughey is terrorizing the neighborhood, systematically beating up all the kids, forcing them to pay money to his "kitty," stand on their heads, and do as he pleases. The gang draws lots to decide who will polish off this pest and get him out of the way. Joe and Farina are the unlucky duo chosen for the task, but before they can approach the bully for a bout, they're told that he's moved out of town. Relieved, they return to the clubhouse, announcing, "The conkerers has come." Joe invents a fantastic story of how they frightened the roughneck into submission, and Farina adds that they threw his body in Coogan Lake. Meanwhile, Toughey, who hasn't left town at all, is chased from a swimming hole by an angry farmer; unable to retrieve his clothes, he keeps out of sight. Then his mother finds his berry-stained sweatshirt by the edge of the river and, thinking the stains are from blood, tells the police that her son has been murdered. Joe and Farina find that their fabricated story has come true, and they make a run for it, trying to avoid the police. Finding Toughey in a white sheet (which he's borrowed from a nearby laundry line) only confirms their fear that he's really dead, and now a ghost. But pretty soon it becomes clear what has really occurred. When the police leave Toughey with the gang, they seize a handy opportunity to beat him up, but they are outdone by his mother, who arrives on the scene and gives her errant son a good licking, while the gang cheers her on.

This routine two-reeler has the distinction of casting *"Our Gang*'s all-American boy," Johnny Downs, as a bully, which he plays quite convincingly, and a delightful "dream sequence" when Joe gives his version of the showdown fight.

Toughey is no ordinary bully. His method is so systematic that he has two blackboards with lists of kids' names on them. The first one is headed "Kids I Have Licked" and the other one reads "Kids I'm Gonna Lick." Talk about organization!

Joe's version of the triumphant battle with Toughey is a lot of fun, with the bully, several heads taller than his opponent, whimpering, "Spare me, Joe—spare me." But Joe and Farina show no mercy, and beat their adversary to a pulp. The glee with which the two "heroes" spin this yarn is contagious; who wouldn't want to be in their position? When news arrives that Toughey is *really* dead, the fibbers' faces suddenly turn white with fear (thanks to an unconvincing special effect). One part of their flight from the cops puts Joe and Farina into a baby carriage that races through the streets of town for a vividly real, and funny, action sequence.

But on the whole, "Telling Whoppers" is a protracted short that takes more time than necessary to make its simple point. In fact, a one-reel home-movie version of the film called "Telling Stories" did the job much better, using only half the original footage.

Sidelights: The film's pressbook carried this item in its "program notes" section. " 'Telling Whoppers' is the title of the latest *Our Gang* comedy classic which will be a feature of the bill ____ at the ____ Theater. The famous laugh-creating youngsters who have made their name a byword for multitudinous mirth the world over are seen at their best in this, their latest picture. Their popularity has become so great that it is a decided handicap to their location work. Anywhere that their director, Robert McGowan, takes them, crowds gather.

"One day recently, important scenes were being shot at a busy corner in Culver City, Cal., and it became necessary to call for additional aid from the police department to keep spectators out of the scenes. It was some job and only after a lot of concentrated effort on the part of the reserves was it possible to go on with the shooting."

57 · BRING HOME THE TURKEY

Two Reels · Produced by Hal Roach · Supervised by F. Richard Jones · Directed by Robert F. McGowan and Anthony Mack · Edited by Richard Currier · Titles by H. M. Walker · Story by Hal E. Roach · Released on January 16, 1927, by Pathé Exchange · Our Gang: Allen "Farina" Hoskins, Joe Cobb, Johnny Downs, Jannie "Mango" Hoskins, Scooter Lowry, Jackie Condon, Peggy Eames, Mildred Kornman, Jay R. Smith, Jean Darling, and Dinah the Mule · The detective, Noah Young; Judge's servant, Lyle Tayo; Orphanage official, Charley Young; Uncle Tom, Tom Wilson

The gang is cruelly mistreated at the Happyland Home orphanage; their only salvation is that kind-hearted Uncle Tom, who lives nearby with his three "children," sneaks them food and tries to look after them. One day, the county officials come to take Uncle Tom's kids away, since he has no legal right to them. Farina, Mango, and Pleurisy end up at the very same orphanage as the gang. When Farina misunderstands the crabby head matron's instructions regarding some chicken ("cut off their heads and we'll eat them for breakfast") and thinks that she means the *kids,* he sends an S.O.S. message to Uncle Tom, who comes to rescue the children that night. After escaping, Tom and the kids set up house in an abandoned old mansion, with Tom "appropriating" food, clothing, and furniture from nearby stores. Finally, the county men locate the house and, after a struggle, round up the kids and Uncle Tom, who must now appear before a judge to answer for his actions. With one fade-out, however, a happy ending is effected as the judge turns the Happyland Home into an entirely different place. The kids have new clothes, friendly supervisors, and Tom himself as chef—while Tom's dog chases the wicked old Happyland trio down the road.

"Bring Home the Turkey" is pretty familiar fare, but it's nicely handled in this well-rounded short. As per *Our Gang* tradition, the three people who run the orphanage are the nastiest cretins on the face of the earth. One man, nicknamed "Old Wart-Head," actually pursues the kids with a bullwhip! It's no wonder that with this kind of attitude, Farina is able to believe that they really *would* cut off their heads and eat them for breakfast.

It's a pleasant bit of irony that Uncle Tom, himself a long way from a life of luxury, is able to provide for the neglected orphans. (It's also significant that this black man is portrayed as the good guy while the whites who run the home, and take away Tom's kids, are the villains). He manages this by "borrowing" the necessities of life wherever he happens to find them. Farina, just a bit suspicious, asks Uncle Tom how and where he manages to get all this food, and Tom points to a sampler on the wall which declares, "The Lord Will Provide." But Farina's eye catches another homily that seems to make more sense: "The Lord Helps Those That Help Themselves." (This two-way philosophizing was apparently inspired by a similar scene in Mary Pickford's *Rebecca of Sunnybrook Farm.*)

"Bring Home the Turkey" has several interesting components that might have been expanded. For one thing, Uncle Tom's home is full of home-made gadgetry reminiscent of inventor Snub Pollard's apartment in the famous Hal Roach comedy *It's a Gift.* With Tom, everything works by some sort of gimmicky locomotion, from an overhead fan to an egg-beater, while the resident pooch runs his forelegs along a treadmill in order to operate the record-player. Still, most of these gag ideas are throwaways, with many possibilities left unexplored.

More important is the abrupt resolution of the story, leaving many questions in even the most unchallenging viewer's mind about how the Happyland Home has been so rapidly and completely transformed. And even though Tom's dog takes off after Old Wart-Head and his cohorts, one would still relish a more vivid close-up enactment of these villains' comeuppance.

The most interesting aspect of "Bring Home the Turkey," which does set it apart from some other *Our Gang* orphanage sagas, is the character of Uncle Tom, who in fact wins more screen time and overall prominence than the kids themselves. One could almost see him becoming a regular character in the series, although prototypes of this friendly adult did appear in many different guises over the years (including Gus Leonard's memorable portrayal of Old Cap in the talkie orphanage story "Mush and Milk").

Black Uncle Tom is played by Tom Wilson, a white actor who specialized in burnt-cork roles like this one. His most memorable characterization, however, was done off-type and without makeup as the suspicious cop who menaces Charlie Chaplin and Jackie Coogan in *The Kid.*

58 · TEN YEARS OLD

Two Reels · Produced by Hal Roach · Supervised by F. Richard Jones · Directed by Anthony Mack · Photographed by Art Lloyd · Edited by Richard Currier · Titles by H. M. Walker · Story by Hal E. Roach · Released on March 13, 1927, by Pathé Exchange · Our Gang: Joe Cobb, Allen "Farina" Hoskins, Bobby "Bonedust" Young, Jackie Condon, Jannie Hoskins, Jean Darling, Mildred Kornman, Jay R. Smith, Johnny Aber, Scooter Lowry, Bret Black, Peggy Eames, and Pal the Dog · Jackie's father, George K. French; Jackie's maid, May Beatty; Joe's mother, Lyle Tayo; Photo used in newspaper, Louise Brooks

Scene from "Ten Years Old."

Joe is left on his own to prepare his tenth birthday party; his mother couldn't afford a cake, so Joe tries to bake one himself. When he isn't looking, his baby sister tosses everything in sight into the batter. The party is called for noon, but by 2:00 no one has yet arrived. The reason: the gang has accepted an invitation to wealthy Jackie's birthday bash, figuring to eat his fancy refreshments first and then to go to Joe's house. Meanwhile, Jackie has upset his elegant household by inviting the scruffy kids of the gang, a sharp contrast to the "sissies" his stepmother asked to attend. When an angry Joe accuses Jackie of breaking up his party, Jackie suggests that Joe bring his cake along with him and combine the celebrations. Joe agrees, and his cake provides a wide range of surprises for the kids—from a bar of soap in the middle of one slice to a mouthful of tacks. But the grand finale comes when Farina presents Joe with his gift, a "kitten" that turns out to be a skunk.

"Ten Years Old" uses many familiar Our Gang themes and elements but fails to use them effectively, although there are some amusing scenes and gags.

The film opens on a note of wistfulness, as Joe's doting mother explains that she can't afford more than 25¢ for ice cream refreshments and warns Joe not to let any bill collectors into the house while she's gone. This element of pathos (which could have resurfaced when the gang deserts Joe's party) disappears at this point. Rich boy Jackie then steals the spotlight, but even the disruption of his parents' stately household is underplayed; there is no confrontation between the rowdy kids and Jackie's snobbish stepmother. The film comes to a sudden conclusion when Farina unveils his gift skunk and everyone faints.

Despite some visual gimmicks typical of director Mack, "Ten Years Old" hasn't much to offer, and it was much better when it was reworked several years later as a talkie called "Birthday Blues."

59 · LOVE MY DOG

Two Reels · Produced by Hal Roach · Directed by Robert F. McGowan · Titles by H. M. Walker · Story by Hal E. Roach · Released on April 17, 1927, by Pathé Exchange · Our Gang: Allen "Farina" Hoskins, Jackie Condon, Scooter Lowry, Joe Cobb, Jay R. Smith, Bobby "Bonedust" Young, Bobby Mallon, and Mildred Kornman · Dog catcher, Charles McMurphy; Office worker, Charley Young; P. Fulton, attorney at law, Stanley (Tiny) Sandford; Attendant at gas chamber, Dick Gilbert

In the midst of the gang's Dog Show, word comes that the dog catchers are on the rampage; a hydrophobia epidemic has forced them to capture all dogs who don't receive an injection, which costs five dollars. Joe and Farina confound the dog catchers for quite a while, twice arranging to open the door on their wagon and set the canines free. But eventually, Farina's dog is nabbed and the grouchy attendant tells him that he's got one hour to raise five bucks or his dog will be killed. By the sheerest of luck, Farina encounters a rich kid who is willing to pay him two bits every time he allows himself to be socked on the nose. Farina stands up to the punishment pretty well, and before long is joined by the rest of the gang for a tremendous sockfest. With five dollars in hand, they race to the Dog Pound, only to be told that they're too late; but when the gas chamber is opened, the pooch is still alive, having had the brains to stick his tail through the gas-pipe and prevent the fumes from coming inside.

There isn't much plot to this two-reeler, so the time is filled by a series of loosely connected episodes that never really tie together: a ventriloquist tries to make Farina think his dog is talking; the gang holds a dog show; they try to scare the dog catchers by making Farina's dog "foam" at the mouth; the mutt saves a baby who has crawled onto the ledge of an office building; and finally we reach the cliffhanger climax with the kids racing to the pound to save Farina's dog.

Here the film employs a device "borrowed" (or more aptly, "stolen") from the stage and screen versions of *Peter Pan*. When all looks lost for the dog and we actually see the gas starting to seep into the tiny chamber, a title card proclaims, "You good people in the audience: Do you want to see this dog die?" If not, we are told to clap our hands. When the situation looks worse, another title reads, "Clap louder," and then "LOUDER!" Not until the kids arrive and go through their motions with the attendant are we shown the dog alive and well.

But while the Hal Roach writers remembered this ploy from *Peter Pan,* they forgot the essence of its appeal: it was the audience clapping that actually saved Tinker Bell. Here, it is the dog's own brain power that comes to the rescue, not our applause, thereby negating the whole idea.

One bright sequence has the gang seeking to foil the dog catchers by disguising their canines as different kinds of animals. Jackie's dog is rigged out with a huge set of udders and told to act like a cow. Scooter and his accoutered pup stroll confidently past a bemused dog catcher, and when the deception doesn't work, Scooter shouts out, "Don't you know a Swiss goat when you see one?"

This film is really Farina's showcase, and he makes good use of it. After some artificial-looking scenes of kids starting to cry when the dog catchers take their pets away, there is an amazing medium close-up of Farina that is held for quite some time as we watch his reaction to one man grappling with his dog inside the office building.

Farina's expression turns from anxiety to horror as he begins to cry and stretch out his arms longingly for his beloved pet; when the dog catcher emerges from the office into the hallway, Farina lunges for his leg and holds on tight, hoping to distract the man long enough so he will drop the dog. This kind of direct and real emotion is part of what gave *Our Gang* its appeal; and these talented kids made such scenes completely believable.

Aside from this, "Love My Dog" is an unexceptional series entry, a bit too meandering to have the impact it should. The whole idea worked much better when resurrected five years later as "The Pooch."

60 · TIRED BUSINESS MEN

Two Reels · Produced by Hal Roach · Directed by Anthony Mack and Charles Oelze · Titles by H. M. Walker · Story by Hal E. Roach · Released on May 15, 1927, by Pathé Exchange · Our Gang: Allen "Farina" Hoskins, Jean Darling, Jackie Condon, Joe Cobb, Jay R. Smith, Scooter Lowry, Jannie Hoskins, Bobby "Bonedust" Young, Bobby Mallon, Johnny Aber, Billy Butts, and Peggy Eames · Officers, Silas D. Wilcox, Charles A. Bachman

The enterprising gang has turned a dilapidated barn into "The Manhattan Club," intended to be their new center of political, social, and animal life. Joe Cobb's just moved into the neighborhood, and since the gang is looking for candidates to initiate for their club, they pounce on Joe like beasts of prey. After undergoing the full rigors, Joe is rejected for membership. His dad, though, is a policeman, and when Joe lets it be known he's kin to the law, the gang is cowed into suffering through the same initiation rites they'd inflicted on him. Meanwhile, a bank robber on the lam named "Blow 'Em Up Barnes" takes refuge in the gang's Manhattan Club, just as Joe's dad

Newcomer Jean Darling serves *Our Gang* veteran Farina in this scene from "Tired Business Men."

and the rest of the police force are converging for the capture. The gang mistakes the men in blue for adversaries, and routs them with a shower of eggs and other debris. Despite this interference, the crook is subdued, and Joe's dad treats the kids to ice cream cones.

"Tired Business Men" is minus Bob McGowan's direction (he was away on vacation), and that's minus plenty. This lackluster film's modest comedy grows mostly out of Charley Oelze's special effects wizardry.

As with other *Our Gangs* cranked out during this period, particularly those of heavy-handed Anthony Mack, "Tired Business Men" suffers from having been shot on dark, unappealing, shabbily dressed sets, and from an immobile camera anchored in place. One doesn't expect luxuriously appointed sets in an *Our Gang* comedy, but they needn't have been so distressingly dingy and cluttered. Either way, kids belong out of doors, and the vitality of McGowan's early Pathé shorts proves the value of location work in those bright and cheery back yards and parks.

61 · BABY BROTHER

Two Reels · Produced by Hal Roach · Directed by Anthony Mack and Charles Oelze · Photographed by Art Lloyd · Edited by Richard Currier · Titles by H. M. Walker · Story by Hal E. Roach · Released on June (?), 1927, by Pathé Exchange · Our Gang: Joe Cobb, Jackie Condon, Allen "Farina" Hoskins, Scooter Lowry, Jean Darling, Jay R. Smith, Bobby "Bonedust" Young, Jannie Hoskins, Mildred Kornman, Bobby "Wheezer" Hutchins, and Donnie "Horatio" Smith · Nursemaid's boy friend, Oliver Hardy; Amorous nursemaid, Anita Garvin; Man with glasses, Ben Hall; Party guests, Symona Boniface, Lyle Tayo; Officers, Ed Brandenberg, Silas D. Wilcox; Gus, one of Barr's midgets, Harry Earles

The automized baby business.

"The story of a rich little boy who had everything he wanted—except a baby brother and a shotgun." Joe is so lonely that all he can think of is having a baby brother to play with. One day, his nursemaid takes him to her neighborhood on the other side of the tracks, where there are plenty of fellows his age. He tells them he's got three dollars, and wants to buy a baby. Farina finds a black woman who's willing to let him mind her baby, so he shrewdly paints the infant white and sells him to Joe.

Meanwhile, the gang has set up a baby-minding operation with assembly-line systems for washing, drying, rocking, and feeding their baby brothers and sisters. When Joe puts his baby through the washer, the white paint comes off, but Joe is happy anyway because the baby calls him papa. Just then, the real mother arrives, sending Joe scurrying home, where he plops the child in his mother's lap. To relieve his anxiety over keeping the baby, his mother and father decide to let Joe in on their "secret"—they're giving him a Shetland pony for Christmas.

"Baby Brother" is a fast-paced, consistently funny short which relies on several standard *Our Gang* devices.

First, Joe is unhappy despite his wealth and plush surroundings. His mother and father are insensitive to his loneliness (his mother even tells him that he looks funny when he cries!) and it takes a down-to-earth nursemaid to realize what he really needs: friends.

Next, the gang's obvious solution to the problem of minding so many babies is to set up an automated "business." This assembly-line system is quite ingenious, with the baby (or victim) sitting in a basket which travels on a treadmill, dipping down into the water at strategic moments; then he is seated on a net placed above a furnace to dry off, and finally he is slid down a chute into a playpen when the job is done. The only ones who don't seem to like this are the babies, who cry and do their best to rebel.

Throughout the short, one is made slightly uncomfortable by the realization that these babies actually *are* unhappy at the treatment they're receiving in the name of comedy. Even though no harm is done, there is an air of manipulation in these sequences that is, in our view, disturbing.

One of the most rebellious babies is a newcomer named Bobby "Wheezer" Hutchins, who enjoyed a long and successful stay with *Our Gang*. He is given a lot of footage in this film, and he proves to be a cunning if unwitting scene stealer. He also establishes an early trademark in this debut appearance: a peculiar penchant for Bronx cheers.

Looking for a baby brother, Joe happens upon Anita Garvin and her gushing boyfriend, Oliver Hardy (in derby and full mustache). Joe embarrasses Anita by asking if she can get him a baby brother, but Hardy is delighted with the prospect, embellishing his playful reaction with a dubious camera look, devilish smiles, and a flirtatious pratfall, all done with a panache only he could bring to the scene!

The film's final joke is likewise aimed more at adult viewers than at children. To assuage Joe's persistent pleas for a baby, his mother and father exchange coy, knowing glances and agree to spill their secret. Father whispers in Joe's ear, and Joe excitedly asks when "it" will arrive. The answer is Christmas. Joe runs to tell the gang, but he doesn't announce the arrival of a baby, as expected; instead he declares that his father is going to buy him a pony! This seems to defeat the film's premise, doing little to revive one's hopes that Joe's parents will be more kind and attentive. Buying a horse is the rich father's solution to Joe's problems. But since Joe seems delighted with the idea, who are we to argue?

62 · CHICKEN FEED

Two Reels · Produced by Hal Roach · Directed by Anthony Mack and Charles Oelze · Titles by H. M. Walker · Story by Hal E. Roach · Released on November 6, 1927, by Pathé Exchange · Our Gang: Joe Cobb, Johnny Downs, Allen "Farina" Hoskins, Jannie "Mango" Hoskins, Jay R. Smith, Scooter Lowry, Bobby "Bonedust" Young, Jackie Condon, Bobby Mallon, Jean Darling, Harry Spear, and Bobby "Wheezer" Hutchins · Animal trainer, Ham Kinsey

Believe it or don't, this is Our Gang. Wonder how long the apparent serenity will last? *Left to right,* Jay R. Smith, Jackie Condon, Joe Cobb, Allen Clay Hoskins, Harry Spear, Jean Darling, and Jannie Hoskins.

The gang attends a local magic show where Johnny Downs seemingly transforms Jean into a rabbit, with the aid of some "magic powder." Joe is determined to learn his secret, so he snatches the powder and experiments on Farina's little sister Mango. He puts her under a wooden box, sprinkled with powder, closes his eyes, and says the magic words. Meanwhile Mango scurries out of the box and a monkey ("Tarzan's youngest was loose") clambers in. When Joe and the gang lift up the box, they think they've hit upon some demon magic, and turn frantic as the monkey clowns around with them. As they try to follow the animal about, it appears to be transformed into a cat (when the chimp dons a Halloween costume), then a bear, and finally a chicken, which they chase to the freight yard, where a hobo is licking his lips and a bunch of feathers lies on the ground. They all think they've seen the last of Mango, but Jay suggests that perhaps they can bring the feathers back to life. They find another empty box, use the powder and the magic words, and this time lift it up to discover a "ghost"—Mango in a white sheet—which sends everyone scurrying down the railroad tracks as the film irises to its closing title.

This unremarkable entry repeats many familiar elements, using a host of dependable gags that seldom surprise, but always please. The monkey is introduced in a protracted and totally irrelevant scene in which it teases a barnyard goose, who manages to get the last laugh by squirting the chimp. The length of this odd and disembodied scene would seem to indicate a need to pad out the short for lack of variations on the basic "plot," which consists of just one joke.

Mango is selected as the "fall guy" for this experiment, just as in the later talkie short "A Lad an' a Lamp" it is Stymie's brother Cotton who becomes a similar victim. Farina is none too happy about his younger sister being chosen for the scheme, and tries to stop the others, who are forced to hold him back while they go through with the project. When the trick backfires, and Joe is unable to return Mango to her original form, no one wants to be responsible—as who would?

The final gag is abrupt and unsatisfying, but with the already overdone series of transformations, as the gang wanders from barnyard to railyard, one could see that the filmmakers were looking for an easy way to finish off the film.

Some of the gags, not to mention the entire premise of the film, are in bad taste, yet apparently the short was considered successful, for the same gags and situations are repeated in later *Our Gangs*.

"Chicken Feed" was slapped together over a two-week period from March 26 to April 10. Although officially credited for the "story," Hal Roach had been away in Europe during most of the early part of 1927, and it wasn't until the final day of shooting on April 10 that Bob McGowan returned to the studio after a three-*month* vacation. This had left Anthony Mack and Charley Oelze to script and create what turned out to be shapeless, lackluster things like "Tired Business Men," "Baby Brother," "Chicken Feed," and coming up next, "Olympic Games." As discussed elsewhere, Anthony Mack's films show little sensitivity, his gags are unsubtle and sometimes tasteless, and his crude stories generally go nowhere. Also, though Charley Oelze was a mechanical wizard, and in Joe Cobb's words, "We couldn't do a film without him," he was *not* a director. The wit and charm Roach and McGowan could provide were sorely missed during this period.

63 · OLYMPIC GAMES

Two Reels · Produced by Hal Roach · Supervised by Robert F. McGowan · Directed by Anthony Mack · Photographed by Art Lloyd · Edited by Richard Currier · Titles by H. M. Walker · Story by Hal E. Roach · Released on September 11, 1927, by Pathé Exchange · Our Gang: Bobby "Wheezer" Hutchins, Joe Cobb, Allen "Farina" Hoskins, Jay R. "Spec" Smith, Jackie Condon, Harry Spear, Mildred Kornman, Peggy Ahearn, Jannie Hoskins, Jean Darling, Scooter Lowry, Johnny Aber, Joseph Metzger, and Pete the Pup

Bob McGowan visits the Gang while on location for "Olympic Games." *Left to right,* Jay R. Smith, Joe Cobb, Jean Darling, Mildred Kornman, Wheezer Hutchins, Farina Hoskins, Jackie Condon, and Harry Spear.

Gracefulness and sportsmanship are hallmarks of most Olympic Games, but not when Our Gang competes in their Backyard-Olympics, where athletic proficiency is *not* a specialty. While everyone tries to master such events as the hurdles, shot put, javelin, broad jump, pole vault, etc., their fumbling efforts seldom meet with success. The athletes' concentration, too, is frequently disturbed by tiny Wheezer, who delights in taunting the gang with "the raspberries" at inopportune moments. Inevitably, the competition winds up with a garbage-tossing slapstick melee.

How director Anthony Mack could do so little with such an intriguing basic concept is a wonder. There is no real story to "Olympic Games," nor is there a buildup to any sort of climax. Everything simply stops after two reels. The gags, too, are ill conceived and poorly executed. In short, the film is a strange mixture of nothing—and lots of it.

Only the byplay between mischievous Wheezer and Petie offers any kind of diversion, and the only solid jokes come from the reliable hand of Beanie Walker. For instance, in sizing up a determined Farina's abilities as a shot-putter, Walker tells us with a title, "Farina's muscles bulged out like bird seed."

With the transition to M-G-M, apparently no one seemed concerned about delivering the usual high standard of *Our Gang* films to Pathé. Unfortunately, after sliding into a slump, the series never really regained its stride until the second season of talking pictures, and the silent M-G-M's are little better than the late Pathés.

Since nothing much is happening on screen, as an offbeat pastime during films like this, it's fun to watch the passersby and vintage autos parading past in the background. Now and then the nonchalant pedestrians and puzzled motorists would stop or slow down to gaze at the *Our Gang* unit on location, probably never realizing that their curiosity would lead to our curiosity about them, many, many years later.

64 · THE GLORIOUS FOURTH

Two Reels · Produced by Hal Roach · Directed by Robert F. McGowan · Titles by H. M. Walker · Story by Hal E. Roach · Released on June 26, 1927, by Pathé Exchange · Our Gang: Joe Cobb, Allen "Farina" Hoskins, Jannie Hoskins, Jackie Condon, Jay R. Smith, Harry Spear, and Pete "Pansy" the Pup · Top-hat inebriate, Charley Chase; Friend of Joe's mother, Dorothy Vernon; Man with monocle, Jack Hill; Officer, Charles A. Bachman; Motorist, Charley Young; Cement worker, William Courtwright; Local residents, Charles Meakin, Al Hallet, Harry Arras, Arthur Millett

Joe's mother operates a fireworks stand, giving the gang access to all sorts of exciting playthings. Farina has to make do with popping paper bags, until the sudden acquisition of 25¢ enables him to buy a massive skyrocket, which plummets right into the middle of the fireworks stand and triggers a minor holocaust. In running from the scene, the kids discover something even more flamboyant: a scientist demonstrating his new Bahama Oil capsules, one thousand times stronger than nitroglycerine. The dog Pansy eats most of the capsules before anyone can stop him, sending everyone in the area running for dear life, fearing that Pansy will explode at any minute. Instead, the dog spits up the pellets, one by one, causing a series of mini-explosions all around the city. In the meantime, the fireworks catastrophe finally catches up with Joe, whose mother gives him a good spanking.

With no more sense of continuity than most two-reelers of this period, "The Glorious Fourth" moves from one sequence to another until the allotted time is up, and then it ends. In the interim there are some funny and well-staged scenes, however.

The individual scenes of Joe and the others setting off firecrackers works as a buildup to the film's highlight, when the whole fireworks stand catches fire. This is one of the most elaborate and amusing sight-gag sequences of this late-silent *Our Gang* period, with a particularly nice cameo by Charley Chase as a drunk who literally stumbles into the line of fire but can't figure out what it is that's continually whirring past his face. Another large-scale gag has a Bahama Oil capsule exploding just as a car drives by, sending the vehicle into space, with a shot of a dozen or more car components floating in the air and crashing to the ground. As for the driver, he's found hanging from a nearby fire escape in a delirious daze.

Another nice if extraneous scene is built into a running gag to top off the film. A worker is finishing off some fresh sidewalk cement. A young woman inadvertently steps into the mushy substance and spoils the finished work; the worker chases her off and fixes up the area. Over the next five minutes, his handiwork is splattered three or four times by the gang running back and forth from their explosive dog. Accelerating this familiar gag idea is the biggest laugh twist, when the gang, a group of military

"Show me the motor, and *I'll* fix it." Is it coincidence that fun went out of the movies at the same time they stopped making running boards?

men and City Fathers testing the Bahama Oil, and a few assorted passersby *all* trample over the fresh pavement—a veritable army that sends the harassed worker into fits of frenzy, topped off when the same army runs through a second time. Now there is nothing left for the worker to do but sit in the fresh cement and play patty-cake with himself.

The only negative factor in "The Glorious Fourth" (aside from its abrupt transitions) is the gang's cruel and unfunny treatment of Farina. At first, they won't let him play with them; then they have fun by tossing firecrackers at him and his sister. Finally, when Farina has the money to buy his own fireworks, Joe "sells" him a skyrocket but sets it off himself, refusing to let Farina come near it. When the rocket destroys the fireworks stand, however, Joe shifts all the blame to Farina—even though Joe gets the whipping at the end of the film from his mother, who supposedly left her boy in charge of the stand. The indefatigable Farina seems to take this harsh treatment in stride, but it is not quite so easy for the audience to ignore the gang's taunting attitude.

"The Glorious Fourth" doesn't so much end as stop, using the spanking and the sidewalk worker's surrender as a convenient conclusion for the film, without bothering to resolve much of anything. This aside, the short moves briskly and features some funny and well-constructed gag sequences, placing it among the better entries from this era.

65 · PLAYIN' HOOKEY

Two Reels · Produced by Hal Roach · Directed by Anthony Mack · Titles by H. M. Walker · Released on January 1, 1928, by Pathé Exchange · Our Gang: Allen "Farina" Hoskins, Jackie Condon, Joe Cobb, Jannie Hoskins, Jay R. Smith, Jean Darling, Harry Spear, Bobby "Wheezer" Hutchins, and Pete the Pup · Moving picture comedy star, Charlie Hall; Movie-makers, Charles Meakin, Lincoln Plummer, Harry Arras; Keystone-ish cops, Ed Brandenberg, Chet Brandenberg, Jack Hill, Arthur Millett

A posed still from "Playin' Hookey." The pies are real. Coincidentally, this film was released but a single day after Laurel & Hardy's *The Battle of the Century*, which featured The Great Pie Fight. Charlie Hall (with derby) had a "pivotal" role there, too.

This film was unavailable for viewing. The following review was printed in *Film Daily* under the headline "Ruining a movie studio": "Pansy, canine actor and member of Our Gang, gets a movie tryout in this picture but fails to do his stuff. When the studio employees endeavor to eject the kids the fun begins, with the youngsters ruining scenes and sets. There is practically nothing new in the comedy business but nevertheless, it's the kind that clicks with laughter and the kids are always entertaining. 'Playin' Hookey' is lots of fun. Anthony Mack directed."

A scrapbook kept by one of the *Our Gang* mothers reveals that this film finished production under the working title "School Is Out."

Side-note: About this time, the Kellogg's cereal com-

pany of Battle Creek, Michigan, announced a promotional tie-in with *Our Gang*, a four-to-six-week advertising campaign to be launched with nationwide newspaper ads in some 350 papers and six magazines (*Photoplay, Physical Culture, Boys Life, Hollands', Liberty,* and *Cosmopolitan*). Mr. W. K. Kellogg himself came to Hal Roach Studios to sign the deal. The commercial slogan was "Our Gang peps up with Pep—the peppy cereal food." Kellogg's planned to blanket the country with 5,000 copies of a 24-sheet poster for billboard use, except in New York, Chicago, and Boston, where the end and side space of streetcars, subways, and elevated trains would be rented. The promotion was so successful, Kellogg's repeated it the following year.

Commented *Film Daily,* "This, in every way, should be

an advertising campaign tie-up of value to every exhibitor playing *Our Gang* comedies. With little effort and comparatively small expense any exhibitor can turn the entire campaign to his own advantage.''

The basic idea was simple: ads would appear with the *Our Gang* kids endorsing Kellogg's cereals. All the theater owner had to do was to arrange with his local newspaper to carry the additional phrase, ''See the Our Gang kids now at the —— Theater in their latest comedy.''

Over the years, Roach tied up with companies selling roller skates, safety stilts, shoes, candy, ice cream, pencils, writing tablets, loose-leaf and composition books, coloring books, crayon sets, balloons, musical instruments, junior sweaters, jump suits, winter outfits, marbles, stamps, calendars, paint sets, coaster wagons, fishing poles, cameras, sporting goods, cowboy suits, greeting cards, firecrackers, clothes hangers, dolls, *Our Gang* Orange Gum, BAB-O Cleaners, Karo Syrup, Maxwell House Coffee, Royal Crown Cola, 7-Up, Bell & Howell photographic equipment, and even *Our Gang* comic strips, and *Our Gang* comic books.*

Presumably these and the many more mass media or window display ads enjoyed the same kind of success the Kellogg's campaign did. Whether or not the tie-in ballyhoo really paid off for the small-town theater owner is difficult to determine, but it did indicate the considerable impact of Our Gang on the American public.

---

* *Our Gang Comics* were drawn for Dell by such noted cartoonists as Walt Kelly and Carl Barks, and outlived the series by six years, through 1949, when the publication's name was changed to *Tom and Jerry* to spotlight instead the popular M-G-M animated series. With *Our Gang*'s television revival in the 1950s, Hal Roach Studios licensed Dell to proffer a new series of comic books, this time entitled *The Little Rascals*.

66 · THE SMILE WINS

Two Reels · Produced by Hal Roach · Directed by Robert F. McGowan · Photographed by Art Lloyd · Edited by Richard Currier · Titles by H. M. Walker · Story by Hal E. Roach and Robert F. McGowan · Released on February 26, 1928, by Pathé Exchange · Our Gang: Allen ''Farina'' Hoskins, Jannie Hoskins, Joe Cobb, Jean Darling, Jackie Condon, Jay R. Smith, Harry Spear, Bobby ''Wheezer'' Hutchins, and Pete the Pup · Character parts unknown, Budd Fine, Lyle Tayo

This film was unavailable for viewing. Apparently an early attempt on McGowan's part to combine comedy and pathos, ''The Smile Wins'' caught reviewers off-guard. *Motion Picture News*'s Chester J. Smith wrote, ''Hal Roach and *Our Gang* go in a bit for the sentimental stuff in this latest of the gang comedies, and it is quite an improvement over the usual all-comedy two-reelers . . . it is mightly good entertainment.

''Farina is the son of an invalid mother who keeps the family alive, despite her condition, by taking in the washing of the neighbors. She is threatened with ejection from her home by a flinty-hearted landlord unless she can produce $200 the following day. Farina, meantime, is in the bad graces of the neighborhood gang, who take it that by his continuous smile he is laughing at them. The gang waylays Farina as he is delivering the laundry and makes a mess of the clean clothes until Joe interrupts. Then the true conditions within Farina's home are learned, and the gang decides to drill for oil in the backyard. They strike a gusher as the grasping landlord appears and rushing to Farina's mother writes her a check for $50,000 for her interest in the property. Farina rushes to the bank, cashes the check, and returns in time to see an irate neighbor berating the grasping landlord for having punched his pipeline. Farina fades out garbed in high hat, swallow-tailed coat and directing his chauffeur to drive him to the new mansion. It is a picture that will bring back renewed confidence in the Roach kids.''

Film Daily's reviewer found the picture ''rather flat,'' however, and commented, ''Below the average for this series. Seems less spontaneous than usual.'' It was inevitable that some would object to the injection of heart-tug elements into *Our Gang*. But McGowan improved on this formula in the next few years and turned his kiddie comedies into something *more:* films with genuine heart and warmth.

''The Smile Wins'' (which had also been the name of a 1923 Paul Parrott short) concluded Hal Roach's *Our Gang* commitment to Pathé Exchange. From now on all the Roach shorts would be upgraded in budget and distributed by Metro-Goldwyn-Mayer, Roach's four-year-old neighbor a few blocks down on Washington Boulevard in Culver City.

Hal Roach had issued product through Pathé since 1914, but when executive Paul Brunet returned to France, the company slid downhill. ''Pathé should have been one of the big companies in the industry,'' Roach recalls, ''and it would have been, had it been run properly . . . . The management was just disgraceful. I never saw a company do so many things wrong so fast.

''For instance, they made a contract with Mack Sennett to make as many pictures as I was making. The trouble was that the theaters didn't want to buy too many pictures from one distributor. So the result was Pathé'd sell my pictures to one theater and sell Sennett's to another: Mack and I were cutting each other's business in half.

''I'd made our new contract with Nick Schenck, of Loew's Theatres, a year and a half before the Pathé agreement expired, and things were getting so bad I would have loved to have been out a year earlier than I was, but we had this obligation to fulfill.''

Asked about his association with Metro Rajah Louis B. Mayer, Mr. Roach recalls, ''I was in New York when I first realized that Pathé was going to have serious management troubles. So I talked to Paramount and Metro,

Christmas at Hal Roach Studios: with the creative forces behind *Our Gang* Comedies gathering for a celebration. *Back row, left to right,* director Bob McGowan, *Our Gang* graduate Mary Kornman, Farina, Wheezer, producer Hal Roach, Mildred Kornman, Jean, Joe, and unsung title writer H. M. "Beanie" Walker. *Front row, left to right,* Harry, Jay R., Pete the Pup, and Jackie. Those Christmas presents aren't props, either. The studio held parties like this every year; the kids could ask Hal Roach for anything they wanted, and get it.

and I liked the deal with Metro much better than the deal with Paramount. Nick Schenck, at that time, was the head of Loew's Theatre Circuit, and also the president of M-G-M, so I made the deal with him because they wanted our pictures for their theaters. Well, Louie Mayer and I were friendly for years, but he never forgave me for not coming to him first and making the deal with him!''

VI THE ROACH M-G-M SILENTS

67 · YALE VS. HARVARD

Two Reels · Produced by Hal Roach · Directed by Robert F. McGowan · Photographed by Art Lloyd · Edited by Richard Currier · Titles by H. M. Walker · Released on September 24, 1927, by M-G-M · Our Gang: Joe Cobb, Jackie Condon, Allen "Farina" Hoskins, Jannie Hoskins, Jay R. Smith, Jean Darling, Harry Spear, and Pete the Pup · Character part unknown, Martha Sleeper

This film was unavailable for viewing. Apparently Hal Roach's first *Our Gang* release through M-G-M won everybody over.

Film Daily exulted, "This is a comedy. By far the most outstanding release among the first releases of the M-G-M new short subject department. The incorrigible youngsters turn to football this time. The gang faces tough competition in the form of the gas house team. Full of cute gags and real comedy value and very much there at the old box office. Hal Roach has again demonstrated that in the *Our Gang* comedies he offers theater owners sure-fire audience material. You can't go wrong on 'Yale vs. Harvard.' ''

Exhibitor's Daily Review wrote, ''Robert McGowan has used a lot of camera tricks and special angle shots in this typical *Our Gang* comedy and the resultant is a production which will add much to the popularity these rascals have already established for themselves. It's a comedy that 'looks like a million dollars.' All the old favorites perform in their accustomed manner. The story will be particularly timely about release date time, September 24, since it deals with an exciting football game.''

Cruickshank in the *Telegraph* called it ''a high-class short, as are all of these series. It is more lavishly produced than the majority of its forerunners and ranks as a wow.''

''Yale vs. Harvard'' gave its distributor plenty to shout about, and one trade-magazine advertisement was headlined ''Touchdown for M-G-M's Our Gang!'' It went on to proclaim, ''Three cheers (and more) for Hal Roach! It's a pleasure to add this wonderful *Our Gang* comedy to M-G-M's Big Time program.'' Yet another ad declared, ''Made to order for the football season! Your audience will *know* you're a showman when you put this on the program right now. Book it quick!'' Theater owners took the advice, and got Our Gang off to a *rushing* start with Metro-Goldwyn-Mayer, even while other titles were still being pitched to theaters by Pathé.

Team photo from "Yale vs. Harvard." Note Petie's four-point stance.

68 · THE OLD WALLOP

Two Reels · Produced by Robert F. McGowan for Hal Roach · Directed by Robert F. McGowan · Photographed by Art Lloyd · Edited by Richard Currier · Titles by H. M. Walker · Released on October 22, 1927, by M-G-M · Our Gang: Bobby "Wheezer" Hutchins, Joe Cobb, Allen "Farina" Hoskins, Jackie Condon, Harry Spear, Jay R. Smith, and Jean Darling · Mother, Anita Garvin

This film was unavailable for viewing. Raymond Ganly reviewed the film when it first came out, for *Motion Picture News*. '' 'Wheezer,' the little chap who is fast taking the place vacated by Farina in Hal Roach's *Our Gang*, stars here. His little act consists in [sic] punching people on the nose and he carries a wallop too (his father is a prize fighter). During the first part of this comedy he punches everyone on the nose, including his brother, Farina, policemen, and passersby who stop to admire him and murmur, 'Nize baby.'

''After they have played on this punching theme for a while, the kids are made to switch their activities to a skyscraper in the construction stage. Farina becomes caught in some of the material and is carried aloft. The gang set out to rescue him and finally do so after various bits of comedy from Fatty, Jackie, and some of the other boys.''

A review of the film's cutting continuity (a detailed transcript of the film's action and text titles filed with the Library of Congress as evidence of copyright) lets us know the opening title, ''The story of a little boy who wanted to be heavyweight champion—he has only two hundred pounds more to go—''

"The Old Wallop."

69 · HEEBEE JEEBEES

Two Reels · Produced by Robert F. McGowan for Hal Roach · Directed by Anthony Mack · Photographed by Art Lloyd · Edited by Richard Currier · Titles by H. M. Walker · Released on November 19, 1927, by M-G-M · Our Gang: Joe Cobb, Allen "Farina" Hoskins, Jean Darling, Bobby "Wheezer" Hutchins, Jackie Condon, Jay R. Smith, Harry Spear, and Pete the Pup · Professor, Bobby Vernon; Wheezer's mother, Dorothy Vernon; Joe's mother, Lyle Tayo; Officer, Charles Bachman

This film was unavailable for viewing. Reprinted here is T. C. Kennedy's original review from *Motion Picture News:* "The personnel of Hal Roach's Gang has undergone several changes since first this now very popular troupe made its appearance. There remains, however, 'Farina,' from the early days, as well as the guiding genius of Robert McGowan. This contribution from the Gang was not directed by McGowan. Anthony Mack is credited with the work. It offers a series of incidents built around the visit of a hypnotist who casts his spell over the town cop, and the members of *Our Gang.* To each one he assigns some animal characteristic, so we have the youngsters behaving like dogs, cats, monkeys, donkeys, etc. They revert to their animal types at odd moments during their presence at an afternoon tea at the home of a society leader. The fruit of these comedy devices is counted in small numbers as laughs go these days, but an effective moment crops up here and there and, with the popularity which the gang enjoys as a basis, this picture may prove amusing fare for the majority."

Moving Picture World was more enthusiastic, reporting that "Hal Roach's *Our Gang* Rascals are given just the proper sort of vehicle to excel themselves in this one, and the way the kids troupe all over the lot is a caution. . . . Lots of pep, fun and entertainment to this one."

The film's cutting continuity reveals that Socrates is quoted in the opening title: "—Little Boys never have to hunt for trouble—it just naturally follows them around—"

Unusual *Our Gang* publicity still. That's director Bob McGowan in the bonnet, sitting on the books.

70 · DOG HEAVEN

Two Reels · Produced by Robert F. McGowan for Hal Roach · Supervised by Robert F. McGowan · Directed by Anthony Mack · Photographed by Art Lloyd · Edited by Richard Currier · Titles by H. M. Walker · Story by Robert F. McGowan · Released on December 17, 1927, by M-G-M · Our Gang: Joe Cobb, Bobby "Wheezer" Hutchins, Jackie Condon, Jay R. Smith, Jean Darling, Mildred Kornman, Allen "Farina" Hoskins, and Pete the Pup · Officer, Charles Bachman; Man in the wheelchair, Charley Young; Lover on park bench, Ed Brandenberg; Lady at accident scene, Lyle Tayo

Pete tries to hang himself, broken-hearted because Joe, his lifelong master, has apparently deserted him. A fellow dog asks Pete to tell him his troubles, and Pete explains how his devoted Joe suddenly turned his attention to a flirtatious young girl, spending all his time and money on her and misunderstanding when Pete saves the girl from drowning—thinking that Pete pushed her in the lake in the first place. The sympathetic dog-friend helps Pete follow

According to the still's original caption, Joe Cobb, "all dressed up for a call on his girl, is undergoing life's most embarrassing moments" in a scene from "Dog Heaven."

through his suicide plans, just as a tearful Joe, realizing he's been wrong, comes to ask Pete's forgiveness. They enjoy a happy reconciliation, and Joe presents Pete with a long-awaited gift: a brand new collar.

"Dog Heaven" is an oddly disjointed two-reeler whose principal interest is in its novelty value, telling the tale through Pete's eyes. Still, one hesitates to dismiss as "novelty" the startling sight of beloved Pete fashioning a noose for himself and praying before slipping it around his neck! Even in jest, this is a rather grim idea for an *Our Gang* comedy, although several such notions crept into the series around this time.

The idea of a fellow dog approaching and asking, "What's the matter, Pete? Family troubles?" is fine, and the illusion of the dogs really conversing is rather remarkable. But the effectiveness of this approach might have been enhanced if Pete were merely despondent, or taking to drink (as he does in another scene). Hanging seems a bit extreme for comic purposes.

Joe's courtship is the most cohesive, and enjoyable, part of the film, which rambles from one flashback sequence to another. The girl flirts with Joe, and when Pete comes alongside and snarls at her cat, Joe angrily tells Pete to go away. Later, Joe plans to call on his girl, dressed to the teeth and carrying flowers. When he goes to buy candy, Pete tries to pull him away, since Joe had been saving money for a new dog-collar. But the collar is forgotten as Joe spends his money for a box of chocolates.

When he arrives at the young lady's house, Joe presents his candy and flowers, and starts petting with the girl, only to find the entire gang stationed on the sidewalk, making fun of his amorous efforts. The sweethearts run to the side of the house, where they won't be seen, but here things go from bad to worse, as Joe's suit starts to fall apart, seam by seam. As he embarrassedly backs away, he trips into a mud puddle for a fitting end to this awkward encounter.

Meanwhile, Pete is disconsolate, finding a bottle of booze and solemnly drinking it down. When Joe finds his dog drunk, he denounces him cruelly. Then, having saved Joe's girl from drowning, Pete is mistaken for a dog who pushed her *into* the lake, and Joe's disgust is complete. For Pete, this is the final straw, and he decides to end it all because "Joe has broken my heart."

A moment later, a bypasser explains to Joe that it was another dog who shoved the girl, and Pete is really a hero. Joe begins to cry, aware that he has hurt his beloved dog; he and the gang try to find the pet to make amends, arriving just in time to stop the hanging and effect a happy reunion between dog and master.

For a punch line, the film returns to an earlier subplot. Pete had explained to his canine pal, "I had an affair with a lady dog from the Follies—I kept it a secret from Joe and the gang." Now, reprieved from suicide, he runs to the side of his lady-friend, only to discover that he's the father of puppies—all sporting rings around their eyes, just like their dad.

As an exercise in the offbeat, "Dog Heaven" is an interesting attempt, and it shows that Hal Roach was seldom afraid of trying something new. But it lacks the strength, either in comedy or in pathos, to make it a memorable success.

Production sidelight: One of the most pleasing aspects of many Hal Roach comedies is the cheerful, picturesque locations Jack Roach used to scout up for his brother's directors. The final quarter of "Dog Heaven," for instance, was shot at sunny Hollenbeck Park, where Harold Lloyd before had filmed scenes for his delightful *Haunted Spooks,* and which Laurel & Hardy would utilize for their boating mayhem a few years later in *Men o' War.* Happily today, almost miraculously, the photogenic tree-lined banks of the lake and walkway bridge remain untouched by onrushing industrial and housing developments. Even if the lovely little park won't stand forever, though, hopefully these films will!

Joe Cobb recalls some shooting difficulties encountered during these park scenes. Strollers would gather around the lake and laugh or applaud the filmmakers, spoiling or disrupting some of the shots. McGowan's trusting solution was to get set up early in the morning, and begin shooting before the onlookers could collect again to watch the crazy antics of comedy movie-makers.

Some production notes kept by Jean Darling's mother disclose that the ever-reliable Charley Oelze co-directed "Dog Heaven" with Anthony Mack, but without credit.

71 · SPOOK SPOOFING

Three Reels · Produced by Robert F. McGowan for Hal Roach · Directed by Robert F. McGowan · Photographed by Art Lloyd · Edited by Richard Currier · Titles by Reed Heustis · Story by Robert F. McGowan · Released on January 14, 1928, by M-G-M · Our Gang: Allen "Farina" Hoskins, Jay R. Smith, Joe Cobb, Jackie Condon, Mildred Kornman, Bobby "Wheezer" Hutchins, Harry Spear, Johnny Aber, Jean Darling, and Pete the Pup · Officer, Charles Bachman; Vendor, Charley Young

35mm frames from "Spook Spoofing."

Farina is brave but superstitious, carrying a special charm he invokes to ward off goblins. Joe, on the other hand, thrives on practical jokes. Abetted by Jay R. (the undertaker's son), Joe and the gang perpetrate an assortment of cruel ghostly jests on Farina. Surpassing the worst gags, Harry pretends to be dead, and Farina congeals in horror as he's advised to bury his "cold and clammy" pal, or he'll be haunted forever. Traditional frights and indignities continue at the graveyard—till a convenient eclipse of the sun and concurrent storming high winds help turn the tables in Farina's favor. The gang's ghostly gadgetry backfires, causing them all to turn tail and scamper off into the end title.

"Spook Spoofing" is more than a little contrived, and at three reels the padding of protracted gags bulges through to the film's detriment.

When critics have rebuffed silent *Our Gang* comedies for shabby treatment of Farina, it's been in large measure owing to exposure to the ubiquitous "Spook Spoofing," and little else. It's dangerous to extend criticism to an entire series because of one isolated film done in bad taste, but the constant showing of this film has done considerable damage to the series' reputation.

Of course, in the 1920s this kind of film was taken very much for granted. Ethnic humor was a staple, and films like this hardly raised an eyebrow. Moreover, the graveyard and old dark house motifs were fixtures of screen comedy. But viewed today, the callous treatment accorded Farina in "Spook Spoofing" allows us precious few opportunities to enjoy the film's atmospheric special effects gags.

72 · RAINY DAYS

Two Reels · Produced by Robert F. McGowan for Hal Roach · Supervised by Robert F. McGowan · Directed by Anthony Mack · Photographed by Art Lloyd · Edited by Richard Currier · Titles by Reed Heustis · Story by Robert F. McGowan · Released on February 11, 1928, by M-G-M · Our Gang: Bobby "Wheezer" Hutchins, Jay R. Smith, Joe Cobb, Allen "Farina" Hoskins, Jackie Condon, Jean Darling, Harry Spear, Mildred Kornman, and Pete the Pup · Wheezer's mother, Lyle Tayo

After breakfast, Jay's mother leaves for the day and charges him with the responsibility of keeping Wheezer and Jean out of trouble while she's gone. With a terrible storm raging outdoors the kids are resigned to spending the day inside. That means trouble. Wheezer and Jean pass the time drawing on the walls with their own special chalk designs. When Jay finds out, he's stunned, and calls on the gang to help him restore the badly defaced walls. New wallpaper is the solution, but they have all sorts of problems preparing a suitable paste (self-rising flour is but one of many ingredients), and soon the entire house and all its furnishings are absolutely drenched in a gooey, sticky mess. The house is still standing, but everything inside is in ruin! Yet after covering the walls, floor, doors, windows, and some of the gang with reams of creeping, dripping wallpaper, when his bewildered mother comes

Lyle Tayo and some of the Gang in "Rainy Days." It was the sausages and Tabasco sauce that did it.

home and surveys the remains, Jay smiles with the pride of accomplishment and asks, "Notice anything, Mom?" as a snakelike piece of wallpaper crawls across the ceiling!

Really not a distinguished comedy, with a few protracted scenes in the early goings, "Rainy Days" nonetheless emerges as a satisfactory second-echelon effort. The gags are not ingenious, but they're serviceable; the story is hardly compelling, but it's workmanlike.

Even if the routines are somewhat predictable, they play well, and evoke satisfactory audience response.

The short scores most on the visual gadgetry gags rigged up by mechanical comedy technician Charley Oelze, who co-directed "Rainy Days" without credit. The costly and time-consuming special effects work—especially the cell and live animation—also contributes to the climactic, paste-dripping episodes: scenes that might be characterized as slapstick that *really* sticks.

73 · EDISON, MARCONI & CO.

Two Reels · Produced by Hal Roach · Supervised by Robert F. McGowan · Directed by Anthony Mack · Photographed by Art Lloyd · Edited by Richard Currier · Titles by H. M. Walker · Released on March 10, 1928, by M-G-M · Our Gang (presumed): Bobby "Wheezer" Hutchins, Joe Cobb, Jackie Condon, Jean Darling, Jay R. Smith, Allen "Farina" Hoskins, Harry Spear, Mildred Kornman, and Pete the Pup

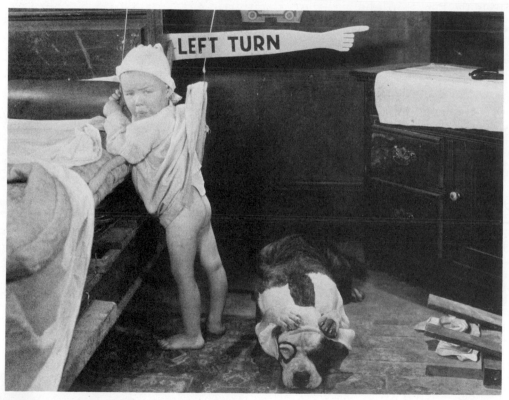

Cheeky comedy is the thing in "Edison, Marconi & Co.," if this still depicting Wheezer's mechanical dressing endeavors is any indication.

This film was not available for viewing. Trade reviews from the time of its release would mark this as a winner.

Chester J. Smith wrote in *Motion Picture News,* "As the title of this picture indicates, the gang is revealed as a band of inventors, of which Jay is the leader. Young 'Wheezer' is his assistant and between them they contrive an automobile of unusual construction, built along the lines of a submarine. It is easy to imagine some of the trick devices that are applied in making the machine function.

"There are eight portholes in this car which has ample room for the 'gang,' and it is self-locking. When they are all within, 'Wheezer' takes the occasion to step on it, and there starts one of the wildest rides ever successfully negotiated. 'Wheezer' proves himself a wizard at driving, and the car plunges through all sorts of traffic, while the 'gang' with heads through portholes wonder just when the crash is coming.

"On plunges the car through hair-raising episodes until a motor cop jumps on the running board and brings it to a temporary halt. As he is writing out a ticket, 'Wheezer' steps on it again, and makes his getaway. There are some extremely funny incidents and situations which should keep almost any audience in an uproar throughout. It is among the best of the *Our Gang* comedies.''

This opinion was echoed by an unnamed reviewer in *Film Daily:* "Here is a fine mechanical gag worked throughout for a merry round of laughs. It seems that Bob McGowan who handles the gang is convinced that you can make a two-reel juvenile comedy amusing, novel, and original. This one is a bell-ringer. If we weren't so hard boiled, we'd rave over it.''

Home-made car contraptions were nothing new for Our Gang even in 1928, but they seemed to provide sure-fire laughs and excitement every time McGowan and technical wizard Charley Oelze cooked one up.

74 · BARNUM & RINGLING, INC.

Two Reels · Silent, with synchronized music track and sound-effects · Produced by Robert F. McGowan for Hal Roach · Directed by Robert F. McGowan · Photographed by Art Lloyd · Edited by Richard Currier · Titles by H. M. Walker · Released on April 7, 1928, by M-G-M · Our Gang: Joe Cobb, Jean Darling, Allen "Farina" Hoskins, Jay R. Smith, Jackie Condon, Harry Spear, Bobby "Wheezer" Hutchins, Mildred Kornman, Johnny Aber, and Pete the Pup · Startled drunk, Oliver Hardy; Lady who sits on the egg, Dorothy Coburn; Hotel manager, William Gillespie; Maid, Edna Marian; Dowager, May Wallace; Desk clerk, George K. French; Lady doing house cleaning, Patsy O'Byrne; Lobby extras, Ham Kinsey, Retta Palmer; Amorous young man, Charles King; One of the hotel detectives, Eugene Pallette

The Ritz-Biltmore Hotel hasn't been the same since a gang of kids moved in for a spell. Aided by bellboy Farina, they decide to put on a circus, complete with a sideshow featuring such acts as Little Egypt, a menagerie full of exotic animals, and a bareback rider in the center ring. A sudden appearance by a startled hotel detective cuts the show short, however, and triggers a hotel-wide chase involving most of the animals, who overrun the place and turn it inside out. In one room, an ostrich causes a drunk to faint dead away, and then samples some of his booze. Eventually, the house dick catches up with the kids, but even he has to laugh along with them when the ostrich enters the scene, hiccoughing and stumbling around in a drunken stupor.

With its many animal accouterments and gadgetry gags, this mild comedy is reminiscent of the earlier and much better "The Big Show," although it's done with more polish and utilizes one additional *Our Gang* mainstay: a scheme by the kids that upsets unsuspecting adults. As the scores of animals run free through the hotel, there are some hilarious moments, including a running gag with a pair of newlyweds persistently trying to have a cozy tête-à-tête, interrupted by disguised dogs, wild pigs, and other assorted beasts, no matter where they go. This kind of humor was reworked in one of the best sequences in "Pups Is Pups" a few years later, at a society pet show.

The pets themselves are a prime attraction in "Barnum & Ringling, Inc.," although the gag possibilities in dressing up ordinary animals to look extraordinary wear thin after a while. Still, it's fun to see a hen on homemade stilts being passed off as a stork, and a cat with a hot-water bottle tied to its tail called a beaver.

An offbeat subplot involves little-rich-girl Jean Darling, who is staying at the hotel, and whose principal hobby is sticking long pins in people when they aren't looking! When bellboy Farina is assigned to play with her, he

Oliver Hardy and Jean Darling clown around near the entrance of the two big Hal Roach stages. Jean's on her way to the "Barnum & Ringling, Inc." set, and while Oliver Hardy works in this picture too, his nightshirt indicates he's heading for scenes in the Laurel & Hardy film *Leave 'em Laughing.*

That's Oliver Hardy holding onto Farina in this intriguing scene which was cut from "Barnum & Ringling, Inc." Also pictured among the crowd are Ham Kinsey (Stan Laurel's double and stand-in), Eugene Pallette, Patsy O'Byrne, Dorothy Coburn, and William Gillespie.

complains that he's still full of holes from the last time they "played" together.

"Barnum & Ringling, Inc." is an unusually handsome production, filmed on the same standing Hal Roach hotel sets which Laurel & Hardy would use within the coming months for their comedy *Double Whoopee,* in which William Gillespie repeated his role as hotel manager.

Other distinctions of "Barnum & Ringling, Inc." include surprise appearances by Charles King and Oliver Hardy.

During the next quarter century, dark-haired, mustachioed Charlie King would become the best "loved" of all B Western heavies, so it's rather odd to see him here as the slim, clean-cut, amorous newlywed.

Oliver Hardy had made fifteen films with Stan Laurel by this time, but there was as yet no official Laurel & Hardy series, so he continued doing bits around the Roach lot in films starring Charley Chase or Max Davidson. In "Barnum & Ringling, Inc." he appears in one scene as a drunk who's startled by the gang's pet ostrich, although production stills would indicate that originally he may have had a larger part in the film, as a detective or policeman of some kind.

Released with music and synchronized sound effects, the surviving original soundtrack of this film features a host of unimaginative animal noises and occasional bursts of cheers and applause from the kiddie crowds in the film, providing a valuable example of primitive attempts to simulate the soon-to-be-realized phenomenon of talking pictures.

75 · FAIR AND MUDDY

Two Reels · Produced by Hal Roach · Supervised by Robert F. McGowan · Directed by Charley Oelze · Photographed by Art Lloyd · Edited by Richard Currier · Titles by H. M. Walker · Released on May 5, 1928, by M-G-M · Our Gang: Joe Cobb, Bobby "Wheezer" Hutchins, Jackie Condon, Jay R. Smith, Mildred Kornman, Harry Spear, Allen "Farina" Hoskins, Jean Darling, and Pete the Pup · Character part unknown, Patsy O'Byrne; Chauffeur, Charles King

This film was not available for viewing. Trade magazine reviewers' opinions seem to have been based on the individual's affinity for pure slapstick, which in some late-1920s circles was a dirty word.

The *Film Daily* critic was enthusiastic: "All the kids will enjoy this, which shows the gang at its mischievous best. . . . An old maid wants to adopt the gang. She takes them on an auto ride, and they succeed in ruining the car and causing the indignant chauffeur to quit the job right there. They get out and meet a bunch of tough kids older than themselves. A mud battle follows, and the old maid steps in and helps them cover themselves with mud

Scene from "Fair and Muddy." That's *the* Charles King (still a few years away from superb B-Western villainy) trying without success to change a tire.

and glory. Pretty mussy at the end, but it's a cinch the kids in the audience will howl themselves almost unconscious.''

However, E. G. Johnston in *Motion Picture News* wrote, ''There's a great deal too much mud-throwing in this Gang comedy . . . . A little mud would have been alright, but when the film develops into just one mud-heave after another it becomes very monotonous entertainment. The story has to do with a child-hating spinster who in order to receive a bequest from a rich uncle must somehow acquire a child of her own by a certain date. . . . The mud throwing turns out to be just the means of softening her attitude toward children and she adopts the whole crew.''

There's no way of judging this film's slapstick except firsthand, but Stan Laurel, James Parrott, or Leo McCarey must have enjoyed it, since they used the same kind of mud melee to climax the very next Laurel & Hardy short, *Should Married Men Go Home?*

The story of this outing seems to hark back to some of *Our Gang*'s earliest efforts. The formula of the gang winning over a cranky old-timer would continue to see active duty into the sound era, most notably in such successful shorts as ''Second Childhood'' and ''Kiddie Cure.''

76 · CRAZY HOUSE

Two Reels · Produced by Robert F. McGowan for Hal Roach · Directed by Robert F. McGowan · Photographed by Art Lloyd · Edited by Richard Currier · Titles by H. M. Walker · Released on June 2, 1928, by M-G-M · Our Gang: Jean Darling, Joe Cobb, Allen "Farina" Hoskins, Mary Ann Jackson, Bobby "Wheezer" Hutchins, Harry Spear, Jackie Condon, Jay R. "Percy" Smith, and Pete the Pup · Jean's mother, May Wallace; Workman, Ed Brandenberg; Officer, Charles A. Bachman

Mary Ann and Jean react to only a few of what must have been thousands of balloons used in the climactic gag of "Crazy House." It's one of the most visually arresting gags on the silent screen. Note the reflection of all the lights used to film this shot.

Poor-little-rich-girl Jean has a large streak of tomboy in her, and she eyes longingly a gang of fighting kids from the window of the mansion where she lives. She invites them to a party that afternoon, while both her parents and the servants are away. Her father has wired the entire house with practical jokes for an April Fool's party he's having that evening. Aware of this, prissy Percy leads the gang down the primrose path so they'll be sure to set off every booby-trap in the place, from an electrified piano bench to rubber hot dogs at lunch. When they get wise, the kids beat Percy to a pulp. Meanwhile, Wheezer inadvertently springs the burglar alarm, sending a squadron of police to the house. Just as they're about to nab the kids, another button is pushed and hundreds of balloons descend from the ceiling, providing a perfect camouflage for the kids to get away. Gathering the balloons around them, they run for the hills.

''Crazy House,'' like many *Our Gang* comedies from this period, suffers from a feeling of contrivance about the whole operation. The film is really resting upon one joke—a house brimming with booby-traps—and having been tipped ahead of time, the unremarkable springing of these traps is supposed to provide two reels of entertainment. It doesn't work, because two or three cotton dinner-rolls are no funnier than one, and the gags don't get much more imaginative than that.

The film's saving grace is its punch line, because the balloons really are unexpected, and, when they come, there are thousands of them, literally covering the entire scene and enabling the kids to escape. The final shot, of each youngster surrounded by multicolored bubbles running down the street, is quite funny.

77 · GROWING PAINS

Two Reels · Produced by Robert F. McGowan for Hal Roach · Supervised by Robert F. McGowan · Directed by Anthony Mack · Photographed by Art Lloyd · Edited by Richard Currier · Titles by H. M. Walker · Story by Robert F. McGowan · Released on September 22, 1928, by M-G-M · Our Gang: Joe Cobb, Jackie Condon, Mary Ann Jackson, Jay R. Smith, Harry Spear, Bobby "Wheezer" Hutchins, Allen "Farina" Hoskins, Jean Darling, and Pete the Pup · Circus giant, John Aassen

This film was unavailable for viewing. Here is the review that originally appeared in *Film Daily:* "Excellent as usual. We never get over our raves about the *Our Gang* comedies. If Hal Roach discontinues them, we, for one, intend registering the loudest squawks we can muster. In this, Mary Ann is the pest of the neighborhood. She just raises hell with the gang, which finally nabs her and licks her plenty. Wheezer, cutest little fellow, is Mary Ann's choice to defend her honor. Mother has told Mary Ann that if Wheezer takes enough cod liver oil he will become a giant. So Mary Ann does the trick. In the meantime, a circus giant comes to board, learns of the plan, and substitutes for Wheezer. From then on, everything happens with the gang finally driving the giant clean out of the neighborhood. A fine comedy. Directed by Anthony Mack."

John Aassen (remembered as the giant from Harold Lloyd's *Why Worry?*) spanks Jean while Mary Ann looks on, in "Growing Pains."

Following a luncheon tendered in his honor, Germany's "Good Will Ambassador," Count Felix von Luckner, gathered outside with some of his new friends at Hal Roach Studios. Squatting in front are studio business manager Benjamin Shipman, unidentified member of the Count's party, and Charley Chase. In the back row are title writer H. M. "Beanie" Walker, director-general Leo McCarey, the Count and Countess, and to the right of Our Gang, another of the Count's party; then Ray Coffin, studio publicity director, Warren Doane, general manager, and Roach directors Hal Yates, James Parrott, Anthony Mack, and Frank Butler. We'd give anything to be able to read the notes on that bulletin board.

78 · OLD GRAY HOSS

Two Reels · Produced by Robert F. McGowan for Hal Roach · Supervised by Robert F. McGowan · Directed by Anthony Mack · Photographed by Art Lloyd · Edited by Richard Currier · Titles by H. M. Walker · Story by Robert F. McGowan · Released on October 20, 1928, by M-G-M · Our Gang: Joe Cobb, Allen "Farina" Hoskins, Bobby "Wheezer" Hutchins, Mary Ann Jackson, Jean Darling, Harry Spear, and Pete the Pup · Chief Cummings, Richard Cummings; Officer Mulligan, Charles Bachman; Creditor, Charley Young; Dowager, Ellinor Van Der Veer; First cab passenger, Mary Gordon; Bearded man, Tenen Holtz

Chief Cummings poses with two of his most charming friends in a posed shot from "Old Gray Hoss."

Retired fire-chief Cummings is reduced to using his faithful horse Duke to run a taxi service, but his loyal friends in Our Gang report to him every morning and continue to treat him like the special person he is. This particular morning the chief is discouraged because a new hotshot cab driver with an automobile is threatening to steal his customers. What's more, the chief owes some money and may have Duke taken away from him. The gang sets out to attract customers, mainly by discouraging people from taking a ride in the new Black and Blue Taxi. They connect a high-voltage wire to the car, giving customers an unexpected shock, they turn the exhaust pipe inside the auto, filling the car with ugly black smoke, and they frustrate the irate driver by hanging a sign reading "Free Rides Today" on the back fender. When the kids see the chief talking with the Black and Blue driver and a local policeman, they think the worst has happened, and run off with Duke. This leads to a long chase through the town—a needless one, they discover, since Officer Mulli-

gan has come through for his old friend Chief Cummings and made good his debt.

A diverting if uninspired comedy from the late-silent era, "Old Gray Hoss" is, like its companion films of this era, long on gimmickry, often without any real point.

Gags involving animated lay-overs seemed to tickle the fancy of director Anthony Mack, and he used them generously. In this film, Wheezer unwittingly hatches some eggs, and the words "Peep! Peep" emanate from the box on which he's sitting. Later, when the cab driver touches his electronically wired car, lightninglike bolts flash dramatically, giving the gag a realistic flavor. Earlier in the film, Mary Ann makes the chief some breakfast pancakes, and inadvertently spills a box of popping-corn into the pan, causing the flapjacks to explode like fireworks on touch.

As clever as these gimmick-gags can be, they wear thin very quickly, and injecting three such scenes into one film is a sure way to kill off the novelty.

Similarly, a running gag with Wheezer is driven into the ground by the end of the fast-moving short. Always in the way, Wheezer is constantly told to "Go sit on an egg!" or "Go roll a peanut!" by one of the older kids . . . prompting the youngster to obediently if grudgingly carry out the order. Instead of milking one gag as a counterpoint to the rest of the story, Wheezer goes through three or four of these routines, and the amount of time spent on each one leads the viewer to surmise that the idea was used to pad out the film. This running-joke also provides the film's incongruous and totally extraneous finale: the chase over, the problem solved, Wheezer is still pestering the older kids, and someone tells him to "Go jump in the lake." He dives off a high bridge, and three of the big kids go after him, hoping to save him from drowning. The three gang members land head-first in a mud-bar directly below the bridge, while Wheezer is shown to be dangling by his suspenders from a ledge just over the railing above.

This bit of elaborate slapstick is needless, but perfectly in keeping with the gags-for-gags'-sake attitude of the film. The diving-into-mud gag had been used many times before, but it doesn't work as well here as in earlier Roach or Sennett films, because it's not quite as funny to see a Joe Cobb or Farina with his head buried in the slimy mess. These are real kids, and likable ones; the gag is too gross to provoke a laugh unless it is done in the totally unreal world of, say, a Sennett Billy Bevan comedy.

Another large-scale slapstick scene is the climactic chase, which does produce some solid laughs in stock situations. The horse-drawn cab races through the city streets, followed close behind by the taxi carrying Chief Cummings and Officer Mulligan. As they race by one intersection, their wagon knocks a pedestrian into an excavation ditch full of muddy water, then the pursuing cab plunges two Good Samaritans into the same watery hole. Some men hoisting a piano to a third-story destination are bumped out of the way and the baby grand smashes on the sidewalk. A photographer with his camera set up in the middle of the street is sent hurling—in very slow motion—into the air. And a fruit stand is completely disrupted, with flying missiles creaming a number of innocent passersby.

Here again, the idea of doing a string of gags takes prominence over doing them *well*. Some of the gooey slapstick is too surefire to be unfunny, but many other shots are done so mechanically that the potential humor is lost.

The most interesting aspect of "Old Gray Hoss" is the continuation of a recurring *Our Gang* theme: the affinity between the kids and elderly people. In a sense, the common bond uniting these two disparate groups is that they are both outcasts of society. Adults no more want to be burdened with the responsibility of paying attention to a fire chief who has "passed his prime" than they want to get involved in the fantasies and schemes of a group of mischievous but well-intentioned kids. This is how it comes to pass that a penniless, forgotten, and aging man is kept young at heart and active by a group of children, while the kids are made to feel part of the grown-up world by working with the distinguished former chief.

The enduring appeal of this alliance made it a natural for inclusion in the *Our Gang* bag of tricks and provided the foundation for many shorts over the years. The sentiment inherent in the situation never failed to make those films particularly appealing entries in the series. This is true even for an unremarkable outing like "Old Gray Hoss."

79 · SCHOOL BEGINS

Two Reels · Produced by Robert F. McGowan for Hal Roach · Directed by Anthony Mack · Photographed by Art Lloyd · Edited by Richard Currier · Titles by H. M. Walker · Story by Robert F. McGowan · Released on November 17, 1928, by M-G-M · Our Gang: Bobby "Wheezer" Hutchins, Harry Spear, Joe Cobb, Allen "Farina" Hoskins, Jean Darling, Mary Ann Jackson, and Pete the Pup

This film was unavailable for viewing.

At the time of its release, Raymond Ganly in *Motion Picture News* declared, "This is one that'll please 'em all. 'Our Gang,' vacation time over, returns to school and everyone will sympathize with the lack of zeal they show, how reluctant they are to pass up the ole swimming hole, the circus, the fishing and the other myriad temptations with which they are beset. The kids are assembled finally in school, after an unpleasant experience for Joe Cobb, who tried to get leave of absence by forging a note from his mother. Class becomes a roughhouse when some seals escape from the circus and visit the schoolhouse. This sequence and, as a matter of fact, all that precedes it, is good."

Film Daily printed this review: "School's on. Harry hates it, frames Farina to deliver a note that his mother has broken both legs and wants him home. Which is swell until mother walks into the classroom. Meanwhile Wheezer, Harry's brother, has been fishing and starts home. Passing a circus, two trained seals smell the fish and follow. Wheezer, in his excitement, begins dropping the fish and finally waddles into the classroom, the seals close on his heels. The excitement is terrific and results in school breaking up for the day. Well gagged and very well done. Has plenty of laughs. Directed by Anthony Mack."

Although *Our Gang* had set earlier stories in the schoolroom, this two-reeler would seem to most closely anticipate the series of classroom-oriented comedies of the early-talkie era. In fact, in "Fish Hooky," "big kids" Joe and Farina tell the little ones how they used to get away with playing hooky when they were little—apparently forgetting to mention that they had problems of their own "back then."

Preschooler Wheezer supposedly answers his fan mail in this publicity shot from "School Begins."

80 · THE SPANKING AGE

Two Reels · Silent, with synchronized music track and sound effects, on disc only · Produced by Hal Roach · Directed by Robert F. McGowan · Photographed by Art Lloyd · Edited by Richard Currier · Titles by H. M. Walker · Story by Robert F. McGowan · Released on December 15, 1928, by M-G-M · Our Gang: Bobby "Wheezer" Hutchins, Joe Cobb, Mary Ann Jackson, Allen "Farina" Hoskins, Harry Spear, Jean Darling, and Pete the Pup

"The Spanking Age": Mary Ann, Wheezer, Jean, Petie, and who knows who else?

This film was unavailable for viewing. Remaining, however, is a brief review from *Film Daily:* "There is nothing in short subjects to outdistance the inimitable, charming antics of the *Our Gang* troupe. Mary Ann and Wheezer,

those adorable kids, hold the center of the stage here as two mistreated step-children who decide on a party of their own. They do so and invite the gang as guests. Mary Ann determines to make a pie and also shrimp salad. From now on figure for yourself what happens. A charming subject and funny to boot. Originally a silent comedy, it now has a synchronized score and effects. They help, but sound or silent, 'The Spanking Age' is there—and how!"

With no print presently available for reappraisal, one is forced to review existing stills to assemble a cast listing. Here, we've identified no adult actors because in every single still, adults (always standing and gesturing) are purposely, inexplicably pictured from the chest down! This, coupled with such favorable reviews, makes the film's unavailability more regrettable.

As motion pictures geared up for sound, Hal Roach announced an agreement with the Victor Company, and by January two big sound stages were to be completed. Talking pictures were still some months away, but hybrid sound was now a reality.

"The Spanking Age" marks the second silent *Our Gang* short for which a disc was made containing a music track and fitted sound effects. The disc, or phonograph record, which played from the inside out, was synchronized with the film's action; it was shipped (in duplicate) to movie theaters to be played along with the film. From the outset, correct synchronization was a problem, and so was breakage or damage during shipping.

81 · ELECTION DAY

Two Reels · Silent · Produced by Hal Roach · Supervised by Robert F. McGowan · Directed by Anthony Mack · Photographed by Art Lloyd · Edited by Richard Currier · Titles by H. M. Walker · Story by Anthony Mack · Released on January 12, 1929, by M-G-M · Our Gang: Allen "Farina" Hoskins, Bobby "Wheezer" Hutchins, Joe Cobb, Jackie Condon, Harry Spear, Jay R. Smith, Mary Ann Jackson, and Pete the Pup · Farina's mother, Louise Beavers; Farina's father, Clarence Muse; man who slips on banana, Ed Brandenberg; Officer, Gene Morgan; Man about town, Ham Kinsey; Lady in town, Retta Palmer; Gangsters, Baldwin Cooke, Jack Hill, Dick Gilbert

Farina and his little sister Pleurisy are caught on the horns of a dilemma: it's election day, and until the votes are counted neither Joe nor Jay will allow them to leave their farmyard. At the same time, the kids' mother expects them to deliver her laundry. Farina and Pleurisy try all sorts of disguises, but none of them really does the trick until a scarecrow masquerade frightens the daylights out of everyone in sight, including their mother and father! When they finally manage to get downtown, they find themselves caught in another battle, between the police

and a crooked group of gangster-politicians (the Pool Room Party) hoping to cause a riot and loot the ballot boxes. A massive shoot-out ensues, with Farina and Pleurisy unwittingly foiling the crooks by finding the "missing" ballots in their laundry wagon and turning them in. This doesn't impress their mother, however, whose only concern is that the laundry hasn't yet been delivered, and spankings are the youngsters' reward.

"Election Day" has about as much to do with elections as "Giants vs. Yanks" had to do with baseball. Opening shots show Jay's campaign sign: "Vote for Jay R. or get a bust on the nose," and Joe's, which reads: "Vote for Joe Cobb or get *two* busts in the nose." Story exposition, however, ends here. Nowhere is it clearly explained why both Jay and Joe are determined to keep Farina from leaving home to do his chores. It takes more than two-thirds into the film before we get a clue: a title card reads, "We gotta catch him before he starts voting." Apparently Farina hadn't voted yet, and each side was afraid he'd vote for the other. Not only is this never clear, but there is no resolution of the whole election idea, either. It's almost as if Roach or McGowan or McCarey viewed the rushes, realized the kiddie election wasn't going anywhere, junked it, and simply switched to the unrelated adult election never even hinted at in the early footage.

The adult election doings are equally fragmented, and the massive shoot-out serves no purpose other than to provide some gratuitous slapstick for the film's final moments. Farina isn't even thanked when he turns in the stolen ballots.

Little Pleurisy, who remains one of the few unidentified *Our Gang* players, has the film's funniest moments, in terms of gags and by virtue of her exuberant, expressive face.

One completely visual gag in "Election Day" was good enough to be reused by Roach staffers in Laurel & Hardy's *Way Out West* nearly a decade later. It's the very effective traveling shot of a huge cloud of dust, supposedly kicked up by Farina's frightened parents as they scurry to leave town. The shot is made by moving a powerful wind machine toward the camera. There are blowers and trays of loose dirt mounted on a dolly, all of which are hidden by the cyclone of dust created in the machine's own path while advancing toward the camera. Then the action is reversed to create a startling illusion on film.

These minor episodes aside, however, "Election Day" has little to recommend it. Even the *Our Gang* kids had trouble rising above mediocre material and lackluster direction such as that of Anthony Mack. Bob McGowan was credited as Supervising Director, but the results on film show that the credit was simply a matter of form. This credit was in vogue during the late 1920s. It was a do-nothing position, and screen credit was often simply a courtesy. Eventually, as Buster Keaton has remarked, title credit for this inflated capacity was "laughed off the screen."

82 · NOISY NOISES

Two Reels · Silent, with synchronized music track and sound effects · Produced by Robert F. McGowan for Hal Roach · Directed by Robert F. McGowan · Photographed by Art Lloyd · Edited by Richard Currier · Titles by Reed Heustis · Story by Robert F. McGowan · Released on February 9, 1929, by M-G-M · Our Gang: Joe Cobb, Allen "Farina" Hoskins, Bobby "Wheezer" Hutchins, Jean Darling, Gordon Thorpe, Mary Ann Jackson, Harry Spear, Bret Black, Jay R. Smith, and Pete the Pup · Joe's mother, Lyle Tayo; Voice coach, Michael Mark; Man practicing the fiddle, Tenen Holtz; Bald man on the stairs, Fred Holmes; Pedestrian, Edith Fortier

Joe has two irritating problems: a painful toothache and having to baby-sit with his brother Rupert, who sits up crying all day. He enlists the aid of the gang, but it seems that every time Rupert finally dozes off, some nearby commotion wakes him up again. When Mother returns home, Joe is able to take his mind off Rupert for a while and concentrate on the toothache instead. He's got a dollar to have the tooth pulled by a local dentist, but Farina convinces him to save the money and let the gang do the work. With one end of a string tied to the tooth and the other wrapped around the tail of canine Pete, the job is swiftly accomplished; but the dollar bill has fallen into the hands of baby brother Wheezer, who sells it to a sharp-eyed youngster for a penny. The gang takes off after the conniving kid for a chase finale.

"Noisy Noises" takes some simple comic ideas and makes the most of them. One could hardly ask for more satisfying results.

Rupert is the cryingest baby either side of the Rockies, but like most such infants, he has a sixth sense about *when* to cry so the effect will be most annoying. Joe tries to rock him to sleep, and the child begins to nap when suddenly a man next door starts practicing his bass fiddle. Snap—Rupert is up and bawling. But when poor, beleaguered Joe rocks the cradle so vigorously that the wooden structure falls apart, Rupert seems downright amused, and even more so when the bumbling older

brother trips over himself trying to transfer him to a baby carriage. The ultimate irony comes when, near the end of the film, Rupert's carriage breaks loose and rolls down a steep hill into the midst of traffic; cars swerve just in time to avoid crashing into the perambulator. As frosting on the cake, a monkey somehow gets into the act and leaps into the runaway carriage next to Rupert, who immediately clings to the animal. And is this obstreperous crybaby shedding tears during such a frightening experience? Of course not. He's having the time of his life, while *Joe* is going crazy.

Entitling this short "Noisy Noises" was doubtless an advertising ploy aimed at sound-conscious exhibitors and the growing legion of box office customers who had been sampling some of the experimental part-talkies over the past year and were clamoring for more. Hal Roach had not yet produced his first talking comedy, but in a primitive attempt to blend sound with moving images, Roach was delivering music and sound effects tracks together with his picture negatives to M-G-M. Though no such recorded tracks or discs for "Noisy Noises" can be located today, the original sound effects and discordant musical instruments (not requiring the same kind of precise synchronization that dialogue did) were probably quite convincing, even startling, for 1929 audiences in the unique position of straddling movies' silent and sound eras.

Jean and Joe in a scene cut from "Noisy Noises."

Some of the "noise" gags are quite funny, and most of them deal with music. The bowing of a bass fiddle next door vibrates all the furniture in the room, while a tuba player's blasts send the curtains on his windows flapping in the air! Best of all is a portly woman who comes for a voice lesson; her teacher, well prepared, has cotton in his ears to shield himself from her crackling coloratura.

"Sounds like murder," says Farina when he hears it. The gang gets her out of the way by sending a mouse scurrying into the room; one look and the lady dives out the apartment window in fright.

One gag used in "Noisy Noises" has always retained a certain fascination, for it falls into the Silent Comedy Lexicon, a *magna carta* of established rules that prevail in comedy films and nowhere else on earth. When the gang is trying to figure out a way to quiet the tuba player, a passing fruit vendor suggests that if they suck on lemons in front of him, his lips will pucker up and he'll be unable to play. This gag (and its first cousin, where someone swallows a dose of "alum" with similar consequences) turns up in countless comedy films, including the *Our Gang* talkie "Mike Fright." Apparently following another nonsequitur comedy precept, the one that holds, "Seeing is believing," Roach gag-writers counted on young viewers simply accepting such nonsense—and of course, we did!

On the other hand, one gag sequence near the end of the film derives its humor from total audience identification. After Farina ties one end of a string to Joe's tooth and the other to Pete's tail, he tells "Round Boy" to stand still as Pete runs after a ball. Naturally, when Pete starts running, Joe can't stand the suspense and has to run after him to keep the rope slack; the idea of standing there and letting the tooth be yanked is too much to bear—as it probably would be for any of us. The tooth is pulled only when Joe is distracted by something else—and then, of course, he doesn't even notice.

83 · THE HOLY TERROR

Two Reels · Silent · Produced by Robert F. McGowan for Hal Roach · Directed by Anthony Mack · Photographed by Art Lloyd · Edited by Richard Currier · Titles by H. M. Walker · Released on March 9, 1929, by M-G-M · Our Gang: Mary Ann Jackson, Joe Cobb, Allen "Farina" Hoskins, Jean Darling, Harry Spear, Bobby "Wheezer" Hutchins, and Pete the Pup

Prints of this film were not available for screening. The cutting continuity discloses the film's opening text title: "The story of a little girl who was bad on Monday, naughty on Tuesday, and terrible on Wednesday—Thursday they called out the marines—" Mary Ann Jackson essays the title role.

Though it's certainly unfair to judge any movie by a transcript of action and titles, "The Holy Terror" seems to have been an empty, routine comedy in the same mediocre vein of Anthony Mack's other work. Perhaps the film plays better than it reads.

Pete the Pup, Jean Darling, and Mary Ann Jackson in a scene from "The Holy Terror."

84 · WIGGLE YOUR EARS

Two Reels · Silent, with synchronized music track, on disc only · Produced by Robert F. McGowan for Hal Roach · Directed by Robert F. McGowan · Photographed by Art Lloyd · Edited by Richard Currier · Titles by H. M. Walker · Story by Robert F. McGowan · Released on April 6, 1929, by M-G-M · Our Gang: Harry Spear, Mary Ann Jackson, Joe Cobb, Bobby "Wheezer" Hutchins, Allen "Farina" Hoskins, Jean Darling, and Pete the Pup

"The story of a little boy who could wiggle his ears. And a little girl who followed him around to watch the wiggling." Mary allows herself to be bullied and abused by Harry for the occasional pleasure of watching him do his ear-wiggle for her. Joe would give anything to receive that kind of attention from Mary, and works like crazy to get his ears to move, without success. When Harry spots flirtatious Jean and tries his specialty on her, she's hooked, and he leaves Mary flat. Mary is distraught, but Farina suggests that she dress up as a flapper to win back her man. She dolls herself up with would-be makeup, fancy clothes, and rolled stockings, but Harry isn't interested; he and Jean are playing that they're married. Then Joe appears and eagerly wiggles his ears for Mary (with the aid of a wad of gum and some string that Wheezer is tugging), and she is enthralled. Now Joe is happy to wait on her hand-and-foot, while Harry finds that "married" life isn't so hot, since he has to play hand-servant to Jean instead of the other way around.

"Wiggle Your Ears" is an amusing but absolutely bizarre two-reeler. One can't help wondering just how McGowan and crew regarded the film, for although the plot situation is clearly a spoof of adult relationships, using kids for comic effect, the young actors take their roles quite seriously and play their parts straight rather than for laughs. Adding to this unsettling feeling is the look of the film, *shot entirely in tight close-up!* Was this intended as a spoof of arty European films of the 1920s, or a case of the cameraman accidentally using a close-up lens?

The answer is not easily determined, for even an action gag such as Pete pulling Harry along the sidewalk by the seat of his pants is shown in such extreme close-up that it's almost difficult to understand what's happening. Other scenes occasionally fall out of focus as the kids move around so close to the camera.

Some of the compositions apparently have a purpose. In the scene of Mary pushing Harry and Jean in his Rolls-Ruff go-cart as the sweethearts eat the ice cream cones Mary has bought, the cone is in focus in the foreground, Mary behind it staring placidly, with Harry and Jean on either side of the frame.

The close-up format also heightens the seriousness of the emotions in the film. When hard-boiled Harry tells Mary, "I'm going to wiggle my ears for Jean from now on," she starts to bawl uncontrollably. What might be cute or funny in the context of another film becomes poignant when shown in such close quarters, although a laugh quickly follows when Mary continues to cry while stuffing part of Joe's doughnut into her mouth. When Joe asks what's wrong she replies through a mouthful of food, "Blub blubbedy glub blub."

The film teeters between humor and pathos; the latter

"Wiggle Your Ears": Metaphorically speaking, hard-boiled Harry's been emasculated. Heart-breaker Jean looks delighted.

was probably not intended, but we care about the kids and don't like to see them get hurt, even though a happy ending is certain to follow. Some of the scenes, like Mary's crying, produce this feeling, while others hit their mark: after Harry tells Mary that he and Jean are going to be married, Mary envisions an elaborate church ceremony with the minister asking, "Do you promise to wiggle your ears for this woman?"

The relationship of Harry and Jean is also explored with an adult sense of satire. Harry rests at her lap on a sofa. When he closes his eyes, Jean's pet cat hops up and starts to lick Harry's face, sending him into waves of ecstasy (we see his legs kicking in the air, then slowly gliding to the floor) before he realizes that he's been fooled.

Mary's humiliation in the opening scenes, where she all but salaams before her hero, is counterpointed by a satisfying conclusion with Joe happily wheeling Mary along in her cart, as Harry wearily does the same for his "wife." The couples meet as they travel in opposite directions on the same street, and Mary says nonchalantly, "Wiggle your ears, Joseph." This makes Harry feel doubly chagrined because his ears are "cramped" and won't move—he's been robbed of his virility.

While "Wiggle Your Ears" is an unexpectedly intriguing subject for older audiences today, who can ap-

Jean and Harry ride along in their Rolls Ruff, as Mary pushes, in this scene from "Wiggle Your Ears."

ranging from $6 to $45, which is surprising in view of how many were printed. The text is superficial, and the scenes they were supposedly shooting that day were never used in any 1929 *Our Gang* comedy; while there are stills for these scenes, they were probably shot specifically for use in this book.

A sampling of random paragraphs: "The studio is tucked away among low, green hills, in a little town called Culver City, just a short drive from Los Angeles. The studio, itself, is a miniature city, with its buildings, streets, sidewalks and tiny factories, where all the things used in the Gang Pictures are made.

"Joe's Dad always comes to the studio with him. The two are great pals since Joe's mother died and left them all alone. Together they go to all the baseball and football games and to the picture shows. . . . Jean's Daddy died when she was just a wee baby, and her mother comes with her to the studio every day. Jean and her mother live all alone.

"A big blue roadster came whizzing down the driveway. Out jumped a man with smiling eyes and hair just beginning to turn gray. Mr. McGowan is his Gang's second Daddy. He has directed their pictures, played with them and loved them for the seven years that they have been amusing all the other little boys and girls in the world."

Preparing for shooting, after having explained the kind of situation he wants the gang to improvise, McGowan is quoted as concluding, "Now let's see you all do it. Just forget the cameras and have a good time."

"Cameras," plural, points up something else interesting. Most Hal Roach silent comedies were shot simultaneously with at least two cameras, from two obviously different vantage points, and sometimes at different (hand-cranked) camera speeds, in order to provide separate original negatives for both domestic issue and foreign release. Close comparison of prints struck from these twin negatives reveals many minor discrepancies, particularly when the different camera negatives were also cut by different editors. All told, it was a practice that made for interesting variations which can sometimes change the tone or tempo of a group of scenes.

preciate the implications of its humor, there is something jarring about the film. *Our Gang* isn't supposed to represent an adult view of life using children as pawns; it's an idealization of youth from a child's point of view. "Wiggle Your Ears" exploits the kids for the sake of sexually oriented humor, and while it's fun as a decided change of pace, it was fortunately one-of-a-kind, for this attitude betrays *Our Gang* and what their comedy was all about.

Sidelight: The first *Our Gang* book. About this time, the Whitman Publishing Company was preparing one million copies of a color-illustrated kids' book for 1929 Christmas sale called *A Story of Our Gang,* subtitled "Romping Through the Hal Roach Comedies." Originally sold for 15 cents apiece, mostly in Woolworth stores, today on the collector market this 22-page book commands prices

85 · FAST FREIGHT

Two Reels · Silent · Produced by Robert F. McGowan for Hal Roach · Supervised by Robert F. McGowan · Directed by Anthony Mack · Photographed by Art Lloyd · Edited by Richard Currier · Titles by H. M. Walker · Story by Robert F. McGowan · Released on May 4, 1929, by M-G-M · Our Gang: Allen "Farina" Hoskins, Joe Cobb, Harry Spear, Mary Ann Jackson, Jean Darling, Bobby "Wheezer" Hutchins, and Pete the Pup · Chief of Police, Robert Dudley; Spooky wall painting, James Finlayson

Farina and his dog Pete are riding the rails. The ingenious youngster can get anything he needs by simply drilling into the railroad car above him and letting the goodies (jelly beans, gumdrops) spill out. During a stopover, he leaves his open-air suspension berth and meets a gang of kids who envy his trip to California, "where the streets are paved with gold" (Farina wants to be a street sweeper). They don old clothes and decide to join him, leaving such drudgeries as music lessons, soap, and baths

behind. The trip is not smooth, however; Farina inadvertently drills his way overhead into a bee cage, releasing a swarm of the insects. At this, the kids leave the train and find themselves stranded in the woods, with night approaching. They take cover in a deserted old house and let their imaginations run wild until they seem to be surrounded by ghosts and other demons. When a local sheriff finds them and announces that he's taking them back home, they're glad to hear it. For Farina, though, it's back to the train, but this time he finds himself locked inside a car full of skeletons and cadavers heading for a medical school!

"Fast Freight" is a contrived outing directed by Anthony Mack that pulls every predictable gag out of the usual bag of tricks. A protracted sequence in the "haunted" house offers no surprises and few laughs. One running gag of Harry Spear continually falling (or being pushed) into a trough of flour and emerging as a "ghost" is repeated so often that it becomes pointless. Farina puts his hat on the floor, where it rests on top of a frog, who leaps about and gives the impression that the hat is haunted.

Even in 1929 these gags must have been wearing thin, although then as now the short may have certain appeal for children. In the greater scheme of *Our Gang*, however, "Fast Freight" is a short where everyone is merely going through his paces.

Wheezer, Jean, Mary Ann, Farina, Joe, Harry, and Pete the Pup in a scene from "Fast Freight."

86 · LITTLE MOTHER

Two Reels · Silent · Produced by Robert F. McGowan for Hal Roach · Directed by Robert F. McGowan · Photographed by Art Lloyd · Edited by Richard Currier · Titles by H. M. Walker · Story by Robert F. McGowan · Released on June 1, 1929, by M-G-M · Our Gang: Bobby "Wheezer" Hutchins, Mary Ann Jackson, Joe Cobb, Harry Spear, Allen "Farina" Hoskins, Jean Darling, Donnie "Beezer" Smith, and Pete the Pup · Father, Warner Richmond; "Mother," Lyle Tayo; Cab driver, Charlie Hall; Skinny man who gets showered, Gene Stone; Bit, Ed Brandenberg

Since their mama has gone to heaven, Wheezer and Beezer are mothered by their resourceful sister Mary Ann, while Pop works as a night watchman. Not only do the kids keep Mary Ann up most of the night, but they prevent Joe next door from sleeping. All the youngsters ever think about is bringing their mama back from heaven, when suddenly one day "she" appears. It's her twin sister, who's come to stay with the family, and seeing the love of the three children, she decides to let them go on believing that she's their real mother.

"Little Mother" is one of Robert McGowan's many *Our Gang* endeavors steeped in sentiment, but its potential here is never realized. He opts for "impossible" sight-gag comedy through the first half of the film, having the two young boys' stomachs suddenly swell (to the size of basketballs), and showing Mary Ann accidentally mixing soap flakes with the baking powder solution she offers them, resulting in a flow of soap bubbles from their lips during the night.

All this is fine in its own way, but it creates a weak foundation for any kind of emotional impact later on. What's more, the story, such as it is, is interrupted by a

Wheezer and Beezer with tummy troubles in a scene from "Little Mother." Beezer is Jay R. Smith's younger brother Donnie.

totally extraneous sequence in which the two youngsters open a fire hydrant, setting loose a water hose which douses everyone in sight. The subsequent scene of the mother's twin sister arriving is shoehorned into a few hurried minutes, with minimal effectiveness for what was intended to be a heart-warming finale.

The beauty of Our Gang was its ability to work equally well with comedy and sentiment; there are classic films in the series from both ends of the spectrum. But mixing the two elements together was a delicate matter, and that delicacy simply didn't enter into the creation of "Little Mother," for all its good intentions.

What remains is a typically charming performance by Mary Ann Jackson, whose knowing sense of comedy bolstered every *Our Gang* film she was in; and an equally pleasing performance by that stalwart Hal Roach regular, Lyle Tayo, as the departed mother (shown in a painting on the wall) and her twin sister.

87 · CAT, DOG & CO.

Two Reels · Silent, with synchronized music track and sound effects, on disc only · Produced by Robert F. McGowan for Hal Roach · Supervised by Robert F. McGowan · Directed by Anthony Mack · Photographed by Art Lloyd · Edited by Richard Currier · Titles by H. M. Walker · Story by Robert F. McGowan · Released on September 14, 1929, by M-G-M · Our Gang: Bobby "Wheezer" Hutchins, Joe Cobb, Allen "Farina" Hoskins, Harry Spear, Jean Darling, Mary Ann Jackson, Donnie "Beezer" Smith, and Pete the Pup · Mrs. President of the Be Kind to Animals Society, Hedda Hopper; Cab driver, Chet Brandenberg; Pedestrians, Jack Hill, Clara Guiol, Dorothy Vernon, Don Sandstrom; Officer, Silas D. Wilcox

"Peruvian Proverb," reads the opening title, "Be kind to all animals—Even an oyster appreciates sympathy." Joe, Harry, and Farina are racing their kiddie cars through the streets. Propulsion is by way of one dogpower under each hood. A lady from the humane society notices this, and persuades the gang they should show reverence for all life. Then the kids' problem becomes one of converting other members of the gang, particularly Wheezer, who isn't convinced until he has a frightening daydream. He sees himself dwarfed by gigantic animal creatures dressed as humans, who as judge and jury advise him he is on trial for cruelty to animals. With the fantasy ended, and Wheezer a believer, the entire gang combines to set loose all the animals in town, sweeping through a dogcatcher's wagon (twice), a poultry market, and an animals' experimental laboratory. Soon the horrified townspeople are confounded with hundreds of giant frogs, dogs, white mice, rats, cats, rabbits, and chickens that overrun Culver City like a plague!

One of the best among late silent *Our Gang* comedies (generally a weak period), "Cat, Dog & Co." is also one of the few skillful films done by Anthony Mack. Presaging the educational shorts Mack would write for M-G-M in the 1940s, "Cat, Dog & Co." teaches a lesson of sorts, but it's one that is entirely incidental to the comedy, as it should be.

Not since *The Dippy Doo Dads*—a novelty series featuring monkeys dressed as humans and spoofing stock movie plots—had Hal Roach lavished such attention on a story that spotlights animals. Wheezer's fantasy sequence, though without the predominantly simian cast of *The Dippy Doo Dads,* is still structured essentially the same, with visual gags like an owl seated on a judge's bench, dressed in a robelike vestment, and with a special talent for the double take prompting most of the laughs.

The special effects in the fantasy sequence are the work of Roy Seawright, later responsible for the marvelous invisibility effects in Hal Roach's three *Topper* comedy features, and later still an associate of renowned cartoon director Tex Avery. Done with giant-size sets and props, and some superimpositions (rather than miniatures), scenes of assorted furry and feathered creatures menacing a tiny Wheezer are surprisingly authentic. The sequence, however, is richer in technique than in comedy, and is carried beyond its essential worth, probably since it required so much effort to produce.

There's also some cunning trick photography that enables us to view a normal-size Wheezer in juxtaposition with his diminutive dream counterpart. Again, the illusion is realistic.

Yet another technical contrivance provides the film with a neat running gag. When Joe comes upon Jean and Mary Ann helping rid a dog of its fleas, he tells them they should never hurt even the smallest living thing. At which point the scene cuts to an animated sequence (again done by Seawright) showing a tiny flea—tiny even in the cartoon segment—leaping into the air and exclaiming, "Hooray! A friend! I'll stick to him!" And stick he does, much to Joe's scratching annoyance as he tries to free himself of this itching nuisance throughout the film.

Mrs. President of the Be Kind to Animals Society is played by Hedda Hopper, who had an undistinguished acting career in films before achieving lasting fame as a powerful Hollywood gossip columnist, along with rival Louella Parsons. (Miss Parsons was quite an *Our Gang* fan and frequently dotted her columns with items on her favorite Gangsters, especially Farina.)

The final third of "Cat, Dog & Co." features a hilarious gag sequence that is crammed with incident and flawlessly edited. Overturning cages and releasing all the pent-up animals in town, the gang transforms Culver City into an open-air menagerie. In a women's shoe store, the salesman fitting a dignified customer laces the shoe and ties the knot with a white rat's tail. Another terror-stricken lady opens her purse and pulls out a handful of mice. Still another exits from an ice cream parlor, gasps at the maelstrom of fury in the street, and jumps ten feet in the air to safety atop the shop's awning.

The camera gives us a panoramic view of a mass of rodents scurrying down the sidewalk as high-stepping shrieking pedestrians try with little success to escape this seeming invasion. The spreading hysteria creates quite a spectacle. The scene changes to six nonchalant pedestrians lined up along a curb waiting for a bus, and then to individual close-ups as their twisting expressions reveal the dawning horror of an army of nibbling little creatures gathering beneath them! The routine was good enough to be reworked just a year later in "Pups is Pups."

Though produced as a silent, this film, like several others, was held out of distribution until after four sound *Our Gang* pictures had been delivered to exhibitors. Though not a talkie, "Cat, Dog & Co." isn't entirely silent either. Surviving prints carry a notice on the film leader for projectionists: "This reel is properly marked for sound effect."

Pete the Pup can't believe his eyes in this scene from "Cat, Dog & Co."

88 · SATURDAY'S LESSON

Two Reels · Silent, with synchronized music track and sound effects, on disc only · Produced by Robert F. McGowan for Hal Roach · Directed by Robert F. McGowan · Photographed by Art Lloyd · Edited by Richard Currier · Titles by H. M. Walker · Story by Robert F. McGowan · Released on November 9, 1929, by M-G-M · Our Gang: Allen "Farina" Hoskins, Joe Cobb, Mary Ann Jackson, Jean Darling, Bobby "Wheezer" Hutchins, Harry Spear, and Pete the Pup · Dr. A. M. Austin, Charley Young; First pedestrian, Ham Kinsey; Second pedestrian, Allen Cavan

On Saturday, the gang dreams of leisure and play away from school, but instead, they are assigned household chores by their mothers, who warn that the Devil will get them if they don't obey. Stealing off to a park together, they scoff at this notion, within earshot of a sandwich-board man dressed as Lucifer to advertise Mephisto Heaters ("Hotter than Hot"). He decides to have some fun, and appears as the Devil to scare them into submission. As a result, the kids race back home to do their chores, with such fervor and diligence that their mothers think they've gone crazy! Then the "Devil" reveals himself to the parents before issuing a final warning to the kids: "Obey your mother! Work for her! Or I'll come back every Saturday!" The gang breathes a collective sigh of relief as he leaves, and vows to follow his command, turning to the camera and declaring, "You little boys and girls out there—let this be a lesson to you." But just to show that even the Devil gets his due, our last view is of Pete the Pup grabbing the bogus Satan by the tail, and refusing to let go.

"Saturday's Lesson" would seem to be a one-joke film, but the material is handled so deftly that the idea sustains this fast-moving two-reeler without any feeling of padding to make a point.

The film opens with Farina's vision of Saturday: seated

A devilish moment from "Saturday's Lesson."

in his best bib and tucker before a tantalizing table piled with luscious food, served to him by a most accommodating butler. Then he wakes up, to find his mother ordering him outside to beat carpets.

In a neighboring kitchen, Harry, Jean, Mary Ann, and Wheezer are forced to eat spinach for breakfast; then the men and women split up to clean the yard and do kitchen chores respectively. "All I do 'round this place is eat spinach and work," Wheezer complains.

While next door, Joe's Saturday is to be occupied splitting wood. He gives up after a few minutes to join his pals in commiserating over their sad lot in life. At this point, the "Devil" comes by and decides to teach the errant children a lesson. Appearing in a puff of smoke (thanks to a pellet he carries with him) he plays his role for all it's worth, causing Farina to faint, and pointing his finger menacingly (into the camera) as he warns, "I'm after you!"

At this, the kids flee home and leap into work in undercranked fast motion. Initially, their mothers are pleased to see the children at work, but after a few minutes, their pleasure turns to concern that something is seriously wrong. Joe's mother is unable to stop him from splitting wood—he won't let go of the ax for fear that the somersaulting ol' Devil-man will punish him. She drags him into the house and brings him castor oil; when he protests, the Devil appears at the window and barks, "You take the castor oil and like it!" With this, Joe downs the entire bottle, sending his mother to phone for a doctor. By the time the doc arrives, Joe is outside again, furiously swinging his hatchet amid an ever-growing pile of wood (by the end of the film, this modest collection has grown to the size of a house).

The situation is the same with the other families. "Mom, please cook us some more spinach," Mary Ann cries to her incredulous mother. And Farina works so hard beating his carpets that they soon are nothing but shreds!

The pace and vigor of this comedy compensate for the pallid "message" being driven home, especially when the kids themselves turn to the camera and issue a direct warning to the children in the audience. Unlike so many later message films, especially in the late-1930s-early-'40s M-G-M period, one accepts this sugar-coated proselytizing cheerfully, because the kids are so endearing, and besides, they've just provided us with twenty minutes of satisfying entertainment—which is more than can be said for most of those later abominations.

"Saturday's Lesson" was the final nontalking *Our Gang* comedy made.

VII   THE ROACH M-G-M TALKIES
(The Little Rascals)

89 · SMALL TALK

Three Reels · All-talking · Produced by Robert F. McGowan for Hal Roach · Directed by Robert F. McGowan · Photographed by Art Lloyd and F. E. Hershey · Edited by Richard Currier · Dialogue by H. M. Walker · Story by Robert F. McGowan · Released on May 18, 1929, by M-G-M · Our Gang: Bobby "Wheezer" Hutchins, Mary Ann Jackson, Joe Cobb, Allen "Farina" Hoskins, Jean Darling, Harry Spear, and Pete the Pup · Wheezer's new mother, Helen Jerome Eddy; Officer in charge, Pat Harmon; Officer, Charles McMurphy; Mrs. Brown of the orphan asylum, Lyle Tayo; Domestic, Edith Fortier*

As orphans, the gang hopes to be placed in happy homes—where spinach isn't on the menu. Wheezer gets adopted by a rich socialite, but Mary Ann is unhappy at being separated from her younger brother, whom she's mothered pretty much by herself. At his palatial new home, Wheezer is gifted with electrical trains, bicycles, and all sorts of fancy toys, but he's lonely for his sister.

While Mother is preoccupied giving a lawn party, the gang—still orphans—breaks into the house to visit their pal Wheezer. Romping through the luxurious home, naturally they get into mischief. Jean finds a strange knob on the wall, and plays around with it, not realizing she's just set off the fire and police alarms. As the two emergency units converge on the home, the Rascals are "captured"

---

* Farina Hoskins's aunt and guardian during the day on the Roach lot.

THE ROACH M-G-M TALKIES (THE LITTLE RASCALS)

and made to explain why they've been prowling around. Wheezer's new mother then realizes Mary Ann's place is with her brother, and so she adopts the two of them together. What's more, she convinces her guests they ought to each adopt one of the Gang orphans—which they do, right on the spot!

A comingling of pathos and humor, "Small Talk" is very much in the overly saccharine vein of "Little Mother" (which was made before "Small Talk," but released after). Individual sequences are touching, but the comedy is mild, and overall the short is somewhat faltering and awkward.

"Small Talk" is set apart from "Little Mother," however, and carries special historical interest since it is the first talking *Our Gang* picture. Dialogue, spoken gag lines, background music, and sound effects would ultimately bring a whole new range to their comedy routines, but the early sound *Our Gang* films like "Small Talk" struggled through a transition period in which they were slow and unsure of themselves. The pacing is usually clumsy, and if anything the use of sound in an empirical film such as "Small Talk" is overly creative, calling attention to itself, and exploiting the novelty of sound for its own sake. Action, slapstick, and situation humor are displaced by gags or props that produce funny noises: a talking parrot, a toy bird that whistles, an auto honking its horn, a dog barking, a gangster blowing his nose, a loud radio, police and fire sirens, and in the film's very first scene (in which the microphone is plainly visible hanging over the kitchen table) the gang is heard playing loud discordant musical instruments.

In 1929, moving pictures and "the movies" had suddenly become talking pictures and "the talkies." Silence wasn't golden any longer. The novelty of sound over the previous two years in some of the Warner Bros. Vitaphone pictures had evolved into a sound revolution that was sweeping through Hollywood: silent films were dead, and commercial movies would have to learn to talk. The box office public was demanding it.

By contemporary standards, one is forced to admit that "Small Talk" and other early sound shorts are not very funny; yet in an academic sense, placed in their proper historical context, they are fascinating to watch. One must try to identify with an audience that had never experienced talking pictures. For them, the miracle wasn't how movies talked, but that they talked at all. It was literally breathtaking to hear an actor say *anything*.

At the time, for instance, Harold Lloyd had just completed production on the silent version of *Welcome Danger,* and in his words, "sound was just coming in, and inconsequential things were getting tremendous laughs—like frying eggs and ice tinkling in a glass. They'd howl at that. So I said, here we're working our heads off trying to get funny ideas, and they're getting them from these sound effects. I said that maybe we had missed the boat and should make *Welcome Danger* over [with sound]." Which is just what he did.

Lloyd fared better than some of his colleagues, for sound killed or crippled many a comedy career. Keaton and Langdon were never the same, while comedy producer Mack Sennett found his slapstick talkies being referred to as "old hat." Chaplin merely ignored sound and continued making silent films with musical accompaniment until *The Great Dictator* in 1940.

In the back of the RCA Victor talking-machine truck, Laurel & Hardy explain a few things to the Gang.

"Small Talk": a scene taking place in Wheezer's new home. The American Flyer train set shown here is today worth thousands of dollars. And what have you up in *your* attic?

From the outset, Hal Roach wasn't concerned with "conquering" sound, as others were. He correctly saw it as a means for expanding comedy styles, rather than changing them. After a compromising period of experimentation, Roach transferred his silent-film formula to the talkies intact, exploring new avenues which might enhance this proven success.

With the release of "Small Talk," Hal Roach was quoted in the *Exhibitor's Herald-World* as saying, "Comedy and short pictures are coming into their own with the talking screen. Unless there should be an unforeseen demand for nontalking pictures, we will continue to make all our comedies with dialogue and sound. People want to laugh, and they want their laughter served to them in the same fast tempo that radio and airplanes have brought into their lives . . . .

"Speech will give our comedy added personality and punch. Too much dialogue must be avoided though. Speedy, obvious action will always be the prime motive of good comedy—we can't depend entirely on dialogue. . . .

"Now that the screen can talk, however, the old hit-or-miss method of making comedies is gone forever. In a talking comedy, you can't start out with a yawn, a pretty girl and a good idea and let the farcical elements develop as you go along. You must have the right dialogue, written concisely, and ready to motivate the action and gags. Of course, with natural comedians like we have, there will always be a certain amount of spontaneous impromptu fun, but there must be a carefully constructed story and speech foundation on which to build."

It would be almost a year before his comedy companies could successfully implement Roach's sound film formula, but when they did, Roach shorts regained their stride and outdistanced competing comedy shorts and features alike. *Our Gang*, Laurel & Hardy, and Charley Chase enjoyed tremendous and renewed popularity in the talkie era.

Simplistic as it may seem, early sound films were advertised as "The marvel of the age! Pictures that talk like living people! Electrifying!" For "Small Talk," the trade blurbs read, "A sensation wherever it is being shown! Until you See and Hear *Our Gang* in their first All-Talking hit 'Small Talk,' you can't know the profit power of the Roach talkies. Many theaters are billing them above the feature. When *Our Gang* made a personal appearance tour they broke every record wherever they played—big cities and small. When you play their charming hit 'Small Talk' you will virtually have an *Our Gang* personal appearance. Three grand reels! Unique, delightful entertainment—and it's only the beginning!"

Reviews were similarly ecstatic. *Film Daily* exulted, "All the charm and delight of the gang that reached out from their silent comedies, plus the brand-new kick of hearing them speak. That should be enough—plus—for any theater. . . . To hear Wheezer and little Mary Ann talk is cunning beyond words. Nab this one."

All of Hal Roach's stars launched their sound careers with pun-ny film titles (Laurel & Hardy's *Unaccustomed as We Are*, Charley Chase's *The Big Squawk*, and *Our Gang*'s "Small Talk," as in *Small* kids *Talk*ing). Then in the gang's second talkie, "Railroadin'," the main title card featured a parody of the famous RCA Victor "His Master's Voice" logo, featuring the Victrola, the dog, and the slogan "Hal Roach Presents His Rascals' Voices . . . in 'Railroadin'.' "

90 · RAILROADIN'

Two Reels · All-talking, sound on disc only · Produced by Robert F. McGowan for Hal Roach · Directed by Robert F. McGowan · Photographed by Art Lloyd and F. E. Hershey · Edited by Richard Currier · Story edited by H. M. Walker · Story by Robert F. McGowan · Released on June 15, 1929, by M-G-M · Our Gang: Allen "Farina" Hoskins, Joe Cobb, Bobby "Wheezer" Hutchins, Mary Ann Jackson, Jean Darling, Norman "Chubby" Chaney, Harry Spear, and Pete the Pup · Joe's father, Otto Fries; Grocery truck driver, Jack Hill; Brakeman, Ed Brandenburg; Limited passenger who stumbles, Bob McGowan; Other passengers, Dorothy Hamilton Darling, Mrs. Norman T. Chaney

Our Gang is spending the day romping around the railroad yards, where Joe and Chubby's dad is an engineer. Farina and Harry are admiring the many engines from a turntable, while Jean, Mary, and Wheezer are pretending to put on a show which, understandably, no one is watching. When Joe's dad breaks for lunch, Harry goads Junior Engineer Joe into taking him up inside the locomotive cab. There they are joined by an uninvited crazy man who releases the brake, starts the engine, then jumps off, leaving the kids to operate the locomotive. Puffing steam and smoke, the drive wheels churning, the engine begins pulling out down the track, with Joe apprehensively peering out the cab window—he hasn't a clue how to stop the thing. Trying to avoid running into the roundhouse, Joe manages to reverse directions and, in the bargain, latches onto the gondola car where the little kids are playing. Then Farina climbs aboard, and the reluctant, frightened passengers wonder what's next as the train picks up speed puffing on down the tracks. Soon they're cruising through the city toward the hazardous open road, inviting hairbreadth escapes from collisions with passing autos and streetcars. Up ahead a grocery truck is stalled on the tracks. The driver tries to flag down the speeding train, but to no avail; it smashes through the vehicle, blasting the contents high into the air in all directions, leaving the looks of an explosion in its wake. Covered with a hail of groceries, Farina's pantomiming prayer, but Wheezer's having a grand time, urging Joe to "step on it." Wheezer hopes they hit an ice cream wagon next. Just then, far in the distance, the frantic kids spot another train bearing

Production crew on location for "Railroadin' ": Otto Fries and Joe Cobb are looking out from the cab window, director McGowan is to their left, and Art Lloyd is lining up the shot behind the camera. Note the assistant beside Lloyd with "idiot" written across his back.

down hard on them from the opposite direction. Farina sounds the whistle in warning. Tension mounts by the second as the camera cuts between shots of the quickly converging locomotives. Inside The Limited, the conductor runs through the coaches screaming about a wild engine streaking toward them! Luckily The Limited reverses direction and backs onto a side track, narrowly escaping disaster as the gang's engine passes by on the main track. At last Joe throws the switch that slows the engine to a steaming halt. A conductor and trainman run up and ask about the gang's wild ride. Joe explains how the crazy man pulled the throttle and jumped off their moving engine. The kids wonder about a reward for stopping the runaway locomotive, and the conductor promises one "from above." Whereupon an egg rolls from some groceries still atop the engine and splatters in Farina's face. "Some reward!" he mutters. Fade out. Fade in. The gang is gathered around as Joe's pop explains what could happen if the kids found themselves aboard a runaway engine. Mary interrupts to point out that Farina's been asleep and didn't hear the story. Before she can wake him, though, a hen on the roof lays an egg that rolls off and (again) clobbers Farina on the forehead, causing him to sit up, wipe his face, and moan "Some reward!? Some reward is right!''

Advertised as another 100 per cent all-dialogue comedy ("They speak for themselves"), "Railroadin' " was a healthy improvement over "Small Talk." Though story exposition might have been tightened a bit, the film is technically expert, and far from routine in conception and execution.

Unfortunately, Our Gang's second appearance before the microphones can be seen only at a disadvantage today, since apparently all duplicate discs (phonograph records) containing the film's soundtrack have been lost, broken, or damaged beyond reclamation, and only the picture negative survives.

At the time, there were two unrelated methods of distributing sound with motion pictures. The competing sound recording systems were Warner Bros.' disc method (Vitaphone), in which the projector was mechanically linked to a record player, and Fox's optical soundtrack method (Movietone), where the sound was printed right on the film stock. For a short while, disc was the more popular method, simply because it was easier for theaters to install quickly, but before long sound-on-film became the accepted format for the entire industry.

Hal Roach's earliest sound product was distributed on disc, but most of the films were either preserved or later transferred to optical negatives. Unfortunately, such important shorts as ''Railroadin' '' and Laurel & Hardy's *Unaccustomed as We Are* were neglected somewhere along the way and exist today only as silent films. Until Blackhawk Films resurrected the negative of these two films and prepared silent adaptations, they weren't seen at all for some forty years.

Luckily, ''Railroadin' '' is one of the few talking films straddling the silent and sound eras that wouldn't stand still for stationary microphones, and makes a much better silent adaptation than would its contemporary releases. If McGowan and Walker had acknowledged natural sound by entitling their first talkie ''Small Talk,'' then ''Railroadin' '' indicated a return to action. Perhaps Roach or McGowan realized the inordinate emphasis on dialogue was depriving movies of their visual impact.* From a review of this film's detailed dialogue cutting continuity, sound was employed only incidentally for special effects, to emphasize certain gags, and to motivate the action. There's even live action coincident with the titles, a device used here far ahead of its time, as the original main title and production credits are superimposed over a scene of a train crossing diagonally in front of the camera.

A real *motion* picture, ''Railroadin' '' is one of the few transitional talkies that wasn't intimidated by the new medium of sound, concentrating on the visual by borrowing sight gags from one of the best Pathé silents, ''The Sun Down Limited.'' Particularly well done are the scenes with Farina sitting on the railroad track, his foot caught in a switch, waving his arms frantically and bobbing up and down while Joe helplessly runs his locomotive back and forth over his prostrate but uninjured pal. An intriguing selection of camera angles, a convincing-looking dummy, and some fine matte work all contribute to the edge-of-seat palm-wringing scenes.

But nothing's as thrilling as the montage of action-charged runaway locomotive scenes on the open road, with the engine roaring through the countryside at full throttle. Skillfully edited, fast-paced, and authentic, the sequence has a striking visual quality—and a few laughs to boot. And while dream endings are generally disappointing, this one is not, because revelation of Farina's dream doesn't interrupt climactic action; it's more of an afterthought than a trick denouement.

---

* Though the silent film died swiftly, many early talkies were static and faltering, and some exhibitors filled the void by reprising the better silent comedies. ''The Fourth Alarm,'' for instance, a fine Pathé silent, was kept busy playing houses in reissue through 1930.

Like the corresponding Laurel & Hardy railroad film, *Berth Marks*, ''Railroadin' '' was filmed on location behind the Samuel Goldwyn studio near Santa Monica Boulevard. Unmistakable landmarks like the huge oil reserve cylinders figure prominently in a number of other comedy films, most notably Charlie Chaplin's *The Kid* in 1921.

''Railroadin' '' introduced roly-poly Norman Chaney, who was christened ''Chubby'' by Bob McGowan, having won a nationwide contest to replace Joe Cobb. Outgrowing the gang wasn't especially traumatic for Joe, who recalls helping Chubby break into his rotund role: ''He adapted gracefully, and we all liked him, he was a nice fellow. As always, everybody tried to be patient with him, coaching him, making it comfortable for him, and you just kind of showed him around, the way I'd worked, and trying out whichever way would be easiest for him.''

Joe Cobb has memories, too, about the conversion from silent films to talkies: ''One trouble was that we'd always worked outside on location quite a bit. We liked to film out of doors, and sound was sensitive, so we had an awful lot of trouble with the neighborhood birds, dogs, cats, even the airplanes, and just about every kind of outdoor interference you can imagine. For a while, someone was always calling the airport, asking for their cooperation so we could shoot. Or sometimes we'd end up by gathering a crowd of onlookers, and they'd be laughing—ruining a scene that way.

''And of course with sound, Bob McGowan couldn't talk to us, directing us verbally through a scene as he liked to do now and then. With talking pictures, we might have to rehearse something two, three times, then we'd be on our own during filming to carry out the idea he'd given us.

''We didn't have written scripts till talkies came along. The older kids with lines would learn their parts, then they'd change the script all around on the set, and you'd give up after a while because by the time they got through changing things you didn't know what was going on and so they'd wind up just telling you what to say before you shot each scene. Later on they'd adhere to the script much more strictly. But scripts were new with talkies.

''In the silent days, McGowan was the only one who knew the whole story for each picture—though I guess it was well planned in advance. We'd sort of gather around him before each scene and he'd give us a little bit of the story before we filmed that scene. And we sometimes didn't shoot in sequence, we might shoot the last scene first, and so forth. Funny thing, I used to think, it took us two weeks to make a picture, and just twenty minutes to show one.''

91 · BOXING GLOVES

Two Reels · Sold to exhibitors as "all-talking," though in fact it's a hybrid · Produced by Hal Roach · Supervised by Robert F. McGowan · Directed by Anthony Mack · Photographed by Art Lloyd and F. E. Hershey · Edited by Richard Currier · Dialogue by H. M. Walker · Story by Hal E. Roach and Robert F. McGowan · Released on September 9, 1929, by M-G-M · Our Gang: Joe Cobb, Norman "Chubby" Chaney, Allen "Farina" Hoskins, Jackie Cooper, Harry Spear, Mary Ann Jackson, Jean Darling, Bobby "Wheezer" Hutchins, Donnie "Beezer" Smith, Bobby Mallon, Billy Schuler, Johnny Aber, and Pete the Pup · Sidewalk diner attendant, Charlie Hall

Harry and Farina are running a boxing arena, but the so-called fights between neighborhood kids are anything but exciting. Farina sets out to find a real match, and discovers Joe and Chubby in the midst of one of their perennial arguments, this one fired by flirtatious Jean. Farina seizes his opportunity and announces a "heavy-wate battle," telling each contender that the other one has agreed to "lie down" in the second round. Neither one is much of a fighter, and Joe wants to leave, but a tough kid in the audience tells him to stay in the ring or he'll have *another* fight on his hands. Then Farina uses his secret weapon, telling Chubby to muss Joe's hair. Nothing makes Joe angrier, and he goes on a rampage, hitting everything in sight, including referee Farina. Eventually, both fighters are knocked out cold, and as Farina announces the decision, a spectator who's tired of the whole thing pelts him with a tomato.

"Boxing Gloves" is not a bad short, but its appeal is severely limited by its awkward use of sound. There is no music over the main title, and most of the footage was shot silent. This seems to have been a time- or money-saving measure and nothing more, since the talkie sequences recorded outdoors sound fine, and there was apparently no barrier to shooting the entire film that way.

Silence in a scene where nothing happens is one thing, but a barren soundtrack when the screen shows a group of kiddie spectators cheering is something else again. It doesn't make sense, and it gives the film a curious, aloof quality that limits its enjoyment. Since sound effects are clearly post-dubbed in one scene, it's difficult to understand why the other silent scenes weren't simply given the same treatment.

The idea of Joe and Chubby as feuding pals is inspired, and their attempts to impress pretty Jean are fun to watch. They race to the nearby sidewalk beanery to buy a bottle of soda pop; when one is racing ahead, the other comes from behind and rips off his opponent's pants, suffering a similar fate himself a few moments later. In racing back and forth, first to buy the pop and then to have it opened, the two rivals eventually crash head-on, sending both bottles smashing onto the sidewalk. At this point they growl at each other in utter contempt; observing the scene, Farina tells Harry, "Now there's a couple of *real* fightin' men." But the two enemies eventually back off, as Harry explains that they've been feuding for years, but they never fight because "Joe can't get mad enough, and Chubby is a-scared." Farina tries to overcome both handicaps at the heavyweight battle.

The fight sequence itself is protracted and directionless, with no set gags but a lot of movement, further flattened by the often-dead soundtrack. The most ingenious moment comes when Chubby is knocked out and experiences a dizzy sensation, indicated by showing the arena swirling around him, as filmed on a merry-go-round device. A few minutes later the same shot is used with Joe in the dizzy position.

Mary Ann is barred from the fight, the ticket-taker explaining that they can't be bothered with women fainting at the sight of blood. Mary Ann replies that she'd like to faint once, to see what it's like, but she is still denied admittance. Not to be put off so easily, she spends the rest of the film trying to get in, and finally does, by abducting Jackie Cooper and taking his place at ringside in male garb.

The kids handle their dialogue quite well, although several flubs are allowed to pass. The worst aspect of "Boxing Gloves," however, is the annoying switchovers from sound to silent footage, with no musical track to make the transitions less apparent. Add to this an abrupt and ineffectual ending, and you have the middling results of a potentially funny short.

92 · LAZY DAYS

Two Reels · All-talking, sound on disc only · Produced by Robert F. McGowan for Hal Roach · Directed by Robert F. McGowan · Photographed by Art Lloyd and F. E. Hershey · Edited by Richard Currier · Story edited by H. M. Walker · Story by Robert F. McGowan · Released on August 15, 1929, by M-G-M · Our Gang: Allen "Farina" Hoskins, Jannie Hoskins, Joe Cobb, Jean Darling, Mary Ann Jackson, Norman "Chubby" Chaney, Bobby "Wheezer" Hutchins, Bobbie Burns, Harry Spear, Pete the Pup, Dinah the Mule, and Elmer the Monkey

Wheezer, Joe, and Chubby in an early-morning stills session before shooting begins on "Lazy Days."

Lazy Farina just barely manages to rouse himself when Joe reports that there's a baby contest in town in which he might win $50. Farina gives his infant brother a bath and dresses him, but on the way downtown he spots a shady tree and can't resist lying down for a while. As he does, Joe and the gang march by and reveal that the show was over a month ago!

True to its name, "Lazy Days" is the most lethargic *Our Gang* comedy ever made. If the sheer novelty of sound was supposed to keep it afloat, that sales point is obviously gone today. Most of the film consists of Farina lolling about, moaning how tired he is, and getting his obedient little sister to wait on him. He's so lazy that when Joe comes along and asks if he'd like to have $50, Farina drawls, "Yeah, I guess I'll take it . . . lay it on that box over yonder."

Farina isn't the only lazy one around; an opening montage shows some of the tiredest barnyard animals ever seen. Some of the lazy gags are fun, but they're presented so lackadaisically that they lose all effectiveness. There is an ingenious *Our Gang* laborsaving device, but this too is mired in the slow-paced comedy: Pete the Pup runs back and forth inside a teetering container, creating a seesaw effect that rocks the baby's cradle and Farina's easy chair at the same time.

As for the baby contest, the single diversion in this one-note film, it scarcely gets launched as a subplot when we're told that it's been and is gone already. The comic possibilities of Joe trying to pass off two-ton Chubby as a baby are nipped in the bud. (Sharp viewers might have known the contest was a bit offbeat, since an advance notice declared, "The Hon. Benjamin Shipman has consented to act as chief judge." Shipman was then the business manager of Hal Roach Studios, and was later to serve Laurel & Hardy in the same capacity.)

All in all, the most appropriate reaction to "Lazy Days" is a loud, long yawn.

93 · BOUNCING BABIES

Two Reels · All-talking, sound on disc only · Produced by Robert F. McGowan for Hal Roach · Directed by Robert F. McGowan · Photographed by Art Lloyd and F. E. Hershey · Edited by Richard Currier · Story edited by H. M. Walker · Story by Robert F. McGowan · Released on October 12, 1929, by M-G-M · Our Gang: Bobby "Wheezer" Hutchins, Jackie Cooper, Joe Cobb, Mary Ann Jackson, Norman "Chubby" Chaney, Allen "Farina" Hoskins, Jean Darling, Harry Spear, Bobby Mallon, Tommy Atkins, and Pete the Pup · The father, Eddie Dunn; Nurse, Lyle Tayo

With a new baby in the house, Wheezer finds that no one pays much attention to him, and he's often left on his own. Tale-spinning Farina tells Wheezer that he once had an unwanted baby brother, and took it back to the hospital, where he traded it for a goat. Wheezer adopts the same plan, unknowingly taking a doll instead of the infant. A nurse plays along with the scheme, alerting Wheezer's mother by phone. When he returns home, his mother and sister Mary Ann are crying uncontrollably about the loss of the baby. Upset, Wheezer tries to retrieve his brother at the hospital, but the nurse tells him that it's too late: they've already sent him back to heaven. Anxious to stop his mother from crying, he asks what he can do, and Mom replies that perhaps if he prays, the angels will bring the baby back. As Wheezer shuts his eyes and prays, Mom brings the child into the room, where he toddles over to his older brother and bops him on the head with a hammer. Opening his eyes, Wheezer sighs, "Well, he's back, all right."

A fairly interesting short based on a keen perception of what goes on inside a child's mind, "Bouncing Babies" (often misnamed "Bounding Babies") is hurt by the ravages of time: existing prints force the barren dialogue (without music) to battle against the roar of static and the general pops and hash of soundtrack noise, making it difficult for the viewer to relax with the film.

This aside, the short stretches what should have been a one-reeler script to twenty minutes. There is a totally irrelevant scene where Farina and Wheezer are scared by some of the other kids in Halloween costumes, and a prolonged scene where Wheezer (forced to make his own breakfast) unwittingly uses plaster of Paris instead of flour to prepare pancakes.

The cleverest aspect of "Bouncing Babies" is a delightful running gag. When Wheezer gets to the corner of a busy intersection, he is literally and figuratively dwarfed by the amount of traffic passing by. In order to acquire some control and be able to cross the street safely, he grabs a light bulb and hurls it to the pavement, producing a sound that causes every driver within blocks to stop his car and step outside to see if one of his tires has blown out! While the traffic comes to a dead halt, Wheezer quietly crosses the street. He pulls this trick three times, with solid success, but a fourth try is timed just as two policemen pull up on motorcycles—prompting a hasty retreat by Wheezer.

There's nothing wrong with "Bouncing Babies" that tighter editing couldn't cure. The perception of a youngster being crowded out of his family's activities by the arrival of a new baby is right on target. How many real-life families have had to face this situation? He wants to be mothered, but when he asks his mom to dress him in the morning, she replies, "You're getting to be a big boy now; you can dress yourself." Later, he complains to Mary Ann, "Before he came, I used to get a little attention; now nobody loves me."

But Wheezer isn't really a bad boy, and he'll even endure a scene-stealing younger brother in order to stop his mother from crying. The hammering reentry of the baby into Wheezer's life nicely sidesteps a phony ending for this short: the audience realizes, as Wheezer must, that while he will face the situation with a bit more maturity in the future, life will never be the same with a new baby in the house.

Farina, Jean, and friends in a scene from "Bouncing Babies."

Footnote: As "Bouncing Babies" was in release around the country, Wall Street laid its famous egg on October 29, and in a single day, the nation was plunged into a depression that brought the ebullient 1920s to a crashing halt, ruining millions of Americans overnight. Small wonder that the next *Our Gang* comedy was entitled "Moan & Groan, Inc."

94 · MOAN & GROAN, INC.

Two Reels · All-talking, sound on film and disc · Produced by Robert F. McGowan for Hal Roach · Directed by Robert F. McGowan · Photographed by Art Lloyd and F. E. Hershey · Edited by Richard Currier · Story edited by H. M. Walker · Story by Robert F. McGowan · Released on December 7, 1929, by M-G-M · Our Gang: Allen "Farina" Hoskins, Mary Ann Jackson, Jackie Cooper, Bobby "Wheezer" Hutchins, Norman "Chubby" Chaney, Jay R. Smith, Bobby Mallon, and Pete the Pup · Kennedy the Cop, Edgar Kennedy; The lunatic, Max Davidson

Kennedy the Cop advises the gang to stay away from the old deserted house on the hill they like to play in. When they ask what they should do instead, he suggests doing what he did as a boy, and try digging for buried treasure. They do exactly that—in the basement of the old house. The creaky, dark mansion is inhabited by a bearded lunatic who pulls hairs from his face in order to produce an eerie howling sound that echoes through the abandoned house. The madman is eccentric but basically harmless, delighting in scaring the kids and pulling spooky pranks. Officer Kennedy makes his way into the house to check up on the gangsters (who are now trapped inside), and prowls around looking for whatever might be haunting the decrepit old place. His index finger is caught in a Japanese finger-trap toy which he repeatedly confuses

with his gun, but upon finding the gang, and the madman, he points his finger and accidentally traps the culprit in the other end of the handcuff for a triumphant finale.

The offbeat "Moan & Groan, Inc." boasts a story outline rich in potential, and the film gets off to a promising start, too, but it never quite clicks and ends up missing the mark. The ominous mood McGowan creates is fine, but the pacing is a trifle deliberate. The story could have been better motivated by a *real* treasure, with Our Gang, Kennedy the Cop, and the lunatic all frantically competing with each other trying to find it. As it is, one wonders what the madman is doing at the old house in the first place.

Any "old house" film, no matter how enjoyable, inevitably runs the risk of being compared with the best of

Max Davidson is the taunting madman and Farina his bemused prey in this wonderfully atmospheric still from Our Gang's haunted-house film, "Moan & Groan, Inc."

playing father to the kids, and when a black woman compliments him on his kindness, he confesses that he likes to have a little fun on the job. Kennedy could be overpowering at times, but he's quite good in this short, especially in dealing with sight gags. Throughout the film, he tries aiming his gun but finds that he's pointing the handcuff trap on his finger instead, with the gun pointed back at himself!

The diminutive Berlin-born Max Davidson once starred in his own series on the Roach lot but is almost completely forgotten today; he deserves at least a passing nod. Some of the Davidson films were directed by no less than Leo McCarey, but they're seldom revived today because they abounded with Jewish stereotypes. Although ethnic humor was common during the 1920s, Hal Roach says that the only reason he discontinued Davidson's series was because the Jewish community objected to it. Otherwise, his films were popular and well received.

"Moan & Groan, Inc." was Max Davidson's only appearance with Our Gang. As the genial madman, he answers every question, from what the time is to where he's hiding, with the same response: "I know . . . *but I won't tell ya!*" This is followed by wild laughter. He makes a most effective bogeyman, especially in the scene where one by one the kids spot him, and the camera shows their pint-sized view of the scruffy demon making faces at them.

Our Gang is almost incidental to the proceedings, acting mainly as an ensemble here and not as individual characters. The major exception is Farina, who has the lion's share of solo footage and is part of a very funny scene in which Davidson serves him an imaginary dinner, and Farina, frightened into obliging his host (the long sharp carving knife *isn't* imaginary) smacks his lips and fusses over an invisible turkey leg. Farina's handling of this scene is comedically superb; for a finishing touch, he tosses pieces of "turkey" to Pete the Pup, who dutifully snaps them up from the air.

Like many frequently lifeless early talkies, "Moan & Groan, Inc." suffers from a barren soundtrack (although "Running Wild" is played under the title cards), a situation to be relieved within the next year as the series began recovering ground rapidly on a number of fronts.

Although this was the sixth all-talking *Our Gang* comedy, the studio was still servicing domestic and export theaters not yet equipped for sound pictures. A negative exists of "Moan & Groan, Inc." in silent form with text titles.

its genre. "Moan & Groan, Inc." may not be a top example, but it's quite satisfactory, and it's to McGowan's credit that he ventured off into material like this for the sake of trying something new.

Most of the performing honors in "Moan & Groan, Inc." go to character actors Edgar Kennedy as the bumbling cop and Max Davidson as the cunning misanthrope. This film marked Kennedy's first appearance as the friendly but inept cop on the beat; he seems to enjoy

95 · SHIVERING SHAKESPEARE

Two Reels · Produced by Robert F. McGowan for Hal Roach · Directed by Anthony Mack · Photographed by Art Lloyd · Edited by Richard Currier · Story edited by H. M. Walker · Story by Robert F. McGowan · Released on January 25, 1930, by M-G-M · Our Gang: Jackie Cooper, Allen "Farina" Hoskins, Norman "Chubby" Chaney, Mary Ann Jackson, Bobby "Wheezer" Hutchins, Donald Haines, Edith Fellows, Gordon Thorpe, Fletcher Tolbert, Jack McHugh, Georgie Billings, Johnny Aber, Douglas "Turkie Egg" Greer, Bobby Mallon, and Pete the Pup · Kennedy the Cop, Edgar Kennedy; Mrs. Funston Evergreen Kennedy, Gertrude Sutton; Boy inside lion costume, Mickey Daniels; Man inside bull costume, Carlton Griffin; Chubby's mother, Lyle Tayo; First man hit with a pie, Ham Kinsey; Man who "resents it," Allen Cavan; Man whose son is splattered, Charles McAvoy; Man in the audience, Charley Young; Lady in the audience, Retta Palmer

Mrs. Funston Evergreen Kennedy brings culture to the community by presenting her version of *Quo Vadis,* called *The Gladiator's Dilemma,* featuring the young members of the Golden Age Dramatic League. Her husband, Kennedy the Cop, is responsible for "special effects," and appears onstage in several roles. Although the proud parents in the audience are oblivious to their children's gaffes, some rowdy kids who were kicked out of the show are not, and they begin hurling eggs at the actors. This erupts into a pie-throwing melee which soon involves all the youthful performers, as well as the audience, and which concludes with the kids pelting the obnoxious Mrs. Kennedy.

The merry Bard of Avon never dreamed on a midsummer's night that his works should be climaxed by the carnage of a gooey pie fight, but Our Gang takes movie liberties with more than just Shakespeare and Roman history in their rendition of "Shivering Shakespeare." A reworking of "Stage Fright," the film offers some interesting comedy ideas, but suffers from awkward pacing and the look of a single joke expanded to fill twenty minutes of screen time.

Divided into three acts, the play moves at a snail's pace, since the kids are unable to get through an entire line of dialogue without prompting from the eager Mrs. Kennedy. Searching for the correct words, Jackie refers to someone being in "the mainspring of his manhood," and Mary Ann speaks of her "kid brother," which Mrs. K. corrects as "youthful brother."

Eventually, the kids grow tired of this constant coaching. Chubby (as Nero) has written prompting notes on his toga, but has used the wrong side, so now he is forced to lift up his "skirt" in order to read the cues, much to the horror of both his mother and Mrs. Kennedy. Finally, he uses his imagination and condenses a high-toned speech into the phrase, "Well, gimme the lowdown," smiling with satisfaction at his skill for improvisation.

"Mary Annicus" is told that Nero wants to marry her, and Mrs. Kennedy cues her speech, "I spurn thy vile heart, o monster, and cast it in the dust." "Well anyway," says Mary Ann, refusing to go through all that, "I won't marry ya." "Farinacus" simply rejects all such prodding and mutters, "I wish that woman would quit bothering me."

After Chubby is splattered with a pie for the third time, his protective mother calls to the assailant, "I saw you!" and then to her son, "Norman, it's that big boy who struck you—now you hit him." Naturally, Chubby's aim is inexact, the wrong party is creamed, and the pie fight begins (for unexplained reasons, there is a pie sale in the back of the auditorium, providing an ample supply of ammunition).

Even the pacing of this comedy scene is unusual. Several pie-tosses are shown in slow-motion, with a silent soundtrack, followed by other direct-hits at normal speed. This likely being the first pie battle to occur in a talkie, the director was probably experimenting with the format, but the results are variable. A most satisfying moment comes when Norman/Chubby inadvertently plasters his own haughty mother!

Despite these oddities in filming and editing, "Shivering Shakespeare" is enjoyable, because it reaffirms several *Our Gang* precepts. Backstage before the show, the gang members are chided by another young thespian who

Propman Bob Saunders had his hands full holding onto pies during shooting for "Shivering Shakespeare." As filmed, the Gang gets plastered with pies but doesn't have a chance to nibble on any. So. . . .

warns, "If you chaps take that attitude toward the drama, you'll all grow up to be rowdies." His stuffiness is greeted by a blast from Wheezer's raspberry whistle. There is nothing wrong with the kids appearing in a play, but they could never cease being kids in order to seriously assume the pose of "young actors."

There is also the ongoing disdain, and inevitable backfiring, of adults taking too great a part in the children's activities. The gang is doing this play to have fun, and the intensity of Mrs. Kennedy's prompting only annoys them—and rightly so. The lady's elaborate preparations in building sets, props, and costumes for her production are all for naught when the highbrow enterprise is reduced to a shambles by the pie-fight. Even Mr. Kennedy gets tired of his wife's carping, and when the kids eye him for permission to shower her with pies, he nods intently.

Most interesting is the basic honesty of the situation shown in the film, for it looks as if this is a real performance, with the kids actually being prompted and coming up with their own substitute lines. Either director Anthony Mack created a real-life situation and encouraged the kids to ad-lib, or they were scrupulously rehearsed to make the situation seem real. It was probably a combination of the two.

Finally, despite the awkward gaps on the soundtrack, particularly in slow-motion scenes, and other gag shots run at silent speed to accelerate the action, there is a keen awareness of sound throughout the film that must have impressed early 1930 audiences. Key gags involve a penny-toy that produces a Bronx cheer, a sheet of metal being used for thunder sound effects, and a hideous orchestra providing sour accompaniment for a brief ballet

interlude. With this emphasis on sound, it seems doubly strange that the final shot of the film should be silent.

So while a pleasurable outing, the film's staging and pacing are somewhat sluggish, leaving a good deal of daylight between the slapstick fracas of "Shivering Shakespeare" and *the* Pie Fight film against which all others are measured, Laurel & Hardy's *Battle of the Century*.

Retreating from the carnage they cause in "Shivering Shakespeare," Our Gang takes time out for studies with their teacher Mrs. Fern Carter. Around the table are Jackie Cooper, Mary Ann Jackson, Wheezer, Chubby, and Farina, all minding their *P*'s and *Q*'s and other things.

96 · THE FIRST SEVEN YEARS

Two Reels · Produced by Robert F. McGowan for Hal Roach · Directed by Robert F. McGowan · Photographed by Art Lloyd · Edited by Richard Currier · Story edited by H. M. Walker · Story by Robert F. McGowan · Released on March 1, 1930, by M-G-M · Our Gang: Jackie Cooper, Donald "Speck" Haines, Mary Ann Jackson, Norman "Chubby" Chaney, Allen "Farina" Hoskins, Bobby "Wheezer" Hutchins, and Pete the Pup · Kennedy the Cop, Edgar Kennedy; Speck's dad, Otto Fries; Grandma, Joy Winthrop

Filming on location in the residential backyards of Culver City, Our Gang huddles around their Spanish language coach, Miss Laurel Peralta, asking advice on lines for a scene in the Spanish edition of "The First Seven Years," entitled "Los Pequeños Papas." That's cameraman Art Lloyd standing next to the recording equipment.

Jackie has eyes for Mary Ann, but doesn't know how to go about acquiring a "wife." Officer Kennedy first advises Jack to try the caveman approach, but Mary Ann turns the tables and beats him up. Then Kennedy suggests that Jackie wash himself, dress up nice, and bring her candy. Just as he's carrying out this plan, a rival enters the picture. Jackie accuses Speck of stealing his girl, and when they square off, Mary Ann interrupts and insists that if they must fight, it should be a duel, just like the storybook she's been reading. The two combatants retire to practice their swordplay, and despite Jackie's fervent attempts to call off the duel, it's soon under way. The swordsmen slash everything in sight (car tires, laundry, barn doors, innocent bystanders) except each other, and finally, Jackie announces that they're going to finish the fight like men—with their fists. Here, Jackie literally has the upper hand, and after a strong sock on the nose, his opponent gives in. When Mary Ann confesses that she always liked Jackie best, Speck punches *her* in the face! This starts Jack on a rampage, and causes Speck to call for help from his pop, who tries to break up the fight. Meanwhile, Jackie's spry old granny has been watching, and comes leaping to the rescue to teach the interfering father a thing or two. She pops him in the nose, and gives him a few swift kicks, to the rousing cheers of the gang.

"The First Seven Years" is the first real "winner" of the sound era, a delightful short that works in every respect, and shows some evidence that the Roach production team was getting the knack of making talkies. The intercutting of silent and sound footage is barely noticeable here, and the use of sound effects (particularly the sound of sheets ripping, in the final duel) is fairly convincing. The only element still missing is music, both for the beginning and end titles, and as background accompaniment during the film. However, this short is so full of action and dialogue that the absence of a music score doesn't seem so acute.

"The First Seven Years" explores the age-old situation of two boys competing for the affections of one girl, with a variety of insightful touches to make it seem vividly real, a page out of anyone's childhood.

While Jackie pulls petals off a daisy, reciting, "She loves me . . . she loves me not," and making eyes at Mary Ann, the young girl pretends to be disinterested, sitting by herself and reading her books. When she overhears Officer Kennedy pitching the caveman idea to Jackie, she rejects the idea of being a piece of property to be acquired so easily, and decides to beat up her predator. When Speck tries a more direct approach, telling her, "Hey, you're a pretty neat lookin' chick," she spurns his advances, claiming, "I wouldn't marry *any* man." Yet when the possibility of a fight develops, Mary Ann changes her tune, and enthusiastically agrees to allow the boys to duel over her, dressing herself as a Fairy Princess to make the whole storybook situation come to life.

As for Jackie, he's too shy to take a blunt approach to love, except when Kennedy eggs him on. He's much more amenable to the idea of bringing her candy and acting polite, although he feels some obligation as a red-blooded young boy to object at first to washing his neck and ears just for a "dame." When it comes to dueling, Jackie feels that discretion is the better part of valor—or more simply, that if winning Mary Ann means getting himself killed, he'll do without Mary Ann.

"The First Seven Years" gives us other nice glimpses into the world of childhood. At first, Jackie is ready to pick a fight with Speck, but when the rival accepts his challenge, he hedges by protesting that Speck is 9 and he's only 8. He enlists a reluctant Chubby to report the fight to Officer Kennedy by reminding him that they signed their names together in blood to be pals forever.

Best of all, when Jackie resigns himself to the fact that he's going to die in the upcoming duel, Wheezer asks, "If you're gonna get killed, can I have that knife?" Jackie hands over his pocket knife, but warns that if the outcome is different, he'll want it back. When the fight is over, he turns to Wheezer and demands the knife, declaring, "I didn't get killed." "Aw gee," moans Wheezer, "I never get a break!"

Adults play an interesting role in the doings of this film. Kennedy the Cop apparently has nothing more pressing on his mind than to stroll around the neighborhood and keep an eye on the kids. He's happy to offer his advice to Jackie on winning a girl, but when the caveman idea goes awry, he has to turn away to keep Jackie from seeing his laughter at the resultant debacle.

When Jackie's mother sees him washing and preparing to dress in his good suit, she asks why, and he explains that he's dressing up to see his girl. "Well, you can see your girl in your play clothes," she says firmly, "This suit is for Sundays." Parents just don't understand these things. Later, in a final, desperate attempt to avoid the duel, Jack calls to his mother to see if there are any errands she wants him to do. "No, dear," she answers. "Mother doesn't need you now. You just continue playing and have a good time." It's no use. Luckily, Granny is a bit more on the ball, providing Jackie with a Sunday suit his father wore years ago, and later coming to his aid when Speck's father steps into the fight.

The key to success in "The First Seven Years," aside from Bob McGowan's sure-footed direction and an expert job of editing and sound recording, is the performances of the kids, who make every line of dialogue, every action, seem real and spontaneous. From Mary Ann's diffidence and elaborate comic "takes" when she's accidentally stuck by a sword, to Speck's final whimpering for his pop, these superb young actors create real-life characters who win our sympathy, our identification, and our laughter.

Even more remarkable is the fact that these kids repeated their roles in foreign language versions of the same short, learning to speak the Spanish, French, and German dialogue phonetically! With the advent of sound, Hollywood studios saw themselves losing their vast export trade; Hal Roach, for one, had always made the largest share of his profits from the higher rentals and volume abroad. Foreign distribution of silent films had been a simple matter of translating and reshooting the titles, but talkies couldn't even be dubbed at this time.

Faced with a major loss of income, coupled with the 20 per cent increment talkies added to production costs, Roach and other producers solved the problem temporarily by hiring language tutors to coach their stars through as many as four separate foreign editions of each film. Highly impractical today, the idea made sense at the time, since Hal Roach comedies weren't talkfests, and blackboards with phonetic dialogue could be placed out of camera range to prompt the stars. Foreign actors were engaged for the incidental roles and helped carry the body of expository dialogue.

Roach explained in 1929, "The principals speak only a word or two anyway, and the best part of a comedy is always a matter of pantomime—actions and expressions. Besides, if they mumble a couple of words in broken lingo it's usually amusing." Each scene was shot first in English, and then immediately afterward in French, Spanish, German, and sometimes Italian. This was an impressive feat for adult performers like Laurel & Hardy, but for the children of *Our Gang* who were still learning to read and write in English, it is nothing less than astounding.

But then, so were the kids.

Hal Roach's all-barkie star, Pete the halo-eyed Pup, tends to fan mail. The studio won't assign him a secretary, so he has to process his varied selection of fan photos himself, which he personalizes with his own distinctive paw print . . . the left front one.

97 · WHEN THE WIND BLOWS

Two Reels. Produced by Robert F. McGowan for Hal Roach; Directed by James W. Horne; Photographed by Art Lloyd; Edited by Richard Currier; Story edited by H. M. Walker; Story by Robert F. McGowan. Released on April 5, 1930, by M-G-M. Our Gang: Jackie Cooper, Bobby "Wheezer" Hutchins, Mary Ann Jackson, Allen "Farina" Hoskins, Norman "Chubby" Chaney, and Pete the Pup. Kennedy the Cop, Edgar Kennedy; Jackie's father, Henry, Charles McAvoy; Chubby's mother, Mary Gordon; Flustered man in shirt sleeves, Chet Brandenberg; Stunt-double for Jackie Cooper, David Sharpe. Cast change for Spanish language version, "Las Fantasmas": Jackie's father, Julian Rivero

Bungling Officer Edgar Kennedy and the *Our Gang* kids in a posed shot from "When the Wind Blows."

"Fine night for a murder," says a passerby to Officer Kennedy, who replies, "Say, nothing ever happens when *I'm* on the beat!" It's pretty much the truth, but on this blustery night the wind, and a prolonged comedy-of-errors create the impression that a prowler is on the loose. It's only Jackie, who's been locked out of his bedroom window. One mishap follows another, with Kennedy running from false alarm to false alarm, until Jackie inadvertently knocks out a *real* burglar, just as the cop arrives on the scene. "Didn't I tell you that Kennedy always gets his man?" he boasts, as Wheezer answers for the whole neighborhood with a loud, blubbering Bronx cheer.

"When the Wind Blows-- is not a terribly funny short, concentrating on action rather than the kids themselves, but it must have been impressive as one of the noisiest comedies to date. The sound track has everything from an orchestral music score (beginning with "That Old Gang of Mine" as theme music, and incorporating such popular songs as "My Man" for background material) to the whistling wind, the clatter of garbage cans and the screaming of various characters on-screen.

There are also some ingenious sound effects which seem fairly obvious today, but which must have been a treat for 1930 audiences. Chubby's snoring is enhanced by a funny slide-whistle effect, and when a flowerpot falls on Officer Kennedy's head, he hears the sound of birds chirping in the trees.

The visual gags are not as clever, with the idea of people getting tangled up in flying laundry and newspapers repeted a few times too often. Other contrived fright-gags, such as Farina's kid brother Hector appearing to be a "ghost" after being doused with flour, were old-hat and unconvincing even in the silent era.

Edgar Kennedy works hard for laughs in "When the Wind Blows," but he has an uphill battle against weak and repetitious material. Although his character is supposed to be a bumbling cop, it becomes trying to watch him do nothing *but* trip over himself and run around in circles for twenty minutes—especially if one's recently viewed his similar nocturnal bungling that same year in Laurel & Hardy's *Night Owls*—probably with the same back-yard fence, the same rattling garbage cans, and the same yowling cats!

Buried in the midst of this overwrought comedy are some nice moments involving the kids. Jackie's father spanks him because he doesn't want to study his schoolwork; when Pop leaves the room, Jackie tosses his book out the window. Later, his parents return to the room, thinking he's asleep, and his father says, "I don't want to lick him, but I want him to learn something—to grow up and have things we never had." Jackie is touched by this obviously sincere sentiment, and he climbs out the window to retrieve his school book. Then the window slams shut, and Jackie's attempts to get back inside start the chain reaction of reports that a prowler is on the loose.

Jackie roams from house to house, trying to find someone who will let him in. When Farina sees him at the window, his nose pressed awkwardly against the pane, he thinks it's a ghost, and hides in terror. Then Jackie climbs a ladder and finds refuge in Mary Ann's room. Following up the resolution of "The First Seven Years," she's just written him a love note. Finding him in her room in the middle of the night, she beams, and says, "I know you love me, but I didn't know you'd spoil your sleep for me."

Less effective are the scenes with Farina in the ramshackle barn he calls home, although there is one typical *Our Gang* contraption: while lying on the floor with his foot in a stirrup, Farina pushes a pedal back and forth and operates a mechanism that both rocks his baby brother's cradle and spins the laundry line at the same time. This clever trick device is also attached to a bell (probably to

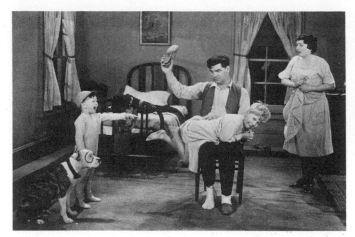 

Jackie Cooper gets paddled by two different fathers in otherwise identical scenes from "When the Wind Blows," *top,* and its Spanish

equivalent, "Las Fantasmas" (*"The Ghosts/Phantoms"*), with Charles McAvoy and Julian Rivero, respectively.

amuse the baby), and when Farina gets scared, he nervously rocks the cradle in double-time, producing a constant clanging that only adds to the commotion and confusion in the neighborhood.

In his lone *Our Gang* endeavor, Roach staff director James Horne went a bit too far in creating such "commotion," and forgot about keeping the film funny, and basically realistic. But in building an eerie comedy around action and sound effects, he did make a film that was more easily adaptable for foreign versions than was "The First Seven Years." Perhaps that's why he was assigned to direct "When the Wind Blows," and its Spanish language equivalent, "Las Fantasmas" (the ghosts, or the phantoms). Horne seemed to have special expertise in this area, and was sometimes given the task of directing

the foreign language versions of Roach shorts and features he hadn't worked on when they were initially shot in English.

James Horne had no particular style as a director, but nevertheless managed to turn out some diverse and outstanding comedies, ranging from his early days at Kalem to Buster Keaton's *College* (1927), Laurel & Hardy's *Big Business* (1929) and *Way Out West* (1937), and Charley Chase's *Looser Than Loose* (1930). Toward the end of his career he slipped into cranking out absolutely bizarre serials for Columbia, which unlike his comedies *are* distinctive and easily set apart from the larger-than-life chapter plays of his contemporaries. His association with *Our Gang* extended, indirectly, to real life when Jackie Cooper married the director's daughter June in 1944.

98 · BEAR SHOOTERS

Two Reels · Produced by Robert F. McGowan for Hal Roach · Directed by Robert F. McGowan · Photographed by Len Powers · Edited by Richard Currier · Story edited by H. M. Walker · Released on May 17, 1930, by M-G-M · Our Gang: Leon "Donald 'Spud' " Janney, Bobby "Wheezer" Hutchins, Allen "Farina" Hoskins, Jackie Cooper, Norman "Chubby" Chaney, Mary Ann Jackson, Pete the Pup, and Dinah the Mule · Spud's mother, Fay Holderness; First bootlegger, Bob, Robert Kortman; Other bootlegger, Charlie, Charlie Hall; Gorilla, Charles Gamora

Probably having heard about "Trader Horn" over on the M-G-M lot, the gang dresses up like African explorers and makes preparations for a hunting excursion. Spud, though, finds he has to stay home and mind Wheezer. It seems Mama's Little Angel has the croup. This threatens to cancel the trip, since everyone's camping equipment is already loaded onto the gang's dilapidated old seesaw wagon, the horsepower for which is Spud's mule, Dinah; and if Spud can't go, neither can Dinah. The situation brightens when Spud cons Mary into coming along to watch Wheezer for him, and soon the expedition is under way. Arriving in the forest, the gang has plans to

trap a bear. Instead, they encounter a large and fearsome gorilla; after an initial scare, the intrepid hunters use their brains and manage to snare him—revealing that inside the animal fur is a man, trying to frighten the kids away from a bootleg operation he and a pal are running from a thatched hut nearby. Jackie brings a bees' nest to keep the "gorilla" occupied, but the swarming insects send the gang running.

"Bear Shooters" opens with a typical Hal Roach title card establishing the premise of the short, a camping trip. "The idea was to shoot wild bears from a distance—say about four or five miles."

Chubby, Jack, and Farina, three intrepid "Bear Shooters" . . . don't you think?

estly pleasing one that scored well at the time with exhibitors and the trade press. *The Motion Picture Herald* reported, "Hal Roach's *Our Gang* unit continues to turn out some of the better short comedies in the industry. The latest proof is 'Bear Shooters.'" *Film Daily* commented, "Fine entertainment! Good comedy with wide appeal. Extremely well done."

Possibly the almost studied lack of dialogue and complicated action was prompted by the foreknowledge that upon completion of the English language version, "Bear Shooters" was to be reworked in at least two foreign languages, French and Spanish (with the separate Spanish negative exported under the title "Los Cazadores de Osos").

The mild comedy of "Bear Shooters" relies mainly on the ever-winning personalities of the kids, and especially their stock-in-trade ability to milk comedic "reactions" with convincingly executed face-twisting double takes.

At an unlikely age, thirteen, successful child actor Leon Janney (formerly Laon Ramon) makes his first and only *Our Gang* appearance as Spud, but fails to leave a favorable impression with his constant repetition of the phrase "Gee whiz!" and his whiny complaints about having to take care of his kid brother. If Hal Roach had been harboring plans to make Janney a featured player in the series, he certainly didn't do anything to build him up in this initial venture.

One of the most memorable aspects of "Bear Shooters" is the gang's wagon, an astounding vehicle which bounces precariously on its hinges, large-spoked wheels swerving from side to side as they turn. Among the carry-on equipment is a bathtub boat that Farina uses for fishing. A horn is sounded by stomping on a pedal which activates a live goose.

Apparently anticipating the possibility of having to defend this last bit of business to humane societies, the cutting continuity for "Bear Shooters" offered this explanation and disclaimer: "Close-up: Goose in cage under driver's footboard. As foot on pedal presses, the plunger underneath footboard apparently presses the goose in the neck. The goose honks. (Note: This is a trained goose, having been coached to stretch its neck and honk. The plunger does not touch the goose's neck.)"

The two bootleggers are played by Robert Kortman, one of the meanest-looking and surliest-sounding villains in moviedom, and Little Charlie Hall (as listed in casting directories), seen to better advantage in dozens of Laurel & Hardy films and countless other Hal Roach comedies over the years.

Besides a lack of bears, this film has precious little action. But unlike the contemporary early-sound short subjects of other studios, there are no windy disquisitions, either. In fact, during the grove scenes it's some loudly chirping birds that dominate the sound track; the kids don't say much at all. So without much action or dialogue there is very little to conceal the fact that nothing is really going on in "Bear Shooters." Between preparations for the trip, and sideline scenes with Wheezer, there's no room left for anything else but the less-than-stirring gorilla climax.

Stuck for a finale, director McGowan resorts to the most timeworn solution possible, with Wheezer bringing a skunk into the proceedings ("Here kitty, kitty, kitty") to send the gang scurrying from the tree-hollow where they've sought refuge from attacking bees. Like the rest of the film, this fade-out gag is acceptable but hardly memorable.

Still, to say the film's story and material is slight is not to say it isn't enjoyable. By any standard, it's not an ambitious or exceptional short, but it is at least a modestly

99 · A TOUGH WINTER

Two Reels · Produced by Robert F. McGowan for Hal Roach · Directed by Robert F. McGowan · Photographed by Art Lloyd · Edited by Richard Currier · Dialogue by H. M. Walker · Story by Robert F. McGowan · Released on June 21, 1930, by M-G-M · Our Gang: Allen "Farina" Hoskins, Mary Ann Jackson, Bobby "Wheezer" Hutchins, Jackie Cooper, Norman "Chubby" Chaney, Beverly Parrish, Tommy Atkins, and Pete the Pup · Stepin Fetchit, Himself; Radio announcer, Lyle Tayo

On a cold, wintry day, the gang helps Stepin Fetchit read a love letter, then he tries to assist them in cleaning up the sloppy remnants of a misguided taffy pull—Wheezer having relayed the wrong ingredients directions from the radio program, as when he calls into the kitchen, "One pound of Lux!"

Plotless and virtually silent, "A Tough Winter" is not an endearing *Our Gang* comedy, nor is its crude, gooey slapstick particularly funny (although scenes with the kids helplessly stuck tight by taffy to walls, furniture, and even themselves generally get some laughs). As a curio, however, the film is fascinating, since it's a showcase for a definitive Stepin Fetchit characterization—Stepin Fetchit, of course, being the unfairly maligned, gangling black comic who holds the patent on what is now labeled *the* racial stereotype in films.

"A Tough Winter" is so much a vehicle for Stepin Fetchit because Hal Roach was planning a comedy series for him, and this piecemeal Rascals short represents the pilot film hastily thrown together to round out the prolific 1929–30 release schedule. Stepin had signed a contract to star in a block of eight Roach comedies (he would earn $350 per week), and the series was even announced in the trade press, but for whatever reasons, the project fell through and the series failed to materialize after the studio's summer break.

Today, "A Tough Winter" is a genuine museum piece. It was almost never aired in the past by local television stations across the country, and the current owners of *Little Rascals* TV rights have now completely withdrawn this film from their package, relegating its exposure to infrequent retrospectives and private screenings.

What modern audiences often fail to recognize in viewing Stepin Fetchit's work is that his characterization was itself a satire. His lethargy and ignorance are comic exaggerations—even his slow-motion speech pattern is part of a rounded routine. Stepin is not just lazy—he is *deviously* lazy, having built all sorts of contraptions to make his daily life less strenuous. He is not terribly intelligent in terms of book learning, but he is chock-full of ingenious schemes to save himself from unnecessary work.

When Farina asks why he can't read his own mail, Stepin explains that he went to night school, and therefore cannot read during the day. After Farina consents to read a recently delivered love letter for him, Stepin decides that he doesn't want the boy to hear what he's reading aloud, so he makes him put cotton in his ears.

The problem with Stepin Fetchit's characterization, to some modern viewers, is that it is *too* convincing. This is of course a backhanded compliment to the actor Lincoln Perry, who no more resembled his screen character off-camera than Stan Laurel resembled his. They were both fine comic artists who created characterizations with whom they became indelibly identified.

It would be ludicrous to deny that Fetchit's characterization contained elements of racism and presented certain stereotype images that did not advance the cause of the black man. But Fetchit's characterization was of someone a bit different from the usual black servant seen in Hollywood films: Stepin created an identity of his own, neither completely subservient nor openly hostile, too slow to be considered a wise guy but too wily to be taken for a fool. There was always more to Fetchit than met the eye.

Frolicking in the backyard "snow" (cornflakes) in this scene from "A Tough Winter" are Petie, Farina, Wheezer, Mary Ann, Jack, and Chubby. Missing from this shot is Charles Foster Kane.

In terms of social history, he made an even more significant mark. Black film historian Donald Bogle has written, "He was . . . the movies' first distinctive black personality. In the early 1930s he was the best known and most successful black actor working in Hollywood . . . the first Negro to receive featured billing." In recent years Fetchit has proclaimed, "When all the Negroes was goin' around straightening their hair and bleaching theirself trying to be white, in them days I was provin' to the world that black was beautiful. *Me.*"

For Hal Roach, there was only one consideration that mattered in hiring the actor: "Stepin Fetchit was a very funny guy," he says simply. "That's why we tried to use him, because he was a *skilled* comic. But he was no funnier or no more of an unreal comic character than W. C. Fields or somebody like that was . . . . Why can't you have a funny colored man if you're going to have a funny white man? But no one understands ethnic humor today, and also, you know, no one understands that there was never a malicious intent in any of this kind of comedy at the time it was made. I mean what's funny is funny, whether it's white or colored or whatever it is. And it wasn't up to me to decide what went over big with an audience, whether it was a colored audience or a white audience or an integrated audience or a European audience or whatever it was. And in fact the colored people in those days got as big a kick out of Stepin Fetchit as anybody. They used to come to the studio every single day, you know, dozens of them, wanted to see him and so on."

"A Tough Winter" was another Hal Roach comedy produced in multiple languages for the foreign trade. With prints of these subjects not presently available for reexamination, one can only imagine how Stepin Fetchit's character was slanted for consumption in France or Germany!

100 · PUPS IS PUPS

Two Reels · Produced by Robert F. McGowan for Hal Roach · Directed by Robert F. McGowan · Photographed by Art Lloyd · Edited by Richard Currier · Dialogue by H. M. Walker · Story by Robert F. McGowan · Released on August 30, 1930, by M-G-M · Our Gang: Bobby "Wheezer" Hutchins, Allen "Farina" Hoskins, Jackie Cooper, Dorothy DeBorba, Norman "Chubby" Chaney, Mary Ann Jackson, Buddy MacDonald, and the Hill Twins · Cement man, Charles McAvoy; Doorman, Silas D. Wilcox; Dorothy's mother, Lyle Tayo; Dr. H. R. White, Allen Cavan; Orchestra leader, playing violin, Charlie Hall; Musician playing bass tuba, William Gillespie; Crowd extras, Chet Brandenberg, Jack Hill; Officer, Harry Bernard

The gang decides to enter a city pet show, since Farina is working there as a page and can sneak their potential prize-winners into the display room. Keeping his pet clean is easier for Jackie than keeping his little sister clean, however; she insists on jumping into a nearby mud puddle at every opportunity. Wheezer has no problem keeping his pet puppies clean; he just has trouble keeping them! Every time they hear the sound of a bell ringing, they run in that direction, causing them to scurry back and forth at the sounds of an ambulance, dinner bell, ice-cream truck, train whistle, bicycle bell, etc. Just when he thinks he's lost the pups, he makes one last effort, ringing a huge church bell, which (belatedly) brings them running back to their happy owner. The gang doesn't fare quite so well, since their unruly pets (everything from a parrot to a pig) cause havoc at the society pet show, sending high-toned ladies running for shelter and causing Farina to lose his job. When day is done, both Wheezer and the gang return to their shantytown playground, where Jackie's sister ignores a brand-new dress and plops herself right back into the mud. Her mother thinks Farina has pushed her in, and in stalking over to scold the "rascal" she loses her balance and topples into the mud herself.

One of those briskly paced films over all too quickly, "Pups Is Pups" is an enchanting short full of quiet charm, and in the *Our Gang* hierarchy a film that must surely rank well near the top. It's also the first entry in the 1930–31 release schedule, marking a time when *Our Gang* was really regaining its stride, and entering the series' finest period.

In disarming simplicity, "Pups Is Pups" spins out its twin reels weaving two story threads and one running (and splashing) joke, the resolution of each providing a whirlwind of gags, one topping the next as the film winds to a close.

The central story concerns the gang's ingenuity at sprucing up its unruly menagerie to compete with the ritzy bluebloods at the pet show, where their innocent knack for upsetting dignity and pomp lays waste all pretensions and fairly pulls the house down in a kind of captivating anarchy.

There's an irresistible spontaneity and innocence in films like "Pups Is Pups," particularly in the warmth and gentleness of the subplot involving a real mainstay of movie magic: kids and their pets. The affection Wheezer feels for his beloved puppies is genuine and is responsible for some of the most cherished moments in this film.

Footnote: In an early scene, the gang reviews a newspaper ad looking for "ten colored boys . . . to act as pages" at the pet show. Jack wants to apply, but Chubby explains dispassionately, "Aw, you can't do that. They

want boys like Farina." His remark bears no malice, but nevertheless the scene has often been cut by TV censors.

In a 1975 newspaper interview, Allen "Farina" Hoskins shared some of his thoughts about race relations in *Our Gang*: "I think that for that time period, and even now, that it was a unique series. They were a bunch of kids, and even though there was a certain amount of stereotyping among the black kids, I'd go as far to say that maybe it was the first time, using the public medium, that kids were shown as just kids with a cross section of what makes up American kids, blacks and whites, and a few others thrown in.

"Even the whites were stereotyped. There was the classic fat boy, the freckle-faced boy, the little blond angel—all the usual stereotypes. But they related to each other as a bunch of kids, doing all the crazy things that kids do.

"There was a certain degree of stereotyping and there was quite a bit of dialect used. We might as well face it, thirty or forty years ago, a lot of our people were talking in dialect and a lot of them are still doing it now."

"I think that Bob McGowan and Hal Roach were ahead of their time; I can't think of anything that compared to the series that showed the equal inner relationships among the races." Conversely, Allen Hoskins is not happy about the black exploitation films of the 1970s. "I think that they build the wrong images for black kids to emulate," he explains. "They've done a lot of harm to the younger blacks who don't have anything to compare them to."

Interlude: Background music. Some of the early talkies were sadly in need of music to enliven dull stretches, a problem fully resolved in "Pups Is Pups," the first *Our Gang* short to employ the delightfully breezy musical background scores one has come to associate with Hal Roach comedies.

In the art of fusing picture and sound, these scores complemented the visuals and dialogue of Roach pictures wonderfully well, adding an essential rhythm and pacing a director or editor was often incapable of achieving on his own.

These colorful themes and melodies have an unmistakable character, and over the years Hal Roach Studios has been besieged with letters requesting copies of the music, to be enjoyed on its own without dialogue or soundtrack action to interfere! (In 1930 the studio did release sheet music of one song featured in a Charley Chase comedy, "Smile When the Raindrops Fall.")

Though they didn't work together as a team, the composers, arrangers, and conductors of Roach's enduringly infectious music scoring were LeRoy Shield and Marvin Hatley.

Evidently LeRoy Shield was not on the Roach payroll, and his talents were secured on a fee basis through the courtesy of NBC in Chicago, where Shield was general music director. He'd come out periodically to Roach's Culver City plant and record maybe fifteen to twenty tunes at one time that would be added to the stock music library for use in the comedies.

In 1929 twenty-four-year-old Marvin Hatley was working at the Hal Roach radio station, and with the advent of talkies, Roach made Hatley the studio music director. In Hatley's words, "I just happened to be in the right place, at the right time, and had a little talent."

He started with a three-piece ensemble known as "The Hal Roach Happy-Go-Lucky Trio" (actually appearing as such in some of Charley Chase's shorts), and grew eventually to a sixty-five-piece orchestra. He composed Laurel & Hardy's "Ku-Ku" theme song, and three of his Roach feature scores were nominated for Academy Awards.

Hatley appeared on camera in "Mike Fright" and "The Pinch Singer," and whenever a kid or an actor had to fake an instrument, Hatley would show him how to hold it and then actually play the instrument himself off-scene, as he could play most everything on anything.

Marvin Hatley has fond recollections of coming down to the *Our Gang* sets, playing with the kids, and watching them work. "What was fun," he recalls, "was writing songs to match the unusual things they'd always be doing in *Our Gang* scripts."

What wasn't fun was the pressure he was under. Hatley's job began when filming was completed and he met with the director and cutter to work out what kinds of background music needed to go where. "The music was done last," Hatley explains. "And when the writers take more time than they're supposed to, then the director takes a little too much time, and finally it gets down to the music man and he's the one that's under pressure. The time was often so short that the musician or composer would go crazy. They'd want you to write as much music as Beethoven wrote in five years, and they'd want it done in a week's time."

Hatley would pick up a cut of the finished film and take it home with him. There he had a studio, a movieola, and tons of music reference material. It was quiet and he could compose without being disturbed. Often he'd work all night long without sleep.

After composing the score there'd be rehearsals at the

"Pups Is Pups," with Wheezer and no pup.

studio and "then we'd take it while it was hot," with Hatley facing his orchestra and watching a print on the screen behind them to achieve proper synchronization as he conducted. Finally, Elmer Raguse and the sound department would mix the recorded music under the dialogue, and the pressure would be off for a while.

"Getting things out in a hurry to the exhibitors was a fact of life we all lived with," Hatley notes. With the constant pressure sometimes a film would bypass Hatley and even the cutter wouldn't have a chance to pull music from stock, resulting in some shorts (the Gang's "Washee Ironee" and Laurel & Hardy's *Their First Mistake* for instance) being released with no incidental scoring except the theme music under the titles. It's our loss.

Victor Hugo once characterized music as expressing that which cannot be put into words and that which cannot remain silent. A precise definition of what the work of LeRoy Shield and Marvin Hatley adds to Hal Roach comedies is certainly beyond our powers. Suffice it to say the contribution is as significant as anyone else's at the studio.

101 · TEACHER'S PET

Two Reels · Produced by Hal Roach · Directed by Robert F. McGowan · Photographed by Art Lloyd · Edited by Richard Currier · Dialogue by H. M. Walker · Story by Robert F. McGowan · Released on October 11, 1930, by M-G-M · Our Gang: Jackie Cooper, Allen "Farina" Hoskins, Norman "Chubby" Chaney, Bobby "Wheezer" Hutchins, Dorothy "Echo" DeBorba, Matthew "Hercules" Beard, Mary Ann Jackson, Buddy MacDonald, Donald Haines, Artye Folz, and Bobby Mallon · Miss Crabtree, June Marlowe; Old man, William Courtwright; Caterers, Baldwin Cooke, Gordon Douglas

On the first day of school, most of Our Gang is moping around the schoolyard, lamenting the loss of Miss McGillicuddy, and dreading the appearance of their new teacher

Miss Crabtree, envisioned as a harridan. Chubby's afraid "There's something goofy with anybody what's got a name like Crabtree." Actually, she's a lovely and charming young blonde, at that moment driving her flashy road-ster toward school. She spots Jack and Wheezer walking along a country road* and offers them a lift. Before she can introduce herself, Jack proudly reveals some of the stunts the gang has planned for "the old battle ax" who'll be their new teacher that day: Chubby's going to bring a flock of red ants, Farina's furnishing some sneezing pow-der, and Bud has a white mouse. Then everyone's going swimming. Miss Crabtree plays along, and the two are the best of chums by the time their chatty ride is over, Jackie remarking, "Gee you're pretty. You're almost as pretty as Miss McGillicuddy—all except in your nose." Miss Crabtree lets Jackie off some blocks before school and he walks the rest of the way, joining the gang outside the one-room schoolhouse. As they rehearse their subversive routine, Jack is distracted by lingering thoughts of the beautiful lady who'd given him the ride, little dreaming she's standing at the window overhead. Soon the school bell rings and everybody files into class. As the elegant Miss Crabtree strides to her desk, Jack shakes the room with a double take, slinks down and looks for a crack in the floor to escape through. Farina wonders what's wrong with his sick-looking pal, and Jack whispers, "That's the pip that gave me the ride, and did I tell her everything!" Jackie tries crawling out of class with a mask on, but Miss Crabtree commands his presence at her desk. Does he remember her? "And how!" Jack moans softly. Showing that she remembers too, Miss Crabtree asks Chubby, Farina, and Buddy to stand: "I understand you have presents for the new teacher." Each rises suspiciously, wondering how she knows their names. As one by one the confederates come forward to deposit their implements of sabotage, they toss off disparaging remarks at Jack, branding him a snitcher and a double-crosser. Things brighten for the rest of the class when Miss Crabtree an-nounces her first day surprise: a get-acquainted party with ice cream and cake. The plotting foursome is told their mothers want them at home right away, just as the caterers arrive. The protesting boys are pushed out the door, where they sit dejected on the steps listening to the happy slurping sounds inside, and berating Jack, who can only plead, "Well gee, fullahs, she didn't wear no sign. How did I know she was Miss Crabtree?" All but Jack resign their egos and go back inside to take their medicine; Jack's too ashamed, he can't ever go back. Crestfallen, he sits down under a tree in the yard and starts to cry, when Miss Crabtree walks over and silently offers him the ice cream and cake she's holding. Grateful for her compassion, between sobs Jackie looks up with deep warmth and sincerity and says, "Gee you're pretty, Miss Crabtree—your prettier 'n Miss McGillicuddy." A storybook ending.

"Teacher's Pet" is one of the most enjoyable *Our Gang* pictures ever made, and one most anybody can identify with instantly. It's lacking Charley Oelze's gadgetry gags, and an action windup, but it's a beautifully struc-tured film drawn from a solid, irresistibly funny story that radiates heart and feeling.

It's easy to admire Bob McGowan's tight, sensitive direction because while there's necessarily some (honest)

Miss Crabtree and happy students in "Teacher's Pet."

sentiment, until the climactic scene it never eclipses the onslaught of situation humor and dry wit. Through it all the kids are incredibly convincing and appealing. If naturalness, spontaneity, and charm are *Our Gang*'s hallmarks, this film may be the series' high point.

Casting twenty-six-year-old June Marlowe as the de-mure Miss Crabtree was a great boon to the series, and set a lucrative pattern for a number of wonderful sequels. "Miss Crabtree" was born Gisela Valaria Goetten and moved to Hollywood from Minnesota in 1925. Chosen as a Wampas Baby Star, she'd been both a Warner's and Universal contractee before landing at Roach, where she also worked with Charley Chase and Laurel & Hardy before marrying a Hollywood businessman and retiring from films. Apart from her role as Miss Crabtree, she's best remembered for a number of *Rin Tin Tin* pictures she did for Warner's and then for Nat Levine's Mascot Pictures.

In vital respects, "Teacher's Pet" brought a lot of firsts. It's the first *Our Gang* appearance for both Miss Crabtree and Matthew (soon "Stymie") Beard; it's the first short to employ what would become *Our Gang*'s theme song; and it's the first real vehicle for Jackie Cooper. It was also the last *Our Gang* escapade produced in separate foreign language versions, the Spanish edition entitled "Comengo La Escuela," though "Senorita Crab-tree" might have been more enticing.

---

* The same winding tree-lined road one most closely associates with Laurel & Hardy's road gang rice-flinging episode in *The Hoose-Gow*.

The series' lilting theme song, "Good Old Days" by LeRoy Shield, is used repeatedly throughout "Teacher's Pet" and would herald every subsequent Roach *Little Rascals* comedy. The tune caught on immediately, and a popular NBC network radio show entitled *Kaltenmeyer's Kindergarten* set lyrics to the melody and adapted it for the airwaves. Then in the *Our Gang*-inspired prison schoolroom episode for Laurel & Hardy's *Pardon Us,* the mood was set by scoring the scene with this same melody.

In another timely innovation, someone at the studio had the idea that they ought to discard main titles, for the same reason they'd discarded the text subtitles used in silent films. Motion pictures could talk now, so in place of introductory title cards, two young ladies would *announce* all the credits on camera! Thus in "Teacher's Pet" the film opens on a stage showing a full proscenium arch with the curtain drawn. Two girls enter from either side of the stage, bow toward the camera, and recite in unison: "Dear Ladies and Gentlemen: Hal Roach presents for your entertainment and approval, His Rascals, in their latest *Our Gang* comedy entitled 'Teacher's Pet.'" Then alternating, girl on left: "Direction by Robert McGowan"—girl on right: "Photography by Art Lloyd"—girl on left: "Edited by Richard Currier"—girl on right: "Recorded by Elmer Raguse"—both girls: "And dialogue by H. M. Walker. We thank you." Curtsy. Fade out.

For a while, all Hal Roach comedies (including the subsequent "School's Out" and "Love Business") presented titles in this fashion before the idea was dropped.

Above all else, "Teacher's Pet" is a showcase for Jackie Cooper. Though the article disagrees with a more recent interview, a magazine quoted Jackie Cooper as having attributed his break in features to the climactic scene in "Teacher's Pet": "That one scene changed my whole life. I had never cried in pictures before, and the director tried all kinds of tricks to get me to cry. He made me believe he was going to shoot Petie, the *Our Gang* dog. Next he had a cop rush onto the lot and pretend that he was going to arrest my mother; and he pretended he was firing an assistant director I liked. I began to cry then, and he got the scene he wanted. Paramount saw it, and it led to *Skippy,* which made more than five million dollars for them." And won Jackie Cooper an Oscar nomination, making him the youngest actor ever so honored.

Hal Roach himself had wanted to produce a feature based on Percy Crosby's famed comic strip character *Skippy,* but Paramount outbid him for the rights. He was reportedly so annoyed that he refused to lend Jackie to Paramount for even a screen test, realizing that "he was the only kid around who could've played *Skippy,*" but he finally relented. After the feature was a hit, Roach sold Cooper's contract to M-G-M for a reported $100,000, believing that the youngster had a much better opportunity in features than in short comedies. He did indeed; like most *Our Gang* kids, Jackie had signed with Roach for an initial salary of $40 a week.

Finally, "Teacher's Pet" is a film to inspire nostalgia, an overworked word perhaps but the right word for the feelings engendered by this wonderful film. With its illusions and graphic imagery, the film is a near-perfect embodiment of a time and spirit we'd all like to return to but can't.

Mary Ann imitates Miss Crabtree.

A trip through "Teacher's Pet" recaptures all the best things about an era and a life-style that were passing even as they were being filmed. Certainly no one thought they were creating any kind of historic record, and location work in those sunny Los Angeles streets, parks, and yards was purely an economic expedient providing a variety of backgrounds at only the cost of transportation. Yet motivations aside, flavorful open-air comedies like this are fascinating for the glimpses they offer of a more innocent time before America accelerated into the Automated Urban Sprawl Age.

Looking back on *Our Gang* in 1975, it's the lost wholesomeness and innocence about the series that strikes Jackie Cooper in somewhat the same way. "Nobody dares do anything like it anymore," he says.

"Economically you can never do it. And the kids today have been exposed to too much. Maybe you could do it with some aborigines who haven't been looking at the Tube. . . . Who knew [then] what was going on in the world? A horse pulled the milkman, I remember that in 1929, in our neighborhood. What did we know? We knew if the guy in the sheriff's uniform came by to stay quiet and hide behind the couch, if you owed any bills; that was a big deal. What else? The radio, and that was about it. The innocence in our youth. . . ."

Today Jackie Cooper has sons who watch the films on television, and he says, "They look at those *Our Gangs,* even the teen-agers, and it's a form of entertainment *they* know will never come back. They don't know why, they don't know how innocent we were, but they sense that it's a different kind of kid up there. My boy says, 'There aren't any kids like that anymore, are there?' They see the driveways, with the two paths of gravel and the grass in between, and they say, 'Where is that?' I say, 'That's right over here where Metro-Goldwyn-Mayer is,' and I've driven them over and some of the houses are still there. I say, '*Every* place used to look like that.' With the little red schoolhouse. . . . Of course, that's all built up now, that's South Robertson Boulevard on the way to the freeway; they tore down all those gorgeous eucalyptus trees where we used to shoot a lot of that stuff and where "Teacher's Pet" was made. But that age of innocence is, looking back at it now, just unbelievable. . . . You look around and you say, 'Where am I going to see that today?'"

It's just one factor that contributes to *Our Gang*'s timeless appeal.

102 · SCHOOL'S OUT

Two Reels · Produced by Hal Roach · Directed by Robert F. McGowan · Photographed by Art Lloyd · Edited by Richard Currier · Dialogue by H. M. Walker · Released on November 22, 1930, by M-G-M · Our Gang: Jackie Cooper, Allen "Farina" Hoskins, Norman "Chubby" Chaney, Mary Ann Jackson, Buddy MacDonald, Bobby "Wheezer" Hutchins, Douglas Greer, Dorothy "Echo" DeBorba, Matthew "Stymie" Beard, Bobby "Bonedust" Young, Donald Haines, Bobby Mallon, and Pete the Pup · Miss Crabtree, June Marlowe; Her brother Jack, Creighton Hale; Lady walking by the stream, Lyle Tayo

Picking up where "Teacher's Pet" left off, Jackie is circulating a "partition" requesting that school stay open for the summer—he's afraid they'll lose Miss Crabtree during the vacation. That morning he asks the teacher if she has any plans to get married, and she tells him that she might, some day. During lunch recess, while Miss Crabtree is away, a stranger comes around asking for her. Worried that he'll marry their teacher, the gang tries to discourage him, Jackie revealing she has two sets of false teeth, and one wooden leg. Bud and Don add that she has two husbands, and twenty-one kids. The bemused stranger takes off, telling the children to let Miss Crabtree know that Jack was asking for her. The gang follows him as he passes the bank of a scenic little creek nearby and decides to go for a swim; they steal his clothes and stash them in the woods so he won't be able to come back. That afternoon, after a hectic class session, Miss Crabtree wonders if the children have seen Jack, her *brother*. The kids confess what they did, dissolving into tears, and Miss Crabtree, shocked at the stories they've told, runs from the classroom, crying. Soon her sobbing turns to uncontrollable laughter, however, when brother Jack appears wearing the only clothes he could find—an ill-fitting dress.

An ideal companion piece to "Teacher's Pet," this short employs the same successful blending of comedy and warmth, derived from appealingly realistic emotions.

Jackie has a crush on his teacher, who gives the children a ride to school every morning. While driving along, they discuss marriage, and Jackie asks if she wouldn't wait until he grows up. Impulsively, she kisses him, provoking a happy combination of pleasure and embarrassment.

The gang rallies to Jack's cause, motivated by the sincere desire to keep Miss Crabtree from getting married. "That's the way we lost Miss McGillicuddy," Chubby reminds his pals. Crowded into Miss Crabtree's roadster, the kids set out the entanglements of marriage for her. Farina warns, "Believe me, married life is sure tough!" Chubby, riding on the running board, reports his granddad died after he was married only seventy-five years. Mary Ann chimes in that she heard her pop say her mom *made* him marry her! And Farina concludes pensively, "I'm never gonna get married—and I'm gonna bring my children up the same way."

Director George Stevens, who was working on the *Boy Friends* comedies at the time, recalled that on the early Roach talkies, "The script was written without any regard for dialogue. The situations were described, with maybe an occasional line. In the silent pictures they'd do the picture and then the titles would be written. Hiram Walker was the title man; he was very funny. So when the dialogue pictures started, the script was written, then it

Gag photo from "School's Out."

went to Walker, and he'd do the dialogue. So the three or four pages of script were here, and eight or ten pages of dialogue were over here. It was sort of non sequitur."

"School's Out" meshes the two elements rather nicely, but does stop for a subplot that enables H. M. "Beanie" Walker to contribute his favored vaudeville patter, with Bonedust selling the other kids trick answers to the day's lessons. Bonedust is sure his answers are correct because he got them out of a book.

The quiz begins with Chubby, who stands, glances down at his desk, and recites the correct answer to the first question. Chubby beams his delight across the room to Bonedust, his enlightened smile as much as saying, "It works!"

Having established that Nathan Hale was an American patriot who gave his life for his country, Miss Crabtree asks Farina to recite Hale's last words before he was hanged. Farina stands sheepishly and answers, "He said . . . uh . . . . 'Brother, this is certainly going to be a lesson to me.' "

Miss Crabtree's open-mouthed astonishment clues Farina he's given the wrong answer. He sits down uneasily, and worried looks descend over the class.

The quiz continues. Miss Crabtree: "On Paul Revere's night ride, what did he say as he stopped his horse in front of the colonial homes?"

Buddy MacDonald stands and acts out the answer: "He said, 'Whoa!' " As Miss Crabtree blinks her surprise, Buddy realizes his answer too was not correct.

out the "long" race to Mrs. Mack's Grocery, the vehicle keeps careening around that same corner or barreling along that same picturesque stretch of road!

The kids are delightfully showcased in a series of vignettes in and around the store. Chubby is a consummate comedian, using his face and body to embellish dialogue jokes. In trying to discourage the sale of Grandma's store, Chubby says authoritatively, "Yeah—everybody's starving to death in *this* town." Pausing to rock back and forth on his heels, he continues with a self-satisfied look, "It's getting me down, too . . . I *used* to be fat!"

Wheezer buys his candy judiciously (paying with slugs) and is resigned to sharing some with his sister, until Shirley Jean Rickert comes along. Exchanging suggestive "eyebrow rolls," winks, and goo-goo eyes, Wheezer snatches the candy from his sister and declares, "Let the lady have some candy," passing it to the flashy blonde. Shirley Jean has little to do in "Helping Grandma," but she makes her scenes count. Recently asked what she thinks when she sees herself in such films, effortlessly stealing scenes, she says candidly, "I still can't stand talented little kids—even if I was one of them!"

Finally, there is a dialogue set piece with Wheezer and Stymie. It seems that Stymie has been sent to the store by his mother with instructions to buy 10¢ worth of *it;* but he doesn't know what "it" is. Since Wheezer has (incredibly) been left in charge, and he can't read either, the youngsters are forced to sample everything in sight, so Stymie can determine what "it" is supposed to be. His traditionally cunning scheme for getting to sample some goodies backfires when the taste treats include gasoline and fertilizer!

Two more of the film's assets, besides the performances of adults Margaret Mann and Oscar Apfel, are a sprightly, intricate music score, full of original themes seldom heard in later Roach shorts, and the naturalness of

"Helping Grandma": Farina and Jack.

the outdoor setting for the film, with the authentic little store situated in a genuine small town, enhancing the believability of the well-worn story line.

Apart from the warm, inviting people inside it, it's significant that Roach used a real general store for his setting, full of the kind of once-familiar elements and detail no one could duplicate today: the glass shades for hurricane lamps, the dry goods on the shelf, the antiquated phone, the rolltop glass counters, the water cooler, the wooden posts, the sagging hardwood floors, and the fountain pens and ink. A real piece of cinéma vérité are the flies that bother the actors in nearly every scene. Count the "A" features you've seen with flies buzzing through the shots! In fact, it's the kind of reality-based setting that the major studios wouldn't have reproduced in such fulsome detail. They sought an escape from reality, while Roach comedies showed us how to laugh at it.

104 · LOVE BUSINESS

Two Reels · Produced by Robert F. McGowan for Hal Roach · Directed by Robert F. McGowan · Photographed by Art Lloyd · Edited by Richard Currier · Dialogue by H. M. Walker · Released on February 14, 1931, by M-G-M · Our Gang: Jackie Cooper, Norman "Chubby" Chaney, Mary Ann Jackson, Bobby "Wheezer" Hutchins, Allen "Farina" Hoskins, Matthew "Stymie" Beard, Dorothy "Echo" DeBorba, Donald Haines, Bobby "Bonedust" Young, Shirley Jean Rickert, and Pete the Pup · Miss Crabtree, June Marlowe; Jackie's mother, May Wallace; Gag photos used, Charley Chase, Thelma Todd, Greta Garbo

Jackie is hopelessly in love with Miss Crabtree. Wheezer can't sleep at night because Jackie talks in his sleep, murmuring, "I love you," and hugging and kissing his brother, who shares the bed. Making matters worse, Miss Crabtree becomes a boarder at Jackie's house, and Chubby comes by to ask her to marry him. Chubby and Miss Crabtree want to be left alone, but Jackie can't stand it, and not only eavesdrops but heckles his amorous adversary. Finally Jackie's mother happens to hear some of Chubby's love recitations, which have a familiar ring to them—and no wonder. Chubby has memorized Mrs.

Cooper's old love letters, which Wheezer sold to him! Mother goes to give Wheezer a good spanking but finds him in bed wearing a catcher's face-mask, with Pete the dog at his side, to protect him from Jackie. Even the angry mother can't help but laugh.

Eschewing the pathos of "Teacher's Pet" and "School's Out," "Love Business" treats us to a completely lighthearted look at the gang's fondness for Miss Crabtree, further exploring Jackie's and Chubby's crush on their teacher. "You're just love-sick, that's all," Farina tells Jack, who replies, "I'm a whole epidemic!"

"Love Business": Pining for Miss Crabtree, Chubby practices making love to a cutout of Greta Garbo. Showing exhibitors how to advertise Hal Roach shorts is the framed photo of a romantic couple who happen to be Thelma Todd and Charley Chase.

Jack isn't exaggerating either, for apparently he can think of nothing but his heartthrob day and night, carrying her picture around with him and mooning over it. Chubby takes a more practical approach, using a giant cutout of Greta Garbo in front of the local movie theater to practice his technique. As he recites words of love from his cribsheets (Mrs. Cooper's letters), Dorothy sits nearby and mocks his dialogue.

"Oh my darling," he murmurs. "Can't you hear my pleas in my whispers?" "Oh my darling," she replies, deadpan, "I hear the fleas in your whiskers." Chubby glowers, hands on hips, at the intruder but presses on: "My heart is filled with joy; I want to skip and dance." "My heart is filled with joy," she repeats. "I want to rip my pants."

Although he is elated when he first hears that Miss Crabtree is moving in, Jackie worries that from now on he'll have to be on his best behavior twenty-four hours a day—washing before every meal, for instance. Sure enough, that night at dinner Mother tells Jackie, sister Mary Ann, and Wheezer to watch Miss Crabtree for tips on etiquette and to do everything she does. This emulation gets out of hand, however, when the schoolteacher tastes her landlady's soup. Unbeknown to everyone but the audience, some mothballs fell into the pot a bit earlier, and now Miss Crabtree has all she can do to keep from spitting up the soup. But the ever-polite young lady tells her hostess that "the soup is a little rich for me," gracefully avoiding another spoonful. Jackie comes more to the point: "It tastes like mothballs!"

As for her young suitors, Miss Crabtree seems to enjoy the charade, and leads them on. When Mary Ann explains that Chubby used to take her out before going cuckoo over the teacher, Miss Crabtree replies that they must be rivals. "Well, I don't know anything about rifles," Mary Ann continues, "but Chubby's coming over here tonight to ask you to marry him!" The little girl seems much relieved when her "rifle" assures her that she has no intentions of marrying Chubby.

Still, the teacher plays along with Jackie, impulsively kissing him when he works up the courage to tell her that she's even prettier than Miss McGillicuddy. She later goes through a similar routine with Chubby, who's leading up to a marriage proposal. "Don't call me Norman," he insists with a broad grin. "Call me Chubsy-Ubsy." She obliges.

In the *Our Gang* version of childhood, it's possible not only to have a teacher as pretty as Miss Crabtree but to have the opportunity of expressing one's feelings—whatever the results. "Love Business" carries schoolboy infatuation to a point few eight-year-olds reach in real life, but the basic emotions are universal enough to give this uproariously funny two-reeler a special appeal for everyone who can remember his or her first crush.

Footnote: The mushy love letters Chubby "bought off of Wheezer" are shown once in close-up, revealing the addressee to be "Miss May Wallace," the real name of the actress who played Wheezer's mother. It's an amusing practice one finds in most Hal Roach pictures.

Focus on Stymie: Director McGowan was learning at

previews what a crowd pleaser Stymie could be, and he was gradually giving Stymie larger and larger set pieces. Coming up in "Little Daddy," he'd be practically the whole show. In "Love Business" the gang is discussing the mixed blessing of Miss Crabtree coming to live with Jack, how he'll have to "slick up" and all, Farina warning him he'll even need to wash his feet. With elaborate decisiveness, Stymie comments, "I wouldn't wash my feet for n-o-*b-o-d-y*."

Recently asked to recount a typical day's regimen for working on an *Our Gang* picture, Stymie Beard gives us this overview: "My mother would take me to the studio early in the morning, and it was like a playground seeing Laurel & Hardy, Charley Chase, all those funny, funny people, and seeing whatever new sets or props or things were built for somebody's next picture. But we'd get there and the first thing I'd do is go to the barber shop, and get my head shaved, because I worked with a bald head. My character called for that—it was Bob McGowan's idea. Everyone would be in costume and ready for shooting around 9:00 A.M., although in the first three hours in the morning or the last three hours in the afternoon we had to have three hours for schooling. We'd have one hour for lunch, and we couldn't work past 6:00 because we were children, but all the rest would be shooting. Sometimes late in the day we could see the rushes, though as kids we really didn't care that much, we weren't so concerned. That's where we'd see Hal Roach, and in the cafeteria, too; he'd let us know when he was close by. He had so much confidence in Bob McGowan, though, he wouldn't come around too much when we were shooting. One parent or guardian had to be somewhere in the background within reach all the time, and they'd ride along with us on location work, too. We'd always be driving around to different spots in the city. We had a big red bus, with *Our Gang* painted on the side."

As for shooting techniques, Stymie explains, "They would try and shoot each film in sequence if they could. It would all depend on availability of sets and location work. Each picture would take five or six days, and we had a shooting schedule and a regular script to stick to. Not for the kids, really, though. They would take maybe three-four lines at a time, then they'd cut the camera. We would go at it very easy. They wouldn't expect us to

Romantic rivals Chubby and Jackie in a scene from "Love Business."

memorize too much. Sometimes my mother would bring home the script and we'd look it over. And sometimes we'd wait till we got to the studio and Mr. McGowan would just play it off the top and take it line by line not knowing what was next. Being kids we muffed a lot of lines, or said them our own way; it happened a lot of the time. But if we said something different, or improvised something, then if it got a laugh and fitted in, they'd keep it. It all depended on just how Mr. McGowan felt. Besides, kids aren't going to hold up too long before they fall down and want to go play and eat ice cream. You know how that is. And we *really* wanted to do that, all the time! In fact, the Good Humor man stayed on the lot and they kept us full of ice cream and Coca-Cola."

Asked if he was aware of how good he was, Stymie explains, laughing heartily, "They used to call me 'One-take Stymie,' I didn't burn up too much film, and I'm very proud of that. But it all just came natural, like most kids five, six, seven years old, I wasn't too aware. A lot of my ability just came from the natural thing, that I guess was a gift from the Good Lord."

105 · LITTLE DADDY

Two Reels · Produced by Robert F. McGowan for Hal Roach · Directed by Robert F. McGowan · Photographed by Art Lloyd · Edited by Richard Currier · Dialogue by H. M. Walker · Released on March 28, 1931, by M-G-M · Our Gang: Matthew "Stymie" Beard, Allen "Farina" Hoskins, Jackie Cooper, Norman "Chubby" Chaney, Bobby "Wheezer" Hutchins, Shirley Jean Rickert, Mary Ann Jackson, Donald Haines, Douglas Greer, Bobby "Bonedust" Young, Dorothy DeBorba, and Pete the Pup · The Parson, George Reed; Orphan asylum agent, Otto Fries; Miss Crabtree, June Marlowe; Singing voice-over for Chubby, Charley Chase

Farina, living alone with Stymie, is acting as his guardian. They seem to be doing all right for themselves, but the authorities decide Stymie ought to be in an orphanage. Reconciled to this adverse fortune, Farina offsets his downbeat mood by throwing a farewell party for Stymie.

When the mountain of sweet eats is all prepared, Farina dispatches *the* Little Rascal to round up the rest of the gang. Stymie, though, has his own designs on this feast and conveniently forgets to invite anyone else, telling Farina that nobody's coming. "And I hope they *don't*,"

Matthew Beard: Stymie.

Stymie adds. "I can eat all this stuff, brother." The gang does arrive, tardy, just in time to eye Stymie polishing off the last morsel of goodies. Their momentary hard feelings are allayed when everyone unites in the anticipated clash with the orphanage official who has come to take Stymie away. A rousing chase ensues, and it remains for Miss Crabtree to (presumably) settle matters.

An *Our Gang* comedy of almost no reputation, "Little Daddy" is a short subject with many nuances to enjoy. It's a real charmer.

The film begins in the black community church. After services, Farina turns in the collection plate, filled mostly with buttons; the pastor wonders how his congregation can keep their pants up.

For a change of pace, there is a soft organ music track beneath the first quarter of "Little Daddy." Roach music composer Marvin Hatley doesn't remember why. It was probably to match the church atmosphere, but whatever the reason, the effect is so enchanting one wishes they'd done it more often.

Another perplexing musical interlude concerns Chubby's entirely gratuitous rendition of "Asleep in the Deep." Perhaps it was an inside joke, since two other concurrently produced Roach subjects both spotlight this unforgettable song: Laurel & Hardy's *Pardon Us* (the snoring business) and Charley Chase's delightful *Rough Seas.* Indeed, it's Charley Chase's basso profundo singing voice that Chubby lip-syncs to in "Little Daddy."

Hal Roach's recollection of this long-ago gag is understandably clouded today, but he believes the whole thing was Chase's idea.

George Stevens—Roach photographer and cameraman, and later one of the industry's most esteemed directors—has said that for years after the advent of sound, "The only pictures we were making at Hal Roach were silent comedies that spoke." One lengthy and completely visual routine in "Little Daddy" certainly bears this out. In fact, the very episode (well into the film) is introduced with a silent-film transition title reading, "Morning."

The routine is a throwback to the gadgetry gags that typified so many of the silent *Our Gangs.* Specifically, it borrows from Snub Pollard's hilarious Hal Roach short of 1923, *It's a Gift,* using Charley Oelze's mechanical genius to design laborsaving devices for the kitchen. No less inspired than a Rube Goldberg cartoon, breakfast for Farina and Stymie is provided by operating a series of mechanized levers, wires, and pulleys. As Farina orchestrates this surprising automation, with a pull here and a tug there, curtains open, milk pours into a pan for a squad of hungry cats, and a chicken lays an egg that rolls down a long spout into a strainer where a hammer neatly cracks it through to a waiting frying pan. Tugging twice more adds salt and pepper.

Another rope flips the water bucket for the morning shower of a reluctant Stymie—who takes his shower fully clothed, wearing a raincoat, and standing under an umbrella, at the same time shouting to Farina in the kitchen, "Burrr! This water sure am cold!"

"Little Daddy" is purely a vehicle for Stymie. With Jackie Cooper on loan from Roach to Paramount for *Skippy,* it was only natural that Bob McGowan would focus on a fresh scene-stealer. Most of the success of this film turns on Stymie's acerbic yet innocent quips. They're totally credible. Stymie somehow manages to do everything with a certain beguiling sparkle. He says funny things, and he says things funny.

The story shell is lined in pathos (*Motion Picture* magazine speculated, "Perhaps the influence of Charlie Chaplin"), but Stymie seizes every opportunity to scatter the melancholy with wisecrack humor. Farina whines something about this being the last breakfast he'll ever fix for Stymie, who says, feet propped on the table while he cleans his teeth with a toothpick, "Well, what do you want me to do, bust out cryin'?"

Despite lines like that, today Stymie recalls "Little Daddy" as "very touching, and one of my favorites."

Unfortunately, the film has been eliminated from the current *Little Rascals* television package. Apparently it is felt that "Little Daddy" presents a demeaning picture of its black characters.

It is sad that such sensitivities can overcome the more important human values of a film like "Little Daddy," which provides a warmth and feeling so lacking in most contemporary children's shows. In their rush to remove

Posed still from "Little Daddy" that doesn't equate with the finished film sequence in which Stymie wants Farina to tell him the story about the boat with all the animals on it. Incidentally, Laurel & Hardy buffs should have little trouble spotting a special pup in this still named Laughing Gravy.

from view a film which portrays black youngsters as being poor and speaking in dialect, some dilettante censors ignore the larger picture: that all the *Our Gang* kids are poor, and that Farina and Stymie, stereotyped dialects notwithstanding, are extremely strong and positive characters. They came off that way in the 1930s, and they still project the same qualities forty years later.

Stymie is one of the most self-reliant characters in the history of *Our Gang*. He can hold his own against any child or adult in the series, just by using his wits, and never does he surrender his basic charm and appeal in the process. Aside from the fact that he is a wily rascal, it's difficult to see any negative connotations that might rub off on an innocent young viewer of the 1970s. Similarly, Farina's devotion to his little brother (not to mention his ingenuity in rigging those household chore devices) builds an affirmative image for this character, certainly more so than the gamblers, pimps, drug-dealers, and violence-oriented detectives who pose as heroes in many recent black movies.

Black film historian Donald Bogle, in his excellent 1973 volume *Toms, Coons, Mulattoes, Mammies and Bucks*, sums up the *Our Gang* comedies this way:

"The *Our Gang* series revolved around a group of lower-middle-class American youngsters making their way through childhood in entertaining ups and downs, ins and outs, as black and white together tried figuring out life and play. Throughout the series the black children spoke in a dialect of the familiar *dats* and *deres* as well as the *I is's, you is's,* and *we was's.* On more than one occasion, Farina was seen banqueting on a colored man's favorite dishes—fried chicken and watermelon. In these respects, the adventures and life styles of the black children conformed to accepted notions and attitudes of the day. But for the most part the approach to the relationships of the black children with the whites was almost as if there were no such thing as race at all. Indeed, the charming sense of *Our Gang* was that all the children were buffoons, forever in scraps and scrapes, forever plagued by setbacks and sidetracks as they set out to have fun, and everyone had his turn at being outwitted."

It seems a shame that others cannot share Bogle's perception of *Our Gang* and what it represents. To censor such a warm and delightful comedy as "Little Daddy" when America is (supposedly) enjoying a new and refreshing openness about race relations is a crime. We might as well burn all existing prints of *Huckleberry Finn* or rewrite Mark Twain's books, for that matter.

And one cannot help but wonder how many so-called "relevant" TV comedies featuring blacks will be able to hold up forty or fifty years from now the way "Little Daddy" does today.

106 · BARGAIN DAY

Two Reels · Produced by Robert F. McGowan for Hal Roach · Directed by Robert F. McGowan · Photographed by Art Lloyd · Edited by Richard Currier · Dialogue by H. M. Walker · Released on May 2, 1931, by M-G-M · Our Gang: Matthew "Stymie" Beard, Shirley Jean Rickert, Bobby "Wheezer" Hutchins, Allen "Farina" Hoskins, Jackie Cooper, Dorothy DeBorba, Donald Haines, Mary Ann Jackson, Norman "Chubby" Chaney, Douglas Greer, and Pete the Pup · Sales clerk, Harry Bernard; Sox customer, Baldwin Cooke; Police captain, Stanley (Tiny) Sandford; Officer, Silas D. Wilcox; Policeman not in uniform, Otto Fries; Voice-over for the monkey, Mickey Daniels

When the gang's baseball equipment is missing, Jackie figures that Wheezer is on another one of his selling sprees, and he's right. Wheezer and Stymie wheel their assorted merchandise to the door of a fancy house where a lonely little rich girl happily invites them in. While Wheezer tries to sell something to the lady of the house, Stymie and Bologna run loose in the mansion, cavorting with the girl's pet monkey. Jackie and the gang arrive, looking for Wheezer, and in touring the house, Chubby decides to try out the reducing-steam cabinet. Meanwhile, Bologna has set off the burglar alarm, and a squadron of police arrive to investigate, rounding up all the kids but discovering that no harm has been done. Cries for help bring them all to Chubby's aid, however, and when he emerges from the reducing cabinet, his clothes are all shrunk and his new top hat looks like a miniature toy on his head.

This modest but amusing two-reeler opens with a close-up of Chubby wearing a silly cap on his head. An adult voice proclaims, "Now there's a hat that could not be duplicated anywhere in the world for the price!" Chubby rejects the idea, however, and rummages (in fast motion) through a score of other hats, looking for just the right one before settling on a fancy dress top hat which figures in the film's closing gag. (The peppy, infectious musical theme used with this sequence is every bit worth identifying: it is LeRoy Shield's "It Is to Laugh.")

Most of the footage in "Bargain Day" is devoted to the younger gangsters, especially the two with "the peddlers' craze." Stymie wheels Wheezer down the street as the would-be merchant sings out to anyone listening, "Who wants to buy something?" A second lesson in salesmanship.

A typical Hal Roach title card introduces "Lonely Little Rich Girl—Mother remembers to leave home every morning—Father forgets to come in at night." Shirley Jean Rickert is ideal as the pampered but friendless youngster, reminiscent of Jean Darling in earlier roles.

As they approach the front door of the mansion, Wheezer cautions Stymie not to show his ignorance, in a brief bit of interplay remindful of Laurel & Hardy out to make a good impression. Stymie obviously thinks his "ignorance" is something different from what Wheezer thinks it is, since he replies with a wry smile, "Uh-uh, brother, I ain't gonna show my ignorance to no-body!"

First lesson in salesmanship in "Bargain Day," as conducted by capable Roach character actor Harry Bernard. Looking on are Chubby, Jackie Cooper, Mary Ann Jackson, Farina, Dorothy De Borba, and Donald Haines.

Their conversation with Shirley dwells perhaps overlong on a play on words as she tells them that her mother has gone over to Watt Street to gad. "What street?" they ask (Wheezer unable to keep a straight face), as the parlay continues for several minutes. Stymie indignantly bleats, "Uh-uh, sista, I can't figure *that* out."

Shirley thinks she recognizes Stymie as the son of the family chauffeur. "Uh-uh, my daddy ain't no chauffeur," he answers, "My daddy's just a crap-shootin' fool!"* (This response is now often deleted from TV prints, along with Stymie's later dice-rolling interludes, pulling for the "eight-er from Decatur.")

Finally, Wheezer gets around to the business at hand and tries to take a professional approach to door-to-door peddling. He succeeds in selling nothing. "Here's a very nice doorknob," he begins. "Would you like to buy *it?*" Maintaining her arm's length role as the customer-housewife, Shirley examines the doorknob and replies, "No, I don't think I want a doorknob—today."

While Wheezer continues his sales pitch, the high-spirited Stymie examines the palatial surroundings, encountering Shirley's playful pet monkey, who bursts forth with a raucous laugh (courtesy of Mickey Daniels)

* At a recent screening attended by Shirley Jean Rickert, she recalled that upon the first take, the line came out, innocently, "My daddy ain't no chauffeur. My daddy's just a crappin' fool!" The entire set collapsed into hysterics, especially since Stymie hadn't intentionally muffed the line. A prize outtake, Hal Roach kept it around to show as a gag. This explains the extra-special glint in Stymie's eye as he does finally successfully deliver the line, and then steals a beaming glance upward, probably at McGowan off-scene, as if to ask, "Did I get it right that time?" Shirley, equally innocent, didn't understand what all the commotion was about and remembers the story today only because her mother used to tell it.

and leads the hapless youngster on a whirlwind chase throughout the house.

When the older members of the gang show up, Farina warns that they're liable to be pinched, unaware that the burglar alarm has already been set off. When the cops arrive, however, kindly chief Tiny Sandford says with a smile, "Only a bunch of kids, fellows; round 'em up." This is easier said than done, but after a brief skirmish the kids are gathered together and the situation is well in hand—except for a stunned Chubby, who concludes after leaving the steam cabinet, "I musta shrunk!"

"Bargain Day" was produced concurrently with Laurel & Hardy's *Another Fine Mess*. They're paced alike, use more or less the same incidental music scoring, and both gain from the same kind of visual design (the high interior sets are impressive).

It's interesting how many Hal Roach comedies shot simultaneously will tie to one another this way (though we'll never know whether the ties were merely cunningly disguised, intentional, or possibly unplanned). Just in this period alone, "Railroadin' " corresponds to *Berth Marks,* "When the Wind Blows" to *Night Owls,* "A Tough Winter" to *Below Zero,* "Teacher's Pet" to *Pardon Us* (the schoolroom scene), and "Dogs Is Dogs," coming up, to *One Good Turn.* The same kind of parallelism holds among the other Roach series, too. People had fun working together at Hal Roach Studios, and the collective result was a uniform, distinctive style of comedy.

"Bargain Day" was budgeted at a mere $19,000 (the range was $20,000 to $30,000 for Roach comedies), and from the looks of it, almost entirely studio made, one wouldn't suppose there'd been a material overrun, but there was. Final negative cost came to $28,600. In looking for hints of production problems, there are scattered lines of dialogue suggesting other marginal sequences that may have been trimmed before release. Continuity is a mite vague. And "Stax" Graves shot an inordinately high number of stills for "Bargain Day," many of which don't equate with footage in the final release. Also, during the closing scenes, the obvious use of two different actors dressed as Jackie Cooper and Donald Haines (by then both at work on *Skippy*) suggests heavy retakes were necessary to reshape the film's climax. (We weren't supposed to notice there were two unknowns posing as Cooper and Haines—it *wasn't* part of the plot.)

Shirley Jean Rickert answered a "Bargain Day" open call and won her first part in an *Our Gang* comedy. She remembers that "The various stars around the Roach lot would drop by from time to time, and the atmosphere on the set was always great." Recalling the craftsmen behind the cameras: "Art Lloyd was a very gentle man who took great pains in photographing the group. I'll always remember Bob McGowan as a very, very lovely man who was, again, all gentleness. Hal Roach was the king in the tower to my memory."

"Uncle Bob" McGowan, adept at distilling the best out of his sundry charges, had a special relationship with Stymie. Recalling McGowan today, Stymie can't say enough kind things about the man. The affection between the two was something few failed to notice. McGowan used to carry Stymie around in his arms when attending to business here and there on the lot.

Stymie, too, remembers the special atmosphere on the Roach lot. "It was a grand place full of laughs all the

time. On the next set would be Laurel & Hardy, and on another set would be Charley Chase and Thelma Todd, or Patsy Kelly and ZaSu Pitts. So you can imagine the kind of fun-filled life we kids had. That was all thrilling. Laurel & Hardy, in particular, were very instrumental with us kids. They used to come over all the time and play with us, make us laugh constantly, Laurel especially, who was my white role model, and a very wonderful kind of guy. I got to wear a derby like he did. Hardy was groovy, but somehow I took to Laurel and he took to me. Later, when I first came to The Club,* I used to go see Laurel, out here in Santa Monica, just before he died. Charley Chase, too, was one of the most delightful, funny men that I've ever known, and that I ever will know in my life. He was a very warm person, very sweet.''

  * ''The Club'' is Synanon, devoted to rehabilitating drug addicts. See the biographies section.

Chubby and standard pensive look in the unforgettable closing scene of "Bargain Day." While attention is riveted on Chubby's shrunken plug hat, it's easy to overlook the two unknowns over his shoulders who are posing as Donald Haines and Jackie Cooper, who left Roach during production to work on *Skippy* at Paramount. Six feet five inches and three hundred pounds, Tiny Sandford, holding Shirley, had once been a child actor in films himself. Believe it or don't!

However, for Stymie, at least, the decidedly make-believe land of Hal Roach Studios served only to provide him with a schizophrenic existence: a stars' pet one place, and the cold realities of near-ghetto life in another place, downtown Los Angeles, where his father was a preacher. His usually cheery voice, and thoughts, grow distant as he recalls, ''When we were at the studio, we were so pampered, and when I went home, on the Lower East Side, my parents had to keep me in so I wouldn't get my face scarred.''

107 · FLY MY KITE

Two Reels · Produced by Robert F. McGowan for Hal Roach · Directed by Robert F. McGowan · Photographed by Art Lloyd · Edited by Richard Currier · Dialogue by H. M. Walker · Released on May 30, 1931, by M-G-M · Our Gang: Allen "Farina" Hoskins, Norman "Chubby" Chaney, Mary Ann Jackson, Matthew "Stymie" Beard, Bobby "Wheezer" Hutchins, Dorothy DeBorba, Shirley Jean Rickert, Georgie Ernest, Dickie Jackson, and Pete the Pup · Mrs. Margaret Mann, "Grandma," Herself; Son-in-law Dan, James Mason; Dan's new wife, Mae Busch; Bond agent, Broderick O'Farrell; Stunt double for Grandma, David Sharpe

In "Fly My Kite" it's the gentler bits of humor that register best. The kids are garbed as Indians to celebrate the Wild West stories Grandma reads them.

Grandma's the bouncy sweetheart of all the youngsters; she reads them pulp fiction, offers kindly advice, and even slips on boxing gloves and spars with them in her living room. Grandma cares for the kids, and they're fiercely loyal to her. At the same time, she has an unfeeling son-in-law named Dan, who wants to fleece her and pack her off to the County Home so he can move in with his new wife. "You're broke, you're old, and you're useless," he tells her coldly. While at Grandma's house, the thieving louse snatches a letter in the mailbox from The Imperial Steel Company advising Grandma to communicate with them immediately concerning some gold bonds she owns. Lusting after the chance for self-aggrandizement, the disreputable son-in-law secretly contacts a bond agent, and learns the old securities are now worth $100,000. Rushing back to steal her fortune, seedy Dan finds Grandma packing her belongings for the Poor Farm. She'd come across those worthless bonds all right, and they finally came in handy for something: she's tied them to the tail of Chubby's kite to help keep it up in the air. Dirty Dan gets excited and races after Chubby out in the field. As they scuffle for possession of the kite, Grandma learns of the gold bonds' true value from the letter Dan has left, and exhorts the gang to run and help Chubby, who with customary aplomb is kicking Dan in the shins: "Hey, what's the big idea? Gimme my kite." As the kids swarm across the sunny field to Chub's rescue, Pete the Pup seizes the ball of string, romping around artfully dodging Dan and piloting the kite himself, managing to keep it fluttering just beyond the crook's reach. Meanwhile, Grandma's

dander is up. She gets a running start and somersaults out of the window on her way to grab the helpful arm of the law down on the corner. By the time help arrives, however, the gang has neatly subdued Grandma's foe, lassoing him around the foot and dragging him over a pile of broken bottles and a board full of upturned nails, then pelting him with rocks and mud when he climbs a telephone pole after the kite, and ultimately sawing the pole down to send the ripe villain plummeting headlong into a pool of mud and final defeat. And with this formidable foe vanquished, Grandma's bonds and future are secured.

An undervalued *Our Gang* long pushed aside, "Fly My Kite" is nonetheless a masterpiece of its corny kind. The appeal here is most certainly to the young at heart, regardless of age, and as such it's a timeless film that deserves its long life.

In the hard days of the Depression, audiences wanted uncomplicated values; they wanted to see an underdog they could identify with triumph over clearcut stock villains like Grandma's son-in-law. The device offered movie-goers a terrific release, because there *was* no single culprit to blame for the Depression.

The dramatic story line was clichéd even in 1931, but it's so skillfully enacted, with such conviction, that one can't help but get caught up in the sorrowful fortunes befalling this down-and-out old lady. Moreover, the sentiment is honest and compelling; few short films would eclipse "Fly My Kite" in its ability to move and involve an audience. It's a comedy to cherish and really warm up to.

Much of the film's allure lies in the mutual affection between the kids and Grandma: it's a rare sweetness often lost in films made today. Their steadfast allegiance to one another is enough to awaken sympathy from even the most callous.

The entire film, particularly the spectacular climax, benefits enormously from an intricate and rousing musical background score. Suspenseful when need be, light and frothy at other times, the scoring both paces the action and punctuates individual gags.

Another plus is an interesting cast. The "ever-popular" Mae Busch was borrowed from Laurel & Hardy roles and makes a brief but distinctively nasty impression as Dan's wife. (They deserve each other.) Son-in-law Dan is despicably played by oily-looking James Mason, no relation (need we say it?) to the British actor of recent times. Mason could usually be found selling guns to the Indians in B Westerns. Margaret Mann endows the film with affecting tenderness in an encore of her role from "Helping Grandma," though it's a characterization she'd done before, most notably as the star of John Ford's wonderful 1928 silent, *Four Sons*. Finally, a nod of appreciation is due to stunt ace Dave Sharpe, who doubles for Grandma in costume to execute some breathtaking leaps and falls (for more on Sharpe, see the write-up for "Ask Grandma," the 1925 blueprint for this film).

Brimming over with class and polish, "Fly My Kite" concluded the consistently outstanding 1930–31 season of *Our Gang* comedies.

In passing, it's worth mentioning that right after "Fly My Kite," both *Our Gang* and Laurel & Hardy contributed their services to an amazing film called *The Stolen Jools,* a star-studded short featuring names like Joan Crawford, Gary Cooper, Buster Keaton, Maurice Chevalier, and some fifty others. It was a fund-raising two-reeler for the National Variety Artists' tuberculosis sanatorium. *Our Gang*'s contribution, like everyone else's, was incidental. The kids are shown slurping ice cream cones on Norma Shearer's front steps when detectives Laurel & Hardy drive up to the house, siren screaming. The kids scatter across the yard. Ollie parks the car and it collapses in a heap. "I *told* you not to make that last payment," he says to Stan, glowering. Fadeout.

James Mason tastes the fruits of Our Gang revenge in "Fly My Kite."

108 · BIG EARS

Two Reels · Produced by Robert F. McGowan for Hal Roach · Directed by Robert F. McGowan · Photographed by Art Lloyd · Edited by Richard Currier · Dialogue by H. M. Walker · Released on August 29, 1931, by M-G-M · Our Gang: Bobby "Wheezer" Hutchins, Matthew "Stymie" Beard, Dorothy DeBorba, Donald Haines, Sherwood Bailey, and Pete the Pup · Wheezer's father, Creighton Hale; Wheezer's mother, Ann Christy; Doctor, Wilfred Lucas; Orderly, Gordon Douglas

Wheezer's parents are squabbling again, and it looks as though they may be heading for the divorce courts. When Wheezer's efforts fail to restore domestic bliss, he seeks Stymie's advice. Together, they decide that if Wheez can manage to get really sick, it might bring his parents back together again. So Stymie feeds him some lard and assorted goodies: "Try another mouthful of that soap." After gorging himself with this stuff, Wheezer does indeed become ill, and asks if Stymie will bring him some medicine. "Sure I will. What kind do you want?" inquires Stymie. "Any kind," says Wheezer, "it's in the bathroom medicine chest." After he samples them all, the doctor is summoned, and the contrivance does succeed in reuniting the quarreling parents.

"Big Ears" is a most unusual *Our Gang* endeavor. Hal Roach doesn't recall the thinking behind the divorce angle, but whatever the reasons, it's resulted in disfavor among some television station program directors, who've censored and shelved the film from their airwaves. It's not that the marital spat is done in poor taste, or is entirely unsuitable for children, but simply that it's the kind of indelicate story not easily explained to kids. In any case, even though the film's sentiment is honest, *Our Gang* stories work much better when they fix on the kids and *their* problems, rather than having the kids meddle in the troubles of adults.

While the basic story may not be to everyone's liking, however, individual sequences are highly charming and delightful; and on a technical level the camera work is at times singularly creative, especially in the use of light and shadow.

Among bright individual sequences, in the early goings there's a carefree romp in the living room, with Wheezer chasing after a playful Petie, who won't let the lad have his cap. Seconds later, out in the yard, more games: they're darting about, dodging one another, or rolling around contesting for a throw rug. As they play together, their affection is obvious and absolutely genuine. The sequence is irresistible, and it's the kind of relaxed and warm throwaway material that many of the best Roach comedies would pause for.

Pete the Pup, in fact, steals nearly every scene he's in, *without* benefit of dialogue. The way his remarkably expressive reactions are intercut with scenes throughout the short, the filmmakers would have it appear that Petie is endowed with special cognitive abilities and understands what's going on around him better than the film's characters do. The canine star seems to be an all-knowing arms-length observer, like the audience, who can see ahead and predict what's going to happen, but who finds himself helpless to explain what is obvious to everyone except the characters on the screen, and who can only react with disapproval or puzzlement when Wheezer or Stymie does something dumb or baffling. He nods his head yes or no to questions, but only Wheezer is smart enough to seek his advice. In the film's closing scenes, though, Petie finds it

Petie and Wheezer push for marital harmony in "Big Ears." In the middle, sharing a brief moment of connubial bliss, are Creighton Hale and Ann Christy.

schedule for the 1931–32 season, and it marked a material change in *Our Gang* personnel. Over the summer break there had been quite a turnover with Jackie Cooper, Chubby Chaney, Mary Ann Jackson, Shirley Jean Rickert, and Farina (after decade of service) all leaving the series. No one could have known that Spanky McFarland would come along and fill the void before the year was out, but in the meantime it gave Beanie Walker plenty of time to concentrate on working up quips for Stymie, many of them incisively funny, especially since Stymie delivered them so effortlessly and naturally, and with such assurance. Counseling Wheezer, Stymie recalls that he once ate two cans of lard, thinking it was ice cream, and that it had made him sick. Wheezer wonders if two cans will do the trick in his case. Stymie explains, "I don't know, the first can didn't make me sick; it was the second can that turned my stomach."

The film's supporting cast is an interesting one. Gordon Douglas was just beginning his career; he was working with *Our Gang* graduates in *The Boy Friends* series elsewhere on the Roach lot, and in a few years he would succeed Gus Meins as the gang's director. Wilfred Lucas was a seasoned veteran in the business, having worked with D. W. Griffith at Biograph and, like Douglas, would spend a lot of time working in Hal Roach pictures over the coming decade. Ann Christy's most distinguished credit came opposite Harold Lloyd in *Speedy* a few years earlier. Creighton Hale had been featured prominently in many leading silent films, including *Way Down East, The Cat and the Canary,* and *The Marriage Circle,* but he worked through the talkies in comparative obscurity. Some of the pictures were still important, but his parts were reduced to unstressed bit roles, as in *The Thin Man* and *One Million B.C.*

hard to remain silent when the vacillating couple promises undying affection for one another. Having heard that before, Petie's ears shoot up in the air, and he sticks out his tongue, letting go with a buzzing Bronx cheer!

"Big Ears" was the first short on the production

109 · SHIVER MY TIMBERS

Two Reels · Produced by Robert F. McGowan for Hal Roach · Directed by Robert F. McGowan · Photographed by Art Lloyd · Edited by Richard Currier · Dialogue by H. M. Walker · Released on October 10, 1931, by M-G-M · Our Gang: Matthew "Stymie" Beard, Bobby "Wheezer" Hutchins, Dorothy DeBorba, Sherwood Bailey, Jerry Tucker, Georgie Ernest, Carolina Beard, and Pete the Pup · The sea captain, Billy Gilbert; Miss Crabtree, June Marlowe; Pirates, Harry Bernard, Dick Gilbert, Cy Slocum, Jack Hill

The gang is playing hooky again; they're down at the docks listening to wild windjammer stories as told by a salty old sea captain. These repeated truancies are naturally upsetting to the schoolteacher, Miss Crabtree, who seeks out the captain and explains why his far-fetched storytelling is harmful to the kids. Determined to cure the gang's fondness for sea adventures, together they plot a scheme whereby the kids will get their wish to sign aboard the captain's ship as pirates and treasure seekers—except that the captain and his mates will try and teach "the little tars" a lesson by scaring them all to death during their first night at sea. But the resourceful Rascals turn the tables and the plan doesn't work out quite as intended.

For the most part, "Shiver My Timbers" relies on the extremely witty dialogue provided by gag writer H. M. Walker, and expertly delivered by Stymie. Though the snappy dialogue does give way to fast-paced action dur-

ing the climactic showdown between Our Gang and the pirates, the film is at its best during quiet exchanges, as when Billy Gilbert tells Stymie of his sea journey round the pole:

Stymie: Is that where the cats come from?
Billy Gilbert: What cats?
Stymie: The polecats! . . . We had a polecat under our house once, and boy did we take a trip.
Wheezer: Oh, you vacated, huh?
Stymie: Vacated nothin', we fumigated!
Much later, after killing two of his mates, Billy Gilbert is blustering around the ship, bragging and trying to intimidate Stymie. . . .
Billy Gilbert (roaring): My feet are bad! My heart is bad! I'm bad all over!
Stymie (unruffled): Boy, that man is bad.

Billy Gilbert spins a yarn for his captive audience.

Our Gang lobby card, illustrated with typical M-G-M theater poster art.

Billy Gilbert: I'm worse than Brute Larson! I'm worse than Captain Kidd!

Stymie: I don't know any of them gentlemen.

Billy Gilbert: Remember, *I'm* the boss!

Stymie: Oh Mr. Boss, we kinda lost our taste for being pi-rates.

Billy Gilbert: Oh ho! So you're going to back out first, eh?

Stymie: Uh-uh, looks like we all going out feet first.

And while the grown-ups frequently retard things, there is one dialogue exchange not involving Stymie or other Gangsters that did produce one of the singularly memorable lines in the annals of film history. The roughneck sea captain is abusing his shipmates to scare the gang, and he calls two grubby seamen over for more derision. Face to face, he growls at them, "What are ya

doin' over there?" Without any hesitation, Harry Bernard shakes his head and answers confidently, "*We don't know,* captain."

Despite isolated sequences like these, however, "Shiver My Timbers" doesn't quite measure up to the promise of its concept. Like Laurel & Hardy's *The Live Ghost,* which it resembles in certain routines and which was made three years later on essentially the same set, "Shiver My Timbers" grows stale and doesn't hold up under repeat viewings. It seems, in fact, that every time an *Our Gang* plot is pegged to the idea of "teaching the kids a lesson," the results are below par.

With little else that's noteworthy, "Shiver My Timbers" does feature an interesting extreme in casting. Billy Gilbert, as the sea captain, indulges his obvious fondness for bravura villainy and loud overacting, offering sharp contrast to the sedate June Marlowe as Miss Crabtree, who, charming though she may be, can barely act at all!

110 · DOGS IS DOGS

Two Reels · Produced by Robert F. McGowan for Hal Roach · Directed by Robert F. McGowan · Photographed by Art Lloyd · Edited by Richard Currier · Dialogue by H. M. Walker · Released on November 21, 1931, by M-G-M · Our Gang: Bobby "Wheezer" Hutchins, Matthew "Stymie" Beard, Sherwood "Spud" Bailey, Dorothy DeBorba, Dickie Jackson, and Pete the Pup · Mr. Brown, Billy Gilbert; Sherwood's mother, Blanche Payson; Wheezer's aunt, Lyle Tayo; Officer, Harry Bernard; Driver, Baldwin Cooke

As their father has seemingly deserted them, Wheezer and Dorothy are forced to live with a mean old step-mother, and her bratty, spoiled son. Not exactly drown-ing the kids in a surfeit of kindness, "Mother" begins her day with a licking for Wheezer, just because the window

was open and Petie happened to jump in bed with him again. After dishing out some more abuse, "Old Hatchet-Face," as Stymie calls her, announces she's going downtown for the morning, and charges Wheezer to look after pampered Sherwood and see that he doesn't get

Pillow fights between a kid and his dog *can* be dangerous, as depicted in this scene from "Dogs Is Dogs" with Pete, "the alley dog," Wheezer, Blanche Payson (as Stan Laurel remarked in "Helpmates," "isn't she sweet?"), tattletale Sherwood V. Bailey, Jr., and his dumb dog Nero, "the pedigree." It looks like another whipping for Wheezer.

dirty. Breakfast goes fine—uninvited Stymie joins the trio and cons Sherwood out of some ham and eggs—but after Sherwood leaves, his own dumb dog shoves him into a deep water well he was peering into. The report is passed to disinterested Wheezer and Stymie, who casually drop by to see what they can do about frightened Sherwood's plight. As a thank-you for pulling him up from his watery confinement, Sherwood blames Petie for killing another of Mr. Brown's chickens, when in fact his own dog Nero is the culprit. An egg shellacking for the enraged, gun-toting Mr. Brown works to no avail, and Petie ends up in the dog pound. It looks like he's a "goner" until Wheezer's loving aunt finally tracks him down at the city pound and gladly pays the two dollars for Pete's license. Wheezer enthuses, "Boy you're swell." Auntie explains that their father has been very ill, and that's why he hasn't been able to come for them. The kindly lady buys a fancy new set of clothes for Dorothy and Wheez, outfits Petie in a special collar, and for good measure plants a swift kick on the cruel stepmother's derriere as she turns to leave. While being escorted to her waiting chauffeur-driven limousine, Wheezer looks around the neighborhood and laments, "Gee I hate to leave my old pal Stymie. I wish he was going with us." Wheezer doesn't know it, but he gets his wish, for as the auto pulls out down the road, there's Stymie, perched in the spare tire on the back of the car, dressed in a new suit himself, and all set for the next adventure!

A short subject one can get awfully fond of, "Dogs Is Dogs" is a winner all the way, both touching and funny, with a vivid set of characters brought to life.

Rare is the child who could watch this film and not become involved with Wheezer's situation. Early in the morning, Pete wakes up his master and happily plays with him in bed. Insufferable Sherwood runs to the kitchen and

says, "Mama, Wheezer's got Pete in bed with him again." "Oh, he *has?*" scowls his mother. "I'll fix him for that!" She stalks into the bedroom and scolds the boy (with a startling close-up of the crabby harridan), following this with a severe spanking, as Sherwood smiles in triumph. Then even beloved Petie is disparaged. Wheezer complains that Sherwood is allowed to play in bed with Nero, but Mother disdainfully replies that Nero is a pedigreed, while Pete is nothing but an alley dog. After she leaves, Wheezer gripes to Sherwood about the way he is treated, and Sherwood smugly replies that this is as it should be, since Wheezer is only a stepson. "*You* haven't got any *real* mother," he flaunts with a smirk. Wheezer pops him on the nose, prompting babyish cries for Mother, who runs to the scene and coddles her precious offspring.

Thus in one introductory scene the stage is set: Wheezer (along with Dorothy and Pete) is the innocent victim of circumstance, his stepbrother is a spoiled brat, and his stepmother is a mean old witch. It now remains for the film to give Wheezer his day in the sun, and the "family" its comeuppance.

"Dogs Is Dogs" bears little relation to "Pups Is Pups," except that it's almost as enjoyable. It's much less visual than "Pups Is Pups," and for that matter most sound *Our Gang* comedies, but the short is nonetheless a jewel, with two clever dialogue segments registering especially well; the first is one of the most delightful bits of chicanery ever devised for the series.

Sherwood's just fixed a lavish breakfast of ham and eggs for himself, but Wheezer and Dorothy are forced to slop down their perennial unfavorite, mush. Adding to the humiliation, Sherwood feeds his leftover ham to Nero, the dog!

Just then, in pops Stymie, who's sure fed up on their mush for his breakfast. "What? Mush again? You know you's the mushiest people I ever did see."

Sherwood says he can't come in, but Stymie—always living by his wits—assures him he just wants to stand around by the door and smell. Then spotting some uncooked ham and eggs, he casually asks Sherwood if he knew that ham and eggs could talk. Sherwood snarls his skepticism, but Stymie leads him on. "Well, I heared 'em talking this morning."

Wheezer can see it's going to be one of Stymie's schemes and with an admiring grin he asks his crafty pal, "What'd they say?"

In a priceless moment, Stymie leans over and says solemnly, "Well, the ham said to the eggs, 'Move over there, white boy, you's crowding me.' "

Wheezer plays along. "Then what'd the eggs say?" he asks.

Stymie tells him, "Ham, I ain't crowding nobody. I'm just nibblin' around in this here grease."

Although it convinces most every kid planted in front of the screen, so far Sherwood isn't buying a particle of it. He tells Stymie he's crazy, so Stymie gives him a wily look and declares, "Yeah, you're one of them wise guys, ain't cha?" Stymie asks Wheezer if he believes it, and the answer comes right back, "Sure I do." He asks Dorothy, too, and whispers, "Say yes." She whispers back, "Yes."

Sherwood takes the bait and brings over the ham and eggs, waiting to hear some conversation. When nothing

happens, Stymie explains pokerfaced, "You gotta kinda mess 'em up . . . in a fryin' pan; *then* they'll talk." A doubting but suckered Sherwood dutifully fries up the ham and eggs, as Stymie coaches him along, "You know you gotta kinda turn 'em over, shuffle 'em around a little bit." When at last the ham and eggs are done, and Stymie can't string this guy along any further, he half apologizes and Sherwood stomps out, leaving with a superior remark that he *knew* all along they couldn't talk. Except that Sherwood has left behind a meal fit for a king—and Stymie, Wheezer, and Dorothy happily gobble it down. His mouth full of food, Wheezer wonders where Stymie ever got such an idea. "Brother," he answers, "I'm full of ideas when I'm hungry." As for the ham and eggs' ability to speak, Stymie concludes, "Well, they're saying hello to my stomach, r-i-i-i-ght now!"

While still at the table, there comes word that Sherwood has fallen into the well. Relaxing in depth for a change, Wheezer mulls over the news, stretches his hands in a yawning gesture, and resolves, "Let's go and see what's the trouble." Stymie agrees they might as well. Sauntering right over, they hear Sherwood crying in a shrill voice, "Mama, mama, mama! . . . I fell in the well!"

Stymie peers over the side, and sizes up the situation, "You fell in the well. Well, well, well. . . . How we gonna get him out?" With a little deliberation, they're certain they need a rope. Stymie grabs a handy length of rope four feet long and dangles it over the thirty-foot-deep well, suggesting, "Catch hold of this, Spud." "I can't reach it," quavers Sherwood in desperation. Without missing a beat, Stymie suggests, "Try jumpin' a little bit."

The two buddies take their time hauling Spud to the surface, and in retaliation, he says that he's going to tell Mama on Wheezer—so Wheezer and Stymie let go of the rope and send Sherwood back to his watery hole. After getting a promise that he won't snitch, Wheezer pulls Spud up once more. Rescued, Spud says smugly, "I am *too* gonna tell," and Wheezer calls after him, "Well, the dunking you got is worth the whipping I'll get!" Clearly, Wheezer takes a philosophical attitude toward survival in this situation.

The performances in "Dogs Is Dogs" are superb. As in "Pups Is Pups," Wheezer's attachment to his dog is be-guiling in its simplicity and sincerity; the opening moments with the two frolicking in bed are sheer delight, and Wheezer's tearful scenes at the dog pound much later are moving. Stymie is in peak form, and with Wheezer, the two are at their best as a team, working beautifully together with uncanny timing, warmth, and comic sensitivity. Their subtle, underplayed scenes couldn't be done any better.

Two fine character performers contribute to the short also. Billy Gilbert, in another loud, stiff role as the irate neighbor gives forth with a few paroxysms of rage amidst being plastered by the gang with his own eggs. He probably realized that to play Mr. Brown for laughs would have taken some of the confrontation edge away from the film. Yet adult viewers can detect tongue slightly in cheek at hearing his off-camera growl, "WHERE IS THAT DOG?" as he comes gunning for Pete. A lustier heavy one couldn't hope to find.

Then there's towering ex-policewoman Blanche Payson (six feet three), who is properly nasty, foul-mouthed, and provoking as the unfeeling stepmother, or as Stymie calls her once, "The Old Pelican." Both she and Sherwood Bailey keep the mother and her bratty son from becoming one-dimensional characters; they are harrowingly real, making their villainy particularly potent.

One special reason for the durability of "Dogs Is Dogs" is that the gang triumphs over such formidable adversaries. Another reason is that Wheezer's happy ending was a soft-pedaled symbol of triumph over the Depression that faced most moviegoers in 1931. Hal Roach never created a plastic utopia as many major studios did during this troubled era; yet he saw no need to fill his films with topical commentary, either. The Roach shorts of this period simply grew out of situations with which everyone could identify, honestly acknowledging the world of frustration outside the theater, but only to entertain, to show an audience how to laugh at it—then as now.

Hal Roach has said, simply, "We just wanted to make people happy. We'd just do things in those films that we personally thought would make 'em laugh. That's all."

That was plenty.

In an era of outstanding *Our Gang* comedies, charming, funny, poignant, and memorable, "Dogs Is Dogs" stands out as one of the best.

111 · READIN' AND WRITIN'

Two Reels · Produced by Robert F. McGowan for Hal Roach · Directed by Robert F. McGowan · Photographed by Art Lloyd · Edited by Richard Currier · Dialogue by H. M. Walker · Released on February 2, 1932, by M-G-M · Our Gang: Kendall "Breezy Brisbane" McComas, Matthew "Stymie" Beard, Bobby "Wheezer" Hutchins, Dorothy DeBorba, Sherwood Bailey, Donald Haines, Carlena "Marmalade" Beard, Pete the Pup, and Dinah the Mule · Miss June Crabtree, June Marlowe; The blacksmith, Otto Fries; The fruit vendor, Harry Bernard; Brisbane's mother, Lyle Tayo; Wheezer's mother, May Wallace

"Readin' and Writin'": Despite mother's protests, Breezy doesn't want to be president. He'd rather be a streetcar conductor because "Boy, do they pick up the nickels!" Lyle Tayo as Mom.

Summer vacation is over, and many of the kids are starting school for the first time. Brisbane's mother sends him off with a parting reminder to study hard so some day he can be President. "I don't wanna be President," he snaps, "I wanna be a streetcar conductor." On the way to school he stops in to see the village blacksmith, who also gives him a pitch about studying, recalling that as a boy he led his class in every subject. "I really wanted to be President," he explains. "And all you turned out to be was a punk blacksmith," says Brisbane with a smirk. The blacksmith warns that "fresh kids like you never amount to anything," and tells of a wise guy he knew who got expelled for playing all sorts of pranks on the teacher and unsuspecting kids. Breezy picks up the cue, hoping that he might get kicked out, too. After he finishes putting tacks on the seats, a foghorn in the wastebasket, gluing Miss Crabtree's books shut, coaching the younger kids with smart-aleck remarks for their new teacher ("H-i-i-i Crabby!"), and leading a mule into the class, Miss Crab-

tree gladly expels him, warning that he cannot come back unless he memorizes a sappy poem recited earlier by Sherwood—"junk" which Brisbane had said he wouldn't read for a million bucks. Free at last, he soon discovers that being out of school during the day is no fun; there aren't any kids around to play with, and he has nowhere to go. After half-hearted attempts at fishing and running a club meeting, he comes back to school and meekly apologizes to Miss Crabtree, begging her not to make him read the poem, especially in front of all his peers in class. She insists, and he recites the silly verse, tears streaming down his face—having learned his lesson for good.

The last of McGowan's schooldays cycle with Miss Crabtree, "Readin' and Writin' " shares with its predecessors a charming knack for combining comedy and sentiment with great success.

The beautifully composed opening scenes of the kids being sent to school are filmed in a lovely soft focus, in actual early-morning sunlight, showing off the woodsy rural community where the stories take place and evoking a rose-colored memory of childhood that may not have really existed, but *should* have. These scenes are filled with an irresistible nostalgia for a simpler time and place, when every mother told her son that he might grow up to be President, and nonschool hours could be spent relaxing in depth at a nearby fishing hole.

The schoolroom scenes bring back more of H. M. Walker's delightfully wheezy jokes. Before class begins, Miss Crabtree asks one young girl, "What is your father doing?" "Twenty years," the girl replies. Later she asks someone to tell what an escalator is, and another girl answers that it's a great big thing that lives in the swamp; they make suitcases out of them. The topper comes when the undaunted teacher tries to demonstrate an arithmetic problem by saying, "Now if a hen laid an egg here, and I laid two over there. . . ." An alert pupil interrupts her and laughs, "I don't think you can do it!"

Sniveling little Sherwood, the worst kind of apple-polisher, goes to the head of the class to read and act out the poem his mother wrote for the occasion: "High up grew a daffodil/I couldn't hardly reach her/Says I to me, I think I will/Pick it for my teacher. . . ." Miss Crabtree listens dutifully and congratulates Sherwood, although her enthusiasm is somewhat reserved.

When Breezy is kicked out of school (leaving with a triumphant "Oh boy!" and self-congratulatory gesture), the mood returns to the soft-focus atmosphere of a morning in the country . . . only now, Brisbane is all alone. He sits on the edge of a stream, as his conscience speaks to him: "Nobody to play with . . . the kids are all in school . . . you can't go home . . . learn that poem . . . learn that poem. . . ."

The passage of time is indicated by repeatedly cutting from classroom activities to Brisbane's listless wanderings. It would have been nice to stretch this segment a bit more, to heighten the impact of the young boy's realization that he's made the wrong decision. Even so, the sequence is quite effective, and by the time he returns to school, Brisbane's apology seems wholly sincere and well founded. The young actor's remarkable performance, reading the sissy daffodil poem while crying at the humiliation of being jeered by his classmates, makes the scene poignantly real. Yet the satisfaction in seeing a wise guy get his just deserts is tempered by our knowledge that Breezy isn't really a bad boy. In fact, because he's so spirited, he's rather a likable sort, and we find ourselves sharing his embarrassment at having to carry out this punishment (with a side glance at Miss Crabtree, smiling sympathetically at her errant pupil come home).

Times have changed since ''Readin' and Writin' '' was made; there are no jobs anymore for blacksmiths or streetcar conductors, or even for people who'd want to make films the way ''Readin' and Writin' '' was made. And many more of us than just Brisbane wouldn't want to be President. School, too, is certainly different in the 1970s than it was in the days of Our Gang's cozy little red schoolhouse, complete even to the curtains around its windows. Yet, after these many years, ''Readin' and Writin' '' retains all the heart, and humor, derived from situations and characterizations anyone can still recognize and identify with, and that made this picture one of the best *Our Gang* comedies of 1932.

The Secret Order of the Winking Eye is now in session.

''Readin' and Writin' '' was Kendall McComas's first *Our Gang* movie. He'd just graduated from Mickey Rooney's competing *Mickey McGuire* kiddie series. It almost worked out like a trade, since Shirley Jean Rickert had just left *Our Gang* to join the low-budget *Toonerville Trolley* troupe.

112 · FREE EATS

Two Reels · Produced by Robert F. McGowan for Hal Roach · Directed by Raymond McCarey · Photographed by Art Lloyd · Edited by Richard Currier · Dialogue by H. M. Walker · Released on February 13, 1932, by M-G-M · Our Gang: Matthew "Stymie" Beard, Bobby "Wheezer" Hutchins, Kendall "Breezy Brisbane" McComas, George "Spanky" McFarland, Donald Haines, Dorothy DeBorba, Sherwood "Spud" Bailey, and Pete the Pup · Head of the family of thieves, Billy Gilbert; His "wife," Elvira, Paul Fix; Mr. Moran, Del Henderson; The detective, Otto Fries; His assistant, Eddie Baker; Officer Flaherty, Harry Bernard; Mrs. Clark, Lillian Elliott; Her friend, May Wallace; Lawn party guests, Belle Hare, Lilyan Irene

A wealthy woman throws a lavish lawn party for poor children, giving a couple of sly crooks the opportunity to pick up some loot, using two midget cronies dressed as babies. Stymie senses something wrong when he hears one of the "infants" talking, but no one believes his story. As the afternoon wears on, the pint-sized pickpockets manage to snatch jewelry from every matron at the party, despite Stymie's repeated warnings that the babies are really "fidgets." When Wheezer and Dorothy learn for themselves that the babies are phony, the whole gang goes after the robbers as they try to open a wall safe. By now the distraught hostess has called the police to investigate her missing valuables, and after nabbing the two adult crooks, the cops catch the gang in the act of retrieving goods from the infant burglars. The chief detective suspects the gang of hanky-panky, refusing to be-

lieve that the babies were responsible. Stymie settles the matter, and clears the gang, by sticking a pin in the rear end of one "toddler," prompting the midget to growl, "Ouch! I'll knock your . . ." before catching himself and reverting to baby-talk. The jig is up, and the gang accepts congratulations.

"Free Eats" presents an ingenious story idea and surrounds it with typically enjoyable *Our Gang* touches.

The opening scene has a society matron complimenting her friend for sponsoring such a worthy party. "I enjoy doing it," she replies, "and then you know, my husband is running for office, and all these little angles help." So much for the kind generosity of rich people.

Then we move to a clearing in the park where the crooks are temporarily camping out, one of them dressed as a woman and smoking a cigar (it's shifty-eyed Paul

Incredibly, the New York State Censors Board ordered Hal Roach and M-G-M to cut "all views of two midgets, dressed as small children, at dial of safe" in "Free Eats." What shocked the censors about other films is no less ridiculous.

Fix, familiar to John Wayne fans as a veteran of more than twenty-five films with Wayne over forty years). Billy Gilbert is berating his crooked partner for bungling their last bank job, when he mistakenly turned on the alarm instead of a light switch. Just then a detective (Otto Fries) drives up in his roadster and asks them if *they've* seen any suspicious characters, falling completely for the bogus wife and especially for the phony infants ("Ga-ga, ga-ga"), who pickpocket his watch. "Couple of nice kids you've got here," he says genially. So much for police alertness.

Billy Gilbert has some funny moments doing elaborate and frantic reactions when he sees his "children" pocketing the watch under the cop's very nose. Gilbert eventually keeps the timepiece, enjoying its tiny alarm, but that same alarm goes off at the end of the film, identifying him to detective Fries, who naturally doesn't remember where he's seen Gilbert before.

In contrast with the detective, who falls for every duplicity, Stymie knows he's dealing with a "mob" from the outset. Worth noting is that it's not the white kids who disclose the ruse, it's Stymie. In fact, no one in the film wants to believe his outlandish story about the disguised "fidgets." "How can a baby talk?" challenges Mrs.

Clark. "Why, with his mouth," Stymie replies. But nobody listens till it's almost too late.

"Free Eats" marks an important first: the debut of George Robert Phillips McFarland—nicknamed "Spanky" by his mother because that's what she was always threatening him with to keep him out of mischief; "Spankee-spankee, mustn't touch," she'd warn.

The three-year-old youngster had been doing some modeling back home in Dallas, Texas, when his aunt mailed a photo to Hal Roach, who arranged for an immediate screen test. James Horne shot it, and actress Dorothy Granger remembers the day they ran it. Horne roamed around corralling everyone on the lot to view the test, urging, "You've *got* to see this." The critical audience of artists in the screening room was captivated with the footage—part of which, Spanky reports, was then used in the next picture, "Spanky."

On November 4, 1931, three months before the release of "Free Eats," Hal Roach signed Spanky to a five-year contract, with his first-year's salary calling for $75 and then $100 a week.

From his early films, Spanky recalls little more than the fact that he was barely able to walk (but then what do *you* remember about your life as a three-year-old?). Though he's barely able to articulate words in "Free Eats," tiny Spanky is featured in an extraneous and protracted scene in which Breezy asks him questions about going to the lawn party that afternoon. Somehow, the discussion drifts into a yarn Spanky tells about horses, airplanes, monkeys, swings, and rats. The raison d'être for this sequence is obvious: to stand still and focus attention on this remarkable, beguiling youngster, who is bursting with energy and imagination and, even better, is absolutely unconscious of the camera.

Apparently, the Hal Roach staff was so enchanted with their new discovery that they didn't mind grinding the story to a halt and letting him ramble for a few minutes. Art Lloyd trained a camera on this newest Gangster for one long uninterruped take, with no one even bothering to cut back to Breezy for his part of their "conversation." Spanky is decked out in the oversized cap and golfing togs that were his trademark for the next year. Surprisingly, he still has that outfit.

This was not a particularly auspicious debut for *Our Gang's* most celebrated player, but Spanky caught on fast, and within a month or two was stealing scenes from everybody in sight.

Later on in the film, there are more extraneous scenes with Spanky petting a monkey. Typically, no one in the gang had the slightest fear of any animal, and apparently Roach and McGowan had learned that the easiest way to win audience identification with an *Our Gang* character, particularly a new one, was simply to earmark a few throwaway scenes that allowed the youngster to frolic all alone with a pet of some kind.

113 · SPANKY

Two Reels · Produced by Robert F. McGowan for Hal Roach · Directed by Robert F. McGowan · Photographed by Art Lloyd · Edited by Richard Currier · Dialogue by H. M. Walker · Story by Hal E. Roach · Released on March 26, 1932, by M-G-M · Our Gang: George "Spanky" McFarland, Kendall "Breezy Brisbane" McComas, Matthew "Stymie" Beard, Dorthy DeBorba, Bobby "Wheezer" Hutchins, Sherwood "Spud" Bailey, Bobby Mallon, Douglas "Speck" Greer, Tommy Bond, and Pete the Pup · Spanky's father, Billy Gilbert

Armed and headed for the window; a posed still that doesn't equate with the action as filmed for "Spanky."

Breezy is supposed to appear as Simon Legree in the gang's production of *Uncle Tom's Cabin,* but his attention is divided between the show and keeping an eye on his baby brother Spanky who has been left in his care for the afternoon. The show is already a shambles; Spanky's horseplay backstage only makes matters worse. When Breezy finally gets the brat to stay in the house, away from the performance, Spanky finds other ways to make noise and get into trouble. His mischief reaches a peak when he inadvertently opens the secret panel where his cheapskate father stashes all his money. Spanky proceeds to take the cash and toss it out a second-story window. At this the *Uncle Tom* audience deserts the show for the excitement in the yard, where it's raining money. Spanky's father arrives in time to chase away the kids, and suddenly contrite, promises that from now on he's going to keep his money in a good strong bank—and spend some of it on his family.

After losing *Skippy* to Paramount and with M-G-M releasing another Jackie Cooper feature, *Sooky,* Hal Roach answered with "Spanky." It's a disjointed film, with interesting elements that have no real connection squashed together into one short. Except for interludes which spotlight Spanky, the story and gags are scene for scene right out of "Uncle Tom's Uncle," a much slicker *Our Gang* production made six years earlier. It seems almost as if Roach and McGowan had mapped out the 1931–32 release schedule, and had slated the season's sixth outing as a reworking of "Uncle Tom's Uncle," but then with the discovery of Spanky McFarland had had to alter situations to fit whatever footage they could get with this exceptional new Little Rascal. (Spanky confirmed recently that scenes from his screen test were actually inserted as a part of this short.)

The film opens as Spanky wakes up in bed and pursues his favorite pastime: killing bugs, first with his popgun and then with a hammer. Pete the Pup joins him in his adventures. Then Spanky's mother arrives and sets up his bath. These scenes have no particular aim or punch line. They merely allow this adorable youngster to fill the screen, laughing and playing to his heart's content. But after several minutes of this—in one of the great transitions of our time—the film leaves such reverie to introduce Spanky's mean ol' pop and get on with the "plot." In the kitchen during breakfast, Spanky is still chasing bugs around with a hammer. "Oh look at the big bug!" he exclaims, and his mother asks what he's doing under the sink. . . .

Spanky (a little put out): I'm bug huntin'.

Mother: Well, never mind those bugs. You just come here and finish your breakfast.

Then Mother peers wistfully off-scene and remarks, "Yes, and I could get rid of those pests—if your father would buy some disinfectant." Just then, the lazy lout (nicely played by Billy Gilbert) strolls into view. Sneering, he offers a stale excuse for his stinginess: "If the bugs can't live on what we live on, let 'em starve to death!"

Mother warns that if she ever finds out where he keeps the money his grandfather left him, she'll spend it all on the children. At this, Pop's expression turns from that of apathy to one of anger—no one's going to touch that money. For expository purposes, we see him cautiously taking a few dollars from his secret-paneled hiding place.

That's the last we see of Pop until the end of the film. The story now moves to the production of *Uncle Tom's Cabin.* The show goes on that afternoon in "the barn" (although geographically the short is never clear about the relationship between Breezy's house and the barn—a few steps seem to connect the two, judging from the way he and Spanky trot back and forth during the film, as if it were a spare room). A full house is on hand for the performance—and all rooting for a flop, too, so they'll have an excuse to do what they really came to do: toss garbage at the actors.

The gang attempts a sincere adaptation of the famous story, but despite elaborate scenery and costumes, very little goes smoothly. The young actors are repeatedly forced to holler instructions backstage in the middle of scenes (covering their mouths with the wrong hand each time), as when a phonograph record playing a Negro

Dorothy as Little Eva, Breezy as Simon Legree (he's cru-el), and Stymie as Uncle Tom in the roles Mary Kornman, Mickey Daniels, and Joe Cobb had in the original "Uncle Tom's Uncle."

spiritual being mouthed by black-faced kids on stage begins to skip, or when a sound-effect toy simulating Little Eva's cough breaks down in the middle of a speech.

Stymie, forced to play both Uncle Tom and Topsy, effects some curious changeovers. When he loses his cotton-white wig for the Tom role, Breezy paints one on his scalp, but Stymie forgets to change his headdress in the next scene, giving little Topsy a bald pate! (Incidentally, Stymie has vivid memories of these scenes today, more than forty years later.)

Spanky's mischief backstage, including dropping an egg on Stymie from the hayloft above, inspires some of the kids in the audience to do likewise, pelting most of the cast members with tomatoes, eggs, and other vegetables. This naturally lessens the dramatic impact of several scenes, as does a mishap in Little Eva's ascent to heaven, when the kids pulling the ropes on her bed have trouble getting organized.

As always, the gang's ingenuity in working out such effects is dazzling. A scene on the ice floes is particularly clever, and shown, in offstage shots, to have been accomplished quite easily, by moving cardboard boxes

back and forth. As elaborate as these preparations can get, they are never beyond the capabilities of a bunch of kids—remarkably inventive, yet real enough to maintain the film's credibility.

What *isn't* credible is the sudden rehabilitation of Spanky's father at the end of the film. After screaming at the kids to drop his money and get lost, and threatening Spanky with a shake of the fist, he tells the gang as they help him pick up the cash that he's going to spend some of the money on his wife and kids from now on. Of course, just as Pop utters his line of repentance, he gets pelted over the head with a heavy load of coins dumped by Spanky from the window above, so we'll know what to think of his sudden transformation! (His promise to put the money in a "good, strong bank" was probably a bit of Depression propaganda aimed at the adults in the audience.)

Then, for another throwaway punchline, we return to the *Uncle Tom* stage where Stymie is caught in Little Eva's rope-pull bed, as a goat runs back and forth in the hayloft pulling Stymie up and down. The scenes reworked from "Uncle Tom's Uncle," such as this last one, aren't done nearly as well.

In an effort to fuse all this with the two other unrelated plot devices—the secret money cache and Spanky's penchant for mischief—the filmmakers gave all three ideas short shrift. Still, though untidy and disjointed, "Spanky" manages to be an enjoyable film.

Incidentally, although he has a blocked memory on many of his *Our Gang* films, Spanky McFarland *does* remember making this one, especially the scenes where he was chasing bugs around with a hammer. "Well, it was a rubber hammer, but Don Sandstrom, who was the propman, was behind that door, and he had this bug on a wire, you know? And the director—it was a silent bit really, and they dubbed in the bangs later—and Bob McGowan, my first director, was in back of the camera saying, 'Hit it, Spanky! Hit it, Spanky!' Well, my father was prone to some pretty strong language, you know, and I had picked it up by osmosis, of course! Anyway, here I was, beating on this bug, and every time I would hit it, well, Don would move it on the wire, and I'd have to keep chasing it. So Bob kept saying, or Mr. McGowan, I should say, kept saying, 'Hit it, Spanky! Hit it, Spanky!' And finally, I just turned around and looked up to him and said, 'If Don'll hold the damn thing still, I *will!*' "

114 • CHOO-CHOO!

Two Reels • Produced by Robert F. McGowan for Hal Roach • Directed by Robert F. McGowan • Photographed by Art Lloyd • Edited by Richard Currier • Dialogue by H. M. Walker • Story by Hal E. Roach • Released on May 7, 1932, by M-G-M • Our Gang: George "Spanky" McFarland, Matthew "Stymie" Beard, Kendall "Breezy Brisbane" McComas, Bobby "Wheezer" Hutchins, Donald Haines, Sherwood "Spud" Bailey, Wally Albright, Georgie Billings, Dorothy DeBorba, Harold "Bouncy" Wertz, and Pete the Pup • Mr. Henderson, Del Henderson; Passenger, Bud Fine; Pullman conductors, Silas D. Wilcox, Harry Bernard; Secretary, Lyle Tayo; Officer, Eddie Baker; Extra on the train, Baldwin Cooke; Dorothy's mother, Belle Hare; Inebriated novelties salesman, Otto Fries; Voice-over for Otto Fries yelling as the bear licks his face, Oliver Hardy

During a stopover, some orphans sneak away from the train that's taking them to their new home, and convince the gang to take their places. The train is forced to leave

without the "missing" children, so when the gang is located wearing the orphans' uniforms, a prissy attendant from Travelers Aid is assigned the task of shepherding them to their destination. The kids manage to make the train ride a living hell for their guardian, and for all the other passengers as well. When they finally arrive at their station, the weary adult is told that he's got the wrong kids—and has to take them right back!

A spirited reworking of one of the Gang's earliest films, "A Pleasant Journey," "Choo-Choo!" represents the most concentrated quantity of mayhem ever produced by Hal Roach's wily Rascals.

Del Henderson, as the finicky clerk in charge of the kids, is a natural target for such tomfoolery; his manner in general, and his overt distaste for children in particular, are tantamount to a written invitation for the kids to run wild. From the beginning of the film to the final shot, Spanky delights in socking Henderson on the nose, later finding a new preoccupation—repeatedly undoing his bow tie.

The kids manage to remove his toupee, squirt him with ink from his own fountain pen, and generally embarrass him every moment of the journey. A young lady sitting nearby feels sorry for him and volunteers to mind Spanky, saying, "Here, let me take care of the sweet little thing." As soon as she gets the youngster back to her seat, he pops her on the nose, and she quickly returns him to Henderson, barking, "Here—take your brat and teach him some manners!"

Henderson's only retort to the passengers is the repeated disclaimer that these are not his children; his only comeback to the kids themselves is a fruity "You make me so angry!"

During the night, things go from bad to worse. Spanky bunks with Henderson, refusing to let him sleep by continually punching him and pulling away the blankets. Into this serene setting comes a drunken novelty salesman, who instead of quietly retiring to his upper berth decides to have some fun, distributing noisemakers to the gang, which they happily demonstrate, waking every passenger in the Pullman car. Just as this dies down, Stymie goes to the freight car to check up on his dog Pete; while untying the pooch he also lets a monkey go free, and in turn the monkey opens the latches to every other cage, loosing a menagerie into the sleeper section of the train, with hens, ponies, a calf, a bear, and the chimp himself scurrying through the various compartments. For a lively finale, the monkey sets off some of the salesman's firecrackers in the middle of the car!

Like the action itself, "Choo-Choo!" is a lively film, but not terribly funny—especially not to a grown-up viewer who may picture himself being victimized by such kiddie tyranny. The commotion in "Choo-Choo!" lacks the kind of comic embellishment to cross the line from being destructive to being funny.

The running gag of Spanky punching every adult in the nose isn't especially hilarious the first time around, and repeating the action twenty or thirty times doesn't enhance the humor. This device was used much better in "Wild Poses," where the punches were used as punctuation to a gag, and where a sharp sound effect made all the difference. One protracted sequence in "Choo-Choo!" with Spanky and Del Henderson in bed provides absolutely no variations on the same joke: again and again Spanky punches the grownup, who makes no attempt to punish the child but continually pulls the blanket back to

"Ooops!" says Wheezer, weapon in hand, as Spanky and Stymie look on, and Del Henderson (the one with the hairpiece askew) peers through a shower of ink for sympathy. Del probably wishes he could trade the mayhem of "Choo-Choo!" for the quiet days at Biograph when he was directing for D. W. Griffith.

its original position, for Spanky to undo and punch him once more.

Even the animals' escape is a rather ordinary sequence, barely touching the comic possibilities inherent in the idea. The forerunner to this segment in "The Big Town" used bizarre insects on the loose, and variations on sleeping passengers wakening to find the little visitors, for maximum impact.

"Choo-Choo!" is very much a formula picture; as such, it is surprising that more laughs weren't elicited from these tried-and-true situations.

Sidelight: Present-day viewers miss a special treat in "Choo-Choo!" Like all other sound *Our Gang* comedies, this one was originally introduced by the roaring M-G-M lion, fading in to a main title card, reading "Our Gang Comedies: Hal Roach presents His Rascals in 'Choo-Choo!' " Normally, the next title card would list all production credits, but this time a unique scene was inserted instead. Heralded by the superimposed slogan "With SPANKY," the newest Little Rascal gestured, said, "Hello, folks!" and laughed, leading into the title card with production credits. This device was repeated in the following *Our Gang* short, "The Pooch."

Since the series almost never accorded screen billing to anyone—character actors, guest stars, or members of the gang—this unusual credit indicates the kind of sensational audience reaction Spanky had won in only two gang outings.

Sadly, the attractive and imaginative main titles for most of the sound *Our Gang* films were obliterated when the films were reissued in the 1950s, first for theaters by Monogram Pictures and then for television by Interstate Television Corporation. Later distributors never bothered to restore the original openings, denying us the pleasure of seeing the films as they were first presented in the 1930s.

115 · THE POOCH

Two Reels · Produced by Robert F. McGowan for Hal Roach · Directed by Robert F. McGowan · Photographed by Art Lloyd · Edited by Richard Currier · Dialogue by H. M. Walker · Story by Hal E. Roach · Released on June 11, 1932, by M-G-M · Our Gang: Matthew "Stymie" Beard, George "Spanky" McFarland, Dorothy DeBorba, Kendall "Breezy Brisbane" McComas, Sherwood "Spud" Bailey, Harold "Bouncy" Wertz, Artye Folz, Dickie Jackson, Bobby "Wheezer" Hutchins, Pete the Pup, and Laughing Gravy (dog) · Dog-catcher, Bud Fine; Officer, Harry Bernard; Diner attendant, Baldwin Cooke; First housewife, Belle Hare; Second housewife, May Wallace; Co-worker at the pound, Dick Gilbert

Stymie and Spanky's devitalized financial condition is little deterrent to their appetites in this sidewalk diner scene with Baldwin Cooke from "The Pooch."

Stymie is in trouble with the gang for stealing a pie, but he wins their thanks and friendship by saving their dogs from capture by the dog-catcher. When the nasty adult hears about this, he retaliates by nabbing Stymie's beloved dog Pete, and snarling coldly, "If you don't have five dollars at the dog pound in a half hour, I'm gonna kill that pooch—understand?" Stymie prays for help from the Lord, and at that very moment, a five-dollar bill is blown from a woman's hand by a gust of wind, carrying it direct to Stymie. A cop goes to retrieve the money, but Stymie is not about to relinquish the bill. A chase ensues, leading to the dog pound, where the impatient dog-catcher—spoiling for revenge—has already put Pete into the gas oven. A co-worker tries to tell him that he can't gas that dog, but he is brushed aside. When Stymie and the gang arrive with the five dollars, the catcher sneers and says, "You're too late; he's dead by now." Stymie bursts into tears, but the coworker returns and says, "Don't you cry, little boy, your dog ain't dead." Then, to the catcher he explains, "I've been trying to tell you, there's no gas in that cylinder!" The catcher opens the oven, revealing a healthy Pete inside . . . ready to take off after this ogre

and mete out some well-deserved retribution.

Another fine comedy with elements of melodrama and heart-tug pathos, "The Pooch" scores in all departments, and is a vast improvement over its blueprint silent equivalent, "Love My Dog."

The opening segments deal with hungry Stymie's attempts to locate food, accompanied by toddling little Spanky and Pete the Pup. At one point Stymie looks at his devoted pet and envisions a long salami, but says reassuringly, "Don't worry, Petie, I ain't gonna eat you up." Stymie and Spanky place a lavish order at a sidewalk diner, but when questioned, they admit that they have no money. "How do you expect to eat?" asks the counter man. "We don't expect to," Stymie replies logically, "We just *want* to."

Stymie uses his wiles to get food elsewhere, supposedly begging for his dog, but winning over a stern old woman who opens her refrigerator to find some leftovers. "Boy, does that dog love cold potatoes and ham," he comments, adding, "He might nibble on that pie!" Who could deny such a cunning beggar?

The matronly benefactor asks if Stymie's dog might like an artichoke, wondering if the bull's-eye pup is a vegetarian. "Uh-uh," Stymie replies, "he's just like me; he's a Methodist."

Stymie recalls having to eat dozens of artichokes to film that scene, and to this day he "can't stand" the vegetable. As he says with a withering look in "The Pooch," after having peeled off all the artichoke leaves looking for the edible portion, "It might choke Artie, but it ain't gonna choke Stymie."

The scenes in "The Pooch" where Stymie bursts into tears are especially effective, since the gesture is so unexpected in this cheerful, self-assured character. He first cries when accused by the gang of stealing their dogs, when in fact he led them out of the dog-catcher's wagon; luckily, Dorothy saw the whole thing and comes to Stymie's defense. He is once again suffused with sobs in begging the dog-catcher not to take Pete away, but the hateful man seems to enjoy the idea of making Stymie unhappy. Finally, there is the shock of being told, by the same villain, that his dog is dead, only to have the healthy pooch emerge triumphantly, poised to take off after the catcher and administer some late-blooming justice.

These poignant moments are highlighted by Stymie's prayer to God where he says that Pete is the only friend he has in this world, and humbly asks for five dollars to save him. When at that very moment, the five-dollar bill blown from the hands of the woman down the street lands several feet in front of him, he exclaims happily, "Boy, that's what I call service!"

116 · HOOK AND LADDER

Two Reels · Produced by Hal Roach · Directed by Robert F. McGowan · Photographed by Hap Depew · Edited by Richard Currier · Dialogue by H. M. Walker · Story by Hal E. Roach and Robert F. McGowan · Released on August 27, 1932, by M-G-M · Our Gang: George "Spanky" McFarland, Dickie Moore, Matthew "Stymie" Beard, Kendall "Breezy Brisbane" McComas, Sherwood "Spud" Bailey, Dorothy DeBorba, Harold "Bouncy" Wertz, Buddy "Speck" MacDonald, Pete the Pup, and Dinah the Mule · Fireman, Gene Morgan; Fire hazard bit, Don Sandstrom

A newspaper story is headlined "Public Asked to Answer All Fire Alarms," citing a manpower shortage and the need for public involvement in fire problems. The gang immediately forms a squadron, converting their barn into an operating firehouse. Dickie Moore is the fire chief, abetted by Stymie, and aggravated by Spanky, who tags along and confounds everything with his mischievous tricks. Dickie advises his crew, "Remember men, we're volunteers, we don't get no pay." Little Spanky pipes up, "What's *that*?! No *pay*?! . . . How *come*?!" But Breezy smooths it over—he doesn't mind ("All I want to do is squirt water") and Stymie chimes in, "That's all right, bring on them fires!" Up on the roof, Breezy becomes the lookout, and when he spots a real fire engine heading out of the station to battle a fire, he sounds the alarm. With some predictable delays, the gang answers the call and piles into *their* fire engines, one of them an amazing contraption that wobbles from side to side as it trundles down the Los Angeles back streets. By the time the three-engine company arrives at the real fire station, the real fire engine is long gone. Now the question is, where's the fire? Fortunately, near the vacated fire station there's a warehouse conveniently burning down. Upstairs, the warehouse is filled with boxes labeled "Dynamite" and "Black Powder." But it doesn't matter, since Stymie can't read, and he tosses the boxes and cans out the window in hopes of saving them! The explosions attract some real firemen to the scene; suspicious at first, they are delighted when Dickie and Breezy tell them they've (somehow) doused a real fire, and promise that each of the kids will receive a reward for such fine work.

"Hook and Ladder" is at times a remarkably clever film, combining sparse but snappy dialogue with some of the more elaborate gimmickry and gadgetry devised on the Roach lot, often punctuated by the kind of superb Roach sound effects one all too frequently takes for granted. That it's a near meticulous reworking of a 1926 silent short, "The Fourth Alarm," explains why "Hook and Ladder" depends mostly on visual gags and has so much the look and feel of a silent comedy. Bob McGowan used to be a fireman, so he was bound to remake what was probably one of his pet stories.

Although the film is full to the brim with typical *Our Gang* machinery, the results are so realistic and effective that some of the fun is lost. While the premise of the *Our Gang* kids as firemen sounds foolproof, the logical resolution of the idea—having them really battle a fire—is not particularly funny. Laughs might have been replaced by thrills in an exciting fire sequence, but in this case the blaze is a rather tepid one, and the one attempt to show Stymie in danger of being burnt by a teasing flame is too

clumsily artificial to provide much excitement.

Most of the machine propulsion in "Hook and Ladder" is of the standard *Our Gang* variety: the "alarm" is sounded by exposing a cat to the company canine, who runs after it pulling a rope that rattles a string of tin cans. Similarly, the chief's car operates by a dog chasing a cat on a treadmill, and one of the hook-and-ladder wagons is driven by a mule following a carrot dangling in front of him. The water pump on one wagon seems to be an actual steam pump, however, and as always in this kind of instance one wonders just how the gang managed to acquire such a contraption. Even in this whimsical world, the credibility is strained.

Dickie wants the gang to act as professional as possible, so he orders everyone to go to bed and "snore—like real firemen" until the alarm sounds, at which point the kids snap to attention, don raincoats and fire hats, and slide down the greased pole to their waiting trucks. Dickie's

kid brother Spanky holds up the works, however, and Dick yells down to his comrades, "I can't get the assistant chief's pants on!"

Spanky is a center of attention throughout the film, with a running gag concerning his medicine. He thinks it's ". . . nasty." Dickie has an alarm clock hanging around Spanky's neck; every half hour it rings to signal the time to give him his dreaded medicine oil. Stymie asks why and Dickie replies, "Worms," prompting his pal to remark that he'd be a great guy to take fishing with them. At the end of the film, Spanky is sitting alone on the curb when the alarm rings. Resigned to his fate, Spanky opens the bottle of medicine oil himself, pours a teaspoonful, but then drinks the bottle dry and deposits the teaspoonful in the grass at his feet. When Dickie arrives and asks what happened to the medicine, Spanky growls, "Aw, I gave it to the worms!" for the film's fade-out punch line.

117 · FREE WHEELING

Two Reels · Produced by Robert F. McGowan for Hal Roach · Directed by Robert F. McGowan · Photographed by Art Lloyd · Edited by Richard Currier · Dialogue by H. M. Walker · Story by Hal E. Roach · Released on October 1, 1932, by M-G-M · Our Gang: Matthew "Stymie" Beard, Dickie Moore, Jacquie Lyn, George "Spanky" McFarland, Kendall "Breezy Brisbane" McComas, Dorothy DeBorba, Douglas Greer, Bobby Mallon, Dinah the Mule, and Elmer the Monkey · Dickie's father, Creighton Hale; Dickie's mother, Lillian Rich; The specialist, Wilfred Lucas; Nurse, Belle Hare; Man who gets socked while asleep by lamppost, Robert A. McGowan (Anthony Mack); Officer sent skyward, Jack Hill; Roadside workers, Ham Kinsey, Dick Gilbert, Harry Bernard

"Free Wheeling": pals Dickie and Stymie.

Rich kid Dickie has a stiff neck and wears a restricting brace for his affliction. His arrogant, overly protective mother has called in physician after physician, but they all hold the same opinion, one shared by Dickie's "Pop" as well: let the kid get out and run and jump and play. Meanwhile, on the other side of the tracks, the enterprising gang has assembled a rickety heap of junk that might pass for an auto, if you didn't look too closely. *They* call it a taxi. It is rigged with gimmicks from front to back,

and the horsepower is furnished from the rear by feisty Dinah the Mule. Stymie's called away from the biz by his mother, though, who sends him up to the "big house" with some laundry. Glad to visit his pal Dickie, Stymie overhears the doctor's advice that the lad get out of the house for some excitement. "If you had some money I think I could excite you," suggests Stymie. Soon they're set to board the taxi for a joyride, when Breezy carelessly leaves a bottle of rubbing alcohol within Dinah's reach. She drinks it down, goes berserk, breaks loose, and chases the big kids down the street. "Look! The mule ran away," cries Stymie. Dickie strains to see, asking, "Where?" Stymie gives his head a chain-wrenching twist and directs his vision "*down there,*" and in the process cures his stiff neck. Still, Dickie's impatient to go for a ride. Stymie never knows what he can't do, and when he hits on an idea, announces excitedly, "We're as good as gone now!" A delivery truck has parked in front of them momentarily, and Stymie hitches the two vehicles together with a rope. The truck then unknowingly tows the cab up and over the crest of a steep hill, where the rope breaks, and the cab begins coasting down the streets of a hilly Los Angeles suburb. As they pick up speed, but without any brakes, the careening adventure becomes one of avoiding whatever they might meet on the road, and the fun comes when they don't. Dickie inquires where they're going, and Stymie blurts out, "I don't know, brother, but we're on our way." Finally, after some hair-raising encounters, they steer into a large haystack, where Dickie's parents coincidentally catch up with them, and all is resolved happily.

Bob McGowan, *seated,* with probably a script in his hip pocket, directs Stymie and Dickie in three brief two-shots to be intercut with Breezy's dialogue to produce an exchange in "Free Wheeling." Breezy is facing them to deliver lines that cue their dialogue. In the film, the taxi is supposed to be parked at the curb, and Dickie and Stymie hop aboard after the conversation. Art Lloyd is peering through his camera preparing the shot (note the Barney used to muffle camera noise). It's curious that no one did anything about the boom mike's shadow cast across Dickie's coat; it appears on film in just the same way it does in this still. It's interesting that during the bright midday sunshine, strong arc lights (barely visible on each flank) were needed as fill light. Note the handful of people gathering up on the hill to watch.

A reworking of the Pathé short "One Wild Ride," "Free Wheeling" succeeds on every level and is among the finest Hal Roach comedies made. It's the kind of endearing, visually memorable film that if seen in childhood is imprinted on one's mind forever. An adult can relate the adventure to his own youth, for in viewing "Free Wheeling" we remember either doing what we see or wanting to have done something inventive and exciting just like it. The appeal is basic and timeless.

Clever visual gags, the flood of sound effects, and dialogue are all executed and pulled together with verve and finesse.

Movies and cars had grown and flourished together, and their happy early partnership is wonderfully illustrated in a film like this. Roach had access to an entire stable of crazy autos in various stages of progression toward the trash heap, and a man named Dale Schrum would provide them to the studio at a cost of $500 per day. He'd insist on driving them himself (if "driving" is quite the word), and there was always some unseen cubbyhole from which he could secretly operate each wreck. (Unfortunately, the budget-saving device of rear projection, or process screen work, flaws some of the climactic chase in "Free Wheeling," just as it would Laurel & Hardy's *County Hospital* that same year.)

Action is nicely complemented by personality spotlights throughout this short. "Free Wheeling" is probably Dickie Moore's best *Our Gang* comedy, and he has some bright gags in the early goings, switching castor oil and pancake syrup on his attractive nurse ("You little rascal," she scolds), and then wrestling her to the ground when she cautions him that he's not strong enough yet to rough it up with Stymie and the gang.

Asked recently if he was really riding in the runaway auto of "Free Wheeling," Dick Moore explained, "Yes! There was a runaway car, and it was steered with a steering wheel by the prop man in the back of the car, who could see through a little kind of tunnel; he was in control of the car, and the wheel we were holding was disengaged. (The whole car was totally rerigged.) I think they undercranked the camera, to get a feeling of great speed, because we weren't going that fast. It was grand, it was wonderful; there was a great haystack they built. The whole thing was on a wooden girder, which they'd pile on, and then it was a tunnel, and then they draped hay on one side and then on the other. I didn't know how they did it, but we had to go through it several times, and each time they had to redrape both sides. That was very enjoyable."

Was he scared? "No. I didn't like that neck brace at all; I didn't like the fact that my movement was encumbered. But no, I wasn't scared."

Dick Moore says today he was intrigued by the mechanical gimmicks in films like "Hook and Ladder," "Birthday Blues," and "Free Wheeling," but adds, surprisingly, "I took them very much for granted, became very blasé, seeing wonders like that at an early age. You could walk through the back lot, and here was this incredible city."

Stymie and Dick play off each other so warmly and so well in "Free Wheeling," it's nice to learn they still have fond recollections of each other. About Stymie, Dick recalls, "I liked him a great deal, he and his family. Personally I remember them best. His mother had us over, made ice cream in the back yard, and cooked dinner for us. Marvelous, lovely day we had; she had a big party one time at their home. I never knew any of the others socially."

The idea of Dickie visiting Stymie is a curious twist on the situation in "Free Wheeling."

Stymie is in good form throughout "Free Wheeling," whether serving as one-man radio station from inside the hood of the taxi or expressing sheer fright by wiggling his ears (a trick often used by Stan Laurel in Roach comedies, accomplished by attaching a thread to each ear with adhesive tape and having someone off-camera pull the threads).

The two toddlers of *Our Gang*, Spanky and Jacquie Lyn, win additional laughs with their completely carefree reaction to the runaway car: they're having a ball and aren't afraid of a thing! "Free Wheeling" marked British Jacquie Lyn's *Our Gang* debut, her charming accent adding yet another dimension to the gang's diversity.

The only negative aspect of "Free Wheeling" is the fact that some TV editors have seen fit to cut the film and remove "offending" racial material—material which is so warm and innocent as to make the accusation ludicrous. When Dickie and his pop agree that he ought to be on his feet, running around with Stymie and the gang, his snooty mother replies, "Stymie? That colored boy?" Yet it is Stymie who cures Dickie's stiff neck—when all the money of his wealthy parents could not—and thus it's Stymie who winds up the hero and wins the plaudits from Dickie's appreciative father at the short's conclusion.

Perhaps it's the fact that there is bluesy jazz music during scenes with Stymie and his "mammy" or the fact that his mother does laundry which bothers some modern-day censors. But there are no racial slurs here, only differences in life-styles which were perfectly common in 1932 and are far from insulting today.

Hal Roach says flatly, "We never had any objections to the *Our Gang* films at the studio, and we always reviewed exhibitor and public reaction carefully. But all the time that we made the *Our Gang*s, with all the colored kids, there was never any theater in the North or the South that ever objected to anything we did." What's more, Roach's films have stood the ultimate test of approval: the test of time.

118 · BIRTHDAY BLUES

Two Reels · Produced by Robert F. McGowan for Hal Roach · Directed by Robert F. McGowan · Photographed by Art Lloyd · Edited by Richard Currier · Released on November 12, 1932, by M-G-M · Our Gang: Dickie Moore, Matthew "Stymie" Beard, George "Spanky" McFarland, Kendall "Breezy Brisbane" McComas, Donald Haines, Jacquie Lyn, Georgie Billings, Carlena Beard, Bobbie "Cotton" Beard, Douglas Greer, Bobby Mallon, Dickie Jackson, Dorothy DeBorba, Marcia Mae Jones, Edith Fellows, and Pete the Pup · Lillian, the kids' mother, Lillian Rich; John, the inconsiderate father, Hooper Atchley; Delivery boy, Gordon Douglas; Proprietor, Harry Bernard; Part cut from the final release print: Officer, Charles McMurphy

Dickie and younger brother Spanky witness an unpleasant breakfast scene on Saturday morning. Their flint-hearted father has forgotten Mother's birthday, for the second year in a row; she's hurt, and to add insult to injury, he refuses to pay for a dress she has ordered C.O.D. Mom runs to her room, crying, and Dickie determines to get enough money to buy her a gift. He and Spanky find a beautiful dress (a "late 1922 model") in a second-hand store for $1.98, but they have no idea of how to raise such a gigantic sum. Stymie suggests that they do as his minister did at church:* bake a cake, put prizes

* Stymie's real-life father was and still is the minister of Los Angeles's Holiness Church.

inside it, and sell slices by advertising surprise gifts in every piece. The kids set out to bake a giant cake, making a shambles of the kitchen and ending up with a strange-looking confection, full of "prizes" like a mousetrap, suspenders, an old shoe, and a scrub-brush, which Spanky and Jacquie dumped into the batter when no one was looking. An irate customer who paid his 10¢ complains to Stymie and starts throwing cake; a melee ensues, just as Dickie's father comes home from work. He chases the kids away and gives Dickie a terrible spanking for what he's done. Then Mom arrives home and Dick explains why he did it, giving her the birthday present. Pop has a change of heart, and next morning goes to church with his family, as Mom proudly wears the old-fashioned dress her son worked so hard to buy . . . and a pair of wobbly shoes the storekeeper threw in for free.

Another of McGowan's sentimental stories from this period, "Birthday Blues" happily spends most of its time on solid gag material, leaving the maudlin moments of opening and closing scenes.

The key segment of the film is baking the cake. Dickie and Stymie try following directions, but they take everything literally. When the cookbook says "whip an egg," they assign Jacquie Lynn to whip an unsuspecting egg just as one would do a naughty pet. "Roll in flour" is a signal for Pete the Pup to gyrate on the floor amid a layer of the white stuff, while another instruction, "set on stove and stir," prompts Stymie to seat himself on the oven while mixing the batter beside him. He's got to stay there till he's "well done."

An indescribable sound effect, something like a tired foghorn, is used to represent the perpetually bulging cake that comes out of the oven like a volcano when all this handiwork is through. Stymie tries to ignore it, and frosts the gigantic cornerstone-looking dessert to serve his impatient customers inside. As he cuts the first slice, he finds some of the bonus gifts baked into the cake, including a hot-water bottle, and exclaims, "This *is* a surprise!"

The homemade-cake sequence has its origins in a nearly identical segment from "Ten Years Old." During this period, the depths of the Depression, in one economy-minded expedient, the Roach plant was reworking whole blocks of silent-film material intact. Charley Chase was doing it, Laurel & Hardy were doing it, but none so heavily (or successfully) as *Our Gang*. "Spanky" had its roots in "Uncle Tom's Uncle," "Choo-Choo!" in "A Pleasant Journey," "The Pooch" in "Love My Dog," "Hook and Ladder" in "The Fourth Alarm," "Birthday Blues" in "Ten Years Old," "Free Wheeling" in "One Wild Ride," and "A Lad an' a Lamp" in "Chicken Feed." That's seven comedies in a row representing sometimes literal remakes of Pathé shorts.

Contrasting the bright, funny cake-baking midsection of "Birthday Blues" is the downbeat nature of its framework sequences. When Pop callously dismisses the fact that it's his wife's birthday, she tells him, "It hurts," and he snaps, "You're just like a kid; next you'll be crying for Santa Claus." The mood here is sad and bitter, and Dickie goes to see his sobbing mother in her bedroom to tell her that *he's* going to give her a birthday present. (As in some other sequences of this kind involving adult actors, neither the dialogue nor the performances are much more than pedestrian, yet they hit just the right note for young viewers, letting them know instantly whether they should like or dislike each character, and serving to propel the kid-related action that consumes the better part of the short.)

At the end of the film, Dickie's father angrily takes the boy over his knee to give him a good whipping, not bothering to ask why he had so many kids in the house making this mess. Then Mother arrives and takes the boy aside to inquire why he would do such a thing. When Dickie says it was to earn money to buy a present, Pop is appropriately embarrassed, and in a triumphal moment of rekindled love, Mother says, "John!" and he murmurs, "Lillian!" Thus, in thirty seconds' time Father changes from an irascible, unpleasant grouch to a loving father and husband. Next morning, he tells his son, "Dick, my

Boyhood pals (and they really were) Dickie Moore and Stymie Beard, in a scene from "Birthday Blues."

boy, that was a great lesson you taught me yesterday— one I'll never forget."

Some viewers may find it hard to swallow the resolution of "Birthday Blues," with Dickie's sharp-tongued, hot-tempered father suddenly seeing the light in a moment of spoken love rivaled only by Stan Freberg's famous soap-opera spoof "John and Marsha." Yet isn't this swift and total contrition the way we'd like to see it happen in our own lives? Wishful thinking? Perhaps, but that's what films are all about.

Dickie Moore looks back today on the heavy sentiment of "Birthday Blues," and comments that making the film was "very affecting. I remember feeling tearful. I didn't analyze it, I don't know why, I didn't articulate it, but I felt it." Asked if he disliked the actor playing his mean father, Dick Moore explains, "No, he was a nice guy, I never thought that way. Instead of going against the situation, you go *with* the situation. But it helped me in terms of relating in a sympathetic way to the character I was playing."

Sometimes McGowan seems to be using the sentiment as counterpoint for gags, most often setting up punch phrases for plain-talking Spanky, as when he accompanies Dickie to find a suitable present for their mother, first suggesting cowboy boots and then a shotgun. "Aw, what would she do with a gun?" Dickie asks. The impudent Spanky fires back, "SHOOT PAPA!"

At theatrical or film-society revivals, this gag never fails to bring absolute screams of laughter. . . . It's no little irony that eleven years later, the actor playing "Papa," veteran B Western heavy Hooper Atchley, took his own life, using a gun to shoot himself in the head.

In a strange way, it points up one reason why "Birthday Blues" works so well. Nobody can ever count on what's going to happen *outside* the theater, but inside, up on that screen, no matter how bad it looks for Dickie or his mom—and sometimes it's pretty grim—things are going to work out fine in the end. It's a sure bet. Every time you see the picture.

"Birthday Blues" features two child actresses who achieved notable success in films during the 1930s and 1940s: Edith Fellows and Marcia Mae Jones. Why didn't these two capable actresses stay in the series any longer than for one or two films? Probably they were too old when they started. In any case, it was no easy task to gain admission into the celebrated gang. The supply far outstripped the demand.

The series was now ten years old, and it was well known around the country that Hal Roach made periodic changes and additions to the gang. The studio would receive close to a thousand pictures from hopeful parents every month, while hundreds more would try to crash the studio gates. Studio statistics showed that approximately 10 per cent of all these moppets would win studio interviews. Less than five per cent of *those* kids would get as far as Hal Roach's office. A screen test followed only for those most exceptional aspirants, and many more failed than passed this test. Each year perhaps four or five candidates would be given single picture "extra" contracts, but only one or two might have that special chemistry to become full-fledged Our Gangers.

Odds against joining *Our Gang,* and staying, were a million to one . . . but Spanky McFarland beat those odds. From thousands of photographs, Hal Roach singled out Spanky's, brought him to the studio from Dallas, Texas, and personally conducted the interview. Success here led to a screen test, which showed Spanky's talent and camera appeal. Next there was a probationary period (up to ninety days) to see if he could adapt to life on a sound stage, and whether he could get along with the rest of the *Our Gang* troupe. If a youngster was camera conscious, or unnerved by the sound-recording equipment and intense lights surrounding movie sets, he'd never make it.

Spanky obviated the probationary period. He completely disregarded filmmaking equipment and won instant acceptance from his peers. What's more, he was a "quick study." Adapting easily, he was the one in a million who really had what it takes.

From that point, success in *Our Gang* would depend on public appeal, and how long the lad's personality could remain untouched by audience adulation and gushing parents. Hal Roach's staff did everything possible to shield youngsters from these two hazards, trying to isolate the kids from publicity blurbs, theatrical screenings, finances, fan mail, and the scores of *Our Gang* enthusiasts who'd crowd around the studio's magic portals every day. If an *Our Gang* star ever discovered he was an *Our Gang* star, he might not be one much longer. Roach requested that no one around the lot show favoritism to any Our Ganger, and parents or guardians had to consent to "keep hands off" during working hours, which included periods for schooling, recreation, and filming.

Stymie Beard explains that parents were there on the lot but segregated from the production unit. "The only time we'd see the parents," he recalls warmly, "is on that rare occasion when one of us would act up, and Mr. McGowan couldn't handle it. He was usually pretty good at dealing with the situation; that's what made him such an amazing man with children. We all loved him. But kids are kids, you know how that is, and once in a while we'd get out of line and have to be chastised. Whenever that happened, he'd turn around and we'd hear him say, 'Bring the mother!' "

McGowan tried to keep the filming like a game, however, in which he was an active participant. He would let the kids work out bits of material, both dialogue and action, for themselves. They could interpret and play such sequences best of all, and the rough edges added to the believability and naturalness of the scenes. There was a script for "Birthday Blues," but it was for the benefit of the director and crew, not the kids.

Later, McGowan would coach Gus Meins and Gordon Douglas (who has a bit part in "Birthday Blues") in the same principles, telling them that a director's technical proficiency meant nothing if he didn't have the confidence and friendship of his young charges. They had to accept him, like the new recruits, as "one of the gang." In this way, he could let them do just what they seemed to be doing—having fun as if there were no camera watching them.

And fun can be contagious.

119 · A LAD AN' A LAMP

Two Reels · Produced by Robert F. McGowan for Hal Roach · Directed by Robert F. McGowan · Photographed by Art Lloyd · Edited by Richard Currier · Released on December 17, 1932, by M-G-M · Our Gang: Matthew "Stymie" Beard, George "Spanky" McFarland, Dickie Moore, Bobbie "Cotton" Beard, Bobby "Wheezer" Hutchins, Dickie Jackson, Dorothy DeBorba, Donald "Toughie" Haines, Georgie Billings, Pete the Pup, and Jiggs the Chimpanzee · Part of the afternoon vaudeville audience, Harry Bowen, James Mason, Jack Hill; Officers, Jack Hill, James C. Morton, Harry Bernard, Dick Gilbert; Construction worker, Dick, Dick Gilbert; Pedestrian, Efe Jackson; Introductory offscreen narration, Lillian Rich; Part cut from the final release print: Store proprietor (as in "Birthday Blues"), Harry Bernard

Wishing and hoping: the opening scene in "A Lad an' a Lamp."

After being read the story of Aladdin and his magic lamp, the gang sets out to find just such an item, abducting every lighting fixture they can lay their hands on. Finally they locate one that resembles the lamp in their storybook. Just as they rub its side, some construction workers nearby set off an explosion, leading the gang to believe that they've hit upon the genuine article. Convening on a sidewalk, they examine the lamp and Stymie wishes for a watermelon; a friendly fruit dealer down the block overhears them and playfully rolls a watermelon down the street. Their amazement is enhanced when a small-time vaudeville magician hears the kids talking and appears before them as the Genie of the lamp. All Spanky keeps wishing is that Stymie's kid brother Cotton should be turned into a monkey. Thanks to a playful chimp from the vaudeville show, this too seems to take place! The monkey wanders off and comes to rest at a sidewalk beanery where Spanky finds him and becomes the sole customer. But the chimp gets bored and takes off down the street, causing minor pandemonium and bringing cops from far and wide to trap him. Stymie stops one officer as he's about to shoot "Cotton," but just then the *real* Cotton emerges from behind the beanery counter, he and Spanky having filled their stomachs to bulging proportions while everyone else was busy.

To say the very least, "A Lad an' a Lamp" is a most unusual film. It combines a wistful kind of fantasy with funny gags, charm, and (alas) a heavy dose of racism. These elements are welded together in a lopsided manner that brings the film to an end, but not to a conclusion, perhaps explained by the fact that H. M. "Beanie" Walker had retired, leaving the unsung position of dialogue director and scenario editor vacant until Frank Butler took over. (For more on Butler, see the entry on "Seeing the World.")

The wonderful fantasy of kids truly believing in a magic lamp is explored at the beginning of the film as each Our Ganger rubs one of the would-be lamps and makes a wish ("I wish there was only two days in the week—Christmas and Saturday," "I wish I didn't have to take a bath every Saturday night," etc.). This feeling is amplified by the introduction of the magician, who is seen playing to a full house so bored by his act that they don't even applaud. Coming offstage, he tells a cohort, "People don't believe in magicians any more, outside of kids." Then, from his second-story window, he hears the gang being bullied by a tough kid who steals their watermelon and laughs at their tale of the lamp. They vow to put the Genie on his trail and chant, "Appear, Genie!" The magician, sensing a perfect cue, drops a smoke pellet and appears in a cloud of dust, playing his role for all it's worth and telling the toughie, "Be gone, villain!" before making his own exit.

Scene from "A Lad an' a Lamp": Spanky asks Jiggs for another pie, warning the chimp to keep his fingers out of this one. After a few Tarzan movies, Jiggs returned to *Our Gang* four years later in "Divot Diggers."

This is a wonderful sequence for kids, and for whimsical adults who still have something of a child inside them, for here is make-believe coming to life.

This mission accomplished, Spanky returns to his original thought, of turning Cotton into a monkey, explaining, "All he needs is a tail." Another smoke pellet, dropped by the mischievous chimp, sends Cotton scurrying so that when the smoke clears the monkey has taken his place. The kids are awed by this transformation; all Stymie can say is, "Ain't Mom gonna be surprised!" Dickie proposes that they sell him to a circus, but dumfounded Dorothy looks on and remarks, "That's funny." "Ain't funny to me, sister," says Stymie, "I gotta sleep with him."

It seems a shame that an amusing idea, skillfully executed, should have to be tainted by unpleasant overtones. If it had been any other member of Our Gang making the transformation, it would still be funny today, but the plain truth is that Cotton (and indirectly Stymie) is the butt of the joke and Dick and Spanky, at least, feel nothing for his dilemma, only pleased that they now have a pet monkey—and thinking of selling him, at that! This theme was reworked from a similarly awkward silent short,

"Chicken Feed," and emerged once again several years later in "Three Smart Boys."

The next, and longest, sequence in the film has Spanky and the monkey at the sidewalk diner, with Spanky rattling off various requests, from a glass of water to a hamburger, and the monkey eagerly obliging, with some slight gaffes such as sticking his fingers in a pie while carrying it over to his customer, at which Spanky complains, "Bring me another one, and keep your fingers out of it!" Spanky, in his cutest period, is shown in a succession of close-ups as he laughs at the chimp's antics, lifting the sequence out of the ordinary monkey-gag variety and giving it real charm.

The plot's loose ends are completely forgotten during this extended sequence, and then hurriedly the film tries to wrap things up, having the chimp run loose down the main street of town and attract a legion of cops who track him to the top of a corner streetlamp,* where he hinders their capture by throwing things down onto their heads. Just as Stymie restrains one policeman from using his gun, we cut back to the beanery, as the real Cotton and Spanky, both the same pint-size, waddle out to the street, their stomachs grossly inflated. They bounce against each other, sending Cotton back to a sitting position for the fade-out.

This final gag doesn't make much sense, but was presumably a way out for the writers. It also leaves a curious aftertaste because despite a quick fade-out, it is clear that Cotton is starting to cry as he stumbles back from Spanky's "bump." Another take where the two kids merely bumped together might have left the film with a fairly amusing finale, but again, the apparent viewpoint toward Cotton was that he was too inconsequential to provoke such sentiments, either on the part of the audience or from the Hal Roach staff. This insensitivity, plus other stereotype gags, really hurts even the funny material that comes along. When all Stymie can wish for is a watermelon (ouch), and Dickie tells him to wish for something big, Stymie responds without a moment's hesitation, "I wish I had a *big* watermelon."

---

* In front of the brownstone building easily recognizable as Laurel & Hardy's "home" in *Pack up Your Troubles*, filmed a few months earlier that year.

120 · FISH HOOKY

Two Reels · Produced by Hal Roach · Directed by Robert F. McGowan · Photographed by Art Lloyd · Edited by Richard Currier · Released on January 28, 1933, by M-G-M · Our Gang: Matthew "Stymie" Beard, Dickie Moore, Bobby "Wheezer" Hutchins, George "Spanky" McFarland, Bobbie "Cotton" Beard, Dickie Jackson, Donald Haines, Mildred Kornman, Georgie Billings, Dorothy DeBorba, and Pete the Pup · Our Gang Graduates: Mickey Daniels, Mary Kornman, Joe Cobb, and Allen "Farina" Hoskins; Amusement park barker, Baldwin Cooke

Dickie, Stymie, Wheezer, and Uh-huh would give anything to get out of going to school, especially when they see the older kids, Joe and Farina, setting out for a day of fishing along the creek. Joe offers to write excuse notes for them. "We used to pull that on Miss Crabtree,"

Farina explains. What the kids don't know is that their teacher, Miss Kornman, has arranged to take the whole class to the Seaside Amusement Park for the day, absolutely free. They find out too late to catch the special bus, but the new truant officer, Mickey Daniels, has stayed

Engaged in boyhood's prime occupation, playing hooky, or in this case, "Fish Hooky," are Cotton, Uh-huh, Wheezer, Stymie, Farina, Joe Cobb, Dickie Moore, and Spanky. Farina joined Our Gang in 1922; Spanky stayed through 1942.

behind to deal with the situation. Without revealing his identity, he tells the disappointed boys that playing hooky could land them in reform school, and he paints a grim picture of life behind bars. Then he offers to drive them to the beach; when they arrive, the kids notice his badge and make a run for it. After a deliberately lengthy chase he rounds them up and brings them to Miss Kornman, who "persuades" him to let them go this time if they promise never to play hooky again. They do and he does.

This lively, enjoyable short adds to a good story and vivid location filming the tantalizing bonus of return appearances by four veteran *Our Gang* members: Joe Cobb and Allen "Farina" Hoskins as the carefree older kids, Mary Kornman as the schoolteacher, and Mickey Daniels as the new truant officer. That this is purely a novelty is emphasized by the fact that none of them is particularly good.

As a child, winsome Mary Kornman had amazing poise and sophistication, which completely disappeared when she grew into a young lady. Her vivacity carried her through the Hal Roach *The Boy Friends* comedies of the early 1930s, but she seems a bit awkward as the schoolmarm in this short.

Mickey Daniels, who developed his own comic formula in *The Boy Friends* series, is equally out of place as the truant officer (especially if one has a clear memory of the kinds of pranks he *used* to pull in shorts like "Circus Fever"). Mickey was much better suited to overgrownjuvenile roles, which he continued to play for the rest of the decade. His repeated attempts to stifle laughter while threatening the kids in this short don't ring true.

Similarly, Joe Cobb's dialogue is poorly delivered in a flat and unconvincing tone of voice. Farina hasn't much to do, but he appears to be the most professional of the group; it isn't difficult to see how he survived in show business while the other kids drifted away from performing.

In fact, "Fish Hooky" is a watershed film for a great many reasons. Here in one short we see the original *Our Gang* kids; it's a nostalgic delight to see them again, but they're clearly past their prime and unable to recapture the spark they created as children. It's nearly the end of the line for Wheezer, too, still young but outgrowing his natural cuteness. On the other hand, "Fish Hooky" represents the prime period for current luminaries Dick and Stymie, and the forecast of things to come with Spanky, just an infant but already a center of attention.

Acting as excuse messenger for the scheming older guys, put-upon Spanky finds Miss Kornman and matter-of-factly announces, "Here's some phony notes from the gang."

The film's most memorable scene, which has more than its share of funny dialogue, is Mickey Daniels's description of reform school. As he paints a chilling picture of this institution, the camera captures close-ups of the kids' astonished reactions. Someone asks what it's like on Sunday, and Mickey replies that on Sunday the prisoners get a break. The camera picks up the kids' faces again, smiling in relief. "They feed 'em spinach instead of bread and water," Mickey explains, prompting more shocked reactions. What about Christmas? "Oh, they're swell to 'em on Christmas," says Mickey, evoking another round

Mickey Daniels and Mary Kornman rejoin Our Gang in this scene from "Fish Hooky."

of happy faces, as he continues, "Everybody gets a brand new sledgehammer." This time, the looks on their faces are devastating.

Later, as the kids try to elude the truant officer at The Seaside Pier, Baldy Cooke* as the barker invites them to try their luck at hitting the bell at the top of a pole. Stymie

* Baldwin Cooke, his wife Alice, and Stan Laurel had combined forces in 1916 to form the long-running vaudeville team known as The Stan Jefferson Trio. The three were reunited at Hal Roach Studios in the late 1920s and throughout the 1930s, where Baldy Cooke and his wife worked in hundreds of Roach comedies. Now in her late eighties, living in Hollywood, and speaking for her late husband, the still sprightly Alice Cooke recalls "Those many, wonderful, never-to-be forgotten years that Baldy and I had working on the Roach lot. It was truly one big and happy family, everyone knew each other, liked each other, and *all* we lived for in those days was fun. And Our Gang: such wonderful kids—liked by everyone on the lot, sometimes a little mischievous but never unruly. Baldy always loved working with them and with Bob McGowan, quite a wonderful man who idolized each kid and was always so good to them, treated them as if they were his own. Just a beautiful man."

turns him down, explaining, "Uhmm-uhmm, not me, brother, I'll be using a hammer soon enough!"

At times, "Fish Hooky" is graced by unusually workmanlike photography and lighting, creating more than a few arresting, almost stunning-looking scenes—that is, provided one is fortunate enough to be screening a 35mm print, or at least a pristine 16mm original. (It goes without saying that aesthetically, almost no film can "leap to life" from a TV screen.)

An important factor in the success of the short is the authentic locations used for filming, from the country roads and little red schoolhouse of the opening scenes to the beachfront amusement park later on.* There are some wonderful almost Cineramalike shots taken aboard the roller coaster, first from the passengers' point of view, then looking back at their reactions to the ride. Other sights and sounds are vividly captured, emphasizing the boys' chagrin at being left out of the fun. A climactic chase with Mickey running after Stymie is shot at silent speed as they careen over, around, and through the various structures at the park.

Fittingly enough, the film's punch line involves the oldest "kids," Mickey and Mary, and the youngest, Spanky. At their first reunion, outside the schoolhouse, Mickey tells Mary he's always been in love with her and asks her to marry him. At the end of the film, with the kids occupied elsewhere, the two grown-ups sneak onto the beach and sit behind a large umbrella. They can't see that Spanky is on the opposite side of the awning, trying to take a nap. Mickey asks Mary for a kiss, and she coyly refuses; he persists, and she holds her ground; he asks again, and finally Spanky barks, "For the love of Pete, kiss him so I can go to sleep!"

* In early 1972, talking long distance with Stymie Beard about this film, he explained how quite coincidentally his home at Synanon overlooked the enthralling amusement park location used in "Fish Hooky." "Sure," he said, "all that is right down the street, just within walking distance, from where we live now. They shot that in what used to be the old Santa Monica Pier. I can look right out my window here and see . . . well, that they're tearing it down now and putting up new construction."

121 · FORGOTTEN BABIES

Two Reels · Produced by Robert F. McGowan for Hal Roach · Directed by Robert F. McGowan · Photographed by Art Lloyd · Edited by Jack Ogilvie · Released on March 11, 1933, by M-G-M · Our Gang: George "Spanky" McFarland, Dickie Moore, Matthew "Stymie" Beard, Bobbie "Cotton" Beard, Tommy McFarland, Tommy Bond, Bobby "Wheezer" Hutchins, Dorothy DeBorba, Dickie Jackson, and Pete the Pup · Telephone operator, Ruth Hiatt; Officers, Harry Bernard, Dick Gilbert; Announcer for radio station NIX, Billy Gilbert; Dr. Nemo, serial character, Billy Gilbert; Nemo's "girl friend" in broadcast, Belle Hare; Phone company official, Belle Hare

The gang is fed up with having to mind their baby brothers and sisters every Saturday when they'd much rather be swimming, so they bamboozle Spanky into baby-sitting for the afternoon. The infants systematically wreck Spanky's house, and by the time the older brothers

return, the frustrated baby sitter has found the only solution to his problem: keeping the hyperactive kiddies in cages!

A meticulous exploitation of a single situation, "Forgotten Babies" is quite an engaging frolic, though one's

Opening gag of "Forgotten Babies," created by clever editing and reworked from "Cradle Robbers." In the foreground are Spanky's younger brother Tommy, *center,* and Stymie's younger brother Bobbie, *right.*

reaction is bound to depend on how cute one finds mischievous youngsters to be . . . and how fond one is of young Spanky, for whom this film is purely a vehicle. Apart from the opening fishing-pole gag sequence, a reprise from "Cradle Robbers," it's all fresh material created to spotlight Spanky.

"Forgotten Babies" offers a reverse twist along the lines of the equally delightful *Brats,* where Laurel & Hardy—who are really children to begin with—have the unwanted task of minding their own sons, who are literally no different than their fathers. The irony of baby sitter and baby behaving essentially alike in *Brats* is also the *Our Gang* contrivance here. Spanky isn't much older (or bigger) or any less childish than the infants *he's* supposed to be minding, but apparently believing that the position can make the "man," Spanky is determined to do a conscientious job—utilizing any means an awfully creative four-year-old can dream up.

What differentiates Spanky from the other toddlers is the gift of speech, whereas the only kid among his charges who knows how to talk is the one who constantly declares, "Remarkable!" (After a while Spanky gets fed up and complains, "Can't you say anything but 'remarkable'?" The boy answers with a determined "Yes!" "Well, for the love of Pete, say it!" says Spanky, and the smiling youngster replies, "Re*mar*kable!")

One tot persists in crawling up the stairs. Spanky can't make him stay put. Thinking over the problem, he spots the solution: "Ah, glue!" he beams, affixing the youngster's rear end to a pool of the sticky stuff on the floor at the foot of the stairs.

Hearing a commotion in the kitchen, Spanky runs in and watches a little girl topple from a tall chair in what must have been a painful fall. The suddenly scrupulous Spanky has no sympathy for her. "Well, it's good enough for you. That's what *you* get for being smart!"

Spanky's also blessed with the gift of gab, and his major attempt to entertain the babies is a long-winded and fully pantomimed story about Tarzan that flows from his fertile imagination. But before long, the kids grow restless and begin to run loose, pulling fish out of their bowl, using a vacuum cleaner (set in reverse) to spray flour around the kitchen, hopping on an upstairs bed until it collapses, knocking over lamps and furniture, breaking china and pottery, and in general making a shambles of the house.

Meanwhile, one child has left the phone off its hook, alongside a radio where a program entitled "The Thirteenth Murder" is just getting started. A telephone operator on the open line hears the radio actors struggling and a man threatening to kill his girl friend, so the call is traced and two cops are sent to the house. Hearing shots, they duck from the windows, but when they go inside they realize what has happened via the radio. At the same time, the gang returns from swimming, and together with the cops, they look for Spanky, who is standing proudly in the kitchen surveying his ultimate handiwork: gluing, strapping, and caging all the babies in one spot where they can't do any more mischief. And the still bright-eyed boy concludes, "Remarkable!"

"Forgotten Babies" amuses throughout, and thanks to Spanky is never once oppressively cute. It's also fun to hear a deliberately hammy Billy Gilbert as the voice of both announcer and featured actor on "The Thirteenth Hour" radio program ("Some know me as Nemo, but I think *you* know me by a different name . . ."). It's really Spanky, though, who commands all the attention, and his delivery of material is something to see. His is not so much a performance as a triumph of film editing, for it seems that every gesture, every reaction, and every line of dialogue were shot independently, after patient coaching from director McGowan—a notable exception being the Tarzan story, which is related pretty much spontaneously and in Spanky's own vernacular.

After this film's release, Hal Roach and Bob McGowan took an extensive European working vacation. Upon arriving in New York, McGowan was cornered by the press corps there, and it produced one of the few interviews we have with him.

In describing his intimate and informal methods for managing the gang, McGowan said he strived only to maintain the confidence and affection of his young troupe. As one picture was completed, previewed and released, the kids were dismissed from their capers, and McGowan, Roach, and the gag writers would go to work on the next epic. When the script was finished, McGowan would gather the gang about him and explain piecemeal segments of the story in their simplest terms. He'd assign "parts," and then let each kid pretty much work out the role for himself. McGowan had found that some of the gang's choicest material had been interpolated spontaneously by the kids, and for that reason, he told the reporter, improvisation was encouraged.

Though some of his 1933 *Our Gang* shorts were still on a par with any he'd ever directed, the strain of working with kids and fighting their parents for twelve years was taking its toll. Hal Roach recalls that McGowan was "an ill man" when he left the series after 1933, returning once two years later to do "Divot Diggers," and then again in the late 1940s to work with another Roach graduate, Bebe Daniels, in producing features for Hal Roach, including one called *Curley,* clearly an *Our Gang* derivative— though an unsuccessful one.

McGowan touched on some of the things gnawing at him in a discussion with one of the New York reporters. "I think it's much harder to direct children than adults," he explained. "It's not merely a question of their undeveloped mentality, but of getting their confidence and cooperation. If you don't have these, you might as well turn over the job to somebody else. There are a lot of problems in making children's comedies that don't crop up in other kinds of directorial work. Of course the kids tire quickly and you can't afford to keep them on the job if they show the least signs of fatigue. Then too, it's hard to get them to settle down to picture making as a serious business. It has to be play for them, but in your own mind you've got to remember it's a business. You want to preserve the carefree spontaneous spirit they start out with, but on the other hand you don't want to reshoot a scene a dozen times simply because the youngsters have been careless about details.

"Naturally dialogue has added to the problem of making the *Our Gang* comedies, although I think the comedies are better now than in the days of silent films. At first the transition was hard. You can't sit on the sidelines and call out, 'Jack, pick up that ball and throw it at Mary!' or 'Open the door quick and duck inside!' All you can do is to make each sequence as short as possible and train the child to remember his lines and actions."

122 · THE KID FROM BORNEO

Two Reels · Produced by Robert F. McGowan for Hal Roach · Directed by Robert F. McGowan · Photographed by Art Lloyd · Edited by Bert Jordan · Released on April 15, 1933, by M-G-M · Our Gang: George "Spanky" McFarland, Dickie Moore, Matthew "Stymie" Beard, Dorothy DeBorba, Tommy Bond, Bobby "Wheezer" Hutchins, Dickie Jackson, and Pete the Pup · The kids' dad, Otto Fries; Kids' mom, May Wallace; Sideshow manager, Harry Bernard; Worker, Dick Gilbert

Spanky's itinerant uncle, who has evidently just seen *King Kong,*[*] returns to his home town with a touring side-show novelty, "The Wild Man From Borneo." Mom loves her brother, but Pop's affections run the other direction, and he won't allow "the tramp" into his house. So Mom sends the kids down to the show to meet their uncle, whom they've never seen. Mistaking the attraction for the impresario, the gang, wide-eyed and foolhardy, tries making friends with the ferocious-looking "Uncle George," unaware they're talking instead to Bumbo, the wild man. Bumbo's temperament belies his vicious appearance, however; he has the mentality of a child and is completely docile, up to a point. The wild man has an enormous craving for candy and, when spotting sweets, he nearly goes into convulsions, grasping and growling,

"YUM-YUM! EAT 'EM UP! EAT 'EM UP!" So when Stymie starts munching on the candy he's brought along, it triggers a long frantic chase, whooping and hollering, back to Spanky's house, where the gang scampers about for their very lives!

"The Kid From Borneo" may not be the most endearing short in *Our Gang*'s golden legacy, but if clocked laughs and the sheer volume of rocking audience response are any measure, this film could well be *Our Gang*'s funniest ever. It's certainly a comedy classic and one that time has touched very little.

In fact, there are no polite little laughs in "The Kid From Borneo," a veritable gag blizzard from start to finish. Even the title is a gag, aping Roach alumnus Leo McCarey's concurrent feature, *The Kid From Spain,* much as *Our Gang*'s "The Awful Tooth" would later poke fun at McCarey's *The Awful Truth.*

_____

[*] Released within the same month as "The Kid From Borneo."

Time is nature's way of keeping everything from happening at once, but nearly everything *seems* to be happening that way in "The Kid From Borneo"—and all of it is pretty funny stuff.

The film is blessed with rich and fruity dialogue but is anchored in visual comedy, too, earning top marks for both. As filmed, the frenetic chase sequences were undercranked to speed up the action and, as always, are enhanced by some resoundingly funny sound effects and a collection of terse, jazzy background tunes. Little Spanky racing and stumbling through Culver City back yards, far behind everyone else, never fails to bring loud approval from audiences.

One sight gag that plays wildly funny involves Stymie suddenly coming face to face with Bumbo in the hallway at Spanky's house. A close-up shows him stunned and gasping in open-mouthed fright as he realizes who he's just walked into. The camera cuts from Bumbo bellowing, "YUM-YUM! EAT 'EM UP! EAT 'EM UP!" to a tight shot of Stymie's feet, which slowly turn inward in fright a full 180° before he has the presence of mind to dash away.

Earlier, when invited to come along and meet the kids' fierce-looking uncle, Stymie declines at first. "Huh-uhhh, brother. I don't want no wild mans nibbling on me!"

Spanky's kitchen confrontation with Bumbo is a comedy wonder. Spank is caught standing in the sink trying to pull down an errant shade, so the two "converse" more or less eyeball to eyeball. Retreating into his house, Spanky had announced no wild man was going to eat *him* up, but now, literally facing up to the situation, he puts it squarely to his huge adversary: "Are you gonna eat me up, Uncle George?" The responding growl is not encouraging, so Spanky warns, "I don't think I'll taste so good. Mom says I'm spoiled."

Spanky cautiously tries to climb down from the sink, "Well, I'll be seein' ya," but Bumbo moves the chair and resolutely growls some more, causing Spanky to launch into a monologue of small talk about the weather, technocracy, and "How's things down in Borneo?" While this is going on, Spank keeps reaching furtively for an iron behind his back, hoping to divert the momentarily tractable monster long enough to conk him on the head. But the scheme doesn't work. Instead, Spanky crashes headlong to the floor (punctuated by sound effects from a tom-tom) when one of his swipes with the iron misses.

More angry than hurt, he sits up and feels for his nose a moment, then, thinking fast, looks up at gigantic "Uncle George" and says, "There's a little snack in the icebox, if you want it." Bumbo eats everything as fast as Spanky can lug it out of the soon-empty refrigerator. "Do you like sardines?" Spank proffers. The answering growl sounds affirmative, so Spank hands them up, and Bumbo gobbles them down, metal container and all, before Spank can add needlessly, "Here's the opener." Bumbo just chews up that crunchy morsel as well.

After a few minutes of this nonsense, Spank's disbelief has him looking up and daring Bumbo with a jug of port wine: "I don't know what this is, but let's see ya drink it."

The dialogue, superbly delivered, is funny enough, but as often happens in *Our Gang* comedies, it's Spanky's pantomimic reactions and gestures that produce the funniest scenes.

"The Kid from Borneo" with wide-eyed Spanky, nonchalantly pacing around the sink in earnest apprehension. "Hello, Uncle George? . . . Well, I'll be seein' ya."

The chatty question Spanky poses about technocracy has always puzzled TV viewers too young to have seen the film when first issued theatrically. It's a dated reference to a theory of social order of the early 1930s whereby scientists and engineers would control and reorganize society in the coming technological age. Most thought it a little silly, and filmmakers had fun with the wacky idea, as in "The Kid From Borneo." Laurel & Hardy tossed off a technocracy gag in *Me and my Pal,* and W. C. Fields did the same in *The Pharmacist.* (Incredibly, all three films were released during the same week in April of 1933.) Legendary animator Ub Iwerks went further, building an entire M-G-M Flip the Frog cartoon around the concept, calling it *Techno-Cracked.*

Unfortunately, "The Kid From Borneo" has been regionally censored through the years, and some TV editors working to cut an expurgated print have wound up with leader, titles, and a few close-ups of Spanky. It's too bad, and hard to understand, since the whole film is so basically innocent.

By contrast, also during 1933, Shirley Temple made a slapdash *Baby Burlesks* comedy for Educational Pictures called "Kid'n' Africa," a purely tasteless thing that calls forth every stereotype whites have created about black Africans. Since she has recently served as United States Ambassador to Ghana, Shirley Temple Black would doubtless shudder in her diplomacy to see "Kid'n' Africa" today. "The Kid From Borneo" is mild by comparison, and on all levels infinitely superior as a film.

Production Sidelight: Considering the whopping expenditures made to produce television shows and motion pictures today, it's astounding to learn that a classic comedy like "The Kid From Borneo" was budgeted for a negative cost of only $21,500. Even the seconds-long commercials currently slotted in *Little Rascals* TV programming can run to multiples of that modest amount.

123 · MUSH AND MILK

Two Reels · Produced by Robert F. McGowan for Hal Roach · Directed by Robert F. McGowan · Photographed by Hap Depew · Edited by Louis McManus · Released on May 27, 1933, by M-G-M · Our Gang: Matthew "Stymie" Beard, Dickie Moore, George "Spanky" McFarland, Tommy Bond, Edith Fellows, Marcia Mae Jones, Dorothy DeBorba, Bobby "Wheezer" Hutchins, Dickie Jackson, Bill Farnum, Olga Therkow, and Pete the Pup · Cap, Gus Leonard; Mr. Brown, the banker, James Finlayson; Waiter, Rolfe Sedan

The kids at the Bleak Hill Boarding School have to endure shivery nights without heat, the rantings of an old lady who runs the prison-like home, and worst of all, mush every day for breakfast. Old Cap, who teaches school in a friendly, informal manner, promises the kids that when his long-awaited back pension comes through, they'll all get out of this place, and live in high style. One day during class the good news comes, and Cap treats the kids to new clothes, new toys, a day at an amusement park, and a fancy French dinner. But in the excitement, he has ordered a French dish called "*porrage*"—mush!

"Mush and Milk" is a delightful short relying on amusing vignettes rather than a strong story line to give it a special appeal. Indeed, the melodramatic possibilities of Cap's pension coming through are roundly ignored—unlike similar situations in "Fly My Kite" or "Helping Grandma," where true suspense and race-for-time episodes were cleverly contrived.

Bleak Hill's headmistress is the most frightening old crone ever recruited for an Our Gang comedy, repeating her role from the forerunner of "Mush and Milk," "Bring Home the Turkey." She's so mean she looks like the realization of an exaggerated Dickens villain, and deserves to be pestered by the flies we see crawling on her shawl. Brandishing a horsewhip, she barks at Dickie and Stymie, "Milk that cow, and if you spill one drop of it, I'll thrash you!" One fully believes she would. The milk is spilled, of course, after the boys use a vacuum cleaner to extract it from the stubborn cow's udders. Dick uses plaster of Paris in water as a substitute, and quietly passes along the message at breakfast, "Don't drink the milk, it's spoiled." But Spank innocently warns Cap's wife, who of course won't *let* them bypass the milk and insists they pour it on their mush, resulting in hardened-plaster breakfast food!

In school, Cap tries asking some geography questions, but is generally defeated by the kids' silly answers. (Asked to use the word "isthmus" in a sentence, Uh-huh declares, "Isthmus be my lucky day.") This lack of knowledge doesn't seem to bother Cap at all; he genially concludes, "Well, we'll pass that up." Instead, he calls for some entertainment: while Spanky holds his nose in disdain, two of the older children do a tap dance, then Spanky recites a jumbled version of "Mary Had a Little Lamb," Stymie supposedly plays Brahms's "Hungarian Dance No. 5" on his harmonica (gesturing furiously to a dubbed soundtrack), and best of all, Tommy Bond decides to sing.

Little Tommy steps to the front of the class, bows, and sings the torch song "Just Friends (Lovers no More)," shocking his classmates with the adult lyrics ("We loved, we laughed, we cried, and suddenly love died . . .") and scowling through the entire rendition. Impossible to capture on paper, this sequence is one of the most memorable

in all Our Gang films—not the least because Tommy really sings the number straight and quite well, all the way through.

During class, the telephone rings and Spanky goes to answer it. Who should be on the other end but James Finlayson, Laurel & Hardy's beloved, pop-eyed nemesis last seen with Our Gang in 1927's "Seeing the World." He begins, "Hello, who is this speaking?" and Spanky squints into the phone and replies, quite logically, "I don't know, I can't see ya!" Finlayson registers a take, but misses the play on words, trying a variant of the same line once again and meeting the same response. Then Finlayson wonders what number he has, and Spank quizzes back, "How many guesses?" Now exasperated, Finlayson asks with a turn, "What is this all about?" and Spanky responds with irritation in kind, "I don't know—*you* started it!" Luckily, Finlayson is finally connected with Cap to tell him that his pension has arrived—nearly four thousand dollars!

The climactic shots at an amusement park are stock footage (coincidentally also used in a Charley Chase short released the very next week, *Arabian Tights*), but the finale takes place inside an elegant restaurant, where Cap orders dinner from Rolfe Sedan, the screen's number-one French headwaiter, who tries to dissuade Cap from his blind choice, to no avail. When the dinner is revealed, Cap asks what he's been served. "Porrage," Sedan replies, "all the children have mush!" And so does the waiter—hurled in his face.

The jubilance of this final sequence is not as meaningful, or as moving, as similar finales in other Our Gang films because the conflict and struggle on the part of Cap and the kids have not been dramatically presented (the old hag notwithstanding). Somehow, the brevity of the establishing scenes in Bleak Hill, along with Cap's lighthearted attitude, give one the vague impression that things are going to turn out all right.

Obscure bit-player Gus Leonard was so ingratiating as Cap that he returned to Our Gang a few years later to enact a similar role in "The Lucky Corner." His little-recognized work at Roach dates back to Harold Lloyd's *Lonesome Luke* films in the teens.

No supporting player ever did more for Hal Roach comedies than Jimmie Finlayson, and his scenes in "Mush and Milk" are delights. The late George Marshall recalled fondly, "Jimmie? Oh, he was beautiful. He loved to chew up the scenery. He had a distinctive element which you could get by [with]. You couldn't do it today, of course. He was, you know, very broad." Stan Laurel once told John McCabe, "He could just lift that eyebrow, and I'd break up."

What "Mush and Milk" may lack in suspense or melodrama, it certainly has in charm and humor, thanks in large part to these two fine comedians, and it leaves a

On the set of "Mush and Milk," with Dorothy, Uh-huh, Tommy, Dickie, holding onto Bob McGowan, who is holding onto Spanky, Olga Therkow and Bill Farnum in the background, and Stymie and Wheezer, appearing in his last *Our Gang* comedy.

Spanky matches wits with Jimmie Finlayson over the phone in "Mush and Milk."

fond and memorable impression . . . as well as a vicarious dislike for mush.

Completing the 1932–33 season, this film also marked Dickie Moore's last appearance with *Our Gang*. He'd been free-lancing quite successfully and was engaged by Roach at the start of the season to—in Dick Moore's words—"hypo the gang a bit, because there'd been a big turnover." He hypoed *Our Gang* considerably, and it's a shame his contract wasn't renewed.

124 · BEDTIME WORRIES

Two Reels · Produced by Robert F. McGowan for Hal Roach · Directed by Robert F. McGowan · Photographed by Hap Depew · Edited by William Terhune · Released on September 9, 1933, by M-G-M · Our Gang: George "Spanky" McFarland, Matthew "Stymie" Beard, Tommy Bond, Jerry Tucker, Georgie Billings, and Pete the Pup · Gay, Spanky's mother, Gay Seabrook; Emerson, Spanky's father, Emerson Treacy; The burglar, Harry Bernard; Officer, Lee Phelps; Radio voice, Billy Bletcher; Stunt double for Gay Seabrook, David Sharpe

A peaceful domestic setting at the Treacy household is disrupted when Spanky sleeps alone for the first time and matches wits with a burglar who gains entrance through his bedroom. Identifying himself as Santa Claus, the late-evening masked visitor is set to make off with all the silverware until the gang happens along and the commotion rouses Spanky's father. Wrestling with the housebreaker, Pop's doing fine until Spanky flings a vase that mistakenly knocks him cold for a few seconds. The neighborhood policeman arrives just in time, though, and as his father comes to, holding his head, Spanky inquires,

"What's the matter, Pop, can't you take it no more?" Then as the cop escorts the kindly burglar to the door, Spanky asks, "Where ya goin', Santy Claus?" "I guess I'm going to jail, son." To which Spanky remarks with a reassuring nod, "I'll come up and see you sometime."

One of Hal Roach's finest examples of situation comedy, on a par with even the Charley Chase-Leo McCarey efforts in the 1920s, "Bedtime Worries" traces an evening at home with a very young Spanky and his parents, who are played nicely by the clever vaudeville and radio team of Emerson Treacy and dizzy but lovable Gay Seabrook,

"Bedtime Worries": Spanky and Santa Claus, making one of his rare movie appearances.

Spanky gets his father's newspaper, slippers, and pipe, and when Pop bursts through the door, he's bubbling with news of his promotion to head shipping clerk down at work. He flings his hat and starts dancing up and down with Gay in jubilation. Spank runs for cover behind the drapes, remarking, "Gee, Pop's gone coo-coo!" An insert of the letter advising Pop of his new responsibilities is signed by "J. W. Burns, manager." It's an inside joke, since J. W. Burns was the long-time manager of the Roach studio's transportation department.

A running gag has inquisitive Spanky trying to figure out what his father does down at the office. When Emerson tells "The Old Timer" he's going to be in charge of shipping clerks, Spanky asks with a frown, "Where you gonna ship 'em, Pop?" "Ship who?" Emerson retorts. "The clerks," answers Spanky. Emerson laughs, "I'm not gonna ship any clerks." Spanky counters, "Well, if you gotta ship clerks, you gotta ship 'em someplace, don't you?"

At this, Pop's impatience to wash up for dinner prompts him to relinquish his part in this discussion to Gay. Mixed-up Mom explains it every which way but the right one, and a frustrated Spanky wonders why Mom can't make up her mind. They both conclude Spanky ought to try getting the answer from his father once more.

In the bathroom, Emerson starts the ball rolling again. "They don't ship clerks," he says. Spanky supposes, "Well, if they did, where would they ship 'em?" Emerson suggests they ought to ship some of those guys in the office to Siberia, "the dumb klucks." Spanky thought they were talking about clerks. "I meant clerks," Emerson exclaims, "but most of 'em are klucks!" "Are you the boss, Pop?" "Yes, sir!" Emerson confirms with beaming pride. Then looking up from the wash bowl, Spanky reasons, "Oh, then you're the Head Kluck, huh?"

Sleeping alone for the first time is a traumatic experience many kids remember. Spanky's "ascaird" of "the

who's sort of a road show version of Gracie Allen. It turns into quite an evening, too, with Spank's father coming home to announce his promotion to shipping clerk manager, Spank's scatterbrained mother trying to explain what "the head kluck" does, followed by a shambles of a dinner, and then Spanky's first night sleeping alone, all capped off by the burglar episode. Spanky understands none of it, but with questions that make perfect sense to any five-year-old, he persists in seriously trying to make sense of it *all*, to the growing annoyance of his beleaguered father.

Well written and well played, the beauty of "Bedtime Worries" is that its gentle domestic portrayal is at the same time as credible and recognizable as it is incisive and hilarious. The situational gags pour forth with unerring accuracy, and except for topical but unstressed tie-ins to a Mae West tag line and Roosevelt's New Deal, the comedy is as fresh and undated as ever.

Films like "Bedtime Worries," and its spin-off "Wild Poses," presage the very staple of commercial television some decades later—the family situation comedy, where the central core of truth depicted in the home setting makes it easy for an audience to identify with the characters, the story, and the jokes. "Bedtime Worries," though, doesn't require a canned laughter track to prove how funny it is, and carries more warmth and comic appeal than any TV "sitcom" could ever boast.

Some bright moments in "Bedtime Worries" include an early scene with Spanky listening wide-eyed to a radio drama in the living room. His mother, preparing dinner, asks Spanky to "dial some nice peppy music 'cause Daddy'll be home in a few minutes." "Okey dokey," he says. Then, just as in Laurel & Hardy's *Busy Bodies,* which was released within the same month, they proceed to tune in one of the stock Hal Roach background music themes—what else?

Spanky with Gay Seabrook and Emerson Treacy in a gag still from "Bedtime Worries."

bogey man,'' as most of us were! His father wants to make a man of him, but Mom's more frightened than Spanky is. She reassures Spank that his guardian angel is right behind him. When they leave the room, he turns to his shadow and warns, ''Better stick around, Guardie, I might need ya!''

Calling out for his parents in the dark, Spanky says he wants a drink of water. Begrudgingly, Emerson drags himself out of bed and obliges with a tall glass of water. Spanky takes but a sip, and Pop complains, ''I thought you were thirsty.'' ''Nope,'' replies Spanky, ''I just wanted to wet my whistle.''

As skillfully directed and convincing as these scenes are, one minor technical slip momentarily tarnishes the authenticity. Although no one should notice these things, as the harried parents pass between bedrooms they flip off the lights, and one can't help but hear the heavy thud of the electrician throwing the master switch that turns off the entire battery of stage lights.

''Bedtime Worries'' was the first entry of the 1933–34 season. As usual there had been some turnover since shooting concluded the previous spring. In presenting a new face, ''Bedtime Worries'' had swept aside ''aging'' *Our Gang* stalwarts Dorothy DeBorba and Wheezer Hutchins, and Dickie Moore had left to resume his prolific career in features. Wally Albright and Scotty Beckett would soon be recruited to pick up the slack, but in the meantime, Spanky McFarland pretty much carried the series. This created a problem, though, since during the year Spanky was often unavailable for shooting. Hal Roach was very profitably loaning him out for feature work in things like *Miss Fane's Baby Is Stolen* with Baby LeRoy, *Kentucky Kernels* with Wheeler and Woolsey, and *O'Shaughnessy's Boy* with Jackie Cooper and Wallace Beery. As a result only six *Our Gang* comedies were produced this season instead of the usual twelve.

125 · WILD POSES

Two Reels · Produced by Robert F. McGowan for Hal Roach · Directed by Robert F. McGowan · Photographed by Francis Corby · Edited by William Terhune · Released on October 28, 1933, by M-G-M · Our Gang: George ''Spanky'' McFarland, Matthew ''Stymie'' Beard, Tommy Bond, Jerry Tucker, and Georgie ''Darby'' Billings · Otto Phocus, the portrait photographer, Franklin Pangborn; Gay, Spanky's mother, Gay Seabrook; Emerson, Spanky's father, Emerson Treacy; ''Children,'' Stan Laurel, Oliver Hardy; Studio portrait used, Hal Roach; Part cut from the final release print: Role unknown, George Stevens, Jr.

Accosting the neighborhood with his sales rigmarole, a door-to-door solicitor convinces the Treacys that they should have their child's picture taken by portrait photographer Otto Phocus. But Spanky is apprehensive about the project, especially when he hears Phocus discussing one picture session when ''I had to shoot that boy nine times,'' and some retouching work where ''I cut an inch off a boy's nose.'' Meanwhile, some other kids roaming around the studio expose Phocus's raw negatives to light and break his lens. This, plus Spanky's belligerence, makes the session a catastrophe. Spanky's most frequent response to the hapless photographer's pleas for cooperation is a crackling punch on the nose. Finally, as a diversion Phocus has Spanky's pop pretend to take his picture with one camera while Phocus secretly does the actual work from another. Through his bird-brained wife's interference, Pop gets tangled up in the camera, sending Spanky into gales of laughter. Phocus takes his shots, convinced he has a set of masterpieces. Once in the darkroom, however, he sees that nothing has turned out, because of the boys' earlier tampering. The provoked family can't stand any more, and turns to leave. ''Oh please,'' begs the sobbing photographer, ''please give me just one more bust!'' Prepared to oblige for once, Spanky walks back over to deliver a final sock on the snoot.

A beautiful essay in frustration, with its story roots in Harry Langdon's *Smile Please,* and Charley Chase's *The Family Group,* ''Wild Poses'' eclipses both, and emerges as an entirely enjoyable short, one that has many unusual things going for it.

First, it throws the figurative spotlight on a delightful comedian, Franklin Pangborn, as the photographer—a rare showcase for an adult performer in this series. Second, it recasts Emerson Treacy and Gay Seabrook as Spanky's parents after their initial appearance in ''Bedtime Worries.'' Third, it features Laurel & Hardy in a brief gag appearance.

Pangborn's pussy-cat face and pansy screen personality had already taken hold with most movie audiences, through frequent appearances in short subjects and feature films, with greater glory yet to come in the films of Preston Sturges and W. C. Fields in the 1940s (he's brilliant as the persevering J. Pinkerton Snoopington in *The Bank Dick*). Wearing a ridiculous smock and beret, the pompous mannerly Pangborn milks his scenes in ''Wild Poses'' for everything they're worth, and finds a worthy opponent in uncooperative Spanky. When he demonstrates how he wants the grouchy youngster to smile for his photo, Pangborn contorts his face into a prissy, cherubic pose, and a frowning Spanky calls out gruffly, ''Hey, Pop, do you see what I see?''

As for Treacy and Seabrook, their personalities seemed to blend quite nicely with Spanky's. This was obviously part of a scheme to make them running characters in the *Our Gang* comedies. Curiously, ''Wild Poses'' was their last appearance. Perhaps it had something to do with Bob McGowan leaving the series after this film and Gus Meins taking over. Whatever the reason, their characterizations counterpoint each other particularly well.

Spanky and his pop have a basic affinity that overcomes minor squabbles and, usually, Spanky's unbelieving looks sympathize with his poor father in moaning over his wife's imbecility. When Pangborn inadvertently squirts Treacy with water during a sitting, Mom explains why to an inquiring Spanky: "Don't be dumb, dear. That's the way they take water-colored pictures." Spanky stares up at her and shakes his head in wonderment at her brain power.

One aspect of the plot that is particularly well handled is Spanky's fear of the portrait camera, which he thinks looks like a cannon. Having heard the photographer speak of "shooting" one boy nine times, and "retouching," which Stymie explains as touching and then touching again, his nervousness is quite understandable. There is then a marvelous sequence of Pangborn rolling the massive camera along the floor toward his "victim." The picture cuts from a first-person shot of Spanky seeing the ominous black monster coming nearer and nearer, to the camera's eye view dollying in toward the frightened boy. In a short that takes an adult's eye-view for most of the proceedings, this is a delightful bit of youthful empathy.

Laurel & Hardy's gag appearance is of course a highlight. Once in discussing with Mr. Roach the casual walk-ons he and his stars often made in each other's films, the subject naturally got around to "Wild Poses." The Laurel & Hardy cameo, it turns out, was Roach's idea. He simply asked if they'd help him follow through on a gag idea he had, and they were happy to do it.

Having played their own children a few years earlier in *Brats,* Laurel & Hardy were well suited for this fleeting sequence involving two babies dressed in nightgowns and bonnets shown fighting over a milk bottle as the photo salesman comes calling. Indeed, the giant chair and wall used in the scene were remnants from the massive set and props constructed for *Brats.*

In a single, medium-long shot lasting some twenty seconds, we see Laurel characteristically grin into the camera while scratching his head, and Hardy, too, looks into the lens as he waves with his pudgy fingers, both as if to say, "Look, it's us!" The Boys' appearance on screen is heralded by incidental music scoring (which incorporates "The Ku-Ku Song"*) out of their recently released feature, *The Devil's Brother.*

Everyone was satisfied with the results, Roach recalls, and McGowan left the sequence in. What prompted the idea? "Well, after all, ours was a comedy studio," Hal Roach explains, "and we always did those walk-ons just for fun."

One more inside joke—just as in *Brats* where The Boys use a gag photo of Jean Harlow, in "Wild Poses" the portrait hanging on the studio wall over Pangborn's right shoulder in the early scenes is a still photo of Hal Roach.

Curiously, as pointed up in Stan Laurel's 1963 letter quoted in the notes for "Seeing The World," Laurel did not recall working in any *Our Gang* film. Hal Roach has said that there was never any rivalry among the units around the lot, and that Laurel, like Charley Chase, would frequently pass on gag ideas to Bob McGowan for use with the gang. Perhaps the brief time spent shooting the vignette during a most prolific and troubled period in Laurel's career contributed to the vagaries of his memory

* For the record, since Stan Laurel was so insistent on it, the Laurel & Hardy theme song was originally called "The Dance of the Cuckoos" and was always so designated by Laurel & Hardy themselves.

Closing scene of "Wild Poses": Between withering looks, dithery photographer Otto Phocus (Franklin Pangborn) pleads for "just one more bust." Spank will be glad to oblige, without punch line, as Gay Seabrook and Emerson Treacy look on and down.

in this instance. Aside from the cross-fertilization of gag ideas, we know from the kids themselves that Laurel & Hardy, like the other Roach stars, would visit the gang during down time on the sets. The question naturally arises, what did Stan Laurel think of *Our Gang?* He had ample opportunity to appraise their product, since he often viewed their rushes each day as well as his own. Stan's biographer, John McCabe, says, "Stan thought *Our Gang* was 'cute'—his word, and a word he meant. He was not a man to use a cute word like 'cute' *unless* he meant it. He thought Spanky was 'cute,' Darla was 'cute,' and said so, warmly. He enjoyed kids very much."

Sidelight: One of Hollywood's greatest directors, George Stevens, had worked for Hal Roach in the 1920s and early 1930s as a staff director and photographer. With a whole host of other Roach alumni, he was currently engaged at RKO on a series that copied Roach's teen-aged version of *Our Gang, The Boy Friends.* It wouldn't be long before Stevens would graduate to features, with Hal Roach loaning him Spanky McFarland for one of his earliest works, *Kentucky Kernels.* A September 5, 1933, press release carried this news of Stevens's son, later the director of the American Film Institute: "Georgie Stevens, Jr., 16 months old, makes his screen debut in 'Wild Poses,' an *Our Gang* comedy. The youngster, according to director Bob McGowan, gives promise of becoming a real 'Gangster' in a few years, and is being groomed for stellar honors." Young Stevens's scenes, however, were inexplicably cut from the finished product and do not appear in "Wild Poses." When we disclosed this information in a letter to George Stevens, Jr., at the AFI in 1971, he wrote back, "I can't tell you how distressed I am to know that someone has finally unearthed documentation of my abbreviated career as an actor. I can only plead, since this took place in 1933, one year after my birth, that I was well below the age of consent at the time."

126 · HI'-NEIGHBOR!

Two Reels · Produced by Hal Roach · Directed by Gus Meins · Photographed by Art Lloyd · Edited by Louis McManus · Released on March 3, 1934, by M-G-M· Our Gang: George "Spanky" McFarland, Wally Albright, Matthew "Stymie" Beard, Scotty Beckett, Jerry Tucker, Jacqueline "Jane" Taylor, Marvin "Bubbles" Trin, Donald Proffitt, Tommy Bupp, Tony Kales, Jean Aulbach, Bobbie "Cotton" Beard, Tommy Bond, and Pete the Pup · Moving men, Stanley (Tiny) Sandford, Jack (Tiny) Ward; Window washer, Charlie Hall; Man watering lawn, Harry Bernard; Pedestrian, Ernie Alexander

When a moving van drives by carrying a shiny new toy fire engine, the gang follows the truck to its destination and greets their new neighbor, a rich kid who couldn't be less interested in them. They try to bribe him for a ride in the fire engine, but nothing works. When Jane comes along, however, she bypasses Wally to admire the beautiful car and is immediately invited for a ride. To show up the snooty new neighbor, Wally boasts that the gang's got a fire engine, too . . . one that will hold *everyone*. To make good on this claim, the gang sets to work building such a vehicle, appropriating wheels, lumber, a hose, a ladder, and other essentials from the neighborhood at large. The finished product is unwieldy but impressive—to everyone but the insufferable rich kid, who calls it "a piece of junk" and discourages Jane from riding on it. Instead, he challenges the gang to race down a steep hill. Before long, the gang's brakes fail, and the rich kid gets nervous with them following so close behind. He crashes against the sidewalk, sending his fair damsel tumbling onto the lawn, while the gang careens down the hill, along a sidewalk, and into a thick hedge (which removes their clothing as they pass through) for a triumphant victory.

Sure-fire *Our Gang* elements combine to make "Hi'-Neighbor!" a delight. First, there is the Type B Rich Kid.

Type A, more familiar, is the wealthy boy who really wants to be part of the scruffy gang. Type B is the kind played here by Jerry Tucker, who's born rich and likes it that way. If Jerry had been born modest, he had evidently outgrown it. When the runny-nosed youngster arrives with the moving van, the gang salutes him with a friendly "Hi, pal!" His reaction is a disdainful once-over, after which he walks away. "What a pal!" comments Spanky. Later trying to pry loose the kids from his shiny new fire engine, Jerry snarls arrogantly, "Look out! Get away from there! Scram!" But Spank persists in leaning on the steering wheel long enough to caution firmly, "Don't rush me, big boy." Then wanting to butter up Jerry for a free ride, Wally offers his "swell pocket knife," but Jerry replies haughtily, "No sir, I've got a *real* pocket knife," taking out his handsome instrument to compare with Wally's weather-beaten sample.

Another of the film's prime ingredients is the Fickle Woman. Jane obviously likes Wally, but when she spots the fire engine, she says admiringly, "Oh, what a beauti-

Our Gang's fire engine in "Hi'-Neighbor!" with schoolteacher Mrs. Fern Carter finding a seat in the rear. Note the pliers serving as safety brake for the front wheel.

ful car!" and goes to meet its owner. Philosopher Spanky strikes a pose and says, "There ya are!" summing up the eternal struggle of love and money. Jane isn't really so bad, however, and as she leaves she tells Wally to bring around his fire engine and she'll ride that one, too. Later, when she and Jerry see the contraption, he doesn't give her a chance to make good her promise, asking, "You don't want to ride in *that* thing, do you?" When she is spilled from his expensive factory-made car down the hill, however, she lets Jerry know what she thinks of him by turning on a nearby sprinkler that gives him a good soaking.

Finally, there is the happiest ingredient of all: the gang going to work on a home-made invention. These kids may not have money, but they have imagination and determination, and that's what counts. Everyone pitches in: "We'll show 'im." Tommy volunteers to get some wheels, and in a panning shot we see just where he's found them: on bicycles, baby carriages, and the like, which are now lame. A nearby window washer suddenly finds himself without a ladder beneath his feet, while a neighborhood moonshiner filling a crock watches the water stop flowing and turns to see his severed hose disappear around the corner. By "borrowing" such items, the kids are able to assemble a full-sized (or is it "over-sized"?) vehicle that really works.

The little kids, Spanky and Scotty, are considered a nuisance by the older fellows, even though Spanky dug up a steering wheel and a bell. No matter where they go in the barn workshop, they're in the way ("This work's for men"), so they sit on the sidelines, wryly observing the others' mistakes. When the job is completed, Wally is jubilant, but Spanky mutters, "You're not so smart." "Why not?" asks Wally. "You can't get it out," Spanky correctly replies. A little detail like this isn't going to stop the gang, however, and by merely knocking down one of the barn walls the engine is freed.

The climactic race combines location footage with process-screen work, but the latter effects seem to have been used only to present close-up action and not to fake the race itself, since long shots show the downhill competition really taking place. This is a most enjoyable and exciting climax for the film, with a funny epilogue as the gang, having left the rich kid behind, inadvertently steers their car onto a sidewalk, knocking unsuspecting pedestrians sky high (in a series of shots of people literally flying into the air) before being stopped by a convenient bush.

Everything clicks in "Hi'-Neighbor!" for the same basic reasons that *Our Gang* itself was successful. Hew-

ing to a proven formula, it delivers the expected, and delightful, results.

Recently, Spanky McFarland commented on "Hi'-Neighbor!" in a newspaper interview: "You couldn't make a series like ours today, the kids are too jaded. Remember, we started out in the Depression years, when building a clubhouse or a home-made fire engine out of junkyard scraps was a fabulous imagination peaker for the kids, especially the way our prop department could put 'em together. Today, if little Jimmy wants a bike or a clubhouse, Dad just goes out and buys him one."

Few films stir a twinge of nostalgia like "Hi'-Neighbor!" However one characterizes it, as a film of comforting illusions, or maybe just wish fulfillment, "Hi'-Neighbor!" is a fascinating exercise in simply recognizing ourselves—through the adventures of *Our Gang*.

Interlude: New Direction. More than four months had passed since the last *Our Gang* comedy had been made. In the interim, besides adding Wally Albright and teaming Scotty Beckett with Spanky, Hal Roach had engaged German-born Gus Meins as the gang's director.

Like more than a few others around Roach, Meins had been a cartoonist, with the Los Angeles *Evening Herald*. He broke into movies in 1919 with Fox, moved to Sennett briefly, and then through the 1920s found a home directing Universal comedies like the *Let George Do It* series. He even directed two of the second-echelon *Our Gang* derivative series. One was *The Newlyweds and Their Baby* series, the other was the *Buster Brown* kid comedies. On both series, Meins alternated direction with Francis Corby, who by 1934 was also on board at Roach, but as a cameraman. Interestingly, the *Buster Brown* comedies were employing and billing the original Pete the Pup in their films, in the part of "Tige."

At Roach, Meins had been piloting some of the best pictures of Laurel & Hardy (*Babes in Toyland*), Charley Chase (*Fallen Arches*), and Thelma Todd and Zasu Pitts (*One Track Minds*, featuring Spanky McFarland). Meins's *Our Gang* films would be witty, tasteful, stylish, and skillfully constructed.

Sadly, Gus Meins left Roach in a clash over production policies on a 1937 feature, *Nobody's Baby*, and committed suicide some years later. Roach music director Marvin Hatley said the news shocked everyone on the lot, and he recalled Meins as "a fine director with a wonderful personality—a very happy sort of person." Asked to assess Gus Meins's talents, Hal Roach has commented, "He was a very good director for the gang, and always did a very good job."

127 · FOR PETE'S SAKE!

Two Reels · Produced by Hal Roach · Directed by Gus Meins · Photographed by Francis Corby · Edited by Ray Snyder · Released on April 14, 1934, by M-G-M · Our Gang: George "Spanky" McFarland, Scotty Beckett, Wally Albright, Matthew "Stymie" Beard, Leonard Kibrick, Marianne Edwards, Jacqueline Taylor, Carlena "Buckwheat" Beard, Billie Thomas, Tommy Bond, Philbrook Lyons, Marvin "Bubbles" Trin, and Pete the Pup · Storekeeper, William Wagner; Man with day off, Fred Holmes; His wife, Lyle Tayo

Bratty Leonard breaks Marianne's doll, and refuses to do anything about it. The little girl has been ill, and older sister Jackie explains that she always takes the doll to sleep with her. Wally and the boys promise to have a new doll in her hands by bedtime, one with eyes that open and close. At the neighborhood novelties store, the cuddly stuffed baby of Marianne's dreams is available for $1.25, a small fortune they don't have. However, Leonard's father, the proprietor, slyly offers to trade the doll for the gang's dog, Pete. Wally tells him sincerely, "Say, I wouldn't trade that dog for your whole darned store," but after an unsuccessful attempt to earn the money by beating rugs, they return and sadly surrender their pet in exchange for the doll. When they accidentally break a vase on their way out, the crabby owner takes the doll back to pay for the damage. Then Pete turns on father and son, scaring them to death and forcing them to beg the gang's help in taking the dog away; Wally agrees, if they can have their doll, and the helpless owner agrees. A last-minute mix-up in dolls is remedied by Pete, who zips back to the store and grabs the correct one from the window display, returning it personally to Marianne for a happy ending.

"For Pete's Sake" is another bull's-eye comedy directed by Gus Meins, perfectly paced and conceived so that every scene fits into place, framed by a running gag: Stymie's little sister Buckwheat getting stuck in awkward places, with sideline observers Scotty and Spanky alerting Stymie to the problem each time.

As usual, the older kids don't want to be bothered when these young ones try to get their attention . . . until it's too late. In the very first scene, they try to warn Wally that the sawdust he's pouring into Marianne's broken doll is landing inside the front of his pants. "He'll never learn," Scotty wryly comments, making the same remark about Stymie, who after rescuing trouble-prone Buckwheat for the third time complains, "This is getting monopomous."

Finally, at the end of the film, after the little sister falls into a basin of water, Stymie takes care of the matter without prompting, hanging the child on a clothesline to dry. "Well," says Scotty triumphantly, "we learned 'em." Thus, the running gag and accompanying remarks provide a perfect punctuation for every segment of the film, as well as a punch line to bring the short to a satisfying conclusion.

The story itself is worked out with equal finesse, starting with a problem that propels the gang into seeking a solution; then a seemingly insoluble dilemma, and a resolution that allows the gang to come out on top with both the dog and the doll, and see the villains get their just deserts.

Leonard is the ideal bully, in a position of power and well aware of it. He "playfully" lassoes Marianne's doll and swings it into the street, where it is crushed by a passing truck—an act of pure meanness without any provocation. To the gang's complaints he sneers, "Aw, it was only an old rag doll," and when Wally insists that he's got to replace it, Leonard answers, "Who's gonna make me?" staring into Wally's eyes while pulling himself up to his full height. Wally knows darn well he doesn't want to fight this bully, but he gulps and says that *he'll* make him. The threats continue, and Spanky remarks, "You guys sure talk a great fight." A call from Leonard's mother cuts short the impending battle.

Only someone as repulsive as Leonard could have a father as seedy as the store owner, played by William Wagner. Leonard even wields persuasive powers over his pop, convincing him that they could use a watchdog like Pete and suggesting the idea of trading doll for dog. Hap-

Storekeeper William Wagner and son Leonard Kibrick confront Wally and the Gang.

pily, both Leonard and his misanthropic father are given their comeuppance when Pete turns on them and causes them to literally climb the walls for dear life, smashing most of the store's contents in the process.

The rug-beating sequence is also fun, with everything going smoothly until Spanky and Scotty rig up a lawn-mowing machine with Pete providing transportation. The eager dog runs loose and "mows" the shag off a long carpet! The kids try to glue back the material before the owner gets wise, but he wakes up from his nap just in time to see what's happened. Chasing after the kids, he trips and falls onto the rug, rising with a face full of carpet!

As an unexpected but pleasing tag for the short, there is a last-minute cliffhanger ending. Just as all seems well and the kids approach Marianne's house, they unwrap their present and discover that it's a black girl doll, inappropriate as a replacement for the blonde youngster. Suddenly Pete snaps into action, darting away and dragging Scotty and Spanky with him, sailing downtown just as Leonard and his father are about to lock up their store. They recoil in horror at the sight of Pete, who barges inside and grabs the right doll from the window, flying back from whence he came, dragging the two boys behind him and causing havoc along the way, bumping into pedestrians, knocking a ladder out from underneath a sign painter, etc., racing back to Marianne's window for the finale.

By now, Spanky and Scotty were established as a team within the gang, their wisecracks working as counterpoint to the main action involving the older kids. (Never caught off-guard, when the gang says, "Look what you did!" after the carpet accident, Spanky replies, "Aw, that could happen to anybody.") This worked so well, in fact, that the next short in the series was built around them and their contrast to the rest of the gang. As for Leonard, he was incorporated into the cast, alternating between good-guy and bad-guy parts; but two years later, director Gus Meins reteamed him with sharkish-smiling William Wagner to perform their father-and-son villainy once more in "The Lucky Corner."

128 · THE FIRST ROUND-UP

Two Reels · Produced by Hal Roach · Directed by Gus Meins · Photographed by Francis Corby · Edited by Ray Snyder · Released on May 5, 1934, by M-G-M · Our Gang: George "Spanky" McFarland, Scotty Beckett, Wally Albright, Matthew "Stymie" Beard, Tommy Bond, Jacqueline Taylor, Cullen Johnson, Billie Thomas, Willie Mae "Buckwheat" Taylor, Philbrook Lyons, Marvin "Bubbles" Trin, and Pete the Pup · Wally's father, Billy Bletcher; Wally's mother, Zoila Conan

The gang plans an elaborate camping trip, roughing it for maybe a week or more, although Wally's father is certain that they'll be back that night after it gets dark. They shun the companionship of Spanky and Scotty, telling them, "You kids'll cry for your mom . . . besides, it's a two-mile walk uphill—you kids'll never make it." The gang plods through the long, long trek to Cherry Creek, only to be greeted there by Spanky and Scotty, who ask, "What took ya so long?" They hitchhiked their way, and Wally admits, "We're not so smart." That sentiment is echoed throughout the evening, as it develops that the little kids are the only ones who remembered to bring food, and are apparently the only ones who thrive on the excitement of the trip. "I hope it don't get much darker," says Stymie,

Scotty and Spanky in "The First Round-Up": "What took ya so long?"

Sleeping under the stars; as the cloak of night descends, smiles vanish on the faces of scared youngsters. These looks of apprehension belong to Willie Mae Taylor, Stymie, Tommy Bond, and Wally Albright, whose tousled hair-style depended on a curling iron, particularly under the hot studio lights that sometimes caused his blond locks to wilt between scenes.

while Spanky asks his pal enthusiastically, "I hope it gets good and dark, don't you?" Darkness only heightens the gang's fear that eerie things are going on, and when thunder and lightning pierce the stormy night, imaginary terrors overcome the kids and they run for home. "They can't take it," says Spanky, as he and Scotty prepare to enjoy the fun. Then a turtle crawls into the creek with their kerosene lamp, and lightning strikes them and their sleeping bag, sending them running down the road with their feet poking out of the bag, thus causing one final nightmarish sight for the unsettled campers.

Unlike some later fishing and camping shorts with "scare" themes, "The First Round-Up" manages to be

real and amusing at the same time, creating atmosphere and situations that an audience can recognize and feel.

For starters, because of the grueling two-mile hike, the gang arrives at their campsite tired and unhappy: this is no way to start an enjoyable outing. Having no food adds to the growing sense of gloom, although after first tantalizing everyone, Scotty generously offers to share his and Spanky's jelly and white bread, causing a momentary mob scene. The coming of darkness is yet another touch of discomfort for the unhearty campers.

Wally tries to muster up some self-deceiving enthusiasm by declaring, "Boy, this is great, ain't it, fellas?" which elicits a half-hearted "yeah" from the others.

As their fire starts to burn out, Wally warns that if someone doesn't get more wood, they'll *really* be in the dark. Stymie answers that there isn't anyone about to go searching for wood at this hour, adding, "This wasn't *my* idea." Thunder and lightning are the last straw, sending the whole group running desperately for the comfort and security of warm beds at home.

As usual, the "dumb little kids" aren't so dumb after all, not only managing to get to the campsite without wearing out themselves or their shoes, but remembering to bring food and a kerosene lamp. Even though Wally has to admit that they were clever in thumbing a ride to camp, he shoos them away from the group, saying, "We don't want any little kids with us." When all eyes turn hungrily toward Spanky and Scotty's bread and jelly, however, Wally changes his tune. "Aren't you kids a little far away from us over there?" he asks sweetly. The kids deadpan their response, Scotty murmuring, "Aw, you don't want any little kids with you."

In one delightful scene, Scotty notices that the lamp casts giant-sized shadows against a nearby rock-face. Spanky runs back and forth waving his arms, to see the results, while a few yards away, Wally sees only the shadow and envisions a monstrous giant coming his way (we share his vision via some clever animation).

Another nighttime illusion has Wally and Stymie frightened by two tiny lights glowing in the dark, approaching their campgrounds. It turns out to be Buckwheat, her eyes having lit up in the blackness of night.

Like most of Gus Meins's two-reelers from this period, "The First Round-Up" has a beginning, a middle, and an end, without the arbitrary padding or gags-for-gags'-sake attitude of many two-reelers. Stuck for an actual punch line, he does take the easy way out: a cut to a close-up of Pete the Pup, having just seen a sleeping bag on four legs running down the road. His eyes go cock-eyed at the sight, rolling wildly in opposite directions (again, with the aid of an animated cartoon layover on the real Pete's face). While hardly the ideal wrap-up for a short, it serves its purpose in providing a tag for the plot itself, which has already been resolved quite neatly.

129 · HONKY DONKEY

Two Reels · Produced by Hal Roach · Directed by Gus Meins · Photographed by Francis Corby · Edited by Bert Jordan · Released on June 2, 1934, by M-G-M · Our Gang: Wally Albright, Matthew "Stymie" Beard, George "Spanky" McFarland, Scotty Beckett, Tommy Bond, Willie Mae "Buckwheat" Taylor, and Philbrook Lyons · Chauffeur, Don Barclay; Realtor, William Wagner; Officer, Charles McAvoy; Household servant, Natalie Moorhead; Maid, Bess Flowers; Bicycle rider, Pete Gordon; Donkey laugh voice-over, Mickey Daniels; Algebra, Dinah the Mule

Wally's doting mother sends her son home from the city with chauffeur Barclay, but the youngster instructs him to take a detour through some alleys so he can meet some roughhouse playmates for a change. At a vacant lot they find the gang enjoying a makeshift merry-go-round with their pet mule Algebra. When the grouchy owner of the lot chases them away, Wally volunteers his spacious home as a new location, and the kids pile in the car, with Algebra bringing up the rear. Later, to save trouble, Algebra is moved to the back seat. Barclay's protests go ignored, yet he's the one who has to unload the mule when they arrive home. The animal starts chasing the chauffeur into the mansion, however, upsetting the household staff and wearing down the harried driver. When Mother returns from her shopping trip she becomes the latest target for Algebra, who chases her outside and into a fountain, where he has the last laugh.

Although the kids are catalysts for the action in "Honky Donkey," most of the attention (and many of the laughs) is generated by the mule, Algebra, and the chauffeur, Don Barclay. This ex-cartoonist came to Hal Roach via the *Ziegfeld Follies,* and spent over a year at the comedy studio bringing his unique off-key characteriza-

"Honky Donkey" is built around Don Barclay.

Unposed still from "Honky Donkey."

is if he hears a bell ringing nearby. Barclay is spectacularly unsuccessful in trying to get the mule out of his limousine, receiving for his troubles a kick on the chin. Spanky and Scotty are sitting on the sidelines watching this episode. "I hope he sneezes," says Scott. "Well, give him time," says Spanky affirmatively. Naturally, Barclay does sneeze, prompting a lengthy chase throughout Wally Albright's palatial home.

As in its companion piece "Washee Ironee," Wally is cast as the archetypal *Our Gang* Rich Kid (Type A). In the opening scene, his mother bundles him up in the back seat of the open car, fussing over the boy and telling him to go straight home, warning, "Don't talk to any strange children." The minute she's out of sight, Wally rips off his blanket and scarf and tells Barclay, "Drive through some alleys." "Alleys?" says the chauffeur incredulously. "Yeah," replies Wally, "and some dirty ones." Like all Type A *Our Gang* Rich Kids, he only wants to have fun with other children his age.

When he comes upon the gang and their mule-drawn merry-go-round, he hollers, "Can I get in on that?" The gang, who never let class distinctions bother them, hollers back, "Sure, come on over!" Then the fun begins.

Wally's pompous mother (who insists on calling him Wallace) gets her comeuppance when she returns home and catches her first sight of the mule at the top of a stairway; she hurriedly jumps onto the banister and slides down, colliding with Barclay at the ground-floor landing. An ill-timed sneeze sends the mule after her, ending with her jumping into an elegant fountain on the front lawn to escape from the rampaging animal, who lets go a whinny in triumph over this silly woman. (This literal last laugh is supplied by way of voice-over from *Our Gang* graduate Mickey Daniels!)

Finally, many of the film's best moments are provided by Spanky and Scotty, the mini-team within the gang. After hatching an idea, Scotty comments, "Have we got brains!" and Spanky says brusquely, "Whaddaya mean, *we?*" This talkative twosome is used as a pleasing counterpoint to Don Barclay's antics throughout "Honky Donkey," with director Meins frequently cutting from Barclay's gags to Spank and Scotty, whose disapproving reactions to Barclay's grandiose bungling *would* generally double the laugh. Instead of simply parading cutesy kiddie routines past the camera, Meins's planned emphasis is on well-rounded, integrated comedy. The result is a balanced and quite amusing two-reeler.

tion to films with Thelma Todd and Patsy Kelly, Billy Gilbert, and British comics Douglas Wakefield, Jack Barty and Billy Nelson, with whom he did a series of *All Star* shorts.

As the high-toned chauffeur he does wonders with his special brand of ostentatious dialogue, as when pleading with the wealthy son, "But my dear Wallace . . . oh goodness gracious," or responding to Spanky and Scott's shenanigans, "Now boys—was that nice?" or remarking to Scott after the lad helps ward off an impending sneeze, "Thank you gigantically." One especially remembers an angry exchange with a policeman, when he concludes by snarling, "Listen, cop, I'm on the verge of disliking you."

The delightfully fruity Barclay also carries most of the burden for visual gags in the film. A premise has been established concerning the mule's behavior: the only way to get him to move is to sneeze, which prompts him to chase the offending party. Then the only way he will stop

130 · MIKE FRIGHT

Two Reels · Produced by Hal Roach · Directed by Gus Meins · Photographed by Kenneth Peach · Edited by Louis McManus · Story by Hal E. Roach · Released on August 25, 1934, by M-G-M · Our Gang: George "Spanky" McFarland, Scotty Beckett, Matthew "Stymie" Beard, Tommy Bond, Alvin Buckelew, Leonard Kibrick, Billy Lee, The Meglin Kiddies, and Pete the Pup · Station manager, James C. Morton; Announcer, William Irving; Mr. Barker, the sponsor, Frank H. LaRue; Elevator operator, Charlie Hall; Radio audition audience, Joe Young, Fern Carter; Piano player, Marvin Hatley

The gang enters a radio audition with its International Silver String Submarine Band. Following a parade of well-rehearsed professional children, their makeshift band seems unlikely to impress the program's potential sponsor, but when he hears their happy, melodic rendition of "The Man on the Flying Trapeze," he's enthusiastic and the boys are hired for the show.

"Mike Fright" may not be one of the funniest *Our*

Gang talkies, but it is one of the most endearing, emphasizing the gang's appeal by contrasting their natural, down-to-earth personalities with the general phoniness of the radio show.

From the opening scene, where radio station manager James C. Morton tries to impress his skeptical sponsor, we can tell that this is Show Business, where exaggeration and the big build-up are king. When Tommy calls the station about signing up for the audition, Morton takes the phone and reacts to the call with admiration and awe. "The International Silver String Submarine Band?" he repeats aloud. "Why, you know them, don't you?" he asks his announcer, who says with a smirk, "I've never heard of them." The undaunted owner tells his sponsor, "Why, they're absolutely wonderful!" Naturally, he's never seen or even heard of the band in his life, but the name *sounds* impressive.

When the gang arrives, dressed in their usual raggedy attire and carting their even raggedier instruments, they tell the receptionist that they are the International Silver String Submarine Band. The startled woman drinks this in and asks, "Are you *sure?*" This prompts an open-mouthed response from the kids, who don't know how to deal with such a question. "Maybe we ain't us," says Scotty, eliciting an Oliver Hardy-ish camera look and grunt of exasperation from his pal Spanky.

Manager Morton is considerably unnerved to find that the impressive-sounding group is actually a bunch of unkempt children, but he tries to hide his apprehension for the sake of the sponsor.

Probably born out of Hal Roach's own frustration in casting *Our Gang* parts, the cutesy acts presented on the program are straight from a typical ego-trip amateur hour. The Two Darling Sisters sing "Jimmy Had a Nickel," mostly out of meter. Another young vocalist offers "I Want to go Back to my Little Grass Shack," garbling most of the lyrics and accompanied by a chorus of pint-sized hula girls. For a finale, a young boy in sailor suit (Billy Lee) tap-dances to a chorus of the song. Head bobbing, arms swinging, and a self-assured expression on his face indicating that he knows he's adorable, this would-be Astaire invites a stare of contempt and disbelief from both Scotty and Spanky—silent cutaway shots which accomplish more than a ream of dialogue possibly could. The next act is a trumpet solo by Little Leonard, egged on by his doting stage mother. As he tries to play "My Wild Irish Rose," he's distracted by Tommy and Alvin sitting on the sidelines sucking some lemons ("They're good for your freckles"); Leonard loses his pucker and stumbles through his rendition, which the announcer cuts short by interrupting, "You have just heard Little Leonard."

At last, it's time for the gang, summoned forth in desperation by the station manager, who has now lost the interest of his sponsor. Just as the money man is about to walk out the station door, he hears the first bars of the gang's song, "The Man on the Flying Trapeze." With penny whistle, kazoo, harmonica, and assorted homemade noisemakers, they are generating more infectious music and natural high spirits than all the other "professional" acts put together.

Why does the gang appeal to the sponsor—and to *us*—so much more than the other kiddie entertainers?

First, they seem to be the only ones who care about

"Mike Fright" still posed to accommodate photographer Stax Graves. In the scene as filmed, the Gang's musical rendition wins the rhapsodic admiration it deserves from William Irving, Frank H. La Rue, and James C. Morton, all with hands over ears for this studio publicity picture.

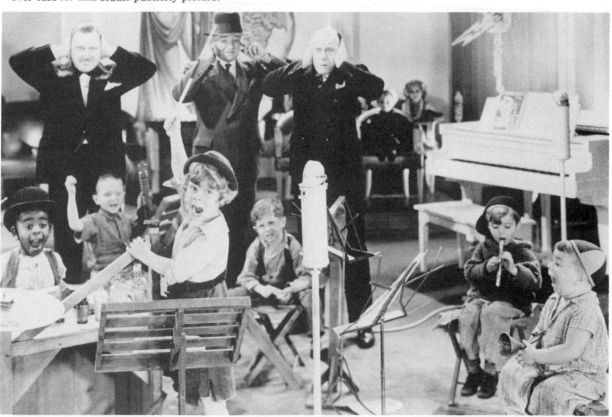

what they're doing. Although Leonard's is the only stage mother we actually see, one can imagine the coaching and prodding that went into the Darling Sisters' memorization (or near memorization) of "Jimmy Had a Nickel," or the hula girls' "Little Grass Shack." Those children have learned their songs by rote, and that's exactly how they sing them.

Second, these children are all trying to imitate or (worse) please adults in one way or another, from the cocky tap dancer to the mumbling vocalists. In a memorable opening shot, one of the Darling Sisters tells another girl, ". . . so the director took one look at me and I got the job just like *that*." (Probably a part in some Shirley Temple picture.) A show-business veteran at the age of eight!

The kids of *Our Gang* are not professional entertainers in this short (although they're clever enough to adopt an impressive-sounding name). They've organized a band for fun, and they've chosen a song that's fun to sing. That same song, of course, had a similar enlivening effect on an adult group in another 1934 film, *It Happened One Night*.

Yet the radio station owner and his announcer have no faith in the gang's prospects beforehand, because they aren't dolled up like the other children, and don't seem to share their sense of professionalism. The radio people *want* those cardboard kids, never realizing that in looking for a "novelty," the greatest novelty of all would be to present engaging children who are *real*, and not doctored in the tricks of the trade by ambitious adults.

In essence, one might say that "Mike Fright" is a character study.

Unfortunately, its gag quotient is rather low, and the one prominent running gag is handled weakly: every time the gang comes near a microphone, they either hit it or knock it over, causing tubes to blow out and drive the harried radio engineer crazy. The timing is off in these cutaways to the engineer, with several reaction shots held too long to be effective. In addition, this unknown player doesn't know how to milk the laugh with comic expressions of frustration and anger. One can picture how funny the sequences would have been if slow-burn Edgar Kennedy were in his place . . . or even blustery Billy Gilbert.

Much better—in fact, he's tremendous—is William Irving as the announcer, whose attempts to preserve

Bobbie Beard, Stymie Beard, Scotty Beckett, Tommy Bond, and Spanky McFarland in 1934.

decorum—and personal dignity—are undermined by the gang. When he tiptoes past the microphone, as an example to the children, Spanky stares at him and snaps, "What's the matter, your feet hurt?" This builds in intensity to the point where Little Leonard's sloppy trumpeting leaves announcer Irving with a look of utter hopelessness on his face.

Actually, watching Leonard and the rest with an impatient smirk, he shares Our Gang's dislike for these polished song-and-dance phonies, but from a different perspective. He's an adult, which means he represents authority, and by nature Our Gang bristles at anyone who exercises authority. Still, because he's a free spirit, unafraid to react the way he *really* feels about things, announcer Irving is the kind of ingenuous guy you'd guess Our Gangers might grow into.

Hardly the first time that the kids of *Our Gang* have encountered professionally cute children, "Mike Fright" was not the last, either. But in the long run, this vivid mirror of two kinds of kids is one of the best.

Tidbits: A special bonus in "Mike Fright" is the appearance of Marvin Hatley, Roach music composer, who spends the two reels seated at a piano to accompany the kiddie acts.

131 · WASHEE IRONEE

Two Reels · Produced by Hal Roach · Directed by James Parrott · Photographed by Francis Corby · Edited by Louis McManus · Released on September 29, 1934, by M-G-M · Our Gang: George "Spanky" McFarland, Scotty Beckett, Wally "Waldo" Albright, Matthew "Stymie" Beard, Jerry Tucker, Dickie Jones, Alvin Buckelew, Leonard Kibrick, Tommy Bond, Jackie White, Yen Wong, Tony Kales, Tommy McFarland, Jacqueline Taylor, Billie Thomas, Willie Mae "Buckwheat" Taylor, Pete the Pup, and Elmer the Monkey · Waldo's mother, Ellinor Van Der Veer; Butler, Sam Adams; Policeman directing traffic, Stanley (Tiny) Sandford; Other officers, James C. Morton, William Irving; Pedestrians, Lester Dorr, Ernie Alexander; Maids of Olympia, Gertrude Astor, Symona Boniface; Man walking by laundry, James Parrott; Dubbing the sneeze, Billy Gilbert

Waldo's high-society mother is having a bridge luncheon for the Maids of Olympia, of which she hopes to be president. She expects Waldo to "enthrall" the gathering of ladies with a violin recital, and sends him off to practice.

But Waldo's eye catches the gang playing football outside, and he joins them instead. When a soaring kickoff comes his way, he catches the ball and runs for a touchdown, landing in a mud puddle just past the goal

A scene from "Washee Ironee." Note Leonard Kibrick, with gag noseguard, behind Petie, playing off type here as a member of the Gang.

posts. He's covered with mud from head to toe, but delighted to be part of the game and the gang, and anxious to make up for a lifetime of behaving. Just then, his mother calls, and Waldo and the rest of the gridiron behemoths sneak into his basement to do a quick and dirty cleaning job. After elaborate procedures, the clothes emerge from the dryer—shrunk beyond recognition. Faced with no alternative, Waldo dons a lamp shade as a kind of skirt and makes his entrance at the party. His mother promptly faints, and simultaneously, the gang barges in. Mother's pet monkey starts teasing Pete, and a melee quickly ensues. When Waldo's mother phones for the police, the gang makes a hasty retreat.

"Washee Ironee," with its unusual pig-Latin title, was the only *Our Gang* two-reeler directed by James Parrott, the brother of Charley Chase and one of the most talented comedy creators on the Hal Roach staff, working often with Chase and Laurel & Hardy. He brought a keen flair for slapstick and sight gags to "Washee Ironee," with delightful results.

The film is loaded with gags, one after another: during the football game, Pete accidentally swallows referee Spanky's whistle, prompting a variety of solutions; soap bubbles from the washing machine float up the dumb waiter into mother's salon, bursting in unlikely places; one bubble causes the butler to sneeze (the whopping explosion dubbed by expert Billy Gilbert); and of course there is the final melee, with vases, cream puffs, and the monkey himself flying around the room.

Best of all is a terrific running gag that provides the film's closing laugh. Early on, when the kids try to figure out how to wash Waldo's clothes, Spanky boards his goat-drawn "ambulance" and, cupping a drinking glass over his mouth, imitates the sound of a siren. Hearing this, traffic cop Tiny Sandford efficiently stops all traffic at a busy intersection to let the vehicle through—only to find a midget-sized homemade buggy weaving between the cars. Flustered, he tries to get traffic moving again. Spanky pulls up in front of a Chinese laundry (just as director Parrott passes by in a cameo), and gets his young friend there to return with him. Again the "siren" is heard, and again the cop halts cars in their screeching tracks only to find Spanky meandering through the traffic; this time he takes out his anger on the drivers and brusquely tells them to get moving.

At the end of the film, with the society party a shambles, Waldo's distraught mother picks up the phone and wails, "Murder! Police!" A squad of officers hops onto a paddy wagon Keystone Cops-style and speeds off down the road, siren blaring. Traffic cop Sandford hears it coming but pauses and smiles, pleased he's wise to the "gag" by now. The camera cuts to the patrol wagon's view of impending disaster as it races toward the busy intersection; a car zips by and a pedestrian jumps out of the way. Then we see the reaction of people on the sidewalk covering their eyes while a fantastic series of unchecked crashing sounds is heard. After a moment, the crowd rushes over to see what's happened, with the camera cutting to a long shot of a monumental pile-up of disabled cars and bewildered drivers, reaching high into the sky, with Sandford teetering atop the pyramidlike heap. Just then, Spanky and the gang pass by in their ambulance; the grim-visaged Sandford shakes his fist at the young troublemaker, and Spanky graciously answers the gesture with Mae West's tag line, "I'll come up and see ya sometime."* Fade-out. This is one of the most elaborate sight gags ever devised for an *Our Gang* comedy—and Parrott (who'd directed Laurel & Hardy's classic *Two Tars,* with its freakish auto parade) knew how to pull it off.

At the same time, the kids almost take a back seat to the gags, with the exception of Spanky, who is featured throughout the film. Wally Albright is pretty much in the position of straight man, except for his climactic entrance wearing the lamp shade. His character here is a standard one in *Our Gang* films harking back to "Saturday Morning" in the early 1920s. In fact, the establishing scene that opens "Washee Ironee" is borrowed from "Saturday Morning." Waldo tries to kiss his mother, but she backs away, saying, "No, no, you'll disarrange me. I'll kiss you later."

Mater, as Waldo calls her, is played by Ellinor Van Der Veer, an unsung lady of comedy who probably never had a bigger part than this one. For ten years the stately Miss Van Der Veer was on the receiving end of pies and other indignities in Hal Roach comedies; her reward was a role

* The second film inside a year to end on this piquant punch line— "Bedtime Worries" having been the first. Obviously, theater audiences loved it. Queried about the verbal if not visual parody recently, Mae West declined comment.

with considerable dialogue in this film, executed quite nicely. Parrott took the believable role of the mother and brought it one step nearer to caricature with a funny scene in the early goings. As Waldo practices his violin in the solarium, she remarks from the next room, "Waldo, your B-flat in the obligato pianissimo needs more staccato." Even the butler winces at this.

Another statuesque actress, Gertrude Astor, is seen briefly at the party, where her bare back is pelted with a cream puff, prompting her to spin around and be splattered with another wad of cream direct in the face. Symona Boniface, placed on this earth to intercept flying pies in Three Stooges films, participates in the gooey indignities too. All of these supporting characters contribute to the success of "Washee Ironee," including the perennial cop Tiny Sandford, given a featured spot with the running gag that closes out this very funny two-reeler.

Billie Thomas makes his third *Our Gang* appearance in "Washee Ironee," but not yet as Buckwheat, who's played here by a girl, Willie Mae Taylor. Who'd have guessed that the modest-looking Billie Thomas would wind up working in most every succeeding *Our Gang* comedy until the series' dissolution a decade later! He's given one good gag in "Washee Ironee." Seated in the bleachers, the youngster is shown watching the game through binoculars made with a pair of soda pop bottles fastened together.

132 · MAMA'S LITTLE PIRATE

Two Reels · Produced by Hal Roach · Directed by Gus Meins · Photographed by Art Lloyd · Edited by Bert Jordan · Released on November 3, 1934, by M-G-M · Our Gang: George "Spanky" McFarland, Scotty Beckett, Matthew "Stymie" Beard, Jerry Tucker, and Billie "Buckwheat" Thomas · Spanky's mother, Claudia Dell; Spanky's father, Joe Young; Voice-over for the giant, Billy Bletcher

At breakfast one morning, Spanky's dad relates a newspaper story of long-lost pirates' treasure having just been salvaged along the California coast. So the adventuresome gang sets out to discover buried riches of their own, despite orders from Spanky's mother not to leave his room for disobeying her. They happen upon an eerie darkened cave that promises mystery, and the wide-eyed youngsters explore its deepest reaches, finally stumbling into a fabulous subterranean room filled with towering furniture and enormous footprints large enough to be buried in. Most intriguing is a gigantic chest, and when Stymie climbs up to flip the lock open, millions of gold coins, rubies, diamond-studded crowns and other gleaming jewels gush out like waters unleashed from a dam, flowing about the room till the kids are literally swimming through glittering wealth. Reveling in their merry triumph, Spanky shouts, "Well men, should we take it all?!" Weighed down with dripping treasure and glory, as they wobble and clank back toward the room's secret entrance, their glee is checked, their muscles tensed by the approaching deep-bass voice sounds of an awesome-looking medieval giant; it's his cavern domicile they've

just disrupted. With wickedly resounding growls, the huge beastlike creature finds the tiny children easy prey, and sets out to capture the appetizing intruders and hang them on meat hooks, one by one. Blanching in fright as the others are captured, Spanky is scampering from his doom when he's awakened from his predicament by the gang's cries outside his window—they're anxious to go to the cave. Bewildered, Spanky realizes the whole thing has been a horrible nightmare.

Wonderful and wonder filled, "Mama's Little Pirate" is one of the most unusual and disarming of all *Our Gang* shorts, a minor classic of the comedy-thrills genre, and a film whose surrealism leaves one lost in admiration.

Beautifully constructed, a mix of comedy and ominous anticipation carries the film's first reel, serving as essential build-up for the fantasy and (unrelieved) suspense one knows is surely coming.

The charming breakfast-table scene at the film's outset wastes little time propelling the story forward, but tosses off a nice quota of gags, too. As Spanky listens open mouthed to his father's newspaper story, he heaps teaspoon after teaspoon of sugar on his oatmeal. Finally realizing what he's done, Spank furtively pours the whole mess into Pop's empty bowl, announces he's finished, and scoots under the table and out the door—anxious to be after the treasure. "That boy's a whirlwind when he gets going," Pop says, as he digs into his oatmeal, stopping short with a sudden sour look.

Hal Roach and his staff did conceive ideas for *Our Gang* films from actual newspaper stories, and some newsworthy event could have inspired "Mama's Little Pirate," just as depicted in the opening sequence. But *Our Gang* films sometimes also show signs of an unconscious patterning after Mark Twain's literary boyhood characterizations, and one can't help but recall *The Adventures of Tom Sawyer* and the chapter that begins, "There comes a time in every rightly constructed boy's life when he has a raging desire to go somewhere and dig for hidden treasure."

And so he does.

Still, angled a third way, the concept for "Mama's Little Pirate" could have been suggested by the pure fantasy of Laurel & Hardy's concurrent *Babes in Toyland* (also directed by Gus Meins). Even if not, the studio-created cave sets certainly are those used in *Babes in Toyland,* having been the underground dominion of sinister "Barnaby" (Henry Brandon) and his army of Bogey-Men.

Coincidentally, Brandon would resurrect his Barnaby characterization for "Our Gang Follies of 1938," another imaginative film again employing the dream contrivance as the pretext for extraordinary fantasizing.

The fantasizing in "Mama's Little Pirate" is abetted by some ingenious double-exposure photography. (There are lots of fancy and costly optical transition wipes, too, adding to the technical polish.) Told to stay in his room ("Aw, a fellah cain't do nothin' "), Spanky's devilish alter ego comes to life and stands next to him arguing that mothers don't know anything about caves, and "If you let her get away with it *this* time, you'll be henpecked the rest of your life. . . . Well, what are we, mice or men?" He's a man, it's decided chin in hand, so out the window he goes.

Later, having listened to his alter ego and regretted it, for a finale Spanky wakes from his dream and knocks his trouble-causing double flat to even the score.

Like the previous year's *King Kong,* "Mama's Little Pirate" wisely withholds what everyone's waiting to see, allowing for the build-up of suspense to overtake comedy by the time the giant makes his startling appearance and changes the pace of the film completely.

As part of the well-designed anticipation, one is led to suspect a giant's imminent presence by the huge furniture and footprints; later thudding footsteps and deep beastlike mutterings promise the worst. Our tense fears are realized when the towering club-toting creature rumbles into the room, but even then the camera cleverly discloses him only from the waist down, having to truck back to reveal the hairy giant in full form—sort of a photographic unmasking.

Underscoring the mood of apprehension through these sequences is some wonderful background music, these particular themes seldom used in Roach pictures and reserved for the few genuinely suspenseful two-reelers the studio made, like George Stevens's brilliant *Boy Friends* comedy *Air Tight.* The nearly identical thrill-music scoring there complements the visuals as nicely as in "Mama's Little Pirate."

The gang size up their hairy foe (played by Jack Earle?) in this scene from "Mama's Little Pirate."

Oddly enough, the ill-tempered giant's threatening grunts and growls (he has no dialogue) are dubbed by five-feet-two Billy Bletcher, who as Wally's father in "The First Round-Up" is the object of a gag about his height. Bletcher's sepulchral tones had also provided the huffing and puffing voice for The Big Bad Wolf in Disney's *Three Little Pigs* the previous year.

In another size dichotomy, as the gang gazes about the giant's quarters and wonders aloud who or what would own such huge things, Spanky and Stymie answer each other with the line, "Well, it certainly ain't no midget." Recently, Spanky McFarland's mother related that the gang's tag-along infant companion in the oversize bonnet was indeed a five-year-old midget who later caught on with one of the major circuses as "The World's Smallest Man."

The contrast between the infant and the giant is remarkable, and the gag writers knew it. Unaware he has visitors, the giant is shown going about his everyday giant-type business in the cave, and each time he picks up something like his huge club, the infant-midget in that funny bonnet is revealed silently hiding behind it.

What gives the gang away though, is not the "baby" popping up all over, but their own avarice when the loot stuffed in Spanky's clothing begins spilling out from his hiding place and attracts the giant's attention.

Summing up one might say that the blending of fantasy and reality was Hollywood's business; Hal Roach added comedy, and intriguing things like "Mama's Little Pirate" are the result.

Henry David Thoreau wrote that the best of all states is

When dreams come true: Spank and Scott sizing up the booty in "Mama's Little Pirate."

years. Claudia Dell (Smith) served the role attractively here, and again in "Anniversary Trouble," though by then she'd taken a new husband, Johnny Arthur—of all people. The lovely Claudia Dell had been Tom Mix's leading lady in the original *Destry Rides Again,* and reportedly served as the original model for Columbia Pictures's statuesque torch lady trademark.

Finally, "Mama's Little Pirate" is the personification of an undervalued comedy device; it's a simple trick, but seldom used elsewhere so often or so well. Hal Roach knew (as his imitators and successors evidently did not) that one could double the laughter on any gag by cutting away and holding briefly on someone else's quiet or broad facial reaction, perhaps embellished by a gesture of some kind. Roach's *Our Gang* pictures are crafted on this formula of "A gag should beget a reaction" and produce two laughs instead of just one.

Pacing and editing have a lot to do with it, too, because much of comedy is carefully measured silence, the spaces in between what's said or done. Frequently it's the scope of the *reaction* to the joke or visual act that makes it funny, not the line or act itself. Often as not, the reaction gets a bigger laugh than what's provoked the reaction, since it allows the audience to relish the gag and then share the response.

Beautifully visual films like "Mama's Little Pirate" are brimming over with raw comic business or setups that cut away to vacant expressions in response, looks of glaring frustration, wide-eyed apprehension, soul-deep resignation, deadpan looks, exchanges of sick looks or pompous, knowing looks, and all often embroidered by subtle gesturing. It's a magic form of silent communication that at its best, and in its way, can be nearly as elegant as the literate dialogue of even a film by James Whale!

That's why, as Spanky McFarland has said, one seldom needed to bother studying scripts; with the advent of sound most everything was shot in shorter takes, and lines of dialogue weren't as essential as the comedy reaction or "take" (what the scripts dubbed "taking it big," or "takems").

to be in dreams awake. And in few films are escapist fantasy elements so vividly realized as in "Mama's Little Pirate": for a handful of minutes at least, it almost makes us believe in make believe.

Random Jottings: Perhaps one isn't supposed to wonder why there was no continuity for Spanky's screen mothers, but he must have had twenty of them over the

133 · SHRIMPS FOR A DAY

Two Reels · Produced by Hal Roach · Directed by Gus Meins · Photographed by Francis Corby · Edited by Louis McManus · Released on December 8, 1934, by M-G-M · Our Gang: George "Spanky" McFarland, Scotty Beckett, Matthew "Stymie" Beard, Billie "Buckwheat" Thomas, Leonard Kibrick, Tommy McFarland, Fred Purner, Jr., Harry Harvey, Jr., Alvin Buckelew, Marialise Gumm,* Marianne Edwards, Jackie White, Jacqueline Taylor, Donald Proffitt, Eileen Bernstein, Jerry Tucker, Delmar Watson, Barbara Goodrich, and Dorian Johnston · Mr. Crutch, Clarence Wilson; Mrs. Crutch, Rosa Gore; Sponsor, Mr. Wade, Wilfred Lucas; Dick, Joe Young; Mary, Doris McMahan; Dick, as a child, George Brasno; Mary, as a child, Olive Brasno; Frightened man on the street, Ray Turner; The butler, Herbert Evans

The children of the Happy Home Orphanage ("Where Kindness Rules") are given a party by Mr. Wade, who sponsors the home. Cantankerous Mr. Crutch, who runs the orphanage, turns into a Santa Claus in front of

wealthy Mr. Wade, his daughter Mary, and her boyfriend Dick. Mary envies the happy children, and when one youngster finds a musty old lamp in the bushes that bears an inscription about magic wishes, she says she'd love to

* Speculation: Could Marialise Gumm be related to The Gumm Sisters (Virginia, Suzy, and Frances), the vaudeville act from Minnesota? Frances Gumm later changed her name to Judy Garland. *Our Gang* periodically employed dancers and extras from a booking agency for child acts known as The Meglin Kiddies, and at one time all three Gumm sisters had indeed signed with this outfit.

enhanced by director Gus Meins's smooth trucking shots and ingenious choice of camera angles, which are used much more effectively in this short than in most others. The camera frequently enables the audience to share a point of view in the most literal sense, from the opening scene, where President Stymie and Treasurer Spanky on the Wood Chucks podium are shot from below, emphasizing the mock importance of the ceremony, to a shot of little Spanky from above—the view of bullyish Leonard Kibrick and the older kids—when they threaten their diminutive treasurer with an "Oh yeah?" and again when they stand by his front gate to prevent an escape. In the final scene, when Pop confesses his error to Spanky, the camera is aimed upward once again, to capture Spanky's reaction and point of view more than his father's as the worm (finally) turns.

The one aspect of "Anniversary Trouble" that doesn't make sense (beyond the question of how someone as likable as Mom could have married anyone like Pop) is why the Wood Chucks elect Spanky Treasurer if they don't trust him in the first place. Apparently, this is a general distrust of anyone holding their money, since Scotty decides to guard Spanky and each of the other members follows suit. What *is* believable, in a comic sense, is that this "ancient and honery" club breaks up within hours of its first meeting.

In many ways, the film's most memorable scene is the one in which Spanky disguises as Buckwheat in order to fool the gang. Buckwheat is depicted here as the daughter of household maid Mandy, delightfully played by Hattie McDaniel,* although Buckwheat's gender evolved into the male category during the coming year, with Billie Thomas continuing in the role. One of Thomas's most endearing yet most perplexing attributes was his garbled speech, and his constant refrain in this film has kept generations of *Little Rascals* fans guessing what he's trying to say. Is it "I'se the man," or "I'se comin'," or maybe a lingering call of "Ice man"? Or something entirely different? We'll never know.

As for Johnny Arthur, a talented comic actor who had starred in his own two-reelers in the 1920s and early 1930s, he was too good to let go after just one *Our Gang* appearance, and the Hal Roach staff called on him again a few years later to play Darla Hood's exasperated father in "Night 'n' Gales" and "Feed 'em and Weep."

---

* She'd win the Academy Award as best supporting actress for her role in *Gone With the Wind* four years later.

135 · BEGINNER'S LUCK

Two Reels · Produced by Hal Roach · Directed by Gus Meins · Photographed by Art Lloyd · Edited by Louis McManus · Released on February 23, 1935, by M-G-M · Our Gang: George "Spanky" McFarland, Scotty Beckett, Matthew "Stymie" Beard, Billie "Buckwheat" Thomas, Marianne Edwards, Carl "Alfalfa" Switzer, Harold "Deadpan/Slim" Switzer, Alvin Buckelew, Donald Proffitt, Sidney Kibrick, Leonard Kibrick, Jackie White, Jerry Tucker, Cecilia Murray, Merrell Strong, Eileen Bernstein, The Meglin Kiddies, The Five Cabin Kids, and Pete the Pup · Piano player, James C. Morton; Master of ceremonies, Tom Herbert; Spanky's mother, Kitty Kelly; Spanky's grandmother, May Wallace; Stage hand, Charlie Hall; Marianne's mother, Ruth Hiatt; Friend of Spanky's mother, Bess Flowers; Studio audience, Ernie Alexander, Fred Holmes, Jack (Tiny) Lipson, Robert McKenzie

Spanky's stage mother has entered him in an amateur contest at the neighborhood theater, where dressed in armor as a gladiator he will recite from Shakespeare ("Friends, Romans, countrymen, lend me your ears . . ."). Worried that if he wins, he'll have to do this for the rest of his life, he tells the gang, and they promise to sit up front that night and heckle him so that he'll be a flop. "All actors are sissies," they agree. Backstage, Spanky meets a sweet girl who really wants to win so she can buy a special dress, but when her turn comes she gets stage fright and runs into the wings crying. Now Spanky changes his mind and wants to win, so he can give the girl his prize money, but he's unable to get his message across to the gang. When he steps onstage, they give him the works, unleashing a barrage of pea-shooter pellets that bounce loudly off his head-to-toe armor. A chorus of hoots and noisemakers greets him next. But Spanky's a real trouper, carrying on despite the royal razz he's receiving, wowing the house with the spectacle he unwittingly makes of himself. Mother won't have her son laughed at, however, and tries to pull Spanky off the stage with a hook from behind the curtain. Amidst approving

howls from the crowd, playful Grandma hoists the curtain, exposing Spanky's mom and ripping her dress off in the process. Spanky quickly pulls a piece of scenery in front of his frozen mother, resulting in her head resting on the cardboard body of an odd-looking ostrich. Despite the ruckus, Spanky wins the prize, for keeping the audience in hysterics.

Designed as a spoof of the radio and theater amateur-night craze then sweeping the country, "Beginner's Luck" is also a hilarious triumph over stuffed shirts in general and stage mothers in particular. (The film's probably a dig at the kind of stage mothers Roach and his *Our Gang* staff had to face all the time.) Spanky's mother apparently seeks some reflected glory in pushing her boy onto the stage, ignoring the fact that he hates every minute of it. She forces him to recite "The Village Smithy" to her ladies' group, and even makes herself obnoxious to the master of ceremonies at the theater, telling him that Spanky is "too much of an artist to open the show."

She is subtly contrasted with the mother of Daisy, the girl Spanky meets backstage. A quiet, plainly dressed woman, she obviously can't afford the luxury of backing

"Beginner's Luck": backstage with master of ceremonies Tom Herbert, Spanky, Spanky's mom (Kitty Kelly), and grandma (May Wallace). When Herbert asks, "Is Barrymore ready yet?" Spanky replies, "Don't rush me, big boy!"

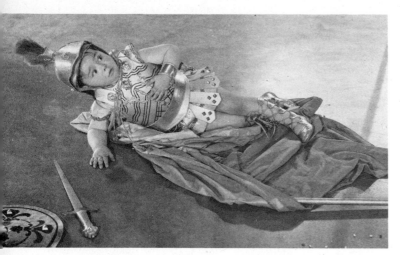

Spanky looks up in disbelief at his mother, *offscreen*, who's reluctantly joined the act during the closing scenes of "Beginner's Luck."

her daughter in a stage career; apparently it is Daisy and not her mother who has the drive to enter this contest. When the young girl runs off the stage crying, her mother is there to comfort her, and not to berate her as an angry stage mother might. When Spanky starts fumbling on the stage, his mother is more upset for herself than for her

son—he is embarrassing *her*. When Daisy gets stage fright, her mother only feels sorry for the girl.

Happily, Spanky's mother gets her comeuppance by making a spectacle of herself—on the stage.

The atmosphere of the amateur night is neatly conveyed by a variety of details, both obvious and subtle. The officious master of ceremonies (played by Hugh Herbert's brother Tom) is constantly bumping into stagehands and getting names confused. When he steps into the spotlight to introduce Spanky, the bulb goes out.

The pianist in the orchestra pit (played to the hilt by James C. Morton) is kept on his toes by the raucous gang seated directly behind him. When they first sound their noisemakers, the force of the blast sends his sheet music flying in all directions. The next time they erupt, he cleverly holds the papers down, only to watch his toupee fly off in a gust of wind. He remains on the wrong end of the action throughout the film.

The kids in the amateur show are typical professional children. The Floradora Dollies do "Honolulu Baby" with the lead singer miles away from the melody and one of the hula dancers completely out of step. Then The Cabin Kids, a popular quintet of black children who appeared in many films, sing close harmony on "Dinah."

"Tom and Jerry, the Arizona Nightingales" are Carl "Alfalfa" Switzer and his brother Harold, doing an infectious version of "She'll Be Comin' Round the Mountain." This was Alfalfa's first *Our Gang* short, and his amusingly determined approach to singing, as well as speaking dialogue, caught the fancy of director Gus Meins, who gave him a considerable amount of attention in this film. Apparently, the Roach staff knew immediately that they had made another "find."

When Spanky balks at being prodded on stage ("Is Barrymore ready yet?"), he unloads at the pompous master of ceremonies, "Why don't you put on the sheepherder?" Alfalfa, then minus most of his teeth, turns with a Jimmie Finlayson squint and shouts back, "Them's fightin' words, partner. We're cowboys from the mountains." Spanky looks away with a smirk, "Huh! From the drugstore!"

The series' knack for showing things from a youngster's point of view was never better put to use than in the scene where Marianne Edwards (as Daisy Dimple) stands onstage, about to perform. As the pianist plays her introduction, her face freezes into immobility. She looks straight ahead and we see, from her point of view, the gaping audience, with faces of wide-eyed strangers superimposed over the broader picture. After a minute of this, she can't stand any more, and runs offstage.

"Beginner's Luck" also boasts one of the best lines of dialogue Spanky ever had. When Grandma scoffs at her daughter's aggressiveness in pushing the boy into an acting career, Mother asks seriously, "What has Clark Gable or Barrymore got that Spanky hasn't?" Spanky looks up at her and snaps, "A mustache!"

136 · TEACHER'S BEAU

Two Reels · Produced by Hal Roach · Directed by Gus Meins · Photographed by Art Lloyd · Edited by Robert Crandall · Released on April 27, 1935, by M-G-M · Our Gang: George "Spanky" McFarland, Carl "Alfalfa" Switzer, Scotty Beckett, Billie "Buckwheat" Thomas, Matthew "Stymie" Beard, Jerry Tucker, Alvin Buckelew, Donald Proffitt, Rex Downing, Harold Switzer, Marianne Edwards, Dorian Johnston, Jackie White, Peggy Lynch, Tommy McFarland, Eileen Bernstein, The Five Cabin Kids, and Pete the Pup · Ralph Wilson, Edward Norris; Miss Jones, Arletta Duncan; Chairman of the board, Billy Bletcher; Party guests, Robert McKenzie, Gus Leonard, Robert (Bobby) Burns, Charlie Hall, Lo Poff, Fred Holmes, Ernie Alexander

On the last day of school, Miss Jones announces that the kids are going to have a new teacher that fall—Mrs. Wilson—because she is getting married. Her fiancé playfully paints a portrait of Mrs. Wilson as a "dried-up mean old woman . . . and you ought to see her teeth!" At the farewell party that night, the gang tries to contrive a way to break up the marriage so Miss Jones will remain their teacher. The idea of making a stirring speech flounders when Alfalfa gets a sore throat; an attempt to scare off the fiancé by having Spanky stand on Alfalfa's shoulders under a long coat and pretend to be a rival boyfriend backfires even worse. Then the kids hear groom-to-be Ralph playfully telling his bride that if her cooking isn't up to par, he'll call off the wedding. The gang thinks the threat is real, and pours entire containers of Tabasco sauce, garlic pepper, and horseradish onto one of the spaghetti platters to make sure Ralph gets a sore mouthful. Then they discover that Ralph is Ralph Wilson, and "Mrs. Wilson" is going to be the very same Miss Jones that fall. Spanky manages to take back the doctored platter, but somehow it lands on the gang's table, and they are forced to eat the fiery concoction. When the plates are clean and the kids are excused, they all make a beeline for the water hose outside, where they do their best to overcome the extra hot dinner. "Well," says the unknowing school-board chairman inside, "it looks like they've had enough!"

"Teacher's Beau" opens on a close-up of a schoolgirl's slate, on which she has written in chalk, "This is the last day of school—hurrah!" Apparently in celebration, some black students (actually the Cabin Kids, who once had their own series of shorts for Educational) are singing "Old MacDonald Had a Farm," with the rest of the class bobbing their heads and singing along. This is about as much schoolroom activity as we get to see before the plot starts rolling with Miss Jones's announcement about the "new" teacher, Mrs. Wilson.

The kiddie comedy of errors makes perfect sense, and flows beautifully from start to finish. There is an echo of earlier outings with Miss Crabtree in the basic premise of "Teacher's Beau," as the kids complain, "Just as we're getting to like her (Miss Jones) she decides to leave us." "Ain't that just like a woman?" adds Alfalfa. They compose a poignant speech to read to the teacher: "My dear beautiful Miss Jones: On account of us liking you so much, we want you to give that Ralph guy the air, before you break all of our hearts."

Although Alfalfa is prevented from reading the speech by a sore throat, some horseradish clears up his voice enough for him to render (in more ways than one) an

Alvin, Scott, Jerry, Spanky, and Alfalfa trying to prevent a marriage that they believe will rob them of their teacher in "Teacher's Beau."

Ozark ballad with his brother Harold, in a move to distract the guests while Spanky hides the specially prepared platter. Unfortunately, the food is resting right in front of a jocular fellow (played by Robert McKenzie) who keeps turning to Spanky and making remarks, instead of keeping his eyes on the stage. Finally Spanky has to tap his far shoulder in order to get him to turn around, so he can make off with the platter.

When Miss Jones fills the gang's plates with the doctored spaghetti, we see a succession of faces in close-up, conveying the alarm with which they greet this volatile meal. "When ya gotta, ya gotta," Spanky declares, as he starts to dig into the food. The other kids make squirmish faces as they eat, while Buckwheat's pigtails go flying in reaction to the hot food. In the final rush for water, Spanky goes right to the outside faucet and drinks so much that his stomach expands like a balloon before our very eyes! This kind of gag was typical for a crew accustomed to rigging such physical distortion gimmicks for Laurel & Hardy.

This was Arletta Duncan's only appearance with *Our Gang,* as the schoolteacher, and indeed she doesn't make as strong an impression as her fiancé, played by Edward Norris, who enjoyed a long career as leading man in B pictures. His performance as the amiable fiancé who jokes with the kids teeters on the edge of coyness but avoids the condescension that some actors brought to such roles in other *Our Gang* shorts. Deep-voiced Billy

Bletcher is the chairman of the school board who proposes a toast to the new couple (revealing to the kids that Miss Jones is to become Mrs. Wilson), while Gus Leonard, the beloved "old Cap" of "Mush and Milk," does a walk-on as another party guest. Robert McKenzie reminds many viewers of Andy Devine in his brief appearance here, although it was not a standard characterization, as he appeared in a wide variety of small roles in many Hal Roach comedies over the years.

Finally, "Teacher's Beau" marks the last appearance of Matthew "Stymie" Beard in an *Our Gang* comedy (except for his guest return in "Reunion in Rhythm"), and it seems a rather sad exit for such a colorful character. Having evolved from a scene-stealing supporting character in 1930 to a principal sidekick in 1931 and then a

major *Our Gang* star through 1934, it's odd to see him, admittedly getting old for his juvenile role, as a *background* player in 1935's "Teacher's Beau," with barely a word of dialogue in the entire short! Such was the irony of this kiddie series, however, that at the age of ten a player was "over the hill," and paving the way for new, younger stars like Spanky and Alfalfa.

On a television talk show one time with successor William "Buckwheat" Thomas, Stymie discussed his feelings about leaving *Our Gang:* "I couldn't understand when I saw they were bringing William along, even though I went through the same thing in replacing Farina. But they brought William out when I was beginning to get too large, and I just had that funny feeling; I heard the footsteps, but I didn't want to go."

137 · SPRUCIN' UP

Two Reels · Produced by Hal Roach · Directed by Gus Meins · Photographed by Art Lloyd · Edited by Louis McManus · Released on June 1, 1935, by M-G-M · Our Gang: George "Spanky" McFarland, Carl "Alfalfa" Switzer, Scotty Beckett, Billie "Buckwheat" Thomas, Marianne Edwards, Alvin Buckelew, Harold Switzer, Donald Proffitt, Dorian Johnston, Jerry "Percy" Tucker, and Pete the Pup · Marianne's father, Mr. Jones, Dick Elliott; Mrs. Jones, Lillian Rich; Real estate agent, James Burtis; Officer Riley, Harry Bernard; Spanky's mother, Leota Lorraine; Scotty's mother, Bess Flowers; Alfalfa's mother, Gertrude Sutton; First pedestrian, Lester Dorr; Second pedestrian, Viola Richard

A tense moment during filming of the third scene of "Sprucin' Up." Propman Bob Saunders and assistant director Gordon Douglas are on either side of the door; Alfalfa and Scotty are flanking director Gus Meins; mother Leota Lorraine is leaning over a puzzled, sleepy Spanky; Pete the Pup is under the covers; and Art Lloyd (without cap) is leaning into the camera. Note the boom mike and arc lamps around the room. If you were an actor, do you suppose any of this would disturb *your* concentration?

The gang is tired of being nagged by their mothers about attending to such bothersome chores as washing their ears, shining their shoes, and combing their hair. But when a pretty young girl moves onto the block, and happens to be the daughter of the new truant officer, these same kids suddenly plunge into neatness activities with surprising zeal. Everyone wants to get on the right side of the truant officer's daughter. Spanky uses his brains to

When a new truant officer moves into the neighborhood, everyone tries to make friends with his daughter, Marianne Edwards. *Left to right* on the curb, Alvin Buckelew, Harold Switzer, Dorian Johnston, Scotty, Spanky, Buckwheat, Alfalfa, and Donald Proffitt. Pete the Pup attends.

make her acquaintance, and eliminate amorous competition, secretly tooting the horn on Mr. Jones's roadster so that he'll come out and chase the other kids away. One rival remains, though—Alfalfa. He's already managed to get inside. How? "Personality, boy, personality," he boasts to Spank. They engage in a battle of wits to win the disinterested young lady's approval, but when this results in a chin-up contest on a curtain rod, they become preoccupied besting one another and fail to notice that the object of their affections is being whisked away by her old boyfriend Percy, literally leaving them hanging in midair.

The creative forces behind the series at this time included Hal Roach, director Gus Meins, assistant director Gordon Douglas, and a fine staff of writers, including Frank Tashlin.* Together, this team produced such subtle, witty, and well-written vehicles as "Sprucin' Up," a polished comedy showcase with more than its share of special moments worth cherishing.

The film opens with a sleepy Spanky feigning illness in bed—and none too convincingly. Mom shakes him to wake up, and with a wry look he says he's awfully sick and can't go to school that day. Mom informs her Little Rascal that it's Saturday, which induces an immediate recovery! Spank pops out of the covers and happily chases Petie around the room. Reveling in his good fortune this bright new day, he begins dressing, dances a bit, and makes up a song, "Oh, it's Saturday! Oh, it's Saturday! Hey nonny, nonny, and a hot-cha-cha!"

Then Spanky tries to leave the house for the day without washing. His mother catches him and asks if he washed. He has to think about it, puzzling, "Let me see. . . ." Mom looks at his ears and complains they're so dirty he could grow potatoes in them. She orders Spank into the bathroom, where he produces a string of homemade sound effects to give the impression that he's scrubbing himself—but Mom's heard that trick before, and joins the cheater to supervise the washing.

Similar scenes are shown with Scotty, who hates to clean his shoes, since they'll only get dirty again, and Alfalfa, who brushed both his teeth but contends that since Tarzan "don't never comb his hair" (especially with hand scoops of lard!) neither should he.

Out on the curb with the gang, Spanky is moaning about having to wash his face and turns to his black pal Buckwheat. "You're lucky!" he says, prompting a wide-eyed double take from the bewildered boy. Although such a gag might be deemed tasteless and/or inappropriate today, it's not; the humor is based on a child's innocence, and not malice, by any means. Buckwheat's marvelous silent reaction take, as if to say, "Boy, are you kidding?" punctuates the gag beautifully. Wisely, the punch phrase is not stressed—it's practically a throwaway—and once Buckwheat reacts, it's over, all nicely done, and they're on to the next bit of business.

Just a short time later, his mind intent on amorous pursuits, Spanky rushes back home to spruce up for the new neighborhood heartthrob, aggressively cleaning out his ears with a squeaking washcloth. To his startled mother, he looks up and declares, "Mom, a potato hasn't got a chance now!"

The competition for Marianne's attention isn't quite as amusing as what's come before, because there's an edge of contrivance to it. First, these scenes involve Marianne, and as attractive as she is, the young lady fights a losing battle to resist stealing glances at the camera, and her performance overall tends to be mechanical. Also, both Spanky and Alfalfa are at a stage in their *Our Gang* careers where they are neither completely spontaneous nor finely polished in their performances. Thus, the scripted material on their game of one-upmanship, to impress the ladylove, is a bit over their heads. The fine

* Later responsible for some of the funniest Warner Bros. cartoons, and then during the 1950s director of many often hilarious features, including *Son of Paleface, The Girl Can't Help It,* and Martin and Lewis's *Artists and Models.*

points of timing are lost, and they are unable to make all of their dialogue sound natural, as if they just made it up on the spot; instead, it sometimes comes off as what it is—a well-written script.

Still, such criticism is relative, as Spanky and Alfalfa shine above dozens of unappealing child actors who have come before and since, and who could never measure up

to their charm and natural talent. Their final showdown with Percy, the smug rich kid played by Jerry Tucker, is very satisfying, and the film's conclusion, with our heroes returning to their ungentlemanly ways, is completely appropriate for *Our Gang*. One gets the idea that Marianne is better suited to a boy like Percy anyhow, and now the gang can stop worrying about having to wash.

138 · THE LUCKY CORNER

Two Reels · Produced by Hal Roach · Directed by Gus Meins · Photographed by Ernest Depew · Edited by Louis McManus · Released on March 14, 1936, by M-G-M · Our Gang: George "Spanky" McFarland, Billie "Buckwheat" Thomas, Scotty Beckett, Carl "Alfalfa" Switzer, Leonard Kibrick, Harold Switzer, Marianne Edwards, Merrell Strong, Alvin Buckelew, Donald Proffitt, Tommy McFarland, Gloria Mann, and Pete the Pup · Grandpa, "Gus," Gus Leonard; Cranky proprietor, William Wagner; Officer, James C. Morton; Painter, Joe Bordeaux; Barber, Charley Young; First customer, Ernie Alexander; "Poisoned" customer, Bobby Dunn; Customer who screams, Art Rowlands; Crowd extras, Fred Holmes, Sam Lufkin, Lester Dorr, Jack (Tiny) Lipson, Jack Hill, Bunny Bronson

Their toy store having been destroyed by Petie the Pup in "For Pete's Sake," William Wagner and his "son" reemerge in the sidewalk diner business. This time, the two clearly drawn meanies are doing their best (their worst) to crowd competition off the block. The "competition" takes the form of a tiny portable lemonade stand run by Scotty Beckett and his grandpa, Gus. Chasing their stand off the corner, bratty Leonard Kibrick snarls, "Get that thing out of here," at which the outsized Spanky retorts, "Don't rush me, Big Boy." Now with their dander up, the gang comes to Grandpa's aid. They stage a makeshift parade and succeed in gathering a crowd of potential customers in front of the stand's new location. Somehow, Alfalfa's off-key rendition of "Little Brown Jug" holds everyone's attention, building to a rousing, crowd-pleasing confrontation with the miserly father and son, highlighted by a scalp-massaging apparatus stuck down Leonard's trousers, who is forced to bounce around on his rear end in time with "Stars and Stripes Forever."

A frequent theme throughout Gus Meins-directed Rascals shorts is one of irreverence for pretentious people, and few illustrate the concept of upsetting stuffed shirts as well as this film. Fast paced, slick and funny, "The Lucky Corner" typifies *Our Gang* at its best: a simple but solid story augmented by comedy that's warm and gentle, witty and visual, and timeless in its appeal. Spanky and Alfalfa divide a lot of the laughs, but Buckwheat also wins his share, and with practically no dialogue. His expressive yet deadpan reactions let one know exactly what he's thinking, even if he can't manage to say it. The production staff rigged up some action gags for him too, and throughout the short (punctuated by a slide whistle in the background) we see him scooting down the sidewalks on cakes of ice, whipping around a barber pole, and zipping through a crowd beneath their legs.

When ol' Gus gets run off his corner, Buckwheat's dad, a bootblack, is more than happy to share space with the little lemonade stand, assuring Gus, "Yes, there's room enough for the both of us." Thus it's another alliance of underdogs: blacks, Grandpa, and a bunch of cheerful and helpful kids, all battling "big" business and a crotchety,

Buckwheat, Alfalfa, and Spanky in "The Lucky Corner."

conceited miser who seems to have the law on his side.

Later, when Gus discovers he's out of sugar for his lemonade mix, Buckwheat's dad offers help again. He sends Buckwheat upstairs with a bowl to bring back the necessary sugar. That he climbs up on the stool and fills the bowl with starch instead of sugar is funny enough, but there's an inside joke that makes the gag doubly amusing. If you watch enough Hal Roach comedies, you begin to wonder about the products with labels showing they're from companies in Elmira, New York. The name crops up with amazing regularity. In this particular scene, the bags of sugar and starch both come from "3 Star Mfg. Co.," in where else but Elmira, New York. Why this

Production shot from "The Lucky Corner." Gus Meins, wearing white cap and sweater, directs Alfalfa in the scene where he stammers through a rendition of "Little Brown Jug." That's assistant director Gordon Douglas hunched in front of the arc with the 60 designation.

devotion to Elmira, New York? It just happened to be Hal Roach's hometown.

The unbeatable Roach stock company makes a hearty contribution to "The Lucky Corner," as well. With all the sour lemonade, many of them get a chance to demonstrate a specialty for spit-takes (a time-honored comedy standby wherein a shock of some kind causes the actor to spit out and spray whatever he's drinking). One Roach regular, Lester Dorr, apparently answered two calls for this film, since he shows up in various scenes wearing different suits of clothes! Maybe the continuity girl was out getting a lemonade.

Another potential source of confusion: "The Lucky Corner" was released one full year after it was completed; it must have puzzled audiences to see Scotty Beckett back in the gang after he'd left for feature roles.

139 · LITTLE PAPA

Two Reels · Produced by Hal Roach · Directed by Gus Meins · Photographed by Harry Forbes · Edited by Louis McManus · Released on September 21, 1935, by M-G-M · Our Gang: George "Spanky" McFarland, Carl "Alfalfa" Switzer, Scotty Beckett, Billie "Buckwheat" Thomas, Donald Proffitt, Alvin Buckelew, Sidney Kibrick, Dickie De Nuet, Baby Patsy Dittemore, Eva Lee "Marvel" Kuney, and Pete the Pup · Mother, Ruth Hiatt

The gang is going to play football when Spanky's mother orders him to stay home and mind the baby. There's one loophole: if the baby goes to sleep, Spanky can put her to bed (and therefore leave the house). Now the trick is to make the baby tired, which turns out to be impossible. Only when Spanky and Alfalfa pretend to go to sleep with the child in bed does she finally drift off to slumberland. Then the kids have a difficult time leaving the room without making a noise that will wake the child. One frustration follows another, and just when all seems solved, and the kids are inflating their football, an air pocket bursts with a bang, waking baby and making it clear that the kids will never get to play football that afternoon.

"Little Papa" is pretty much a misfire. Laughs are few and far between, and the overall concept of the short, depicting a series of unresolved frustrations, does not lend itself to a successful outcome in the *Our Gang* format.

The main problem is that the baby (actually quite an adorable child) is playing straight man, while the gang is supposed to be getting laughs. This puts them into the position of comedians, which they are not. Their resulting dialogue and gestures are wholly contrived, from the first scene to the last. As the kids are leaving for the day, a woman's voice calls, "Spank-eee!" Spanky and Alfalfa jolt to a halt and make wincing gestures. Spanky declares, "That's my mom!" while Alfalfa unconvincingly groans, "Everything happens to us!"

After a while, "Little Papa" develops into a reshaping of an idea used as the second half of *Their First Mistake,* George Marshall's Laurel & Hardy short with The Boys trying to put an infant to sleep, with equal unsuccess. And midway through "Little Papa" Spanky and Alfalfa begin to take on the characteristics of Laurel & Hardy. When Alfalfa goes to completely close a window shade, Spanky brushes him aside and announces, "*I'll do* it.'' Whereupon that shade, and both others in the room, flap into the air, making a tremendous racket. Later, the boys manage to tie their shoelaces together, and at one point, when Spanky tries to free his sleeping sister from his sweater, he manages to tangle up Alfalfa instead. When Alfalfa gets stuck in a closet and the doorknob falls off, he shoves it back in place, poking Spanky in the face on the other side of the door. This is pure Laurel & Hardy material, except that director Gus Meins should have realized that Spanky and Alfalfa are not Stan and Ollie,

and watching them struggle with a sweater simply isn't that funny. It isn't *Our Gang* humor. (One final reminder of L & H comes when Alfalfa tries singing, ''Go to Sleep, My Baby,'' just as Oliver Hardy had done to his children in the comedy *Brats* a few years earlier—except that Ollie sang better than Alfalfa.)

Oddly enough, the Hal Roach staff seemed to like the plot of ''Little Papa,'' because it was reworked just a few years later as ''Canned Fishing,'' with somewhat better results.

140 · LITTLE SINNER

Two Reels · Produced by Hal Roach · Directed by Gus Meins · Photographed by Francis Corby · Edited by Louis McManus · Released on October 26, 1935, by M-G-M · Our Gang: George ''Spanky'' McFarland, Billie ''Buckwheat'' Thomas, Eugene ''Porky'' Lee, Carl ''Alfalfa'' Switzer, Sidney Kibrick, Jerry Tucker, Donald Proffitt, and Rex Downing · Property owner, Clarence Wilson

Porky (making his debut at just two years of age) and Spanky plotting new duplicity in "Little Sinner."

Spanky decides to skip Sunday school in order to try out his new fishing rod. ''Boys who don't go to Sunday school is bad,'' Alfalfa declares, and Sid adds, ''Something's going to happen to you!'' but Spanky ignores their warnings, strolling away with his kid brother Porky and wide-eyed Buckwheat. Nothing seems to go right for the would-be fisherman, who is chased away from the river by a crabby caretaker. Wandering into the woods nearby, Spanky soon gets a strong dose of shivery atmosphere: an eclipse of the sun turns the sky suddenly dark, while a nearby baptism sends shouts of ''Hallelujah!'' and the ominous chant of a black chorus through the air. Pretty

soon Spanky is running for dear life. Crestfallen, and perspiring heavily, he manages to arrive back at the church just in time to race through the front door and follow the departing congregation through the exit, where the minister, referring to his sermon, asks, ''Well, Spank, did you learn a good lesson?'' ''And how!'' replies the frightened youngster.

A timely Halloween release, ''Little Sinner'' seems like a fine idea for an *Our Gang* short, but one ingredient is missing: believability. Actually, the film is a pleasant diversion and has good intentions, but one never quite accepts the situation as being real. From the kids' righteous warnings that he'll be sorry for skipping Sunday school to Spanky's growing fright while walking through the woods, ''Little Sinner'' seems to be telling the audience that this is all a charade to teach the errant boy a lesson.

The excitement and fear of being in the woods when the sky turns dark and ominous voices begin to sing in the distance could have been built into a tremendous sequence, but somehow director Gus Meins was unable to create a convincing atmosphere that would enable the audience to share Spanky's feelings. As a result, his emotions seem a bit contrived, simply means to an end of pointing up a moral.

Even the religious hysteria of the black baptism scenes is not woven into the film very convincingly. A long shot of the crowd waiting on the riverbank is almost certainly stock footage, interspersed with close-ups of individuals being dunked in the water and arising with shouts of belief and confirmation. Spanky's only contact with these people, however, is when he sees two Mantan Moreland types running through the woods in white outfits, stopping dead in their tracks and suddenly declaring, ''Hallelujah!''

Still, while the filmed realization of the story lacks zip and somewhat disappoints as a whole, to its credit there are some stylish touches to ''Little Sinner'' that make one want to watch it more than once . . . the quiet charm of the beautifully composed scenes by the lake on a bright Sunday morning . . . the smooth tracking shots through the woods as the kids look for a fishing spot where someone like cantankerous Clarence Wilson can't disturb them . . . the entrancing spiritual "Poor Mourner's Found a Hiding Place," sung while the frightened kids grin weakly to reassure one another and trek deeper into the darkening forest . . . and the running (or maybe toddling) gag of little Porky stuffing his mouth with whatever he can get his hands on—fruit, worms, flowers, even live fish.

Perhaps "Little Sinner" needs to be viewed under the guiding postulate that the sum of its parts *can* exceed the whole.

The succession of titles like "Little Papa" and "Little Sinner" was probably designed to cash in on Shirley Temple's (truly) unbelievable success in her concurrent string of syrupy features with titles such as *Little Miss Marker, The Little Colonel, Our Little Girl,* and *The Littlest Rebel.*

"Little Papa" and "Little Sinner" are two things Shirley Temple could *never* have been.

Sidelight: During production of the 1935 Laurel & Hardy feature *Bonnie Scotland,* Stan Laurel and the studio temporarily parted friendly company. Various reasons were given, but the fact of the matter was that half of Hal Roach's starring comedy team was not working. Perhaps as a bargaining ploy in renegotiating Laurel's contract, Hal Roach announced at this time that the Laurel & Hardy series was going to be replaced by another, called *The Hardys,* a family situation comedy to feature Oliver Hardy and Patsy Kelly as parents of Spanky McFarland. Of course, Laurel & Hardy eventually reunited, making further conjecture about *The Hardys* pointless.

Unfortunately, the recollections of Hal Roach, Spanky McFarland, and Patsy Kelly cannot provide us with further details, but the still photo released by the studio to publicize the new series was a composite, indicating that the three stars probably never gathered together on a sound stage to begin filming.

In a piece of real understatement, the trio's chemistry seemed right, and the series could have been glorious, but then we would have been deprived of all the wonderful Laurel & Hardy films yet to come . . . and who would have replaced beguiling Spanky in *Our Gang?*

141 · OUR GANG FOLLIES OF 1936

Two Reels · Produced by Hal Roach · Directed by Gus Meins · Photographed by Art Lloyd · Edited by Bert Jordan · Released on November 30, 1935, by M-G-M · Our Gang: George "Spanky" McFarland, Carl "Alfalfa" Switzer, Scotty Beckett, Billie "Buckwheat" Thomas, Dickie Jones, Eugene "Porky" Lee, Darla "Cookie" Hood, Philip Hurlic, Jackie White, Donald Proffitt, Harold Switzer, Sidney Kibrick, Jerry Tucker, Dickie De Nuet, Marvin Trin, Leonard Kibrick, Delmar Watson, Janet Comerford, Joan Gray, Jackie Banning, Patty Kelly, Rex Downing, Joyce Kay, Lona McDowell, Junior Kavanaugh, Garret Joplin, Ten Meglin Kiddies, The Bryan Sisters, The Bud Murray Dancers, and Elmer the Monkey

The gang stages a neighborhood musical revue. Hal Roach's miniature answer to M-G-M's *Broadway Melody of 1936,* "Follies" really has no plot at all. But the song and dance novelty acts are varied and unusually entertaining, the kids are convincing, the nonstop lively and loud musical background scoring is well above average, and there are some serviceable running gags to tie the fast-moving short together.

In keeping with the movie musical's high "camp" genre, "Follies" is presented tongue in cheek, sometimes as unreal as it is funny. It's not clear how the kids could have produced such a polished show in their cellar theater all by themselves, but that is the suggestion. (The show is produced by and for neighborhood kids. Not a single adult appears in the film.) Spanky, though, as master of ceremonies, tips us from the start that it's all in fun, exchanging dialogue in rhyme and song with a crowd outside, and crooning, "Step up kids, if you want to know, about the swell stuff, in this show. There's singin', dancin', and hotcha, too. It's only a penny—it won't break you."

Happily unpretentious, the kids run through their specialty numbers with just the right mix of individual character appeal and artless natural talent, though with the rough edges still very much in evidence. Professional, ultracutesy kiddie acts would have ruined the film's charm. So none of the acts are *too* cleverly staged, and indeed it's the unpolished naturalness and even amateur feel of the various routines that provide much of the short's appeal: little things like the kids in the audience cheering all the goofs. Or Buckwheat taking a serious approach to lighting the footlights while Porky toddles along behind to blow them out. Or the kids in the audience recognizing Buckwheat onstage as the curtain goes up and yelling together, "H'yah, Buckwheat!" causing him to drop his "character," which isn't so important anyway, beam at the recognition, and wave his greeting to the roaring audience.

The novelty acts, spaced with backstage running gags, are themselves very entertaining. Frequently the routines are gently impudent caricatures of current screen stars, but with no ornate choreography, no mobile camera, and no lavish production numbers; in short, none of the tinsel and glitter of an opulent musical spectacular, but some funny stuff nevertheless.

The musical format is really a beautifully conceived vehicle for Alfalfa, and he renders the first ballyhoo number—a spoof of the title song from Gene Autry's currently popular Western musical feature *Comin' Round the Mountain.* Still cast and costumed in the series as "a cowboy from the drugstore," and with his hillbilly drawl very much intact, Alfalfa was the perfect selection to parody the latest vogue in motion pictures, the "singing cowboy." One needn't be aware of this rather specific

Crooners Alfalfa and Bing Crosby share a melody on the set of "Pennies from Heaven," with Darla, Buckwheat, Spanky, and *Our Gang* alumna Edith Fellows.

takeoff to enjoy the sequence, though. It's humor that is more basic than topical, developing naturally out of the characters.

An ensemble of hula beauties follows Alfalfa, dancing none too well to "Honolulu Baby," a clever Marvin Hatley tune trotted out periodically and used in many Roach Studio films.

A second chorus line, this one bigger but no better, officially opens the homemade variety show. They greet a disbelieving audience with the deathless lyric, "Hello, hello, hello. We hope you like our show. Hello, hello, hello."

The Bryan Sisters sing an engaging corn-pone ditty, "How You Gonna Keep 'em Down on the Farm?" But the big-dollar acts are still to come.

Darla Hood, discovered and hastily written into the film during production, clicks in her *Our Gang* debut as the billboard girl, and sings "I'll Never Say 'Never Again' Again." She was too young to remember much about making it, but today brackets "Follies" as one of her two favorite *Our Gang* shorts.

"The Ghost Frolic," with its dancing, rattling skeletons and jaunty waltz-time melody, succeeds in being both offbeat and even chilling, if measured by the intercut reactions of wide-eyed, startled kids embracing each other in the darkened audience!

Returning minus his cowboy outfit, Alfalfa joins Darla and unknowingly parodies crooners for the first time, aping "Pinky" Tomlin's popular hit, "The Object of my Affection." Darla seemed impressed during the serenade, but though it's unstressed, we know how Alfalfa really feels about girls when he exits backstage and passes by Scotty and Spank and says, "Boy, I'm glad that's all over with."

The intended highlight of the program is to feature "The Flory-Dory Sixtette," a play on Broadway's famous *Flora Dora Sextette*. But the girls are late, forcing Spanky to reshuffle the acts. They never do arrive, so in desperation and to resounding chants of "We want the Flory-Dories!" Spanky and the gang put on the girls' costumes, and in the finest *42nd Street* tradition try to finish the show as best they can. No one but Spanky knows the girls' routine, though everything will be okay so long as they all watch Spanky and do exactly as he does. Buckwheat's nemesis monkey finds his way into the bustle of Spanky's costume, however, and starts wielding a long needle just as the music of "Narcissus" begins, soon bringing the short to a predictable but rollicking finish.

Studio publicity for "Follies" highlighted Spanky's debut as a crooning M.C., but reviewers were quick to single out Alfalfa, "the talented youngster with plenty of missing teeth," as the Roach Rascal who steals the show. Some critics noted shrewdly that the musical format and finale was a follow-up to the amateur-night story in "Beginner's Luck," the big commercial and critical *Our Gang* success released earlier in the year. Generally, critics' response to *Our Gang*'s musical innovation was quite favorable. Louis Sobol in *The New York Evening Journal* wrote, "A bow to Hal Roach for unearthing another set of amazingly precocious child stars for his new series of *Our Gang* pics—the current one at the Capitol Theater is a howl from start to finish." "Follies" was held over and played for at least three weeks at the Capitol. A number of trade reviews advised exhibitors they could profitably advertise "Our Gang Follies" with the feature film in their marquee play-up outside theaters.

Other trade press comments: Jack Harrower in *The Film Daily,* "A wow! A riot! This special short should wow 'em wherever the *Our Gang* aggregation are known and loved. And that's practically everywhere!" *Motion Picture Daily* said, "Hal Roach has produced a swell singing, dancing musical in two reels, using the talents of his famous gang to the utmost for entertainment and laughs. Should get unusual box-office response." And *Daily Variety* wrote, "Sure fire! First musical short featuring *Our Gang* players is an ambitious undertaking, providing eighteen minutes of solid entertainment. Direction expert, and featured players great. Will click on any program."

"Follies" *was* a high-budget *Our Gang* comedy, with an advertised cast of one hundred kids and an unusually long shooting schedule of three weeks. It came at a time when Hal Roach was casting about for new ideas in the *Our Gang* screen unit. Roach's pet series had always been *Our Gang,* and even in 1935 when the program feature was squeezing out of the short subject, Roach would still spend the extra time and money to extract an ambitious short from an idea he believed in. Roach promised that two-reel revues like "Follies" would be an annual event, but the only official sequel wasn't to be released for another two years.

142 · DIVOT DIGGERS

Two Reels · Produced by Hal Roach · Directed by Robert F. McGowan · Photographed by Francis Corby · Edited by Louis McManus · Released on February 8, 1936, by M-G-M · Our Gang: George "Spanky" McFarland, Carl "Alfalfa" Switzer, Billie "Buckwheat" Thomas, Eugene "Porky" Lee, Darla Hood, Harold Switzer, Baby Patsy May, Pete the Pup, and Jiggs the Chimpanzee · Mr. Hatfield, the caddy master, Jack Hatfield; Caddy, Leonard Kibrick; Caddy, Matty Roubert; First golfer to tee off, Thomas Pogue; Second golfer, David Thursby; Third golfer, Billy Bletcher; Golfer completing the foursome, Tom Dugan; Tractor driver, Hubert Diltz; Golfer left sprawling, Jack Hill; Gibberish voice-over for Jiggs, Russ Powell

Taking advantage of a sunny spring day, Our Gang is out running riot over a golf course. How they ever got onto the country club is a mystery, but they're there digging divots nonetheless. No one has a care in the world, and life couldn't be sweeter. Buckwheat's the caddy, carrying doubles for Darla and Spanky. When Spanky's ladling spoon "club" won't help him whack his way out of a sand trap, he just picks up the ball and throws it toward the pin while no one's looking. Walking to the green, resourceful Spanky carefully takes the cover off his putter—a long-handled hammer. Porky is carrying Alfalfa's bag, and he's earnestly recording zeroes on his slate for each time Alfalfa fans on a swing from behind the sand bunker *he's* buried in. Spraying sand like a snow blower, but not the least upset by it, Alfalfa finally lifts a lucky shot to the green, and gladly exchanges his pitching wedge (a shovel) for his putting iron (a billiard cue). Chalking up and taking aim from a prone position, Alfalfa lags his putt a wee bit short, but cagey Porky guides the shot into the cup with a blast from his trusty bean-shooter. Meanwhile, back at the clubhouse, the caddies, protesting their low rates, walk off the course, leaving a desperate caddy master to scout up some substitutes for the next foursome anxious to tee off. Anyone will do. He settles for even less, rounding up Our Gang when one of Spanky's slicing drives upends the harried caddy master as he tries to cross the fairway. These kids make an aggregation of bag-toters like this unlucky foursome's never seen, and their unorthodox caddying turns the golfers' game into a frustrating shambles, all climaxed by a wild chase over the golf course's rolling hills when Jiggs, the gang's pet chimp, takes after the golfers in a runaway lawn-mowing tractor. No one is safe in the chimp's path, including the gang, who lean on a fence at the crest of the hill, breaking it down and turning it into a sort of sled that whizzes them downhill, clearing the fairway of golfers and clubs alike, knocking them high into the air and leaving the dazed duffers sprawling in the sled's wake!

Busby Berkeley may have had his *Gold Diggers,* but Hal Roach scored a bull's-eye casting his kids as "Divot Diggers" in this delightful short. The last *Our Gang* picture directed by series mentor Bob McGowan, it's also one of his finest and most enduring efforts, a happy movie brimming with sight gags, carefree fun, heart, action, peppy background music—a film in which forty laughs to a reel is par.

Disarming in its simplicity, "Divot Diggers" is one of those ideal *Our Gang* comedies that succeeds on several levels. It offers a broad base of identification, even for those who never caddied as a kid or played golf later on. This is basic visual comedy, made doubly funny by frequent cutaways to close-up reactions of the gang.

Gangway! Spanky McFarland, Tom Pogue, and Alfalfa's brother Harold Switzer in "Divot Diggers."

In the film's opening scenes, there's a vicarious adventure in the gang's efforts to fashion their own amusement. Somehow, they're having great fun playing lousy golf, all by themselves, and using makeshift implements ill-designed for the purpose. Later, as the kids are recruited as inexpert bag-toters, you can watch from a different (safe and superior) point of view, laughing at the golfers' abundant misfortune—because none of it is happening to you!

As one flustered golfer tees up and addresses the ball, Buckwheat's shoes squeak, Jiggs the Chimp starts thumbing his lips and sputtering unintelligibly, and Baby Patsy pops a balloon in the poor guy's ear during his backswing! Another member of the group (character comedian Tom Dugan) finds that the monkey is *his* caddy. On one hole, he wastes forty-six shots before sinking his putt, and when he finally does, the ball pops out of its hole, propelled by a frog resting underneath! At this, Dugan goes berserk and breaks his putter over his knee. Following his master's cue, Jiggs dutifully begins taking clubs from Dugan's bag and cracking them in two.

It's likely Dugan had a hand in writing "Divot Diggers." Listed as a scenarist on the Roach payroll, the Dublin-born actor also turned up in one of Charley Chase's golf-related pictures, *Poker at Eight.* Other possible contributors to the gag fest: Chase's brother James Parrott, prolific supporting comic Charlie Hall, famed circus clown Felix Adler, silent star Harry Langdon, John Guedel (later the producer of Groucho Marx's TV show), Carl Harbaugh (who coauthored some of Buster

"Divot Diggers," with Jiggs and Spanky.

Keaton's silent masterpieces), Frank Butler (later to win an Oscar for *Going My Way*) and, by two reports, Frank Tashlin, at the outset of his career as a distinguished writer-director. With all this gag-writing talent at Roach in 1936, no wonder "Divot Diggers" has such a high laugh quotient.

Golf was a particularly inspiring subject for the staff, growing out of an annual studio event explained by Hal Roach: "Every year, more or less, we used to have a golf tournament at the studio, and everybody played, no matter how bad. Now Babe (Oliver) Hardy and Bob McGowan and I used to play a bit of golf out at Lakeside [Country Club], but Hardy was the best golfer around, and he used to win the thing nearly every time and get the trophy. We'd all play and have a good time. Once in a while someone'd get an idea for a picture from the thing. One year it would be Charley Chase, another year Laurel & Hardy , or the Gang, and so on." The Chase outing is a particularly delightful one called *All Teed Up* (1930), co-starring Thelma Todd.

Adding to the fun of "Divot Diggers" is a lively incidental music score that enhances the film with its own rhythmic pacing. Studio music cue sheets provide us with titles to some of these jaunty tunes: "Cuckoo Waltz" (a Nathaniel Shilkret composition), "Buckwheat's March," "Alfalfa's March" (composed and orchestrated by Marvin Hatley), "Colonel Buckshot," "Miss Crabtree," "Sliding," "Slouching," "Dash and Dot," "Gangway Charley," "Riding Along," "On a Sunny Afternoon," "We're Out for Fun," and "Flivver Flops" (all written by LeRoy Shield). Some of these were library themes, their names revealing their sources from earlier Hal Roach films (Colonel Buckshot was a character in the 1930 Laurel & Hardy film *Another Fine Mess*), while many of the compositions recorded for "Divot Diggers" were used as background scoring for a concurrent reissue of the L & H comedy *Brats,* which had been musicless when first issued in 1930.

Astute *Our Gang* viewers will notice that Darla Hood has blond tresses in this short. The reason is that her hair was bleached for her role in the Laurel & Hardy feature *The Bohemian Girl*. Originally Darla had been cast to play Thelma Todd as a child; with Miss Todd wearing a dark wig, Darla was a perfect choice for the role. The actress's death in early stages of production caused a hasty rewrite of the film and the sudden casting of blond Jacqueline Wells in the role of Darla grown up. So . . . brunette Darla became a blonde, at Westmore's Beauty Salon in Hollywood, where she met Shirley Temple, the only time Darla crossed paths with the actress who had bid unsuccessfully for the *Our Gang* leading lady role. Darla's natural hair coloring hadn't been restored when "Divot Diggers" started filming.

Of Laurel & Hardy, Darla recalls, "They were so marvelous, Hardy was a bit more serious, and reserved, but Laurel apparently just loved children, and he'd always pick me up, and hold me, play games. I remember one time I wanted to sit and make mud pies, and he sat right down on the ground with me and helped me mold my mud pies! After filming *The Bohemian Girl,* we'd take turns visiting each other's sets. If the Gang wasn't shooting, we could walk up real close and watch Laurel & Hardy, or anyone on the Roach lot, as long as we behaved ourselves, which we did now and then! Of course the back lot there at Roach was the greatest playground any kid could ever have."

Darla has no clear recollection of "Divot Diggers," but she has some clear observations on the series itself: "Our films were based on the kinds of activities kids would normally be involved in anyway; the only thing is that the studio provided us with the sets, props, costumes, and everything else to go with it all. For the longest time, I wasn't even aware that I was being photographed. I was so young it was like living in a dream world, and I hardly remember the first few pictures I did, and I wasn't even aware that they were movies. Even when I was making my screen test, they just kept telling me, well do this and that, and I thought I was sort of performing just for them. I didn't understand what a motion picture camera was, or what it was doing in the way of recording my actions."

Spanky McFarland agrees, again pointing up the *Our Gang* comedies' unstudied quality. "I was making pictures before my memory process started, and before I could walk. It was the only way of life I knew. For a long, long time I thought every kid grew up making pictures. Before adolescence, I really didn't think too much about being in the movies. I was actually eight or nine years old before I realized all kids weren't in the movies, and I never had any friends other than the Gang. It wasn't like a job—but it wasn't exactly like playing either." (In late 1935, *Collier's* magazine asked Spanky his age. "Six," he said. And how long had he been working in motion pictures? "Seven years," answered Spank.)

Bob McGowan and successor Gus Meins sometimes filmed the series in what amounted to a modified, supervised "candid camera" technique. Kids, like people, are most interesting when they don't know they're being watched. Of course, Roach staffers didn't conceal their filmmaking equipment, but its presence was unstressed and its purpose downplayed as much as possible. With proper direction, this method allowed the kids' true, ingratiating personalities to shine through on film essentially unadulterated. It enabled McGowan to capture the unaffected innocence that was *Our Gang's* hallmark; and it was precisely the loss of this feeling that made the later films in the series seem so contrived and heartless.

Hal Roach's fundamental theory of comedy is based on the innocence of children. Ultimately and always we care about what we did as kids, what we would have liked to do, and what we *still* would do if we could recapture that youthful innocence. Hal Roach maintains that the top comedians, from Charlie Chaplin right through to Bill

Cosby, have always tried to capture that childlike feeling, and this is the basis of their great success. Roach's *Our Gang* series used actual kids to communicate the same feeling; this is why it was so important that the youngsters in *Our Gang* come across as real kids—talented, personable kids just being themselves.

An interesting parallel between "Divot Diggers" and real life (some years later) involves Spanky, who in the film boasts that he shot a seventy-four. "Seventy-four strokes for eighteen holes?" "No!" says Spank. "That was just for the first hole. But I cut it down to sixty-four for the second." Well, in recent years his golfing has improved considerably, and since 1971 he has hosted the annual Spanky McFarland Celebrity Golf Classic in Marion, Indiana, attended by sports and entertainment luminaries ranging from baseball great Bob Feller to bunnies from *Playboy* magazine. Entrants have also included pals Jackie Coogan, and Stymie Beard, who today characterizes Spank as "still the same, always in charge, doing everything for everybody, running around saying 'Just relax, let me do it for you.' " Tournament proceeds are distributed to charities.

Interlude: Director's Swan Song. More than two years back, kindly "Uncle Bob" McGowan (as his press notices called him) had relinquished his lengthy affiliation with *Our Gang*. At the time he was tired, ill, but financially secure at age fifty-one, and wanted to engage in other, less strenuous projects. He remained at his home studio for a time, and between relaxing at the Masquers' Club and Lakeside Golf Club, he managed to find time to direct a funny Hal Roach *All Star* comedy, "Crook's Tour," and contributed gags to Laurel & Hardy's *Babes in Toyland*. Then he accepted a position with Paramount, writing, producing, and directing some generally undistinguished features and shorts, including some one-reel kid comedies featuring W. C. Fields's nemesis, Baby LeRoy. One of these was called *Babes in Hollywood*.

Accounting for the director's return to *Our Gang* in 1936, the "Divot Diggers" pressbook dubiously quotes McGowan as bemoaning, "I just couldn't stand being away from the kids any longer. I couldn't have missed members of my own immediate family more than I missed the Gang. After working with youngsters for twelve years it seemed strange to be telling adults what to do and when to do it. As a matter of fact, every once in a while, I would catch myself mumbling baby talk to some big lumbering actor, so I thought it was time to quit and return to my first and only real love." If true, why was this film McGowan's last *Our Gang* assignment? The answer is unclear.

Increasingly studio-bound under the direction of Gus Meins, the Gang was brought back outdoors by McGowan for "Divot Diggers." It's easy to admire his tight, tidy direction—there's hardly a wasted moment in the film—showing that McGowan's skills had not atrophied. What's most striking is that "Divot Diggers" doesn't overlap with any other known McGowan work, and boasts some original touches besides, all serving to indicate that he'd recharged his batteries for a fresh start. More's the pity he didn't continue his association with the Gang at this point.

He worked infrequently after 1936. Hal Roach recalls that "after Bob left us he did practically nothing. He was just worn out." McGowan's inactivity probably explains why he didn't mind when his (less talented) nephew An-

thony Mack used the name Robert A. McGowan to write the new series of *Our Gang* comedies over at M-G-M.

Later, together with other Roach graduates like Fred Guiol and Bebe Daniels, McGowan did return to Roach off and on in the 1940s to help produce feature films and those awkward "streamliners" for the studio, including two mediocre *Our Gang*-derivative features in color: *Curley* (1947), also known as *The Hal Roach Comedy Carnival,* and *Who Killed "Doc" Robbin* (1948).

In 1952, McGowan, cameraman Art Lloyd, and grown Our Gangers Mickey Daniels, Jackie Condon, Farina Hoskins, Joe Cobb, and Johnny Downs were reunited for a poorly staged episode of Art Baker's television program *You Asked for It.* A slapdash affair, it didn't begin to exploit the possibilities of an *Our Gang* reunion, but was a nostalgic treat nonetheless.

Three years later, in 1955, McGowan died of cancer in Santa Monica, at age seventy-two.

Hal Roach remembers Bob McGowan as "a very delightful kind of a guy to know and be with. I made a vacation trip to Europe with him once, and we had loads of fun. Bob had a great sense of humor. He always called me 'Boss.' After each picture he'd come up and say, 'Well, Boss, what do we do next?' Bob was always a top director, head and shoulders above most others in the business. He was great on the silent pictures, then when sound came in he had trouble for a while because he couldn't talk to the kids off-scene while he was directing. It was tough on him, but he adjusted. Overall, though others like Gus Meins and Gordon Douglas were very talented, I'd have to say Bob was the best director the Gang ever had."

143 · THE PINCH SINGER

Two Reels · Produced by Hal Roach · Directed by Fred Newmeyer · Photographed by Art Lloyd · Edited by Louis McManus · Released on January 4, 1936, by M-G-M · Our Gang: Carl "Alfalfa" Switzer, George "Spanky" McFarland, Darla Hood, Billie "Buckwheat" Thomas, Eugene "Porky" Lee, Dickie DeNuet, Billy Winderlout, Jerry Tucker, Marianne Edwards, Sidney Kibrick, Peggy Lynch, Harold Switzer, Dorian Johnston, Junior Kavanaugh, Dickie Jones, Jackie Morrow, Harry McCabe, Betty Cox, Rex Downing, Delmar Watson, Warner Weidler, George Weidler, Walt Weidler, Bud Murray's Dancers, and Pete the Pup · Music conductor, Marvin Hatley; Radio announcer, Blair Davies; Information girl, Gail Goodson; Elevator boy, Eddie Craven; Druggist, Charlie Hall; Audience extras, Charlie Hall, Chet Brandenberg, Lester Dorr; Pages, Bill Madsen, David Sharpe

A prize of fifty dollars inspires the gang's Eagles Club to find a singer who can win a radio station amateur contest that afternoon. Auditions are held before a capacity kiddie audience in the clubhouse, with Spanky moderating and assistant Pete the Pup poised awaiting Spank's wink as the cue for striking a loser's gong with a mallet tied to his tail. One kid objects to being "hooked" so abruptly: "I just already got started." "Oh, no," Spanky delights in telling him, "you mean you just finished." Darla is chosen as the prime candidate, despite Alfalfa's persistent efforts. She is set to meet Spanky at the station later that day, but when the time comes, she's nowhere in sight. Spanky goes to look for her, and in his absence, Alfalfa decides to perform in Darla's place ("I'll *do* it!"), singing her song, "I'm in the Mood for Love." Listening back in the clubhouse, dozens of Our Gangers rush out to the local drugstore's battery of pay telephones, phoning in a ton of votes for Alfalfa, with the result that this dark-horse contestant (who was hooted off the clubhouse stage three times that morning) saves the day and wins the fifty dollar prize.

Out of which probably had to be paid a whopping reimbursement for the drugstore phone calls.

If, as Truman Capote says, failure is the condiment that gives success its flavor, crooner Alfalfa feasted on a tasty mouthful in "The Pinch Singer." As a film, however, "The Pinch Singer" was fed too many sweets, and without the proper nutrients never grew into the kind of healthy comedy it might have been.

Of *Our Gang*'s three radio contest shorts for Roach, "The Pinch Singer" is probably the weakest. The music is sprightly and delightful but the kids perhaps too cute and story exposition notably deficient. Most of the blame must go to director Fred Newmeyer, making his official credited debut with the series on this film (he'd worked on the very first *Our Gang* comedy in 1922).

A boyhood chum of Bob McGowan's in Denver, Newmeyer was by this time a veteran comedy director, having worked for many years with Harold Lloyd, directing such classic films as *Grandma's Boy, The Freshman,* and *Safety Last*. He branched out into other feature films (once directing W. C. Fields) but by the mid-1930s was working on Poverty Row. Having started his successful career with Hal Roach in the late teens, he now returned to Roach for a job, and worked on several *Our Gang* comedies, including the feature-length "General Spanky."

What Newmeyer apparently didn't realize was that the stars of *Our Gang,* although extremely talented, were still children, requiring a special kind of direction to make

Spanky and Darla arrive just in time to be too late, in this closing scene from "The Pinch Singer."

their planned movements and dialogue seem spontaneous. Bob McGowan, Gus Meins, and later Gordon Douglas mastered this technique of working with the kids, but Newmeyer did not, as evidenced by this two-reeler.

A great deal of the dialogue and gesturing is hopelessly contrived, much like the later M-G-M *Our Gang* shorts. As Alfalfa and Buckwheat audition for the club, the kids laugh and cheer them in a forced, unconvincing manner—precisely the way a group of kids would act if someone told them to laugh on cue, without actually giving them anything to laugh at. The camera repeatedly cuts to reaction shots of Spanky making broad, knowing gestures; when Buckwheat's whistling is exposed as a fraud (he's got Porky playing a phonograph nearby), Spanky says, "Hey kids, let's give Buckwheat a big, great big hand, because he had us all fooled then!" (Even a good director would have had trouble getting anyone to sound convincing with that kind of dialogue.)

Worst of all is the finale. After Alfalfa has unexpectedly won the prize money, Spanky and Darla arrive on the scene. Spanky is about to scold Alfalfa, but when he hears about the prize, he says, "Say pal, I knew you could do that all the time. Besides, I was just telling Darla, you're the best singer in the whole wide world. . . .'' Alfalfa interrupts Spanky's hot-air speech by giving him a taste of his own medicine, and ringing the audition gong he's concealed in his briefcase. At this point what do the three kids do? They lock arms, snuggle up together and smile blissfully for the camera in an ''aren't-we-cute'' pose for the fade-out. Apparently, Newmeyer missed an essential point of the series. One need only look back to ''Mike Fright,'' from 1934, or ahead to the excellent and compact one-reeler ''Framing Youth'' in 1937, to see how this same material should have been treated.

There are other interesting side notes to ''The Pinch Singer.'' Looking at the film out of context, it comes as a surprise that the gang doesn't immediately think of Alfalfa when they want a singer. Although he is by now one of the gang's main characters (sort of displacing Scotty Beckett, who'd just left the series), Alfalfa hadn't yet solidified his image as a ''crooner,'' even with his song numbers in ''Beginner's Luck,'' ''Teacher's Beau,'' and ''Our Gang Follies of 1936.'' It was in the coming year that Alfalfa's singing became a fixture of the series and an integral part of story lines.

Alfalfa's singing, and his sincere attitude toward performing, are equally interesting in this short. His audition song is ''On the Road to Californy,'' a folk song with his brother backing him up on accordion, creating the same enjoyable country-western feeling as the songs they had done in earlier films; Alfalfa's love songs were to come later. When he goes on the air to sing Darla's number, ''I'm in the Mood for Love,'' he is uncertain, forgets words, loses the beat, and summons up a falsetto to reach half the notes. Then in an effort to induce Alfalfa to conclude his unending number, the microphone begins to sink, forcing Alfalfa to stoop down with it to finish his

song! This innocence is a far cry from the superconfident crooner of later *Our Gang* comedies, when Alfalfa *knows* he's funny and his character appeal varies inversely.

Several professional-school kiddie acts are seen in the course of the radio program. One blackfaced group called The Plantation Trio sings ''Five Foot Two'' (''Has Anybody Seen My Gal?''). A top-hatted troupe does ''The Broadway Melody,'' led by a well-scrubbed young man belting out the theme from M-G-M's famous early-talkie musical. An instrumental trio plays a saxophone version of a number written for an earlier Hal Roach *All Star* comedy, *Mixed Nuts,* while the song's composer, studio musical director Marvin Hatley, leads the on-camera orchestra (cued by an announcer who proclaims, ''Take it away, Marvin!''). Earlier, Buckwheat mimes to a 78 rpm recording of ''The Whistler and his Dog.''

Music aside, ''The Pinch Singer'' demonstrates that the *Our Gang* kids were like any actors working in films—they needed a good director.

Footnotes: ''The Pinch Singer'' is Darla Hood's third *Little Rascals* appearance. She'd been christened ''Cookie, Our Gang's Sweetheart,'' for ''Follies,'' but nobody'd call her that, using her real name, Darla, instead.

In another deplorable example of how cavalier TV editors and syndicators have sometimes slashed *Our Gang* films, ''The Pinch Singer'' almost never turns up intact on television or for other revival showings. With all that's missing from expurgated prints, one might be led to believe the film is actually a one-reeler. In the bargain, the original titles are usually obliterated, too; the as-always interesting artwork on the main titles having shown a silhouetted radio tower with pulsating radio waves.

144 · SECOND CHILDHOOD

Two Reels · Produced by Hal Roach · Directed by Gus Meins · Photographed by Francis Corby · Edited by Louis McManus · Released on April 11, 1936, by M-G-M · Our Gang: George ''Spanky'' McFarland, Carl ''Alfalfa'' Switzer, Darla Hood, Dickie DeNuet, Eugene ''Porky'' Lee, and Billie ''Buckwheat'' Thomas · Grandma, Zeffie Tilbury; Hobson, the butler, Sidney Bracey; Maid, Greta Gould

Apparently without friends or kin, a crotchety old woman is ''celebrating'' her sixty-fifth birthday in her usual cantankerous manner, complaining about the morning sunshine and browbeating her well-meaning servants as they ply her with pills to restore her health. Suddenly a toy airplane flies through her window and buzzes overhead in her dining room (''Get the Flit!'' she cries) before crashing against a vase and coming to a halt. Spanky comes looking for the plane and is told that he'll have to pay seventy-five cents for the broken vase. Spanky replies that he and his pals haven't got that much money, but they could earn their way by cleaning up the yard, to ''make this place look like somebody really lives in it.'' The old lady represses a smile and goes along with the idea, already becoming fond of the children but reluctant to admit it. Before long she's doing more work than they are, showing them how to mow the lawn, then challenging

Alfalfa on his singing of ''Oh Susannah.'' She is intrigued with Spanky's slingshot and when an accidental shot smashes a bottle of pills, she's delighted, and decides to pulverize every capsule container on the premises. Now she's really fired up, and Grandma demands to borrow a pair of roller skates. Spanky is wary, but the enlivened old lady proclaims, ''When you gotta, you gotta!'' and starts careening around the house, out of control. On one pass she latches onto a serving cart on which the gang is sitting, pulling it along with her. It lands next to an indoor fountain, dumping the kids into the water. When she sees how much fun they have playing in the ''pool,'' Grandma says, ''For twenty years I've wondered what that thing was for,'' takes a running leap, and dives in with the kids, happier than she's ever been before. Coming up spouting water, the gang hugs her, saying, ''You're all right, Grandma!''

What "Second Childhood" may lack in credibility is compensated by the sheer fun of this fast-moving film.

Zeffie Tilbury is engaging as the Miss Havisham-like elderly lady, but her nasty nature is never really convincing; from the start it's clear that she and the kids will get along.* The reason is simple: she is tired of being coddled by her servants, and Spanky is the first person in the household to talk back and say what's on his mind. Protesting that the seventy-five-cent broken vase has only a twenty-five-cent price tag on it, butler Hobson blurts out, "Such impudence!" Grandma interjects, though, "Hobson, I'm taking care of this," and Spanky chimes in, "Yes, she's taking care of this, Hobson."

When the butler brings his eccentric employer her morning pills and insists that she must get well, Grandma puts up a fuss and barks, "I'll stay sick just as long as I want to." Later, however, Spanky declares, "Those pills are a lot of baloney!" and gets Grandma to admit that she never felt better in her life.

Grandma's transition from foe to friend is nicely handled. After she upbraids the gang in the initial encounter over the toy airplane, we catch a glimpse of the old lady smiling to herself, our first hint that things aren't as bad as they seem. To Spanky she's just "an old crab," but later when she joins him and Alfalfa in energetically mowing the lawn, he says, "You know, Grandma, you're a pretty swell guy," to which she replies, "I'm nothing of the sort," her mask of ill humor refusing to acknowledge that she's actually having fun for a change.

As she's mowing, Alfalfa begins to sing "Oh Susannah," completely disregarding the actual melody. Grandma wonders if he doesn't feel well, but Alfalfa smilingly objects, "I'm singin'!" Grandma advises him that he isn't paid to sing, and he doesn't know the song besides. "I guess I do," he complains. "You guess again," Grandma says sternly. Spanky explains, "Grandma, you cain't tell him nothing about singing. He's been singin' that stuff ever since he was a kid." After a few more songful false starts, the trio adjourns to the piano inside where they work out the melody and lyrics. As the threesome is happily singing, Spanky's slingshot catches on the edge of the piano bench, and snaps against Grandma's derriere just in time to spark her toward a high-note finale.

This provides a perfect introduction to the slingshot, which captures Grandma's fancy and really gets her into the spirit of playing with her new-found friends. Borrowing some of Spanky's marbles, she gleefully shoots down every pill bottle in the house. When this game is over, the momentum is tremendous, and the spry old woman seeks another challenge: roller skates. Even Spanky has his doubts about this, but Grandma chides him as she did her butler earlier, snapping, "Oh, don't be an old fogey; you're only young once!"

The use of a double for Zeffie Tilbury is all too obvious in the skating scenes, but a valiant attempt is made to

Buckwheat, in character for "Second Childhood."

make it look real by intercutting excellent process-screen work of Grandma sailing around corners, chased by her distraught servants.

The kids' handling of dialogue in "Second Childhood" seems more stilted than usual, perhaps because they are pitted against such a canny professional as Miss Tilbury, yet one is willing to go along with the contrivances in this film because as a whole it works so very well.

The secret of "Second Childhood" is charm, and that can make up for flaws that might seem more serious in other, less entertaining films.

Supposedly celebrating her sixty-fifth birthday in "Second Childhood," Miss Tilbury was actually an agile, peppy seventy-three, and lived to be eighty-two. Like Margaret Mann, her predecessor Grandma for an earlier generation of Our Gangers, she too was a veteran of John Ford films, later working in both *The Grapes of Wrath* and *Tobacco Road*.

At a theater screening with Spanky McFarland in 1973, he had fond recollections of "Second Childhood" and thought the short was quite funny, particularly liking Grandma's romp on roller skates and her running jump into the garden pond at the end. A large, rollicking, applauding audience then confirmed his opinion as they viewed the film. The ovation for this sequence was the biggest of the evening.

Surprisingly, George McFarland today can watch his own films with what he calls complete detachment. But he still enjoys them. "It's interesting to look at yourself when you were decades younger," he says, "and it's sure nice to be remembered, but I don't go into waves of ecstasy." He views the Gang shorts purely as entertainment, and apart from his participation in them. "The only time I really personally look at a part or a scene I did,"

---

* Except for Buckwheat, who in the film's first few days of production steered shy of Miss Tilbury, since he found it difficult to believe that her scripted sharp remarks and cross disposition were not the lady's true character. . . . It's surprising what miracles a few candy bars and peanuts can work, though.

Spank explains, "is if I acted badly, or overacted, or made a mistake. Then I might wince a little."

Sidelight: No one promotes movies the way they used to. A press-book exploitation idea for "Second Childhood" suggested, "A ballyhoo that should attract no end of attention on downtown streets would be a conserva-

tively dressed old woman carefully made-up to resemble the sixty-five-year-old Grandma in the film, who would circulate through the business and shopping areas on roller skates, carrying a small placard announcing 'Second Childhood.'"

Wonder if anyone ever did that?

145 · ARBOR DAY

Two Reels · Produced by Hal Roach · Directed by Fred Newmeyer · Photographed by Milton Krasner · Edited by Bert Jordan · Released on May 2, 1936, by M-G-M · Our Gang: George "Spanky" McFarland, Carl "Alfalfa" Switzer, Darla Hood, Billie "Buckwheat" Thomas, and Harold Switzer · Girl midget, Olive Brasno; Boy midget, George Brasno; Buckwheat's mother, Hattie McDaniel; Mr. Cass, the principal, Maurice Cass; Mr. Smithers, the truant officer, George Guhl; Lady after an autograph, May Wallace; Miss Argyle, teacher, Kathryn Sheldon; Miss Lawrence, playing piano, Rosina Lawrence; Murphy, the side show barker, Dick Rush; Atmosphere extras, Rolfe Sedan, Bobby Dunn

Two sideshow midgets find that the only way they can get some time off is to fool their boss, dress as children, and run away . . . but Smithers, the hard-working truant officer, thinks they are kids playing hooky and carts them off to school, where they sit through an Arbor Day pageant begrudgingly performed by the gang, and then volunteer to contribute a song. When the song evolves into a vaudeville shimmy number, the principal calls a halt: ("Positively shocking!"), just as the sideshow owner turns up and explains that the "children" are really midgets. Smithers is fired and the midgets are escorted back to their sideshow.

Not uproarious, but subtly funny, "Arbor Day" is an engaging piece of fluff built around a school pageant. What makes it unusual, especially for this period of *Our Gang* films, is that the pageant looks real, complete with "original" lyrics and music by one of the teachers, choreography, costumes, and a general aura of amateurishness that makes it most disarming. Fred Newmeyer, who made the overly studied "The Pinch Singer" earlier in 1936, swung to the other extreme with this entry and landed right on target.

In fact, the performance is so vivdly evocative of school plays we have all experienced that one would almost bet that the Hal Roach writers cribbed this entire sequence from a bona fide grade-school pageant. First there is a tree-planting ceremony, with Spanky reluctantly speaking the words: "Men may come and men may go/but I have heard them say/Big oaks from little acorns grow/So we have Arbor Day." Then there is a song-and-dance recital, with the girls dressed as the spirit of Mother Nature, and the boys as "sturdy oaks . . . really hardy blokes."

When the time comes for Buckwheat to deliver his one line, he stammers, and looks out to his mother in the audience, who loudly prompts him, "With plow and spade, the hole is made." Happy his mother knew the line, Buckwheat applauds and exudes, "Yep! 'at's it!"

Later, when Spanky, as a woodsman, threatens to cut down a tree, Alfalfa stops him and explains why he must cherish the oak, by singing Joyce Kilmer's "Trees," in what has to rate as the poem's all-time worst rendition. Even this is acknowledged within the film; as Alfalfa garbles the words and strains for the high notes of the song,

Alfalfa feeding Spanky his lines in "Arbor Day."

truant officer Smithers starts to doze off, and Spanky shakes his head in weary disgust, while the emotional teacher in charge of the play finds tears in her eyes.

The entire ceremony is framed by the wordy eloquence of school principal Maurice Cass, a character actor who was born to play headmasters and orchestra conductors, which is precisely what he did for nearly thirty years in Hollywood. His dowdy speech making is perfectly attuned to the atmosphere of the school pageant. "If I may be permitted to be facetious," he declares coyly at the end of his long-winded recitation, "On with the dance— let joy be unconfined!"

George and Olive Brasno, who were ideally cast as pint-sized replicas of the young-adult couple in "Shrimps for a Day," return as worldly-wise sideshow midgets, which they actually were, performing between film jobs in

Buster Shaver's vaudeville act. The diminutive twosome was engaged for "Arbor Day" at fifteen hundred per week, no little sum. The film's only disappointment is that when the Brasnos finally do their number, they get through just a few lines (which aren't easily intelligible) before Principal Cass cuts them off. It would have been fun to see their whole act, and we are anticipating just that at this point in the film. No wonder George calls as he's being carried away, "Come over and see a *good* show some time!"

146 · BORED OF EDUCATION

One Reel · Produced by Hal Roach · Directed by Gordon Douglas · Photographed by Art Lloyd · Edited by William Randall · Released on August 29, 1936, by M-G-M · Our Gang: George "Spanky" McFarland, Carl "Alfalfa" Switzer, Eugene "Porky" Lee, Billie "Buckwheat" Thomas, Darla Hood, Sidney Kibrick, Harold Switzer, Donald Proffitt, Dickie DeNuet, Dorian Johnston, and Pete the Pup · Miss Lawrence, the new teacher, Rosina Lawrence; Ice cream attendant, Jack Egan

"With vacation over, thousands of smiling, happy children return to school"—but Our Gang is neither happy nor smiling. All they want to do is find a way to skip the first day of class—especially since they're going to have a new teacher, who's sure to be an old crab. Spanky hatches an idea and rigs a phony toothache for Alfalfa, blowing up a balloon inside his cheek to make it look real. Meanwhile, the pretty new teacher, Miss Lawrence, overhears their scheme and decides to teach them a lesson. When Alfalfa refrains from singing "Good Morning" in class, Miss Lawrence innocently asks what's wrong, and told about his toothache, gives the groaning faker permission to go home, and encourages Spanky to accompany him. Just as they leave, a Good Humor delivery man comes along with ice cream bars for the entire class, a little surprise engineered by the teacher. Now Spanky has to find a way to get himself and Alfalfa back *into* class; he pops the balloon inside Alfalfa's cheek and tries to pull it out, but it snaps back into Alfalfa's throat. Trying to cough it up, he gulps it back down instead. Clutching his throat with a pained expression, he realizes "I swallowed it!" "Aw, that's nothin'," Spanky assures his pal. "I swallowed lots of things when I was a kid. Come on." So fully "cured," at least to Spanky's satisfaction, Alfalfa is led back into class, where Spanky accounts for his recovery: "Funny thing, teacher, he's all well now." Miss Lawrence insists that he must sing before getting his treat, so Alfalfa launches into "Believe Me, if All Those Endearing Young Charms," with the balloon stopper providing a whistling sound every time he inhales! He manages to get through the song, however, and Spanky and Alfalfa finally get their share of the ice cream from this kind—and clever—new teacher.

"Bored of Education" was almost never made. When the previous season's cycle of Our Gang comedies had concluded with "Arbor Day," there was speculation that the celebrated series might be suspended, despite its popularity.

With movie theaters literally dropping their shorts in favor of the double feature, Hal Roach had resigned himself to producing a new brand of ambitious, top-grade feature-length films. Our Gang was nearly a casualty in this purge, as the Laurel & Hardy and Charley Chase shorts had been. Our Gang, though, was a favorite with M-G-M, and Louis B. Mayer convinced Hal Roach to continue making the lucrative comedies by agreeing to accept the shorter episodes and agreeing to distribute the Our Gang feature test, "General Spanky." Luckily, the series' farewell was postponed.

The new season of shorter length Our Gang pictures was announced to the trades with this offbeat press release: "Certainly this year, in addition to his new feature production enterprise, there will be 12 single-reel Hal Roach Our Gang comedies. The public just wouldn't stand for a discontinuance of Our Gang. Might as well abolish baseball!

"Of course Spanky will continue to star in Our Gang comedies now being made by as spry a troupe of youngsters as ever gathered under the Klieg lights. You'll find Alfalfa there, too, as he's got all those things that make folks chuckle and a weirder voice than ever!

"It is to be emphasized the Our Gang comedies are in 1-reel each now and definitely a bright spot on any program."

Somehow, remarkably, this initial Gang single-reeler won the series its only Academy Award, as the best short subject of 1936.

One can only wonder how such a comparatively lackluster entry managed to win when so many more deserving Our Gang films had been bypassed through the years. Perhaps it was because Our Gang hadn't yet won an Academy Award, and the series appeared to be nearing an end. Or possibly the studio lobbied hard for recognition that year. Whatever, the award seems to have been a product of whim and timing, rather than strictly a consideration of merit. While a pleasant short, "Bored of Education" is hardly an outstanding one.

Most surprised of all was the film's director, young Gordon Douglas. Although he had been with the Roach studio for several years, working in the casting office, the prop room, as assistant cutter, as assistant director, and as part-time actor (in some earlier Our Gang and Boy Friends shorts) his name had appeared as director only twice before, on undistinguished Irvin S. Cobb shorts in Roach's All Star series. This was his first important assignment, and, significantly, it was the first Our Gang short in the new one-reel (ten-minute) format, after years of comedies twice that length. When his maiden effort in the series won an Academy Award, Douglas was elated. "I figured if at twenty-two I could get an Oscar, I had this town made," he recalls.

But reviewed today, the film "Bored of Education" doesn't stand up to earlier *Our Gang* efforts or to Douglas's later films in the series. The young filmmaker was still learning his own lessons, in a sense, when he made "Bored of Education." Each successive film showed a firmer grasp of timing within each scene, and overall pacing within the ten-minute format. In addition, Douglas got to know the kids much better and elicited more convincing performances from them.

"Bored of Education" suffers most in comparison with "Teacher's Pet," the superb 1930 two-reeler from which it was derived. The warmth, sincerity, and poignancy of "Teacher's Pet" are not to be found in this more streamlined edition. Miss Lawrence's gesture in handing the two would-be truants their ice-cream sticks at the end of Alfalfa's song can hardly compare with the reconciliation between Miss Crabtree and a weeping Jackie Cooper in "Teacher's Pet," but even without the comparison, one feels no real resolution in the ending of "Bored of Education." The kids haven't really learned much of a lesson, since they got away with their scheme and didn't suffer for it, and it doesn't appear that they've drawn any closer to Miss Lawrence because of the incident. One fully expects them to try something else another day—and, of course, they do.

Within one year, Gordon Douglas nailed down the one-reel *Our Gang*s and directed a series of slick, entertaining films that were near-perfect in construction and pacing. He has gone on to become a successful director of feature films, with *Come Fill the Cup, Them!, Young at Heart, Tony Rome,* and *Harlow* among his credits. But after all these years he still harbors special feelings about the Hal Roach studio. "It was a marvelous family. Everybody was there to make the picture as good, and as fast as possible . . . and as funny. Nobody was there to hurt anybody else. I've never run into as many nice people in one spot as at Hal Roach."

Just as it was Douglas's directorial debut with *Our Gang,* "Bored of Education" marked Rosina Lawrence's debut as *Our Gang*'s schoolteacher, in the first serious attempt to revive the role popularized by June Marlowe six years earlier. Hal Roach was grooming Rosina Lawrence for big things, casting her opposite Charley Chase in *Neighborhood House,* Laurel & Hardy in *Way Out West,* and Jack Haley in *Pick a Star.* The young actress had looks and talent (she sang and danced well, having learned to dance as a child to combat a spinal paralysis), but somehow she never quite made the splash the studio expected. Roach publicist Dick Hurley believes it was because she wouldn't go out and "push," as other movie protégés found they had to.

"Rosina told me a couple of times how much she enjoyed working with the kids," Hurley recalls. "She was actually the filmic prototype of the pretty schoolteacher, and oddly enough it seemed she would have been very content just tutoring the kids between scenes. She was all sweetness, the same off-screen as on." In real life, Miss Lawrence retired from the screen, married a judge, and raised children of her own.

Production Footnotes: From script to screen, "Bored of Education" underwent surprisingly few alterations. By

The faces tell the story; frames from "Bored of Education."

this time, each short was scripted fairly tightly, and Spanky McFarland recalls that the only improvisation during on-the-set rehearsals involved motions and rhythms, and occasionally dialogue, in order to make it sound natural for whoever had to deliver the lines. Usually the director would encourage the kids to iron out awkward dialogue that didn't sound right to them, or seemed somehow unnatural. "Well, how would *you* say it?" they might ask. The technique fostered spontaneity, and the charming rough edges only enhanced the films' believability.

In "Bored of Education," the camera setups and pan shots, the cuts, actions, reactions, attitudes, and dialogue were all executed essentially as set forth in the eight-page shooting script. However, one running gag was excised; it involved Spanky's repeated characterization of the new teacher as an old owl, calling for Buckwheat "takems" (as the script labeled such exaggerated reactions) each time Spanky mimes an owl's look and imitates the "Hoo! Hoo!" sound it makes. In turn, each time the script would also call for a cut to an amused Rosina, "as she takes it big," too. In the release print, the only trace of this gag is a single scene in class with Spanky drawing an owl on a slate ("the new teacher") and showing his handiwork to Alfalfa, thereby eliciting an exchange of approving nods between the two Rascals.

147 · TWO TOO YOUNG

One Reel · Produced by Hal Roach · Directed by Gordon Douglas · Photographed by Art Lloyd · Edited by William Ziegler · Released on September 26, 1936, by M-G-M · Our Gang: George "Spanky" McFarland, Carl "Alfalfa" Switzer, Eugene "Porky" Lee, Billie "Buckwheat" Thomas, Donald Proffitt, Jerry Tucker, Dickie De Nuet, Sidney Kibrick, Rex Downing, Joe Strauch, Jr., and Harold Switzer · The teacher, Rosina Lawrence

Spanky and Alfalfa gesture their agreement over some new duplicity as Rosina Lawrence looks on thoughtfully in this posed still from "Two Too Young."

Buckwheat and Porky have some firecrackers, and Spanky and Alfalfa are determined to get them. The direct approach—being overly pleasant while offering to swap a water pistol and magnifying glass—fails. Then Spanky perches on Alfalfa's shoulders, dons a hat, phony mustache, and a long black coat, to pose as a wobbly G-man and demand the goods. This scheme works, more or less, but just as the two connivers are about to set off the explosions, class is called back in session—Buckwheat cleverly rings the recess bell early. Alfalfa tucks the firecrackers in his back pocket, and while he stands to recite, Porky trains the magnifying glass on Alfalfa's back pocket; with the help of the sun, the firecrackers start to smoke and ignite, and Porky and Buckwheat have the last laugh while Alfalfa runs around in circles yelling and holding onto his flaming backside.

This tight-knit, well-made one-reeler sets its sights modestly and comes up with a pleasing if not overwhelming comedy. As in many of these one-reelers, the burden of a flimsy plot is carried admirably by the winning personalities of the central characters. Here, Buckwheat and Porky are the "little kids," too young (in Spanky's opinion) to have the responsibility (or is it the fun?) of setting off some firecrackers. Alfalfa winds up the pawn in brainy Spanky's plans.

Porky and Buckwheat were featured together in a host of shorts following this one, always with the same basic notion, that despite their incoherent speech and reticent nature, they aren't as gullible as they seem. Time and

time again, these little kids, apparent pushovers, somehow turn the tables and get even with their older and supposedly wiser pals.

There are some nice touches in "Two Too Young": Buckwheat and Porky's lengthy, whispered debate whether or not to trade the firecrackers, ending with a loud, firm one-word decision ("No") . . . Spanky's idea to cut off Alfalfa's cowlick with a sickle and use it for a mustache (Alfalfa's frozen reaction: "I'm ruined!") . . . the setup of G-man Spanky's conversation with Buckwheat, who seesaws up to Spanky's eye level and down again throughout the scene . . . and the timing of the climactic explosions, while Alfalfa is reciting "The Charge of the Light Brigade." As he intones the words, "Cannons to the left of me," the first firecracker goes off. By the time he reaches "volleyed and thundered," the whole packet is on fire, causing havoc in the classroom as Alfalfa scoots about frantically, finally locating a basin of water just outside and plopping down for some sizzling relief.

Only the fade-out fails to hit the bull's-eye. Standing on the steps outside the little schoolhouse, Spanky has watched Alfalfa's dunking to douse the firecrackers, and turns to find Porky and Buckwheat smiling at each other triumphantly. Slowly he begins to smile himself, and then bursts out laughing, joined by the rest of his classmates. Manufacturing artificial laughter is one of the toughest jobs *Our Gang* directors had to face, and even the skilled Gordon Douglas couldn't make his finale totally convincing. Furthermore, there is always the feeling that such conclusions are convenient excuses to end a film, brought in when no one can think of anything else.

Actually, in this case, the Roach scenarists had thought of something else, as documented in the film's shooting script. The intended version involved Rosina's use of a fire extinguisher and Spanky's misuse of a water pistol filled with ink. Perhaps this scripted version was indeed shot, previewed, and abandoned, when measured audience response proved it unsatisfactory, forcing a hasty rewrite to utilize the group-laughter routine instead.

But this is carping about an otherwise enjoyable short, with pretty Rosina Lawrence (accorded special billing in the film's original titles) doing a nice job once more as the schoolteacher.

As with the larger part of the post-McGowan *Our Gang* films, the sixteen-page shooting script for "Two Too Young" is surprisingly detailed and shows little variation from conception to final release print. Here the film's final sequence was altered from script to screen, and the rock and teeter-totter gag was used later than intended by the writers, but otherwise "Two Too Young" was filmed virtually as written.

One example: at the short's outset, Rosina is pacing her

students through a boring penmanship lesson, complete with the rhythmic, scratching sound effects produced by a roomful of fountain pens working in circular movements. While Porky and Buckwheat are practicing dutifully, dipping their pens into inkwells (remember those?), using blotters, and so on, Alfalfa is writing a note to tell Spanky about the firecrackers, making a paper airplane out of it, then blowing it from his desk across to Spanky. From this point, here's how the next few scenes were written:

10
_____

CLOSE SHOT—SPANKY. His head is way over on one side, leaning lazily on his hand as he leisurely does the lesson with obvious finger movement. The airplane drops on the desk in front of his nose. He hardly stirs from his lazy position as he unfolds the note with one hand. This is a little difficult, but he couldn't think of using both hands because one is busy holding up his head. He keeps his eye on the teacher until he scans the words rapidly, his lips moving as he reads. His face lights up. He looks off and nods slyly at Alfalfa, waves his index finger in a definite sign as to say "Check!"

11
_____

CLOSE SHOT—ALFALFA. Nodding back, Alfalfa returns the "check" sign.

SOUND: Bell rings.

He immediately comes to polite attention, straightens desk.

12
_____

MEDIUM SHOT—TEACHER. At desk ringing hand bell.

ROSINA: *All right, children—*
prepare for recess.

13
_____

BACK SHOT—SCHOOLROOM. All of the children stand up beside their desks.

ROSINA: *Now walk quietly like*
little ladies and gentlemen.

She gives the bell another ring. The kids dash out as fast as their feet will carry them, yelling all the way.

14
_____

CLOSE SHOT—ROSINA. Smiling as the kids leave.

One other interesting feature about *Our Gang* scripts: each has a liberal sprinkling of slapstick jargon indigenous to the colorful comedy heritage on the Hal Roach lot. Though no such argot was used in the sequence just excerpted, it's rare when a page from a Roach script won't employ terms like the "108" (a staggering pratfall), the "burn" (an angry reaction), the "slow burn" (as in E-d-g-a-r K-e-n-n-e-d-y), the "takem" (a pronounced facial reaction—Spanky and Buckwheat execute it often in "Two Too Young"), and the "double takem," or "taking it big" (slight initial reaction, hesitation, then full, wide-eyed comprehension that builds). Charley Chase originated the phrase "fig bar" for a particular kind of business he frequently employed, though Oliver Hardy and Alfalfa Switzer came to excel at it as well. An Alfalfa "fig bar" calls for an exaggerated coyness and a series of embarrassment pauses at talking with some charmer, usually Darla Hood, and especially while being paid a compliment, whether deserved or not!

148 · PAY AS YOU EXIT

One Reel · Produced by Hal Roach · Directed by Gordon Douglas · Photographed by Walter Lundin · Edited by William Ziegler · Released on October 24, 1936, by M-G-M · Our Gang: George "Spanky" McFarland, Carl "Alfalfa" Switzer, Eugene "Porky" Lee, Billie "Buckwheat" Thomas, Darla Hood, Sidney Kibrick, Harold Switzer, Rex Downing, Bobs Watson, Robert Winkler, Marvin Trin, and Joe Cobb

Despite an energetic come-on, the local kids are reluctant to invest a penny to see the gang's matinee of "Romeo and Juliet," so ticket taker Alfalfa proposes an idea: if they like the show, they can pay as they exit. He tells Spanky that the risk is small since he's playing Romeo, but matinee-idol Alfalfa has been eating onions again (to

"Step right up and buy your tickets. Don't crowd."

improve his voice) and this repels leading lady Darla, who walks out after the first act. Spanky stalls for time while Alfalfa finds a new Juliet; the show continues with Buckwheat as the new leading lady! When Alfalfa climbs the ladder to "her" balcony, he starts to teeter precariously. Spanky rings down the curtain, but Alfalfa and the ladder fall right through the drapery onto the stage, as the kids file out. "Great idea, pay as they exit," Spanky grumbles. "That's just what they did," Alfalfa replies triumphantly, pouring the pennies into Spanky's hands, and offering his pal an onion.

"Pay as You Exit" is a fast-moving short with some pleasingly inventive frills on the usual *Our Gang* putting-on-a-show formula. A kid-lettered sign outside the barn proclaims the matinee of "Romyo and Juliet, by Spanky and Shakespeer." Alfalfa's box office is actually an old car door, enabling him to roll up a window which reads "Sold Out" after the kids go inside.

As usual, the gang has made elaborate preparations for their performance in the barn-theater. Porky sits at a phonograph and provides appropriate background music* for every scene. Painted backdrops and period costumes set the mood for Shakespeare's love story. Spanky and

* Long-sought titles for familiar melodies include, in order, "In My Canoe," "Furioso," "He Peddled his Bristles to Women," and "Walking the Deck"—all stock themes from the Hal Roach music library.

Alfalfa even fight a well-staged duel to the death (with Spanky spoiling his performance as a corpse by standing up to take a bow). The only anachronism is the sudden appearance of Buckwheat as a Nubian slave to announce, "Miss Juliet, your Pappy's comin'."

When Alfalfa proposes love to Juliet, she recoils and asks, "Have you been eating onions?" The rest of their scene is played with the fair damsel holding her nose. When she walks out in the middle of the show, Spanky tells Alfalfa, "I'll do my old act and stall 'em off." Spanky's "old act" (presumably dating back to his days in vaudeville?) is a strongman routine where the realism of his weight lifting is enhanced by having Porky drop cannonballs backstage in synchronization with Spanky's dropping weights to the floor (a momentary slip, dropping one of the lead balls when Spanky tosses away his handkerchief, goes unnoticed by the audience). The strongman is defrauded, however, when his stagehand cleans up after the act and blithely picks up the "hundred-pound weights" to cart them offstage. Innocent Porky doesn't realize what he's done, and when Spanky says a sarcastic "Thanks a lot," Porky replies characteristically, "O-tay!"

Alfalfa's replacement leading lady is first revealed when he asks, "Juliet, where art thou?" and "she" replies, "Here I is!" The jubilant crowd shouts, "It's Buckwheat!" and gives him an ovation, which he happily acknowledges. After Alfalfa's ladder falls away from the balcony one time, he asks Buckwheat to hold onto it, but the sudden whiff of onions makes him forget, and Alfalfa plunges to an unexpected finale.

Exactly when everyone had the opportunity to rush up and give Alfalfa their pennies is a point of time and logic the viewer is not supposed to consider. When Alfalfa produces the ticket money, the major conflict of the plot is resolved, and one simply doesn't ask foolish questions . . . well, maybe just one. Off in the wings, is Porky's devilish, knowing grin as the film fades to its end title supposed to mean something special that's eluded us? A warehouse in Nebraska has been reserved for letters of explication we expect to pour in.

A final note on "Pay as You Exit" involves the casting of Joe Cobb as one of the neighborhood kids. Absent from the series since "Fish Hooky" in 1933, Joe towers over the other children and looks a little mature for the group. In fact, his bulk smashes the front-row bench in half! Joe would find more appropriate surroundings the following year in the gang's "Reunion in Rhythm."

149 · SPOOKY HOOKY

One Reel · Produced by Hal Roach · Directed by Gordon Douglas · Photographed by Art Lloyd · Edited by William Ziegler · Story by Hal E. Roach · Released on December 5, 1936, by M-G-M · Our Gang: Billie "Buckwheat" Thomas, Eugene "Porky" Lee, George "Spanky" McFarland, Carl "Alfalfa" Switzer, and Von the Dog · Miss Jones, Rosina Lawrence; Sam, the janitor, Dudley Dickerson

The circus is coming to town for one day only, a day when the gang has to go to school. But Spanky has a plan: he's written a doctor's note excusing them all from school the next day because of colds, and he has Buckwheat and

Porky place it on the teacher's desk at the end of the afternoon so she'll see it first thing in the morning. Then they learn that Miss Jones plans to take the class to the circus anyway! By now the school is locked, and the note is already in its place, so the kids return that night to break into the building and retrieve their letter. Lightning, thunder, and darkness make the escapade a scary one, and by staying out in the rain that night the four would-be truants find themselves with *real* colds the next morning, keeping them from school, and the circus.

Like the slick new top-grade features the Roach plant was then introducing (including ghostly items such as *Topper*), "Spooky Hooky" and most other one-reelers of this period share a brisk pacing and sure-footed sense of storytelling that makes them winners from start to finish. Nothing is rushed, yet there is no time wasted: the plot is presented and carried through with perfect timing.

Miss Jones is, as always, the perfect schoolteacher: pretty, pleasant, and genuinely concerned about her students. When Spanky and Alfalfa display their phony coughing and sneezing symptoms as warnings that they may be sick the next day, she reveals her surprise of planning to attend the circus and hopes they get better so they can come too. Thus the frustration of having hatched this scheme needlessly is coupled with the notion of having tried to pull a fast one on someone as nice as she.

The main concern of the four burglars that night is spooks; Spanky takes a brave, no-nonsense stance on the matter ("I told you once before, there ain't such things like spooks"), yet in the end he's as frightened as the others at the possibility of a ghost or skeleton creeping up behind them. On the other hand, Porky (with a crafty mind behind that bland exterior), is so far removed from this that he pretends to *be* a spook, to scare his friends, by donning a white sheet, carrying around a noisemaker, and breaking lightbulbs in a class lab room.

Buckwheat gets the biggest scares, having to wait outside and act as lookout for the others. The darkness, a nearby hoot owl, and the noisemaker Porky left behind all contribute to his growing fright, prompting him to join the gang inside. A short time later, after hiding behind a drapery, Buckwheat tiptoes back into the open and finds a

life-sized skeleton clinging to his back! By now the janitor has been awakened, and at the sight of Buckwheat and the skeleton, he leaps through the front door of the schoolhouse, followed by the kids, who have managed to retrieve their note amid this ruckus.

Next morning, however, we see the results on a screen split into four equal sections, with the same scene taking place in four bedrooms: Spanky, Alfalfa, Buckwheat, and Porky are being given cold remedy oil by their mothers, who intone in unison, "For the last time, you can't go to school today!"

Although it has no real laugh-getting qualities, "Spooky Hooky" is thoroughly engaging and enjoyable, easily one of the best and most skillful *Our Gang* one-reelers. Its possibilities are fully realized by director Gordon Douglas, and its soft-sell moral is abundantly clear: even on a petty scale, crime doesn't pay.

150 · GENERAL SPANKY

Seventy-one minutes, 6,426 feet · Produced by Hal Roach · Production managed by Sidney S. Van Keuran · Directed by Fred Newmeyer and Gordon Douglas · Photographed by Walter Lundin and Art Lloyd · Edited by Ray Snyder · Original story and screenplay by John Guedel, Richard Flournoy, Carl Harbaugh, and Hal Yates · Musical score by Marvin Hatley · Sound recorded by Elmer A. Raguse and William Randall · Special effects by Roy Seawright · Settings by Arthur I. Royce and William I. Stevens · Casting by Joe Rivkin · Released on December 11, 1936, by M-G-M · Our Gang: George "Spanky" McFarland, Billie "Buckwheat" Thomas, Carl "Alfalfa" Switzer, Harold Switzer, Jerry Tucker, Flaette Roberts, Eugene "Porky" Lee, Rex Downing, Dickie De Nuet, and Von the Dog · Marshall Valient, Phillips Holmes; Yankee General, Ralph Morgan; Simmons, crooked gambler, Irving Pichel; Louella Blanchard, Rosina Lawrence; Boat captain, James Burtis; "Mammy" Cornelia, Louise Beavers; Colonel Blanchard, Hobart Bosworth; 2nd Lieutenant, Carl Voss; 1st Lieutenant, Buddy Roosevelt; Captain Haden, Walter Gregory; Henry, lazy slave, Willie (Sleep 'n' Eat) Best; General's aide, Jack Daugherty; Overseer, Robert Middlemass; Slavemasters, Henry Hall, Hooper Atchley; Bit parts, Karl Hackett, Frank H. LaRue, Ernie Alexander, Jack Hill, Ham Kinsey, Jack Cooper, Slim Whittaker, Harry Bernard, Alex Finlayson, Harry Strang, Richard Neill, Portia Lanning

With a setting in the Old South at the time of the Civil War, Spanky is an orphan who earns his livelihood shining shoes on a Mississippi riverboat. As an overseer disembarks with his consignment of slaves, he mistakenly

loses track of Buckwheat, who teams up with Spanky. Upstream, the young pair incur the wrath of Simmons, a crooked gambler, and flee to a nearby plantation, where Spanky is reunited with an old friend, Marshall Valient,

Spanky and Alfalfa (General Nuisance and Major Annoyance) direct battle in this scene from *General Spanky*. Forming the rest of this fighting machine are Jerry Tucker, Harold Switzer, unidentified, and Buckwheat.

who is preparing to march off to war. Valient commissions Spanky to protect the womenfolk—especially beautiful Louella—while the Southern forces are away. Spanky organizes a kid army that sure enough is pressed into action to defend the plantation against the attacking Yankee regulars, led by the same sinister cardsharp Spanky had encountered on the river. With their makeshift implements the gang fortifies a hill and tricks the Union army in battle until Simmons is discredited in front of his superiors, and Valient, who's been wounded, can be reunited with Louella. The gang even makes friends with a Northern general.

Basically a burlesque melodrama of the Civil War, the comedy in "General Spanky" is mild, and the slight material is stretched rather thin at times. The plan was to combine the charm and picturesque beauty of the Old South with a satirical yet at times dramatic look at the Civil War, all mounted on the story of a boy and his love-struck hero—but it doesn't quite come off. None of these fairly disparate ideas is explored fully—as a short subject would do—nor is any one of them compelling enough by itself to rivet audience interest, so that coupled with the film's leisurely pace there's no opportunity to get anything really going.

Coming as it did on the heels of Shirley Temple's successes in the plantation and Civil War–based Fox features *The Little Colonel* and *The Littlest Rebel* the previous year, Hal Roach had decided *Our Gang* might do well to defend the Confederacy too.

The announcement in *The Motion Picture Herald* carried the blurb: "If this turns out the way Hal Roach thinks it will, you've got a new electric light name to challenge *any* existing juvenile star. Good as he was in those merry short subjects Spanky McFarland's got a lot of talent and winsomeness that can only be brought out fully in a full-length feature with character building and story construction. In putting Spanky into a big feature production Mr. Roach really follows the logical develop-

ment of this grand youngster with audiences and showmen. The deciding factor was Spanky's personal appearance tour when he literally wowed them! So here's his feature debut and it's getting every chance in the way of production, etc. It's a swell comedy and a big role for the little fellow!"

Well, it wasn't really Spanky's feature debut. In addition to other features mentioned earlier, he had most recently been lent out for the prestige Technicolor film *The Trail of the Lonesome Pine*. The inference from the ad is that Spanky's new feature would signal the end of "those merry short subjects." Hal Roach has confirmed that this was indeed the plan. Of course, it didn't work out.

With the market for expensive one- and two-reelers beginning to thin as double features grew apace, Roach wanted to test his already waning roster of short-subject stars in features. Laurel & Hardy had made the transition some time ago. In an extraordinary loss, Thelma Todd had just died, but her partner Patsy Kelly was working successfully in Roach features. Charley Chase's pilot feature for Roach, *Neighborhood House,* was cut down to short-subject length for release (originally titled *Bank Night,* pressure from the Bank Night Corporation of America had forced Roach to tone down the material and cut the film from its initial length).

Hal Roach wanted to move *Our Gang* into features, too, but the box-office response just wasn't solid enough to warrant a second try. Mr. Roach explains, "Well, the idea was that these kids had a play fort, then the Northern Army came along and thought the thing was on the square, so they attacked. But the audience wouldn't believe it, and so it just didn't work. The comedy part of the picture, involving the kids, was all right. I think it was Gordon Douglas who directed that part. But putting in the other story, the North-South conflict, was a mistake, and it was this dramatic part of the picture that slowed it way down. Besides, as I say, it was unconvincing, too. So I was basically unhappy with it, though that's a long story."

The first and only *Our Gang* feature was a radical departure from anything Roach had previously done with the Gang. There hadn't been a single other period picture in the series' history, and taking the kids out of their backyard element and dropping them into a feature film with a lot of adults and adult problems proved an unsatisfactory experiment.

The film's simple and disjointed story, without an exciting climax, dealt another blow to the test feature. The film's director, Gordon Douglas, comments, "In those days, you didn't have to have too much story in a two-reeler, but you had to have a lot of story in a feature. Now today, a lot of features don't have too much story—they're just set up with people. But Hal Roach features in the early days suffered from too little story, for that time; the audiences then wanted a beginning, a middle, and an end."

Another vital difference between "General Spanky" and the *Our Gang* shorts was one of attitude. On the one hand, much of the acting by adults in the cast is condescending, indicating an attempt to aim the film strictly at juvenile audiences. At the same time, however, a romantic subplot is introduced, which then as now was certain to bore any red-blooded child (not to mention most adults, in this case).

When it is viewed today, the film is seen to suffer from references to ''slave masters,'' ''pickaninnies,'' and the like. Upon discovering that he's lost, Buckwheat attaches himself to Spanky, knowing that a slave without a master is likely to be shot.

Even with all this, ''General Spanky'' has things to recommend it. The not-so-belligerent warfare is amusing at times, and Spanky and Buckwheat make a fine team, causing plenty of mischief and making a monkey out of screen ''heavy'' Irving Pichel.

''General Spanky'' is also a very well-made film. It was nominated for an Academy Award for best sound recording of 1936, and production values are high. It's a handsome-looking film, and it benefits from liberal use of Civil War stock-footage from such films as Buster Keaton's *The General* and D. W. Griffith's *Abraham Lincoln.*

The location work, too, is convincing and picturesque. With trees growing down to the water's edge, and its stream winding round the bends, Jack Roach chose the Sacramento River to capture the atmosphere of the Mississippi River and the flavor of the Old South. Hal Roach's brother then chartered an old stern-wheel steamboat, *The Cherokee,* and every morning for a week the cast and crew answered early morning calls and gathered at 7:00 A.M. to begin shooting while the steamer cruised up and down a scenic eight-mile stretch, while a squadron of studio cars followed along on the riverbank.

''General Spanky'' is interesting mainly as a curio.

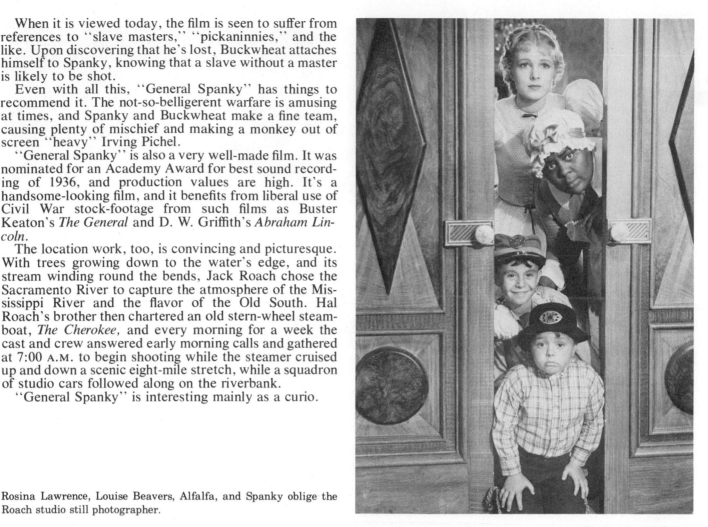

Rosina Lawrence, Louise Beavers, Alfalfa, and Spanky oblige the Roach studio still photographer.

151 · REUNION IN RHYTHM

One Reel · Produced by Hal Roach · Directed by Gordon Douglas · Photographed by Art Lloyd · Edited by William Ziegler · Released on January 9, 1937, by M-G-M · Our Gang: George "Spanky" McFarland, Darla Hood, Billie "Buckwheat" Thomas, Carl "Alfalfa" Switzer, Sidney Kibrick, Harold Switzer, Georgia Jean LaRue, Eugene "Porky" Lee, and Pete the Pup · Our Gang Graduates: Mickey Daniels, Mary Kornman, Joe Cobb, and Matthew "Stymie" Beard · Miss Jones, the teacher, Rosina Lawrence; Band leader, Ernie Alexander

As part of a class reunion at the Adams Street Grammar School, the gang stages a musical show. ''The Toy Shop at Midnight'' depicts two toy dolls coming to life, as Darla sings ''Baby Face'' to Porky. In ''The Gay White Way,'' Spanky and a chorus of top-hatted boys and girls dance and sing ''Broadway Rhythm.'' Buckwheat, who is merely supposed to display special cards announcing each scene, yearns to be an actor and makes several valiant attempts to recite ''Little Jack Horner,'' until Spanky finally puts adhesive tape over his mouth so he won't ad-lib. The last sequence, ''Hopeless Love,'' has Georgia walking out on sweetheart farmboy Alfalfa, singing ''Going Hollywood,'' followed by Alfalfa's musical reply ''I'm Through with Love.'' For a finale, the gang assembles on stage, singing to the tune of ''Auld Lang Syne,'' ''Our show is through/We hope that you/enjoyed our little play. If it brought a smile/it was worthwhile/and we'll try again some day.''

The opening scene of ''Reunion in Rhythm'' shows the crowd assembled for a class reunion singing ''Auld Lang Syne.'' The camera tracks along one table where four former *Our Gang* members toast their young successors with milk: Stymie Beard and Buckwheat, Joe Cobb and Porky, Mary Kornman and Darla, and Mickey Daniels with Alfalfa. Schoolteacher Miss Jones is at the head of the table with Spanky. This warmly nostalgic opening is, alas, the sum total of the alumni's contribution to the short, with the exception of one gag involving Mickey Daniels, who's just as funny as ever.

Miss Jones introduces Mickey, as former class presi-

Nostalgia, 1937-style, as *Our Gang* graduates rejoin the cast for the special production "Reunion in Rhythm." *Left to Right,* Rosina Lawrence, Spanky, Mickey Daniels, Alfalfa, Mary Kornman, Darla, Joe Cobb, Porky, Buckwheat, and Stymie Beard (by then no longer shaving his head).

dent, and persuades the reluctant returnee to make a speech. Standing and striking a serious pose, he muses, "When I first came to this school, I was nothing but a bashful, freckle-faced boy. [Pause] Look at me now!" The response is obvious but made twice as ludicrous by Mary Kornman's reaction and the sounding of a fanfare by the band nearby. Mickey thinks they're making fun of him, but Miss Jones explains that this is the signal for the show to start.

This introductory reunion footage seems to be impromptu and is not well integrated with the material that follows. Possibly it was an afterthought, someone's brainstorm during production, since it would seem that this film was originally intended to have been "Our Gang Follies of 1937," a title which was announced in the trade press but which did not materialize. Indeed, the "Reunion" Broadway and Forty-second Street set includes a flat picturing a "Follies Night Club."

None of the living participants in this production can recall just why this reunion was so halfhearted. It was certainly not meant to slight the returning gang members. Hal Roach always looked out for his people in a way no other motion picture company, big or small, ever did (for instance, the then-nineteen-year-old Joe Cobb had been touring the country as master of ceremonies for *Our Gang*'s frequent live stage appearances).

But it does seem a shame that the Roach team couldn't have devised an expanded plot that would have made better use of this cast, perhaps contrasting the mischief of the older kids with this present group, or making use of flashbacks as was done in *Too Many Women* five years earlier when Mickey Daniels and Mary Kornman took time out in this *Boy Friends* comedy to flip through a scrapbook that came to life with scenes from their silent *Our Gang* shorts.

As for the show itself in "Reunion in Rhythm," it is brisk and enjoyable, but suspiciously slick for an *Our Gang* production. The scenery alone in the toy shop and Broadway sequences is quite lavish and professional, not to mention a smartly dressed chorus line, and full orchestrations that are reminful of Roach's prestigious feature

films. In this the show goes somewhat against the grain of the gang's heritage of barnyards and makeshift equipment. What's more, the performances themselves border on those of the well-scrubbed theatrical kiddies disdained in so many earlier comedies like "Mike Fright" and "Beginner's Luck." The cardinal difference between those kids and the gang, of course, is talent, genuine and pure . . . although Spanky does look a bit uncomfortable in his role as a pint-sized Fred Astaire.

At the time this short was being made, material was being gathered for a book called *Of All Places,* published in 1937. Supposedly a kid's-eye view of Hollywood studios, it is full of surprising insight and detail. A few excerpts:

"Alfalfa has a long stick of hair sticking up on his head and every minute somebody like the painter or the carpenter or the photographer or someone working around would stick it up again for him. The Hal Roach studio was like being home, although it was on a sound stage, where everyone was working but having a good time. Nothing seemed to be a matter of life and death. Our Gang acts, but they don't seem to be not real. They seem to be what they are. The director . . . sits on the floor and talks to the Gang and tells them what to do and they go over and do it. The extras were the ones who made the mistakes. They were kids all dressed up in smoking and cabaret costumes, and some were in street clothes and rode around on scooters, but they were always making mistakes.

"Alfalfa was a traffic cop directing traffic on Broadway and 42nd Street, New York City, and he did it over and over again while these other kids made mistakes because they didn't get around the scenery in time on the scooters. But the director never got mad once . . . It seemed remarkable to us that there were no fights at all on the sets and they all seem to get along.

"Everybody seems to be happy on the Hal Roach sets. We did not see anyone being bored. The *Our Gang* set looked a little like a picnic, and if the lights and cameras had not been there we would have thought so."

152 · GLOVE TAPS

One Reel · Produced by Hal Roach · Directed by Gordon Douglas · Photographed by Art Lloyd · Edited by William Ziegler · Released on February 20, 1937, by M-G-M · Our Gang: Tommy "Butch" Bond, Carl "Alfalfa" Switzer, George "Spanky" McFarland, Billie "Buckwheat" Thomas, Eugene "Porky" Lee, Sidney "Woim" Kibrick, Jerry Tucker, Harold Switzer, Darwood Kaye, Rex Downing, Larry Harris, Hugh Chapman, Donald Proffitt, Darla Hood, and Robert Winkler

It's Friday afternoon, and there's a new kid in the neighborhood, a tough guy named Butch. He and his scruffy pal, "The Woim," stop by for a look at the school they'll have to attend. Just then the bell rings and class lets out. The gang files past and Alfalfa moans something about "the strain," and taking a "good rest over the weekend." Butch quickly demands everyone's attention and, pacing back and forth, announces with a defiant scowl that starting Monday, *he's* the Big Shot around here. He usually proves it by licking every kid on the block but, to save time, he'll just take on whoever's toughest. Spanky asks for time to train, gets it, then volunteers a reluctant Alfalfa as Class Pugilist ("Who, *me?*"). Alfalfa's never struck a man in his life, but he needn't worry, Spanky assures his frightened pal, as Spank has a book that tells all about it, called *How to Be a Fighter in 10 Easy Lessons.* Simple? With less than a day to prepare, Spanky puts the Neighborhood Underweight Champion through his paces: roadwork (tugging Spanky along on a wagon), a bone-crunching rubdown ("Aw, there's no rest for the weary"), and some shadow boxing (first round to the shadow). Yet it remains for the smallest fry, Porky and Buckwheat, to save the day. When comes the appointed hour, there's a big crowd of kids at ringside set to cheer on their sentimental favorite, "The Oklahoma Wildcat" (though Butch takes one look and disparagingly dubs his opponent "The Thin Man"). In the second round, Butch toys with his prey for a time and then, poised near the ropes, is about to separate Alfalfa from his senses, when from behind the curtainlike canvas hanging near ringside, the concealed twosome of Porky and Buckwheat finally connects with a well-aimed loaded glove attached to the end of a big club they're swinging—knocking Butch cold and leaving Alfalfa the victor, as his chest-beating Tarzan yell confirms.

Without any meddling adults around to foul things up, "Glove Taps" is profoundly true to one of boyhood's most deep-seated fantasies—licking the neighborhood bully. Fast-paced and totally satisfying, "Glove Taps" can be enjoyed over and over again; it's practically therapeutic.

Spanky's misplaced confidence in Alfalfa's boxing ability is always a source of wonderment. Noting in his book that a fighter has to have confidence, Spanky asks "The Champ" if he has any. "I don't *think* so," Alfalfa says slowly, scratching his head. "Well, after you lick Buckwheat, you'll have plenty," Spanky assures him. Except that Alfalfa's sparring partner promptly knocks all the incipient confidence right out of him with just a single well-measured wallop that sends "The Champ" off to dream land—in a prone position.

As in later shorts, Spanky's trumped-up reassurances to his hapless fighter in the face of such overwhelming odds are probably less a case of misplaced confidence

The "Oklahoma Wildcat" mixes it up with Butch in this scene from "Glove Taps." Whoever dressed this set will win no awards for art direction.

than a concealed attitude of "better him than me!" As his opportunist manager, Spanky would stick by his pal as long as he could keep conning Alfalfa to do the dirty work, hoping all the while that by some miracle Alfalfa might manage to win out, and a miracle is usually what it took.

Particularly funny through all this are Porky and Buckwheat, "the little kids," teamed much as Spanky and Scotty had been a few years earlier. Always in the background, practically ignored by the big kids, in a sense the wily twosome takes the audience's part. They seem to be one step ahead of everyone else in the picture, reacting to Alfalfa's ineptitude or Spanky's malarkey with a timely exchange of disapproving frowns or knowing shakes of the head. And of course they take care of Butch when no one else can.

Two other factors help make "Glove Taps" such a hit—superbly rhythmic musical scoring and the return of Tommy Bond to *Our Gang* as Butch.

Marvin Hatley's music complements and fits the visuals as well as the dialogue in this short. All but two of the film's snappy, flavorful tunes can also be enjoyed in the concurrently produced Laurel & Hardy feature *Way Out West,* which that year received an Academy Award nomination for Best Music Scoring, a distinction that might have been conferred on many of the *Our Gang* films since they utilized the same material. (Much of the music from "Glove Taps" and "Hearts Are Thumps" also appeared on the soundtracks of two other Laurel & Hardy films, *Perfect Day* and *Blotto,* which were provided with full background scoring for the first time when reissued successively in 1937.)

Through someone's signal oversight, Tommy Bond hadn't worked in an *Our Gang* comedy in two and one half years. As he explained recently, "I started out with the Gang in 1932–33, and then my contract ran out and they didn't pick up the option. So during the interim, I free-lanced in shorts and features with other studios, coming back now and then to do a few things at Roach, too, but not with the Gang. Actually, there were problems when I first joined the Gang, since Bob McGowan was still directing then, and I didn't care too much for him, because he was the kind of a guy who had his favorites, and then the rest of the kids he just let go, and they wouldn't get much to do. But then by the time the studio was looking for a tough guy, and Hal Roach, Sr., wanted me back, Gordon Douglas had taken over directing, and of the six or so *Our Gang* directors I worked for, I think Gordon Douglas was my favorite. He was terrific, and it was Gordon who directed 'Glove Taps.' Well, he's still directing—quite a big director now."

Tommy Bond never played the tough guy during his first *Our Gang* stint, though between Roach contracts he was every bit the devilish Rascal in a funny Charley Chase comedy called *I'll Take Vanilla,* which is what Hal Roach remembered when casting the role of the bully in "Glove Taps."

"Hal Roach, Sr., was a wonderful man, just a great guy," Tommy Bond recalls, "and it was Mr. Roach who got me back with the Gang. He was actually the one who'd cast the Gang parts. You would have to go upstairs to this tremendous office he had. He didn't usually come down unless they needed him on a set, or he was directing certain scenes in a picture. But Mr. Roach was the guy who picked all the kids in the Gang. He was really fantastic with kids; he was just that type of guy. He would ask you things like, 'Can you look tough? Can you fight?' And he'd say, 'Make a mean face for me,' and all that sort of thing. He defined your character for you, and then you signed the contract with Hal Roach, right there in his office."

Asked if he was really a tough guy—as kids camped in front of TV sets, *we* always thought he was—Tommy Bond answers today in a deep and rugged yet extremely friendly voice, "No, no. I was anything but. Alfalfa and Spanky and I were always the best of friends, really, the three of us, and we got along beautifully together. We'd joke about the scenes that we'd have to play where I'd tweak Alfalfa's nose, knock him on his can, and all that kind of stuff, you know. We'd always laugh about it afterward. It was great fun. Of course people outside the studio who were just watching movies in the theaters would think that we hated each other and that I was really a mean kid."

153 · HEARTS ARE THUMPS

One Reel · Produced by Hal Roach · Directed by Gordon Douglas · Photographed by Art Lloyd · Edited by Bert Jordan · Released on April 3, 1937, by M-G-M · Our Gang: Carl "Alfalfa" Switzer, George "Spanky" McFarland, Darla Hood, Billie "Buckwheat" Thomas, Sidney Kibrick, Darwood "Waldo" Kaye, Eugene "Porky" Lee, Beverly Lorraine Smith, Shirley "Henrietta" Coates, and Robert Winkler · Miss Jones, the teacher, Rosina Lawrence

Valentine's Day is a lot of hooey so far as Spanky, Buckwheat, and Alfalfa are concerned. They decide to start the He-Man Woman-Haters' Club to make their displeasure official. But when Darla walks by and winks at Alfalfa, he forgets about his vow and goes after her, accepting an invitation to lunch and exchanging valentines. Spanky wants to teach this Romeo a lesson, so while Alfalfa is off with Darla at the swings, he substitutes soap for cheese in his sandwich, and liquid soap for whipped cream in the cream puff. In class that afternoon, when the teacher asks Darla to play the piano, she agrees if Alfalfa will sing. He takes a drink of water first, so that with every line of "Let Me Call You Sweetheart," a raft of soap bubbles flows from his mouth! At the finish of the song, Alfalfa runs out of the classroom, and Spanky triumphantly tears up his lovelorn pal's valentine from Darla.

"Hearts Are Thumps" (often misnamed "Hearts Are Trumps") is another fast-moving, entirely satisfying one-reeler that is built on a single, simple idea. Also, it's yet another short that benefits tremendously from the superb musical background scoring of Marvin Hatley.

One is never quite sure why Alfalfa goes along with his pals in the renunciation of women, since he hasn't indicated such tendencies before. Nevertheless, he repeats Spanky's improvised oath: "We, the He-Man Woman-Haters' Club, promise not to fall for this Valentine business, because girls are the bunk." All it takes, however, is goo-goo eyes from Darla to set Alfalfa's heart quite literally a-thumping, and that's the end of his involvement with the club. As he tells Spanky, "I have to live my own life."

Darla, of course, is no dummy. She knows how to go after her man, combining flirtatiousness with food and telling Alfalfa that she likes him above all the others because "you have *personality*." His face lights up like a thousand-watt bulb as he replies, "*Have* I?"

When Alfalfa starts to eat Darla's sandwich (as doctored by Spanky) he chokes on the soapy substance, contorting his face in obvious pain. When he tries to make a tactful comment to Darla, she haughtily replies that if he doesn't want to eat her lunch, she knows plenty of boys who will. Alfalfa immediately begs her to let him finish the lunch, promising to eat every bite. "Pretty please?" she asks. "Pretty please," he replies sheepishly, resigning himself to finish the sandwich and cream puff.

Our Gang and Rosina Lawrence on the interior school set perusing what else but a casting directory, between scenes of "Hearts Are Thumps."

Later, when Miss Jones asks Darla to play the piano, she in turn asks Alfalfa to sing with her. He replies that he'd rather not . . . he isn't in the mood. Spanky leans toward him, aping Darla, and says mockingly, "Pretty please!" and goads Alfalfa into agreeing to sing.

It's easy to take a sequence like the bubble-song for granted, but aside from the wonder of movie special effects to make the gag seem real, there is the skill of Alfalfa and the other kids in pretending to play with, and react to, imaginary bubbles on-screen (the animated bubbles were added to the picture after the live-action scenes were finished). Alfalfa's exaggerated emphasis of the words in his song, especially at the end of each phrase, widen his mouth and make more logical the thrust that propels the bubbles to emerge, a group at a time. His wide-eyed amazement and discomfort at the results are those of a skilled comic actor—who just happens to be 9 years old.

Laughter evoked by Alfalfa's mime and music is doubled, too, each time the camera cuts away to a broadly smiling Spanky and Buckwheat, who are content to sit back and relish the crooner's struggles. The camera cuts

to a stunned Darla, also, though one may wonder whether she's bewildered as to what's made Alfalfa become a bubble machine, or whether it's simply that she can't figure out where the violins are coming from that gradually merge with her piano accompaniment!

Of course, Spanky's momentary victory over "women" doesn't keep Alfalfa from becoming increasingly fond of Darla, as their on-again, off-again sweetheart relationship formed the basis for more and more story lines during the coming year of *Our Gang* films.

As a behind-the-scenes footnote to the theme of this picture, it is curious to learn that Darla Hood today admits to having had a slight crush on Spanky, rather than Alfalfa. Spanky, of course, was never linked romantically with Darla on screen, and in front of the cameras was seldom a Lothario of *any* kind. "He was by far, though, at least to my girlish eyes, the most likable of the gang regulars," Darla says. "It was Alfalfa who was the dominating one, and so was his father, who pushed Alfie and his brother Harold into prominence, and encouraged Alfie's sometimes arrogant and unruly behavior around the lot. Spanky may have gotten along with him, but I was terrified of him. In regard to Spanky, though, I always felt a certain kindliness and generosity; I guess I always had a gentle feeling for Spanky, who after all was the real pro of the gang in every way.

"None of us socialized off the set except for an occasional birthday party. I believe the parents were mostly to blame—as you know how kids are—they love anyone and everyone unless they learn prejudices from their parents. I recall that Alfie's and Spanky's fathers fought continually over billing, salaries, and star status between their sons. Very much unlike his screen character, Tommy Bond, of all, seemed most 'normal,' perhaps because he was a semiregular *Our Gang* member and missed the jealousy and constant status-seeking conflicts the Switzers and the McFarlands went through. Honestly, I must say that these are my impressions, but as I was three-four years younger than Spanky and Alfalfa, as well as being the only girl around, I did feel a little left out of their activities, and perhaps never fully understood these kinds of things."

154 · THREE SMART BOYS

One Reel · Produced by Hal Roach · Directed by Gordon Douglas · Photographed by Art Lloyd · Edited by William Ziegler · Released on May 13, 1937, by M-G-M · Our Gang: George "Spanky" McFarland, Carl "Alfalfa" Switzer, Billie "Buckwheat" Thomas, Eugene "Porky" Lee, Darwood "Waldo" Kaye, Darla Hood, and Shirley Coates · The veterinary doctor, O. T. Hertz, Sidney Bracey; The assistant, Jack Egan; Teacher, Miss Lawrence, Rosina Lawrence; Superintendent, Miss Witherspoon, Nora Cecil

Outside the teacher's window, three unwilling scholars overhear the superintendent of schools tell Miss Lawrence, who wants to attend her sister's wedding, that nothing short of an epidemic would justify closing the school. Alfalfa wonders what an epidemic is, cueing Spanky to remark with mischievous delight, "That's just what we're going to have now." Thinking it's a sure-fire prescription for a hooky holiday, Spanky shows Alfalfa and Buckwheat how to paint their faces with spots, then

plants inflated footballs in their stomachs. With symptoms like that, the neighborhood doctor is certain to want to close the school. Trouble is, the kids go to a veterinary performing an experiment with a monkey. Severely suspicious, the doctor "treats" Buckwheat first, and from the double-edged conversation they overhear out in the waiting room, Spanky and Alfalfa believe Dr. Hertz has used a serum to turn poor Buckwheat into a monkey. Their fears are realized when left alone to prowl about the empty office they find a monkey romping around in Buckwheat's discarded sweater. Meanwhile, Porky, who's not put off by Spanky's lofty dismissals, keeps traipsing after the gang trying to deliver a note from Waldo. It seems an epidemic is unnecessary: the superintendent changed her mind and approved the school's closing for a few days. The gang inescapably learns the news just as Buckwheat emerges untriumphant from the sack he's been hiding in—he's not a monkey after all!

"Three Smart Boys" (the title spoofing Henry Koster's concurrent delightful feature *Three Smart Girls*) has its roots in "A Lad an' a Lamp" (1933) and "Circus Fever" (1925), which had just been resurrected and scaled into "Spooky Hooky," too. "Three Smart Boys," though, owes its existence to an actual flu epidemic that swept through Hollywood around Christmas. More of the Roach roster was sick at home than working, and it developed that the studio was closed down tight for weeks. Bed-sore gag writers had plenty of time to think about the "hilarity" of an epidemic, and "Three Smart Boys" is the result. It's a brisk, diverting picture, mildly amusing, but hardly inspired, rather too economically made perhaps, and a film that certainly never takes itself seriously.

And small wonder. For starters, there's unsung character player Sidney Bracey as the veterinarian, evidently having left Grandma's employ as the butler in "Second Childhood." (Bracey was a favorite of glittering artists like King Vidor and Buster Keaton, who used him often and well in their features. Bracey looks much younger than his sixty years in "Three Smart Boys.") It would take a character like Bracey to depart from his empty, unlocked office in the middle of the day, leaving a hyperactive monkey and three little rascals inside to roam around poking into whatever they might find. And if these three penniless truants are his only patients—no one else seems to be around—the doctor must enjoy a very low standard of living.

Then there's Spanky's contrivance of slapping dark paint over his and Alfalfa's faces with a fly swatter to simulate a plague of some kind. Of course the spots don't show on Buckwheat, and somehow without guile they resort to using white paint for the desired effect.

This gag, coupled with the plot device of Buckwheat's supposed simian transformation, is responsible for this episode having been quite drastically trimmed in television syndication markets.

Laurel & Hardy's *Dirty Work* has never been suppressed because Laurel inadvertently turns Hardy into a chimpanzee; but apparently because Buckwheat is black and Hardy is not, censors construe the parallel idea in "Three Smart Boys" differently.

Robert Klein, a popular monologist and the kind of stand-up comic who only "reports" comedy, has long poked fun at the presumptive bad taste of spraying Buckwheat's face with white paint (though from the rest of his *Our Gang* routine it would seem he cherishes the series). The criticisms bother Spanky McFarland, who recently commented on the paint gag for a newspaper story: "That's not degrading, that's just funny. I've looked at the scrapbooks. There's me, Stymie, the bulldog, and Alfalfa going to school together in 1935, the first integrated class in the country."

Then on a late 1974 national television talk show where

"Three Smart Boys": concocting an epidemic and leaving a few tires flat.

More monkeyshines in "The Smart Boys," with Buckwheat, Sidney Bracey, and Jack Egan.

they were both guests, Spanky McFarland asked Billie "Buckwheat" Thomas if he felt at all demeaned working in "Three Smart Boys." Billie Thomas responded genially, "I remember the picture quite well. They had to do something, so white measles was white measles. Moneywise, it felt pretty good. It was a job, and it was a nice living."

With a knack for knowing just what to say and how to say it, Stymie Beard, also a guest, followed up by adding, "That was all some forty years ago, and as children we didn't have too much feelings then about it. I look at it as having been mostly a fun thing; we were just a group of kids who were having *fun*. We all stayed together, and 'partied' together. We were all *together*. I felt it was great."

And people like Stymie tried to help make it so.

155 · RUSHIN' BALLET

One Reel · Produced by Hal Roach for M-G-M · Directed by Gordon Douglas · Photographed by Art Lloyd · Edited by William Ziegler · Released on April 24, 1937, by M-G-M · Our Gang: George "Spanky" McFarland, Tommy "Butch" Bond, Carl "Alfalfa" Switzer, Billie "Buckwheat" Thomas, Eugene "Porky" Lee, Sidney "Woim" Kibrick, Darwood "Waldo" Kaye, Harold Switzer, Darla Hood, and Maria Ayres · Harried dance recital teacher, Kathryn Sheldon; Audience extra, Fred Holmes

With the help of his rabbit's foot (and some very tricky animation), Buckwheat wins another marbles game with Porky. But the fun ends for both when tough guys Butch and The Woim show up and for no good reason smear their faces with some handy tomatoes. Porky and Buckwheat report their grievance to the Sekret Revengers Club, where the two resident ministers of justice are Spanky and Alfalfa. Setting out to right the wrong, Alfalfa takes the first initiative and confronts the two bullies for facts about the offense. Amused for a while, Butch confesses his guilt but then throttles Alfalfa and defies him to do anything about it. Suddenly terrified, and with good reason, Alfalfa forces an apologetic smile, says good-bye, tips his cap, and cowers back to Spanky, who has a plan of his own. This time they pelt their adversaries with more tomatoes, and the chase is on. Spanky and Alfalfa retreat into a prissy dancing school during the midst of a performance, and to foil their pursuers they don wigs and ballet skirts. The disguise works so well that the graceless pair soon find themselves onstage ruining the next terpsichorean frolic. To the delight of his audience, Alfalfa takes an encore, but with dawning horror discovers he is alone onstage with Butch and The Woim, now masquerading in adagio costumes. The choreo-graphed knockabout that ensues concludes with Alfalfa being twirled aloft and casually tossed into the wings with a dull thud. Blissfully unaware of their fate, Butch and The Woim are taking their bows when Porky and Buckwheat, passive observers through all this, decide to settle the matter for themselves—the way it began—with another pair of accurately tossed ripe tomatoes. Dignity restored, they stroll off together arm in arm with furtive, knowing smiles.

Lively and fast, with the usual quota of Alfalfa's malapropisms, as well as his unintentionally muffed lines, "Rushin' Ballet" is a winning short. Skillfully edited and consistently paced, there isn't a moment's footage wasted on anything but gags. Lots of gags. Constrained to a single reel, it didn't pay to concentrate on anything *but* gags.

One gag that seldom fails has the two bullies rout Spanky and Alfalfa into the dancing school's spacious dressing room, where they change into girls' ballet costumes and strike poses as mannequins. Butch trounces in, look around and snarls, "All right. Where are you guys?" Without a moment's hesitation, helpful Alfalfa advises, "There's nobody down here but 'cept us dummies." Spanky prolongs the laugh with a resigned grimace at his pal's stupidity. Luckily they hold their poses, because Butch never figures it all out anyhow.

"Rushin' Ballet" features an interesting variation on the kids' relationships. The characterizations are clearly drawn and enable us to recognize much of ourselves—where we want to. The youngest but brightest pair, Porky and Buckwheat, don't try to combat the biggest and toughest pair, Butch (whose sarcastic, bravura villainy really makes the short work) and The Woim. After the tomato-smearing indignity, Buckwheat only wrinkles his face and consoles his partner with a look. He takes it in stride, and unruffled, he warns Butch, "You be sorry."

They bring their problem to Spanky and Alfalfa, the well-meaning but inept pair. These two are helpless, but they don't know it. Pompous Spanky can't decide whether "you kids" are still young enough to need his condescending protection. Buckwheat knows his age, but Porky isn't so sure:

Spanky: How old are you?
Porky: Huh?
Spanky: I said, "How *old* are you?"
Porky (barely whispers): Three . . . three or so.

In the end, of course, the self-appointed bungling protectors need all the help they can manage, while the two little kids—not old enough to know they should be terrified of Butch—win well-ordered climactic retribution with little effort at all. It was seldom that easy for the rest of us, so the vicarious requital is satisfying.

156 · ROAMIN' HOLIDAY

One Reel · Produced by Hal Roach · Directed by Gordon Douglas · Photographed by Art Lloyd · Edited by William Ziegler · Released on June 12, 1937, by M-G-M · Our Gang: George "Spanky" McFarland, Carl "Alfalfa" Switzer, Eugene "Porky" Lee, Billie "Buckwheat" Thomas, Darla Hood, Pete the Pup, and Von the Dog · Hiram Jenks, Fred Holmes; Mrs. Jenks, May Wallace

Annoyed that they have to spend their valuable time doing such juvenile chores as baby-sitting, Spanky and Alfalfa decide to run away from home, with Porky and Buckwheat tagging along. When they arrive in the tiny town of Jenksville, they're starving, and they notice that the proprietors of a neighborhood bakery enjoy feeding stray dogs. Spanky and Alfalfa bring their pooch into the store and ask if the kindly couple has any cookies to spare; instead, the lady in charge gives them a bag of dog biscuits, which wasn't exactly the idea. Undaunted, Buckwheat and Porky try the same routine, not realizing that the dog *they're* towing inside belongs to the good-natured hubby and wife behind the counter, who decide to have some fun. The youngsters are given a full array of pastries and cakes, ostensibly for their dog, and then when they've eaten them all, Mr. Hi Jenks, who also happens to be the constable, demands to know who's paying for the food. Since none of the gang has any money, the officer "arrests" them, puts them in striped suits and has them work on the rock pile, to learn their lesson for running away. As he's about to round up "ya rascals" and drive them home, they try to escape, getting tangled up with the barnyard animals and finally being chased off by a swarm of bees, which heads them in the right direction—back home.

Unlike the best one-reelers, this outdoor comedy seems rushed and condensed, as if ten minutes wasn't enough to carry out the idea. The announcement that they're running away dissolves to a picture of the gang already on the road, carrying packs fastened to sticks in hobo fashion. There is no real feeling of distance when they arrive in the small town, except for Spanky's remark that they're tired and hungry. Most abrupt of all is the final chase, with a quick scene inside the barn where, as Spanky and Alfalfa hide inside a wicker container, a rooster tugs on Alfalfa's cowlick, which is standing up through the top of the basket. As soon as the constable shows up, however, the kids are out the door and suddenly writhing in the midst of a bee farm, which gets them on their feet and running down the road to the strains of "There's No Place Like Home" on the soundtrack. (Fiddles atypically predominate the background music throughout, literally underscoring the film's rural setting.)

Usually, plots involving eye-winking adults who are about to teach the kids a lesson are unbearably coy and unfunny. Perhaps because this film moves so quickly, or because the adults (May Wallace and Fred Holmes) are so engaging, this feeling never dominates "Roamin' Holiday." Besides, the gang's scheme is so transparent that it would take an imbecile to fall for their line. The constable, after hearing the kids speculate that "our mothers are plenty sorry now," decides that it's his duty to teach them "a durn good lesson." When he arrests the

Alfalfa and country friends on location for "Roamin' Holiday."

runaways, he charges them with everything in the book, including "five counts of frequency."

All the dialogue in the film is entertaining, from Buckwheat's request for food for "his" dog ("He likes chewin' gum, don't he, Porky?" "Ylass!" confirms Porky) to Alfalfa's exclamation when the rooster pulls out his stand-up thatch of hair, "He's got it: my personality!"

Alfalfa's cowlick also figures in the film's major sight gag, in the opening scene when Spanky and Alfalfa are walking their baby brothers. Spanky complains about his, but Alfalfa says he's got it twice as bad: there in his carriage are twins, both sporting identical hairdos with a part down the middle and a cowlick standing stiff in back, just like their older brother, who sighs, "How could a fella with my looks have brothers with faces like them?"

Good material, hurried along, makes "Roamin' Holiday" a pleasant but unremarkable one-reeler in the series.

157 · NIGHT 'N' GALES

One Reel · Produced by Hal Roach · Directed by Gordon Douglas · Photographed by Art Lloyd · Edited by William Ziegler · Released on July 24, 1937, by M-G-M · Our Gang: Darla Hood, George "Spanky" McFarland, Carl "Alfalfa" Switzer, Billie "Buckwheat" Thomas, Eugene "Porky" Lee, and Gary "Junior" Jasgar · Arthur Hood, Darla's father, Johnny Arthur

Mrs. Virginia McFarland and her favorite child movie star.

Darla and her mother.

A peaceful evening at the Hood household is disrupted by The Four Nitengales, a supposed singing group composed of Spanky, Alfalfa, Porky and Buckwheat. Needless to say, their rendition of the one song they know, "Home, Sweet Home," is dreadful. Even Junior plugs his ears. Mr. Hood is particularly relieved when after an hour of such torture, they're set to leave. "You must come back and harmonize again, *some*time," he warns. Very much to Mr. Hood's chagrin, they find there is a storm raging outside, and Darla's mother invites the gang to spend the night. Alfalfa is delighted: "You know Darla, this is the first time I've ever slept at your house." The four boys bunk with Mr. Hood, who of course can't stand them. They, on the other hand, think he's "pixilated." Predictably, everything that happens from this point only confirms each side's bad opinion of the other. "I'd rather sleep with a bunch of porcupines," complains Mr. Hood. With a perfectly straight face, Alfalfa counters, "Where you gonna find a porcupine this hour of the night?"

A very funny and polished short, "Night 'n' Gales" is brimful with inventive gags of all varieties. The dialogue is clever, and some photography and editing tricks aid the visuals: undercranking, frame cutting, double exposures, animation, etc.

When Alfalfa swats a moth that lands on Johnny Arthur's nose with his own slipper, the poor man decides he's had enough and heads downstairs to sleep by himself. Scooping up a bearskin rug off the floor for his blanket, he plops down on the living-room sofa. But even in his dreams he can't escape the Little Rascals, as—to the stylized incidental scoring of "Funny and Mysterious"*—they suddenly appear through the dark in miniature, standing around the rim of the couch in double exposure. Outfitted as devils with horns and a tail, they begin laughing and poking the slumbering "bear" with their pitchforks. The furry phantom roused from his nightmare, he stalks in his sleep back up the stairs—a sure bet to cause more havoc when the "bear" stumbles back into bed with the kids.

Johnny Arthur, one of filmdom's great pansies, scores high again in his second *Our Gang* short, working as counterpoint to the kids' antics. His characterization here seems to have somewhat an affinity with Charley Chase. As the henpecked hubby, Johnny Arthur, like Chase, finds himself on one of those never-ending trips from bad to worse!

Assembled with a lot of assurance, "Night 'n' Gales" has an efficient, effortless look to it, and was good enough to inspire a sequel, "Feed 'em and Weep."

* Used memorably the following year in Laurel & Hardy's escapade on the swaying rope bridge with *their* furry friend—a gorilla. It's the highlight scene in *Swiss Miss*, made famous in writings by John McCabe and James Agee.

158 · FISHY TALES

One Reel · Produced by Hal Roach · Directed by Gordon Douglas · Photographed by Art Lloyd · Edited by William Ziegler · Released on August 28, 1937, by M-G-M · Our Gang: Tommy "Butch" Bond, Carl "Alfalfa" Switzer, George "Spanky" McFarland, Eugene "Porky" Lee, Billie "Buckwheat" Thomas, Harold Switzer, Tommy McFarland, Darwood "Waldo" Kaye, Darla Hood, Gary "Junior" Jasgar, Sidney "Woim" Kibrick, Dickie De Nuet, and Dorian Johnston

While performing a William Tell stunt with his popgun, Alfalfa inadvertently sends a suction-cup dart smack onto Butch's nose. Just as a fight is averted, playful Junior fires the gun again, planting another dart on the back of Butch's head. This time there's no way out of a fight, except for Alfalfa to "faint," but Butch promises to return later and settle his account. In the meantime, Spanky sends the bully a note explaining that Alfalfa has dislocated his shin bone and is incapacitated. Butch comes to see for himself, and finds Alfalfa in bed, his right leg an unfeeling limb. That's because the "leg" is really a lengthy fish stuffed inside a long black stocking, while Alfalfa's right leg is dangling through a hole in the bed. But when a crab and then several cats get to work on the exposed leg, Alfalfa is undone, and Butch gives chase, with Spanky urging his pal to "Run, Alfalfa, run!"

"Fishy Tales" is yet another slickly made, totally enjoyable one-reeler directed by Gordon Douglas. The director gets his kicks early on by setting up a pair of enjoyable mirror views, showing William Tell/Alfalfa lining up a backward shot at Buckwheat, and then also revealing the unexpected results—pinning Butch right on the nose. Another delightful trick shot involves Alfalfa's first firing, as his suction-cup dart zooms right into the camera, darkening the screen while the picture flips to the reverse angle, showing the projectile soar away from the lens and land on the apple sitting on Buckwheat's head. The animation used to accomplish this trick is impeccable.

Not much time is spent with Junior, but as usual, he is the so-called innocent cause of all this mayhem. It's he who fires the pistol a second time, hitting Butch, and it's he sitting under Alfalfa's bed who overturns a pail of crabs, setting them free. What's more, the usually stony-faced youngster actually laughs out loud at Alfalfa's predicament!

Equally familiar is Spanky and Alfalfa's overconfidence when they know they've got one up on Butch. It's not enough that the bully buys their charade of Alfalfa being in bed; Spanky has to paint a picture of Alfalfa having obtained his injury while defending Butch's honor against someone who called him yellow. Of course, this bold-faced lie only makes Butch that much angrier when the ruse is uncovered.

As the aimless tough Butch, Tommy Bond is delightfully convincing as usual and steals all honors again. He's once more paired with rowdy sidekick The Woim, played by Sid Kibrick, younger brother of oily Len Kibrick, another notorious *Our Gang* scourge.

Butch seems to revel in his own scowling villainy, taking sadistic glee impatiently rattling off his lines, as when Alfalfa faints, and Butch snorts with neck extended and ruffled brow, "BRING THAT MUG TO, 'cause I'm coming back, and when I DO I'm going to bounce him around like a rubber ball—GET ME?! . . . Out of my way; come on, Woim."

Fast, funny, and original, "Fishy Tales" is hardly a classic, but at the same time ranks as a flawless entry in the *Our Gang* series.

159 · FRAMING YOUTH

One Reel · Produced by Hal Roach · Directed by Gordon Douglas · Photographed by Art Lloyd · Edited by William Ziegler · Released on September 11, 1937, by M-G-M · Our Gang: George "Spanky" McFarland, Carl "Alfalfa" Switzer, Tommy "Butch" Bond, Billie "Buckwheat" Thomas, Eugene "Porky" Lee, Darla Hood, and Gary Jasgar · Radio announcer, Jack Mulhall; Usher, Ernie Alexander; Singing voice-over, Olive Brasno

Alfalfa has been training for weeks at Spanky's Voice Studio to enter a radio talent contest, but the morning of the program, Butch arrives and threatens Spanky with a beating if he allows Alfalfa to show up. Without the competition, Butch is a sure winner playing his violin. Spanky wants to save his skin, so he convinces Alfalfa that his voice is gone, due to a frog in the throat (actually a *real* frog inside the muffler he's wearing). The disheartened Alfalfa listens to the contest on the radio and murmurs, "I'd rather take a beating than to have this happen . . .

and the worst thing is that I let my own pals down." Spanky blurts out, "No you didn't—*I* let *you* down." He rushes Alfalfa to the radio station just as Butch is being declared the winner; the judges agree to let Alfalfa perform, however, and during his song Butch takes Spanky outside to settle the score. Spanky has taken the muffler with him, but the frog has lodged itself in Alfalfa's shirtfront, providing a most unusual accompaniment to his singing. The audience loves it, and Alfalfa is judged the winner. Spanky returns from the hallway to congratu-

A publicity photo for "Framing Youth."

late Alfalfa, looking a bit mussed up and sporting a black eye. "What happened?" his pal inquires. "Ask *him*," says Spanky, pointing to Butch, who somehow got the worst of the licking, displaying two shiners!

"Framing Youth" is a short and sweet. Despite its brief running time, there is introductory material, exposition, a crisis, a climax, and an ideal conclusion. Everything clicks.

The Voice Studio (Alfalfa, crooner; Spanky, manager) is a fascinating operation, housed in the gang's barn-headquarters. Junior sits just inside the outer gate, and when a horn sounds, he opens the door to allow Spanky to ride in on his bicycle. After making an adjustment in the billing on the front door (listing his name first instead of Alfalfa's), Spanky steps inside and greets First Office

Boy Buckwheat and Second Office Boy Porky. Just outside his office sits switchboard operator and receptionist Darla, who says brightly, "Good morning, boss," and arranges a vase of flowers on his desk.

When Butch arrives and tries to talk to Alfalfa, who is vocalizing at the piano, the crooner tells him to see his manager. First he must go through the office red tape, however. "I'll see if he's in," says Buckwheat, picking up his telephone and ringing Porky, who is seated right next to him. Porky doesn't move, and Buckwheat says impatiently, "Why don't you answer the phone, Porky?" He finally does, and Buckwheat announces, "Mr. Butch to see Mr. Spanky." "I'll see if he's in," says Porky, who in turn telephones Darla, who relays the message to Spanky himself. The busy executive instructs Darla, "Tell him I'm not in," but by now Butch has barged inside and the jig is up.

Alfalfa, whose nervous characteristics sometimes overlapped into the area of hammyness, is utterly delightful in this short. When Spanky and the boys pretend that they can't hear him because he's lost his voice, he seems genuinely distraught. And when he mopes over the radio contest, his disappointment is touchingly real.

Director Gordon Douglas builds an admirable amount of tension as the boys sit in their office listening to the contest, their somber faces superimposed over the radio speaker. The silence is excruciating, and when Alfalfa starts to speak remorsefully about his failure, Spanky can't take any more.

As usual, Alfalfa sings a song introduced by Bing Crosby, "Just an Echo in the Valley," with every "yoo-hoo" in the lyric accompanied by two croaks of the frog. During the sequence when the boys listen to the radio contest, there are snatches of Marvin Hatley's "Honolulu Baby" from "Mike Fright" and Olive Brasno's rendition of "The Ice Cream Song" from "Shrimps for a Day," proving once more that the Hal Roach studio was nothing if not resourceful.

160 · THE PIGSKIN PALOOKA

One Reel · Produced by Hal Roach · Directed by Gordon Douglas · Photographed by Art Lloyd · Edited by William Ziegler · Released on October 23, 1937, by M-G-M · Our Gang: Carl "Alfalfa" Switzer, George "Spanky" McFarland, Dickie Jones, Darla Hood, Eugene "Porky" Lee, Billie "Buckwheat" Thomas, Harold Switzer, Tommy McFarland, Barry Downing, Rex Downing, Payne Johnson, Cullen Johnson, Sidney Kibrick, Alvin Buckelew, Marvin Trin, Gary "Junior" Jasgar, Freddie Walburn, Delmar Watson, Darwood "Waldo" Kaye, Larry Harris, Charles Flickinger, Donald Proffitt, Hugh Chapman, Billy Ray Smith, Leon Holland, Priscilla Lyon, and Pete the Pup

To curry favor with Darla, Alfalfa has been writing home from military school telling her that he's a big football hero, even though he's never played a game in his life. The subterfuge backfires when Alfalfa comes home on a weekend and finds himself recruited for a game with Spanky's *All Stars,* which touts him as a hero, "The Tarzan of Football." Although he tries to stay out of the action as much as possible, Alfalfa's bumbling inadvertently wins the game, and makes him a *real* hero to the gang.

Released to coincide with the kickoff of the football season across the land, and with its title a play on the previous year's Fox feature *Pigskin Parade* (which featured Judy Garland and Johnny Downs), "The Pigskin Palooka" presents one of the few occasions when an *Our Gang* one-reeler is so tightly packed with story and gags that one almost wishes it were longer, to allow more breathing room. From the opening shot, with Alfalfa posing in a "borrowed" football uniform for a photo at school, to the climactic game, there's not a wasted sec-

Porky, Gary, and a pale substitute for the original Pete the Pup wait on the sidelines in a scene from "The Pigskin Palooka."

Alfalfa's to the 40, the 50, the 60, the 70 . . . .

in his long johns, without even bothering to put his clothes back on. A close-up of his letter dissolves (via an optical effect) into a scene of the crowd awaiting Alfalfa's arrival at the train station that weekend. And after he is carried off on the shoulders of his admirers, the camera focuses on two tough-guy members of the opposing team who linger behind to discuss their plans to "get" Alfalfa in the game that afternoon.

In the game itself, Alfalfa is aghast and confused, sporting an appropriately lopsided uniform, yet the reluctant gridiron hero can't seem to do anything *wrong*. He carelessly tosses a helmet into the air, but it collides with the ball and prevents the other team from converting a point-after-touchdown. Later, as crushing defenders charge across the line of scrimmage, his frightened, last-minute desperation pass to Spanky results in a TD as Spanky and Buckwheat scramble downfield and into the end zone.

Perhaps only a dyed-in-the-wool nonathlete could completely sympathize with (and find credible) Alfalfa's predicament and share his fear and frustration on the football field. Yet this is part of the *Our Gang* tradition, empathizing with the underdog who somehow comes out on top, and it is certainly a key factor in any audience's enjoyment of "The Pigskin Palooka."

After several misadventures, Alfalfa tries to get excused from the game, but Spanky says, "You've got to make one of your famous single-handed touchdowns for us!" This is accomplished only after Alfalfa returns to the bench; the timekeeper has been eating bananas, and in a frenzied moment, the banana peels funnel unnoticed into the back of Alfalfa's pants. At the same time, two tough guys on the opposing team put a wad of chewing gum on the football so he won't be able to arc another surprise pass. The joint result: the ball is thrown to Alfalfa, who finds he can't get rid of it; fleeing for his life, he happens to run in the direction of the goal line, as the banana peels drop out of his pants one by one, causing the chasing tacklers to slip and fall to the ground. Alfalfa electrifies the grandstand as he "sprints" the length of the field to score the winning touchdown just as the gun sounds! Even here, no time is wasted in hoisting Alfalfa to the shoulders of his surging fans, as the band that's been playing throughout the game shifts into the *Our Gang* theme to close out a breathless but most entertaining short.

ond. In fact, director Gordon Douglas had to cram so much into ten minutes that he apparently worked twice as hard at tying scenes together and getting as much out of each sequence as possible.

For example, in the opening scene, after the real football captain finds Alfalfa posing in his uniform and demands it back, Alfalfa goes to write Darla another letter

161 · MAIL AND FEMALE

One Reel · Produced by Hal Roach · Directed by Fred Newmeyer · Photographed by Art Lloyd · Edited by William Ziegler · Released on November 13, 1937, by M-G-M · Our Gang: Carl "Alfalfa" Switzer, George "Spanky" McFarland, Darla Hood, Billie "Buckwheat" Thomas, Eugene "Porky" Lee, Alvin "Spike" Buckelew, Harold Switzer, Tommy McFarland, Darwood "Waldo" Kaye, Freddie Walburn, Hugh Chapman, Robert Winkler, and Joe "Corky" Geil.

In the eternal battle against women, Spanky *will* believe his greatest supporter is Alfalfa. That's why, when the gang isn't invited to the MacGillicudy girls' party,

Spanky's indignation causes him to organize a He-Man Woman-Haters' Club, and designate Alfalfa president, "because *he hates women*." That's all greeted with

A tense moment from "Male and Female" . . . but Porky doesn't seem to think so.

cheers, but Alfalfa isn't there to share in his moment of triumph; he's off writing a love note to Darla, which he asks Porky and Buckwheat to deliver, cautioning, "Keep it under your hat—get me?" Later, when he happens into the clubhouse, Alfalfa is pleased to learn he's been named president—of something—and takes full charge of everything, appointing tough-guy Spike as sergeant at arms, who vows to enforce the rules of the club with a sturdy paddle. . . . This guy means business, so Alfalfa leans over and asks, "By the way, Spanky, what am I president of?" When he finds out, he decides to remember some important business he has to do—retrieve that note! He rushes to Darla's house, and asks for his love letter. She doesn't know what he means, but when he sees the gang coming down the street, the romantic interlude is cut short, and Alfalfa pleads for a place to hide. Porky and

Buckwheat have unwittingly disclosed where he's gone, and Spanky and Spike are on their way to administer appropriate discipline. Darla assures them no one else is home, but they look around anyway. Then Alfalfa emerges in a frilly dress and blond wig as Cousin Amelia. Shining up to the older boys, she somehow wins them over (Darla can't believe it either). Porky and Buckwheat are more committed to their ideals, though, and also aren't so easily taken in, as revealed by cutaway shots of the two of them wrinkling their faces and shaking their heads at this nonsense. When Darla passes the cookies, Buckwheat declines: "No thanks, we're woman-haters, aren't we Porky?" who answers, "Yassh." When Amelia leaves the room and reappears as He-Man Woman-Hater Alfalfa, with paddle in hand, everyone is forced to line up for their swats. One by one, they ignominiously take their punishment, until Buckwheat bends over, and the unde-livered love note falls out of his hat. Realizing the decep-tion is over, Alfalfa makes a hasty getaway through an open window, landing in a pond and cueing those inevita-ble buckets of water hurled from off-screen for the film's finale.

"Mail and Female" is a thoroughly enjoyable romp, fast-paced, tightly scripted, and full of fine, underplayed situational humor that holds up today as well as ever. In fact, even apart from its fresh humor, "Mail and Female" is one of those rare 1930s pictures that remains absolutely undated, with surprisingly neither dialogue, nor props, nor costumes even hinting at when the film was made. Simply, it's the kind of slick, efficient, durable comedy where everything works and one seldom tires of repeated viewings.

162 · OUR GANG FOLLIES OF 1938

Two Reels · Produced by Hal Roach for M-G-M · Directed by Gordon Douglas · Photographed by Art Lloyd · Ed-ited by William Ziegler · Released on December 18, 1937, by M-G-M · Our Gang: George "Spanky" McFarland, Carl "Alfalfa" Switzer, Eugene "Porky" Lee, Darla Hood, Billie "Buckwheat" Thomas, Dickie Jones, Tommy McFarland, Harold Switzer, Alvin Buckelew, Darwood Kaye, Kenneth Wilson, Philip MacMahon, Annabella Logan, Georgia Jean LaRue, Ada Lynn, Josephine Roberts, Joe "Corky" Geil, Charles Flickinger, Raymond Rayhill Powell, Billy Mindy, Frances Bowling, David Freeman, Patsy Currier, Gloria Hurst, Bobbie Hickman, Tommy Braunger, Jimmy Sommerville, Robert Winkler, Betsy Gay, Bobs Watson, and Philip Hurlic · Opera impresario, Barnaby, Henry Brandon; Stenographer, Miss Jones, Wilma Cox; Singer, Gino Corrado; Piano player, Winstead (Doodles) Weaver

The gang is staging a musical show in their kid-rigged cellar theater (customers get there by sliding down a coal chute). Spanky's in charge, Darla's the female vocalist, and Buckwheat's the Stokowski-inspired band leader, but the kid patrons' rapt admiration is reserved for Al-falfa. Announced as "The King of Crooners" to a ga-ga audience, Alfalfa strides onstage and bellows, "I'm the barber of Seville." Spanky rings down the curtain to a chorus of catcalls; Alfalfa's burned and explains that from now on he won't waste a voice like his on anything less than opera. Quitting the show, he and companion Porky haunt an opera company until with mock serious-ness Barnaby, the impresario, signs him to a contract, effective twenty years later. They check their watches. As Alfalfa triumphantly returns backstage to flaunt his

secure operatic future at Spanky, he's warned he'll wind up singing in the street for pennies. Unruffled, Alfalfa settles back in an easy chair, and dreams the twenty years have elapsed: he swaggers down a wintry Broadway, and sees neon lights flashing his name wherever he looks. Debuting in *The Barber of Seville,* his first lusty aria is greeted with boos, and overdressed kids in a side theater box mug sourly and begin heaving some convenient ripe vegetables on stage. The curtain falls, and Alfalfa departs in disgrace, but the villainous Barnaby, now stooped and gray, won't relinquish the ironclad contract, and hands Alfalfa a tin cup to sing in the streets. Plodding through the snow, braced against the weather, he and Porky hap-pen upon prominent Club Spanky. Just then the immacu-lately dressed proprietor arrives in a chauffeured Austin

Alfalfa thinks he's "The Barber of Seville."

car, and steps out to drop a coin in Alfalfa's cup. "Why, Spanky!" Alfalfa exclaims. Invited inside Spanky's plush cabaret, the dazed Alfalfa is treated to a fancy floor show featuring songstress Darla and that King of Swing, "Cab" Buckwheat—both now rich and making "hundreds and thousands of dollars." Alfalfa's encouraged to croon, but, when he finally tosses aside his pride and consents, in steps the leering Barnaby to drag him back to the streets. By now Alfalfa's screaming that he doesn't want to sing opera, he just wants to croon. At that moment the scene blurs woozily, Alfalfa awakens and realizes it's all been a terrible dream; he's still backstage at the gang's little production, and with renewed confidence he gladly returns to the show to sing (Bing Crosby's) "Learn to Croon" for a happy, off-key, "just murmur boo-boo-boo-boo-boo" ending.

"Our Gang Follies of 1938" is a delightful change-of-pace film, perhaps the best of the mini-musicals, and with its huge cast, full orchestra score, elegant costuming, and richly dressed sets certainly the most elaborate.

The film's considerable production values and radical departure in format are pleasing, though puzzling, as is the question of why the studio made this glossy one-shot return to the two-reel format ("Our Gang Follies of 1938" is the last two-reeler Hal Roach Studios would ever make).

One area of conjecture revolves around M-G-M's interest in acquiring or at least perpetuating *Our Gang* as one of the few remaining profitable series of live-action short subjects. Possibly either the Roach studio wanted an impressive entry to boost the stock in its *Our Gang* property for possible sale to M-G-M, or Metro sensed the potential for a high-grossing picture and wanted to participate in funding an ambitious short musical that would more than return Metro's investment at the box office.

The film's original titles tell a story in themselves. Instead of the usual "Hal Roach Presents," this one picture only is introduced by the roaring "lion head" trademark and dissolves to a title reading: "Metro-Goldwyn-Mayer Presents 'Our Gang Follies of 1938,' a Hal Roach Production." And the leader at the beginning and end of each 35mm reel is labeled "Our Gang Follies of 1938/A Metro-Goldwyn-Mayer Musical." Usually the designation was simply "Hal Roach Comedy," and indeed subsequent one-reelers resumed this mode of identification, and also reverted to the "Hal Roach Presents" credit line.

For whatever reasons, "Follies of 1938" was produced and regarded as a special picture, and special production credits were listed: S. S. Van Keuren as associate producer, Bud Murray as dance director, and Marvin Hatley as musical director. (Incidentally, the charming theme song introducing the film is a different orchestration of one of Hatley's recurring themes throughout Laurel & Hardy's *Way Out West* entitled "Stagecoach Conversation.")

Movie musicals of the 1930s were incredibly lavish, and for *Our Gang's* spoof to work (and it does) the film would have to reach beyond a standard parody of backstage intrigue and temperament, and *somehow* approach the extravaganza and wonderful absurdity associated with things like M-G-M's *Broadway Melody*. The dream contrivance neatly sidestepped the credibility problem of why scruffy back-yards-kids are costumed to the teeth and romping around deluxe movie musicals sets, but then the problem became what kind of sets should they be? Spectacular? Fashionable? Wild fantasy?

Since of the cast of more than one hundred all but the four members of the laughable Cosmopolitan Opera House are kids, it was decided that instead of duplicating a pretentious Warners or M-G-M musicals set, Club Spanky would be designed to conform to what a kid's idea of a nightspot ought to be like, resulting in impressionistic backdrops and things like the decorations representing out-size dishes of ice cream and peppermint stick candy.

Refreshments served the kid patronage at Club Spanky are mostly luscious-looking ice cream cones, sodas, and sundaes topped with jelly beans, though instead of the genuine confections, which under the hot studio lights would've melted faster than any kid could've eaten them, these delicacies were actually mashed potatoes whipped up with cotton to look like the real thing. This way, at least no one would eat the props.

Blending in with the larger than life atmosphere is Henry Brandon as the enjoyably menacing "Barnaby" (so named in the script, if not on screen), repeating the lecherous character of the same name he'd created in *Babes in Toyland,* his first film, at age twenty-one. His superb "Barnaby" villainy soon led to such sinister roles as Captain Lasca in *Buck Rogers,* and the evil Chinese mastermind, Fu Manchu, in the Republic serial *Drums of Fu Manchu.*

As counterpoint to Barnaby's Scroogelike shenanigans, there are some bright and cheeky musical production numbers: Spanky and Darla alternating choruses of "King Alfalfa" ("You may love the voice of Vallee/And think Bing's the swellest thing/But when it comes to crooning/Alfalfa is the King!"); Ella Logan's Scotch

Impresario Barnaby (Henry Brandon) with Porky and Alfalfa in "Our Gang Follies of 1938."

niece belting out "Loch Lomond"; "Cab" (Calloway) Buckwheat leading his orchestra through a hot rendition of "Follow the Leader"; Darla, Porky, and ensemble performing the snappy song "The Love Bug Will Get You If You Don't Watch Out"; Georgia Jean LaRue and Phil MacMahon combining on two engaging tunes, "That Foolish Feeling" and "There's No Two Ways About It"; and then everyone joining in for the "Wedding March" smash finale. Dandies, all.

Finally, a review of the "Follies of 1938" shooting script points up some interesting things about *Our Gang* filmmaking. Since this particular copy of the forty-one-page script was kept by the script clerk, it's replete with marginal notes concerning the continuity of attitudes, and positioning (particularly props) from one scene to the next: whether Spanky's wearing a hat, whether Alfalfa's playing his concertina, what hand Porky's holding the atomizer in (for spraying Alfalfa's gifted throat)—all things we take for granted, until spotting a goof on the screen.

Perhaps the most interesting aspect of *Our Gang* scripts is the degree to which the nuance of emotions portrayed in facial reactions is already spelled out precisely on paper before shooting ever begins. Directors McGowan, Meins, or Douglas knew pretty much what would work, and then went out and captured it on film. Take for instance the following *planned* scene descriptions extracted from the script:

33
_____

FULL SHOT—BACKSTAGE NEAR DOOR. Spanky is pacing the floor in a dither.

> VOICES (Off-scene): *We want Alfalfa! We want Alfalfa!*

Alfalfa is seen through the glass pane of the door as he arrives exterior on landing, smugly self-satisfied. Spanky turns to retrace his steps and catches a glimpse of Alfalfa, does a delayed double take and dashes for the door gleefully. Throwing the door open, he grabs Alfalfa and pulls him into the room, fairly bouncing with excitement and relief. Porky enters and closes the door.

> SPANKY: *Gee, I'm glad you changed your mind and came back. Listen to 'em yell! Go out there, boy, and croon for 'em—*

Alfalfa, enjoying the situation, expands with satisfaction, and shakes his head with an oily smile.

34
_____

TWO SHOT—SPANKY AND ALFALFA—PANNING. Spanky urges Alfalfa on with a push. Alfalfa pridefully, daintily removes Spanky's hands from his arm.

> ALFALFA (Snootily): *Just a minute——*
> SPANKY (Reacts, injured, unbelieving, dumbfounded): *What's the matter?*
> ALFALFA (Definitely): *I told you before— my crooning days are over.*

Spanky gives him a hurt, resentful look.

> SPANKY (Quietly): *Oh! So you still feel that way about it, huh?—Okay.*

Spanky stalks out toward waiting dancers, off-scene. CAMERA PANS OVER to TWO SHOT—ALFALFA AND PORKY. They exchange looks of smug enjoyment.

> SOUND: Off-scene, crowd calling for Alfalfa

Though one can find slight differences in the filmed scenes, they were shot virtually as scripted.

163 · CANNED FISHING

One Reel · Produced by Hal Roach · Directed by Gordon Douglas · Photographed by Art Lloyd · Edited by William Ziegler · Released on February 12, 1938, by M-G-M · Our Gang: George "Spanky" McFarland, Carl "Alfalfa" Switzer, Billie "Buckwheat" Thomas, Eugene "Porky" Lee, and Gary "Junior" Jasgar · Spanky's mother, Wilma Cox

Spanky discusses a scene from "Canned Fishing" with his director, Gordon Douglas (back to camera), as Alfalfa and Buckwheat consider the point being made. The coats indicate it must have been chilly during shooting. The production assistant working on Alfalfa's errant hair is unidentified.

Alfalfa has spent the night at Spanky's, in anticipation of a scheme for getting out of going to school the next morning: Spanky places a block of ice on Alfalfa's chest, and tries to convince mother that Alfalfa's got a chill. While Mom goes for a hot water bottle, the doorbell rings, and she finds Porky and Buckwheat outside, asking if their pals are ready to go fishing. Now aware of their scheme, Mom plans to teach the two recalcitrants a lesson. She insists that Alfalfa stay home from school, and allows Spanky to stay with him so she can go shopping. Everything works to schedule, except that Mom leaves bratty Junior behind for the boys to watch. Before they can do a thing, Spanky and Alfalfa find Junior playing in the sooty incinerator; in their attempt to clean him up, they get locked in a steam cabinet, and Buckwheat gets stuck in a washing machine! Mom returns to find all three boys in a state of frenzy, and as she frees them they grab their books and hurry off to school, proclaiming, "No more hooky for us!"

"Canned Fishing" is neither plausible nor convincing. Its sole asset, along with a number of one-reel films directed by Gordon Douglas, is that it *moves,* from beginning to end. Unfortunately, it also carries the theme of an adult deciding to teach-these-kids-a-lesson, which seldom paves the way for good *Our Gang* comedy.

The nicest part of the rather conventional phony-illness scheme is the payoff with Porky and Buckwheat spilling the beans to Spanky's mother. Buckwheat asks for Alfalfa, who's supposed to be ready to go fishing. When Mom expresses surprise, Buckwheat replies brightly, "Yeah, he's gonna play hooky." The alert mother catches on and tells the boys to come back a bit later. When she leaves them, Buckwheat turns to his companion and asks innocently, "Do you think we did anything wrong?" "I don't think so," Porky answers.

Yet this same wide-eyed Buckwheat is not so dumb as to be fooled when Spanky and Alfalfa try to get him to stay with Junior while they go fishing—absurdly presenting the idea as if they're doing Buckwheat a big favor.

All in all, the most interesting aspect of this forgettable outing is Junior himself. Never in the history of *Our Gang* has there been a more emotionless child. Studio publicists realized this, and the twenty-six-month-old youngster was ballyhooed in the trades as "a vest-pocket edition of Buster Keaton." His frozen face expresses absolutely nothing, whether he's playing a scene on his own or being talked to by Spanky, as when he and Alfalfa push the youngster through a tiny opening in the steam cabinet, hoping he will climb out and open the door for them. Not only doesn't Junior help the captive duo, but he turns on the heat, leaving them to "stuffocate," in Alfalfa's words.

The contrivance that puts the boys into this situation is so silly as to challenge the gullibility of the youngest viewer. Seeing that Junior has climbed into the open cabinet, Spanky announces that they'll have to go in after him to pull him out. Only two grade-A dumbbells could arrange to climb all the way into a small cabinet, ostensibly to remove a young child, and somehow avoid noticing that the cabinet door is closing behind them. It would take a similar lack of brain power to devise the idea of having Buckwheat "demonstrate" for Junior how much fun it is to sit in a washing machine, and then run off and leave the demonstrator with no way of getting out. Yet this is how "Canned Fishing" presents our "heroes." It's somewhat a betrayal of the whole *Our Gang* idea; yet it all seems so false and shallow (like the kids' final announcement, "No more hooky for us!") that one can't get too alarmed.

What *is* disturbing is that other films followed in the same vein, gnawing away at everything that had made *Our Gang* so good.

164 · BEAR FACTS

One Reel · Produced by Hal Roach · Directed by Gordon Douglas · Photographed by Art Lloyd · Edited by William Ziegler · Released on March 5, 1938, by M-G-M · Our Gang: Carl "Alfalfa" Switzer, George "Spanky" McFarland, Darla Hood, Billie "Buckwheat" Thomas, Eugene "Porky" Lee, and Elmer the Monkey

Spanky and Alfalfa bemoan the fact that there's nothing to do around town except play checkers, while Porky and Buckwheat apparently have nothing to do but sit and watch them. Then the two younger kids spot some newcomers moving into the neighborhood: a circus owner and his pretty daughter. When Alfalfa hears the news, he's certain that his magnetic personality will persuade the daughter to have her father hire the gang as animal trainers, enabling them to travel and see more of life. Calling on Darla, the boys sit open-mouthed as Alfalfa spins a tall tale about his great abilities at hypnotizing wild bears into submission. In order to teach Alfalfa and the others a lesson, Darla's father dresses in a bear outfit to test the young boy's prowess. After a few shaky minutes, Alfalfa and the gang scramble away from the house to return to their clubhouse haven and the game of checkers.

"Bear Facts" is slickly made and enjoyable, if marred by the never-too-funny notion of an adult having a laugh at the expense of the gang. In this instance, it's more a case of just deserts, however, since Alfalfa has gone to such extremes in fabricating his story of jungle conquests, shown in a flashback sequence in which the intrepid hunter who laughs at danger ("Alfalfa never turns back!") stares down three husky bears. When the picture returns to Darla's living room, the wide-eyed look of awe and shock on Buckwheat's face at hearing this story is priceless.

Darla's father has heard the story, too, and steps in to congratulate Alfalfa and offer him and his friends jobs with the circus. Then he takes Darla outside, divulges his plan and says, "I don't think they'll want to run away with any circus when we get through with them."

Darla's traditional coyness is on display in "Bear Facts," from her expression at being greeted with flowers to her reaction when Alfalfa says, "Gee but you're pretty." In best dainty-damsel tradition, she turns her head away in mock modesty at the compliment. But apparently Darla is not so easily taken in, for she shares her father's delight in scaring the boys away. When they leap through the living-room window to escape, Father looks after them and says, "Well, I guess we cured their circus fever." "And how," says Darla gleefully, "look at them run!"

According to a press book story for *Bear Facts*, during production Gordon Douglas entrusted Spanky with the 16mm Keystone camera he's shown holding in this still. Spanky then supposedly filmed one of the "deepest Africa" scenes concurrently with Art Lloyd, and when the rushes were screened amateur Spanky's low-angle grinding had captured special top lighting that Lloyd had missed in 35mm, so they reshot the scene. Anyhow, of such things are movie press books made.

A saving grace of this final segment is Alfalfa's truly funny attempt to train the bogus bear. Darla plays a record for dance music,* and Alfalfa teaches the surprisingly cooperative beast to do a toe dance; when he tries to tiptoe away, however, the unwilling trainer is recaptured by the bear, who enthusiastically goes into a waltz!

If "Bear Facts" has less to offer in terms of story, humor, or involvement, than the better *Our Gang* efforts, it shares with other one-reelers of this period a rapid pacing and professional polish that makes it easy-to-take entertainment . . . and there's nothing wrong with that.

* Immediately recognizable as "Nightfall," the Marvin Hatley background music used during the camping-out scenes in Laurel & Hardy's *Way Out West*.

165 · THREE MEN IN A TUB

One Reel · Produced by Hal Roach · Directed by Nate Watt · Photographed by Art Lloyd · Edited by William Ziegler · Released on March 26, 1938, by M-G-M · Our Gang: Darwood "Waldo" Kaye, Carl "Alfalfa" Switzer, Darla Hood, Billie "Buckwheat" Thomas, George "Spanky" McFarland, Eugene "Porky" Lee, Jerry Tucker, Sheila Brown, Harold Switzer, Gary "Junior" Jasgar, and Tommy McFarland

Darla hasn't joined the gang on a picnic outing, supposedly staying home to mind the baby. Alfalfa is angry but not suspicious, telling Spanky that "she wouldn't even look at another man." Just then, wealthy Waldo rides by the lake front in his motorboat, with Darla luxuriating in the back seat, loving every minute. Alfalfa is distraught, but Spanky hatches a scheme to give the new Romeo some competition: they challenge him to a race for the championship of Toluca Lake, and hastily assemble a makeshift craft propelled by a Rube Goldberg-ish system involving some ducks and an open umbrella. Waldo laughs at the amateurish opposition, but they give him a run for his money, and when he takes the lead, his boat suddenly springs a leak. As the flustered

Preparing for the unveiling scene in "Three Men in a Tub" are Porky, Buckwheat, and Spanky (Alfalfa's under the sheet). The three are reviewing their lines and cues with script girl Ellen Corby, whose husband at the time was Roach photographer Francis Corby. Ms. Corby later carved out quite a career for herself, working as a character actress in films like *Shane, Vertigo,* and *Little Women,* writing screenplays for Hopalong Cassidy westerns, and starring as Granny on the CBS television series *The Waltons.*

captain consults his boating manual, Darla shrieks for help and is dramatically rescued by Alfalfa. While Waldo is perplexed at how the leak could have occurred, Alfalfa's unsung cronies Porky and Buckwheat smile together as they produce the missing cork-stopper!

Pretty much a compact reworking of "Hi'-Neighbor!''—with motorboats serving as the central props instead of fire engines—"Three Men in a Tub" has a fine sense of story and pacing that packs a fully developed plot into ten minutes, with no feeling of abruptness or condensation from its lengthier antecedent.

The roles of wounded lover, fickle female, and cocky suitor are played for all they're worth in this short, almost hinting that the whole episode is just a facade. Alfalfa is crushed at the sight of his girl with someone else, and moans, "After all I've done for her, she's let me down for a man with a yacht . . . a speed man." Throughout the short, Alfalfa mugs relentlessly, with director Nate Watt (a moonlighting second-unit director) even supplying medium close-ups to emphasize these moments, as at the unveiling of his new boat where Alfalfa gloats for the crowd, then gets tangled up in the sheet that was covering the mystery vessel.

Darla has cruelly deserted Alfalfa, but while she continually gushes lines like, "Oh Waldo, you're simply divine," she is clearly more interested in what Waldo has to offer than in Waldo himself: flowery compliments, boxes of candy, a spiffy boat to cruise around in, and a secure place on his pedestal. When the ship starts to leak, Waldo is more concerned with his motor than with her, leaving the field open for Alfalfa to save the damsel in distress. "My hero!" she cries, happy to be the center of attention once more.

Waldo is at his most insufferable. When Darla exclaims, "Oh Waldo, your boat is beautiful," he replies diffidently, "She's a very trim craft." In his natty formal boating attire and horn-rimmed Harold Lloyd glasses, he is the antithesis of the unspoiled Our Gangers.

The production values of this short are first-rate. While there is much outdoor location footage around the lake, the process-screen shots during the racing sequence are so good that they might go undetected (except for dialogue echoes that give away scenes made in the studio tank), which is more than can be said for other Hal Roach films where the shoddiest rear-projection is allowed to pass muster.

Director Nate Watt had come to Roach from a stint as director of the early Paramount Hopalong Cassidy Westerns, which were noted for their fine use of exteriors; possibly it was his eye for detail that resulted in such a fine finished product. Watt alternated between second-grade assignments as director, and top-drawer films like *All Quiet on the Western Front, Rain, The Front Page,* and *Of Mice and Men,* where he worked as assistant director for Lewis Milestone.

Phony-looking sequences on the water could have sunk ''Three Men in a Tub.'' As it is, the boating scenes work because like all good comedy scenes, they seem real.

166 · CAME THE BRAWN

One Reel · Produced by Hal Roach · Directed by Gordon Douglas · Photographed by Art Lloyd · Edited by William Ziegler · Story by Hal E. Roach · Released on April 16, 1938, by M-G-M · Our Gang: Carl "Alfalfa" Switzer, Tommy "Butch" Bond, George "Spanky" McFarland, Eugene "Porky" Lee, Billie "Buckwheat" Thomas, Darla Hood, Darwood "Waldo" Kaye, Sidney "Woim" Kibrick, Alvin Buckelew, Patsy Currier, Raymond Rayhill Powell, Billy Mindy, Betsy Gay, Joe "Corky" Geil, Harold Switzer, and Tommy McFarland

''Wildcat'' Alfalfa is set to wrestle the Masked Marvel this afternoon at Promoter Spanky's arena, but it's a fixed fight, of course, and Alfalfa has yet to choose an opponent weak enough for him to overcome. First he selects Porky, but in a preliminary match the tiny youngster has Alfalfa pinned to the mat in a matter of seconds. Then Alfalfa finds a sure-fire weakling he *knows* he can lick: poetry-reading Waldo . . . who's always tripping over things. The match rehearsal concluded, Alfalfa visits Darla secure in the knowledge that he'll win the big fight, but he brags a bit too much in front of Butch, his rival for Darla's affections, inspiring the bully to sneak into the Masked Marvel's dressing room and force Waldo to switch places with him, a hood covering his face to maintain the surprise. Once in the ring, Alfalfa is clearly in trouble, and gets the scare of his life when Butch unmasks himself. Then Porky and Buckwheat do some poking underneath the wrestling ring and manage to catch hold of Butch's Marvel suit, ripping it off completely, leaving him cowering under a sheet of canvas, unable to show himself. Alfalfa demands that he stand up and finish the fight, but Butch is forced to concede. The fight is his, but much to Alfalfa's chagrin, Darla isn't—she's given him up for Waldo and his poetry.

With its story line resurrected and scaled down from ''Boxing Gloves,'' made nine years earlier, and ''The Champeen,'' made *sixteen* years earlier, ''Came the Brawn'' is a breezily amusing, if somewhat illogical, *Our Gang* comedy. How Alfalfa could pass himself off as even a third-rate fighter when he's unable to out-wrestle a child like Porky is a mystery. Yet what he lacks in brawn he makes up for in bravado. As Spanky announces that the (phony) Masked Marvel has never been defeated in the ring, Alfalfa boasts, ''That doesn't phrase me a bit!'' He is even so bold as to make threats to Butch, where in other films he would slink away at the mere mention of the bully's name.

Most likely it is love that takes Alfalfa to such heights of presumed power, although the adoration of Darla is whimsical at best. When Butch turns up in a Little Lord Fauntleroy outfit, Darla says it looks silly. Butch protests that she told him to buy it that morning, so he'd be a gentleman, but Darla disinterestedly replies that since then she's changed her mind and fallen in love with he-men. Similarly, at the end of the film, Alfalfa finds Darla hanging on Waldo's every word (courtesy of Shakespeare), and telling him, ''I like boys of refinement.''

It's unlikely that fickle women enter into the lives of most eight-year-olds, except in the mock-adult world of *Our Gang,* yet fickleness became Darla's principal characteristic in the late 1930s. And as any Hollywood hero could tell you, the more aloof a leading lady becomes, the more vigorous his pursuit of her, this too becoming a standard *Our Gang* plot fixture.

In fact, the only disruptive element of ''Came the Brawn,'' a slick and funny if not outstanding *Our Gang* entry, is the final shot, where Alfalfa watches Darla walk away with Waldo and declares, ''To think she'd do this to me—I'll never speak to another girl again as long as I live.'' Then, to the camera, he adds, ''Good night, folks.''

What possessed director Gordon Douglas to betray the fantasy world of this film series and have Alfalfa acknowledge his audience is beyond our ken. Most likely it was simply a means of breaking the monotony of one ten-minute short after another cut from the same cloth—a one-time gimmick that was never used again.

Yet the notion itself could never have occurred to the *Our Gang* filmmakers of an earlier time, when warmth, sincerity, and believability were the goals of every short. Only in the midst of more streamlined and contrived comic outings in the late 1930s would the idea of admitting that it's all a charade have come to pass.

Caught off-guard for this informal shot—Darla and Alfalfa.

167 · FEED 'EM AND WEEP

One Reel · Produced by Hal Roach · Directed by Gordon Douglas · Photographed by Norbert Brodine · Edited by William Ziegler · Released on May 7, 1938, by M-G-M · Our Gang: Carl "Alfalfa" Switzer, Eugene "Porky" Lee, Darla Hood, Philip Hurlic, and Gary "Junior" Jasgar · Darla's father, Johnny Arthur; Darla's mother, Wilma Cox

Mr. Hood is celebrating his 32nd birthday just the way he pleases—with a quiet dinner at home. But before he can sip his first spoonful of soup, Alfalfa, Porky, and Philip arrive to present their birthday greetings in song and gifts (a frog, a duck, and a cat). These hungry well-wishers completely disrupt the dinner, preventing the beleaguered Mr. Hood from taking one bite of his food. Just when it seems that he'll finally get to eat some of his own birthday cake, yet another intruder arrives, carrying a message to Alfalfa that his parents want him to come home. Percy, the messenger, manages to take Mr. Hood's piece of cake with him as he zips out of the house on his tricycle, frustrating the Birthday Boy to such a degree that he stalks out, announcing his intention to go to a restaurant! Alfalfa and his pals follow him out the door, totally oblivious of what they've done to wreck a potentially serene birthday celebration.

Naturally, the star attraction of "Feed 'em and Weep" is Johnny Arthur, repeating his role as Darla's father from the previous year's "Night 'n' Gales." Even in this briskly paced one-reeler, we are given ample indication of his personality. He calls his wife "Mama," and explains that he's especially hungry since all he had to eat that day was a lettuce sandwich on gluten bread.

Although he has a low boiling point, Mr. Hood can hardly be blamed for going crazy with these pests interrupting his dinner. When he finally gets to taste his soup, it's ice cold. "Well, why didn't ya eat it when it was hot?" Alfalfa asks, sending Mr. Hood running to the kitchen moaning, "Mama! Oh, Mama!" "And to think that this should happen to me on my natal anniversary," he complains. The kids even blow out the candles on his cake for him.

It may be difficult to believe that Alfalfa and friends are completely unaware that they grate on Mr. Hood's nerves, but anyone who has been around children would readily recognize the innocent annoyance caused by two young boys fighting over something (in this case, Alfalfa and Philip bickering over Tarzan being stronger than Flash Gordon, or vice versa) repeating their claims of "He is!" and "He isn't!" over and over again.

Porky and Darla.

Alfalfa also contributes an ear-splitting rendition of "Many Happy Returns of the Day" to the celebration, with ever-dutiful Darla accompanying him on the piano. Wilma Cox is fine as Mrs. Hood, much more tolerant of the boys than her husband, and not totally sympathetic to his outbursts of frustration. "John!" she reprimands. "Don't lose your temper!"

But as mentioned before, "Feed 'em and Weep" is primarily a vehicle for Johnny Arthur, and not so much for other players, especially the depleted Gang, who come off as a trio of slightly obnoxious brats.

"Feed 'em and Weep" is minus Buckwheat, Butch, and Waldo, being also the first of the five shorts made without Spanky McFarland. His absence left a void in the series, though for some time Alfalfa had marginally supplanted Spanky as *Our Gang*'s lead character. The stories are more often about Alfalfa's problems, feature Alfalfa's parents, etc., while Spanky is relegated to the role of Alfalfa's slightly brighter sidekick and steadying influence.

168 · THE AWFUL TOOTH

One Reel · Produced by Hal Roach · Directed by Nate Watt · Photographed by Norbert Brodine · Edited by William Ziegler · Released on May 28, 1938, by M-G-M · Our Gang: Carl "Alfalfa" Switzer, Billie "Buckwheat" Thomas, Eugene "Porky" Lee, Alvin "Spike" Buckelew, and Pete the Pup · Dr. Schwartz, Jack Norton

In their devitalized financial condition, the gang needs $3 for a catcher's mitt, but the club treasury is 20¢ short. When Buckwheat tells the others that he got a dime by putting a tooth under his pillow, Alfalfa reasons that they could amass a small fortune by having *all* their teeth pulled out. They go to see Dr. Schwartz, the dentist, for just such an operation, but he and his nurse decide to frighten the kids out of such a silly scheme by making the dental work sound as horrifying as possible. The scare treatment works, and in return for coming to their senses, the good doctor presents the gang with two new baseballs, a glove, and a catcher's mitt.

Very much a lesser *Our Gang*, ''The Awful Tooth'' derives its title from Leo McCarey's popular feature film of 1937 *The Awful Truth;* to say that this is the cleverest part of the dispirited short gives some indication of its general quality.

There's nothing wrong with ''The Awful Tooth'' that a good dose of humor wouldn't cure. The trouble is that the basic premise involves a dentist and his nurse having a laugh on the kids, precisely the opposite notion of *Our Gang's* basic foundation. The appeal of the series was built up over many years by showing mischievous youngsters defying such authority-figures as dentists.

Making matters worse, the dentist and his nurse can hardly control their enjoyment of the situation. ''I'm going to put on a show for those little schemers that will change their minds in a hurry,'' Dr. Schwartz says gleefully. Playing his role to the hilt, he gathers a formidable array of tools, including a hacksaw and a mallet, and tells Alfalfa that they might as well ''get the suffering over with.'' Every time he catches his nurse's eye, he can't help smiling, and when she isn't in the room, he resorts to smiling to himself. In the outer office, when Buckwheat becomes so scared that he begins to pray, the nurse bursts into laughter! Pretty funny, eh?

Finally pop-eyed Alfalfa can stand no more, and tells the doctor that he's changed his mind, and wants to keep his teeth. Suddenly our slap-happy dentist turns sober-faced and replies stoically, ''That's right, son, you take good care of your teeth, and hold onto them as long as you can.''

Then, in the outer office, the doctor asks his nurse if he didn't hear the Good Fairy come by. She replies in the affirmative and produces a boxful of baseball equipment the Fairy left for the boys, adding tactfully, ''He said you can give him the teeth later, when they come out naturally.''

Thus, an *Our Gang* film has been used to promote dental health at the expense of good comedy. This being the next-to-last Hal Roach short in the series, ''The Awful Tooth'' stands as an unfortunate harbinger of things to come at M-G-M, where moralizing got completely out of

At the Hollywood Wax Museum the *Our Gang* exhibit is based on a scene from ''The Awful Tooth.'' On the next set, through the door where Buckwheat's standing, is Buster Keaton, suffering from a toothache. Photo by Jordan Young.

hand. At the same time, one wonders just what good this dentist accomplished by convincing four gullible youngsters that dental work is the most terrifying torture on earth.

Easily the most interesting aspect of this film is the unusual casting of Jack Norton as the dentist. Norton was typecast as movies' foremost drunk, staggering his way through untold scores of films in the 1930s and 1940s, usually in small (and sometimes infinitesimal) roles, only occasionally playing straight parts. His showy performance as the dentist here may have been one of his largest roles, as well as his least typical. Adding to the paradox, Norton's closest competitor as most celebrated screen imbiber was Arthur Housman, who worked frequently at this same studio with Laurel & Hardy in the 1930s.

169 · HIDE AND SHRIEK

One Reel · Produced by Hal Roach · Directed by Gordon Douglas · Edited by William Ziegler · Released on June 18, 1938, by M-G-M · Our Gang: Carl "Alfalfa" Switzer, Billie "Buckwheat" Thomas, Eugene "Porky" Lee, Darla Hood, and Gary "Junior" Jasgar · Janitor, Fred Holmes; Voice on the record, Billy Bletcher

''Hide and Shriek'' casts Alfalfa in the role of ''X-10 . . . Sooper Slooth.'' Sporting a deer-stalker cap and reading cheap detective magazines, X-10 hires Porky (X-6) and Buckwheat (X-6½) as deputies, and dispatches them to

sleuth up a mystery. The detective agency's first client is Darla, whose box of candy seems to have disappeared. The two deputies round up a pair of guilty-looking suspects (they're innocent, of course), but when they refuse to talk, X-10 lets them go, reminding his aides with impressive determination that a felon always returns to the scene of his crime. Donning disguises, with stealthy haste the three junior detectives trail the suspects to the cab of a truck, and then seek cover in some large cartons, which, unknown to them, are consigned to the haunted house of an amusement pier! Upon delivery, the gang comes out of hiding goggle-eyed with fright. Alfalfa pulls what he thinks is a light switch, activating the fun-house machinations. A recorded voice laughs wickedly and warns, "Many enter this evil house, but few depart alive." Locked in a darkened room, they are confronted by assorted swooping goblins and skeletons, eerie lights, fiendish laughter, a ghoulish organ, and trick machinery torture—such as a moving buzz saw aimed right at their necks! They set off every booby trap in the place before finally being deposited outside. Fleeing back to headquarters they pass Darla, who announces wide-eyed that she found the missing candy in her doll carriage, "Just where I left it." The case solved, Darla is sharing her candy with the two "crooks," and offers Alfalfa some. Peering out of his doorway, still shuddering, Alfie pleads, "Don't ever mention candy or detectives to me again!" and hangs a sign on the door declaring, "Out of Bizzness."

With its sleuthing misadventures theme possibly inspired by the initial Basil Rathbone Sherlock Holmes film being produced concurrently on the Fox lot, "Hide and Shriek" offers some fresh story slants and emerges as a brisk and clever comedy. The short is intended as a spoof, so it really doesn't matter that its haunted-house scenes give off a definite air of contrivance. Unlike "Mama's Little Pirate" or "Spooky Hooky," which created memorable auras of stark tension and genuine fright, one need not be convinced by the film's artificial situations in order to enjoy it; and fortunately, the film is so well made that one can be entertained without necessarily being persuaded by it.

"Hide and Shriek" is the final Roach Our Gang comedy. Frequently, the last entry in a series of pictures is assembled hastily, with little care, and a low budget, simply to fulfull a commitment so as to be done with it and go on to something else. This film is a happy exception to that rule; not only is it better than the two shorts which preceded it, but it's easily better than any of the fifty-two M-G-M-produced comedies that followed. In a way, it says something special about Hal Roach.

A rare, surviving shooting script for "Hide and Shriek" provides some interesting information concerning the film's production. The cover discloses that S. S. Van Kueran, Hal Roach's cousin, served as production manager, a capacity never credited on screen, and one Van Kueran held on the Roach lot from the mid-1930s through the 1950s, winding up his career supervising things such as Roach's Amos 'n' Andy TV series. The story department (room 29, it says), working with director Gordon Douglas and his production staff, pulled together the shooting script from the preliminary "treatments" over three days—May 9 through May 11. This left another fifty or so days for shooting, cutting, scoring, previewing, as well as a cushion for things like exploitation and retakes (which were rare in an Our Gang film) before the film's general theatrical release on June 18. The twenty-one-page script is surprisingly detailed, denoting whether there should be interior or exterior shooting, de-

scribing every camera setup, advising whether there should be a master shot, medium close-up, two shot, insert, or panning shot, noting where special techniques such as reverse cranking are to be used, and listing all intended optical effects and transitions (swish pan, wipe-dissolve, etc.). The dialogue, too, conforms very much to what's actually used in the film. Spanky McFarland recalls that the variations from script to screen were most often the kids' own malapropisms. For instance, Alfalfa's scripted line, "Now what would Sherlock Holmes do?" emerged as "Now what would Sherlock's Home do in a case like this?"

The script also uses comedy shorthand and refers to one gimmick-prop as an "Oelze gag." Through the years, Charley Oelze had been responsible for rigging all the gag props and mechanical gadgetry in the studio's films. He and Hal Roach had worked together on the very first Our Gang comedy, and here they were, seventeen years later, still together, making their last one. As filmmaking and styles of comedy had changed over the years, the Our Gang pictures had changed, too, gradually shifting away from fast-moving stories and elaborate props, to simpler situations that allowed stronger focus on the kids' personalities. Oelze's contributions to the films had diminished accordingly, but Roach, who always watched out for his friends, kept Oelze on until he retired.

Not only was "Hide and Shriek" the final Our Gang comedy its creator would make, but it was also the last short subject of any kind produced by Hal Roach Studios. One wonders about the final scene of "Hide and Shriek" where Alfalfa hangs the sign on his door that reads "Out of Bizzness."

After delivering just one more Laurel & Hardy feature, Block-Heads, Roach would also conclude his twelve-year distribution arrangements with M-G-M, thus drawing another curtain on an era of prolific and superb comedy creation. In late May, with production winding down on "Hide and Shriek," Hal Roach sold the entire Our Gang company to M-G-M and announced that he was joining United Artists, intending to produce comedy features exclusively.

Hal Roach explains, "The market for short comedies was beginning to dry up, and we had to slowly drop them. Later, I tried to bring them back in a way with my 'streamliners,' which ran fifty or so minutes, on the theory that if features could grow as they had from five reels to ten reels, then shorts could grow twice their size, too, from twenty minutes to forty minutes. The streamliners were very successful until I was called back into the army for the war. Anyway, I was giving more and more of my attention to feature-length comedies in the 1930s, not only with Laurel & Hardy, but we tried Our Gang and Charley Chase in features, and there were the Topper films, and so on.

"Now I was against the double-feature setup from the start, but it had always been my feeling that it was unfair to high-ranking comedians to keep all story vehicles as shorts with a twenty- to twenty-five-minute limitation; I mean, that's a big reason why we originally branched into features with Harold Lloyd in the first place. When I saw our people could sustain full-length feature pictures, we'd make 'em, but from the start we were specializing in feature quality short subjects, and fought the industry trend toward double features. But in the end, when we had been squeezed down to just the *Our Gang* one-reelers, I could see the writing on the wall.

"You see, Metro had been releasing our short comedies for a long time, and they were our distributing agents. But they made their own features; they were not interested in Hal Roach making features for them, and in order to keep the studio going, we had to do feature productions. So it was at that time that I sold Metro the *Our Gang* unit, because they wanted me to continue making the one-reelers. But as I say, our style of comedy was changing from two-reelers to full-length features, and even though it's still comedy, the mechanics involved are not quite the same. In many cases you need different workmen and different players. So with the profit margins getting tighter on the Gang one-reelers, because of the rising cost, and our bookings leveling off, well, I couldn't see a good future for the series. Anyway, shorts were now being crowded out by double bills, and even the cartoons, which were cheaper to make and becoming popular. Well, Metro still thought that there was a strong demand for *Our Gang* in the theaters, and that's why they bought me out. If they hadn't bought me out, though, I would have been forced to discontinue them anyway."

If M-G-M, which loomed as the most powerful studio in the industry, wanted to continue the *Our Gang* series, and had Roach's entire *Our Gang* company to start with and build on, why did they turn out product so far beneath the standard achieved at Hal Roach Studios? In Mr. Roach's words, "Well, they had thousands of people at Metro, but they didn't have anybody down there to supervise the films and take any interest in their production in the same way I had. And I could see that, I mean fairly quickly, from the *kind* of films and stories they were doing. Nobody over there knew comedy, whereas at our studio, we specialized in comedy—that's all we did."

The Boss—Hal E. Roach.

VIII   THE M-G-M TALKIES

170 · THE LITTLE RANGER

One Reel · Produced by Jack Chertok for M-G-M · Directed by Gordon Douglas · Photographed by Robert Pittack · Screenplay by Hal Law and Robert A. McGowan · Released on August 6, 1938, by M-G-M · Our Gang: Carl "Alfalfa" Switzer, Darla Hood, Tommy "Butch" Bond, Billie "Buckwheat" Thomas, Eugene "Porky" Lee, Shirley "Muggsy" Coates, Darwood "Waldo" Kaye, Sidney "Woim" Kibrick, Alvin Buckelew, Harold Switzer, Becky Bohanon, and Tommy McFarland

Alfalfa is waiting for Darla outside the local movie house; when she arrives on Butch's arm, he's upset, and accepts Muggsy's eager invitation to accompany her instead. Once inside, Alfalfa dozes off and dreams that he and the gang have taken the place of Fearless Bill and the other horse opera characters on-screen. Villain Butch kidnaps Darla and takes her to his hide-out; Alfalfa—guitar in hand—is left hanging from a tree, but manages to escape, riding to Darla's rescue, closely followed by sheriffs Porky and Buckwheat. After a major brawl, Butch manages to get the drop on all three heroes and leaves them tied up in the room with a keg of dynamite about to explode. Given the choice of marrying Butch or remaining with the doomed cowboys, Darla instantly chooses to marry Butch. Then who should come along to save the day but Muggsy, who tosses the TNT out the window just in the nick of time. At that, Alfalfa wakes up and, with renewed confidence, tweaks Butch in the nose and spurns Darla's sudden attention, walking off with Muggsy instead, telling her that he should have realized all along that she was the girl for him.

"The Little Ranger" is a fine example of what could, and should, have been done with *Our Gang* at their new headquarters, the M-G-M lot. This bright and entertaining one-reeler has all the elements that had made *Our Gang* a success in the first place, plus the typically fine production values the Metro studio had to offer, making it doubly aggravating to see how the studio allowed these films to deteriorate within the next few years.

Co-scripters Hal Law and Robert A. McGowan turned in a good job, both being Hal Roach veterans familiar with the series. Law began his career as a twenty-four-year-old script clerk with Mack Sennett in 1928, then moved to Roach in the early 1930s, where he wrote and occasionally directed pictures, mostly for Charley Chase. Robert Anthony McGowan, nephew of the series' mentor, had directed the silent *Our Gang* shorts for several years under the name of Anthony Mack. Yet he and Law were also responsible for many of the series' later scripts which brought the series to its absolute nadir.

171 · PARTY FEVER

One Reel · Produced by Jack Chertok for M-G-M · Directed by George Sidney · Photographed by Robert Pittack · Screenplay by Howard Dimsdale · Released on August 27, 1938, by M-G-M · Our Gang: Tommy "Butch" Bond, Carl "Alfalfa" Switzer, Darla Hood, Darwood "Waldo" Kaye, Eugene "Porky" Lee, Billie "Buckwheat" Thomas, Sidney "Woim" Kibrick, Harold Switzer, and Pete the Pup · Mayor, "Uncle Frank," Frank Jaquet

Waldo asks Darla to accompany him to the Strawberry Festival, but she explains that Alfalfa and Butch have already asked her and are fighting it out between themselves. Waldo proposes a solution to the problem: a junior mayor is about to be appointed for Boys' Week, and whoever wins the honor will get to take Darla to the festival. Butch and Alfalfa wage a heated campaign for kiddie support. First, Alfalfa pitches a clean-up campaign, foiled by Butch's dirty work; then Butch throws a giant marshmallow roast with free food; but Alfalfa tops him by taking off in a skywriting balloon, thereby capturing the biggest crowd of all. Finally, the big day comes, and the mayor announces his choice for junior mayor, explaining, "Honesty and faithful service will always win out over sensationalism." With that, he bestows the honor upon Waldo for his essay on good government, and the lad blurts out, "Thanks, Uncle Frank."

"Party Fever" is an entertaining short which benefits from first-class production; it's directed and photographed with unusual effectiveness. Credit must go to the series' new director George Sidney, spreading his wings as a short-subject director after having held a variety of odd jobs on the Metro lot. He would go on to direct such major M-G-M features as *Anchors Aweigh, The Harvey Girls, Annie Get Your Gun, Show Boat,* and *Scaramouche.*

Concerning the production of his *Our Gang* shorts at M-G-M, he recently recalled, "Writing, preparation, budgeting, shooting, and editing were done with the same thoroughness as a feature. From the idea to the answer print would be several months. We had access to most facilities so long as we did not get in the way. . . . The *Our Gang* scripts were completely planned to the most minute detail, and it is very possible that doing that series conditioned me to hate all kids. At the time I was only seven years older than the oldest kid. They didn't know . . . neither did I." It was a far cry from Bob McGowan's attitude toward Our Gang . . . and the results showed on-screen in subsequent shorts.

172 · ALADDIN'S LANTERN

One Reel · Produced by Jack Chertok for M-G-M · Directed by Gordon Douglas · Photographed by Robert Pittack · Screenplay by Hal Law and Robert A. McGowan · Released on September 17, 1938, by M-G-M · Our Gang: Carl "Alfalfa" Switzer, Darla Hood, George "Spanky" McFarland, Eugene "Porky" Lee, Billie "Buckwheat" Thomas, Darwood "Waldo" Kaye, Gary Jasgar, Joe "Corky" Geil, Alvin Buckelew, Harold Switzer, Peggy Lynch, and Marylyn Astor Thorpe

The gang stages a show about Aladdin and his lamp, but from the very start, Buckwheat and Porky try to crash the production with their song and soft-shoe rendition of "Strolling Through the Park One Day." In the show, Aladdin displays his magic lamp to lonely Caliph Spanky, who asks for dancers and gets a chorus line led by Darla, singing, "Your Broadway and Mine." The proceedings are interrupted again by Porky and Buckwheat, and Darla is so insulted that she quits the show. Alfalfa seats the two troublemakers backstage and tells them, "No matter what happens, don't move!" Spanky dresses in Darla's costume to finish the second act, in which Alfalfa arrives on his magic carpet (tied to a pulley) and sings, "I'll Take You Home Again, Darleen." During the song a playful monkey pulls the carpet directly over Alfalfa's lamp, holding a lit candle. The burning sensation gives Alfalfa's song a frantic edge, and when it's over he runs from the stage, his backside on fire! "Don't just sit there like dopes," Spanky barks at Porky and Buckwheat, "Can't you do anything to help?" "Yes!" they reply, running onstage to continue their song and dance. Meanwhile, Alfalfa finds refuge by sinking his derriere into a water-filled washing machine. "What a relief." He sighs. "And what a show," moans Spanky.

"Aladdin's Lantern" is virtually indistinguishable from a Hal Roach entry, largely because it rehashes earlier *Our Gang* put-on-a-show stories. Unfortunately, it was director Gordon Douglas's last film in the series. He left M-G-M to return to Roach, preferring the atmosphere at his home studio and feeling that M-G-M "involved the kids with adult problems [in the films], and I think it was a mistake . . . they were going back to mortgage-on-the-farm plots. And we never made fun in the Roach days of any physical deformities, and Metro did, in a few pictures I remember."

The loss of Douglas was a major blow. The kids in the series had liked and trusted him, and moviegoers in the audience had responded to his work as they never would to the M-G-M product that followed.

Director Gordon Douglas considers Billie "Buckwheat" Thomas's opinion in this candid shot taken on the set of "Alladin's Lantern."

173 · MEN IN FRIGHT

One Reel · Produced by Jack Chertok for M-G-M · Directed by George Sidney · Story by Carl Dudley and Marty Schwartz · Screenplay by Hal Law and Robert A. McGowan · Released on October 15, 1938, by M-G-M · Our Gang: George "Spanky" McFarland, Carl "Alfalfa" Switzer, Eugene "Porky" Lee, Darla Hood, Billie "Buckwheat" Thomas, Gary Jasgar, and Sonny Bupp · Elevator operator, Ray Turner; Darla's mother, Bess Flowers; Sonny's mother, Barbara Bedford; Hospital orderlies, Jack Rice, Don Castle; Nurses, Mary MacLaren, Margaret Bert, Nell Craig

The gang visits Darla in the hospital, bringing a picnic basket full of goodies, knowing full well that she is recuperating from a tonsillectomy and won't be able to help devour the feast. While waiting outside her room, Alfalfa is approached by a wily young patient who gives him a dime to change clothes. Alfalfa, in hospital gown, waits for the kid to come back from "taking a walk," not realizing he is fleeing the hospital to escape surgery! An orderly arrives to take Alfalfa to the operating room, but the crisis is happily forestalled when an open container of laughing gas sends the orderly (and Alfalfa) out of the elevator in a slow-motion state of bliss. A dousing with water returns Alfalfa to reality, and he and the other kids dig into their picnic basket. They dig a little too deep, however, and end up with phenomenal stomachaches. All of them are committed to the children's ward, while Darla is able to

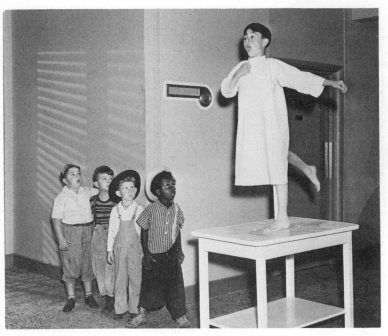

Scene from "Men in Fright."

leave with her mother. She promises to visit them the next day, but they tell her, "Just bring flowers."

This enjoyable short combines the top-notch M-G-M production values with the spirit that characterized the Hal Roach comedies; it represents the best of both worlds in an amusing and imaginative little film.

Alfalfa's tipsy bout with laughing gas is particularly amusing, his light-headedness inspiring him to swing from the chandelier in Darla's room before crashing back to earth. There is also an ingenious animated scene of Alfalfa's stomach as a hot dog starts a fight with a lump of ice cream, precipitating the massive tummy ache that concludes this short.

The hospital set, and faces, are reminiscent of M-G-M's *Dr. Kildare* films, with Nell Craig appearing briefly as a nurse, as she did in the *Kildare* series. Even the title of this short is a spoof of the M-G-M feature *Men in White,* which had already been burlesqued by the Three Stooges several years back as *Men in Black.*

What really sets this apart from many later M-G-M shorts is its point of view. The aim of the film is fun, with no messages or morals to impart. The incidents that occur are shown from the kids' outlook and not from that of condescending adults. This is *Our Gang* as it was meant to be.

174 · FOOTBALL ROMEO

One Reel · Produced by Jack Chertok for M-G-M · Directed by George Sidney · Photographed by Clyde DeVinna · Screenplay by Hal Law, Robert A. McGowan, and Jack White · Released on November 12, 1938, by M-G-M · Our Gang: Carl "Alfalfa" Switzer, George "Spanky" McFarland, Tommy "Butch" Bond, Darla Hood, Eugene "Porky" Lee, Gary Jasgar, Sidney "Woim" Kibrick, Robert Winkler, Joe "Corky" Geil, and Billie "Buckwheat" Thomas · Darla's mother, Barbara Bedford

Alfalfa believes there's more to life than becoming a football hero. When he decides not to suit up for the vital game againstButch's Assassins, lovelorn Darla plots to induce him to play. Parading in front of his home with Butch, she hopes to make him jealous, but this only convinces Alfalfa he should become a hermit. Darla receives his mushy farewell love poem, and then his mother sends a note back to Alfalfa, advising her recluse son that if he doesn't play, Darla is going to read his maudlin ode to a bleacher full of football fans. Alfalfa is none too thrilled with this prospect, so he dashes home, dons his grid togs, and charges into the game. When he asks Darla for the love letter, she tells him it's between the laces of the football, so that if he wants it, he'll have to "go get it" during the game. With that incentive, the complexion of the game changes. Rallying behind both Alfalfa's inspired defensive pursuit and his rushing game, the gang overcomes a two touchdown deficit and wins the contest, with Alfalfa racing sixty yards on an interception for the final

score. At last, with the game over, he has enough time to pry loose the note, which reads, "I kept your poem, here's one from me, I like you best, do you still like me? [Signed] Darla . . . P.S. Butch is a *dope!*"

The second of Alfalfa's three gridiron epics, "Football Romeo" isn't bad at all. It's fast paced, full of action, and the kids obviously still believe in what they're doing. The technical expertise and polish of the M-G-M plant is quite evident, too, as shown in the sets, lighting, photography, sound recording, etc. George Sidney's direction in some of these early M-G-M's is practically imperceptible from Gordon Douglas's work. Sequences move well, the kids maintain an aura of spontaneity, but few things *really* impress.

He's not credited on screen, but in the press book Jack White, veteran comedy producer-director, is listed as having worked on the story. White directed many Three Stooges shorts under the pseudonym Preston Black.

175 · PRACTICAL JOKERS

One Reel · Produced by Jack Chertok for M-G-M · Directed by George Sidney · Screenplay by Hal Law and Robert A. McGowan · Released on December 17, 1938, by M-G-M · Our Gang: Tommy "Butch" Bond, Carl "Alfalfa" Switzer, George "Spanky" McFarland, Darla Hood, Eugene "Porky" Lee, Billie "Buckwheat" Thomas, Becky Bohanon, Grace Bohanon, and Gary Jasgar · Butch's mom, Marie Blake

Butch, scourge of the neighborhood, has been perpetrating all sorts of dirty tricks on the gang, particularly Alfalfa, who seems to fall for booby traps easier than the rest. Looking ahead toward Butch's birthday party that afternoon, the gang sees a way to reciprocate in kind and get even with this prankster. Intercepting the birthday cake, they substitute a firecracker for one of the candles. Their scheme literally backfires, though, and explodes right in their faces when Butch's mom innocently asks Alfalfa to sing a birthday song while holding the lighted cake with its sputtering firecracker-candle. With the explosion, pastry is splattered everywhere, but Alfalfa finds he doesn't mind so awfully much; it's pineapple cake, he discovers, and that tastes good!

A complacent Metro entry of little pretension, "Practical Jokers" tosses off a few predictable discomfiture gags, "builds" to one of Alfalfa's increasingly unfunny, squeaky tunes, and then calls it a reel.

Inexplicably, in at least two instances M-G-M television syndicators have failed to deliver air prints of "Practical Jokers," even though the subject is listed in the Metro contract. It's not censorable material (is it?!), nor is the film "lost," so why is it withheld?

Wide-eyed scene in "Practical Jokers" as Buckwheat, Porky, Spanky, and Alfalfa watch as Butch's mom, Marie Blake, lights the explosive candle.

176 · ALFALFA'S AUNT

One Reel · Produced by Jack Chertok for M-G-M · Directed by George Sidney · Photographed by Jackson Rose · Screenplay by Hal Law and Robert A. McGowan · Released on January 7, 1939, by M-G-M · Our Gang: Carl "Alfalfa" Switzer, George "Spanky" McFarland, Billie "Buckwheat" Thomas, Eugene "Porky" Lee, and Gary Jasgar · Title role, Marie Blake; Alfalfa's mother, Barbara Bedford; Alfalfa's father, William Newell

Alfalfa's Aunt Penelope comes to visit the family; last year's pursuits as a sculptress are forgotten, and now she fancies herself a writer of murder mysteries. Alfalfa reads a page from her manuscript written in the form of a letter which says that "only my nephew stands between me and the Switzer millions," and that he will be murdered at the stroke of nine! With his parents out of the house, Alfalfa turns to the gang for help, and they unwittingly succeed in frightening Aunt Penelope as much as she's scared them with her eerie threat. Just then Alfalfa's mom and dad come home, and the whole situation is explained. Alfalfa is about to apologize to his aunt, who's decided to leave this "madhouse," but Dad is so happy to be rid of his freeloading sister-in-law that he presents Alf with a crisp dollar bill as a reward.

"Alfalfa's Aunt" is rather good; its obvious comedy-mystery plotting is enhanced by superior camera work and evocative lighting, giving the film a chilling atmosphere (when appropriate) that makes the whole thing work.

It's a perfect night for a murder, with the wind blowing outside and a cat screeching in the dark. At the stroke of nine, Porky is busy in the bathroom eliminating all the poisonous medicine bottles; at the sound of breaking glass, Aunt Penelope screams, Alfalfa leaps out of bed, and Buckwheat's hair stands on end. The kids' surreptitious movements around the house give Penelope the shivers, with her sister and brother-in-law arriving home just in the nick of time to turn on the lights and expose the whole situation, a major comedy of errors.

Director George Sidney makes a worthy effort to fill the film with sight gags, all too rare in these M-G-M shorts: when Porky sniffs a bottle of smelling salts, his hat goes flying in the air; as mentioned before, the sound of screaming sets Buckwheat's hair on end; and when Penelope comes to Alfalfa's room to see if he's asleep, his pals run in fast motion to hide before she can open the door.

177 · TINY TROUBLES

One Reel · Produced by Jack Chertok for M-G-M · Directed by George Sidney · Photographed by Al Gilks · Screenplay by Hal Law and Robert A. McGowan · Released on February 18, 1939, by M-G-M · Our Gang: Carl "Alfalfa" Switzer, George "Spanky" McFarland, Darla Hood, Billie "Buckwheat" Thomas, Eugene "Porky" Lee, Edward Marazoni, and Jimmy Marazoni · Officer Clancy, Emory Parnell; Officer O'Brien, Lee Phelps; The judge, Fred Kelsey; Light Fingered Lester, Jerry Maren/Marenghi; Myrtle, Sue Moore; Alfalfa's mother, Barbara Bedford

Alfalfa's baby brother never stops crying. So Alf endeavors to trade the little nuisance for a quieter model. The "infant" he receives in exchange turns out to be "Light-Fingered Lester," a midget who dresses in baby clothes to fool his pickpocket victims. Fleeing from the police, Lester plays along with the gang, until later at Alfalfa's home when he cracks open a bottle of beer and begins taunting the kids. Before the gang can reverse matters, the police break in and haul the whole bunch to the courthouse. The judge can see the kids aren't part of Lester's mob, but he decides to place them on probation and teach them a lesson for having such foolish notions

Porky squares off with midget Jerry Maren between scenes of "Tiny Troubles."

about baby brothers. If this ever happens again, the judge warns, "I'll sentence you with every sentence in the book."

Woefully thin stuff, "Tiny Troubles" suffers from many troubles. A shapeless reworking of the central idea in "Bouncing Babies," it represents the first really bad M-G-M *Our Gang* short. Somehow the production staff expected an audience to swallow the idea that eleven-year-old Alfalfa and ten-year-old Spanky couldn't tell the difference between an infant and a midget dressed as one. If this was supposed to be funny, it isn't. Embarrassment displaces laughter.

Midget Jerry Maren appeared that same year in *At the Circus* with the Marx Brothers, and as a Munchkin in *The Wizard of Oz*. He was still active in television through the 1970s.

Cinematographer Alfred Gilks later won an Academy Award for color camerawork on M-G-M's *An American in Paris* (1951), reemphasizing the fact that no matter how cold and wooden the performances and scripts might become, the studio's *Our Gang* shorts always boasted the finest production money could buy. But no one at M-G-M really *cared* about the films, and no Metro budget ever allowed for that.

178 · DUEL PERSONALITIES

One Reel · Produced by Jack Chertok for M-G-M · Directed by George Sidney · Photographed by Jackson Rose · Screenplay by Hal Law and Robert A. McGowan · Released on March 11, 1939, by M-G-M · Our Gang: Carl "Alfalfa" Switzer, George "Spanky" McFarland, Darla Hood, Tommy "Butch" Bond, Eugene "Porky" Lee, Billie "Buckwheat" Thomas, Sidney "Woim" Kibrick, Darwood "Waldo" Kaye, Shirley "Muggsy" Coates, Priscilla Lyon, Ruth Tobey, Allan Randall, and Becky Bohanon · Prof. William Delmore, hypnotist, John Davidson; Hypnotist's assistant, Phillip Terry; Goofy assistant, Winstead (Doodles) Weaver; Man in crowd, Lester Dorr; Woman in crowd, Marry Milford

A famous hypnotist does a sidewalk demonstration in Greenpoint, and the gang goes to see the display. Alfalfa then volunteers himself as a subject, mistaking the word "skeptical" to mean timid. The hypnotist convinces Alfalfa that he is d'Artagnan, and tells him that he should not let a rival (in this case Butch) steal his girl away from him. Still in character when Butch walks by, Alfalfa challenges him to a duel later that day. Darla is thrilled about the boys fighting over her, but Muggsy reminds her that one of them might get killed; she runs to stop them from dueling, but arrives at the gang's headquarters just in time to hear Butch hatching a scheme with Alfalfa. He tells his adversary that no girl is worth duelling over, so instead, they will fight with guns (cap pistols), both fall to the ground, and whichever one Darla rushes to will be declared the winner, and her permanent beau. Darla, who's overheard the conversation, has a plan of her own, and when the two boys fall to the ground, wounded, she surveys the situation and calls for Waldo to take her to the show. "Don't forget to bury them," she calls over her shoulder as she walks away with the last laugh.

Possibly inspired by the screen's revived interest in swashbucklers, with Errol Flynn's *Adventures of Robin Hood* (the previous year) and *The Three Musketeers* with the Ritz Brothers (the same year) leading the way, "Duel Personalities" is short, sweet, and to the point, presenting the gang in familiar surroundings with a good story, and not posing awkwardly with a saccharine script.

Darla and Alfalfa's on-again off-again romance is treated with just the right touch of mock melodrama. After being snubbed by his girl, Spanky asks Alfalfa, "Why don't you forget about her," and the sorry swain replies mournfully, "If I only could!" Later, when the duel is arranged, Darla proclaims, "This is the most romantic thing I ever heard of," as she rushes off to brag

Still believing he is the spirited reincarnation of D'Artagnan, Alfalfa is about to challenge archrival Butch (de Rochefort) over the affections of Darla. She loves it. Butch and Spanky can't figure it out.

about it to her girl friends. It's important to note that Darla doesn't really care that two mortal enemies are vying for her favor; what matters is that they do it in public.

One of the nicer aspects of this short is the casting of John Davidson as the hypnotist; well-known to serial fans from his frequent character roles in films like *Dick Tracy* *vs. Crime Inc.* and *The Adventures of Captain Marvel*, Davidson presented just the right blend of theatricality and believability to suit this role.

It's astounding to think that the same people who would make the loathsome ''Dog Daze'' a few months later could turn out a short as pleasing as this one. One wonders why they couldn't do it more often.

179 · CLOWN PRINCES

One Reel · Produced by Jack Chertok for M-G-M · Directed by George Sidney · Photographed by Jackson Rose · Edited by Roy Brickner · Screenplay by Hal Law and Robert A. McGowan · Released on April 15, 1939, by M-G-M · Our Gang: Carl "Alfalfa" Switzer, George "Spanky" McFarland, Darla Hood, Eugene "Porky" Lee, Billie "Buckwheat" Thomas, Shirley "Muggsy" Coates, Harold Switzer, Gary Jasgar, Joe "Corky" Geil, Hugh Chapman, Freddie Chapman, Larry Harris, and Payne Johnson · The landlord, Clarence Wilson

The gang stages a circus performance to help Porky's parents pay their rent. Ringmaster Spanky introduces weird caged animal attractions at the sideshow, including The Wild Man from Borneo (Buckwheat) and the Head Without a Body (Porky). Inside the big top there are acrobats (Spanky and Leonard), followed by Darla's lion-taming routine (domestic pets outfitted in furs), and topped off with Daredevil Alfalfa's swinging rendition of ''The Man on the Flying Trapeze.'' He's held aloft with a pulley powered by a mule harnessed outside the barn, causing a hectic climax when the animal is stung by a bee and goes berserk.

Originally entitled ''Circus Capers,'' this above-average Metro effort features some authentic visual gags, some clever dialogue jokes, and some borrowing from earlier films such as ''Spanky'' and ''Barnum & Ringling, Inc.''

Today, with the benefit of hindsight, both Spanky and Darla agree that the M-G-M shorts, even at their best, are a full grade below the Hal Roach productions. Darla Hood explains, ''When we moved over to M-G-M, we knew something had changed, I mean even the kids felt it, and I remember Spanky and Alfalfa particularly sensed it. Instead of playing, having fun under a director's supervision, as we'd done back at the Roach lot, we suddenly became aware that we were supposed to be performing. After a few M-G-M shorts, I knew what I was doing, I knew I was acting; before, I didn't know it. That's the difference. I'm not sure if it was the atmosphere there, or the direction, or our ages, but we'd become actors.

''Some of the films were overproduced, especially the junior Busby Berkeley-dance things. Also, it seemed like

Ta-da! Spanky and Leonard are a couple of swell acrobats in this scene from ''Clown Princes.''

there were so many more executives around telling everybody what to do. It was just a whole different idea. The M-G-M pictures were carefully thought out, planned, and rehearsed, and they were beautifully made, but they're nowhere the same as the Hal Roach comedies, that's for sure.''

180 · COUSIN WILBUR

One Reel · Produced by Jack Chertok for M-G-M · Directed by George Sidney · Edited by Roy Brickner · Screenplay by Hal Law and Robert A. McGowan · Released on April 29, 1939, by M-G-M · Our Gang: Scotty "Cousin Wilbur" Beckett, George "Spanky" McFarland, Carl "Alfalfa" Switzer, Darla Hood, Tommy "Butch" Bond, Sidney "Woim" Kibrick, Eugene "Porky" Lee, Billie "Buckwheat" Thomas, Darwood "Waldo" Kaye, Phillip Hurlic, Harold Switzer, Payne Johnson, Gary Jasgar, Freddie Chapman, and Tommy McFarland · Wilbur's Aunt Martha, Mary Currier

Alfalfa reluctantly introduces the gang to his prissy cousin Wilbur, who inquires why the All 4 One Club has only four members; learning that the organization offers no incentives, Wilbur suggests that the club become a benevolent society, offering accident insurance. Before long, the club's membership (and treasury) is swelling as all the neighborhood kids eagerly pay their 2¢ dues in order to qualify to collect 1¢ for a busted nose or 2¢ for a black eye. But Butch and Woim decide to muscle in, ruining the gang by punching everyone in sight and forcing the club to pay out the entire treasury. Wilbur is blamed for the incident, and Alfalfa sends him home, but just outside the clubhouse, he's pulled into a fight by Butch and Woim—who soon come running to Spanky and Alfalfa pleading for insurance coverage to protect them from Wilbur, who's a fighting firebrand! In appreciation for his good services, Wilbur is made honorary president of the All 4 One Club, and cousin Alfalfa now beams proudly at his brainy relative.

An adjunct to "Alfalfa's Aunt," "Cousin Wilbur" boasts a novel story idea that's smoothly executed by director George Sidney. The notion of the gang tackling the ambitious adult machinery of insurance is a natural . . . and the film has added interest because of Scotty Beckett's return to *Our Gang*.

Cousin Wilbur is a far cry from Spanky's tattered sidekick, but in the years that had passed since Scotty's last *Our Gang* short, he had become one of the finest child actors in Hollywood, equally adept at emotional drama and light comedy. Even in the role of Wilbur, he's just too likable to really irritate the viewer, as tunnel-visioned

Spanky, Alfalfa, and Scotty Beckett, returning to *Our Gang* for the title role in "Cousin Wilbur."

Waldo might have done in the same situation. Cousin Wilbur seems quite pleasant for all his fancy talk and immaculate dress, and it doesn't take him long to ingratiate himself with the gang, and with us.

Unfortunately, M-G-M let him go, after a thankless bit in "Dog Daze," while obnoxious newcomers joined the troupe. It was *Our Gang*'s loss.

181 · JOY SCOUTS

One Reel · Produced by Jack Chertok for M-G-M · Directed by Edward Cahn · Photographed by Ray June · Edited by Roy Brickner · Screenplay by Hal Law and Robert A. McGowan · Released on June 24, 1939, by M-G-M · Our Gang: Carl "Alfalfa" Switzer, George "Spanky" McFarland, Eugene "Porky" Lee, Billie "Buckwheat" Thomas, and Mickey Gubitosi · The scoutmaster, Forbes Murray; Boy Scout patrol, The Clark Gable-sponsored Los Angeles Boy Scout Troop No. 59

The gang wishes to enter a Boy Scouts interpatrol meet, but the scoutmaster tells them they're too young, so the envious kids stomp off on a camping excursion of their own. The expedition proves to be one misadventure after another, though, as they pitch their tent in a hole for a temporarily dormant mammoth geyser, burn the bacon and fish they try to cook, get caught in a rainstorm, and stumble into some poison ivy. Having learned their lesson from these calamities, the gang is thankful when rescued by the scoutmaster and his unit, who promise to teach the kids the right way to camp when they get a little older.

"Joy Scouts" goes beyond mediocrity to rate a position as one of the worst *Our Gang* shorts produced thus far.

It boasts two distinctions. First, it was director Edward L. Cahn's initial *Our Gang* entry. A former editor, he became a prolific director of B-pictures through the 1960s. His *Our Gang* shorts were nothing to cheer about, but he did good work on other short-subject series at M-G-M.

The other debut in "Joy Scouts" is that of Robert Blake. In a recent talk-show interview, the star of *Barretta* recalled, "I was an extra. My brother and sister and I came out here to Hollywood and . . . used to get half-a-buck a day, except we couldn't make it on that, because my mother and father weren't working. So I found out that you could make more money if you talked. So we were extras on the *Our Gang* set, and they had this little rummy that couldn't say the lines, and the director said, 'Well, what are we gonna do here, the kid's gotta say this.' So I said, 'I can say that.' I said it, got the job, and became a regular from that. My real name was Mickey Gubitosi, so they called my character Mickey."

Although he emerged as a fine actor in the 1960s and 1970s, his histrionics in *Our Gang* were soon to play a part in the series' demise.

182 · DOG DAZE

One Reel · Produced by M-G-M · Directed by George Sidney · Photographed by Harold Marzorati · Edited by Tom Biggart · Original story and screenplay by Alfred Giebler · Released on July 1, 1939, by M-G-M · Our Gang: George "Spanky" McFarland, Carl "Alfalfa" Switzer, Darla Hood, Billie "Buckwheat" Thomas, Eugene "Porky" Lee, Tommy "Butch" Bond, Sidney "Woim" Kibrick, and Scotty "Cousin Wilbur" Beckett · Precinct officer Riley, Wade Boteler; Officer Sweeney, Lee Phelps; Captain Pindle, John Power

Sid Kibrick, Tommy Bond, Alfalfa, Darla, Spanky, Porky, and Buckwheat in a scene from "Dog Daze."

The gang owes 37¢ to Butch's loan-shark operation; they had to borrow the money to help care for a stray dog with two broken legs. The dog turns out to be a police mascot, and a grateful officer gives the kids a dollar for their kindness in caring for the canine. Before they can spend the money, however, a neighborhood goat eats the dollar bill! Desperate for money to repay Butch, Alfalfa has an idea: if they got a dollar for taking care of one stray dog, they'll make more money going into the business on a large scale. Soon the townspeople are up in arms with dozens of dogs reported missing; the gang's scheme has backfired disastrously. The dogs are returned and the owners satisfied, but the police officers in charge explain to the kids that "you can't sell kindness." They've learned their lesson, and in return, the officers present them with a terrific new kiddie-car for aiding their precious mascot.

Another story-with-a-message, the real horror in this film is the mannered performances of the kids. Every line of dialogue, every reaction is embellished with contrived facial expressions: the snapping of fingers to indicate the coming of an idea, rubbing a hand against the side of the face to indicate despair, and other gestures that went out with the last touring company of *Uncle Tom's Cabin*. To make matters worse, director George Sidney even cuts to close-ups of Buckwheat, emphasizing his exaggerated, stagelike reactions and making them doubly embarrassing to watch. Oddly enough, this phony posturing is not limited to the kids; most of the adults in this short are equally bad.

When in the early 1940s a new group of kids populated *Our Gang*, this kind of plastic performing became the norm, but it is distressing to see such artificiality in Spanky, Alfalfa, Darla, and other series stalwarts.

Scotty Beckett makes his second and final *Our Gang* return appearance as Cousin Wilbur, sort of an erudite, pantywaist character. He's not really a member of the gang, but rather a scholarly sidelines observer who is always either answering questions for the pet-napping kids, or explaining their behavior and stratagems to grownups.

183 · AUTO ANTICS

One Reel · Produced by Jack Chertok for M-G-M · Directed by Edward Cahn · Photographed by Harold Marzorati · Edited by Roy Brickner · Screenplay by Hal Law and Robert A. McGowan · Released on July 22, 1939, by M-G-M · Our Gang: Tommy "Butch" Bond, Darla Hood, Carl "Alfalfa" Switzer, George "Spanky" McFarland, Billie "Buckwheat" Thomas, Eugene "Porky" Lee, Sidney "Woim" Kibrick, and Mickey Gubitosi · Mayor, Major James H. McNamara; The dog catcher, Joe Whitehead; Luke, Baldwin Cooke

Hoping to win the Kidmobile Race Classic, Spanky and Alfalfa rig their souped-up entry with special rocket propulsion. But when Butch secretly observes this invention, he plots a way to sabotage their auto; while the gang is preparing for the gala event, he fetches a dogcatcher who rounds up the neighborhood pet, Whiskers. Unless the kids can raise the necessary $3, Whiskers will be destroyed—an added incentive for winning the race and its cash prize that afternoon. As everyone crowds around the back of the dogcatcher's truck, Butch and his accomplice, The Woim, sneak over and reverse the superchargers on Spanky and Alfalfa's machine. During the soapbox derby, Butch has run most of his competition into the ditch, but Spanky and Alfalfa remain. Deciding it's time to turn on their superchargers, they discover with some alarm that their invention is propelling them back up the hill, so Alfalfa jumps on the hood and pilots the racer backwards—to a smashing victory. Darla's told the mayor about Whiskers's predicament, so, with the prize money in hand, everyone rushes to the dogpound in the mayor's escorted car, just in time to rescue their canine friend.

With many surefire ingredients, "Auto Antics" never lives up to its potential. If the M-G-M filmmakers' lack of enthusiasm showed in these shorts, so perhaps did growing tensions on the set, with the kiddie stars beginning to show signs of temperament. Darla Hood recalls an early scene in "Auto Antics" where everyone is pleading with the dogcatcher. "We were just supposed to hang onto the back of the truck as it pulled out down the road," she

A posed still from "Auto Antics."

says. "But Alfalfa was in one of his little moods that time, and he'd louse up every single take. We had made *thirty-two* takes, and I guess even the one they eventually used wasn't quite right, because on the last take, with all of us hanging onto the back of this truck, I passed out from the exhaust fumes and they had to take me to the hospital."

184 · CAPTAIN SPANKY'S SHOW BOAT

One Reel · Produced by Jack Chertok for M-G-M · Directed by Edward Cahn · Photographed by Robert Pittack · Edited by Roy Brickner · Screenplay by Hal Law and Robert A. McGowan · Released on September 9, 1939, by M-G-M · Our Gang: George "Spanky" McFarland, Tommy "Butch" Bond, Darla Hood, Carl "Alfalfa" Switzer, Sidney "Woim" Kibrick, Billie "Buckwheat" Thomas, Darwood "Waldo" Kaye, Clyde Wilson, Shirley "Muggsy" Coates, and Mickey Gubitosi

Butch wants to sing in Spanky's new production, but Spanky explains that they already have their singer—Alfalfa. So Butch and Woim attend the gala performance, and when Alfalfa starts to sing, Butch creeps backstage to arrange some sort of "accident." He unplugs the player-piano accompanying the song, but Spanky quickly restores the power. Then Butch cuts a rope which he thinks will send a chandelier toppling onto Alfalfa's head. Instead, it loosens a sandbag which knocks Butch cold, enabling Alfalfa to finish his song uninterrupted.

"Captain Spanky's Show Boat" is a tired rehash of earlier *Our Gang* ideas, as the kids stage a production of " 'Out in the Snow You Go'—by speshul permission of Spanky's uncle" (the latter reference unexplained, which is probably just as well).

The "meller drammer" is just what one would expect, with Spanky in the Simon Legree role, and Alfalfa in white whiskers as the plantation owner who must sacrifice his goody-goody daughter (Darla) in order to forestall the mortgage. Then a compromise is reached: Alfalfa

Darla Hood dressed in crinolines for her part as the goody-goody heroine in "Captain Spanky's Show Boat" heads for an M-G-M sound stage and shooting for the next scene.

will race his horse Grey Beauty against Spanky's nag Black Satan for the mortgage. The race is simulated by some clever stage devices (perhaps a bit *too* clever for a bunch of kids to have engineered). The whole show is a far cry from the clumsy inventiveness of "Uncle Tom's Uncle" or its remake, "Spanky."

The play is preceded by "Darla and her Dancin' Buddies" in an old-fashioned song and soft-shoe number, and followed by Alfalfa's strained rendition of Irish tenor John McCormack's "I Hear You Calling Me," ending on a grotesque close-up of the freckle-faced singer. The humor inherent in Alfalfa's sour renditions of old songs diminishes with each successive film.

The kiddie audience in this short reacts loudly to the entire production, but it's unlikely that a similar movie audience could muster the same enthusiasm for "Captain Spanky's Show Boat." . . . Singularly dull.

185 · DAD FOR A DAY

One Reel · Produced by Jack Chertok for M-G-M · Directed by Edward Cahn · Photographed by Jackson Rose · Edited by Roy Brickner · Screenplay by Hal Law and Robert A. McGowan · Released on October 21, 1939, by M-G-M · Our Gang: Mickey Gubitosi, George "Spanky" McFarland, Carl "Alfalfa" Switzer, Billie "Buckwheat" Thomas, Darwood "Waldo" Kaye, and Tommy McFarland · Title role, Bill Henry, Louis Jean Heydt; Mickey's mother, Mary Baker, Peggy Shannon; Gas station patron, Tom Herbert; Receptionist, Mary Treen; Mr. Kincaid, father of triplets, Milton Parsons; Father who presents award, Arthur Q. Bryan; Extra at the hospital, Walter Sande

M-G-M publicity tells us that Clark Gable is Buckwheat's favorite. Believe it or don't!

In planning their Father and Sons Day Picnic, the gang has forgotten that Mickey has no father; he feels left out of this all-important event. The gang prevails on friendly Mr. Henry, who runs the gas station next to Mickey's mother's coffee shop, to be "dad for a day." The picnic is a huge success, Mickey and Mr. Henry have a great time, and when day is done Mr. Henry works up the nerve to ask Mickey's mom to marry him—which he's wanted to do for three years.

"Dad for a Day" comes closer to being "heartwarming" than many other M-G-M endeavors but falls short of the mark because of Mickey Gubitosi. When the gang announces the Father-Son picnic, Mickey immediately starts blubbering, and therein lies an essential difference between the M-G-M and Hal Roach philosophies. The Roach films weren't afraid of sentiment, but they had kids who could make an audience *care* about them and their plight. When for special reasons Farina or Jackie Cooper would cry, we would be moved; but the Roach staff held such scenes in reserve, and the last things these kids indulged in was self-pity. Mickey Gubitosi, on the other hand, manages to be insipid whether he's crying or even smiling!

Louis Jean Heydt does a fine job as bashful Mr. Henry, and Peggy Shannon is pretty and appealing in her few scenes as Mickey's mother. The scripting is skillful, telescoping the story line into a smooth-flowing, unhurried narrative, with some nice touches (like Mr. Henry's fondness for coffee, particularly "Mrs. Baker's") giving the film a polish too often missing from these ten-minute reels. But a great deal of *Our Gang*'s success has to do with *charm,* and that's the missing ingredient from this short's main character.

Interestingly, Robert Blake (Mickey Gubitosi) says today that his own children are more impressed with his *Our Gang* films than with anything else he's done . . . but reports that he makes them watch the series in another room where he won't be bothered. Who could blame him?

186 · TIME OUT FOR LESSONS

One Reel · Produced by Jack Chertok for M-G-M · Directed by Edward Cahn and Bud Murray · Photographed by Robert Planck · Edited by Ralph E. Goldstein · Screenplay by Hal Law and Robert A. McGowan · Released on December 2, 1939, by M-G-M · Our Gang: Carl "Alfalfa" Switzer, George "Spanky" McFarland, Darla Hood, Mickey Gubitosi, Billie "Buckwheat" Thomas, Shirley "Muggsy" Coates, Sidney Kibrick, Darwood "Waldo" Kaye, Jackie Horner, Hugh Chapman, Valerie Lee, Paul Hilton, Harold Switzer, and Tommy McFarland · Alfalfa's father, Si Wills

Alfalfa is about to practice a new football play with the gang when his father asks to speak to him alone about the poor grades on his new report card. Pop explains that he and Mrs. Switzer have been planning to give Alfalfa a college education, but without better grades this won't be possible. Alfalfa thinks that being able to play football will serve him well in college, but his father asks him to envision this situation: he's the gridiron king of Hayle University, but just before the biggest game of the season, his professor announces that he's been ruled ineligible to play because of poor grades. "You've not only failed your friends," the professor intones, "but yourself as well." The make-believe story has a profound effect on Alfalfa, and when the gang arrives to work on their new team play, he explains that he can't join them until he's finished studying. But Alfalfa's pop encourages him to continue with football—just so long as he doesn't neglect his studying in the process. Alfalfa leaves with his pals, proclaiming, "Listen, Gang, from now on we take time out for lessons!"

Here's another of the M-G-M morals series, better suited for showing in the schoolroom of a reformatory than in theaters.

The major question about these lesson-teaching exercises is Where did the idea originate? Did scripters Hal Law and Robert A. McGowan simply fall into such a pattern by themselves, or did some studio executive (perhaps Louis B. Mayer himself) dictate the policy? Whatever the case, it's difficult to understand how the studio could have hoped to milk the same idea over and over again with repeated success.

Love-struck Muggsy swoons as Alfalfa glides by, but Darla sees things a little more clearly in this scene from "Time Out for Lessons," originally titled "Learn to Play."

"Time Out for Lessons" even borrows the clichés of feature-length college films, with leading-lady Darla singing at a pregame pep rally and Alfalfa's bookish roommate warning him about taking time to study, etc. It's shallow, false, and unmoving, but worst of all, it's not funny . . . and this was *supposed* to be a comedy series!

187 · ALFALFA'S DOUBLE

One Reel · Produced by Jack Chertok for M-G-M · Directed by Edward Cahn · Photographed by Sidney Wagner · Edited by Albert Akst · Screenplay by Hal Law and Robert A. McGowan · Released on January 20, 1940, by M-G-M · Our Gang: Carl "Alfalfa" Switzer, George "Spanky" McFarland, Darla Hood, Billie "Buckwheat" Thomas, and Mickey Gubitosi · Inebriated railway agent, Hank Mann; Alfalfa's mother, Barbara Bedford; Governess, Anne O'Neal; Willoughby, Milton Parsons

A wealthy young lad who looks just like Alfalfa comes to Greenpoint; when they meet, they decide to switch places. Alfalfa can't wait to lead the life of luxury he envisions Cornelius enjoying, while Corny is eager to rough it up with Our Gang. But Alfalfa discovers that Cornelius's life is conducted on a strict agenda, with naps, dancing lessons, baths, and such; while Cornelius, trying to get the gang to do his yard cleanup for him by treating them to ice cream sodas, forgets that as Alfalfa (and wearing his clothes) he has no money in his pockets any more.

Each boy returns to his former identity, a little more content than when he started on this adventure.

"Alfalfa's Double" is a smoothly executed, passably entertaining version of *The Prince and the Pauper,* but as with so many promising ideas from this period, one can't help but wonder what Hal Roach's staff of gagmen would have done with it. As always, the purpose here seems to lean more toward teaching a lesson (the grass is always greener) than creating a truly funny *Our Gang* comedy.

While the double-exposure work is excellent, both in

Trick still for "Alfalfa's Double."

daylight and interior settings (the only fault: Alfalfa and Cornelius are *always* standing four feet apart), Carl Switzer is not able to carry off the dual role as well as one might like. His Cornelius is too adaptable and down to earth to make the two characterizations seem like totally different people. In other words, Alfalfa has a hard time playing the part of Waldo. "Our resemblance is rather striking," Cornelius says upon first meeting Alfalfa. "Yeah, and we look alike, too," replies his new friend.

Even a scene rife with comic possibilities, where Alfalfa tries his best to get through Corny's dance lesson, isn't that funny.

In fact, "Alfalfa's Double" has everything going for it—a good story, quality production values—except humor.

188 · BUBBLING TROUBLES

One Reel · Produced by Jack Chertok and Richard Goldstone for M-G-M · Directed by Edward Cahn · Photographed by Clyde DeVinna · Edited by Ralph E. Goldstein · Screenplay by Hal Law and Robert A. McGowan · Released on May 25, 1940, by M-G-M · Our Gang: Carl "Alfalfa" Switzer, Darla Hood, Mickey Gubitosi, George "Spanky" McFarland, Billie "Buckwheat" Thomas, and Tommy "Butch" Bond · Alfalfa's mother, Barbara Bedford; Alfalfa's father, William Newell; Butch's father, Hank Mann; Explosives worker, Harry Strang

It's spring, and Darla's two romantic swains, Alfalfa and Butch, once again try and outdo each other for her favor. His appetite gone, Alfalfa can't think of anything but Darla. Mom serves alphabet soup, but Alf can only spell out D-a-r-l-a with his spoon. Misunderstanding the ailment, Alfalfa's dad prepares a stomach remedy, called "Settles-itt Powders." Later, in Butch's garage-laboratory, everyone is impressed when Butch is seemingly able to manufacture dynamite. Recognizing the preparation as mere "Settles-itt Powders," Alfalfa defies Butch to let him drink this explosive concoction. When he gulps it down, Alfalfa's stomach suddenly swells to freakish proportions; the powders hadn't been mixed properly. His frantic pals bind pillows to Alfalfa's feet and gingerly walk him to a secluded spot where he'll be safe till they can secure aid. Sure enough, as they leave, there's a real dynamite explosion nearby, and the dejected troupe heads for Alfalfa's home to break the news

that he won't be home for dinner. Alfalfa, meanwhile, scared by the explosion, has trotted home where Dad fixes him up again, this time with a dose of bicarb. When the gang discovers Alf is okay, Darla rushes to embrace him, but Alfalfa trips and falls on his distended stomach, and like a sputtering balloon, his gusty deflation is so powerful that it rips out the entire front wall of his home!

Borrowing some from *Sneak Easily*, Gus Meins's Thelma Todd comedy for Hal Roach, "Bubbling Troubles" (previewed as "In Love Again") is very good at comedy externals, from the exploding jackknife car gag to the elaborate windstorm house demolition at the finish—which incidentally doesn't appear to be a glass shot. And some of Clyde DeVinna's trick photography (showing first Darla and then interloper Butch in Alfalfa's soup) is amusing too. But the gang's lifeless performances take the edge off this comedy potential. There's no characterization at the base of this comedy.

Eureka!

Hank Mann goes for a ride in this explosive scene from "Bubbling Troubles."

189 · THE BIG PREMIERE

One Reel · Produced by Jack Chertok and Richard Goldstone for M-G-M · Directed by Edward Cahn · Photographed by Paul Vogel · Edited by Adrienne Fazan · Screenplay by Hal Law and Robert A. McGowan · Released on March 9, 1940, by M-G-M · Our Gang: George "Spanky" McFarland, Carl "Alfalfa" Switzer, Darla Hood, Billie "Buckwheat" Thomas, Mickey Gubitosi, Darwood "Waldo" Kaye, Shirley "Muggsy" Coates, Harold Switzer, Clyde Wilson, and Larry Harris · Officer, Eddie Gribbon; Doorman, John Dilson; Imra Acacia, Ethelreda Leopold

After being chased away from a big Hollywood premiere, the gang decides to stage one of its own at the clubhouse, complete with spotlights, crowds, and a radio announcer (Spanky) to introduce the stars. There's only one mishap, when Buckwheat gets stuck in a box of cement as he tries to leave his footprints. Inside, the gang unveils *The Mysteeryus Mistry,* as filmed by Waldo with his home-movie camera. The kids provide their own dialogue in person, standing next to the screen. Unfortunately, the picture comes to a sudden halt just as Alfalfa's song begins; it seems that Waldo ran out of film. So Alfalfa continues his song "live" for the large kiddie audience, getting through the ballad even when he swallows an egg and emits a live baby chick from his mouth!

"The Big Premiere" is a noble attempt to revive the kind of slapstick and sight-gag comedy that put *Our Gang* on the map. The results are pretty good, and if not up to the level of quality one would expect from the Hal Roach team, at least it's a notch above the usual M-G-M product.

The real-life premiere takes place at Los Angeles's Carthay Circle Theater, where a new star, "Imra Acacia," is being feted at the debut of her new movie *Gun Boats.* While a radio announcer babbles all the usual clichés one hears on such occasions, the dainty Miss Acacia places her footprints in cement for posterity. But when the gang breaks through the security barriers to say hello to Waldo across the courtyard, a cop chases after them and slides into the cement, splattering the blond starlet's chic gown with goo.

Such comedy action is sparse at the gang's own premiere, with director Edward Cahn trying to get as much mileage as possible out of Buckwheat's predicament being stuck teetering in a vat of cement, and leaning to and fro while his feet remain anchored.

190 · ALL ABOUT HASH

One Reel · Produced by Jack Chertok and Richard Goldstone for M-G-M · Directed by Edward Cahn · Photographed by Clyde DeVinna · Edited by Adrienne Fazan · Screenplay by Hal Law and Robert A. McGowan · Released on March 30, 1940, by M-G-M · Our Gang: Mickey Gubitosi, George "Spanky" McFarland, Carl "Alfalfa" Switzer, Darla Hood, Billie "Buckwheat" Thomas, Janet Burston, and Tommy McFarland · Mickey's father, Louis Jean Heydt; Mickey's mother, Peggy Shannon; Alfalfa's father, William Newell; Alfalfa's mother, Barbara Bedford; Radio announcer, Ferris Taylor

Mickey is upset, and he tells the gang his problem. Every Sunday night his family has roast beef for dinner, and every Monday night his mother makes hash from the leftovers. His father hates hash, and so the dinner hour becomes the stage for a bitter argument that leaves Mickey crying. The gang decides to teach Mickey's parents a lesson by using their problem as the subject for a skit to be performed on a radio amateur hour. Naturally, the parents are listening to the broadcast, and when they hear their own situation dramatized, they realize how wrong they've been and make up for good.

Despite its typical M-G-M message formula, "All About Hash" wouldn't be so intolerable if not for one ingredient: the work of Mickey Gubitosi.

From his entrance in the first scene, in which he whines, "I got a sort of a headache—down here" (pointing to his heart), to the scene in which his face is superimposed over a radio speaker as he blubbers about how much he loves his parents when they don't fight, one is hard pressed to feel any sympathy for such a loud and obnoxious child. There is a limit for cloying sentimentality. This is it.

There is one scene that's particularly bad in which Mickey goes to wash up for dinner and, emerging from the bathroom with a broad grin on his face, hears the argument erupting inside. He stops dead in his tracks, and his unconvincing smile puckers into an equally unconvincing mask of tears. There's nothing real or heart-tugging about such a contrived performance.

There are other things to pick on in this film (including a nauseating wind-up-doll rendition of "Tippi Tippi Tin" at the amateur contest by highly unpromising little Janet Burston), but there's just no sense in wasting additional time and space on this short here. Enough time was wasted in filming it.

191 · THE NEW PUPIL

One Reel · Produced by Jack Chertok and Richard Goldstone for M-G-M · Directed by Edward Cahn · Photographed by Paul Vogel · Edited by Ralph E. Goldstein · Screenplay by Hal Law and Robert A. McGowan · Released on April 27, 1940, by M-G-M · Our Gang: George "Spanky" McFarland, Carl "Alfalfa" Switzer, Darla Hood, Juanita "Sally" Quigley, Mickey Gubitosi, Billie "Buckwheat" Thomas, Billy "Froggy" Laughlin, Darwood "Waldo" Kaye, and Patsy Currier · Sally's mother, May McAvoy; Schoolteacher, Anne O'Neal

A pretty new pupil named Sally makes Spanky and Alfalfa ignore their lunch date with Darla and fawn over her instead. But Sally considers them pests and leaves them flat, going to sit with Darla and making friends with her by explaining that she doesn't like boys. The two girls then plot to teach fickle Spanky and Alfalfa a lesson. Turning on her flirtatious charm, Sally invites both boys to her house later that day and, when they arrive, persuades them to don women's clothes and play tea party with her. Just then, the whole gang appears from behind a garden hedge to laugh at the two would-be suitors, whose embarrassment is painful. The next day they beg Darla's forgiveness and rejoin her for lunch. "Beauty is only skin deep," Alfalfa concludes, "but old friends are thicker than water."

Not only is "The New Pupil" embarrassing for Spanky and Alfalfa, but it's also pretty difficult for an audience to stomach. Female masquerades are usually pretty grim in themselves, but what's worse is making fools of kids one used to identify with and admire.

When the teacher introduces Sally, Alfalfa, sighing, says, "Gosh, ain't she purty?" Mickey, sitting behind him, shrugs, uninterested—the most intelligent thing he's ever done. Sally is one of those unbearable Miss Perfection types that no one wants to know in real life, played by Juanita Quigley in one of two *Our Gang* appearances. (A former child star at Universal, she later became a Roman Catholic nun but, with papal dispensation, renounced her vows after thirteen years and married a man who had studied for the priesthood; as of this writing both are teaching at Villanova University.)

At the foundation of this short's failure is the same lack of understanding that spoiled many an M-G-M *Our Gang* short. When Darla sees her boyfriends lunching with Sally, the camera pulls in as her lips begin to tremble and she breaks down crying! Melodrama was not the idea of this series, but the M-G-M directors and writers seemed to recognize only the broadest forms of emotion, from forced laughter to crocodile tears.

"The New Pupil" . . . It's not that funny.

192 · GOIN' FISHIN'

One Reel · Produced by Jack Chertok and Richard Goldstone for M-G-M· · Directed by Edward Cahn · Photographed by Jackson Rose · Edited by Adrienne Fazan · Screenplay by Hal Law and Robert A. McGowan · Released on October 26, 1940, by M-G-M · Our Gang: Carl "Alfalfa" Switzer, George "Spanky" McFarland, Billie "Buckwheat" Thomas, and Mickey Gubitosi · Bus conductor, Paul Hurst; Police officer, Robert Emmett Homans; Woman on bus, Anne O'Neal; Man on bus, Arthur Hoyt

The gang camps out on a city sidewalk overnight in order to catch the earliest morning bus for a fishing trip to the East River. The bus arrives before dawn, and the kids, encumbered by fishing equipment, climb to the upper deck while Mickey hunts for the fares to pay an impatient conductor. When he cannot find the money, the conductor orders the kids off the bus, but as they climb down again, Mickey discovers the money in his shoe. After this lengthy delay, the gang finds that they're on the wrong bus; this one is going to the *West* River. The conductor, and a cop, try to persuade the kids that the fishing is just as good in the West River, and they finally prevail. Ready to pull out at last, they drive only a few feet when a sudden stop sends Spanky's pack over the side of the bus, and the implements inside cause a flat tire when the bus runs over it. This means *another* delay, and by the time the bus is ready to leave, with a pack of angry riders, the

Anglers doing a little angling over the cost of transportation in "Goin' Fishin'." *Top to bottom,* they are Mickey, Leonard, Buckwheat, Spanky, Paul Hurst, and Alfalfa.

sun has come up and the kids decide that it's too late to go fishing. As they get off the bus, it speeds away in a blur, rid of the gang for good.

"Goin' Fishin' " is a very entertaining set-piece, one of the best M-G-M shorts in the series. Although it is a study in frustration, the situations are never stretched beyond the point of credibility. The kids mean no harm, and their bungling is entirely believable; so is the mounting frustration of conductor Paul Hurst, wearing his customary scowling slow-burn throughout. Incidentally, this character actor receives special billing for this film.

Viewed today, the short has the added nostalgia of seeing double-decker buses, and illustrating both their joys and handicaps. The kids want to sit on top to enjoy the view, but getting there with a load of equipment is decidedly *not* half the fun.

"Goin' Fishin' " has the virtue of simplicity, and very simply speaking, it is a lot of fun to watch.

193 · GOOD BAD BOYS

One Reel · Produced by Jack Chertok and Richard Goldstone for M-G-M · Directed by Edward Cahn · Photographed by Jackson Rose · Edited by Leon Bourgeau · Screenplay by Hal Law and Robert A. McGowan · Released on September 7, 1940, by M-G-M · Our Gang: George "Spanky" McFarland, Carl "Alfalfa" Switzer, Billie "Buckwheat" Thomas, Freddie "Slicker" Walburn, and Mickey Gubitosi · Store proprietor, Mr. Stephens, Byron Foulger; Burglar, Al Hill; Judge Kincaid, George Lessey; Court official, Joe Young; Judge's aid, Hugh Beaumont; Alfalfa's father, William Newell; Alfalfa's mother, Barbara Bedford; Officer, Emmett Vogan; Freddie's mother, Margaret Bert; Mrs. Wilson, Leila McIntyre; Banker, Harry Strang

Alfalfa and Slicker with Byron Foulger in a scene from "Good Bad Boys."

Alfalfa has been unfairly blamed, and punished, for stealing, so in revenge he announces that he's going to become a real crook; the rest of the gang is with him, except for Spanky, who decides to teach his pals a lesson. Mrs. Wilson has just offered him 25¢ to haul away some junk, so he leads the gang to think that they're burglarizing her house. The would-be criminals are scared to death as they flee back to the clubhouse with the loot. Meanwhile, local cops are chasing a real robber who has sought refuge near the clubhouse barn. When the police approach and start shooting, Alfalfa and his pals walk out of the barn with their hands up, confessing their crime. Next day in juvenile court they are about to be arraigned when Spanky arrives with Mrs. Wilson to explain the whole situation. The judge admonishes Alfalfa's father for wrongly punishing the boy without giving him a chance to explain, and dismisses the gang when he sees how truly remorseful they are. They all buy ice cream cones with the 25¢ Mrs. Wilson gave them, and when Alfalfa says it tastes good, Spanky replies earnestly, "*Anything* tastes good if you *earn* it."

"Good Bad Boys" is another of those Sunday-school-lecture films with no redeeming value other than the lesson it supposedly teaches. The premise and execution of the story are obvious and heavy handed, and like most of these moralizing shorts, it is totally without humor.

The one amusing aspect of "Good Bad Boys" is that watching Al Hill as the small-time crook brings to mind his similar role (and identical "costume") in W. C. Fields's classic *The Bank Dick* made that same year. Now *that* was funny.

194 · WALDO'S LAST STAND

One Reel · Produced by Jack Chertok and Richard Goldstone for M-G-M · Directed by Edward Cahn and Steven Granger · Photographed by Jackson Rose · Edited by Albert Akst · Screenplay by Hal Law and Robert A. McGowan · Released on October 5, 1940, by M-G-M · Our Gang: Darwood "Waldo" Kaye, George "Spanky" McFarland, Billy "Froggy" Laughlin, Carl "Alfalfa" Switzer, Billie "Buckwheat" Thomas, Darla Hood, Mickey Gubitosi, Janet Burston, Clyde Wilson, Patsy Anne Thompson, Bobby Sommers, Patsy Irish, Lavonne Battle, Betty Jean Striegler, Jackie Krenk, Helen Guthrie, Shirley Jean Doble, Patricia Wheeler, and Donna Jean Edmonsond

Waldo has no customers at his lemonade stand, so Spanky suggests that they stage a floor show to attract people. The barn is refurbished as a daytime nightclub, with Darla leading a chorus line in the opening number, the Singing Waiters performing barbershop nonharmony, and a miniature Floradora Sextette Finale. The club's one and only customer, however, refuses to buy lemonade throughout the show, despite Spanky's constant badgering and such subtle inducements as salted crackers and a floor heater turned on beneath the unsuspecting victim. Finally the lone patron stalks out without having purchased a single thing. Then it occurs to the gang why they couldn't attract any other customers: every kid in the neighborhood was working in the show!

A real clinker, the film's one joke is intended to be newcomer Froggy's lack of interest in Waldo's lemonade. Silent and deadpan throughout the short, Froggy shrugs refusals at each gracious offer until at last he speaks for the first time with his surprise Popeye-the-Sailor trick voice, telling everyone, "I don't have no money, and besides, it's too hot in here."

When an M-G-M series entry reworks an idea used before by Hal Roach, it becomes especially clear how much better the Roach comedies were. This same situation was the basis of "The Lucky Corner," which is infinitely superior to "Waldo's Last Stand."

The main difference, besides the contrived acting of the gang regulars, is the introduction of elaborately costumed, singing-dancing, cutesy kiddies from Professional

Buckwheat, Waldo, Spanky, Leonard, and Mickey discussing a sales strategem in "Waldo's Last Stand."

Children's School during the floor show. These well-scrubbed youngsters, eyes and teeth aglow, would be enough to torpedo any film's success. Add to this the first-grade-level acting approach of the gang, and you have all the ingredients for a loser. When pondering Waldo's sales shortage, Spanky suddenly bursts forth with the idea, "What that lemonade needs is a floor show," and Mickey unspontaneously (and unconvincingly) replies, "That's a swell idea!"

195 · KIDDIE CURE

One Reel · Produced by Jack Chertok and Richard Goldstone for M-G-M · Directed by Edward Cahn · Photographed by Jackson Rose · Edited by Leon Bourgeau · Screenplay by Hal Law and Robert A. McGowan · Released on November 23, 1940, by M-G-M · Our Gang: George "Spanky" McFarland, Carl "Alfalfa" Switzer, Darla Hood, Billie "Buckwheat" Thomas, Mickey Gubitosi, Billy "Froggy" Laughlin, Rollie "Tisket" Jones, and Bobby "Tasket" Jones · Mr. Bill Morton, Thurston Hall; Mrs. Julia Morton, Josephine Whittell; Evans the butler, Gerald Oliver Smith; Dr. Malcolm Scott, Edwin Stanley; Parts cut from the final release print: Ballplayers with Morton's Mugs, Hugh Chapman, Freddie Chapman

While playing sandlot baseball, one *Our Gang* slugger cracks an errant drive through a window in the house adjacent to their field. The homeowner, Mr. Morton, is a blustery hypochondriac, whose doctor has just advised his wife that what he needs to do is adopt some kids. Having overheard this disastrous notion, Mr. Morton concocts a plan to frighten off the gang when they come by to claim their ball. Pretending to be crazy, he tosses things around and overturns his own furniture, hoping to dissuade his wife when she returns by blaming the wreckage on the miscreant kids. The scheme backfires, though, when in the ensuing wild chases and bedlam throughout the large house, Alfalfa's little brothers eat some of Morton's "strongest" pills. Not realizing they're only candy, Morton is understandably distraught and phones his doctor with the emergency; the doctor arrives in time to assure the flustered patient that the pills are harmless, simply make-believe pills prescribed for a make-believe ill-

ness. Thinking about it for a moment, the suddenly cured hypochondriac ▓▓▓▓▓ that he feels fine and that all the shenaniga▓▓▓▓▓▓▓ have done him some good.

One of ▓▓▓▓▓▓▓ worth seeing more than once, "Kiddie ▓▓▓▓▓ m bright scripting, fine production, ▓▓▓▓▓▓ performance from character actor Thu▓▓▓▓▓ ankerous Mr. Morton.

It also ▓▓▓▓▓▓ ast *Our Gang* appearance. At thirteen h▓▓▓▓▓▓ oldest "kid" in the gang, but one wond▓▓▓▓▓ only reason he left the series. According▓▓▓▓▓ worked with Alfalfa, once *Our Gang* moved over to Metro, the precocious youngster started exhibiting temperament and caused trouble on the set from time to time. Robert Blake recalls Alfalfa staging some formidable pranks on the M-G-M lot. Whatever the case, Carl Switzer's life and career were plagued by problems and frustration after he left the series. To the time of his death, *Our Gang* remained his major achievement.

196 · FIGHTIN' FOOLS

One Reel · Produced by M-G-M · Directed by Edward Cahn · Photographed by Clyde DeVinna · Screenplay by Hal Law and Robert A. McGowan · Released on January 25, 1941, by M-G-M · Our Gang: George "Spanky" McFarland, Billy "Froggy" Laughlin, Billie "Buckwheat" Thomas, Mickey Gubitosi, Billy Ray "Boxcar" Smith, Freddie "Slicker" Walburn, and Joe "Tubby" Strauch, Jr.

Slicker and his bunch are always playing dirty tricks on the gang, but tying the gang's clothes in knots while they're swimming is one indignity too many. Spanky declares war and challenges Slicker's bunch to a battle, fought mainly with flying tomatoes, Limburger cheese, and watermelons. Some of Spanky's soldiers are ready to quit after being plastered in the face, but he rallies their support for a final aerial barrage attack which forces Slicker and his cronies to surrender. As punishment, they are forced to painfully unknot the gang's clothes, while Froggy warns, "Never do unto others what we'll make you undo!"

"Fightin' Fools" is a promising but ultimately pedestrian outing for the gang. The idea of a kiddie war is sound, but after one tomato is thrown, the well of gag ideas seems to evaporate, and with it the film. The problem with "Fightin' Fools" is the same one shared by so many other M-G-M shorts in this series: it isn't funny.

The film's one major attempt at humor falls flat not because of a poor idea but because of poor execution. During the opening sequence at the swimming hole, Tubby is reluctant to dive in. Taunted by the gang, he finally relents and makes the jump, his tremendous bulk splashing all the water out of the pond and leaving the gang high and dry! Unfortunately, this clever-sounding gag is accomplished with an optical effect showing a cascade of water in front of the camera, which in no way convinces the viewer that this jet stream has actually come from the pond. Director Edward Cahn just didn't realize that a gag isn't funny unless it seems *real*. He would have done well to screen some earlier Hal Roach comedies for examples.

Incidentally, the boy playing Tubby, Joe Strauch, Jr., had been Spanky's stand-in at the Hal Roach studio. At the time of this short he was appearing in Gene Autry's Westerns as Tadpole, a miniature replica of Gene's sidekick Frog Millhouse (Smiley Burnette).

197 · BABY BLUES

One Reel · Produced by M-G-M · Directed by Edward Cahn · Photographed by Jackson Rose · Edited by Leon Bourgeau · Screenplay by Hal Law and Robert A. McGowan · Released on February 15, 1941, by M-G-M · Our Gang: Mickey Gubitosi, George "Spanky" McFarland, Billy "Froggy" Laughlin, Billie "Buckwheat" Thomas, Janet Burston, Betty Scott, Freddie "Bully" Chapman, Billy Ray Smith, and Edward Soo Hoo · Zoo attendant, Hank Mann; Receptionist, Margaret Bert; Mickey's father, William Edmunds; Lee Wong's father, Eddie Lee; Lee Wong's mother, Jennie Lee

Scene from "Baby Blues." The still caption indicates that the film's working title had been "Too Many Sisters."

The Gubitosi household is in disorder, with Mama expecting a new baby. Mickey and his two sisters fight over their improvised breakfast (strawberry shortcake) while Papa tries to quiet them down. Mickey goes into the living room to read for a while and comes upon a statistic that every fourth child born is Chinese. Mickey fears that his new brother will be an Oriental, and he runs to tell the gang this terrible news, but Spanky explains that there's nothing wrong with the Chinese. To prove his point, he takes Mickey and the gang to meet his friend Lee Wong, whose mother invites them for lunch and whose behavior proves beyond a doubt that there's no real difference between people, as long as they're regular fellas. Then Mickey goes home and gets the worst news of all: "The doctor brought twins, and they're all girls!"

As a morality play, "Baby Blues" has a few good notions but strangles them with half-baked ideas of brotherhood and overwrought performances by the gang. From the opening scene in which we hear Mickey intoning the words, "HEEYYY, WHAT KIND OF BREAKFAST IS THIS?" there is a certain amount of apathy for the problems of this whiny, loudmouthed boy. "GOLLY," he exclaims after reading the Chinese statistic, ''I GOTTA TELL THE GANG ABOUT THIS!''

After unsuccessfully trying to head off the doctor before he goes to Mickey's home, then attempting to locate the stork making the delivery, Spanky announces the idea of taking Mickey to meet Lee Wong, a ''swell guy'' whose father presses Spanky's father's shirts. Lee is being taunted by some pretty unconvincing street kids who ask, ''Where's your pigtails?'' They try to pick a fight, but the gang chases them off. Lee and his parents bridge the gap between Old World manners and a New World life-style. The kids are worried that Mrs. Wong may serve birds' nests or rats' tails for lunch, but instead she prepares a luscious order of ham and eggs. Mickey and the gang leave the Wong household with renewed respect for their Chinese friend.

198 · YE OLDE MINSTRELS

One Reel · Produced by M-G-M · Directed by Edward Cahn and Bud Murray · Photographed by Jackson Rose · Edited by Albert Akst · Story by Sam Baerwitz · Released on March 18, 1941, by M-G-M · Our Gang: George "Spanky" McFarland, Darla Hood, Billie "Buckwheat" Thomas, Mickey Gubitosi, Billy "Froggy" Laughlin, Joline Karol, Jackie Salling, David Polonsky, Valerie Lee, Marlene Mains, and Bobby Browning · Minstrel Maestro Walter Wills, Himself

The gang wants to raise money to help the Red Cross, but Spanky is reluctant to stage another show since their last effort, to promote Waldo's lemonade, was a flop. Then Froggy suggests that they enlist the aid of his uncle to put on a minstrel show. They do, and the resulting benefit program is a great success.

''Ye Olde Minstrels'' is a virtually plotless short, in essence a ten-minute musical revue. That the show is somewhat depersonalized and beyond the scope of a small group of youngsters to have staged—even with the help of an old codger like Froggy's uncle—is not supposed to concern us. Nor is the question of why an adult audience would sit through a thing like this when they could go to a movie theater and see an M-G-M feature.

The ensemble opens with ''Carry Me Back to Old Virginny,'' cutting in close-ups of Spanky, Darla, and Buckwheat singing to remind us that they're still there. Then the group does a tambourine specialty, and a gimmicky number tap dancing in place while seated, as precision-timed spotlights create geometric patterns within the pyramid-shaped bleacher holding the thirty-five participants.

Froggy is then featured on ''When De Profundis Sang Low C,'' in an endurance test of our ability to withstand this grating voice. After Spanky announces that the show has netted $208.40 for the Red Cross, he introduces Froggy's uncle, Walter Wills, in a salute to the famous minstrel man George Primrose. In closing, the group sings ''Auld Lang Syne,'' as the enthusiastic theater audience joins in.

This is a curious short, even for the M-G-M minimusical formula, since the gang figures almost incidentally in the actual performance. One close-up each is about all we get of Darla and Buckwheat, while the only solo spot of the show is given to Froggy, of all people. Mickey and Froggy do some unfunny patter jokes with interlocutor Spanky, while the finale goes to ''uncle'' Walter Wills, in a dull rendition of ''Lazy Moon.''

If the show had been done on a smaller scale, it might have afforded more opportunity to the supposed stars of the film. After all, it is supposed to be an *Our Gang* comedy.

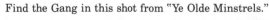

Find the Gang in this shot from "Ye Olde Minstrels."

199 · COME BACK, MISS PIPPS

One Reel · Produced by M-G-M · Directed by Edward Cahn · Photographed by Clyde DeVinna · Edited by Leon Bourgeau · Screenplay by Hal Law and Robert A. McGowan · Released on October 25, 1941, by M-G-M · Our Gang: Darla Hood, George "Spanky" McFarland, Billy "Froggy" Laughlin, Mickey Gubitosi, Billie "Buckwheat" Thomas, Leon Tyler, Teresa Mae Glass, and Tommy McFarland · Alonzo K. Pratt, school board chairman, Clarence Wilson; Miss Pipps, teacher, Sara Haden; Mr. Swenson, caretaker, Christian Rub; Froggy's father, Billy Bletcher; Attorney Arthur Prince, Byron Foulger; Angry parent, Barbara Bedford

To dramatize their feelings for the unjustly ousted Miss Pipps, the Gang offers a playlet depicting the school board chairman as the Simon Legree they know him to be . . . 1 × 1 = 2?

Hatchet-faced school board chairman Mr. Pratt fires devoted schoolteacher Miss Pipps when he discovers her celebrating Mickey's birthday on school time—even though the class had finished its work ahead of schedule. In protest, the gang stages a play for the parents of the town, and members of the school board, portraying Mr. Pratt as Simon Legree and revealing the truth about their board chairman. As a result, Pratt is demoted to school gardener, while *former* gardener Mr. Swenson is promoted to the top position. And just to show that the reinstated Miss Pipps and her class realize that everyone is human, a birthday party is thrown for Mr. Pratt himself.

"Come Back, Miss Pipps" is one of the more effective mini-melodramas of the M-G-M period, largely because of perfect casting in the adult roles . . . or perhaps we should say typecasting, for that's really what it is.

Sara Haden, the wise and serene aunt from M-G-M's *Andy Hardy* series, has the role of Miss Pipps, the wise and serene schoolteacher who really cares about her children. Christian Rub, the archetypal kindly-old-Swede (best remembered as the model and voice for Geppetto in Disney's *Pinocchio*) is ideal in the role of school gardener Swenson, who conspires with the kids to get even with Mr. Pratt. And Pratt himself is played by none other than Clarence Wilson, well remembered for earlier *Our Gang* villainy in "Little Sinner" and "Shrimps for a Day," and mean as ever in this welcome reappearance.

Somebody once observed that in many cases, "trite is right," and that phrase certainly suits "Come Back, Miss Pipps," which works within its modest boundaries because of casting that in another situation might be considered hackneyed. The need to imbue this *Our Gang* outing with larger-than-life characters, rather than performances with insightful nuances, makes this formula a success.

200 · 1-2-3 GO!

One Reel · Produced by M-G-M · Directed by Edward Cahn · Photographed by Jackson Rose · Edited by Leon Bourgeau · Screenplay by Hal Law and Robert A. McGowan · Released on April 26, 1941, by M-G-M · Our Gang: George "Spanky" McFarland, Billy "Froggy" Laughlin, Mickey Gubitosi, Billie "Buckwheat" Thomas, and Freddie Walburn · Mayor of Greenpoint, John Dilson; Man at accident scene, Joe Young; Cab driver, William Tannen; Pair of pedestrians, Anne O'Neal, Arthur Hoyt; Nurses, May McAvoy, Barbara Bedford, Margaret Bert

During a baseball game, Mickey runs out into the street to catch a fly ball and is struck by a car. When the gang goes to visit him in the hospital, they realize how many kids are injured by automobiles, and decide to do something about it by starting the 1-2-3-Go Safety Society. The club encourages children, and adults as well, to take extra precautions before crossing the street. The idea catches on like wildfire, and is endorsed by the Board of Education, the police commissioner, and the mayor, who presents the gang with a special citation at a radio broadcast.

This short completely abandons entertainment in order to preach a cause. Admittedly, this is a worthy cause, but before M-G-M took over, the *Our Gang* comedies never could have been mistaken for educational films.

All the stops are pulled out. When Mickey lies in the street after being hit, he looks up toward Spanky and says weakly, "I . . . caught . . . it, fellas," the kind of dialogue one would expect in the death scene from a bad B movie. Later, in pitching the idea of the Safety Club, Spanky's speeches become incredibly pedantic. He explains to the other kids that the hospital ward is filled with youngsters who have been injured "because they, too, were careless." This sounds like a political speech, not the words of an *Our Gang* kid.

Endorsements by the police, the mayor, and the Board of Education are appropriate in the context of this public-service tract. But a few years earlier the gang's only connection with the mayor would have been a baseball inadvertently thrown through his window.

Suddenly aware that there has been no humor in the short, however, the creators of "1-2-3 Go!" decide to close with a gag. Froggy is asked to speak to the supposed national radio audience, but his voice only causes the microphone wires to explode, until he adopts a falsetto to make his little speech.

Simply hilarious.

Buckwheat, Froggy, Spanky, and Mickey (Robert Blake)

Darla Hood, in her last *Our Gang* appearance, with Froggy Laughlin, both toeing their marks (note the chalk on the floor) for a scene in "Wedding Worries."

the spanking-finale geared more for adults in the audience than for kids . . . just like the whole series at this point.

One final note: "Wedding Worries" was Darla Hood's last *Our Gang* short.

201 · ROBO[T]

One Reel · Produced by M-G-M · Directed by Edward C[ahn ·] Bourgeau · Screenplay by Hal Law and Robert A. McGov[an ·] George "Spanky" McFarland, Billy "Froggy" Laughlin, [Darla] Hood, Freddie "Slicker" Walburn, and Billy Ray "Bo[xcar] father, Billy Bletcher; Froggy's mother, Julia, Margaret

After seeing a department store demonstration of Volto, "the almost-human robot," the gang decides to build a mechanical man who will do all their chores. Slicker tells them they will need some "invisible rays," which quite naturally he will sell them. While the kids go to fetch the cash, Slicker fits Boxcar into the robot suit the gang has built. When they return and feed their robot some of the special "rays," he starts to move and obediently follows Froggy's wish that he mow the lawn. On a signal from Slicker the "robot" goes berserk, however, running at triple speed and mowing down everything in sight, including the flowers and plants on Froggy's lawn. Just then, Froggy's mom and dad come home; when Froggy explains the whole story, his dad pulls off the robot's head and exposes Boxcar underneath. Dad then orders him and Slicker to return the money and join the gang in cleaning up the yard.

The basic idea of "Robot Wrecks" isn't bad, and the kiddie fantasy of building your own robot has great possibilities. All of this potential goes down the drain, however, thanks to overwrought performances, a poor script, and direction to match.

Although Slicker has portrayed adversaries in previous shorts, the gang swallows his offer to sell the invisible rays wholeheartedly, repeatedly exclaiming lines like, "It was swell of Slicker to sell us his rays!" Too bad there wasn't anyone around to offer them the Brooklyn Bridge.

All of this is topped by a general phoniness in the way the short was filmed. The gang's obviously dubbed voices

[FACES] OLD AND NEW

[Directed by Edwar]d Cahn · Photographed by Jackson Rose · Edited by Leon [· Produced by M-]G-M · Our Gang: George "Spanky" McFarland, Mickey [Gubi]ton, Eddie Ehrhardt, Roger Morris, Sheila Brown, Billy [Fro]d, Patricia Wheeler, Donna Jean Edmonsond, and Lavonne

OUR GANG in ROBOT WRECKS

Directed by EDWARD CAHN

but featuring unnamed youngsters in examples of dances from various eras. The young boy and girl who do the jitterbug and boogie-woogie are excellent, as are most of the dance ensemble.

But watching talented young dancers is not the purpose of *Our Gang,* or so it seemed before M-G-M went to work on them. "Melodies Old and New" is more pleasant than some minimusicals in this series, but it remains as contrived and superfluous as most of the other entries—with and without music—from this Metro period.

205 · GOING TO PRESS

One reel · Produced by M-G-M · Directed by Edward Cahn · Photographed by Walter Lundin · Edited by Leon Bourgeau · Screenplay by Hal Law and Robert A. McGowan · Released on March 7, 1942, by M-G-M · Our Gang: George "Spanky" McFarland, Billy "Froggy" Laughlin, Mickey Gubitosi, Billie "Buckwheat" Thomas, Billy Ray "Boxcar" Smith, and Freddie Chapman · Frank, Darryl Hickman; Sally, Juanita Quigley

Spanky, Mickey (Robert Blake), Buckwheat, and Froggy.

The gang publishes a crusading neighborhood newspaper called *The Greenpoint Flash,* and in the best journalistic tradition, they vow to track down the mysterious leader of the Gas House Gang, juvenile delinquents running a so-called protection society and harassing the local kids: if you don't *join* up, you get *beat* up. Their efforts are supported by Frank, whose good-guy appearance and manners make him an unlikely suspect; yet he is the nefarious Gas House boss, whom "no human being has ever seen." The gang sets a trap for him by claiming to have damaging evidence in their safe, and leaving the office empty while they go on a fishing trip. The decoy works, Frank tries to loot the safe and is caught quite literally red-handed; the gang makes him sign a confession and prints an extra edition to announce the news, but immediately afterward is forced to close down. The reason: a neighborhood goat has eaten their printer's type.

"Going to Press" is one of the best M-G-M shorts, combining imagination with satire for happy results. The operation of the newspaper harks back to the earliest *Our Gang* pictures, as the kids convert a barn into their idea of what a city room looks like. There is an "intercom," and one kid wears the various hats of Janitor, Copy Boy, and "Noosboy," depending on current demands.

Blended with this is a sharp spoof of racketeer movies, with the kids taking their roles very seriously. When the Gas House boss orders his henchmen to take Froggy for a ride, they do—with Froggy perched in the front-end basket of his bicycle.

Darryl Hickman, a popular and successful child actor of the 1940s, is excellent in his "guest star" role as the mystery hood; it's a pity that this was his only *Our Gang* appearance. In recent years he has worked as a producer, writer, and actor both in television and on the New York theater scene. His younger brother Dwayne Hickman became TV's *Dobie Gillis.*

206 · DON'T LIE

One Reel · Produced by M-G-M · Directed by Edward Cahn · Photographed by Walter Lundin · Edited by Leon Bourgeau · Screenplay by Hal Law and Robert A. McGowan · Released on April 4, 1942, by M-G-M · Our Gang: Billie "Buckwheat" Thomas, George "Spanky" McFarland, Billy "Froggy" Laughlin, and Mickey Gubitosi · Circus official, Emmett Vogan

Since Buckwheat is a chronic liar, the gang doesn't believe him when he says he's seen a monkey-spook near the haunted house. In order to teach him a lesson about lying, they dress Froggy as a chimp and take Buckwheat to the haunted house for a good scare. Pretty soon the *real* monkey shows up and has them all on the run, until a man arrives from the circus to reclaim his lost animal-star.

If there's anything worse than an *Our Gang* comedy

with adults trying to teach the kids a lesson, it's an episode with the *kids* trying to teach someone a lesson. The superior attitudes taken by Spanky, Mickey, and Froggy are astonishing considering their own track record. Where do they come off lecturing Buckwheat about telling the truth?

Equally surprising is the idea of these four boys being scared witless by an obviously playful monkey. Having hosted several menageries' worth of animals over the years, it seems inconsistent for them to be so frightened of one medium-sized chimp—Spanky, particularly, since he spent many of his early Rascals films sharing scenes with monkeys.

The film's "haunted" house is fairly short on terror. In fact, it seems more dirty than scary.

"Halfhearted" is probably the best description of this short. Even a comic conclusion with all four boys crashing through barn wall cutouts while running away from an escaped lion has such a mechanical air about it that it fails to get a laugh. In this, the finale matches the rest of the film—completely unconvincing, uninteresting, and unfunny.

Spanky, Mickey (Robert Blake), and adversary in "Don't Lie."

207 · SURPRISED PARTIES

One Reel · Produced by M-G-M · Directed by Edward Cahn · Photographed by Walter Ludin · Edited by Leon Bourgeau · Screenplay by Hal Law and Robert A. McGowan · Released on May 30, 1942, by M-G-M · Our Gang: Billy "Froggy" Laughlin, George "Spanky" McFarland, Janet Burston, Billie "Buckwheat" Thomas, Mickey Gubitosi, Leon Tyler, Robert Ferrero, and Frank Ward · Froggy's mother, Margaret Bert

At the conclusion of a birthday party for one of the kids, Froggy is crying. The gang asks why and he complains that he almost never gets a birthday party, since he was born on February 29 during a leap year. With that, the gang decides to host a surprise party for Froggy. When he finds them in the midst of preparations, they pretend to kick him out of the club in order to preserve the surprise element of the big celebration. Froggy doesn't take this lightly, however, and plans his revenge by sneaking into the clubhouse and planting a series of booby traps. Then he shows up at the party dressed as a girl. When he discovers that the party was for him, he shoves other kids away from the games and sets off all the booby traps himself. But upon learning what has happened, the gang forgives him and restores him as guest of honor. Froggy sets off one last trap—a water-spouting chicken— and, as he is doused with water, exclaims, "This is the happiest day of my life!"

Once more, good comic possibilities are destroyed by saccharine treatment. Any *Our Gang* film that opens with one of the kids crying is in trouble right away. Froggy remains so annoying throughout that it's a wonder he wasn't permanently expelled from the gang.

Not that the others are any better. The acting is hopelessly contrived and at times inept. Atmosphere kids stare into the camera, while Janet, seated next to Froggy before he cuts open the rigged chicken, inexcusably anticipates the water-spray gag and moves away.

Worst of all, the booby traps Froggy springs simply aren't funny. What a field day the Hal Roach staff could have had devising elaborate gadgets and slapstick contraptions. But at M-G-M this didn't seem so important. Froggy's being squirted in the face is a limp closing to a lame short, and his claim that this is the happiest day of his life conjures up pictures of a harrowingly dreary existence by comparison.

208 · DOIN' THEIR BIT

One Reel · Produced by M-G-M · Directed by Herbert Glazer · Photographed by Jackson Rose · Edited by Leon Bourgeau · Released on July 18, 1942, by M-G-M · Our Gang: George "Spanky" McFarland, Billy "Froggy" Laughlin, Janet Burston, Billie "Buckwheat" Thomas, Mickey Gubitosi, Billy Finnegan, Freddie Walburn, Freddie Chapman, Jackie Salling, Lawrence Long, Jr., Valerie Lee, and Billy Ray Smith · Walter Wills, Himself; Miss Liberty, Beverly Hudson

Mr. Wills hears the mayor of Greenpoint making a radio speech about the fine work the USO is doing in entertaining soldiers overseas, but reminds citizens that many soldiers stationed in small U.S. towns are being neglected. Inspired by the talk, Mr. Wills persuades the gang to put on a show for local servicemen, billed as Our Gang's Junior USO. The program opens with a line of tap-dancing boys in military garb, followed by Janet singing, "I Love a Man in a Uniform." Then Spanky and Froggy do a skit entitled "A Day in Camp." Everyone joins in the big finale, "The Allies on Parade," for a patriotic conclusion that wins a rousing response from the soldier audience.

There is virtually no plot in this wartime musical short, but that isn't the only missing ingredient. The show itself is a coy and plastic idea of an *Our Gang* production, without any heart, humor—or talent.

The opening Bud Murray-staged tap-dance number features a group of well-rehearsed young boys, but the song that follows shows Janet Burston at her worst—perpetually off-key and doggedly cute in singing her big

number. Judging from the applause this generates, the soldiers in the audience must have been truly starved for entertainment.

The comedy skit with Froggy as a soldier and Spanky as his officer is merely a rehash of old vaudeville patter, updated with references to "killing the Japs"; not particularly funny if done by adults and less so when attacked by kids.

The finale, "Allies on Parade," is an unabashed flag-waver intended as a wartime morale booster; its success is difficult to judge today, but without the timeliness it seems merely a well-staged kiddie ensemble as Miss Liberty sings a patriotic song while youngsters representing various countries march past in formation.

One must try to appreciate this film in the context of its time, but even the most charitable outlook leaves only one conclusion: this alternately cute and stale little revue couldn't have had much appeal for youngsters weaned on earlier and better *Our Gang* comedies. It certainly doesn't today.

209 · ROVER'S BIG CHANCE

One Reel · Produced by M-G-M · Directed by Herbert Glazer · Photographed by Jackson Rose · Edited by Leon Bourgeau · Screenplay by Hal Law and Robert A. McGowan · Released on August 22, 1942, by M-G-M · Our Gang: Bobby "Mickey" Blake,* Billy "Froggy" Laughlin, Janet Burston, George "Spanky" McFarland, Billie "Buckwheat" Thomas, Freddie Chapman, Bobby Anderson, Clyde "Fatty" Demback, and Billy Finnegan · J. D. Broderick, casting director, Byron Shores; Bill Patterson, director, Horace (later Stephen) McNally; Studio clerk, Barbara Bedford; Professor Ventriloko, Hugh McCormick

* About this time, Robert Blake anglicized his screen name, changing from Mickey Gubitosi to Bobby Blake, so he could play parts like "Little Beaver" in the *Red Ryder* series.

"Rover's Big Chance": trying to persuade us this is a comedy, the director (Horace McNally) explains to Rover's managers that when he said he was going to "shoot" Rover, he meant with a camera, not a gun. A real highlight. Byron Shores looks on.

On his way to work at glamorous Mammoth Studios, the casting director's car suffers a flat tire. While his driver makes the change, he watches a sand-lot baseball game, noticing a little dog has been inserted at second base. Impressed (the dog's a "good glove"), he arranges for a screen test. The rigorous scene requires the dog to bark, and after one unsuccessful coaxing by the director, and a second failing try by Our Gang ("his last chance"), the dog's career is over and, mercifully, so is the short.

If this picture sounds dumb on paper, it's worse on film, where its triteness really shines through. There's not a single believable scene. Kids-and-pets is an *Our Gang* formula that had been rather successful down through the years, but never at M-G-M.

Moving from "Doin' Their Bit" to "Rover's Big Chance" is like standing in the dregs, and then wallowing in it. Together, these two shorts demonstrate that the current *Our Gang* troupe couldn't or wouldn't sing, dance, act, or amuse, and did them all equally well. One has to wonder, too, if the director and writers were ever kids themselves.

"Rover's Big Chance" is just one more Metro "comedy" potboiler that proves the worth of the Roach style by repudiating it, and is hardly worth discussing.

What's next. . . .

210 · MIGHTY LAK A GOAT

One Reel · Produced by M-G-M · Directed by Herbert Glazer · Photographed by Jackson Rose · Edited by Leon Bourgeau · Screenplay by Hal Law and Robert A. McGowan · Released on October 10, 1942, by M-G-M · Our Gang: George "Spanky" McFarland, Billie "Buckwheat" Thomas, Billy "Froggy" Laughlin, and Bobby "Mickey" Blake · Schoolteacher, Anne O'Neal; Bus driver, William Tannen; Bus passenger, Charlie Sullivan; Girl at the Bijou box office, Ava Gardner; Matinee movie patrons, Joe Yule, Sr., George K. French; Officer, Lee Phelps; Chapter-play actors: Detective King, Robert Emmett O'Connor; Banker Stone, John Dilson

After a discourteous motorist splashes mud all over the gang on their way to school, Froggy takes them home and mixes some cleaning fluid with his chemistry set. The mud is removed, but in its place is a horrible smell that makes the kids instantly unpopular. A driver refuses to let them on his bus, and when they finally arrive at school, the whole class files out in rapid motion, while the teacher dismisses the gang for the rest of the day. With a free afternoon, Mickey, Spanky, Buckwheat, and Froggy decide to take in a movie, starring their hero Detective King. As they enter the darkened theater, the customers, overcome by the awful aroma, begin to leave until the only patron left besides the gang is a man with a cold in his nose. Even the actors on-screen can't stand the smell, walking off-camera and leaving the movie set empty! Finally, four cops wearing gas masks unceremoniously pluck the kids out of the theater, and the clothes are buried underground to put a definite end to the problem.

"Mighty Lak a Goat" is one of the more engaging M-G-M *Our Gangs*, with a truly funny premise. Of course, the "wildest" reaction to the gang's unpleasant odor is a bus pulling away at double speed; repeating the same gag idea, a classful of kids files out of the room in fast motion. The topper is the departure of the actors appearing on-screen in Chapter 33 of the Climax Pictures serial *Don't Open That Door*. But one yearns for the silent-comedy zaniness that would have greeted the same situation—people leaping in the air, flowers wilting, other comic chain reactions. This kind of humor was unknown at Metro, sad to say. The genuine comedy that is contained in this short is somewhat dispelled by a weak and unrewarding punch line.

This short does have one asset unique to a studio like M-G-M, however. The studio often placed young starlets and actors into its short subjects, and this one features the beautiful Ava Gardner as the movie cashier. She was then married to the studio's top juvenile star, Mickey Rooney.

211 · UNEXPECTED RICHES

One Reel · Produced by M-G-M · Directed by Herbert Glazer · Photographed by Charles Schoenbaum · Edited by Leon Bourgeau · Screenplay by Hal Law and Robert A. McGowan · Released on November 28, 1942, by M-G-M · Our Gang: George "Spanky" McFarland, Bobby "Mickey" Blake, Billy "Froggy" Laughlin, Billie "Buckwheat" Thomas, and Barry "Ken" Downing · Ken's father, Emmett Vogan; Mickey's father, Ernie Alexander; Mickey's mother, Margaret Bert; Extras in Froggy's dream, Symona Boniface, Stanley Logan; Bits in Buckwheat's dream, Willa Pearl Curtis, Ernestine Wade

A fortune from a penny-weighing machine predicts unexpected riches for the gang. Another kid hears them talking about it, so later when he's assigned to dig a hole for a shade tree his father wants to plant, he draws up a treasure map and slips it into the gang's clubhouse. They fall for the scheme and follow instructions right to the tree-site, where they bargain with the boy and even pay him a dime for the privilege of digging a hole. As they dig, they

While Buckwheat and Spanky (in his final *Our Gang* film) dig for Captain Kidd's treasure, it seems that Mickey and Froggy, as the original still caption notes, "believe in sitting on their shovels, instead of leaning on them."

dream about what they'll do with their money. Mickey, being a devoted child, buys his mom and pop a glorious mansion. Froggy presents the United States with a brand-new battleship, pooh-poohing official thanks and promising that when this one wears out he'll buy another. Buckwheat pictures himself riding through the black section of town in a chauffeur-driven limousine, dispensing watermelon and fried chicken to one and all. But these fantasies come to an abrupt end when the scheming kid's father discovers what's going on. He chastises his son but tells the gang that since he was going to pay his boy $1.50 for the work, *they* have now earned that sum—making the prediction of unexpected riches come true after all.

This story line borrows a page from Tom Sawyer, who tricked neighborhood kids into whitewashing a fence for him, and spices up the original idea by showing the gang's dreams of untold wealth (curiously omitting Spanky's visions, perhaps because this was his last *Our Gang* short).

The dreams conform to the individual kids' established personality traits. It figures that Mickey would be a do-gooder and treat his parents to an extravagant gift, while it's equally logical that Froggy would want to build *himself* up by making a grandstand play. But Buckwheat's dream comes closer in concept to the kind of things an earlier Gang would have thought about. The ultimate fantasy existence was depicted as Freetown in the silent short "Young Sherlocks," where new clothes, free food and toys, and no adults in sight were the order of the day!

212 · BENJAMIN FRANKLIN, JR.

One Reel · Produced by M-G-M · Directed by Herbert Glazer · Photographed by Charles Schoenbaum · Edited by Leon Bourgeau · Screenplay by Hal Law and Robert A. McGowan · Released on January 30, 1943, by M-G-M · Our Gang: Bobby "Mickey" Blake, Billy "Froggy" Laughlin, Billie "Buckwheat" Thomas, Janet Burston, Mickey "Happy" Laughlin, Barry Downing, Valeria Lee, Billy Ray Smith, Frank Ward, and Dickie Hall · John, Mickey's father, Ernie Alexander; Martha, Mickey's mother, Margaret Bert; Janet's mother, Barbara Bedford

A couple of thousand neighborhood kids gather in the clubhouse for a general complaint session concerning how the war is encroaching upon their lives. Everyone registers his gripes, then with no minds of their own, they entrust to the five *Our Gang* principals the task of deciding what everyone else should do about present conditions. After a week's deliberation, the gang does indeed have an answer for wartime shortages and hardships—in the form of a play. Mickey's been reading *Poor Richard's Almanac,* a guidebook of American philosophy by Benjamin Franklin, and the gang dramatizes what Mickey has learned about the patriotism involved in making sac-

Republic's *Johnny Doughboy* (1943): the story of a child star who outgrows his roles in kiddie pictures. Left to right, Bobby Breen, Alfalfa Switzer, Robert Coogan (Jackie's younger brother), and Spanky McFarland. By this time, Spanky and Alfalfa had both outgrown *Our Gang* and left it.

rifices. At the skit's conclusion, one kid in the audience stands up and speaks for everyone when he says, "The gang sure proved that squawkin' ain't right!"

From the company that gave you "Time Out for Lessons," "Doin' Their Bit," and the ever-popular "Don't Lie" comes "Benjamin Franklin, Jr.," which is so bad it's embarrassing.

The direction and acting, in fact, may be the worst yet—a new low. The cast appears very much aware that they're working in a "comedy," and in trying to persuade us to think we're watching something funny, they exaggerate their actions, their expressions, and their dialogue.

Films like this one helped seal the lid on the series' coffin.

213 · FAMILY TROUBLES

One Reel · Produced by M-G-M · Directed by Herbert Glazer · Photographed by Walter Lundin · Edited by Leon Bourgeau · Screenplay by Hal Law and Robert A. McGowan · Released on April 3, 1943, by M-G-M · Our Gang: Janet Burston, Bobby "Mickey" Blake, Billy "Froggy" Laughlin, Billie "Buckwheat" Thomas, Mickey "Happy" Laughlin, and Dickie Hall · Mrs. Jones, Sarah Padden; Mr. Tom Jones, Harry C. Bradley; Aunt Aurelia, Elspeth Dudgeon; Janet's sister, Aurelia, Beverly Hudson; Janet's father, Byron Shores; Janet's mother, Barbara Bedford

Janet is running away from home; she's been neglected lately, and has the idea that her parents don't love her any more. The gang volunteers to help her get "adapted," proposing kindly Mr. and Mrs. Jones as prospective parents. Mrs. Jones decides to teach the kids a lesson; she agrees to adopt Janet, but immediately drops her smile and puts the girl to work scrubbing the floor in order to earn her keep. Janet is crushed, and the boys are stunned; when Mrs. Jones leaves the room to call Janet's parents, the gang slips away with the girl to their hide-out in a nearby cave. Living there is no easier, and eventually they bring Janet back home for a happy reunion. Janet's mother apologizes for being thoughtless, and promises that it will never happen again.

Like "Surprised Parties," this short gets off on the wrong foot with a close-up of Janet drowning in tears; from here, things can only get worse, and they do. After a tear-choked flashback showing Janet being ignored by her family, she sets off with the gang to be adopted. This talented youngster manages to be as obnoxious when smiling as she was when crying. When Mickey asks the Joneses, "How would you like to have a little girl in your home?" Janet chimes in, "A very *nice* little girl, too!" Indeed.

Of course, it isn't long before Janet is bawling again, while scrubbing the kitchen floor, crying, "Why did I ever leave home?" just in case the youngsters in the audience haven't gotten the message already. In the file of M-G-M's let's-teach-these-kids-a-lesson films, this short ranks as one of the worst.

Another trait this film shares with many M-G-M entries is a completely unrelated punch line gag, shoehorned into the script in order to end on a laugh—at least, that's the intention. During the family reunion, Froggy chirps, "All's well that ends well, I always say." "Froggy," says Janet's father, for no apparent reason, "Shakespeare said that." "He *did?*" replies Froggy, "Shucks!"

Labeling this the film's comic high point gives some indication of the general quality of what came beforehand.

214 · ELECTION DAZE

One Reel · Produced by M-G-M · Directed by Herbert Glazer · Photographed by Robert L. Surtees · Edited by Leon Bourgeau · Screenplay by Hal Law and Robert A. McGowan · Released on July 31, 1943, by M-G-M · Our Gang: Bobby "Mickey" Blake, Billy "Froggy" Laughlin, Billie "Buckwheat" Thomas, Janet Burston, Dickie Hall, Freddie Chapman, Robert Ferrero, Billy Ray Smith, Mickey "Happy" Laughlin, Buz Buckley, Jackie Horner, Robert Anderson, Frank Lester Ward, Tommy Tucker, and Valerie Lee

It's election time at the One for All and All for One Club. President Mickey seems a shoo-in for reelection, but Froggy decides to run against him. The first ballot results in a tie vote, so the candidates postpone the election one day to allow for campaign speeches. Incumbent prexy Mickey entices his public by offering free lemonade, while Froggy doles out free jelly beans with his oratory. When the next election is held, however, the results are the same: another tie. As a solution, the club splits in half, operating on equal halves of the clubhouse floor, with Mickey leading his constituents and Froggy in charge of his supporters. This only leads to chaos though, and Buckwheat reminds everyone what happened when the country split during the Civil War. So one final election is taken to reunite the club, and this time Mickey, Froggy, and Buckwheat receive but one vote each, resulting in a sweeping plurality for write-in candidate Janet, who immediately announces a whole new slate of ladylike special events for future meetings, ". . . and every Saturday morning will be visiting day for dolls!"

A pointless short with a more pointless conclusion, "Election Daze" was released in the midst of the wartime presidential campaign between Thomas Dewey and Franklin D. Roosevelt, and was just about as funny.

The single noteworthy aspect of this film is that it was photographed by Academy Award-winning cameraman Robert Surtees (*King Solomon's Mines, Quo Vadis,*

"I have come here to tell you all about it . . . when you think of jelly beans, think of me."

Mogambo, The Graduate, Summer of '42, The Sting), but even that isn't much of a recommendation for this ridiculous short.

Despite the tired pun in the spelling of "Election Daze," this film is more of an election doze.

215 · CALLING ALL KIDS

One Reel · Produced by M-G-M · Directed by Sam Baerwitz · Photographed by Jackson Rose · Edited by Leon Bourgeau · Story by Sam Baerwitz · Released on April 24, 1943, by M-G-M · Our Gang: Billy "Froggy" Laughlin, Billie "Buckwheat" Thomas, Bobby "Mickey" Blake, Janet Burston, Jackie Horner, Marlene Mains, and Marlene Kinghorn · NBC radio announcer, Mark Daniels; Voice-over for Buckwheat, Eddie (Rochester) Anderson

The gang stages a military salute for a radio and in-person audience, featuring songs, a recruiting skit with Mickey and Froggy, a series of celebrity impressions, and a flag-waving finale.

"Calling All Kids" has nothing to do with *Our Gang,* or with the kind of films audiences once associated with the series. What's more, the film is laden with camera trickery which one isn't supposed to notice during the "live" performance, adding an unpleasant air of phoniness to the proceedings. Froggy walks behind a curtain to change costumes, and does so only after an obvious camera cut. Buckwheat does an "impression" of Eddie "Rochester" Anderson which is accomplished by dubbing the real An-

derson's voice on the soundtrack. For the finale, a screen suddenly appears behind the kids with footage of marching troops, as the kids sing lyrics like "We don't mind working hard and paying taxes, if they get rid of the Japs and Axis." That this show could never have been conceived and prepared by a group of young children was not supposed to concern audiences of 1943.

But, as in the earlier "Doin' Their Bit," this phoniness *does* concern viewers today, especially those who care about *Our Gang.* An announcer who opens the short declares, "Take it away, Our Gang!" And we echo that sentiment with regard to this film: take it away.

Pitched as a musical mélange in the George M. Cohan tradition, "Calling All Kids" is another morale effort, featuring takeoffs on Hollywood stars. *Left to right,* they're supposed to be Judy Garland (Marlene Kinghorn), Virginia O'Brien (Marlene Mains), Eleanor Powell (Jackie Horner), Jack Benny's valet Rochester (Buckwheat), and for a good-neighbor note (that's what the press book says!) Carmen Miranda, Brazilian Bonfire (Janet Burston). The unidentified lad on the far right impersonates Fred Astaire.

216 · FARM HANDS

One Reel · Produced by M-G-M · Directed by Herbert Glazer · Photographed by Jackson Rose · Edited by Leon Bourgeau · Screenplay by Hal Law and Robert A. McGowan · Released on June 19, 1943, by M-G-M · Our Gang: Bobby "Mickey" Blake, Billy "Froggy" Laughlin, Billie "Buckwheat" Thomas, and Mickey "Happy" Laughlin · Mickey's Dad, Murray Alper

Mickey's Uncle George invites the gang to spend a weekend on his farm; they are awakened the first morning by a rooster at their window, signalling the start of a day doing chores. Unfortunately, the boys' enthusiasm is not matched by their know-how. Buckwheat places two empty milk bottles underneath a cow's udder and expects the rest to take care of itself; Mickey and Froggy think that serving the chickens "mash" means they should mash up a sack of chicken feed. Froggy then drops some of his jumping beans into the feed mixture, providing an eye-popping sight a few minutes later—hopping hens. Finally a runaway mule sends the foursome scattering; they seek refuge on top of a pile of hay, while Uncle George calms down the playful animal. Before they know what's happening, however, the kids are swallowed with the hay into a baling machine, and in a moment's time they are deposited through a chute encased in square bundles of hay. When the mule acts up again, they zip off into the horizon. Uncle George calls, "Children, come on back," but they shout, "We'll write you a letter!" as they head for the hills.

A very weak film. Still, if nothing else, "Farm Hands" has some action, and a different backdrop, to set it apart from other entries of this period. But it shares with those others an almost complete lack of amusing material. Buckwheat's set-piece with the cow, for instance, has no

In this scene from "Farm Hands," the cow is supposed to put the cream in the little bottle and the milk in the big one. *Left to right,* Froggy, Buckwheat, and Mickey (Robert Blake) are laughing just about as hard as we are.

laughs because nothing happens. He expects the cow to milk itself, and that's the joke; prolonging this idea doesn't improve it. Even a sure-fire gag like Mickey being lowered into the well to get water, being pulled to the top and then allowed to fall back, is wrecked because the joke isn't followed through. There's no splash, or reaction shot of his pals, or any water flying through the air; it's as if director Herbert Glazer was afraid of a little slapstick comedy. The only gag that works in the whole film is the shot of the chickens hopping in the air, having swallowed the jumping beans. And even that's pretty limp.

The film's finale, with the kids encased in bales of hay, is an ingenious gag idea, but this too is weakened by being treated realistically. With no sense of exaggeration, or build-up to this laugh, it becomes an intriguing but basically oddball shot, with Mickey's uncle George and his father pulling the boys through the chute asking if they're hurt.

Yet the same director that wouldn't use the hay-baler for an impossible but broadly funny kind of gag is perfectly willing to use under cranking to make the mule, and kids, run at double-speed. This was M-G-M's idea of good clean comedy.

217 · LITTLE MISS PINKERTON

One Reel · Produced by M-G-M · Directed by Herbert Glazer · Photographed by Jackson Rose · Edited by Leon Bourgeau · Screenplay by Hal Law and Robert A. McGowan · Released on September 18, 1943, by M-G-M · Our Gang: Janet Burston, Bobby "Mickey" Blake, Billie 'Buckwheat" Thomas, and Billy "Froggy" Laughlin · Burglar, Joe, Norman Willis; The dumb guy, Pete, Dick Rich; Irish cop, Robert Emmett O'Connor

Froggy, Mickey, and Buckwheat at the kidnappers' lair in "Little Miss Pinkerton." The crooks are Norman Willis and Dick Rich.

The Greenpoint Department Store is staging a display window murder-mystery promotion. Dummies are strewn about, with clues placed nearby. Whoever can identify the murderer wins $100 in prize money. But there's always such a big crowd around the window that the gang can never get close enough to study the clues. The store is closed on Sunday, so the kindly old janitor promises to let the kids inside then to examine the display as long as they'd like. That day, though, the janitor is murdered by a pair of real crooks who are robbing the store's safe. The burglars dump the body in the display window and discover the gang has heard everything. Janet hides, but the rest of the youngsters are taken hostage. At first, the police won't listen to Janet's story, so the amateur sleuth rounds up all the kids she can find and tries to rescue her captive friends. Eventually, it's the police, with Janet's aid, who give chase and apprehend the criminals in time to save the gang.

Running just about a reel too long, "Little Miss Pinkerton" is another M-G-M factory second, with a ridiculous premise, and poorly executed. A *real* murder in an *Our Gang comedy*? And of a sweet old man who befriends the kids?

But a misfire story, undirected by Herbert Glazer, is far from being the film's only shortcoming. The unlikely M-G-M screenplays are made more difficult to swallow when overacted out by increasingly unlikable young performers. Our Ganger Janet Burston, more than the rest, suffers from a severe and persistent case of "the cutes." Her dialogue and delivery here are so stilted and contrived that it's just plain uncomfortable to watch. No one could possibly identify with these kids, except maybe the boobs who wrote the stories.

218 · THREE SMART GUYS

One Reel · Produced by M-G-M · Directed by Edward Cahn · Photographed by Jackson Rose · Edited by John D. Faure · Screenplay by Hal Law and Robert A. McGowan · Released on October 23, 1943, by M-G-M · Our Gang: Billy "Froggy" Laughlin, Bobby "Mickey" Blake, Billie "Buckwheat" Thomas, Janet Burston, Eleanor Taylor, and Marlene Kisker · Schoolmarm, Marta Linden; Wise old fisherman, Edward Fielding

Mickey, Froggy, and Buckwheat would rather go fishing than stay in school, so they plan to disrupt the class and get themselves sent home. The teacher catches on, however, and makes them stay after school instead. Next morning they plan on playing hooky and meet at their favorite fishing spot bright and early. As inept anglers, they catch the attention of an older man, who scolds them and explains that in order to catch the biggest fish in the world—success—the only bait is study. The boys get the message and scramble off just in time for school.

A hack reworking of the basic plot idea in "Readin' and Writin'," this film is rambling and unfunny. No opportunity is missed to hammer across the film's important message. When the boys tell ever-obnoxious Janet that they plan to skip school to go fishing, she replies with astonishment, "That would be playing hooky!" After they leave, she declares to no one in particular, "*They* think

they're smart—*I* think they're foolish."

There is one first-rate sight gag when Froggy and Buckwheat's lines get tangled on opposite sides of a dock, and they tug each other back and forth in total defiance of the laws of gravity. But this is smothered by inept performances that deaden even the pleasure of this comic moment.

By far the most ingenious aspect of the film comes when the kids are ordered by their teacher to write "I will be a good pupil" on the blackboard one hundred times. Froggy concocts a work-saving system by wedging three pieces of chalk into an eraser and writing three sentences simultaneously! This kind of comic invention stays in a viewer's mind far longer than the supposed lesson being taught. But the powers at M-G-M didn't seem to agree.

In short, "Three Smart Guys" is one dull film.

219 · RADIO BUGS

One Reel · Produced by M-G-M · Directed by Cyril Endfield · Photographed by Walter Lundin · Edited by Leon Bourgeau · Screenplay by Hal Law and Robert A. McGowan · Released on April 1, 1944, by M-G-M · Our Gang: Billy "Froggy" Laughlin, Bobby "Mickey" Blake, Billie "Buckwheat" Thomas, and Janet Burston · Shakespearean actor, Brandon Hurst; Mr. Jasper, bookshop proprietor, Pete Sosso; Pain-Killer Kilroy, the dentist, Morris Ankrum; *Kant-Fall Cake Hour* radio host, Tiny Hanlon; Audience extra, Robert (Bobby) Burns; Morticians, Walter Soderling, Erville Alderson; Dental patients, Fern Emmett, Chester Clute, Jack (Tiny) Lipson, Joe Yule, Sr.; Radio voice-over, Red Skelton; Part cut from the final release print: Town banker, Charles K. French

Looking for a sponsor, the Gang thinks they've found one in the waiting room of a dentist's office in this scene from "Radio Bugs." The patients are Joe Yule (Mickey Rooney's father), Fern Emmett, Jack (Tiny) Lipson, and Chester Clute.

After listening to Red Skelton's radio show with his parents, Froggy dreams of being a popular and successful radio comedian. He enlists the support of the gang, they buy an old joke-book, and go to a dentist's office to audition their material and hopefully obtain sponsorship to go on the radio. Their noisy performance only causes havoc

in the waiting room. Then the words of a hammy Shakespearean actor persuade them to abandon comedy in favor of the Bard. They try out this material on the three owners of a funeral home, but find that their attempts at drama only make their listeners laugh hysterically. Frustrated, they leave the building and find a man-in-the-street interview being conducted on the sidewalk. The reporter asks the kids what they think is the crying need of radio today. In unison they shout, "A sponsor!"

There is only one thing wrong with this short: it isn't funny. After an opening scene in which some wartime morale dialogue is shoehorned in (Froggy's father notes what a fine job comedians are doing entertaining the soldiers, and the close of Skelton's broadcast adds a reminder that "it's bonds or bondage") the plot plods along to its unamusing punch line.

The premise is not bad, and with the old set of kids under the Hal Roach banner it might have been enjoyable. But the kids' so-called comedy routine for already pained dental patients is only loud and obnoxious, and their rendering of Shakespeare is more so. There is a calculatedness in all of the kids' actions that makes it clear they are not the ingenuous youngsters the plot would have one believe them to be. Janet Burston, who often finds it necessary to shout her dialogue, is especially guilty of this, but unfortunately, it applies to every aspect of these later films.

220 · DANCING ROMEO

One Reel · Produced by M-G-M · Directed by Cyril Endfield · Photographed by Charles Salerno, Jr. · Edited by Leon Bourgeau · Screenplay by Hal Law and Robert A. McGowan · Released on April 29, 1944, by M-G-M · Our Gang: Billy "Froggy" Laughlin, Bobby "Mickey" Blake, Janet Burston, Billie "Buckwheat" Thomas, Valerie "Marilyn" Lee, Bobby "Gerald" Browning, Billy Ray Smith, Frank Ward, and Dickie Hall

Worried over his lack of terpsichorean talent, Froggy is planning desperate measures as Buckwheat, Mickey, and Janet look on in this scene from "Dancing Romeo."

Froggy has a crush on Marilyn, who tells him, "Dancing is more important to me than anything else." At first,

Froggy is disheartened, but then he realizes that he's simply got to learn how to dance. He announces a solo dance recital, and impresses everyone with his grace and skill. No wonder—his fantastic "leaps" are accomplished by having Mickey and Buckwheat yank him up in the air on a barely visible wire and pulley apparatus. Marilyn's dancing partner Gerald exposes the fraud, but when Froggy explains that he only did it for her, Marilyn tells him that she loves him . . . and he faints dead away.

The problem with "Dancing Romeo" is Froggy. The film's idea is good, and might have made a more entertaining short were it not for the almost unbearably abrasive Froggy in the leading role. His doggedly uncomic delivery of lines virtually destroys a credible story.

Seen to much better advantage are Valerie Lee as Marilyn and Bobby Browning as Gerald, doing a remarkably mature dance routine to Tchaikovsky's "Sleeping Beauty Waltz." Unfortunately, Miss Lee's thespian talent is somewhat less inspiring.

Cyril (Cy) Endfield, who directed the last three M-G-M shorts in the series, was one of many directors receiving on-the-job training. He went on to a prolific career writing and directing B pictures, and has done some above-average work more recently in England, including *Mysterious Island, Zulu,* and *Sands of the Kalahiri.* One can assume without fear of contradiction that he would not place "Dancing Romeo" among his major works.

It was the last *Our Gang* comedy to be released by M-G-M, after which the studio let this once valuable property quietly expire . . . officially.

221 · TALE OF A DOG

One Reel · Produced by M-G-M · Directed by Cyril Endfield · Photographed by Charles Salerno, Jr. · Edited by Leon Bourgeau · Screenplay by Hal Law and Robert A. McGowan · Released on April 15, 1944, as an M-G-M Miniature · Our Gang: Billie "Buckwheat" Thomas, Cordell "Big Shot" Hickman, Bobby "Mickey" Blake, Janet Burston, Billy "Froggy" Laughlin, and Dickie Hall · Dr. Parkson, Emmett Vogan; Buckwheat's mother, Willa Pearl Curtis; Alarmed citizen, Margaret Bert; Prissy gossipers, Anita Bolster, Dorothy Neumann, Fern Emmett

When Mickey, Froggy, and Janet overhear Big Shot and Buckwheat talking about giving smallpox to the gang, they run in horror—not realizing that "Smallpox" is the name of a dog. Froggy calls the Board of Health to report this emergency, and then spreads the word to every kid in town that Buckwheat and Big Shot have smallpox and plan to spread it around. Before long, the city is overrun with panic and outlandish rumors. When the doctor from the Board of Health finally locates Buckwheat, he learns the truth about "Smallpox." The kids are given a stern lecture by the mayor of Greenpoint, and sent on their way. The dog is renamed Spotty, and that's that.

The essence of this film can best be conveyed by quoting from the climactic scene in the mayor's office. He tells the gang that they are responsible for the worst day in Greenpoint history, having incited a panic.

Mickey replies, "I can see now that that's where we were wrong. If we'd been more careful and learned everything about it, we wouldn't be here, disgraced and in trouble."

The mayor says he's glad they've learned a lesson, and tells the children, and their parents, "I trust that you . . . have learned how repeating unconfirmed rumors and jumping to conclusions can be a danger to you, your city, and even your country."

With that, class is dismissed . . . and so is Our Gang, for on this heavy-handed note, the story of a once-great comedy series comes to an end. "Tale of a Dog" was the last short made in the M-G-M series. And although the film itself ends with a joke (the dog "talks," with the aid of an animation trick), the humor is as limp as the effectiveness of the message being preached by the mayor—a thinly veiled reference to wartime propaganda about keeping your mouth shut for fear of exposing information to enemy agents ("Loose lips sink ships").

Exactly why M-G-M threw in the towel at this point is not known. According to *Motion Picture Herald*'s annual poll of breadwinning short subjects, *Our Gang* still rated

The final scene in the final *Our Gang* comedy made, "Tale of a Dog." *Left to right,* Billie Thomas, Cordell Hickman, Robert Blake, Janet Burston, and Billy Laughlin.

high with theater owners. Perhaps it was felt that the series had run its course (which had been true for about five years) . . . or it may have been part of the general phasing-out of short subjects at the studio, for during this decade such other long-running series as *Crime Does Not Pay* and *John Nesbitt's Passing Parade* were discontinued.

Happily, it was just a few years hence that Hal Roach arranged to reissue some of the classic shorts of the 1930s period, enabling a new generation of youngsters to enjoy those timeless comedies, and hopefully, to erase the memory of the bleak M-G-M period when a successful and unique film property was beaten into the ground.

IX THE LITTLE RASCALS TELEVISION REVIVAL

The warm feeling of a huge theater audience laughing together spontaneously through the latest *Our Gang* comedy is a thing of the past, but the films are still with us, even if often blithely cut, and reduced to the belittling dimensions of a nineteen-inch TV tube.

Despite these handicaps, *The Little Rascals* are more popular today than ever. Kids and grown-up kids alike cherish the films with a fervor offered few other series. It's not just nostalgia, either. Children who don't have any conception of what life was like in the 1920s and

1930s can still identify with the kids of *Our Gang,* some forty to fifty years later. TV personality Orson Bean says, "I watch the *Our Gang* comedies every single day—today! My kid puts them on, and if he doesn't, I do. I think they're the finest thing since *Gone With the Wind.* I just flip over them. All of the boys were doing Oliver Hardy, with the double takes and all. I think they're genuine works of art; I'm not kidding. I think they're *so* wonderful."

Our Gang was only off movie palace screens a few years when television sprang up in the late 1940s, hungry for product. The Hal Roach backlog of short subjects was ideal for video programming, and the studio began parceling off rights to keep TV sets glowing.

What's happened since has brought *Our Gang* legions of new admirers, and also left a tangled legal mess that would challenge the most competent contracts attorney. The *Our Gang* property has been kicked around through more irresponsible hands than a park grounds football.

Even Hal Roach Studios found it difficult to follow the shuffle of assignments, litigation, and contract modifications. A 1955 Roach inter-office memo tried to reconstruct some of the legal maneuverings, gave up, and caused the writer to conclude by asking, "What did we do with the other fifty-one *Our Gangs* theatrically when we got them back?"

The maneuverings and confusion began in 1938, when, as covered in the notes for "Hide and Shriek," Roach sold the entire *Our Gang* films backlog (with the exception of the silent Pathés) and all of the unit's current talent contracts to Loew's (M-G-M).

In 1949 Roach reobtained an assignment of copyrights to the films, but Loew's retained all rights to produce, distribute, and exhibit films under the title *Our Gang.* Loew's also retained their own backlog of fifty-two Metro-produced *Our Gang* comedies, and Roach agreed to remove the roaring M-G-M lion head trademark, the small reclining lion and torch insignia trademark, as well as the names and titles of Metro-Goldwyn-Mayer, Loew's Incorporated, and *Our Gang* from all prints Roach would reissue.

Hal Roach Studios, though, was not going to reissue the series. The Roach plant had tied its fortunes to television production, and would merely sell or license rerelease rights, thereby collecting a pile of cash up front and saddling someone else with the problems of financing and promoting a reissue.

Enter Major Difficulty. Through the years, the series had been known jointly by two names, *Our Gang* (the title of the series' first film), and secondarily, *Hal Roach's Rascals* (the series' original title). Both names had frequently been used in tandem for studio publicity and for identifying the series on main title cards shot for the films.* Now neither one could be used. M-G-M owned the designation *Our Gang,* and the new series packager was not about to provide free advertising for a competitor, so the "Hal Roach" part of *Hal Roach's Rascals* was out, too.

Since the new distributor would be contractually bound to remake all of those glorious original title cards anyway,

Hal Roach decided to rechristen the series with a brand-new name: *The Little Rascals,* an appellation that did turn up now and again in the films' dialogue ("Free Wheeling," for example).

With that decided, the studio could begin peddling rights to the renamed *Little Rascals* property. Roach had already licensed most of his backlog—the Laurel & Hardys, the Charley Chases, and the rest—to a rerelease theatrical and television distributor, Film Classics. *The Little Rascals* was originally contracted for Film Classics, too, but by 1951 when Roach had finally resecured the rights and was able to deliver the negatives, Film Classics was declaring bankruptcy.

The Film Classics successor was Regal Television, which was overloaded with short product and decided not to incur the expense of printing up and distributing *The Little Rascals* backlog. So the leased rights then passed through Superb Television to a consortium headed by producer Jack Dietz and on to independent distributor Joe Auerbach in 1952.

For starters, Auerbach licensed Official Films for the 16mm nontheatrical home-movie market, and Monogram Pictures for the 35mm theatrical reissue and 16mm television syndication rights.

Due to contractual restrictions, the television revival didn't explode until 1955, but Monogram embarked on a theatrical reissue immediately.

The accretion of age only proved the films' undated qualities. Audiences which had never been exposed to the classic Roach *Our Gangs* of the 1930s responded favorably, as did trade papers like *Variety,* and Monogram kept the shorts in very profitable release for a number of years, splicing several of the musical-revue episodes together in 1959 to comprise a makeshift feature film called *Little Rascals Varieties.*

But as the films flourished through the 1950s theatrical and television revivals, multiple licensing caused plenty of behind-the-scenes confusion. Monogram Pictures changed its corporate name to Allied Artists, and the company's video arm was known as Inter-State Television, explaining why one often sees prints carrying these three seemingly unrelated introductory titles.

Unfortunately, when these various licensees (including Official Films) replaced the original distributor, main, and interior production credit titles with those bearing their own company logo, they often did so on 35mm preservation fine-grain negatives instead of on dupe negs and 16mm masters that should have been used to service print orders, thus depriving future audiences from enjoying the clever title design and artwork of the originals.

To boot, in their carelessness, these same companies mistitled some of the films: "Hearts Are Thumps" became "Hearts Are Trumps"; "Bouncing Babies" became "Bounding Babies"; "Arbor Day" became "Arbor Days"; "Bargain Day" became "Bargain Days"; "Hi'-Neighbor!" became "Hi Neighbor"; "Our Gang Follies of 1936" became "Little Rascals Follies"; "Our Gang Follies of 1938" became "Follies of 1938."

Even worse is what happened to the silent Pathé *Our Gangs* when they were retrieved from the vaults. Besides carving the films to a fare-thee-well, their syndicators often chopped out *all* titles: main titles, text titles, everything, totally obscuring the origins and contents of the films. Viewers not only didn't know what they were watching, but what was happening besides.

---

* The one curious exception was at the outset of the 1931–32 season, when instead of Hal Roach presenting "His Rascals in an Our Gang Comedy," Hal Roach presented "The Little Pirates" in first "Big Ears" and then "Shiver My Timbers."

In New York, Officer Joe Bolton brought the Rascals to home viewers over WPIX-TV.

In St. Paul and Minneapolis, kids of the 1950s were introduced to The Little Rascals over WCCO-TV, up in a tree house, by "Axel" (Clellan Card) and "Carmen" (Mary Davies).

Video rights to the sixty-six Pathés were divided between National Telepix, who called their package *The Mischief Makers,* and a second distributor who labeled theirs *Those Lovable Scallawags With Their Gangs.*

M-G-M television joined the syndication sweepstakes, too, with their backlog of fifty-two shorts, the only *Our Gang* comedies that could still be advertised and exhibited as such.

Complicating things further was the fact that over the years Roach licensed various home-movie companies to issue 8mm and 16mm copies of certain of his *Our Gang* films, under such unimaginative package titles as *Kids and Pets* and *Famous Kid Comedies.* Some of these entrepreneurs (and bootleggers, too) issued condensed versions of original two-reel films and gave them new titles.

The confusion didn't end there, however. Each of these revivals was launched with spectacularly uninformed press material. Right from the start, Monogram, for instance, insisted that their two-reelers included Mickey Daniels, Joe Cobb, Jackie Condon, Sunshine Sammy, and Mary Kornman, none of whom appeared in the talkies (discounting reunion appearances as grownups). Just as bad, a press book for the films actually identified photos of Chubby Chaney as Joe Cobb, Stymie Beard as Sunshine Sammy, and Jean Darling as Mary Kornman! The only truthful claim in Monogram's entire press book was the campaign slogan that pegged *The Little Rascals* as "the kids who made the whole world laugh."

Unfortunately, this trend of scholarliness has followed *The Little Rascals* ever since. Distributors don't know anything about the films, or who is in them, and they don't bother taking the trouble to learn.

The current television distributor, King World Productions, issued a campaign book which did things like picking up the most notorious *Our Gang* impostors and misidentifying "Pups Is Pups" as "Pets Is Pets."

Is it any wonder the history of *Our Gang* is such a mess?

Despite the shoddy way the series has been handled, *The Little Rascals* television revival has been and continues to be a phenomenal success story, currently pulling leading demographics in over one hundred television markets across the country, many of them having telecast the series continuously since first offered in 1955. Not only does the series continue to outperform all other children's programming, but according to Michael G. King of King World Productions, it draws more adult viewership than kids. Not really too surprising.

What *is* surprising is that during the early 1970s, heightened sensitivity to racial stereotypes inspired angry reaction to *The Little Rascals* in some cities. Television stations which had been running the films for nearly twenty years suddenly found themselves the target for attacks. King World Productions feared that the controversy might drive the Rascals off television if something wasn't done, and they invested the time and money to reedit the series, removing racial and other gags thought to be in bad taste.

Some twenty-minute episodes were cut by as much as ten minutes, while others ("Little Daddy," "The Kid From Borneo," "A Tough Winter," "Lazy Days," "Little Sinner," "A Lad an' a Lamp," "Moan & Groan,

Inc.," "Big Ears") were eliminated from the TV package altogether. Representatives of the NAACP were called in to approve the laundered prints, and they even issued statements on the positive and "nonracial" aspects of *The Little Rascals.*

While *Our Gang* buffs deplore the censorship of these films (leaving certain stories senseless), it cannot be denied that King's decision to edit the series has kept the films alive in many TV markets which were ready to bounce the "controversial" series.

Many purists, though, tired of watching incomplete prints constantly interrupted in the middle of scenes by commercials for the Cumquat Institute of America, or

Burger Doodle, and the like, turn to home-movie companies like Blackhawk Films (yet another Roach licensee) for uncut 8mm and 16mm prints.

In either case, for that isolated stodgy parent not cut from the same cloth as Orson Bean who wonders why his son sits and watches those "old movies," Junior has an answer for him: "They're new to me, Dad."

Note: As of this writing, prints are available for television programming through King World Productions, 903 Mountain Avenue, Berkley Heights, N.J. 07922, and are offered for nontheatrical and home-movie use to the general public through Blackhawk Films, Davenport, Iowa, 52808.

APPENDIXES

A · NOTES ON BIG IMPOSTORS OF LITTLE RASCALS

Not long ago, *Los Angeles Herald-Examiner* columnist James Bacon wrote, "If my mail is any indication, the most popular star in the world today is not Robert Redford. It's Spanky McFarland. . . . You can't imagine how many letters I received asking me to check a story that Spanky had died in a Denver hospital. Not true. There were a dozen other stories about Spanky, the cute fat boy of *Our Gang.* Some said he was a millionaire. Others said he was pumping gas in a station in Lubbock, Texas."

Why on earth should there be such confusion about George "Spanky" McFarland, who is alive, well, and very visible on television shows and college campuses? Because within these United States there is a thriving industry comprised of people who find instant fame by claiming to have been members of *Our Gang.* Interest in these ex-movie kids is phenomenal, as Bacon reported. Richard Lamparski, author of the popular *Whatever Became Of . . .?* series, says that nothing brings in so much mail as *Our Gang.*

At the same time, nothing is the subject of so much misinformation. Hardly a week passes that some newspaper, magazine, or television show doesn't carry a story about a supposed *Our Gang* kid, now residing in a small town, or carrying on a show-business career, or having just died. The authors' clipping files are bulging with bogus stories of this kind, some of which are carried to an incredible extreme. How is this possible?

First, one must suppose that in small towns, garrulous old-timers who have nothing better to do try out this ploy to attract attention. One can just picture an oldster draw-

ing on his pipe and rocking easily on the front porch as he talks to a reporter for the *Centerville Sun.* "Yep," he says, smiling, "I played the bully in the old *Our Gang* films for five or six years back in the silent days. Made two hundred eighty-three films.* Had a lot of fun. They wanted to sign me for another six years but the money wasn't good enough."

The small town reporter has no cause to doubt the old-timer . . . and besides, there is no way to check the facts. There has not been (until now) any thorough book on *Our Gang,* and the Hal Roach studio files are indecipherable to most and generally inaccessible besides. So the story gets printed, perhaps picked up by a major wire-service, and another name enters the *Our Gang* clipping files.

Well-known people in big towns are guilty of the same trick, however. Comic actor Eddie Bracken's official biography states that he was in the *Our Gang* shorts many years ago. When interviewed for *Film Fan Monthly* in 1966 he was asked about this, and said that he was in a *rival* children's series called *The Kiddie Troupers.* Somewhere along the line, a press agent must have made the switch. After all, who would know the difference?

Nanette Fabray's bio has also credited her with these early appearances, but she has been careful to explain that she was merely an extra in these shorts, never a featured player.

* No exaggeration. One prominent impostor actually stated, in print, and more than once, that he'd appeared in two hundred eighty-three *Our Gang* comedies. The established fact that only two hundred twenty-one films were made in the series' entire twenty-three-year history didn't seem to bother him.

One can thus reason that many other people who claim to have been Gang members were really in another kiddie series, or perhaps crowd extras and not starring players in *Our Gang*. But for them it's easier and more rewarding to stretch the truth.

How can we tell which people are phonies and which are bona fide Gangsters? First, we have the facts at our disposal: actual names of the children who starred in the films (not stage names), their real backgrounds, studio talent contracts, studio production records, and pertinent data and stories from trade papers, press books, original still captions, and casting directories. All together it's a pretty tight web of evidence.

Second, and as important as anything else, we've studied the films, and know them pretty well—though even casual buffs only remotely familiar with the series can nail a phony by the self-aggrandizing misinformation and contradictions he (or she) spouts. Bogus Little Rascals often claim they played "Freckles," or "Fatso," or "Smelly," or some other nonexistent character in the series. They exaggerate the length of their stay with the Gang into impossible numbers, they confuse dates and whereabouts of so-called colleagues, and the films they allegedly appeared in are conveniently unnamed. In fact, when cornered, this species has a clear nonrecollection of film titles and their stories. "One of them had something to do with a little girl and a dog," Mr. X (not his real name) will blithely tell you. "I do remember that." And nothing else.

One hilarious 1967 column from a Minneapolis newspaper includes an interview with a gentleman working as a nightclub singer, who claims to have been in *Our Gang*.

"He was the original 'Freckles' in the original 'Our Gang' of the silent films," wrote the columnist, "in the days when Joe Cobb was the fat boy, Dickie Moore was the good kid and Farina was the first young Negro comic.

" 'Carl (Alfalfa) Switzer replaced me in the cast when I was eleven,' Mr. X said. 'That's when Spanky McFarland took over as the fat boy and Buckwheat went in to replace Farina.

" 'Hal Roach directed us himself . . . with a megaphone, you know.'

"Mr. X said it used to take three to five months to shoot a thirty-minute short subject. 'And we all had con-

Impostor? No, this is Spanky's stand-in, Joe Strauch, Jr., who had incidental roles in *Our Gang* films over the years.

tracts paying us $75 a week. That would be like $750 a week today.' "

The Minneapolis columnist swallowed Mr. X's routine word for word, although every statement he made was incorrect (there never was a character called Freckles, Joe Cobb was in the silents while Dickie Moore was only in talkies, Hal Roach didn't direct the films, Farina wasn't the first black kid in the series and he wasn't replaced by Buckwheat, they never spent anywhere near three to five months filming a short, etc., etc., etc.). Yet this is entirely typical of the hogwash dispensed by so-called *Our Gang* kiddies—and published in newspapers and magazines all the time.

Some prominent alumni, like Spanky McFarland, Darla Hood, Porky Lee, Buckwheat Thomas, and Johnny Downs, have been the victims of outrageous swindlers actually claiming their names! Is there no higher aspiration in American life than purporting to be an *Our Gang* kid?

Even one of Raquel Welch's husbands was linked with the series. One can appreciate the scope of this compulsion to trade on an *Our Gang* identity when being married to the world's premier sex goddess isn't enough, and greater satisfaction comes in assuming the (figurative) posture of a grown *Our Gang* kid.

The information that follows on the *real Our Gang* members, has been accumulated from ten years of diligent research by both authors. We can confidently state that the distressingly large number of other men and women claiming to have been stars in the *Our Gang* series are out-and-out phonies . . . and if we've spoiled their one claim to fame, we're not terribly sorry. We're too busy paying tribute to the real kids to waste our time with cranks who just want some undeserved attention.

B · REGULAR OUR GANGERS

A 1974 photo of Joe Cobb and Bob Davis.

JOE COBB (Joe Frank Cobb)

Born in Shawnee, Oklahoma, November 7, 1917. First short, at age five, "The Big Show," last short "Bouncing Babies." Appeared in eighty-six Our Gang comedies over seven years (excluding three return appearances during the 1930s).

Joe Cobb long carried great weight in the Our Gang troupe, and his jolly naiveté brought a special spark to the series that Hal Roach was never able to recapture in "fat-boy" successors, though Roach kept searching up until the last year he produced the series.

Joe Cobb recounts his Our Gang entree: "My dad and I were vacationing in Los Angeles. He thought we'd make the rounds of the studios, and of course we eventually stopped at Hal Roach's. We drove into the parking lot just as the noon whistle blew, and so the casting people took us right out to lunch with them. That same afternoon they put me through wardrobe upstairs, and I started immediately working on a picture called 'A Tough Winter' with Snub Pollard, Marie Mosquini, and Jimmie Finlayson, who played the landlord—naturally evicting everybody. I played Marie's little brother.

"Well, the whole thing left me flabbergasted—just speechless. Good thing it was a silent picture. Charley Parrott (before he was Charley Chase) was the director on this picture, a very patient easy-going kind of guy, and after we finished he installed me with Our Gang, since he was the supervising director for Our Gang at the time (this was all in September of 1922). In fact, Chase was dabbling in everything at the studio then, and I think he used to write some of the gags for the Gang.

"At Roach everybody did a little bit of everything. It was a small studio, but a happy studio. We had a lot of funny people, and because it was a comedy studio and a family studio, you always went to work with a good feeling, and went home the same way. The atmosphere was so informal and friendly, if your family was around one

day, Roach'd try and give them something to do in a picture, extra work, or maybe a small part where they could work you in. Wonderful place. The people were just so nice."

After leaving the Gang, Joe was engaged by the studio again in 1936 to serve as master of ceremonies for Our Gang's publicity tours. He then sought out minor roles in things like Tuxedo Junction for Republic and Where Did You Get That Girl? for Universal before going into defense work as an assembler in 1942. He's been employed at what is now Rockwell International in Los Angeles for some thirty years.

Today he lives across the street from Bob Davis, transportation director at Roach for forty years, and the man who beginning in 1922 used to drive Joe Cobb and the rest of the Gangsters and crew to wherever their Los Angeles location work might take them that day.

Joe never did get much taller than he was in 1930s Our Gang cameos like "Fish Hooky," "Pay as You Exit," and "Reunion Rhythm"; he stands about five feet tall today, though he's a bit slimmer than during his film career.

Most important, Joe Cobb's a real gentleman, and just as likable as ever.

JACKIE CONDON

Born in Los Angeles, California, March 25, 1918. First short, at age four, "Our Gang," last short "Election Day." Appeared in seventy-eight Our Gang comedies over seven years.

One of the original Our Gang, mischief-making, tousle-haired Jackie Condon was a sturdy Rascal regular for nearly the duration of the silents. Through the years he's gathered with other Gang alumni for periodic reunions, but was never able to cash in on his Our Gang success and get back into theatrical work after leaving the series, though he tried comebacks as recently as the 1950s. In a decided coincidence, he works today with Joe Cobb at Rockwell International in Los Angeles.

JOHNNY DOWNS (John Morey Downs)

Born in Brooklyn, New York, October 10, 1913. First short, at age nine, "The Champeen," last short "Chicken Feed." Appeared in twenty-three Our Gang comedies over five years.

Johnny Downs was a shining example of the all-American boy in Hollywood movies for nearly twenty years—although during his Our Gang stint he frequently played a bully.

The son of a Navy lieutenant (Morey H. Downs), Johnny moved to San Diego with his family while still a child, and became interested in acting. With his obliging mother, he made the rounds of Hollywood studios in the early 1920s, and because of his fresh good looks, was cast in small roles. At the Hal Roach studio he was put to

Our Gang past and present gathered for their Fifteenth Anniversary. *Back row,* Allen "Farina" Hoskins, director Gordon Douglas, schoolteacher Fern Carter, Joe Cobb, Mary Kornman, assistant director Hal Roach, Jr., Johnny Downs, director Fred Newmeyer, and Jackie Condon. Front row, Billie "Buckwheat" Thomas, Baby Patsy May, Spanky McFarland, Alfalfa Switzer, and Darla Hood.

work with Charley Chase and Glenn Tryon before being initiated into *Our Gang* as a regular.

Johnny brushed up on his singing and dancing during *Our Gang* vaudeville tours, and after leaving the series, he and Mary Kornman continued to work together onstage. He landed juvenile roles in such Broadway shows as *Growing Pains* and *Strike Me Pink* (with Jimmy Durante) before returning to Hollywood to play Little Boy Blue in Hal Roach's *Babes in Toyland.* Then as a young leading man, he starred in an endless succession of lightweight musicals, including *Pigskin Parade, College Holiday, Junior Prom, Turn off the Moon, Hold That Co-ed, Hawaiian Nights, Melody and Moonlight,* and *Harvest Rhythm.* He returned to Hal Roach Studios for yet another songathon, *All-American Co-ed,* in 1941. Occasional nonsinging roles came his way, in films like *So Red the Rose, Algiers, A Child Is Born,* and *Adam Had Four Sons,* but producers and audiences alike identified Johnny almost exclusively with his campus musicals.

In the 1940s his Hollywood career dried up. Looking back, he once explained, "I was the college boy type, a sort of second generation Buddy Rogers. A war was shaping up ann producers and the public suddenly wanted its heroes to act and look more like Bogart and Cagney." He left California for New York, played in one hit show, *Are You With IT,* then did the best he could (supporting a wife and four children) touring in vaudeville, playing summer stock, doing occasional television work.

In the early 1950s he enjoyed a brief movie comeback, landing roles in *Here Come the Girls, Call me Madam, The stars and Stripes Forever, Cruisin' Down the River,* and *The Caddy.* Since that time he has worked as a television host in California, retaining his boyish good looks even in his 50s.

(Ironically, another fellow with boyish good looks who lives in New York has been successfully identifying himself as Johnny Downs, much to the embarrassment of several authors and TV hosts who have believed the man and featured him in interviews.)

Over the years, Johnny remained friendly with his *Our Gang* co-star Mary Kornman. When he was offered a job in an Audie Murphy movie, *Column South,* he was told he'd have to ride a horse. He quickly called Mary, who coached him at her ranch until his riding was up to par.

Recalling his *Our Gang* days, Johnny Downs sayd, "It was a memorable experience. I think we had a privileged childhood working in those films. It was great fun, and certainly had no ill effects on my life."

A good family man (now a grandfather) who worked hard at his craft, Johnny Downs practiced in real life the virtues he projected for so many years in movies as a clean-cut, all-AMerican boy.

"STYMIE" BEARD (Matthew Beard, Jr.)

Born in Los Angeles, California, January 1, 1925. First short, at age five, "Teacher's Pet," last short "Teacher's Beau". Appeared in thirty-six *Our Gang* comedies over five years (excluding "The Stolen Jools" and the later cameo appearance in "Reunion in Rhythm").

If not Spanky, perhaps *Our Gang*'s best-loved character was (and is) derby-hatted Stymie. His beguiling personality and tantalizing smile brightened every scene he did—and usually stole effortlessly. Stymie often seemed detached, but he could generally outsmart or outmaneuver any adversary. He tossed off snappy dialogue with assurance, and above all could register a shrewd variety of double takes.

It was mid-1930 when some friends of Stymie's father told him Hal Roach was interviewing black kids to replace Farina. The studio had tested an incredible three hundred fifty kids vying for the part before Stymie walked onto the stage, looked around nonchalantly, rolled his big expressive eyes, and prompted Bob McGowan to conclude, "That's who I want, sign him up for five years." They never even got to the screen test.

Instead of the ponderous management meetings that produced stars' names like Rock Hudson, Tab Hunter or

Matthew "Stymie" Beard at Synanon in 1973.

Spanky and Stymie at the Spanky McFarland Celebrity Golf Classic in 1975.

Kitty Litter at other studios, Hal Roach let his director and crew name the *Our Gang* kids, and the names usually meant something. Butch was tough, Chubby was chubby, Porky was too, and so on.

They called Stymie "Hercules" at first, but it didn't stick. Instead, Stymie explains today, "Bob McGowan decided on the name 'Stymie' because I was always in the way. I would get on the set and be so excited and curious over what was going on, looking at the props and gimmicks at the wrong time that I was always underfoot, interfering. And Mr. McGowan used to get frustrated and motion, 'Get that kid out of the way so we can shoot.' So he came up with this line after a while, 'Well boy, this kid's beautiful, but he stymies me all the time.' That's how the name came."

Stymie stayed over five years. They were *Our Gang*'s best years, and some of Stymie's happiest years. "We had fun doing the films," Stymie recalls. "Aside from an occasional scrap, the kids got along very well. It was a wonderful experience."

The magic of movies bestows a degree of immortality, and we can treasure "forever" the frozen illusions and dazzling eternally young faces we visit over and over up on the screen. Sometimes, though, the benignly arrested development can be unsettling when we know what the Fates have dealt our motion-picture favorites. Among other things, it shakes us back to an awareness of our own transience.

When he was graduated from *Our Gang,* where he'd helped support his thirteen brothers and sisters, Stymie entered the public school system in the ghetto section of Los Angeles. He also free-lanced in some twenty features, winning small parts in *Jezebel* with Bette Davis, *Stormy Weather* with Lena Horne, and *Captain Blood* with Errol Flynn (who took him fishing once). Mostly, though, he just wanted to fit in and be accepted as one of the guys. He dropped out of school in the eleventh grade when "the guys" drifted into drugs and street life. His acting background "helped" him here, for he found he'd have to play a role to survive on the streets, too. It was not to be pleasant.

Stymie's mild flirtation with marijuana at age sixteen paved the way to a quarter-century long narcotics-induced nightmare that found him in and out of prisons, trying everything and chasing addiction and degradation most of his adult life. Even outside jail he was never free, a prisoner to his heroin habit, committing small crimes to support it, which only landed him behind bars again.

The many lost years are all a blur for Stymie today.

In the mid-1960s Stymie Beard miraculously resurrected his future—at Synanon, the California community providing a unique alternative life style for drug addicts. He'd staggered into Synanon in desperation, a sick, sick man. He originally intended to stay only two weeks, but endured the agonies of withdrawal symptoms, got himself together again, and wound up staying seven years. Strung out on drugs no longer, he'd made it back and began forging a new life.

One of those happiest for his rehabilitation is his father, a long-time minister in Los Angeles. Mr. Beard is never so happy though, as when Stymie brings his Synanon choir to sing at Church. Stymie exudes, "My father just *glows* when we come to sing. Once again we have a wonderful father-and-son relationship, and especially great birthday celebrations—we were both born on New Year's Day."

Even more recently, Stymie's been making a show-business comeback. He's won roles in features like *Truck Turner* (as a jail guard) and *It's Good to Be Alive* (the Roy Campanella story), and TV shows like *Good Times, Maude,* and *Sanford and Son* with Redd Foxx. He's also had speaking engagements and he's done some *Our Gang* commercials and personal appearances with Spanky McFarland, whom he hadn't seen for thirty-five years.

Not content basking in the glow of rediscovery, Stymie harnesses the attention he's received to share his own horror story in the hopes that he can save others from traveling the narcotics road he took. "It was the neighborhood, the ghetto," Stymie says. "It had nothing to do with my Hollywood experience."

Stymie the Little Rascal is always happy in the face of troubles, always saying that indefinably "right thing" that makes audiences applaud its agreement. Childhood litheness has given way to rather expansive girth, but Stymie the fifty-some-year-old man has enduring appeal too; he talks freely about his past problems, and he's as ingratiating as ever. The deep warmth and the twinkle in his eye are still there, and he's an inspiration to anyone who may someday try to recover from adversity and despair.

Strangely enough, Stymie's younger brother Bobbie, who played "Cotton," and who never said a word in all the *Our Gang* films he made, is today an auctioneer for a Los Angeles auction dealer. Stymie reports he's *quite* a speaker today.

"SPANKY" McFARLAND (George Robert Phillips McFarland)

Born in Dallas, Texas, October 2, 1928. First short, at age three, "Free Eats," last short "Unexpected Riches." Appeared in ninety-five *Our Gang* comedies over eleven years.

It's hard to believe Spanky McFarland is edging middle age. These days Spanky is happily married and lives near Fort Worth, Texas, where as George McFarland he is area manager of the commercial contract division of Philco-Ford television. He's very good at what he does, and proud of the fact that "Nobody buys TV sets from me because I'm Spanky McFarland." He doesn't deny he's Spanky, but doesn't broadcast it, either. Philco-Ford hired George, and they promoted George, not Spanky.

As far as he's concerned, "Spanky" happened a long time ago. "That's dust," he says, and he trades on the Spanky name only for occasional weekend personal appearances at college campuses around the country. His in-person *Our Gang* reminiscences, however, are always on *his* terms, and represent the extent of his show-biz comeback aspirations. He's happy in the business world, and while he's still "show business oriented," being in sales, he insists he is glad to be out of the theatrical fray with all its headaches and insecurity.

(Spanky, too, is plagued by impostors—quite a few of them. A 1974 feature entitled *Moonrunners* boasted a "Spanky McFarland" in its cast. It was not *Our Gang*'s Spanky. Nor did the real Spanky have any affiliation with the rock group of the late 1960s called "Spanky and Our Gang." Darla Hood says that over the years five different impostors have introduced themselves to her as Spanky. Apparently for some, pretending to be Spanky McFarland is an attractive calling in life.)

Meeting George "Spanky" McFarland today, one is impressed by two things. First, his prosperous, well-groomed appearance. Still stocky, and standing about five feet five, he dresses stylishly, and *looks* successful. "Not many people recognize me," he says. Second, one can't help but be struck by his confidently self-sufficient attitude. He's personable, engaging, and candid, but he's a "loner," and he likes it that way.

He was evidently independent as a kid, too. "Interviewers never got anywhere with Spanky," newspaper reporter Paul Harrison wrote. "He'll shake hands politely enough. But after that, he's about as garrulous as Garbo. It doesn't seem to be shyness. He's just bored."

Called before the cameras, he'd grumble, "Aw, nuts." When he understood the scene and was ready for shooting, he'd remark, "Okay, Toots."

Gordon Douglas describes Spanky as having been "a kid with a good brain that the other youngsters looked up to." Bob McGowan called him "a natural," declaring at the time that "he's the first genius I've directed since Jackie Cooper."

Genius or not, he was a kid like most kids. One 1936 news story reported, "Spanky still gets spanked occasionally. Sometimes for swearing. Adults around the Roach studio have been trained for years to avoid profanity, but the kid star has picked up an impressive vocabulary somewhere."

While still with *Our Gang,* Spank did a fair amount of loan-out work in features: *Day of Reckoning* (1933) for M-G-M; *Miss Fane's Baby Is Stolen* (1934) with Baby LeRoy for Paramount; George Stevens's *Kentucky Kernels* (1935), starring Wheeler and Woolsey (Spanky played "Spanky") for RKO-Radio; *O'Shaughnessy's Boy* (1935) with Jackie Cooper and Wallace Beery for M-G-M; the early Technicolor film *Trail of the Lonesome Pine* (1936) for Paramount; *Varsity Show* (1937) with Dick Powell (Spank was billed as George McFarland) for Warner Bros.; and *Peck's Bad Boy with the Circus* (1938) featuring Billy Gilbert and Edgar Kennedy, for RKO.

Right after leaving *Our Gang* there was an incidental role reuniting Spanky and Alfalfa in Republic's *Johnny Doughboy* (1943), but then the parts dried up.

Between 1944 and 1966, when he joined Philco Ford, George McFarland's life took quite a few twists. He moved back to Texas, joined the Air Force, received a hardship discharge, and then found himself broke—after having worked hard for twenty-one of his twenty-four years. "It was the worst time of my life," he says in heavy Texas drawl, "but it taught me a lot."

Picking up the pieces, he worked at a soft drink plant, a hamburger stand, and even made popsicles. Then came a 1958 stint as host of a television show in Tulsa, Oklahoma, running *Our Gang* movies, wearing beanie, short pants, and all. He was seeking an opportunity to show he was a competent actor, but nobody would give him one. To casting directors and three generations of moviegoers, he was "still a chubby little boy with a lisping voice," he lamented at the time. "You'd think, with a name like mine, I'd be a natural for a network kiddie show emcee. But uh-uh."

Mike Douglas reunites Darla Hood and Spanky McFarland on his TV show in late 1973.

Back to a dizzying variety of nondescript occupations outside the entertainment business: he sold wine, then appliances in Oklahoma, got into oil promoting, the restaurant business, other things. Finally his flair for sales led to ultimate success at Philco-Ford.

Spanky has mostly fond but hazy recollections of the series. "I had a ball," he'll admit grudgingly. He has every right to be embittered about getting no residuals for TV reruns, but he's not. "I have no regrets. Even though it was a job, we had a pretty good time making those comedies. As a kid I had most everything I wanted, and we had a good life. When it was over it was over.

"I wouldn't take a million dollars for the experience, and I wouldn't take a penny to do it again. If I knew then what I know now, I wouldn't have done it. I would have finished school and gone to college, and by now I'd be the president of some corporation.

"But I do have to admit when I walk down the aisle at the beginning of our [personal appearance] shows and the folks stand up and cheer, I get all choked up. It's nice to be remembered."

There is not a whole lot of "Spanky the kid star" left in George McFarland. But that's not altogether a bad thing. Certainly not for him; he's doing quite nicely, thank you. Besides, in a world full of people pretending to be something they're not, it's refreshing to find a guy without any pretense like George McFarland. He speaks his mind, but he's sincere. He's a man's man, and he's been his own man all his life.

Yet much like little Spanky, he's still plucky, talented, pleasantly grumpy, "in charge," and likable withal.

For the record, Spank's younger brother Tom worked irregularly and without fanfare in *Our Gang* nearly as long as Spanky did, but he seldom had lines, and usually served only as an extra. He lives in Dallas.

HARRY SPEAR

Born in Los Angeles, California, December 16, 1921. First short, at age five, "Chicken Feed," last short "Bouncing Babies." Appeared in thirty-one *Our Gang* comedies over two years.

Information about Harry Spear ends with his studio bio, which credits only a few Buck Jones Westerns for Fox before joining the Rascals.

What's worse, when an *Our Gang* impostor died some years ago, one of the wire services mistakenly printed a photo of Harry Spear with the obit, muddying the waters all the more.

So who can say what's become of Harry Spear? All other *Our Gang* alumni have completely lost track of him, and efforts to trace reports that he'd become either a banker or a surgeon were unavailing.

DARLA HOOD (Darla Jean Hood)

Born in Leedey, Oklahoma, November 4, 1931. First short, at age four, "Our Gang Follies of 1936," last short "Wedding Worries." Appeared in fifty *Our Gang* comedies over six years.

Her mother made up the name Dorla, then somebody at the studio misspelled it Darla; everyone liked the name, and it stuck. Since then lots of parents have liked "Darla," too, and named their daughters for *Our Gang*'s heartthrob. Darla named her own daughter Darla Jo.

Her father was a banker, but her mother encouraged Darla's talents with singing and dancing lessons in nearby Oklahoma City. Her teacher took special interest in Darla, bringing her along on a trip to New York City, where one night at the Edison Hotel in Times Square the band leader invited her to sing and conduct the orchestra. The crowd loved it. Roach casting director Joe Rivkin happened to be dining in the audience, and he arranged for an immediate screen test in New York; Hal Roach liked the test, whisked Darla to Hollywood, signed her to a seven-year pact beginning at $75 a week, and had her hastily written into "Our Gang Follies of 1936," by then well along in production.

From then on she was a fixture as *Our Gang*'s leading lady, and within the year she was eagerly snapped up for jobs in other units around the Roach lot: Charley Chase used her in *Neighborhood House,* and Stan Laurel liked her radiant innocence and cast her in the title role for *The Bohemian Girl.*

When six years later she was graduated from a career as *Our Gang*'s sweetheart, there came a difficult period of adjustment. "I had trouble associating with people not in show business," she explains. Like most *Little Rascals* alumni she found it hard to understand why the world had stopped worshipping her at twelve. She was well able to cope with her plunge from the limelight, however, and while never regaining full-flung stardom, she has been quietly successful over the past two decades as a behind-the-scenes performer in the entertainment business. "Quietly," though, is perhaps a misnomer.

As a teen-ager she formed a vocal group with her first husband called "Darla Hood and the Enchanters." They did background and off-scene music for lots of late 1940s films, including Joseph L. Mankiewicz's classic *A Letter to Three Wives* in 1948, and also Ken Murray's Academy Award winning *Bill and Coo.* This led to an audition for *Ken Murray's Blackouts,* which turned out to be the longest-running stage play in the history of the theater. During runs at the El Capitan in Hollywood and the Ziegfeld Theatre on Broadway, Darla managed to find time to work as a featured artist on both Ken Murray's television series, and Paul Whiteman's program as well.

Since then, she's had quite a range of experience. She was a regular on Merv Griffin's one-time ABC radio show; she's written song lyrics, and as a songstress has cut nearly a dozen recordings; her nightclub act has brought her bookings at the Copacabana in New York, the Cocoanut Grove in Hollywood, and the Sahara in Las Vegas; and movie roles have included *The Bat* (1959), where she was cast as a pretty secretary in this Vincent Price thriller.

Groucho Marx and Jack Benny both enjoyed *Our Gang,* and Darla did a number of guest shots with each on their television shows in the 1950s. Benny would feature a periodic *Our Gang* sketch with himself as Alfalfa, Don Wilson as Spanky, Eddie "Rochester" Anderson as Buckwheat, and Dennis Day as Waldo. Sometimes funny, it was always interesting.

In 1957 she married artists' manager and music publisher Jose Granson, and about this time began cashing in on her unusual three octave range voice, doing voice-over and on-camera television commercials. Noisy ones. Tons of them. She's one of the Campbell Soup kids, she does the Tiny Tears doll voice and the Chicken-of-the-Sea mermaid jingle. Some weird things, too. Her career as a vocal impressionist has brought her jobs as an abominable snowman, a salad, and one time an ad agency called to ask if she could do the voice for a sore toe. She thought the guy was putting her on, and asked him, "So which foot, left or right?" The caller answered, "I don't know, I'll find out and get back to you." He did both, and she got the job.

Her trick voice specialty has also brought her work dubbing current television shows and feature films, *The Towering Inferno* among them.

Living currently in North Hollywood, she's still cute and cuddly at only five feet one and one-half, and unmistakable as the Darla Hood of *Our Gang,* yet she too has been troubled by impostors. Like the others, her impostors appear to be boobs, yet so must be the news reporters who print their fabricated stories. They are hilarious, nearly everything is wrong, and one couldn't make up something half as funny—unless of course he or she was a fraud too.

One dear soul in Philadelphia, claiming to be Darla Hood, went to the trouble of finding out Darla's parents' names, and was even giving reporters her grandmother's name. An irrefutable presumption of identity, right? No one was so perplexed about this poor soul's aberrations as Darla's grandmother, who sent Darla one of the articles with a note inscribed, "I'm *not* this lady's grandmother. Who is she?"

Darla is amused, too, by the glut of fan mail she still receives. In recent years it's been mostly from young adults, but adoring preadolescent boys write too, proposing marriage, "when you grow up." Noting the resurgent interest in the *Our Gang* series over television, one fan recently informed her, "You've been revived again." Another wrote, "I've loved you since I was six, and now I'm nine." Darla signs stills for admiring youngsters, "From one Little Rascal to another."

Darla holds happy memories as *Our Gang*'s leading lady. "I had a very happy childhood," she says. "It may sound like a strange life—but since it was my life for as long as I can remember, I loved it." She was sometimes terrified of prankish Alfalfa, who was a big tease and made her the object of some practical jokes as he grew older, but she enjoyed Spanky's company, commenting, "Spanky was always delightful, and still is."

She notes, too, that working for Hal Roach was something very special: "At Christmas time, Mr. Roach would ask each kid individually what he wanted as a gift. It was an annual *Our Gang* tradition, and you could have anything you wanted. Mr. Roach would find it or build it. One year I asked for a doll house, and he misunderstood and thought I meant a playhouse. So the prop department constructed a ten-by-twelve-foot playhouse that they moved into my backyard with a moving truck. It was completely decorated and furnished with my-sized furniture that I could arrange and rearrange. We made it into a neighborhood clubhouse and used to sleep out overnight. It was fantastic."

Darla with Groucho Marx on his TV show.

Don Wilson as Spanky, Jack Benny as Alfalfa, and Darla as herself in a comic re-creation of *Our Gang*.

MARY ANN JACKSON

Born in Los Angeles, California, January 14, 1923. First short, at age five, "Crazy House," last short "Fly My Kite." Appeared in thirty-two *Our Gang* comedies over three years.

Having starred with Raymond McKee and Ruth Hiatt in Mack Sennett's *Smith Family* series for two years, Mary Ann Jackson brought her Dutch-cut hair, freckles and delightfully impish characterization to *Our Gang* in 1928. A tomboy and happily never a "leading lady," she stayed through 1931, though her mother and younger brother Dick remained on the Roach lot doing extra work and bit parts through at least 1933 (they both appear in "A Lad an' a Lamp").

As a kid, Jackie Cooper admits to having been "desperately in love" with Mary Ann Jackson, who at last report, in 1960, was living in Santa Monica, California, with her husband (not Jackie Cooper) and two children.

DOROTHY "ECHO" DeBORBA (Dorothy Betty Jean DeBorba)

Born in Los Angeles, California, 1925. First short, at age five, "Pups Is Pups," last short "Mush and Milk." Appeared in twenty-four *Our Gang* comedies over three years.

A little bundle of curls, pep, and mischief was Dorothy DeBorba. Though never once addressed as such on screen, her official studio nickname was "Echo," since in early Rascals pictures she was cast as Chubby's younger sister, with a smart-alecky compulsion to repeat as best she could whatever he'd say. "Teacher's Pet" and "Love Business" are notable examples.

She came from a show-business background. Her mother was a singer-dancer, and her father was a drummer in Paul Whiteman's band.

In 1975 the San Francisco *Examiner* reported she was very happy working as a senior clerk in the school of journalism at UC-Berkeley, where she'd been for nine years since obtaining a divorce in Billings, Montana, and moving back up the coast with her two children.

Of her *Our Gang* days she says, "It wasn't really much fun, working every day and going to school besides. By the age of ten, of course, the movie careers of most of us were finished."

"WHEEZER" HUTCHINS (Bobby Hutchins)

Born March 29, 1925. First short, at age two, "Baby Brother," last short "Mush and Milk." Appeared in fifty-eight *Our Gang* comedies over six years.

Artless scene-stealer "Wheezer" joined *Our Gang* from Gus Meins's competing *Buster Brown* comedies in 1927. Most of the kids who worked with Wheezer remember surprisingly little about him today, and even less is known about his personal life after leaving the Gang. He was killed in a training camp accident during World War II.

Our Gang in 1931: Farina Hoskins, Pete the Pup, Chubby Chaney, Jackie Cooper, Mary Ann Jackson, Dorothy De Borba, and Wheezer Hutchins.

MARY KORNMAN

Born in Idaho Falls, Idaho, 1917. First short, at age five, "Young Sherlocks," last short, "The Fourth Alarm." Appeared in forty-one *Our Gang* comedies over four years (excluding two return appearances during the 1930s).

Precocious, blond-haired Mary Kornman was the daughter of Hal Roach's still-photo cameraman, Gene Kornman (later one of the foremost Broadway showgirl photographers in the 1930s and 1940s). Hal Roach liked Mary and cast her as leading lady in the series soon after it was launched. Her younger sister Mildred Jean was recruited for the series at the end of Mary's stint, but never caught on as Mary had.

As an *Our Gang* alumna, like so many others, she toured in vaudeville for three years, with time out to attend Beverly Hills High School. Teaming with Mickey Daniels in 1929, they made one of the funniest *Voice of Hollywood* shorts, then returned to the Hal Roach lot the following year to co-star in *The Boy Friends* series for two years, and stayed around for special *Our Gang* homecomings in "Fish Hooky" (1933) and "Reunion in Rhythm" (1937). Curiously, as a child Mary had the mature assurance and occasional sauciness of actresses years her senior, while as a petite (five feet two) young lady in the 1930s, she projected a naive, childlike quality that was perhaps less appealing, though not without its own charm. In either case, she was often alluring.

Attempts to establish herself as an ingenue in the 1930s led to occasional good roles in major films like *College Humor* at Paramount (photographed by her first husband, noted Hollywood cinematographer Leo Tover, with credits including *The Day The Earth Stood Still, I'm No Angel,* and *The Sun Also Rises*). She did win leading-lady assignments in some Bing Crosby shorts, but mainly she worked in low-budget films like *Picture Brides, The Quitter, The Calling of Dan Matthews,* and *Queen of the Jungle,* a laughable cheapie in which she had the title role. In one big picture, *Flying Down to Rio,* the first Astaire-Rogers film, pretty little Mary Kornman sizes up her distaff competition and delivers this deathless line, "What have those South Americans got below the equator that we don't have?" One of her more unusual roles had Mary as the love interest for John Wayne in an unremarkable B Western, *Desert Trail.* Separating from Tover, she retired to private life, and married Ralph McCutcheon, who supplied livestock to Hollywood studios (they owned the TV program *Fury*). Mary became an expert horsewoman herself. In the 1960s she told Vernon Scott, "It was fun being a Gang member. It was play. I have no regrets. . . . We didn't have to be talented. Just kids. All we did was make big eyes and do reactions—which is natural for kids. . . . I think we had a privileged childhood working in those films."

On June 1, 1973, she died at age fifty-six in Glendale, California, of cancer.

Mary with Edward Chandler and John Wayne in the 1935 Western *Desert Trail.*

JAY R. SMITH

First short, "Boys Will Be Joys," last short "Moan & Groan, Inc." Appeared in thirty-six *Our Gang* comedies over four years.

Arrow-narrow Jay R. Smith was *Our Gang*'s original skinny kid—he could tread water in a hose. A recent letter from Jay R. disclosed that he was signed to replace Mickey Daniels in the series since he rivaled Mickey for freckles.

After *Our Gang,* he had a few walk-ons in Roach's *The Boy Friends* series, then left motion pictures. He lives today in Kailua, Hawaii.

MICKEY DANIELS (Richard Daniels, Jr.)

Born in Rock Springs, Wyoming, 1916. First short, at age six, "Young Sherlocks," last short "Thundering Fleas." Appeared in forty-nine *Our Gang* comedies over four years (not counting three appearances during the 1930s).

In typical Hal Roach Studios fashion, freckle-faced Mickey Daniels was recommended for the *Our Gang* troupe by Roach's still photographer, the father of Mary Kornman! The Danielses and the Kornmans were family friends. The ever-animated Mickey Daniels and his character actor dad signed their first contracts with Hal Roach in 1922. Mickey was paid $37.50 per week during his first six months on the lot, but was up to $175 by 1924. Richard Daniels, Sr., started at $5 a day, and often joined his son in front of the *Our Gang* cameras. Either Mickey or his dad worked in most all of Harold Lloyd's features for Hal Roach. Mickey's brother Leonard joined the Roach forces too, working in the transportation department for at least twenty years.

During high school, Mickey returned to movies, and to Hal Roach, for *The Boy Friends* series, fifteen short sub-

Scene from the *Boy Friends* comedy *Doctor's Orders* with Dorothy Granger, Mickey Daniels, Gertie Messinger, Dave Sharpe, Grady Sutton, and Mary Kornman.

jects made between 1930 and 1932 which depicted an adolescent kind of *Our Gang* and which reunited Mickey with Mary Kornman, as well as a number of other silent *Our Gang* stars. Later, Mickey and Mary got together again for a pair of nostalgic *Our Gang* shorts: "Fish Hooky" (1933) and "Reunion in Rhythm" (1937). Three years after the demise of *The Boy Friends,* some of the stars regrouped to continue their misadventures as *The Young*

Friends in a trio of inexpensive states-rights features, each shot in less than a week: "Adventurous Knights," "Roaring Roads," and "A Social Error." The cast was composed of Mickey Daniels, David Sharpe, another *Our Gang* alumnus, and his then wife, Gertie Messenger, herself star of the Fox *Sunshine Kiddies,* the original kid-picture series made during the mid-teens.

Also during the 1930s, Mickey Daniels became a familiar face, and voice (through his inimitable horse-whinny laugh) in such feature films as *This Day and Age, Magnificent Obsession, Pennies From Heaven, Strike me Pink, The Great Ziegfeld,* and then in the early 1940s, *Li'l Abner* with Buster Keaton, and *Miss Polly* with ZaSu Pitts. After the war, he was disenchanted with films, and entered the construction engineering field in Pearl Harbor, which eventually took him to Africa, "in search of the good life." He's been traveling the globe ever since. In late 1966 an Associated Press reporter caught up with him in Tasmania, where he was materials supervisor for the Bechtel Pacific Corp., constructing an iron ore mine. Reported as fifty years old, he was using the name Mike Daniels. "I have a home, a daughter, a grandson, and an ex-wife in Los Angeles, but I don't get home often," he said.

Joe Cobb says he hasn't seen Mickey Daniels since a 1950s *Our Gang* TV program reunion.

Mickey Daniels today.

NORMAN "CHUBBY" CHANEY (Norman Myers Chaney)

Born in Baltimore, Maryland, January 18, 1918. First short, at age eleven, "Railroadin'," last short "Fly My Kite." Appeared in eighteen *Our Gang* comedies over two years.

When Joe Cobb showed signs of outgrowing *Our Gang,* Hal Roach decided to find another rotund youngster to replace him, and to get as much publicity mileage as possible out of the search, a nationwide contest was held.

Naturally, it is difficult to separate fact from fancy in researching a publicity stunt like this, but Norman Chaney reportedly topped a list of 20,000 entrants in the 1928 competition. When Jack Roach, the studio casting director, broke the news to Norman, he blurted out, "Mister, are you just kidding me because I'm fat?" Roach wasn't kidding, and "Chubby" Chaney launched his screen career in early 1929, an "overnight star."

The changing of the guard was celebrated in publicity photos and stories, and an entire film, "Boxing Gloves," was contrived to feature the two fat-boys of *Our Gang* before Joe Cobb retired and Chubby took his place. Not even a full year younger than Joe Cobb when he came to Roach, Norman was three feet eleven inches tall and weighed in at one hundred thirteen pounds.

His natural flair for comic dialogue and open, friendly personality made him an instant hit in *Our Gang,* playing Nero in "Shivering Shakespeare," fighting a duel in "The First Seven Years," and paying a courtship call on schoolteacher Miss Crabtree in "Love Business," among other comedy chores.

But at the end of the 1930–31 season, Chubby was dropped from *Our Gang;* he was getting too old, and too big, to be cute any more. Apparently Norman's mother and father (neither with a show-business background—his dad was an electrical worker) did not attempt to channel their son into a more extensive movie career; he returned to his native Maryland to continue school and live with his family.

His weight continued to increase as the boy grew into his teens, expanding to about three hundred pounds. In 1935 he became ill and underwent an operation for a glandular ailment at Johns Hopkins Hospital; his weight dropped to one hundred thirty-six pounds, and he remained gravely ill, dying on May 29, 1936 at the home of his grandparents in Baltimore. He was eighteen.

According to a *New York Times* obituary, Norman's grades in school when he joined *Our Gang* were excellent, except in deportment. "That's low," he explained, "because I make the other kids laugh so easily." Just as he did in *Our Gang.*

TOMMY "BUTCH" BOND

Born in Dallas, Texas, September 16, 1927. First short, at age four, "Spanky," last short "Bubbling Trouble." Appeared in twenty-seven *Our Gang* comedies over eight years.

As *Our Gang's* pliable bully "Butch," Tommy Bond is one of the series' handful of truly memorable characters. The notes for "Glove Taps" trace his growth from a soft-spoken peripheral Our Ganger to full-fledged glowering meanie, but it's worth adding here that with the possible exception of Farina, Tommy Bond is the only Little Rascal who got better at what he was doing as he grew older.

Elsewhere around the Roach lot during the 1930s, he worked with Charley Chase on *The Cracked Iceman* and *I'll Take Vanilla;* he's the brat playing football in the apartment in Laurel & Hardy's *Block-Heads,* and like

Norman "Chubby" Chaney is initiated into Our Gang by Joe Cobb
and the kids, while director Bob McGowan tries to avert trouble.

most everyone else in *Our Gang* in 1934, he did the Eddie
Cantor musical *Kid Millions* over at Goldwyn, appearing
in the color sequence at the ice cream factory.

Between Rascal roles he free-lanced in quite a few Columbia B features (like *City Streets*) and short subjects
(starring comics like Andy Clyde and Monty Collins). He
worked a lot of network radio programs, too, with performers such as Bert Lahr, Joe E. Brown, and Edward
Everett Horton.

His favorite role came in a 1944 Republic programmer
Man From Frisco, with Michael O'Shea and Dan Duryca.
He enjoyed it because it was a sympathetic role, "and it
gave me a chance to play somebody other than a villain,"
he says.

After the war he had small parts in *Tokyo Joe* (1949)
with Humphrey Bogart, *Any Number Can Play* (1949)
with Clark Gable, and *Call Me Mister* (1951) with Betty
Grable. His most interesting roles, though, came in two
Superman serials, and PRC's *Gas House Kids* series.

Tommy played boyish star photographer Jimmy Olsen
of the Metropolis Daily Planet in a pair of fifteen episode
chapter plays for Columbia: *Superman* (1948), and *Atom
Man vs. Superman* (1950). Noel Neill portrayed Lois
Lane, and Kirk Alyn was mild-mannered reporter Clark
Kent, also known to everyone else in the world but Lois
and Jimmy as Superman.

In 1947 he'd been reunited with Alfalfa for two pleasant
low-budget features: *The Gas House Kids Go West* and
The Gas House Kids in Hollywood. They were vehicles for
Alfalfa, and Tommy was cast as his chummy sidekick,
totally repudiating their previous *Our Gang* adversary
relationship.

On film, Alfalfa still looked like Alfalfa, but Tommy,
now the shorter of the two, didn't suggest much of his
former wizened, puckish character. In the Gang, Hal
Roach wanted the kids to cultivate long hair styles, so
they'd look like moppets. After the service, though,

Tommy's hair was close-cropped, and he just didn't resemble tough guy "Butch" anymore.

Today, Tommy Bond talks warmly of his off-screen
relationship with Alfalfa. "We were the best of friends,
knew each other for many years. Alfalfa was just a coun-

Young adult portrait of Tommy Bond.

try boy. I don't think he ever wore shoes till he came out
to California and broke into the Gang. We used to go coon
hunting together, believe it or not, in Topanga Canyon.
He had some coon dogs and we'd put them in the trunk of
his Cadillac and we'd go coon hunting all night. We always had a lot of fun together, as kids and after we grew
up, an awful lot of fun."

In 1951 Tommy Bond was graduated from Los Angeles
State College with a Bachelor of Arts degree in theater
arts. Two weeks later he began working for KTTV in
Hollywood, Channel 11. Today he's in charge of proper-

Tommy Bond as Jimmy Olsen, with Perry White (Pierre Watkin), Superman (Kirk Alyn), and Lois Lane (Noel Neill) in the Columbia *Superman* serial.

ties there and at the parent corporation Metromedia's Los Angeles production center, serving its scores of outlets across the country. He's also happily married to a former Miss California.

Explaining his career decision, Tommy says, "I decided I was going to get out of the acting bit and go into television because there's a lot more security to the business on the other side of the camera. Some of the kids couldn't make that transition, though, because a lot of them had ego problems. Myself, I could never stand the thought of being inactive, and sitting by the phone waiting for an agent to call with a part, and I love the business, so I decided I'd get on the other side of it."

Reminiscing about his *Our Gang* career, he says today, "The Roach studio was like a big family. It was a small studio compared to Metro and Twentieth, yet it was just like a big family. My mother and grandmother were on the lot with me one day, watching filming for the Gang, and the assistant director came running over from the Thelma Todd-Patsy Kelly comedy they were doing and shouted, 'Hey, we need some more extras for the audience over here—do you want to be extras in the picture?' It sounded like fun to them, so they went over and did it. It was almost like a carnival atmosphere. Laurel & Hardy had a little car that they drove around the lot, a funny little car for visiting everyone. They were really great guys. And Charley Chase—there was a prince, a real sweetheart of a guy.

"There was a kind of a flavor to the movies in those days, and particularly those Roach movies, that they've lost now. Now it's all a factory, a real factory. But back then the movie business was the only business out here. No industry, no conglomerates, just the movies and radio. That was it. Hollywood was it. There was nothing else.

"I wish somebody could duplicate that same feeling in movies today, but they're not doing it. I don't think it's possible anymore, really. I guess it's the times we're living in nowadays that change people, even though I think the whole country wants to get back to those kinds of films and days again."

Tommy Bond, Alfalfa Switzer, and bony friend in *The Gas House Kids in Hollywood* (1947).

"ALFALFA" SWITZER (Carl Switzer)

Born in Paris, Illinois, August 8, 1927. First short, at age seven, "Beginner's Luck," last short "Kiddie Cure." Appeared in sixty-one *Our Gang* comedies over six years.

Carl Switzer and his older brother Harold had won quite a little recognition singing at auctions and other functions near their parents' farm in Illinois, so when visiting their grandparents in California, it made sense to seek an audition at the Hal Roach plant. One needed a pass to get inside, though, something the Switzers didn't have. However, just outside the studio gate was the Our Gang Cafe, the commissary cafeteria where everyone on the lot ate, and which was open to the public. So the boys marched in one noon, began performing their hillbilly harmonizing and captivated everybody, including Hal Roach, who that day had them hastily written into the current *Our Gang* picture, aptly titled "Beginner's Luck."

Harold was nicknamed both "Slim" and "Deadpan." As an Illinois farm boy, "Alfalfa" was perfect for Carl. It's a name Will Rogers had used for one of his country characters in the silent series he'd done for Hal Roach.

Alfalfa's trademarks were his unpredictably squeaky singing voice, his bug-eyed double-take, and his unruly cowlick, waxed to stand up straight under the studio lights. Coupled with a load of personality and talent, Alfalfa captured the imagination of American movie-goers like few other child stars have done before or since.

Leaving *Our Gang,* Alfalfa's career soon went into eclipse, though he did star in a picture marking Elizabeth Taylor's debut, *There's One Born Every Minute,* then worked with a few *Our Gang* veterans in Republic's *Barnyard Follies,* and starred again in *The Great Mike.* He was the hub of two low-budget series of program features designed to capitalize on his *Our Gang* background, one called *The Reg'lar Fellers,* and the other, in the late 1940s, *The Gas House Kids,* which reunited Alfalfa with his long time *Our Gang* adversary Tommy "Butch" Bond.

His only work in really important features came in bit roles. He was given an incidental part in Leo McCarey's *Going my Way* (1944); he had a run-on in *It's a Wonderful Life* (1946), and he was a bellhop in *State of the Union* (1948), both films by Frank Capra, who'd written for *Our Gang* in the 1920s. Then he was a messenger in *A Letter to Three Wives* (1948), a busboy in the Tracy-Hepburn vehicle *Pat and Mike* (1952), and a co-pilot in John Wayne's *The High and the Mighty* (1954).

Also in 1954 Alfalfa played a century-old Indian in William Wellman's *Track of the Cat.* Two years later he won a recurring role in Roy Rogers's TV show, and then in 1958 he had a nice featured part in his final film, Stanley Kramer's engrossing *The Defiant Ones.* As the picture went into release, Alfalfa told reporter Erskine Johnson, "I look just like I did when I was a kid. It's hard for a child actor to start working again. I've never played a part over nineteen. I'm always a teen-ager and there haven't been many jobs until recently. I'll see how this turns out. If this doesn't do it for me, nothing will. I go all the way through the picture."

Through the years, Alfalfa would augment his acting income by tending bar, and serving as a fishing and big-game hunting guide in Northern California. Henry Fonda and Roy Rogers were regular customers. Switzer would haunt movie producers' offices for acting assignments, but as Darla Hood recounts, "They used to say to him, 'Hey, Alfalfa, sing off-key for us.' It used to drive him crazy."

Tragedy began stalking Alfalfa Switzer. In January of 1958 an unknown assailant shot and wounded him as he climbed into his car. The ambush was never resolved. Thirteen months later, in 1959, at age thirty-one, Alfalfa Switzer was shot to death in a fray over $50 allegedly owed him by his ex-partner in the big-game hunting business. The shooting was ruled justifiable homicide at the coroner's inquest. Alfalfa had threatened his ex-partner with a knife.

Carl "Alfalfa" Switzer at age twenty.

It was a sad ending for someone who'd brought so much laughter to others.

"FARINA" HOSKINS (Allen Clayton Hoskins, Jr.)

Born in Boston, Massachusetts, August 9, 1920. First short, at age one, "Fire Fighters," last short "Fly My Kite." Appeared in one hundred five *Our Gang* comedies over nine years (excluding "The Stolen Jools" and the later cameo role in "Fish Hooky").

Reportedly named for a breakfast cereal because a Roach studio exec thought he was as chubby and agreeable as breakfast "mush," Farina appeared in more *Our Gang* comedies than anyone else in the series. He worked in all but two of the silent shorts and, since he was skillful with dialogue, made two seasons of talkies as well.

In part, his longevity is attributable to timing: he started at less than two fingers of age, supposedly having been discovered in Watts by Ernie Morrison and his father. A more important reason was the youngster's enduring popularity. Farina and Joe Cobb had been the two most popular Our Gangers before the advent of sound—both with movie audiences and with the boss, Hal Roach, who comments today, "They were both excellent, and so well-behaved, too. But I think Farina particularly was one of the finest natural actors we had in the Gang. He could cry great big tears in just a few seconds. You'd think his heart was breaking, then they'd cut the camera and he'd be back playing again."

Farina was called on to deliver his sobbing routine even in the last Rascals film he made, "Fly My Kite," a real two-handkerchief picture. He finally left the series because, as quoted in a 1975 newspaper interview, "I was too big, my voice changed, and I was no longer a cute little black kid." His last Hal Roach contract called for compensation of $350 a week, much more than anyone else was getting. Most everyone in the Gang started at $40 per week.

After his *Our Gang* swan song cameo in "The Stolen Jools," the first part he took was in one of Tiffany's single-reel *Voice of Hollywood* shorts, this intriguing

Allen Clayton (Farina) Hoskins in the 1950s.

episode (number 13) also featuring Jackie Cooper, Thelma Todd and John Wayne. Farina was the studio emcee. Then he repudiated his *Our Gang* trademark for a role supporting Joe E. Brown in Warner Bros.' feature comedy *You Said a Mouthful:* he cut off the upswept pigtails he'd worn for movie cameras since 1922. After playing "Smoke" in *Mayor of Hell* (1933) with James Cagney, parts became hard to win. With his younger sister Jannie (who'd done more than a score of Rascals pictures herself), Farina reportedly developed a vaudeville act, and did movie bit roles between engagements (e.g., he has one scene shaking hands with William Powell in M-G-M's 1936 feature *After the Thin Man*). Through the years he retained an *Our Gang* affiliation, turning out for reunion parties at the studio, and even participating in the Gang's 1936 personal appearance tour.

Shortly came the war. *Time* magazine juxtaposed "then and now" photos showing a tiny Farina with melting grin and a husky close-cropped army private named Allen Clay Hoskins.

After service in the South Pacific, it was back to Hal Roach Studios auditioning for a featured part in Roach's *Amos 'n' Andy* television series. He didn't get it. Al Hoskins had majored in drama at Los Angeles City College, but acting jobs were scarce.

Appearing on the *Our Gang* reunion episode of TV's *You Asked for It* series in the early 1950s, Farina was asked if he was still in theatrical work. "Well, not now," he said with that smile that never dimmed. "I was for a while, but about four years ago I decided I'd like to eat regular."

Hoskins then went into "hiding" as he calls it. He began working with mentally handicapped people. "I didn't get to do what I wanted to do," he recently explained, "so I did something I could live with."

In Los Angeles his *Our Gang* past kept intruding and threatening his present, so he moved near San Francisco, changed careers, and began quietly building a distinguished record of achievement for himself in the rehabilitation field. A licensed psychological technician, Al Hoskins ("Not Farina," he'll tell you) is presently supervising director of adult workshop programs at the Alameda County Association for the Mentally Retarded. He's resolutely proud of finding fulfillment without once trading on the name of Farina.

"Give me the rejects," Hoskins says. "I can work with people who are nobodies. I love these people."

Married with six children, he's also currently involved in a radio series, and heads up his own company for creative projects, called Alfran.

In his words, he "stayed buried for a long, long time," but accepted public recognition again in 1975 when together with company like Sidney Poitier he was inducted into The Black Filmmakers' Hall of Fame.

Al Hoskins appears to be a man who doesn't live in the past, but says his *Our Gang* days were exciting ones. His working relationships with the kids were "some good, some bad."

On the issue of race relations, he says he didn't encounter discrimination until World War II, in the army, which was still segregated. Our Gang never was. "They related to each other as a bunch of kids," Al Hoskins says. "The message, I think, was that we're all just people, sometimes good and sometimes bad."

MICKEY GUBITOSI—now ROBERT BLAKE—(Michael James Vijencio Gubitosi)

Born in Nutley, New Jersey, September 18, 1933. First short, at age five, "Joy Scouts," last short "Tale of a Dog." Appeared in forty *Our Gang* comedies over five years.

In a remarkable turnaround, one of *Our Gang's* few really unappealing characters emerged as one of the series' few really fine actors in later life: Robert Blake.

Joining *Our Gang* as Mickey Gubitosi, he Anglicized his professional name and became Bobby Blake. From that point his character in the series was called Mickey Blake.

As Mickey Gubitosi he was whiny and obnoxious. As Bobby "Mickey" Blake he was unconvincing and obnoxious. As Robert Blake he made *In Cold Blood, Electra Glide in Blue,* and won an Emmy as TV's *Baretta.*

Between this nadir and nirvana was a rough climb with plenty of treacherous detours, few of which have remained secrets, since Robert Blake has exploded as the most exciting and outspoken talk-show guest since Don Rickles in the late 1960s. Frank and unashamed, he'll confess anything. "I've sold dope, used it, snorted it, done everything you can do to it," he revealed to a stunned Merv Griffin and a television audience of four million. Robert Blake's late-night chatter is usually sensational, and audiences love it.

His own childhood, though, was a drag, and he far from loved it.

At two, he was working in a song-and-dance act called "The Three Little Hillbillies" with his father and sister in Nutley, New Jersey. It flopped. His parents were so poor they'd send him out to steal milk in the mornings.

Then came relocation to Los Angeles, and *Our Gang.* "I wasn't a child star," Robert Blake has said more than once, "I was a child laborer.

"In the morning my mother would deliver me [to the M-G-M studios] like a dog on a leash. See, I had four rummies to support, I mean my family you understand. My father jumped off the boat and he just hung around the house singing Caruso records and wearing a cape. I think he wanted to be Valentino or something. And my mother's sitting in the dressing room out to lunch with the sewing needles, right? She gave her life to Jesus. And so anyway they all had to eat.

"I was like most child performers, I acted only because I was told to and you can hardly consider what I did acting. I didn't like it. It was no kind of life. Forcing a kid to become a performer is one of the worst things that can happen to a child. It's turning them into adults when they're still youngsters."

Surprisingly, though, Robert Blake doesn't believe enforced child labor shaped his emotional character. "I was just an unhappy kid," he says. "If I hadn't been on a set, I would have been grumpy wherever I was."

After *Our Gang* came a continuing role in Republic's above-average Western action series *Red Ryder,* starring William Elliott. Bobby Blake played the Indian boy sidekick, Little Beaver. "The commode of my life," he says today.

Through a tortured childhood, there were some bright spots. Working with Laurel & Hardy was a small one. Bobby Blake played a capsule-happy brat in their 1944 feature *The Big Noise,* probably the second-worst film Laurel & Hardy ever made. Even so, "They were terrific," Blake recalls. "I liked them a lot. The set was an absolutely hysterical place. It's a thing about if you're funny and crazy behind the lines, it'll work in front of the lines, too. And they were off kilter from morning till night."

There was one short period where Bobby Blake was very happy as an actor. "I went to Warner Bros.," he says, "and I got to work with like Eddie G. [Robinson], and Garfield, and Bogart, and the big cat, Sydney Greenstreet."

In the 1948 classic, *The Treasure of the Sierra Madre,* Robert Blake's the Mexican boy who sells Bogart the winning lottery ticket. Also at Warners he worked in Jack Benny's notorious *The Horn Blows at Midnight.*

Then at age sixteen, with home life no better, and having toiled in scores of feature films apart from *Our Gang,* it all caught up with him. As he tells it, "I just checked out of life, man." After being expelled from five Los Angeles high schools in two years, he decided to continue his education learning about booze and narcotics. And for a while, he just kept on skidding.

Much of his earnings had supported his family, but the Jackie Coogan law helped provide a $16,000 nest egg that he claimed on his twenty-first birthday "after nineteen years of 'schlepping'," he says ruefully. "I spent a deuce on a car, and the rest went into therapy. I could've shot it in my arm like some other folks I knew, but I'd beat that rap. So I spent the rest trying to get my head unbent, or trying to learn how to live with the bent head that I had."

His salvation was to rediscover acting, although it was a seesaw struggle, and he got burned more than once. He worked irregularly from the late 1950s in movies and television (*The Purple Gang, PT 109, The Richard Boone Show*), but his hardline values, integrity, and bluntness cost him good roles. He wouldn't compromise over something he believed in. One time he punched out a director. Even after finally streaking to the top with his shattering performance as the death-row killer in Truman Capote's *In Cold Blood,* his mercurial personality sometimes dictated a self-destructive existence. He let slip the lead in *Lenny* to Dustin Hoffman, and lost out to James Caan in *Funny Lady* out of a pique when Barbra Streisand

Bobby Blake as Little Beaver, Alice Fleming as The Duchess in one of the popular Red Ryder films of the 1940s.

Robert Blake as Perry Wilson, with Scott Wilson in a scene from *In Cold Blood.*

made him audition for the role.

When he signed to do *Baretta,* ABC executives—"the suits," Blake calls them—told him how to dress, how to behave, and how to do the show. "I told them to get a chimpanzee and give him a banana and have him do it," Blake said. They left him alone. . . .

. . . Until the time when as Baretta the cop he decided that instead of shoving a suspect up against the wall to make him talk, he'd stick the guy's head in a toilet. "That's what a cop did to me once," Blake said, "and it happens all the time." The argument lasted for days, and Blake lost. They cut the scene.

He philosophizes, "I try not to follow, lead, or join," and adds, "I don't have to act in disaster films—my whole life has been a disaster."

Yet with all the setbacks have come some impressive post-*In Cold Blood* triumphs: overshadowing Robert Redford in *Tell Them Willie Boy is Here,* and the wonderfully played motorcycle cop Big John Wintergreen in *Electra Glide in Blue.* Neither picture was the smash commercial success it should have been, but *Baretta* has certainly won both critical and popular acclaim.

Though the concomitants of success have mitigated the insecurity and bitterness he harbors from his childhood, Robert Blake is still moody, introspective, and spends time with "the head man" getting psychiatric help.

What is it about being a child actor that leaves such scars few can overcome? (Even Robert Blake kids about "going bonkers" again.) Talking about the sad ends of Scotty Beckett and Alfalfa Switzer, Blake told Johnny Carson on *The Tonight Show,* "A lot of it has to do with being in a unique environment, and when you leave the studio at the end of the day, you can't recreate that environment, cause man, it's fantasy; little kids can't find it in the real world." He pauses, milking the moment. "Yeah, Alfie [Switzer] got snuffed out with a shotgun. I remember that. A lot of them. . . . I've been on borrowed time since I was nineteen years old."

JACKIE DAVIS (John H. Davis, M.D.)

Born in Los Angeles, California. First short, "Young Sherlocks," last short "Derby Day." Appeared in nineteen *Our Gang* comedies over two years.

The younger brother of Mildred Davis, Harold Lloyd's leading lady and later his wife, Jackie Davis was *Our Gang's* first tough guy. In "Derby Day," the young scrapper is introduced by a title predicting his future: "Jack—some neighbors say he'll be hanged when he grows up—others hope it will be sooner." Coincidentally, it was his last film; after Harold Lloyd eloped with Mildred Davis, he pulled his young brother-in-law out of the series and sent him off to military school. Not to belabor the suspense, evidently Jack enjoyed lessons better than laughs, and grew up to be a prominent physician in West Los Angeles.

Our Gang happy endings aren't always just dreamstuff.

DARWOOD "WALDO" KAYE (Darwood Kenneth Smith)

Born in Fort Collins, Colorado. First short, "Glove Taps," last short "Waldo's Last Stand." Appeared in twenty-one *Our Gang* comedies over four years.

Pedantic "Waldo" was *Our Gang's* lone exponent of academia. Fitted with Harold Lloyd-type horn-rimmed glasses, he was skinny and scholarly and perfect as the sissy who'd set his wits against Alfalfa and Butch and walk away with their femme fatale prize—Darla.

In Hollywood for a vacation during 1936, Waldo's father registered him with central casting, bringing parts in *The Plot Thickens* with ZaSu Pitts, and George Stevens's *Quality Street,* starring Katharine Hepburn. While still with the Gang he appeared in *Gone With the Wind.* Then later with Alfalfa and Muggsy he did Republic's *Barnyard Follies.* During the 1940s he had incidental roles in dozens of features, including M-G-M's *Best Foot Forward* (he played "Killer"), Clarence Brown's *The Human Comedy,* and Del Lord's *Kansas City Kitty* for Columbia in 1944.

After serving in the army, he decided on a career in the ministry. As Elder Darwood Kenneth Smith he is now a missionary with the Seventh-Day Adventist church. As-

sisted by his wife and four sons, he's already completed twelve years of missionary work in Thailand. Still erudite, he's recently earned a Master's degree in theology at Michigan State.

Coincidentally, as "Waldo" he'd portrayed a minister in the dream sequence for "The Little Ranger."

DICKIE MOORE (John Richard Moore)

Born in Los Angeles, California, September 12, 1925. First short, at age six, "Hook and Ladder," last short "Mush and Milk." Appeared in eight *Our Gang* comedies in his one season with the series.

Dickie Moore made his screen debut at the age of eleven months, playing John Barrymore as an infant in *The Beloved Rogue* (1927). With this auspicious beginning, Dickie's mother took him to auditions, and he started working regularly at age four.

Before long, this wide-eyed youngster was a prominent screen actor, working in as many as twelve feature films in one year! Among his early credits were Cecil B. De-Mille's *The Squaw Man, So Big* with Barbara Stanwyck, *The Star Witness* and *The Expert* with Chic Sale, and *Blonde Venus* with Marlene Dietrich.

In 1932, Hal Roach recruited him for *Our Gang,* where he became a most endearing leading man for the next year, and struck up a warm off-screen friendship with costar "Stymie" Beard. His proven success in films had entitled him to a contract calling for $225 a week, more than five times the amount most Our Gangers started at.

After one year, however, Dickie left for the monetarily "greener" pastures of feature films, and starred in the title role of *Oliver Twist,* had the lead in *Little Men,* and won supporting parts in *Man's Castle* with Spencer Tracy, *Peter Ibbetson* with Gary Cooper, *The Story of Louis Pasteur* and *The Life of Emile Zola* with Paul Muni, and *The Bride Wore Red* with Joan Crawford.

As a teen-ager, Dickie appeared with Gary Cooper in *Sergeant York,* one of his favorite film experiences; as young Don Ameche in Ernst Lubitsch's *Heaven Can Wait,* another favorite; and as the boyfriend who gives Shirley Temple her first screen kiss in *Miss Annie Rooney* (1942).

After serving in World War II and attending college (majoring in journalism) Dickie Moore became Dick Moore, had a good role in *Out of the Past* with Robert Mitchum, and then he co-produced, co-directed and acted in a two-reel short subject called *The Boy and the Eagle* that was nominated for an Academy Award in 1949. Later the same year he relocated in New York. Working in the theater, as actor and director, he became involved with Actors Equity, the prominent theatrical guild, and became editor of their magazine, eventually assuming the larger role of public relations counsel, a post he held for seven years. His last of more than eighty feature-length films was *The Member of the Wedding,* released in 1953.

After the Equity stint he formed his own public-relations office, which he maintains today, editing the journal of AFTRA (the American Federation of Television and Radio Artists), producing industrial shows, and supervising other accounts.

Dick had problems of competing with his past

Adolescent Dickie Moore with Shirley Temple in *Miss Annie Rooney* (1942).

achievements as a child actor, but overcame these hurdles to build a successful life. Though he believes his child star experience "was much more beneficial than injurious," he also says, "I enjoy my life. I would never go back and redo a moment of it. There were difficult times . . . but I think there are difficult times for people who *don't* have that background.

"I think performers have a real need to be made aware of the fact that their gifts and talents have a residual use. I'm always interested in anybody's story where they have managed to beat the odds and come out doing something they want to do, and still be able to utilize their backgrounds. It's worked for me."

An introspective man, Dick Moore has one of the more thoughtful analyses of the problems confronting grown child stars: "People have a tendency to remember you as you were," he says. "And, unless you're careful, you have a tendency to remember you as you were, too."

"BUCKWHEAT" THOMAS (William Henry Thomas, Jr.)

Born in Los Angeles, California, 1931. First short, at age three, "For Pete's Sake," last short "Tale of a Dog." Appeared in ninety-three *Our Gang* comedies over ten years.

Along with Farina, Spanky, and Joe Cobb, probably the most durable of all Little Rascals, Billie "Buckwheat" Thomas first crashed the *Our Gang* ranks because his mother wanted it that way. "I started out when I was three years old," Thomas explains. "My mother just took me out to the studio on a regular interview day, and they needed a person, and that was it." The combination of a bewitching smile and deep luminous eyes won Hal Roach's favor and a film contract starting at $40 per week.

Modeled after Farina, the Buckwheat character was pigtailed, named for a breakfast food, wore the same old patched gingham clothing, and for a while Buckwheat's sex, like Farina's, was a matter of national speculation.

Shy and well liked around the *Our Gang* sets, he en-

joyed what he was doing, and told Darla Hood recently that any racial hurdles one might imagine never bothered him.

Thomas dropped out of show business after his M-G-M contract expired, and for decades not even his *Our Gang* colleagues knew what had become of him. At last, Billie Thomas's whereabouts were disclosed in late 1974; living in Los Angeles, he'd been working for Technicolor as a film technician for some twenty years. As a hobby, he's a citizen's band "ham" radio operator.

As the proverb goes, widely circulated reports of Buckwheat leading a jazz combo, or dying in a plane crash flying emergency rations to Biafra, are premature and greatly exaggerated, respectively.

Like other popular Our Gangers, Billie's essential identity has been plagued by people who claim to have been "Buckwheat" and were not. One aggressive impostor's line has paved the way to a feature story in *Ebony* magazine, and TV guest shots on Steve Allen's talk show and also *I've Got a Secret*. Little did they know he had a secret.

Stymie Beard's sister Carlena held the role for one film, Willie Mae Taylor for three, but in all others, covering eleven years, the "Buckwheat" characterization was irrefutably Billie Thomas and Billie Thomas only.

"PORKY" LEE (Eugene Lee)

Born in Texas, 1933. First short, at age two, "Little Sinner," last short "Auto Antics." Appeared in forty-two *Our Gang* comedies over four years.

Eugene Lee's mother sent his photograph to Hal Roach, who was so struck by the resemblance to Spanky that he arranged for a screen test which led to the lad being cast as Spanky's kid brother in "Little Sinner." After this successful trial appearance, "Porky" was placed under long-term contract.

When he left *Our Gang*, he also left show business. He has chosen not to exploit his past movie career, and is today a teacher in Texas.

Parenthetically, during the 1960s one gentleman began holding himself out as *Our Gang's* "Porky" in some specious self-promotional publicity and for a book he wrote. In recent years, after being confronted with some bizarre juxtapositions of fact, he seems to have retreated from his claims.

ERNIE "SUNSHINE SAMMY/BOOKER T." MORRISON (Frederick Ernest Morrison)

Born in New Orleans, Louisiana, in 1914. First short, at age seven, "Our Gang," last short "Cradle Robbers." Appeared in twenty-eight *Our Gang* comedies over three years.

The very first and oldest of the original *Our Gang* contingent, Ernie Morrison was already working in shorts and features around Hollywood when Hal Roach conceived *His Rascals*. Since 1919, as brightly smiling "Sunshine Sammy," the youngster had been adding spice to

The East Side Kids: Stanley Clements, Sunshine Sammy, Billy Benedict, Bobby Jordan, Huntz Hall, Leo Gorcey, and Bobby Stone meet no less than Ava Gardner (and Rick Vallin) in a scene from *Ghosts on the Loose* (1943). The previous year, Ava Gardner had worked in *Our Gang*'s "Mighty Lak a Goat."

Roach's Harold Lloyd, Paul (James) Parrott, and Snub Pollard comedies. He possessed the high skill of screen exuberance. By late 1921 he was spun off into his own *Sunshine Sammy* series, though only one entry was produced, "The Pickaninny." It's probably an *Our Gang* precursor, but one can't be sure since the film is considered lost and its scant reviews are imprecise. Hopefully the film's standards surpassed that of its flinch-causing title. In any case, Ernie Morrison's unwitting role in *Our Gang*'s inception should not be overlooked.

In 1924, when offered a lucrative three-year vaudeville pact, Sunshine Sammy (or more probably his father and manager) did not evince interest in making movies for less money, and left *Our Gang* after the first twenty-eight episodes. He remained on the vaudeville circuit at least until the early 1930s, where he was billed as "Sunshine Sammy—*Our Gang* star."

He wasn't heard from again in movies until he joined a *Dead End Kids* splinter group at Monogram Pictures in the early 1940s. *The Dead End Kids* genealogy is labyrinthine, but Ernie Morrison joined the clan of brawling rowdies only briefly, appearing in most of the early *East Side Kids* pictures. Co-featured were Leo and David Gorcey, Huntz Hall, Gabriel Dell, Bobby Jordan (all originals from Sidney Kingsley's Broadway play *Dead End*) and Donald Haines, another *Our Gang* graduate. Listed on the credits as Sunshine Sammy Morrison, he played a character named "Scruno," a fast-talking devil's advocate type. Others in the mongrel-like pack were "Mugs" and "Glimpy," so "Scruno" wasn't the only piquant moniker. "Scruno" *was* the only black kid in the series, however.

Some of the *East Side Kids* pictures Sunshine Sammy made during his nearly four years with the series (1940–

43) included *Spooks Run Wild, Ghosts on the Loose* (both with Bela Lugosi), *The Ghost Creeps, Smart Alecks, Mr. Wise Guy, Let's Get Tough, Boys of the City, Clancy Street Boys, 'Neath Brooklyn Bridge, Flying Wild* and *Kid Dynamite.* The films were every bit as outrageous as their titles, and date horribly today. They were all cheaply made, fractured the English language, and told the same story every time. But the rough edges (mightily rough) are somehow appealing, and the series for many remains undefinably enjoyable.

Ernie Morrison retired from show business in the 1950s, and in the early 1970s was reported working in the missile and aerospace industry in Los Angeles.

JACKIE COOPER (John Cooper or Cooperman, Jr.)

Born in Los Angeles, California, September 15, 1922. First short, at age six "Boxing Gloves," last short "Bargain Day." Appeared in fifteen *Our Gang* comedies over two years.

With his father Jack Cooper in silent-film comedies, it was almost inevitable that young Jack should venture into show business, and at age three he made his screen debut in some Lloyd Hamilton shorts. Then his parents separated, his father died young, and it was his mother, working in the music department at Fox, who secretly arranged for a successful Fox *Movietone Follies* audition. No one knew the two were related till Jackie won the part. This led to a short but amusing role in the early Fox talkie *Sunny Side Up,* which brought him to the attention of Hal Roach.

Roach's own greatest talent may have been recognizing talent in others, confirming it, and nourishing it. In Jackie Cooper, Roach saw more than just the pouty bee-stung lower lip that was to be the youngster's lifelong trademark, and he signed him in July of 1929 to a two-year contract. The "good little bad boy," as Roach saw him, quickly became the star of the series. Gifted yet unaffected, he was a natural, blessed with a photographic memory as well as a genuine acting instinct that carried him through comedy as well as pathos.

Jackie's tenure with *Our Gang* came to an end in 1931 when he won the leading role in *Skippy* at Paramount. This feature film based on the popular comic strip earned Jackie an Academy Award nomination, and a Best Director Award for his uncle, Norman Taurog. The youngster was an overnight sensation, co-starring later that year with Wallace Beery in another Oscar-winning feature, *The Champ.* Beery and Cooper reteamed during the next few years in such other tear festivals as *The Bowery, Treasure Island,* and *O'Shaughnessy's Boy,* a 1935 film in which Jackie was billed second as "Stubby," and incredibly, Spanky McFarland was billed third in the part of "Stubby as a child." The best kid stars, it seems, were worthy of youthful counterparts in their pictures.

Without Beery (or Spanky), Jackie's career flourished through other 1930s features including *Young Donovan's Kid, Dinky, Sooky* with Robert Coogan, and the 1934 remake of older brother Jackie Coogan's *Peck's Bad Boy.*

Jackie Cooper's early success was phenomenal. He made over a million dollars. Everything he did was news. In late 1931 M-G-M released a special one-reel short called *Jackie Cooper's Christmas Party,* featuring Beery, Lionel Barrymore, Marion Davies, Clark Gable, and other lesser lights looking for work around Metro.

One of the movie magazines broke a story that Jackie Cooper was in truth a midget. It was hard to squelch and lots of readers swallowed the notion. No kid actor could be *that* good, could he?

Although his talent never dimmed, Jackie found starring roles increasingly scarce in the late 1930s, and he moved from prestigious M-G-M and Paramount to Universal and Monogram so he could continue working. Occasionally he landed a plum, like the co-starring role in *The Return of Frank James* (1940), with Henry Fonda, and he scored a certain success creating the screen role of Henry Aldrich in *What a Life!* and *Life With Henry.* He even starred in a twelve-chapter serial, *Scouts to the Rescue.* At least one film, *Glamour Boy* with Darryl Hickman, traded on his former child stardom, while other films paired him with female counterparts from the child-star ranks (Bonita Granville in *Gallant Sons,* Judy Garland in *Ziegfeld Girl,* Jane Withers in *Her First Beau*). W. S. Van Dyke's *The Devil Is a Sissy* (1936) cast him with Freddie Bartholomew and Mickey Rooney, with routine results.

Through all this he later realized he'd never had a chance to act, or even find out whether he *could* act. "Kids don't act," he says. "Anyway they didn't in the movies when I was a kid. One kid has a unique voice, another has a disarming smile, another has a pathetic kisser and looks underprivileged. Whenever they want a certain quality in a kid, they hire one who has it. And if you're successful, nobody wants you to change. After a while you get conditioned, and it's a miracle if you ever amount to anything as an adult actor."

He served in the Navy during World War II, where life was suddenly not so easy anymore. He was forced to compete, and found he could. The experience matured him, and when he returned to Hollywood, he got serious about his trade. Trouble is, no producer would give him an opportunity to grow up as an actor. His career plunged as he made a pair of featherweight Monogram pictures, *Kilroy Was Here* (1947), and *French Leave* (1948), interesting only for twice pairing him with Jackie Coogan. They were so bad, he says, they drove him to the New York stage to practice his craft and prove he could act. Turning down $100,000 for a series of Western features, he refused to let Hollywood continue merchandising him as a personality instead of an actor.

His first comeback success came as Ensign Pulver in the road company version of the original Broadway play, *Mr. Roberts.*

In 1955, after paying his dues with more stage work, two starring Broadway plays, and lots of live television, he returned to Hollywood to direct and star in the half-hour TV sit-com *The People's Choice.* He played "Sock" Miller, lived in a trailer home, and shared the laughs with a sleepy-eyed basset hound who talked to the audience by way of droll, sexy off-screen voice-over. Cleo got more close-ups than "Sock" did. The show was a big hit, lasting three years.

In 1959 he fell back on his Navy background a second time to launch another even more successful TV series, *Hennessy,* where he played a Navy doctor. *Hennessy* ran three seasons, too, and was showered with awards, including a citation from the American Medical Associa-

Jackie Cooper and Judy Garland on the M-G-M lot in the late 1930s.

Jackie Cooper and Patricia Breslin with "Cleo," from the TV series *The People's Choice.*

tion. Jackie Cooper was twice nominated for an Emmy for his performance in the title role. Again he often directed, and coproduced besides.

After *Hennessy* his growing expertise behind the camera led to his appointment as vice-president in charge of production for Screen Gems, the television arm of Columbia Pictures, where he had responsibility both for programs on the air, and any number of pilots vying for slots with the networks. He tried to revive an *Our Gang* series, without success.

Lured in front of a camera from time to time, he continued to score points as a director in the early 1970s (the feature film *Stand Up and Be Counted,* an Emmy-winning episode of *M*A*S*H**) before returning to performing on a major scale with guest appearances on many leading TV shows, a meaty role in the horror/sci-fi film, *Chosen Survivors,* and a new series of his own, *Mobile One.*

There's a story behind his Emmy for *M*A*S*H.* In *Gallant Sons* (1940) he'd worked with Gene Reynolds, another young actor. Reynolds hadn't been in *Our Gang,* but he had appeared in a Bob McGowan feature, *Too Many Parents,* as well as *Boys Town* and *Young Tom Edison,* both directed by Jackie Cooper's uncle, Norman Taurog. Their paths crossed again while Jackie Cooper was working in *Hennessy,* and he gave Reynolds his first opportunity to direct. Reynolds was a casting director at NBC, and Cooper said, "As an actor I figured he'd make a good director." Since then Reynolds has been a successful producer-director, with shows like *Hogan's Heroes* and the irreverent *M*A*S*H* (for 20th Century-Fox) to his credit. Eventually Reynolds returned the favor by assigning Jackie Cooper to direct the (Emmy-winning) *M*A*S*H* episode. In a final twist, the office at Fox where Jackie Cooper's mother was a secretary is now the office of the secretary to . . . Gene Reynolds.

Jackie Cooper has one child from his first marriage, and three from his third and lasting union, to the former Barbara Kraus; they have been married since 1954. They hit it off right away, despite the fact that she had not seen a single one of his films at the time they met. He liked that.

Through the years Jackie Cooper has pursued many varied interests. He races sports cars like a pro and plays the drums like a pro (so say other pros), he's an accomplished skeet shooter, he learned how to box with skill as a boy, he's a licensed pilot, owns his own airplane, sails boats, and is a commander in the naval reserve. He raises an exotic species of tropical fish, used to raise quarter horses, and his wife says he'd make a great chef. He taught her how to cook. With all his avocations, and his career success besides, he still finds time to screen movies at home for his family once or twice a week at his Beverly Hills mansion.

The most prominent *Our Gang* alumnus still active in show business, Jackie says of his career, "As much as I've directed, and horsed around with different parts of this business, once you're an actor, you're always an actor. You can stay out of the water for ten years, but if you fall in, you can swim. It never leaves you."

He still prefers directing, though. "I don't know an actor who has worked as long as I have who would not rather be a director," he says. "A motion picture camera is the greatest toy ever invented for a man."

Particularly for the boy inside of the man.

JEAN DARLING (Dorothy Jean LeVake)

Born in Santa Monica, California, August 23, 1922. First short, at age four, "Seeing the World," last short "Bouncing Babies." Appeared in thirty-five *Our Gang* comedies over three years.

If a name ever suited a little girl it was Jean Darling. The beautiful blond, blue-eyed youngster was spotted on the street one day by the wife of Hal Roach's assistant general manager, L. A. French, who recommended her for *Our Gang.* She remained with the troupe not only in films but in vaudeville, touring the RKO-Orpheum Theatre circuit through the early 1930s with fellow Gangsters Harry Spear, Scooter Lowry, and Peggy Eames. Jean returned to the Hal Roach studio in 1934 to play Curly Locks in Laurel & Hardy's *Babes in Toyland,* and appeared in Monogram's production of *Jane Eyre* that same year.

After graduating from Miss Long's Professional Children's School in Hollywood, she began to study singing seriously and in 1940 was awarded a scholarship by the New York Municipal Opera Association. Around the same time, M-G-M offered her a role opposite Mickey Rooney in one of his *Andy Hardy* films, but spurning both Hollywood and the operatic stage, Jean (who was voted queen of her senior class at the City College of New York) turned to Broadway instead, making her debut in *Count Me In,* and scoring a major success as Carrie in Rodgers and Hammerstein's *Carousel* (she can be heard on the still-available cast album).

A fan photo of Jean Darling from 1933.

Jean also won many fans on a lengthy USO tour during World War II, boosting her popularity on both radio and television during the late 1940s and early 1950s. Her work in CBS radio serials included *Hilltop House,* and *Road of Life,* while on television she had local shows of her own, and one NBC network program from New York, *Have a Date With Jean Darling.* In 1961 Jean was working in an improvisation troupe with George Segal in New York's Village.

Some years back Jean Darling told a reporter from *Pageant,* "It's bad enough for an adult—to be on top one day, and just another performer the next. For a child, it's disastrous. When I was a child, I got to thinking I was a little god. I lived in a world of glorious make-believe, surrounded by people who oohed and ahed, and I was sure I was everything they said I was. I must be. Otherwise why would they stand around saying it? That sort of thing could have destroyed me. It did destroy so many others. I sometimes think the fact that I was spared was just plain magic."

In 1954 Jean married Reuben Bowen, whose stage name is Kajar the Magician; they have one son, and live in New York.

"FROGGY" LAUGHLIN (Billy Laughlin and also McLaughlin)

First short, "The New Pupil," last short "Tale of a Dog." Appeared in twenty-nine *Our Gang* comedies over four years.

"Froggy" Laughlin, a favorite with kids for his weird glasses and deep "Popeye" trick voice (not dubbed, he could really talk that way), was killed in a motor scooter accident near Huntington Beach, California, in the early 1950s.

SCOTTY BECKETT (Scott Hastings Beckett)

Born in Oakland, California, October 4, 1929. First short, at age four, "Hi'-Neighbor!" last short "Our Gang Follies of 1936." Appeared in fifteen *Our Gang* comedies over two years (not counting two return appearances at M-G-M).

Scotty and his family moved to Los Angeles when he was three. He came to the attention of a casting director and made his debut in a 1933 drama, *Gallant Lady,* starring Ann Harding and Clive Brook. Interestingly, Scotty played a boy of three in the film, and was succeeded in the story by Dickie Moore, playing the same boy, aged six. The next year, Scotty followed Dickie into *Our Gang.* They finally appeared together in Marilyn Monroe's first film, *Dangerous Years,* made in 1947.

One of the cutest child actors ever, Scotty was interviewed for *Our Gang* in January of 1934. Hal Roach thought the cherub-faced youngster had a wistful Jackie Coogan-ish quality about him, and had a long-term contract drawn up immediately. It was decided Scotty should be teamed with Spanky McFarland, and their interplay highlighted many mid-1930s *Little Rascals* films. Scotty's usual attire was an oversized turtle neck sweater and baseball cap worn sideways, both remindful of garb worn

Scotty Beckett and Betty Sullivan (Ed's daughter) at the Stork Club in Manhattan in 1948.

by the waiflike character Jackie Coogan played in his early films, dating from *The Kid* in 1920.

After his tenure with *Our Gang,* Scotty won increasingly prominent roles in major Hollywood films, usually playing the star's son, or the hero as a boy. Among his major credits: *Dante's Inferno* with Spencer Tracy, *Anthony Adverse* with Fredric March, *The Charge of the Light Brigade* with Errol Flynn, *Conquest* with Greta Garbo, *Marie Antoinette* with Norma Shearer, and *Kings Row,* playing Robert Cummings as a child.

Scotty attended Los Angeles High School, and took time off from film assignments to try his luck on the stage. Adolescence didn't seem to hamper his career, as he won such important roles as that of young Al Jolson in *The Jolson Story,* and Junior in the long-running radio show *The Life of Riley.* He attended the University of Southern California, but dropped out when the combined work load of school and movies became too great.

Although he was working steadily at M-G-M in such films as *A Date With Judy* (as Elizabeth Taylor's brother), *Battleground,* and *The Happy Years* (with fellow child-stars Dean Stockwell and Darryl Hickman), his life grew increasingly tumultuous in the late 1940s and early 1950s.

In 1948 he was arrested on suspicion of drunk driving. The following year he eloped with Beverly Baker, a tennis star, but their marriage dissolved within a period of months. A second marriage produced one son, Scott, Jr., and this alliance seemed to last, but in 1954 he ran afoul of the law again, once for passing a bad check and once for carrying a concealed weapon.

Ironically, that same year Scotty's career took an upward turn as he was cast as Winky, the comic sidekick in the popular TV show *Rocky Jones, Space Ranger.* Unfortunately, this was Beckett's last regular work.

Scotty Beckett at the time of an arrest in 1959.

The last ten years of his life were filled with unpleasant stories of divorce, violence, drugs, and arrests. After more or less giving up show business, he tried selling real estate, then cars, and twice enrolled at universities with the intention of becoming a medical doctor. He checked into a Hollywood nursing home on May 8, 1968, needing medical attention himself after suffering a serious beating. He died two days later. Although pills and a note were found, no conclusion was made by the coroner as to the exact cause of death. He was just thirty-eight years old.

It was a particularly sad end for someone who as a child had shown so much easy charm and talent.

WALLY ALBRIGHT (Walton Albright, Jr.)

Born in Burbank, California, September 3, 1925. First short, at age six, "Choo-Choo!" last short "Washee Ironee." Appeared in six *Our Gang* comedies over two years.

Wally Albright served *Little Rascals* capers only fleetingly, but well. He made his mark as the well-meaning lead character in Gus Meins's earliest *Our Gang* entries.

A sampling of his extensive work away from the Gang includes *Thunder* (1929) with Lon Chaney, Sr., *The Single Standard* (1929) with Greta Garbo, *The Trespasser* (1929) with Gloria Swanson, Fox's first sound version of *Rebecca of Sunnybrook Farm* (1932), *Mr. Skitch* (1933) with Will Rogers (Wally played his son), two Rowland V. Lee classics: *Zoo in Budapest* (1933) and *The Count of Monte Cristo* (1934), Michael Curtiz's *Black Fury* (1935), John Ford's *The Grapes of Wrath* (1940), and even some B Westerns: Tim McCoy's *End of the Trail* (1933) and Gene Autry's *Mexicali Rose* (1939). In 1945 he was still listed in casting directories under the "younger leading men" section, but parts by then were mostly fringe roles, and he quit motion pictures soon thereafter.

After service in the Navy, he pursued an interest in water sports, winning national championships and setting world records in trick water-skiing and speedboat racing. (He'd build his own boats, presumably with more skill than he could construct fire engines!) He's won some five hundred trophies through the years for athletic prowess in various sports. He owns and pilots his own airplane, too.

A successful businessman, he lives today in Thermal, California, and operates a trucking firm that packages and ships produce throughout the state.

Wally Albright is another quiet exception to the fantasy that sensation-seeking writers try to create about most *Our Gang* alumni finding only failure and ruination in adult life. Hal Roach acknowledges the tragedies that have befallen some, but maintains that if you followed any number of other kids through their lives, "you would find the same percentage of them have troubles in later life."

Wally Albright, for one, is happy, prosperous, and still pretty adventuresome.

C · THE REST: THEIR GLORIES AND THEIR RUIN

Others who met with *Our Gang* fleetingly or incidentally deserve acknowledgment in passing, too. They are "the rest."

There are a few important child stars like Darryl Hickman, and Juanita Quigley who joined the Gang only briefly, and are covered elsewhere. One who's not is Leon Janney; in recent years he's become a prominent and prolific New York-based actor on stage, television, and radio, where his voice is familiar on scores of commercials.

As for the rest of the rest, many are scattered wide. Like Our Gangers already covered, time has treated some fiercely, some happily. On balance, a few have experienced their measure of ruin, but more have adjusted and survived. Some have even prospered.

Some we've frankly been unable to trace. Their subsequent lives and careers are a mystery. Most of the kids today share only a common memory, and lost touch with each other when they left the series. It's not surprising. Shirley Jean Rickert says, "It's like the kids you went to kindergarten with—you probably don't know many of them now." Among those for whom our sleuthing has regrettably drawn the proverbial blank are Kendall "Breezy Brisbane" McComas, Andy Samuels, Jacquie Lyn, Marianne Edwards, Alvin Buckelew, Donald Haines, Sherwood V. Bailey, Jr., and of course the pair we can't even identify, Leonard(?) and the character known only as "Uh-huh." Whatever's become of them, they have sealed up their pasts pretty tightly. One can hope they achieved the success their early lives pointed to, though the odds were clearly against them. Many grown Our Gangers haven't fared too well, especially those who tried to stay in the business.

The inability to retain childhood stardom and talent through adolescence and into adulthood was certainly not unique to *Our Gang,* though. The most popular child stars in movie history—Jackie Coogan, Shirley Temple—suddenly found themselves gangly teen-agers one day, bereft of the cuteness that had made them stars, and, briefly, in danger of becoming young has-beens.

For his own charges, Hal Roach was powerless to do anything about this situation, although he showed a devotion and loyalty rare in Hollywood producers. *Our Gang* graduates were always welcome at his studio, and he found jobs for them wherever possible. As best he could he tried to shield the kids from the harshness of Hollywood life, and most Our Gangers look back today on their one-time boss with respect and fondness; some of them know just how special he was in comparison with other studio rajahs.

All child stars bore heavy crosses: if not at Hal Roach Studios then later in life. "Nobody outside the profession has any idea what it was like," Darryl Hickman noted recently. "To survive in Hollywood you've got to have a shaft of steel right up your back. It must be flexible enough to bend but not brittle enough to break. Jackie Cooper has got it. He's tough and he survived. Most of the others didn't. None of our stories is very pretty."

Among "the rest," another who survived, and is herself very pretty, is Jackie Lynn (Jacqueline) Taylor, who appeared in five *Little Rascals* films in her one season with the series in 1934. One of the kids who leads quite a visible adult life, she is today Dr. Hope Taylor Fries, D.D., president of the nondenominational Academy of Infinite Metaphysics. She's also worked steadily through the years as a Southern California television personality, and has been the host of an extremely popular *Little Rascals* program syndicated out of San Diego. During the 1950s she was a colleague of Johnny Downs at a San Diego television station. This Jackie Lynn, though, is not to be confused with Jacquie Lyn (Dufton), the English actress who made a lasting impression in some 1932 *Little Rascals* pix, and also in Laurel & Hardy's *Pack up Your Troubles.*

Others?

Tough guys Leonard and Sidney Kibrick live in the Los Angeles area. Incidentally, Sid Kibrick ("The Woim") appears as one of the little kids in Samuel Goldwyn's 1937 classic, *Dead End.*

Jerry Tucker was wounded in World War II, overcame a slight disability, and is now an engineer with RCA Communications in New York.

We have no doubt that Janet Burston saved moviegoers many headaches when she left acting and ultimately became a housewife.

Eugene "Pineapple" Jackson, who succeeded Sunshine Sammy for a handful of early silent pictures, has worked without fanfare through the years in television and movies (even Gene Autry Westerns), gaining the most recognition for continuing roles as Uncle Lou on Diahann Carroll's TV program *Julia,* and as a driver on M-G-M TV's long-running *Daktari* series. He's also

Wally Albright, Tommy Bond, Jackie Taylor, and Stymie Beard go over their lessons with Mrs. Fern Carter in 1934.

played nightclubs for years with his Jackson Trio. Presently he runs a stage workshop in Compton, California. Ironically, Roach named the youngster "Pineapple" for his clutch of hair; today he's bald.

Dickie Jones worked irregularly in the Gang for about four years. He found more work, though, in B Westerns starring George O'Brien, Kermit Maynard, William Boyd, Hoot Gibson, Tim McCoy, and Buck Jones. By 1950 he was working regularly in Gene Autry's last theatrical Westerns, and when Autry moved to television, Dickie Jones went with him. Producer Autry first paired him with Jock Mahoney for a popular juvenile action TV series called *The Range Rider.* Dickie was later spun-off into his own Western series, *Buffalo Bill, Jr.,* which ran up into the late 1950s. Both video series were made under Autry's Flying A Productions, and were marked by spectacular daredevil stunting and riding that hasn't once been duplicated on television since.

Dickie Jones also played Humphrey Bogart's son in *The Black Legion* (1936), and worked in George Marshall's 1939 version of *Destry Rides Again,* Ernst Lubitsch's *Heaven Can Wait* (1943), and John Wayne's *Sands of Iwo Jima* (1949). Most interestingly, he did the voice of Pinocchio for Walt Disney's full-length cartoon feature. Later he did the voice of Henry Aldrich for the popular network radio series.

According to his former partner Jock Mahoney, for the last fifteen years Dickie Jones has been selling real estate and doing appraisals in the Southern California area, and making a bundle at it.

Shirley Jean Rickert was the cute little blonde with the spit curls. Today she's a charming, attractive businesswoman. Between then and now she's had a colorful career as an eye-filling exotic dancer, a stripper. Her professional name was "Gilda and Her Crowning Glory." Though now divorced, Shirley Jean still uses her married name, Measures. Intently studying stills from her burlesque days, one concludes she measures up quite nicely.

She jumped *Our Gang* in 1931 for the competing Mickey

McGuire comedies starring Mickey Rooney. She played Tomboy Tailor. In 1934 she turned up as an Indian heiress in one of John Wayne's early horse operas for Monogram, 'Neath Arizona Skies, also featuring Gabby Hayes. Then the film roles evaporated. She reveled in driving a truck for the air corps during World War II, then on through the 1940s she did movie bits and choreography. She was a dancer in some wonderful screen musicals like Royal Wedding (1951) and Singin' in the Rain (1952), but they led nowhere. When she left burlesque, she moved into secretarial work, then legitimate stage work on the East Coast, both as an actress and a businesswoman on the theater staff. "I've never been as happy as I am these days," she says.

While stripping on the night club circuit as "Gilda," Shirley Jean met her share of Our Gang phonies. "Almost every town I played had a bartender that used to be Spanky," she says. "I never bothered with any of them—why embarrass them?"

Some unhappy endings. . . . At times, it does seem tragedy has swept through Our Gang. Certainly the specter of death at an early age has loomed over some. Besides Chubby, Alfalfa, Scotty, Froggy, and Wheezer, peripheral Our Gangers like Helen Parrish and Robert Young died while only in their mid-thirties.

Helen Parrish brushed with Our Gang for only a few moments, but had been moderately successful later as an ingenue in films. She married producer John Guedel, credited on the screenplay for "General Spanky." She died of cancer in 1959.

Bobby (later Clifton) Young played "Bonedust" off and on from the late Pathé period up through the Miss Crabtree talkies. As an adult he was active in top-level postwar pictures: Bogart's Dark Passage (1947), Raoul Walsh's Pursued (1947), Joan Crawford's Possessed (1947), Robert Mitchum's Blood on the Moon (1948), and Rosalind Russell's A Woman of Distinction (1950). He worked as a villain in lots of Republic B Westerns, particularly two with Roy Rogers, Trails of Robin Hood and Bells of Coronado. But he was also a comedy semi-regular in the wonderful Joe McDoakes short subjects for Warner Bros. He died in a 1951 Los Angeles hotel fire that started when he fell asleep smoking in bed. He'd been recently divorced.

For certain others, a prosperous, exciting beginning in life proved a hindrance to a normal existence later on. When they tried to rekindle movie careers as adults, and failed, they sold out their dreams to other pursuits. One young lady who'd worked in some of the McGowan talkies was placed on probation in 1956 after a jury convicted her on two counts of embezzling $6,267 from a bank. She couldn't cope with an unglamorous life.

The rest of the troops have wrapped themselves with the cover of anonymity, sliding back into oblivion as rapidly as they'd risen to prominence. Chances are they've done as the others have with their eclectic skills: they've married magicians, they've died young, they've become salesmen, actors, alcoholics, Campbell Soup kids, doctors, embezzlers, popsicle makers, Pinocchio, businessmen, dope fiends, ministers, strip-tease artists, housewives, hunting guides, auctioneers, teachers, laborers, and grandparents ready for social security. Of one sobering thing we are sure. Mortality embraces them all.

Except, we can hope, on film.

Shirley Jean Rickert as Gilda in her burlesque days. Pulchritude aplenty.

Shirley Jean today.

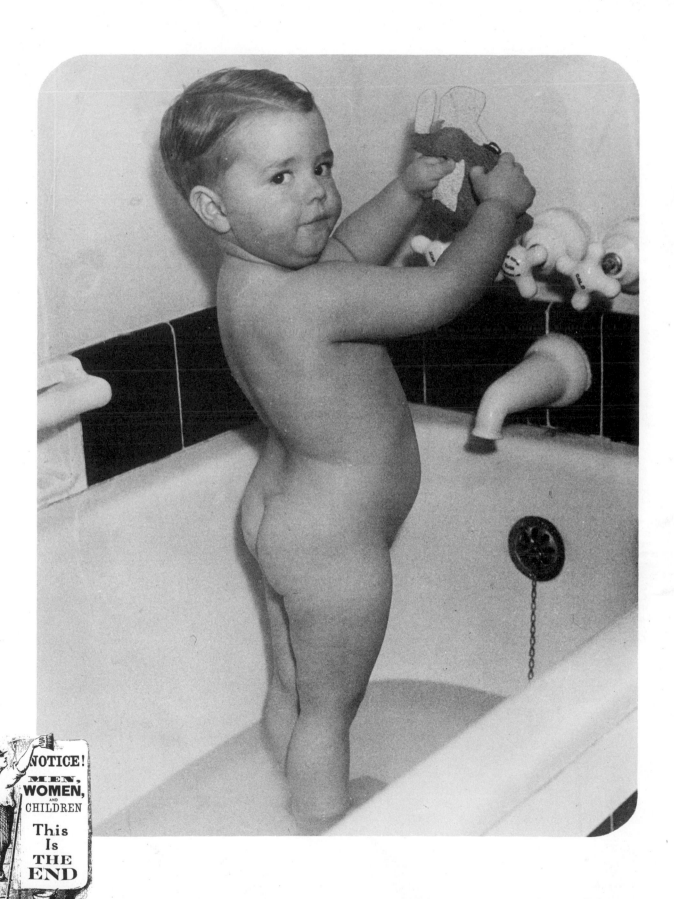

NOTICE!
MEN,
WOMEN,
AND
CHILDREN

This
Is
THE
END

INDEX

Boldface numbers refer to discussions of movies.